RUSSIA

NORWAY FINLAND
SWEDEN ESTONIA
LATVIA
LITHUANIA
GERMANY POLAND BELARUS
CZ.
AUS. UKRAINE
HUNG. ROMANIA MOLDOVA
ITALY B.H. YU.
ALBANIA BULGARIA
MAC.
GREECE TURKEY ARMENIA
MALTA CYPRUS AZERBAIJAN
TUNISIA SYRIA
LEBANON
ISRAEL JORDAN
EGYPT KUWAIT
LIBYA SAUDI
ARABIA
NIGER CHAD SUDAN
BENIN ERITREA YEMEN
NIGERIA CENTRAL DJIBOUTI
AFRICAN REP. ETHIOPIA
CAMEROON
GABON UGANDA KENYA
RWANDA
CONGO ZAIRE
BURUNDI
TANZANIA
ANGOLA
ZAMBIA MALAWI
NAMIBIA ZIMBABWE
BOTSWANA MADAGASCAR

KAZAKHSTAN
MONGOLIA
UZBEKISTAN
KYRGYZSTAN
GEORGIA
TAJIKISTAN
TURKMENISTAN
IRAQ IRAN AFGHANISTAN
BAHRAIN PEOPLE'S REPUBLIC OF CHINA
QATAR PAKISTAN BHUTAN
UNITED OMAN NEPAL
ARAB EMIRATES BANGLADESH
INDIA MYANMAR
(BURMA)
SOMALIA MALDIVES
SRI LANKA THAILAND
CAMBODIA
(KAMPUCHEA)
SEYCHELLES
COMOROS
MAURITIUS

N. KOREA
S. KOREA JAPAN

TAIWAN

LAOS
VIETNAM
PHILIPPINES
BRUNEI
MALAYSIA
SINGAPORE
INDONESIA

PACIFIC OCEAN

Mariana
Islands
Guam

Belau
Caroline Islands

Wake I.

Marshall
Islands

KIRIBATI

NAURU

PAPUA
NEW
GUINEA

SOLOMON IS.
TUVALU

VANUATU

FIJI

New Caledonia

AUSTRALIA

NEW
ZEALAND

INDIAN OCEAN

MOZAMBIQUE
SWAZILAND
SOUTH
AFRICA LESOTHO

ABBREVIATIONS

AUS.   AUSTRIA
BEL.   BELGIUM
B. H.   BOSNIA AND HERZEGOVINA
CR.   CROATIA
CZ.   CZECH REPUBLIC
DEN.   DENMARK
HUNG.   HUNGARY
LUX.   LUXEMBOURG
MAC.   FORMER YUGOSLAV REPUBLIC
       OF MACEDONIA
NETH.   NETHERLANDS
SLK.   SLOVAKIA
SLN.   SLOVENIA
SWITZ.   SWITZERLAND
YU.   YUGOSLAVIA

20°E   40°E   60°E   80°E   100°E   120°E   140°E   160°E

THE HUMAN POLITY

**A Comparative Introduction
to Political Science**

Fourth Edition

KAY LAWSON
San Francisco State University

Houghton Mifflin Company   Boston   New York

Editor-in-Chief: Jean Woy
Senior Sponsoring Editor: Paul A. Smith
Senior Associate Editor: Melissa Mashburn
Senior Project Editor: Charline Lake
Associate Production/Design Coordinator: Jennifer Meyer
Senior Manufacturing Coordinator: Priscilla J. Bailey
Marketing Associate: Amanda Rappaport

Cover design: Linda Manly Wade, Wade Design
Cover image: Linda Manly Wade

For Trevor Robert Wallace

Printed in the U.S.A.

Library of Congress Catalog Card Number: 96-76922

Student Text ISBN: 0-395-74356-7
Examination Copy ISBN: 0-395-84388-X

123456789-DH-00 99 98 97 96

CONTENTS

11   Justice Under the Law   394

PART V
ALTERNATIVE ARENAS OF GOVERNMENT   433

12   Accessible Government: Local and Provincial Politics   434

13 International Relations 464

14 Regime Change in the Human Polity 506

PREFACE

AS WERE ITS PREDECESSORS, the fourth edition of *The Human Polity* is based on the latest edition of the human polity — the world of interconnected and interdependent governments in which we live. Once again, that world has refused to stand still. Four years ago we could only attempt to describe some of the massive changes begun in 1989, and wonder where they were taking us. Now patterns have begun to emerge: the overwhelming triumph of capitalism, the shift to free elections, the substitution of limited but real and relentless warfare and terrorist activity for our former fear of worldwide cataclysmic holocaust, the rise of religious fundamentalism, the new and conflicting struggles to define the roles of women, the acceleration of the race between responsible environmentalism and planetary meltdown, the growing difficulty of solving our problems within the nation state.

Who could possibly keep up? Yet it is the challenge of political science not only to keep up but to make sense, and *The Human Polity* tries to do both. It continues to be a book about politics and about the study of politics in a world that is increasingly and irreversibly interdependent. The human polity is the polity — the political community — to which we all belong merely by virtue of living together on the globe. At the same time that we proudly give our first loyalties to the separate nation states that lay claim to our citizenship, we also recognize that there are problems we can resolve only in unison with the citizens of other states. The study of politics has thus become the study of the web of life on our planet.

The complexities of political science are an outgrowth and an accompaniment to the increasingly complex scope of politics itself. Complexity is interesting, and does not in itself make something difficult. We can respect the complexity of politics and at the same time write about it clearly, using a familiar vocabulary and explaining new terms in a context that makes their meaning immediately comprehensible and easy to remember. The style of *The Human Polity* is one of informal but respectful dialogue between author and reader. Direct questions are occasionally posed in the text in order to stimulate the students' interest and to prompt them to apply their steadily increasing knowledge of political science to the more familiar experiences of their own lives. Students who take this opportunity to "talk back" to the author will find that as a consequence they are better prepared to enter into class discussions and to recall what they have read. Both normative and practical problems are raised throughout the book, in a manner intended not only to inform but also to encourage students to form their own opinions and make their own recommendations for change.

Features of the Book

The Human Polity offers a full and comprehensive introduction to political science. It describes the nature of the discipline, explains the ways in which political scientists study politics, and offers introductory treatment of all the major topics we normally think of as constituting political science. Chapter 1 considers the meanings of interdependence, the nature of politics and polities, and the methods of political science. Succeeding chapters cover the language of politics, the chief political ideologies, the relationships between politics and economics and between politics and culture, the ways in which individuals can and do act in politics, political groups, political parties, executive leadership, the work of legislatures, executive bureaucracies, the judiciary and systems of law, local and provincial government, international relations, and the present era of post cold war regime change.

The fourth edition is slightly shorter than earlier editions, and the number of chapters has been reduced from sixteen to fourteen. However, all the topics treated in the third edition are discussed in this edition as well. The study of groups now has a chapter of its own (Chapter 7). The study of the media is now found in the chapter on political parties, partly because we cannot understand what is happening to the world's parties without understanding how they have been affected by the communications revolution and partly because the increasing political significance of the media becomes especially apparent as we consider the interaction between these two forces today (Chapter 8). The study of bureaucracy is now back where I always thought it should be: in the chapter on executive power, which is, after all, the power that exercises the closest control over the bureaucrats (Chapter 10). A formerly separate chapter on different ways power is sometimes exercised extraconstitutionally by business, church, military, and other forces has been broken up and its parts have been incorporated as appropriate in other chapters, especially in the chapter on groups. Teachers familiar with — and, I hope, happy with — previous editions need not worry: every topic is still *here* — and more besides.

The *Instructor's Manual with Test Items*, written by W. D. Kay of Northeastern University, provides a chapter outline, a chapter overview, questions for class discussion, and an annotated list of additional readings for each chapter. The test items include essay questions for each chapter and approximately 35 multiple-choice items per chapter. A computerized test generation program containing all the printed test items is also available.

New to the Fourth Edition

Although the same subjects are treated, they are not always treated in exactly the same way. The world does not stop changing, so neither can *The Human Polity*. The chapter on political ideologies now has less to say about the many varieties of socialism and communism, but includes an important new section in which the claims of feminism, ethnic nationalism and religious fundamentalism to stand as separate ideologies are treated. (Hint: only two of the three meet all the criteria). Besides giving important information about each of these three ever more common modes of approaching political realities, this section should help students understand the importance of having a clear workable definition of what we mean by any political concept — in this case, ideology (Chapter 3). The chapter on political economy takes up new global issues as well as updates those treated in earlier editions (Chapter 4). Our study of the reciprocal relationship between politics and culture gives more attention to questions of ethnicity and race than in the past (Chapter 5). The section on how the individual act of voting is transformed into power differently by different electoral systems is clearer and more thorough now (Chapter 6). The examination of the role of interest groups in politics has been brought into better congruity with today's world by looking at wider range of such organizations' activities (Chapter 7). Giving political parties a whole chapter of their own was immensely satisfying to an author who specializes in that subject; incorporating the love-hate relationship between parties and the media taught the expert to look at her own subject with new eyes; avoiding jargonistic specialist talk was the same challenge it always is (Chapter 8). Chapters 9 through 13, always well received in the past, cover the same materials — the only obvious topical change is the above-mentioned combination of the former two chapters on the executive and bureaucracy (Chapter 10).

Chapter 14 gives this edition an entirely new and I think extremely exciting conclusion. The changes initiated in the world in 1989 have now reached the point where preliminary first assessments of the new regimes are possible; "Regime Change and the Human Polity" attempts to make those assessments. The chapter looks first at the criteria for establishing democracy, and expert opinion regarding the possibility and means of doing so. It then considers specific kinds of transitions that have been taking place: from communism to democracy and capitalism (Russia, Eastern and Central Europe); from communism toward capitalism (China); from noncommunist authoritarian rule to democracy (Africa and Latin America). A third section looks at the widely varying impact such change has on certain categories of individuals, such as the newly rich, the newly poor, women, and those of us who live in stable democracies. The chapter concludes by looking at new evidence of the meaning of these changes for three kinds of international activities: international governance, international organization on behalf of specific interests, and international business. The findings are often surprising and dramatic, especially for those who are just beginning to realize how profoundly the human polity shapes the everyday life of every one of us.

As in earlier editions, examples and contemporary scholarship are used to highlight important points and clarify difficult concepts. Even more than in earlier editions, these examples and scholarly references have been brought up to date — a text that will carry us from one millennium to the next cannot draw its materials from a distant past. The fourth edition **is** up to date (a simple claim which required more hours of hard work than you want to know, or my assistants and I want to remember). As before, a few of the examples are personal, drawing from my own experience or asking the students to reflect on their own, as a way of helping readers realize the relevance of topics and issues they might otherwise regard as remote or arcane.

Acknowledgments

This book is itself always the product of interdependence. I have leaned often and with profit on the work of student assistants, who, in exchange for remuneration far from equal to their labors, helped me get the books I needed from libraries, find many of the examples, and work up several of the charts and tables. For this new edition, I have had the benefit of working once again with Paul Anderson, who provided such invaluable help on the third edition and did no less for the fourth, as well as with Tina Nasseri, Dana Polk, and Lori Smersfelt, all of whom worked very hard and often under very heavy pressure. As in previous editions, they and I could draw on the earlier excellent work of former assistants: Janet Ciarico, Andrea Rommële, Ann Loepfer and Regan Fordyce for the third edition; Marisa Kelly for the second edition; and Andrea Bonime, Robin Davis, Mark Dorfman, Paula Fleming, Lynne Laidlaw, Adrienne Levey, James McGuire, Alan Vlautin, and Cynthia Witman for the first.

It is also a pleasure to thank the following reviewers, whose thoughtful comments and careful critiques have helped to guide the manuscript's development:

Bruce Berg, Fordham University
Chris Hamilton, Western Kentucky University
Ted G. Jelen, Illinois Benedictine College
Brian Loveman, San Diego State University
Daniel E. Ponder, University of Colorado at Colorado Springs
David E. Schmitt, Northeastern University
Jocelyn D. Shadforth, University of Louisville
Charles E. Strikwerda, Calvin College

Also as before, this edition owes a great deal to the support of family and friends. To the former I have been pleased beyond measure to welcome the addition of Trevor Robert Wallace, to whom this edition is so very happily dedicated. Is there any better support for any intellectual activity than the sheer delight of turning it off from time to time and chatting cheerfully with a beloved child? Is there any better way of keeping faith in the capacity of the human polity to overcome its distressing woes than to welcome one of its brand new members into your arms?

Finally, as always, I willingly take responsibility for the book's faults but insist on my share of any praise for its merits. I hope the effort that I and others have given to making this new edition a lively and interesting introduction to the ever-changing world of politics and political science will seem well worthwhile, especially to the students for whom *The Human Polity* is *their* introduction to political science.

                                                                      Kay Lawson

Thinking About Politics

1 Politics and the Human Polity

THE MEANING OF THE HUMAN POLITY
The Challenge of Interdependence
The Task at Hand

THE SCOPE OF POLITICS

THE SCOPE OF POLITICAL SCIENCE
The Puzzle of Political Science
Six Approaches to the Study of Political Puzzles
    Studying Political Behavior
    Studying Political Structures and Functions
    Studying Political Phenomena
    Studying Political Ideas
    Studying Political Documents
    Studying the Political Future
Normative versus Empirical Political Puzzles

SUMMARY AND CONCLUSION

TODAY THE WORLD OF nations is more interdependent than ever. Increasingly, our lives and welfare depend on developments beyond our nation's borders, however well secured those borders may be and however strong the social and economic systems within those borders. The need to preserve and replenish the limited resources of our planet while meeting the massive energy demands of advanced civilization, and the need to develop and expand this civilization while protecting it from the destructive havoc our own technology has made possible, are needs we can meet only collectively and cooperatively. We can no longer comfortably assume that "we" means "we Americans" or "we Swiss" or "we Japanese" when such matters are to be resolved. More and more often, "we" means "we humans," and "our" problems, resources, and efforts are those of the species, not of any single nation state. We live in the human polity.

THE MEANING OF THE HUMAN POLITY

What is the human polity? *Polity* is a word with several meanings. It can mean a state or any society that has an organized government. More generally, it refers to a "body politic" — that is, any group of persons who have some form of political relationship with one another. The *human polity* is a polity in the second sense. It includes all the people presently living on the planet who have become so interdependent that they now constitute a body politic.

However, the *human polity* is made up of separate polities in the first sense of the word, too — individual nation-states. It is to these states that most people pledge their loyalty. For this reason, the capacity of human beings to interact effectively across national boundaries depends very much on what goes on inside those boundaries. If the citizens of individual polities are able to address their internal problems efficiently, equitably, and cooperatively, then they will be able to address the problems that extend into the international arena. On the other hand, citizens of individual polities that suffer from severe internal conflict and dissent, inequitable distribution of inadequate national resources, inappropriate or outmoded political institutions, and/or exploitative intervention by other polities in their own affairs must inevitably find it difficult to function effectively in the world at large.

Unfortunately, there is no nation in the world that does not suffer from one or more of these problems, a fact that influences the nature of the human polity in which we all must live. To understand that larger polity, we must therefore, learn to recognize and understand these problems as they manifest themselves in our own nation, in other nations, and in international relations. Once we have a better understanding of the politics and government of individual nation-states, we will be better able to deal with the complexities produced by the increasing global interdependence of those separate polities.

It may seem obvious that in any enterprise, knowledge of the parts (individual nation-states and their political components) is essential to an understanding of the whole (the human polity) and that the whole will inevitably be greater than the mere sum of all the parts. However, it is not necessarily obvious that increasing interdependence produces complexities. Let us take a closer look at that association.

The Challenge of Interdependence

The word *complexities* was chosen carefully. Although interdependence will increasingly bind all states together and make their individual security, especially their economic fortunes, dependent on one another, this increased interdependence does not necessarily make our problems more *difficult.*[1] In fact, the more interdependent we become, the more we recognize our shared interests and our need to work together to meet those interests. Still, the very conditions that make it imperative for us to cooperate — and thus make it easier to do so — tend to make that work considerably more complex.

Today, economic change tends to be global in scope. Changing interest rates, growth rates, and rates of unemployment and inflation in one nation mean related changes in many other nations as well. If the international market goes into a decline (as it did beginning with the oil crisis of 1973), almost every nation is affected. If the stock market of a major nation suffers a sudden drop, as it did in the United States in October 1987 and in Japan in April 1992, all other major markets are likely to respond, recognizing that the affected nation may now buy fewer exports, invest less abroad, and possibly be less competitive in the international market as smaller manufacturers are squeezed out by more conservative banking practices. If the economic system of a superpower ceases to function with at least minimal success (as was the case in the former Soviet Union in 1989), a chain reaction of change can result extending far beyond its borders, as other nations consider the prospects for their own markets and political stability and react accordingly. The imminent failure of a trading partner can provoke the stronger partner to take drastic steps to prop up an economy other than its own. When failing investor confidence sent the currency of Mexico into a free fall in early 1995, the Clinton administration and the U.S. Congress were quick to take remedial action, firmly in agreement that "if Mexico's economic growth slows or stops because of this crisis, the impact on trade, on immigration and the whole strategy of spreading free trade in the region could be enormous."[2]

In the past, it might have been possible for stronger nations to retreat to isolationist policies when the economies of other nations were in danger, and even today such ideas have their appeal. But stronger nations need the income they receive from exports and from overseas investment. They also need conditions for peaceful trade, a state of affairs not likely to be fostered by protectionist policies: "If goods cannot cross borders, soldiers will" goes the cliché, and Renato Ruggiero of the World Trade Organization argues further, "Protectionism is a road that leads to economic nationalism [which] can easily transform itself into political nationalism."[3] Leonard Silk carries the argument to its logical conclusion in our increasingly interdependent world: "Protectionism and an aggressive nationalism . . . as the world has learned over and over, endanger both peace and prosperity."[4]

The complexities produced by global interdependence are particularly apparent in the species' most fundamental quest: the maintenance of our planet as an environment fit for human habitation. In this domain, we have been slow to recognize not only that solutions must depend on international cooperation, but even that we have a problem, and one of the most serious dimensions. As early as 1962, Rachel Carson was attracting attention with her book *Silent Spring*, a study of the damage done by the indiscriminate use of pesticides, and her work was preceded and followed by many others.[5] More and more authors have attempted to call our attention to the pressures of our ever-increasing global population, the blindly selfish use of agricultural and industrial methods that destroy and/or pollute as they produce, the decline of our natural resource base, and our steadfast

insistence on pursuing the objects of individual and national greed —
sometimes through the use of weapons that do even more damage to the
earth than to our enemies. All these factors place our collective home in
greater danger than any natural disaster is ever likely to do.[6]

The message has been loud and clear for over thirty years, and often the
solutions that must be adopted are as unambiguous as the problems they
address. But these problems cannot be solved by single individuals, or even
by single nations. Motivated individuals can recycle and avoid environ-
mentally destructive behavior and nations can pass laws and establish agencies, but finally a worldwide effort of staggering dimensions is required. It
is not merely that the task of saving the planet is complex and expensive;
the task also poses extremely difficult social and political problems on an
international scale. To illustrate this dilemma, let us look at our need for fuel.

The fuel problem is in fact made up of many different problems. One
problem is that energy demand is constantly growing, particularly in developing nations. The global forecast is that the demand for all forms of
fuel (oil, gas, coal, nuclear, and "other") will increase at an average rate of
2.3 percent between now and 2010. A second problem is that the nations
likely to experience the greatest increase in the need for energy are developing nations (their needs are projected at a 4.3% annual growth rate for
the same period of time), but these are the very nations likely to have the
greatest difficulty paying for the fuel they need (and if they do not get it,
they will not be "developing"; they will be simply "poor"). A third and
related problem is that in the past many of the energy needs of developing
nations were met by noncommercial means (such as the use of animals for
transportation and of gathered fuels for domestic cooking and heating),
but that now, as populations move to the cities and traditional energy
sources are becoming exhausted or impractical, the demand for commercial fuels in nations with large populations like China and India is steadily
growing. The fourth problem is that many of the standard sources of commercial energy, such as hydroelectric power, petroleum and natural gas,
will have been developed to capacity by the mid-twenty-first century.
There will be no way to meet the rising need by increasing use of available
sources of these forms of fuel, which in turn will force greater reliance on
coal and nuclear fission energy. A fifth problem, and the one that makes
this complex case so appropriate to consider here, is that commercial fossil
fuel development and consumption is having a massive negative impact on
the habitability of our planet. Acid rain and other forms of air and water
pollution, radiation emissions caused by accidents in nuclear energy plants
and the faulty disposal of hazardous waste, and dangerous changes in climate resulting from the release of excessive carbon dioxide into the atmosphere are only a few of the environmental disasters caused by the frantic
global rush to energy self-sufficiency.

All of these interrelated problems are compounded because no single
nation, acting alone, can possibly solve them all, even for itself. With ex-

When political planning for the environment goes awry, private efforts are unlikely to suffice. Here Ethiopians seek to dig a well in a dry river bed after the government failed to respond to a long drought. (© Chris Steele — Perkins/Magnum)

pensive environmental controls in place, self-sufficiency in energy may or may not be possible for one nation alone, but even the most fortunate and responsible of nations is affected by the damage done to the global atmosphere by other nations that cannot or will not follow suit. Daniel A. Dreyfus and Ann B. Ashby say it as well as any. They insist that a "cavalier approach" to global energy consumption is no longer viable:

> In terms of the environmental impacts of energy use . . . there is no distinction among the economic or political persuasions of the users. A ton of coal burned in China . . . has the same physical consequences as one burned in the United States. . . . No single action or nation can greatly influence the energy outlook. Rather, a global effort must take advantage of numerous opportunities to make small progress wherever they occur. . . . An unprecedented degree of international cooperation will be required to apply the scarce available resources to the most promising opportunities without regard to political boundaries.[7]

Of course, there are many other examples of interdependence. Some of its effects constitute what can only be termed "negative interdependence." Military expenditures may grow to unreasonable proportions of national budgets in a world tangled in a web of defensive pacts: Iraq spent 27.4 percent of its gross national product on military expenditures in 1990, and in that year just prior to the outbreak of the Gulf War every other Middle

Eastern nation also spent well above the global mean of 3.8 percent (Israel spent 13%, Jordan 12.2%, Qatar 12.5%, Oman 17.9%, Saudi Arabia 14%, Syria 13.5%, and Yemen 14.9%).[8] Or home industries may suffer when economic treaties give too favored a status to foreign competitors. In other cases, one nation may accrue benefits while the other realizes only costs; the interdependence relationship is asymmetrical.

At other times, the effect of interdependence may be strongly positive, as when two or more nations recognize their mutual need for a period of peaceful coexistence in order to restore economies damaged by war. The present relatively good relations between France and Germany grew out of such a recognition after World War II, and today the French remain particularly aware that German markets and German military security are crucial to France's own prosperity and safety.[9]

In any case, it is important, as Robert Keohane and Joseph Nye remind us, not to succumb to "interdependence rhetoric" while recognizing that nearly every problem we attempt to solve, and nearly every action we endeavor to promote, forces us to consider, sooner or later, the effects our plans will have on those beyond our borders — and the effects their responses will have on us and other peoples.[10]

These effects may be very great indeed, and there is nothing to guarantee that overall the net results will be positive. R. J. Barry Jones' earlier concern that the growth of interdependence may serve to "create such frictions, sensitivities and worrying vulnerabilities as to generate disharmony and potential conflict" often seems to be proving only too well founded. It is equally hard to disagree with Terry L. Beibel's observation that the factors creating interdependence are also making "all states' borders highly permeable and their peoples vulnerable, [as well as] drastically reducing the ability of governments to solve problems at home."[11]

Indeed, there are only too many signs of our globally inadequate response to the challenges posed by this vast and amazing transformation in the nature of the world we must live in. Continued and often genocidal warfare, brutal acts of terrorism, growing unemployment, poverty, and homelessness in the world at large along with a seemingly uncontrollable international drug trade are only some of the sad signs of our inability, so far, to take back positive control of our collective destinies. Yet if we can, however slowly and painfully, learn to accept the complexity of the world we now live in, and the consequent necessity of moving more carefully and compassionately to pursue the goals we cannot help sharing across the planet, our chances for success are great. We have the technical capacity to acquire the information we need to put all the resources of our planet and our human intelligence to work for our collective good.

Will we ever decide to do exactly that? What choice will we humans make? Will we cast aside our responsibilities as citizens in the human polity, forget the quest for answers as soon as we see that they will not be easily or selfishly found, and allow those we cannot hold accountable to squander our goods and destroy our future? Or will we organize our resources — natural and intellectual — and establish democratic, equitable, and efficient control of our shared life on this planet?

The Task at Hand   You will not find the answers to these questions in this book. What you will find is an introduction to a field of study, political science, that is hard at work on the puzzles these questions pose. *The Human Polity* introduces you to all of political science, and invites you to pay particular attention to the way these questions of interdependence arise in the study of politics. To accomplish this task, in Part I we begin by looking first at the scope of politics and then at the scope of political science itself. We will consider the means political scientists have developed (and are constantly improving) to organize the study of questions like those we have been talking about, the conceptual language they employ to clarify the intricacies of these matters, and the variety of ideological perspectives they and others use to evaluate the world of politics.

With these tools in hand, political scientists have begun to find some answers to the questions that intrigue us all and that must be answered if we are to understand the nature of the human polity and its prospects for the future. For example, they know something about the impact of social relationships and economic resources on the human condition and on the political choices that citizens make in endeavoring to improve that condition. They know how to identify popular opinions on an issue, how individual opinions sometimes coalesce into "public opinion," and how citizens around the world participate (or do not participate) in their nations' politics and governments, either individually or via political organizations. Political scientists have investigated the constitutional structures and decision-making processes of nearly every existent government and can speak with some authority on questions of political leadership, the legislative functions of government, the bureaucratic organization of different states, and the judicial process. Political scientists have also studied arenas of government other than the nation-state, from local government bodies to international organizations to those unofficial agencies — such as multinational corporations and religious institutions — that sometimes take a powerful yet unacknowledged part in the work of governing nations.

Studying human interaction is not like studying the physical laws of the universe. There are no fixed principles we can use to predict with certainty how human beings will interact in the future. We can, however, identify some of the more common kinds of change in human relationships over time and consider what these changes may mean for the human polity. And we can remember at all times that our problems are seldom merely national in scope. As the example of fuel made clear, the interdependence of nations is profound, yet at the same time there are national and natural forces at work that shape our lives regardless of the policies of other nations. The human polity cannot be understood only in terms of international interdependence; neither can it be understood without recognizing the impact of such interdependence, an effort we will make throughout this book.

We turn now to the first of our tasks, an exploration of the scope of politics in the human polity.

THE SCOPE OF POLITICS

> The first civilizations arose in the fertile alluvial basins of the major rivers that water the otherwise arid plains of southern Asia, draining from the mountain fringes where agriculture first began. These more complex societies were the natural outcome of the increasing organization needed to make use of these problematic, but potentially highly fertile, lowland environments. . . . These societies had many features in common: the development of cities, writing, large public buildings, and the political apparatus of the modern state. They all stemmed from the need to organize local production and long-distance trade.[12]

Around the year 3,500 B.C.E., human beings, attracted by the fertility of lands enriched by the periodic floodwaters of the Euphrates and Tigris rivers, began to settle in large numbers in the area now referred to as the Middle East. To do so, they had to solve two problems. They had to control the supply of water to avoid both flood and drought, and they had to maintain a supply of raw materials that were not abundant in the area, especially metals and wood. By this stage of human evolution, the necessary technological expertise existed: men and women knew how to irrigate and how to transport materials. But now these activities had to be carried out over a vast area. The work of thousands had to be planned, directed, and coordinated. It was time to get better organized. It was time to invent the state.

The earliest states were small — so small they are usually referred to as **city-states**, small polities seldom larger in population or area than a medium-sized city of today. Over the centuries, the continued quest for material abundance and political power led to the emergence of larger polities, such as empires, composed of numerous smaller polities that maintained their own identities but were subjugated to a larger power, and, eventually, **nation-states**, in which the inhabitants of numerous subunits now recognized and accepted a common citizenship.

About 5,500 years after the first small city-state was formed, in the year a new calendar numbered 1945, the members of many of these nation-states found themselves emerging from the most devastating war ever waged on the planet. By then, the technology of battle had evolved to the point where a single weapon could lay waste to vast areas, killing and maiming thousands with one blow. Codes of behavior had been cast aside, and whole peoples had been threatened with torture and extinction. At this stage of human evolution, men and women had begun to acquire some rudimentary knowledge of how to devise and instill codes of behavior that would ensure peaceful coexistence among nations. The need to apply this knowledge was more desperate than ever before, and the penalty for failure had become unthinkably cruel. It was time to get better organized. It was time to establish an international organization that every nation in the world would wish to join.

Politics is a means of organizing collective human activity. The city-state, the empire, the nation-state, and the United Nations are four of the more complex forms of that kind of organization. But politics has been with us since before the first city-state was formed. It has been practiced ever since human beings began living and working together. Decisions had to be made about how to build shelters, how to secure food, and how to ward off predators. Making those important collective decisions, and resolving the conflicting demands about how they should be made, was humanity's first venture into the difficult art and science of politics.

Even today, politics is part and parcel of nearly all human interactions. In daily life, we use the word to refer to almost any collective decision-making process, especially if there is a hint of struggle and controversy over "who gets what, when, how." One common definition sees politics as simply the allocation of scarce resources, using the word *scarce* to mean "not unlimited."[13] Since most resources are limited in some fashion, such a definition covers many ordinary activities remote from the realm of government and law. When you start a new job, you may find yourself involved in "office politics" about who performs particular tasks, who gets certain supplies or accommodations, and above all, who makes the most money. When you try to persuade your instructor to postpone the date of an examination (worrying about the allocation of your time and the eventual allocation of good grades), you may say you "are doing a little politicking." But in the study of political science, the word usually has a more restricted meaning. For a political scientist, **politics** means seeking and using the power of the state to make allocations of scarce resources throughout a given polity.

In this book we will use that more restricted meaning of the term — a meaning that still covers a very wide range of human activities. Political decisions govern almost everything we do and everything done to us. The requirement that drops be put in the newborn baby's eyes to protect her or him from venereal disease stems from a political decision, as does the requirement that bodies be buried in containers made of specified materials. Between the cradle and the grave, we live our lives in the midst of politics. The British baby swallows a formula of cow's milk and vitamins because the European Community allows such products to be sold, although marketing is seriously restricted; the baby in Papua, New Guinea does not because the government of her nation has made their sale illegal out of

Population control in Indonesia. Politics can influence every aspect of our lives. Here a group of young men are being given a lesson in family planning in the village of Sala. (UPI/Corbis-Bettman)

concern that facilities and training will be inadequate to keep such products healthful.[14]

And so it goes through life. It is government policy that ensures that the female child in Canada will routinely enroll in elementary school along with her male peers, whereas her counterpart in most Third World nations has only about a 50 percent chance of getting an education.[15] Marriages are not legal in Mauritania without a religious ceremony; in France they are not legal without the endorsement of the civil authorities.[16] The government pays married couples to produce babies in Belgium (because that country is still trying to recover from the population losses suffered in two world wars), while the government of China (population over 1 billion) reduces by 15 percent the salary of any couple having more than a single child.[17] Statutory retirement age is 65 for both men and women in Sweden, 60 for men and 58 for women in Japan, and 55 for men and 50 for women in Turkey.[18]

We are, in short, a most political species. Furthermore, we are steadily becoming *more* political. One of the most interesting questions in the study of politics is not who has power, but simply how much power there is.[19]

We live in an era in which political power is constantly expanding as more and more people (nearly 5 billion) lead more and more complex lives, and as these lives require some kind of political order if minimal standards of well-being are to be achieved and maintained.[20]

In meeting this constantly growing need for political order, we have gradually accumulated some mastery of the skills of political organization — more than is sometimes realized. A familiar cliché suggests that we have been much more successful at learning to manipulate the physical properties of our environment than in dealing with the social attributes of humankind: "We can put a man on the moon but we cannot stop the exploitation of one man by another." However, not all clichés bear close inspection, and this is one that does not stand up well to careful scrutiny. When we consider how difficult the task, and how much we actually have achieved, we may find reason to take some pride in our accomplishments to date in coping with the social problems of the human polity, however much remains to be done.

Of course, we obviously still have a very long way to go in developing our skills of interaction and, equally important, in learning to apply these skills to our collective betterment — just as we still have much to learn in our efforts to master the physical environment for our common good. Amassing political power in itself solves nothing, for it can be (and often is) used against the needs and wishes of the majority of humankind. It is all too true that we have not yet learned how to eliminate the exploitation of one person by another. Nevertheless, it is important to see that we have come a long way since our first tentative efforts in cooperative social life about 5,500 years ago. Although it may not always seem to be the case, the fact that we now have a better understanding of how to acquire and use the resources that *produce* political power is obviously a key step in the task of learning to use that power well.

It is a task that does not necessarily get easier as we go along. Wherever we live and work, we do so in an increasingly complex world. If you are reading inside a building, look up from this book and count the different human-made objects in your range of vision. Chances are you did not finish the chore; it would take too long. Consider the processes of producing and distributing these goods, consider the uses such items are put to all over the globe; consider the debates, the problems, the open hostilities that have developed among peoples over the exchange of material goods. Then think of the abundance of styles and practices we have developed in other aspects of our daily lives — in religion, social customs, language usage, ethnic identities — and think of the disputes and rivalries these have produced. The rich variety of the human experience is exciting, challenging, and fascinating. It also constantly produces conflicts that political processes can help resolve.

Thus, we live in an era when the temptation to seek political solutions for our difficult problems is nearly irresistible. Our lives are not becoming more simple, and the need to coordinate our activities in some harmonious fashion is not growing less urgent. The more we rely on political processes to accomplish these ends, the more the political sphere will grow. Political power is like muscle power. Give it work to do, and it will grow larger and stronger.

THE SCOPE OF POLITICAL SCIENCE

Political science is the study of politics. This means the work of political science is to seek the answers to a number of important questions: What attitudes and values produce political conflict and dissent? What political organizations are active in the struggle to achieve political consensus? What is the nature of the socioeconomic relationships inside a polity? How adequate are resources to meet needs, how equitably are resources distributed, and how are material interests pursued, protected, or changed by the course of public policy? What are the constitutional structures and the decision-making procedures of each nation, and how well suited are they to that nation's needs? What internal structures and procedures exist for the debate and resolution of problems with other nations? What assistance is available from international agencies and the international community at large?

Political science does not have all the answers to these questions, but it does have some, and, what is more important, it has the means of finding others. Becoming a political scientist means joining a community of people who work on just these sorts of questions.

Like politics itself, the work of political science has developed over the centuries, expanding and subdividing. Scholars, critics, playwrights, correspondents, and poets have been observing and commenting on political processes since pen was first put to paper (or stylus to tablet). Confucius wrote on moral and ethical issues relevant to the concept of authority as early as 500 B.C.E. In 450 B.C.E., Herodotus' history of the Persian Wars included his reflections on the issue of tyranny versus the rule of law, and Aristophanes wrote *Lysistrata*, an antiwar play, in 412 B.C.E.

Over the years the focus of political studies has changed and expanded. The subfields of political science have multiplied accordingly. To our original study of political philosophy (now more commonly termed *political theory*) we have added, one by one, constitutional law, public administration, international relations, American government, comparative government (by which we really mean the study of foreign governments), political behavior (the study of political attitudes as well as political acts), political economy, political organizations, and urban politics. In addition, some of us devote most of our time to studying and developing the methodology of political science, while others are interested in such newer, less well-established areas

'I'm part of a Rapid
Bewilderment Force - I fail
to understand events as soon
as they've happened'

(Matt/The Telegraph, London/Rothco)

of study as *biopolitics* (the study of how the physical characteristics and conditions of political actors may sometimes influence their behavior).

The Puzzles of Political Science

How do political scientists do their work? They often begin with very ordinary activities: They read what other people have to say, they follow current events, they note what appear to them to be certain interesting tendencies, they wonder why such things are happening, and they wonder what will happen next. What makes a political scientist different, however, is the capacity and the will to make systematic inquiries into a political puzzle. The political scientist does not simply say, "Hmm, I see by the paper that our president has vowed to save the American worker from the competition of cheap foreign imports while at the same time protecting the principle of free trade. That's a good trick," and turn the page. The political scientist tries to solve the puzzle such a statement presents.

But what is that puzzle? When we stop to think about it, this statement, like almost every statement about politics, is replete with puzzles. Think about it for a moment. An American president promises to save American workers while encouraging the freedom of international trade that threatens the livelihood of many of them. What do you think is puzzling about that promise? (Write your answer.) Does it seem to you that what you just wrote is the only possible answer? In fact, we all differ in how we perceive political reality, and thus in how we formulate the puzzles it poses. Just consider some of the possibilities:

1. What puzzles me is what endangered workers think about this announcement. Did this president win the steelworkers' vote? Is he likely to do so again?
2. What puzzles me is how the *president* can do anything to save jobs. Isn't it the work of the legislature to make the laws and of the president to carry them out?
3. What puzzles me is why the president suddenly made this nod to the protectionists. He has always been strongly committed to free trade. Is it because an election is coming up, or has he decided the effects of foreign competition are so harsh they require a serious change of direction?
4. What puzzles me is the perennial conflict between policies that help, in the short term, to solve a national problem, and long-term policies that seem necessary if we are ever going to have a human polity that is economically stable and at least minimally responsive to the needs of human beings everywhere. Must we always sacrifice the needy of another nation to care for the needy at home?
5. What I don't understand is how the president can act as if all the trade treaties we have made with various nations can simply be set aside at will. Are our agreements no longer worth the paper they are written on?
6. What puzzles me is what the impact of protectionism — if that is the policy we really adopt — is going to be on those nations whose economies depend on cheap exports to the United States. Will our policies destabilize those economies, and, as a consequence, those polities? Will there be other effects in international relations stemming from these changes?

As you can see, how we formulate our puzzles makes a big difference in the questions we ask and in the work we need to do to find answers to them. Just as not all political scientists study the same subfield, so not all of them puzzle about political phenomena in the same way. Some kinds of questions interest you, other kinds interest me, and across the room our good friend Bob is probably thinking about this same problem in some entirely different way — or simply doesn't care at all.

How we formulate the problems we wish to study as political scientists also has some relationship to the subfields that interest us. Wondering about how workers will react at the polls or about whether or not policy statements are governed by upcoming elections are questions about political behavior as well as about American government. Those interested in constitutional law might worry about presidential interference in the legislative domain, and so might political scientists whose studies are concentrated in American government or public administration. The philosophical tone of the fourth puzzle suggests the work of political theorists, but political economists might want to claim this puzzle as their own since it stresses the relationship between politics and economics, whereas those interested in comparative politics will appreciate the focus here and in puzzle 6 on the internal affairs of other nations. Arguing for the validity of international treaties suggests an interest in international affairs, as does considering the impact of the president's decision on the welfare of foreign states.

Six Approaches to the Study of Political Puzzles

The way we puzzle over political phenomena does more than reveal which subfields of political science are likely to interest us most. It is also strongly related to our method of inquiry and the approach we take in our quest for an answer. There are six main approaches to the study of politics: (1) behavioral, (2) structural-functional, (3) phenomenological, (4) philosophical, (5) documentary, and (6) predictive. Each of the preceding six puzzles is related to one of these approaches.

Studying Political Behavior   "What puzzles me is what endangered workers think about this announcement." The **behavioral approach** to politics means focusing on how individuals act politically and seeking explanations for that behavior within those individuals. Behavioralists are not especially interested in what the rules say or what philosophers recommend about political action. They want to know what human beings really do when they act politically — that is, when they discuss politics, vote, contact government officials, demonstrate, riot, or otherwise act out their political convictions.

Once political scientists have what seems to them to be reliable evidence about the facts of political behavior, they want to know what motivated that behavior. What does the actor feel, believe, or think about politics that caused him or her to act in that particular way? Sometimes the behavioralist carries the inquiry another step: What factors seem to be associated with having those particular feelings, beliefs, and opinions? Does growing up in a certain kind of home or having a certain kind of job influence what kind of a political actor a person will be?

How can this kind of information be gathered? A key method for the behaviorialist is survey research — that is, research that studies a large number of individuals, finding out, by asking them, about their political behavior (voting, joining groups, writing letters, and so on). Such research permits the acquisition of a great many answers, often in simple, uniform format (*yes, no, often, one, two . . . five*), and these answers may in turn be subjected to complex statistical analysis, permitting the researcher to draw far-reaching conclusions about political behavior and its causes with considerable confidence. In the United States we know, for example, not only the characteristics most commonly associated with voting but also what other kinds of political participation voters engage in, how much more likely they are to do so than nonvoters, and what difference various kinds of voter registration arrangements are likely to make in voter turnout.[21] Such knowledge does not always tell us what to do next — we have not yet been able to increase the number of people who vote in the United States — but it does give us an important part of the factual base we need.

The behavioral approach is appropriate when the puzzle at hand requires and permits the accumulation of information about human behavior and its motives. It helps if that data can be gathered in discrete but uniform bits, permitting statistical analysis. The study of the personality of a single political actor, however, may be as important — and is every bit as "behavioral" — as the study of hundreds of voters.

Studying Political Structures and Functions   "Isn't it the work of the legislature to make the laws and of the president to carry them out?" When political scientists adopt the **structural-functional approach**, they focus on the important political roles established in a society, what functions they perform, and how the carrying out of these roles influences the quality of life.

Structural-functionalism is an approach that was first developed by anthropologists looking for ways to free themselves from Western biases when studying non-Western cultures. It soon became clear to such scholars that different structures might well perform different functions in different societies. For example, religious institutions might have the function of conducting seasonal ceremonies to ensure that planting and harvesting are done at the appropriate times of the year as well as the functions of setting codes of interpersonal behavior and guiding believers to presumed eternal happiness. Even where familiar political structures seem to be missing, closer observation might reveal that very familiar functions are still being performed, although through other structures. For example, there may be nothing that calls itself a political party, but when the members of the club Mr. X belongs to are busily asking everyone to vote for him, while those in the club Ms. Y belongs to are equally active on her behalf, then at least one of the key functions of parties — campaigning on behalf of chosen candidates — is not neglected.

The structural-functional approach helps us focus on what is really happening. It tells us to look at structures objectively: What are their role occupants really doing? It reminds us that certain functions are probably being performed even when persons with positions inside the structures normally responsible for them are not doing the job: Someone is creating political issues, someone is choosing the leaders, someone is making rules for society, someone is carrying them out, someone is deciding disputes arising under those rules. Who is doing what, in what office or role, and with what effect?

Structural-functionalists are sometimes accused of finding functions for every structure that exists and thereby implicitly defending that structure, no matter how unfortunate its effects. Where others might study the Spanish Inquisition as an example of religious intolerance, for example, the functionalist might consider it an interesting illustration of how religious bodies can take over the government functions of making and carrying out the laws and settling disputes. But this does not mean the functionalist *approves* of the takeover. Understanding how particular structures perform essential functions is obviously important, regardless of our opinion of their worth. Furthermore, if in fact we strongly disapprove of what is being done by persons within a particular structure, knowing what they offer to those who support them (i.e., what functions they fulfill) is essential before we offer our recommendations for replacing the structure within which they work. Practicing structural-functionalists may have a bias (or may not), but the method itself seems reasonably neutral.

A further testimony to the usefulness of this mode of analysis is the rapid growth of a "new" subfield in political science, known as the "new institutionalism." As we will see in Chapter 2, *institutions* are *structures*. In political science as in botany, a rose by any other name sometimes does smell sweeter, whatever William Shakespeare may have had to say on the subject.[22]

Studying Political Phenomena   "What puzzles me is why the president suddenly gave this nod to the protectionists. He has always been strongly committed to free trade." One criticism often leveled at the two approaches we have considered so far is that they are not useful for considering political change. Behavioralists rely on opinion polls that may be useless two days after they are taken. How many Soviet citizens do you suppose felt exactly the same about the likelihood of their nation making a peaceful change to a capitalistic market system before, during, and after the attempted coup d'état by old guard communists in 1991? The structural-functionalist determination that a structure does or does not perform a particular function may be equally shortsighted. The role of the Guinean Confederation Générale du Travail, an early trade union in what later became the west African nation of Guinea, changed with dramatic speed when that union staged the first successful strike by black workers in west Africa. Shortly thereafter, the trade union became the nation's leading political party.[23] In such cases, goes the critique, what is missing is any allowance for change. An approach to politics that does not find a way to take into account the inevitability of change can never get more than a fleeting hold on the slippery facts of political reality.

The **phenomenological approach** to the study of politics does not suffer from the same problem. It begins with an interest in change. The question this approach asks first and foremost is: What are the causes of a significant change in a political system? Specifically, what are the events (the *phenomena*) that led up to that change, and which of these were significant in producing that change?

As the preceding discussion suggests, the political scientist gives a broad interpretation to what constitutes a political phenomenon. For the political scientist, a political phenomenon is any event that affects the right to allocate scarce resources. It may be one brief happening, or it may be the general consequence or outcome of a series of interrelated political acts. Nearly everyone would agree that the American Revolution was a political phenomenon, but it might take a political scientist to see the development of commercial wealth in the United States early in the nineteenth century as a political phenomenon, one that forced significant changes in the authoritative allocation of resources as the people who acquired such wealth successfully insisted on their right to share political power and as the right to vote ceased to depend exclusively on the ownership of land.

Note that in the effort to find the roots of major change, the student of phenomena inevitably asks and answers numerous questions that could properly be considered the work of the behavioralist and the structural-functionalist. What sets this approach apart is its commitment to the study of structures, functions, behavior, and events *over time*.

Studying Political Ideas   "Must we always sacrifice the needy of another nation to care for the needy at home?" The **philosophical approach** to the study of politics focuses on the meanings of political life. Like the behavioralist approach, this mode of study is closely associated with a single subfield of political science, in this case *political theory* (so-called even though theory is in fact used in every subfield of the discipline). Typically, the political theorist is interested in general questions relevant to politics. What are the limits on the exercise of political power, if any? What are the various meanings of *representation* in the political arena? Can the apparent conflict between economically sound versus humanely caring public policy ever be resolved?

All such questions have specific applications. When we argue about whether any conditions exist under which investigative agencies like the FBI should be allowed to tap private telephones, we are arguing about the limits that should be imposed on political power. If we are angered when one of our senators votes his or her conscience, even though that vote is contrary to known popular opinion in our state, we are expressing an opinion about the meaning we prefer to see given the concept of representation in the political arena. The controversy over whether or not the American public debt can be reduced while maintaining programs for social welfare reflects the eternal conflict between good budget management and social responsibility in the making of public policy.

The political philosopher seldom makes more than passing reference, however, to specific problems illustrative of the more general question under consideration. The emphasis in this approach to the study of politics is on examining the work of other philosophers who have grappled in a useful — or at least an interesting — way with the topic at hand and then endeavoring to deduce one's own logical conclusions. Sometimes this form of study involves simply allowing the comments of accepted classical authors, carefully selected, to make the desired point. In other cases, political scientists using this approach make their own arguments, backed up by authoritative citations. Sometimes the theorist's chief object is to offer a new interpretation of a classic text. In other cases, the object is to draw together the comments of several political philosophers on a particular matter of interest to the political scientist.

Because they place so much emphasis on political ideas — their own and others' — political philosophers are often criticized for having too little awareness of the real world, for worrying too much about what should be and too little about what is. But, in fact, all political scientists have values that guide the work they do. The political philosopher differs in placing greater emphasis on general ideas and values and in keeping alive the arguments for and against their application.

Studying Political Documents   "What I don't understand is how the president can act as if all the trade treaties we have made with various nations can simply be set aside at will." The art and practice of reading **political documents**, from constitutions to campaign speeches, is one of the oldest forms of political science — and currently one of the least appreciated. Political scientists have learned the hard way that documents cannot always be trusted as guides to political practice. Constitutional and statutory law, treaties, party statutes and platforms, leaders' speeches and memoirs, records of legislative proceedings, authorized biographies, judicial decisions, and newspaper accounts of political happenings are among the forms of the written word that political scientists have discovered they must approach with caution. They offer rich lodes of information about politicians' intent and officeholders' official commitments, but often only fragmentary evidence of motivation and practice, and they are sometimes replete with self-serving distortions of the truth.

Even a constitution, the "highest law of the land," is not always to be trusted as an infallible guide to reality. No constitution did a better job, on paper, of protecting democratic principles than did that of the Union of Soviet Socialist Republics (USSR), yet nothing in that constitution could effectively block Joseph Stalin from transforming the Soviet government into an instrument of personal tyranny. Similarly, Adolf Hitler came to power under the terms of the well-respected constitution of the Weimar Republic of Germany.[24] Democratic nations have also shown surprising gaps between constitutional theory and political practice. Charles de Gaulle refused to take power in France in 1958 until he was assured that he would have the right to rewrite that nation's constitution, yet only four years later he blithely put through a major constitutional change (direct election of the president) by popular referendum, in bold contravention of his own prescribed method of constitutional amendment.

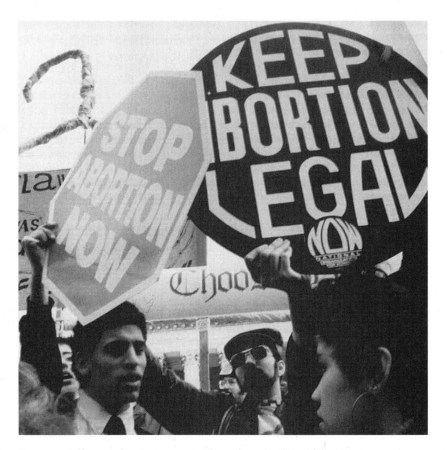

Documents become key instruments of our shared political life. Here representatives of both sides of the abortion issue argue for and against the Roe v. Wade decision long after it was issued. (UPI/Corbis-Bettmann)

Nevertheless, studying political documents remains an important and useful mode of inquiry in political science. As long as such pronouncements are not openly repudiated or revised, any violation of their provisions invites attention and protest. Political scientists who explicate the meaning of such materials may well make the fact of such violation clear for the first time and provide a means of holding officials accountable to their word — and to their words. Or they may simply make clear how ambiguous certain key clauses in important documents may be, such as the wording of the idea of maintaining the separation of church and state, contained in the First Amendment to the U.S. Constitution.[25]

Furthermore, we need to ask how much sense it makes to accord greater credibility to forms of evidence other than official documents. Why believe an unofficial commentator more readily than an official one? Are not nonofficials sometimes just as strongly motivated to distort the truth as those in authority? And why believe that the spoken word, even when uttered in the sheltered confines of the personal interview, is necessarily more reliable than words committed to the greater permanence and accessibility of print? The fact is that political truth is difficult to come by, and we need every useful method we can devise to track it down.

Studying the Political Future   "What puzzles me is what the impact of protectionism — if that is the policy we really adopt — is going to be on those nations whose economies depend on cheap exports to the United States." In a sense, every political scientist studies the future, and all the approaches thus far discussed can be applied to the study of the future. Our interest in politics is sharply honed by our desire to be prepared for what might be coming next. But some political scientists take the responsibility to make well-founded **predictions** about the feared or hoped-for events of the future more seriously than do others.

Efforts to predict the future must necessarily be based on our knowledge of the past. We cannot predict the future from the present — not if we use that term literally. How much does any of us know about what is happening right now? We need time to acquire information, organize it, assimilate it, and make sense of it — and by then the present will be the past. However, the time-honored certitude that "the past is prologue" has been shaken by the course of events in the twentieth century. Too often and too obviously the past has proved an untrustworthy guide. Soviet suppression of eastern European revolutionary movements in Hungary in 1956 and in Czechoslovakia in 1968 would never have led us to expect the USSR would offer active support to new movements to overthrow the state in those two nations in 1989. Periodic angry denunciation of the NATO pact and its members by members of the Warsaw Pact of the eastern bloc did little to prepare us for the day in 1992 when many of the latter would seek to join the former, having dissolved their own alliance the year before.

I used to teach the politics of South Africa in one of my courses but gave it up, too disheartened by what seemed the ever-tightening hold of the white supremacists on that nation's destiny. Yes, I knew something about Nelson Mandela, a brave leader in an island jail, but little did I dream that someday you would, too, and that you would learn about him not in a college course but on the front page of your newspaper. Our species' capacity for rapid change that shatters old patterns of political relationships forever — a capacity that seems to have grown only stronger as our century draws to its close — has been a major stimulus to the effort to find ways to use information about the past more systematically to predict the future. One such way is by building **models**.

What is a model? Scratch fifty political scientists and you will probably find fifty different definitions. Let me try to offer a fifty-first here, one that encompasses most of what is said in the other fifty. To begin with, a model is an imitation of something that is, or that is thought to be, or that might someday be. It is an *ideal* in the Platonic sense — that is, a representation of the essence of the subject, not the best possible version. Thus, a model is also a simplification. It does not tell the whole truth about a subject, nor does it purport to do so.

Models are not used only in the study of the future. They can be used in all the approaches of politics that we have looked at so far. Models, as any child with glue-covered fingers and leftover extra parts can tell you, can be material objects. The models of political scientists, however, almost never are. They are abstract — verbal, mathematical, or diagrammatic descriptions or imitations of reality. For example, political scientists have formulated verbal models of political development, trying to help us understand how the relationship between political and economic factors will affect a nation's ability to develop and to modernize. Some development models suggest that modernization requires the centralization of political power, others stress the need for a division of labor (leading to a division of political power), and still others argue that development will never take place until the poor nations of the world free themselves from dependency on richer nations whose only goal is to continue to exploit them.[26]

Statistical models are used to predict electoral outcomes, among other things. Suppose you had wanted to know what the chances of the Liberal Democratic Party of Russia, led by hardliner nationalist Vladimir V. Zhirinovsky, were likely to be in the parliamentary elections of 1993. In fact, the Zhirinovsky party took over 24 percent of the vote in that election, more than any other single party, a result that First Deputy Minister Yegor T. Gaider termed "a big and unpleasant surprise." The controversial leader of this party, often labeled a fascist by his opponents (but see Chapter 3 for a better definition of fascism), campaigned on a platform of law and order and the restoration of Russia's imperial legacy. He said he wanted to "stop the outflow of assistance from Russia, stop the conversion of the military industry and deal a crushing blow to crime." These issues were obviously important to a large minority of Russian voters, and the postelection comments of the government were rueful: "We saw the threat posed by the radical extremists too late, and we didn't reorient the focus of our campaign quickly," said Mr. Gaider, whose party, Russia's Choice, had first been favored to win but in fact took 10 percent less of the vote than the Liberal Democratic Party.[27]

The election surprised Gaider, most Russians, and most of the rest of the world, but it probably would not have surprised political scientists who knew how to use statistical models. Before the election they would have gathered as much information as possible about public opinion on the issues of the day, the strength of party identification (unlikely to be strong when most of the parties were new), and the personal popularity of the candidates. They would have fed all this information into a computer and, using formulas drawn from probability theory, would have produced a statistical model, a **simulation** of the actual election. If their work had been well done, they would have known that the issues of fighting crime and restoring lost prestige would have a strong appeal in postcommunist Russia, stronger than the platform of any of the parties favoring continuation of economic and governmental reforms. (As it turned out, these parties were forced to form an often uncomfortable coalition with each other to maintain control of the Russian parliament).

Game theory is a kind of modeling that is both verbal and mathematical. It uses the model of the game to predict the political future. Any game has players who play to win, rules, and information. Game theorists use this model and imagine politicians as players; international treaties, laws, and electoral systems as rules; known political conditions as information; and desired political outcomes as what the players are trying to win. Using this model, they attempt to deduce the decisions the players will make to move rationally toward their goals.[28]

Yet another kind of modeling, one that is both verbal and diagrammatic, is found in **political systems analysis,** a form of analysis suitable for the study of whole nations.[29] Studying whole nations as political systems means treating them as structures with interdependent parts and exploring the relationships among those parts. Figure 1.1 offers an example of the kind of diagram this form of analysis uses. To understand the diagram and this way of studying politics, let us work our way through it, beginning with ourselves — that is, with "members of a polity." We citizens do not come into the political system untouched by life — we have all been shaped by our "nonpolitical environments" as well as by the dominant "political culture and patterns of political socialization." Now follow the arrows on the diagram, moving left and upward. "Feedback" means that once we take on the identity of "member of a polity," we inevitably find some way of letting those in positions of authority know what we think of their performance. We may do this simply by keeping quiet, thereby letting the government know that its work is at least being tolerated, if only for the time being. Or we may provide more substantive "inputs," expressing our "support" (for example, by voting to reelect the same men and women to office again and again, or by paying our taxes without protest) or making "demands" (for example, by forming new pressure groups or parties, or by using those that exist to carry our wishes for different policies into the arenas of power). Those who receive these inputs, the "authorities," convert them into "outputs" by making and enforcing policies, laws, and decisions, or simply by passing on information. Much of this output becomes a kind of "feedback" to the citizens, who are expected to obey the laws, suffer punishments for criminal offenses, accept the rewards good government brings, and so forth. The ways we experience the impact of government in our daily lives enter into our consciousness, become part of our citizen selves, and help shape what we have to say to that government and how we choose to say it. The systems loop is complete; the spiraling history of the political system continues on its way.

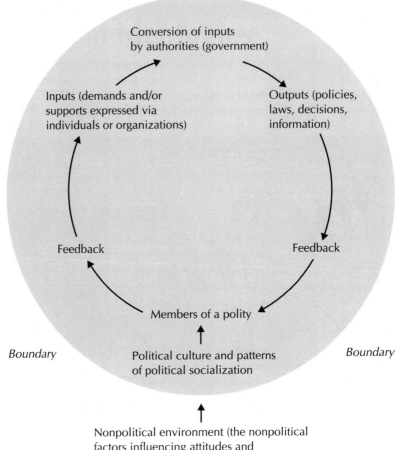

Conversion of inputs
by authorities (government)

Inputs (demands and/or
supports expressed via
individuals or organizations)

Outputs (policies,
laws, decisions,
information)

Feedback

Feedback

Members of a polity

Boundary

Political culture and patterns
of political socialization

Boundary

Nonpolitical environment (the nonpolitical
factors influencing attitudes and
behavior of citizens and authorities)

FIGURE 1.1   **The Nation as Political System**

Some critics have argued that the systems model overemphasizes the interdependence of the parts of any given political system and fails to distinguish among parts that are more or less important to ensuring the successful functioning of the whole system. Others point out that it underestimates the interdependence of different political systems and of their citizens: Where does something like the loss of American jobs caused by the competition of government-subsidized firms in other nations fit in the political system diagram? And still others object to the language of systems analysis, arguing that words like *input, output,* and *feedback* are scarcely suitable for conveying the rich spectrum of shared social life that makes up today's world of nations.

How good are the various approaches to the study of political science?

Do they really work to solve political puzzles? That depends on what you mean by work. If you mean, "Are political scientists able to figure out what is really going on behind the superficial appearance of political phenomena?" the answer is, "Yes, quite often." But if you mean, "Can they come up with lasting solutions to the puzzles of politics?" the answer is almost certainly, "No." As we have already had occasion to point out, political life is both complex and constantly changing. One plus one is likely to remain two for all eternity, but the factors causing political phenomena to take the form they do may well disappear and be replaced by others — or they may not. What is most likely to happen as a result of a political scientist's work on a puzzle is that the puzzle will become a little less puzzling — at least for a while.

Normative versus Empirical Political Puzzles

One further distinction needs to be drawn about political puzzles: the difference between those that are normative and those that are empirical. A *normative* puzzle is a puzzle about values. Facts will be pertinent, of course, but the final solution of the puzzle is one that depends on what standards, or **norms**, an individual, a group, or a social system decides to apply to the facts uncovered. When we find instances of political corruption, we seldom think it is enough merely to describe the mechanics by which bribes exchanged hands. The study of the political causes of warfare, terrorism, poverty, or famine cannot fail to evoke our compassion for those who suffer and our hope that revealing the facts will somehow produce positive change. Political scientists cannot and do not work in a normative void.

Nevertheless, at various times political scientists have been tempted to rule the consideration of normative puzzles out of order. In the throes of the "behavioral revolution" of the 1960s, many political scientists were persuaded that the more scientific their discipline could be made, the less concern anyone who worked in it would have with matters of moral choice. I remember asking once about the propriety of dishonest manipulation of public opinion in a course on the tactics of political persuasion, only to be told by my professor (then a leading behavioralist) that if I wanted to pursue that kind of question perhaps I had better go take a course in ethics.

The question of the proper role of normative considerations, if any, in the work of the political scientist is still an open one, although few practitioners would now go as far as the professor just cited. Most political scientists now recognize that in political science, as in all the sciences, the very decision that a puzzle is interesting and worthwhile is itself a normative one — as is the contention that "should" should not be part of political science! Furthermore, almost every article and book in the field begins with an effort, explicit or implicit, to persuade the reader that the subject matters, and most end by noting the implications the findings have for one or more widely cherished values (such as popular representation, freedom, or peace on earth). When David Geller offers a study of the "impact of political system structure on probability patterns of internal disorder" that employs some of the discipline's most difficult and sophisticated modes of statistical analysis, he nevertheless makes it very clear that what interests him are the "forms and patterns of political conflict" and, in particular, whether "violence breeds violence."[30] Geller never tells us he favors the reduction of violence, but we feel pretty confident that he does, and that his choice of topic is at least in part related to what he considers to be an important normative quest.

In any case, there is now a widespread conviction that the political scientist "should" confront and acknowledge his or her own normative biases and then pursue the work at hand as objectively as possible. I may have a strong bias against government interference in personal freedom and also a strong bias in favor of my own country. Unless I confront those biases very clearly, it may be difficult if not impossible for me to recognize infringements on personal freedom in my own country with the same ease that I ferret them out in other nations.

Thus, the normative component of the puzzles of political science requires special attention and consciousness. It is not going to disappear. Politics itself is largely concerned with the establishment and implementation of values and the distribution of resources, and those who care enough to study politics are not likely to be individuals coldly unmoved by questions of right and wrong. All we can do — and all we "should" do, to my way of thinking — is acknowledge the values that inevitably underlie our work and prevent them, if we can, from distorting our perception of the facts.

The puzzles of politics are large and formidable, and, given the constancy of change, it is true we may never find absolute solutions for any of them. But the recognition of that complexity is itself an encouraging sign of progress. Political scientists no longer simply label nations as "totalitarian," "democratic," and "developing," as if such labels in themselves tell us exactly what amount of individual liberty, political participation, bureaucratic centralization, or industrialization of production we might confidently expect to find. We know that simply tacking on labels does not do the job. We have been working hard to improve our methods of inquiry and to acquire a body of significant and readily applicable knowledge. Much of this book is devoted to summarizing the knowledge political scientists have acquired. Our work is not done — but if it were, what would be the fun of studying how to do it?

SUMMARY AND CONCLUSION

The human polity is the world of politics. In a time of increasing international interdependence, we have all become members of a global body politic as well as citizens of individual nation-states. This means that the only way we will be able to cope with the problems of today's world is to study not only our own nation's politics but those of other nations as well, and the relationships among nations. This increased interdependence does not necessarily make our problems harder to solve, since it can have the effect of making cooperative work with other nations an easier task, but it does increase their complexity. Still, if we learn to accept that complexity and move carefully as we pursue the goals we cannot help sharing, our chances of being able to put all the resources of our planet to work for our collective benefit are good. Whether or not we will do so remains to be seen. We may well be at the most significant crossroads our species has ever faced.

Political science is the study of politics. Politics is a means of organizing collective human activity. The city-state, the empire, the nation-state, and the United Nations are four of the more complex forms of that kind of organization, but politics has been with us ever since human beings first began living and working together. Today, politics is part and parcel of nearly all human interactions, and political power is constantly expanding.

The scope of political science is vast, and the puzzles of political science are all interrelated. Political scientists need one another's work, and that work is divided into subfields. Political theory, constitutional law, public administration, American government, and comparative government are some of the oldest. More recent additions include political behavior, international relations, methodology, political economy, political organizations, and biopolitics. These may or may not endure; political science changes and evolves.

Men and women constantly make observations about what interests and perplexes them about politics. Political scientists treat these observations as puzzles and set to work to understand them. To do so, they use various approaches, singly or in combination: behavioralism, structural-functionalism, phenomenology, the study of ideas, the study of documents, and prediction. Whatever the approach, the political scientist inevitably confronts normative questions, questions that are related to our values. This cannot be avoided. Politics itself is concerned with the establishment and implementation of values, and those who care enough to study politics are likely to be people who care deeply about questions of right and wrong. We should, however, make an effort to acknowledge our values and to prevent them from distorting our perception of the facts.

In this chapter we have only begun the introduction to political science that is the task this book has set for itself. A key aspect of that task is to explain the terms and concepts political scientists use to describe the phenomena of politics, and this is the vocabulary we turn to in Chapter 2, "The Language of Politics."

Selected Readings

Cohen, Mitchell and Nicole Fermon, eds. *Princeton Readings in Political Thought* (Princeton: Princeton University Press, 1996). A survey of writings on western political thought that have influenced current society and politics.

Crotty, William, ed. *Political Science: Looking to the Fu-*

ture: *The Theory and Practice of Political Science*, vol. 1 (Evanston: Northwestern University Press, 1992). This book of essays offers a useful overview of political science theories and methods.

Edelman, Murray J. *Constructing the Political Spectacle* (Chicago: University of Chicago Press, 1988). An examination of political psychology, symbolism in politics, and sociolinguistics.

Farr, James, John S. Dryzek and Stephen T. Leonard, eds. *Political Science in History: Research, Programs and Political Traditions* (Cambridge, MA: Cambridge University Press, 1995). Essays by political scientists on the history of the field of political science.

Hall, John A., ed. *States in History* (New York: Basil Blackwell, 1986). A series of articles examining the state throughout history. The state as it existed during the time of hunters and gatherers to the time of the polis and to the present era of supranationals is discussed.

Johnson, Janet Buttolph. *Political Science Research Methods* (Washington, D.C.: Congressional Quarterly Press, 1986). An examination of political science research techniques ranging from formulation of the questions posed to statistical analysis and observation. Uses case studies.

Lasswell, Harold D. *The Analysis of Political Behavior: An Empirical Approach* (New York: Oxford University Press, 1947). One of the early explanations of behavioralism, by a leading practitioner.

Ordeshook, Peter C. *Models of Strategic Choice in Politics* (Ann Arbor: University of Michigan Press, 1989). A collection of articles on the application of mathematical models to political science.

Parsons, Wayne. *Public Policy: An Introduction to the Theory and Practice of Policy Analysis* (Gloucestershire: Edward Elger, 1995). A detailed study of the theory and practice of public policy that provides a good introduction to the role of government.

Purvis, Hoyt. *Interdependence: An Introduction to International Affairs.* (Chicago: Harcourt Brace Jovanovich, 1992.) Uses established principles and theories of international relations to study emerging interdependence in contemporary world politics. Analyzes environmental questions, population trends, advances in communications and technology.

Ricci, David M. *The Tragedy of Political Science* (New Haven: Yale University Press, 1984). Considers the historical development of political science. Urges more emphasis on political thought.

Ross, Marc Howard. *The Management of Conflict: Inter-* *pretations and Interests in Comparative Perspective* (New Haven: Yale University Press, 1993). A comparative study of political conflicts and solutions worldwide.

Tansey, Stephen D. *Politics, the Basics* (London: Routledge, 1995). An historical survey of politics that is a useful resource for those new to the field or seeking a review.

Wilentz, Sean, ed. *Rites of Power* (Philadelphia: University of Pennsylvania Press, 1985). A collection of ten essays on symbolism and politics throughout history.

Notes

1. John Spanier, *Games Nations Play*, 6th ed. (Washington, D.C.: Congressional Quarterly Press, 1987), 651.
2. *New York Times*, 13 Jan. 1995, A1, and 10 Mar. 1995, D1.
3. Renato Ruggiero, "Agenda for Trade," *Financial Times*, 5 Oct. 1994, 22.
4. Leonard Silk, "Dangers of Slow Growth," *Foreign Affairs* 72, no. 1 (1992): 167–82.
5. Rachel Carson, *Silent Spring* (Boston: Houghton Mifflin, 1962).
6. For U.S. Vice President Albert Gore, "the consequences of unrestrained exploitation" of the earth are now "every bit as unthinkable as the consequences of unrestrained nuclear war." *Earth in the Balance: Ecology and the Human Spirit* (Boston: Houghton Mifflin, 1992), p. 31. See also Richard A. Falk, *This Endangered Planet: Prospects and Proposals for Human Survival* (New York: Vintage, 1971), pp. 1–92.
7. Daniel A. Dreyfus and Anne B. Ashby, "Fueling Our Global Future," *Environment* 32, no. 4 (May 1990): I have drawn heavily on this excellent article for the preceding discussion.
8. Ruth Leger Sivart, *World Military and Social Expenditures* (Washington D.C.: World Priorities, 1993), p. 44.
9. *Christian Science Monitor*, 22 Jan. 1988, 10.
10. Robert O. Keohane and Joseph S. Nye, *Power and Interdependence: World Politics in Transition* (Boston: Little, Brown, 1977). See also Robert O. Keohane, *After Hegemony: Cooperation and Discord in the World Political Economy* (Princeton: Princeton University Press, 1984).
11. R. J. Barry Jones, "The Definition and Identifica-

tion of Interdependence," in R. J. Barry Jones and Peter Willetts, eds., *Interdependence on Trial* (London: Frances Pinter, 1984), p. 19, and Terry L. Beibel, "Internal Affairs and International Relations in the Post–Cold War World," *Washington Quarterly*, 16, no. 3 (Summer 1993): 13.

12. Geoffrey Barraclough, *Times Atlas of World History* (Maplewood, N.J.: Hammond, 1979), p. 52.

13. Harold D. Lasswell, *Politics: Who Gets What, When, How* (Cleveland: World Publishing Company, 1958); and David Easton, *A Systems Analysis of Political Life* (New York: John Wiley and Sons, 1965), p. 21.

14. "Govt. to Restrict Baby Milk Ads," *Marketing*, 9 Dec. 1993, 11, plus information supplied by Douglas Clement of INFACT, 15 July 1981.

15. Susan Tiano, "Gender, Work and World Capitalism: Third World Women's Role in Development," in Beth B. Hess and Myra Marx Ferree, eds., *Analyzing Gender* (Newbury Park, Calif.: Sage, 1987), pp. 223–24.

16. Claire Anthony, *Love Law: Love, Sex and Marriage, and the World* (London: BBC Publications, 1986), pp. 73, 122.

17. James C. F. Wang, *Contemporary Chinese Politics*, 2nd ed. (Englewood Cliffs, N.J.: Prentice Hall, 1985), pp. 235–36.

18. *Social Security Programs Throughout the World — 1993* (Washington, D.C.: U.S. Department of Health and Human Services, 1994), pp. 175, 310, and 332.

19. Samuel Huntington, *Political Order in Changing Societies* (New Haven, Conn.: Yale University Press, 1968), p. 1.

20. A. M. Carr-Saunders, *World Population: Past Growth and Present Trends* (Oxford: Clarendon Press, 1936), p. 42; and *The World Almanac and Book of Facts 1988* (New York: Pharos Books, 1987), p. 522.

21. Michael M. Gant and Norman R. Luttbeg, *American Electoral Behavior: 1952–1988* (Itasca, Ill.: Peacock, 1991) and Steven J. Rosenstone and John Mark Hansen, *Mobilization, Participation and Democracy in America* (New York: Macmillan, 1993).

22. William Shakespeare, *Romeo and Juliet*, act 2, sc. 2, lines 43–44.

23. Claude Rivière, *Guinea: The Mobilization of a People*, trans. Virginia Thompson and Richard Adloff (Ithaca, N.Y.: Cornell University Press, 1977).

24. On the Soviet constitution, see Robert LeFevre, *Constitutional Government in Soviet Russia: The Constitution of the USSR* (New York: Exposition Press, 1962). On that of the Weimar Republic, see Herbert Kraus, *The Crisis of German Democracy: A Study of the Spirit of the Constitution of Weimar* (Princeton, N.J.: Princeton University Press, 1932).

25. See, for example, Robert S. Alley, *School Prayer: The Court, The Congress, and The First Amendment* (Amherst, N.Y.: Prometheus, 1994).

26. Samuel H. Beer, *Modern Political Development* (Boston: Little, Brown, 1966) p. 25; Immanuel Wallerstein, *The Modern World System* vols. 1 and 2 (New York: Academic Press, 1980).

27. Celestine Bohlen, "The Russian Vote: Nationalists Move Far Out in Front in Russian Voting," *New York Times*, 14 Dec. 1993, 1.

28. For further discussion of game theory as it relates to international politics, see Duncan Snidal, "The Game Theory of International Politics," *World Politics* 38, no. 1 (Oct. 1985): 25–57; and R. Harrison Wagner, "The Theory of Games and the Balance of Power," *World Politics* 38, no. 4 (July 1986): 546–76.

29. The concept of the political system has been most fully developed by David Easton in *A Framework for Political Analysis* (Englewood Cliffs, N.J.: Prentice Hall, 1965). See also his *An Analysis of Political Structure* (New York: Routledge, 1990). For another, more imaginative use, see Karl W. Deutsch, *The Nerves of Government* (New York: The Free Press, 1966).

30. David S. Geller, "The Impact of Political System Structure on Probability Patterns of Internal Disorder," *American Journal of Political Science* 31, no. 2 (May 1987): 217–33.

2 The Language of Politics

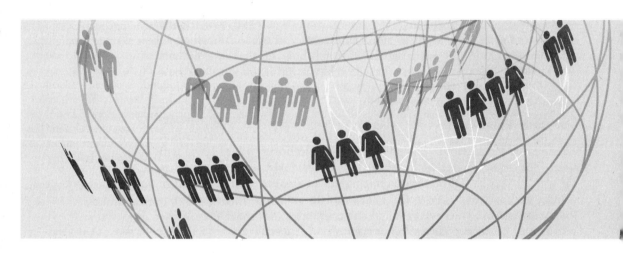

CONCEPTS THAT NAME STRUCTURES
Organizations
Institutions
States
Systems

CONCEPTUALIZING RELATIONSHIPS OF CONTROL
Power
Influence
Authority
Legitimacy
Linkage

POLITICAL CONCEPTS REGARDING THE QUALITY OF LIFE
Equality
Freedom
Order
Progress

INSIGHT VERSUS JARGON IN THE STUDY OF POLITICAL SCIENCE

SUMMARY AND CONCLUSION

W HEN AN ASPECT OF our experience interests us, we begin to develop language for talking about it. The words we choose are
not important in themselves. We might decide to call the people
who decide disputes "munchkins" or "sweethearts" instead of "judges."
What is essential is that a name, once we settle on it, always refer to the
same aspect of our experience. The *concept* is important — in this case, the
idea that some people have the job of making authoritative decisions in
disputes between other people.

Some names, as in the preceding example, refer to concepts or phenomena that we have little or no trouble recognizing. We can see them
and touch them. We can confirm their existence *ad lapidum* — that is, in the
same way we can confirm the existence of a stone, by looking at it, touch-
ing it, picking it up, or giving it a kick. (Most of these are not seriously
recommended when verifying the existence of judges.) Other concepts are
more difficult or even impossible to confirm through single sensory perceptions. We develop an awareness of what seems to us an important component of the nature of reality, and we pick what seems like a good name
for it. That way we can at least talk about it and describe it more carefully.
We may discover that we were wrong. The divine right of kings to rule,
the unseen hand of the free market, and the biological inferiority of
women and of nonwhite races are all examples of concepts that have been

developed, explored, found inadequate, and abandoned by most social scientists.

The study of politics is rich with language about concepts. Some political scientists argue persuasively that our discipline is still too young for us to have achieved full agreement on the concepts we use and the language we employ. However, we do agree on the meanings of many important terms and are unanimously persuaded that these terms refer to phenomena that really do exist.[1] Such terms can be divided for convenience into three categories: those that name kinds of structures, those that name relationships of control, and those that name certain qualities of daily life that are subject to political determination. We cannot review all the accepted terms, but we will consider some of the more important examples in each category.

CONCEPTS THAT NAME STRUCTURES

As used in the social sciences, the word **structure** itself refers to a concept. It denotes a set of patterned role relationships. Any time human beings interact by adopting specific roles and carrying out those roles in a specific way, they have created a structure. Four structures that particularly interest political scientists are organizations, institutions, states, and systems.

Organizations

An **organization** is a body of persons working together in a structured way to achieve a specific purpose. In the case of a political organization, that purpose is political. Interest groups, political parties, candidates' campaign organizations, revolutionary movements, and even terrorist groups are examples of political organizations. Political organizations may be long lived or short lived, large or small, important or unimportant. Such seemingly nonpolitical organizations as flower clubs, hobby associations, and poetry reading groups may find themselves temporarily politicized under certain circumstances. If the park in which the city's finest chrysanthemums are grown is threatened by the extension of the freeway, the members of the flower club may find themselves devoting much of their time to lobbying the state legislature and engaging in various tactics to enlist public opinion on their side. Under these circumstances, the club will have become, for the time being, a political organization.

Institutions

When a structure becomes an institution, its activities are widely viewed as helping to meet one or more of the basic needs of a society. An **institution** is a structure with established, important functions to perform, well-specified roles for carrying out those functions; and a clear set of rules for governing the relationships between the people who occupy those roles.

Organizations may be institutions, but not all are — and not all institutions are organizations. The members of an organization may have a common purpose, but they may not be viewed by society as having an important function; the people working through an institution may have a common and important function to perform, but they may not have a common purpose. A single political party is an organization; political parties, collectively, may or may not have the status of institutions in a given polity. If they are routinely expected to carry out such important functions as recruiting political leaders in a particular way, political parties in that system have achieved the status of institution.

Any given institution may be wholly or partly political, or absolutely nonpolitical. Courts, legislatures, civil services, and political parties are examples of wholly political institutions. Most institutions are at least partly political; when the occasion arises, they will engage as institutions in the political process. Many of the world's corporations, trade unions, and educational and religious institutions routinely commit a portion of their resources and attention to attempts to influence political decisions.

Institutions are important to political scientists because most significant political action takes place within and between institutions. This action is performed by individuals playing the roles assigned by their institutions, usually in accordance with the rules and established modes of procedure of those institutions. This is true whether we are speaking of the king of Norway or a crime syndicate's hit man. Role players *can* act contrary to the stated purposes and precepts of their institutions, and can even do so with the full consent of their superiors. Political scientists have thus learned not to take written rules too literally.

It is also wrong to imagine all institutions as fixed, rigid, ossified structures. Effective institutions are the ones that can adapt successfully to changing conditions. The U.S. Supreme Court and the Catholic church are examples of institutions that maintain power by making some effective adaptations to changing conditions. The communist parties of eastern Europe that came tumbling down soon after the Berlin Wall are examples of institutions that did not. When the Argentine military junta that ruled from 1975 to 1983 refused to respond to popular demand for democratization and undertook instead to suppress opposition by torture and murder, to engage in an ill-fated venture to retake the Falkland Islands from Great Britain, and to pursue economic policies that produced an inflation rate of over 600 percent, it demonstrated that it was an institution incapable of adjusting effectively to change.[2] What about the British monarchy? Is this an institution that is failing, as its current representatives behave in scandalous fashion and as the British public becomes ever more aware not only of these deficiencies but also of the high cost to them of maintaining an institution the citizens of so many other nations find, at best, amusingly archaic?

States

A **state** is a structure that has the legal right to make rules that are binding over a given population within a given territory. As such, it has geographic as well as political characteristics. A state is a political institution, but it differs from other political institutions in having **sovereignty** — that is, it has the power to make decisions that cannot be overruled by any other body.

This definition may seem reasonable and clear enough, but in practice the term *state* is often very ambiguous. There is no better example of this ambiguity than the practice of referring to the constituent units of the federal system of government in the United States as *states*. These units were never *sovereign states* — although some of them nearly met the conditions of that definition in the few years between the Declaration of Independence and the adoption of the present Constitution.

Other problems with the concept emerge when we consider states with constitutions that specifically allow for the contingency of ceding some of the nation's decision-making power to a supernational body. The constitutions of the African states of Ghana and Guinea had such clauses when those states first achieved independence, because it was hoped that a larger African state would be formed in the near future. The Organization of African Unity was formed in 1963, but it is not a state and does not require its member states to cede any measure of their sovereignty as a condition for joining.[3] On the other hand, the European Economic Community has evolved to the point where it now routinely expects its interdependent member states to obey its collective decisions in matters reaching far beyond simple economic pacts. Most of the member states' constitutions do not allow for this infringement on the sovereignty of the state, but their silence on the matter does not make the change any less real. The French, who are perhaps more likely than other peoples to insist on a rational match between what they say and what they do, added an appropriate sovereignty-ceding amendment to their constitution before voting to ratify the EC's Treaty of Maastricht in 1992.[4]

Finally, certain geographical entities are states only by legal definition and international courtesy. Lesotho, Monaco, and Panama are "states" that remained under the nearly absolute power of a neighboring or surrounding state long after achieving legal independence. What is the true status of the ex-Soviet republics of Eurasia: Armenia, Azerbaijan, Belarus, Georgia, Kazakhstan, Kyrgystan, Moldova, Tajikistan, Turkmenistan, the Ukraine, and Uzbekistan?[5] Do the Baltic states of Estonia, Latvia, and Lithuania have the resources to practice the absolute independence they so boldly claimed when the Soviet Union collapsed?

Nevertheless, whatever answer we give these difficult questions and however remote political practice may sometimes appear to be from theory, the study of international relations and of the interdependence of the various units that make up the human polity seems impossible without recourse to the concept of the state.

Systems

A **system** is a structure all of whose parts are interrelated, so that a change in one part means a change in all. A political system is a system that deals with political matters. Any structure with interdependent parts that deals with political matters is a political system.[6]

As we have already noted in Chapter 1, the concept of a political system gives us a useful way to organize the study of politics and to remind ourselves of the importance of the multitude of elements that constitute a polity. As you may have already figured out, organizations, institutions, and states are all systems. The term *system* can be used to refer to any level of political order. We can conceive of the human polity as a single political system and study the interrelationships among a multitude of individuals and institutions throughout the world — or we can treat the local ten-member Republican Women's Club as a political system and try to figure out the basis on which its collective decisions are made and the impact those decisions have on the members.

CONCEPTUALIZING RELATIONSHIPS OF CONTROL

Engaging in politics means engaging in efforts to control the acts of others. Many of the key concepts of political science have to do with relationships of control. Here we will briefly consider five: power, influence, authority, legitimacy, and linkage.

Power

We are usually ready to endorse such glib comments as "Power is the very heart of politics." In fact, however, the concept of **power** is one of the most difficult to define. Robert Dahl has pointed out three common fallacies in the analysis of power. The "lump-of-power" fallacy is the mistaken assumption that power comes in lump sums and cannot be shared, so all one needs to ask is: Who's in charge? "Confounding power with resources" is what we do when we take literally such aphorisms as "Money is power." Money may be a resource on which power rests, but the two are different entities. Finally, "confounding power with rewards and deprivations" happens if we look beyond the powerful act to its ultimate consequences for the people it has been exercised for or against. One consequence of a law calling for lower defense expenditures may mean fewer jobs in California, but "reducing the number of jobs" is *not* power.[7]

What, then, *is* power? Dahl suggests that power means getting others to comply "by creating the prospect of severe sanctions for noncompliance."[8] He quotes Harold Lasswell and Abraham Kaplan to the same effect. "It is the threat of sanctions which differentiates power from influence in general. Power is a special case of the exercise of influence: it is the process of affecting policies of others with the help of (actual or threatened) severe deprivations for nonconformity with the policies intended."[9] When Adolf Hitler forced significant changes in the foreign policy of the British prime minister Neville Chamberlain by making clear the devastation he was prepared to wreak, that was power. When President Franklin Roosevelt persuaded the U.S. Supreme Court to stop declaring New Deal legislation

"At least we always know who's in charge around here."

(Drawing by W. B. Park; © 1983 The New Yorker Magazine, Inc.)

unconstitutional by threatening to induce Congress to increase the number of justices so he could "pack" the Court with fellow liberals, and the Court promptly ceased to find that kind of legislation questionable, that was power.

Thus defined, power involves two parties and two steps. In the first step, party A threatens unpleasant consequences if party B acts or does not act thus and so. In the second step, party B acts as party A wishes *because* party A has made the specified threat. It is a relationship of control. Sometimes the power relationship is interestingly reciprocal. The 1995 decisions of the British to withdraw troops from Northern Ireland and of the Irish Republican Army to end its acts of guerrilla warfare were clearly both made in partial response to the continued "deprivations" the other had threatened and imposed.

Dahl's formulation seems to place chief emphasis on the *threat* of sanctions; although Lasswell and Kaplan mention *actual* deprivations, Dahl himself does not. In today's world, however, power is all too frequently achieved only when threats have been carried out. Iraq withdrew from

Kuwait in 1991 only after the Gulf War had taken some 100,000 Iraqi lives. Both the British Army and the Irish Republican Army had carried out many murderous threats against one another before making mutual concessions to the other's power. And most commentators on the war in the Balkans believe that a major reason it became such a long, drawn-out, and bloody affair was because so often the threats made by the United States, by the North Atlantic Organization, by the European Community, and by the United Nations were either not carried out or were carried out with such minor damages that neither Serbs nor Bosnians, Christians nor Muslims, found the sanctions sufficiently compelling. Not every leader or nation yields to even the most believable threats; if in doubt, consider the fierce resistance so long waged by the fighters for Chechen independence inside the boundaries of contemporary Russia. Nor does agreement reached after threats of violence have been carried out always endure, as the cases of Ireland and the Middle East have made clear.[10]

Influence

Whether exercised by threat or use of force, power is a limited method, one that cannot be used effectively in all relationships. Political scientists have lately been giving more attention to a broader relationship of control: **influence**. Again following Dahl, we can say that influence includes all cases when one party's desires affect the behavior of another party. As just noted, power is a form of influence. But influence can take place without the threat of sanctions or use of force, as well as without the promise of personal rewards. The neoconservative economists whose arguments lent scholarly credence to the policies of Britain's prime minister, Margaret Thatcher, exercised influence in that government, as did their counterparts during the presidency of Ronald Reagan in the United States. The articulate witness who persuades a committee of the U.S. Congress to support (or not support) a proposed bill authorizing increased arms exports to a Latin American dictatorship about to be tumbled from power by revolutionary insurrection is exercising influence. The Islamic religious leaders known as *marabouts* who convince the president of the west African state of Senegal that they can increase his popularity by supporting him, and who promise to do so as long as he does not depart from the moderate policies of his predecessor, are men of influence.

Where does influence come from? Why do some people have the form of influence we call power? As we can deduce from the preceding examples, influence over political decisions is not confined to public officials. This is true even of power. Organized groups of voters can make threats (such as refusing to help with campaign costs) that have the effect of changing policy; revolutionary or terrorist movements can succeed in changing the allocation of resources by their threats of continued violence.

Differences in capacity to influence public policy can be traced to a wide number of factors. More money, more information, more friends, more skill in the art of persuasion, more weapons, better organization, a better job, better means of communication, and stronger motivation are all attributes that — depending on other circumstances — can give one person more influence over public policy than others who are less well endowed. One important resource for the exercise of influence is *not* on this list, however, and that is the occupancy of public office. Public office is, after all, the proper home of political decisions. If one occupies a public office, one is authorized to make certain political decisions. One has authority.

Authority

Authority is the right to exercise the power and influence of a given position that comes from having been placed in that position according to regular, known, and widely accepted procedures. We sometimes speak of "the authorities" as if they were remote figures, self-created, hopelessly beyond our reach. It is a misuse of language, however, to confuse those who usurp political power by means of force or trickery with those who have obtained such power by accepted means. In a democratic system, accepted means are normally either elections or appointments by elected officials. Citizens in such a system who are not content with the performance of "the authorities" have means of redress that go considerably beyond angry expostulation about remote figures of power. If enough of them agree, they can throw the rascals out.

The means of acquiring authority vary greatly. An Indian president must be elected by an electoral college consisting of the elected members of the Indian Parliament and the state legislatures, by means of a complicated system of weighted voting.[11] A Japanese prime minister must win the approval of the leaders of all factions of the party that wins the most seats in the Diet, Japan's legislative body.[12] An Australian aboriginal headman comes to his office through traditional paths of kinship.[13] A French judge must have studied for and passed a competitive exam; only those who do best will receive appointments from the Ministry of Justice.[14]

A sign that significant change is taking place in any country is a shift in the rules for authorizing access to political power. The declaration of American revolutionaries that British agents had no authority to collect taxes from subjects who were not represented in British decision-making processes initiated a set of changes leading to the formation of a new nation. Some older inhabitants of the African continent have witnessed an amazing series of changes in the procedures for authorizing leadership. The precondition for attaining the right to rule in many parts of Africa has shifted over the past century from (1) place in the kinship lineage to (2) position as representative of foreign conquerors to (3) good behavior as "native administrator" (the title given African chiefs willing to serve as agents of colonial rule) to (4) "reasonableness" and "representativeness" (when leadership shifted to Africans who represented key groups that were willing to make the transition to independence on colonial terms) to (5) number of votes (in the early days of independence) to (6) having the backing

Authority versus legitimacy. As Chairman of the Joint Chiefs of Staff, Colin Powell had *authority* to make key decisions in the Gulf War of 1991. His style and demeanor during that event gave his leadership *legitimacy* as well, to the point where he was considered a likely prospect as U.S. presidential or vice-presidential nominee in 1996 (until he himself decided not to pursue a career in politics). (UPI/Bettmann)

of armed strength (as the first military coups took place and/or personal dictatorships were established), and back again to (7) number of votes (when the military returned power to civilian hands or other leaders, keen to reduce corruption and improve the nation's eligibility for foreign aid, forced the dictators out of office and reestablished democratic elections).[15]

Legitimacy

Legitimacy means having the approval of others. It is the condition of being regarded as correctly placed in a particular role and as carrying out the functions of that role correctly (whether or not one is actually doing so). Political legitimacy means having widespread approval for the way one exercises political power. Under normal circumstances, authority gives legitimacy to power; it is possible, however, to have authority but lack legitimacy. If a president is seen as failing to take adequate steps to resolve an economic crisis, such as a wildly fluctuating financial market or a seemingly unending recession, he or she may lose legitimacy without losing authority. The authority to rule and the power to rule legitimately may rest in different hands. If a king is insane, a grateful people may permit the cardinal to rule and grant his orders legitimacy. In some circumstances, no duly constituted authority may be able to take charge when leadership is required. Isolated survivors of catastrophes accept as legitimate the orders of someone whose directions make sense and save lives; they will worry later about who should be "authorized" to take charge of the little polity they may be forced to create.

Standards of legitimacy do not always change with standards for achieving authority. When communist political systems were established in the nations of eastern Europe, the new rulers placed strong emphasis on single-party rule, centralized at the top. As long as they remained in power, gaining a position of authority was possible only by working through that single party and receiving its approval for one's candidacy, which would then be uncontested in the pro forma election that followed. The new rulers also worked hard to change their nations' standards of legitimacy, stressing the importance of reducing ethnic rivalries and eliminating organized religion (which had often played a powerful role in the earlier political systems). To all appearances, their efforts were successful, or largely so. Yet as soon as the communist systems began to crumble and fall, both ethnic identity and religious guidance resumed their former function as legitimizing agencies. In postcommunist states, the various peoples who originally formed these polities are now once again granting legitimacy on the basis of answers to the age-old questions: Is this leader one of ours? Does he or she come from the same ethnic group and have the same religious faith? In ex-Yugoslavia, the answers to these questions have assumed such overriding importance that hundreds of thousands of lives have been lost when the answer seemed "wrong" and the questioners have had the armed might to insist on *their* standards of legitimacy.[16]

In any case, the distinction between legitimacy and authority is an important one to keep in mind. When the exhortation "Question authority!" is widely uttered and widely followed, existing authorities are in danger of losing their legitimacy. When the people authorized to rule lose legitimacy, the chances are good that an attempt will be made to replace them with others; if a change in the basis of authority is required to replace the people who have authority, that change may well be made. On such foundations do revolutions rise.

Linkage

In all relationships of control, there is an element of linkage. **Linkage** has been given two meanings in political science — meanings that at first seem quite different from each other but that are in reality closely related. Scholars, diplomats, and journalists interested in international relations have used the term *linkage* to point out the ways in which decisions in one nation may force desired decisions in another. For example, a donor nation may "link" the decision to continue foreign aid to a recipient nation's decision to allow greater freedom of speech.[17] Those who study domestic political processes use the term to refer to the way pressure groups, political parties, and electoral processes connect the general public with the leaders who make policy decisions.[18] What both definitions have in common is an emphasis on the connections between one political unit and another, on the way decisions made at one level (for example, by a nation's own voters or by the leaders of another nation) influence those made at another level (for example, by the first nation's leaders).

Domestic linkage can be either *upward* or *downward*.[19] (See Figure 2.1.) **Participatory linkage** is an example of upward linkage. It occurs when citizens are able to take part directly in government decision making. The traditional New England town meeting is an example of that kind of linkage, at least in theory.

Policy-responsive linkage is another form of upward linkage. It is present when there is some way to ensure that leadership decisions will be responsive to the views of ordinary citizens, although not made by them. Representative government can be a form of policy-responsive linkage, but only when the representatives are clearly chosen (or removed from office) at least partially on the basis of their stands on policy questions.

Clientelistic linkage is both upward and downward. It takes place when leaders offer specific rewards in exchange for support. When this kind of linkage is dominant, citizens are not expected to concern themselves with matters of national policy, but they *are* expected to favor those officials who see to it that jobs, roads, or other material benefits flow from the government to them. They are the "clients" who "buy" such benefits with their votes or their support rather than with money. So long as Turkey was a single-party system, Turkish peasants' entire political participation consisted of voting as local notables instructed; the latter held all the important positions in the party, the bureaucracy, and the parliament, but they were expected to use those positions to mediate with the central authorities to whom they had access, improving life for "their" villagers. Even today, says Ayse Gunes-Ayata, Turkish members of Parliament "routinely spend every morning responding to demands. . . . Most of them keep files for each client, registering all favors rendered so they can claim favors in return; some of these records are even computerized."[20]

Directive linkage is downward linkage. It is the way leaders maintain control over followers. Such control may be coercive, exercised by secret police or by other armed forces; or it may be manipulative, exercised by control of the media, the schools, or other agents of instruction.

It is, of course, possible to combine forms of linkage in any given polity. Some citizens may be linked to their government by their own participa-

A. Participatory linkage between citizen and state (upward)
Citizen takes active role as member of government advisory board, candidate for office, active member of political organization

B. Policy-responsive linkage between citizen and state (upward)
Citizens choose government to carry out their wishes; candidates for office campaign on program incorporating citizen wishes

C. Clientelistic linkage between citizen and state (upward and downward)
Citizen exchanges vote for material rewards for community or self

D. Directive linkage between citizen and state (downward)
Citizen complies with government policy under threat of force; citizen is educated by government to accept and comply with policy

FIGURE 2.1   **Four Kinds of Linkage Between Citizen and State**

tion in it, others by their power to compel changes in policy, others by their willingness to give their votes in exchange for material favors, and still others by constraint, as they unthinkingly accept their leaders' propaganda efforts or live in fear of physical coercion. What interests political scientists is the degree to which each form of linkage is present, if at all, and why.

POLITICAL CONCEPTS REGARDING THE QUALITY OF LIFE

Politics is a fascinating subject in and of itself, but the reason most of us care enough about politics to study it is both more personal and more global. We are well aware that the quality of the life we lead together is strongly influenced by the quality of our politics. We rely heavily on political processes to organize our interactions with one another. We know we need one another to live and prosper, but we do not always find that aspect of the human condition entirely satisfactory. Four questions in particular are likely to concern us here: How different are we, or should we be, from one another? How free from control by one another are we, or should we be? How peaceful, stable, and orderly can we make our interactions with one another? How can we act together to provide an atmosphere in which new ideas — ideas that might lead to improved conditions for us all — can be permitted to develop and challenge our established ways of doing things?

Puzzling over these questions has given rise to the concepts of equality, freedom, order, and progress. Although these terms refer to qualities of daily life that, in practice, are inextricably meshed, I will endeavor here to treat them one by one. (My purpose is simply to explore what aspect of reality each of these words denotes. The ways different forms of government endeavor to cope with the problems they pose will be considered in Chapter 3.)

Equality

Contemporary political systems nearly all give at least lip service to some version of the happy thought that all men are created equal. Some even go so far as to include women in this blessing. Rational observers may protest that there are obvious differences, from birth, in the physical and intellectual abilities of human beings. However, most of us are willing to grant that there are important ways in which we all *are* created equal, if we focus not on our abilities but our needs. All of us need shelter, food, sleep, safety, various forms of social responsiveness (love, sex, affection, kindness, respect) and interesting activity. We may even agree that this fundamental **equality** in neediness is more important in determining the role of government than innate or acquired differences in abilities.[21]

Political equality means an equal right to participate in the political

Slums and high-rise housing in Caracas, Venezuela. Such inequities in status and prosperity are met throughout the world. (Peter Menzel/Stock Boston)

process and to be treated fairly by it. When Oliver Cromwell's momentarily victorious troops sat around the campfire on the fields of Putney during the English Civil War debating the order of the future society they intended to establish, one eloquent soul argued for political equality (as opposed to basing the right to vote on the possession of property) on the grounds that government affects everyone. "Verily," he said, "I do believe that the poorest he that is in England hath a life to live as the richest he."[22] In the seventeenth century such a notion was nothing short of radical, and in the twentieth century its implications are still not accepted everywhere. The right to vote and to hold office is hemmed in with numerous restrictions, and equal treatment under the laws is routinely denied women, children, aliens, and racial and religious minorities in various parts of the world.

Social equality is the right to be treated as a social equal, at least with respect to one's basic characteristics and needs. When governments attempt to outlaw discrimination in housing, jobs, and education on the basis of race, religion, or sex, they are asserting that such differences do not make some persons more socially worthy than others. Constitutional provisions that forbid governments to grant titles of nobility, laws that establish egalitarian standards of salutation ("citizen," "comrade"); and judicial rulings that limit the right of private associations to grant or deny membership privileges are all motivated by the belief that government has a role to play in ensuring that if we cannot all be truly equal socially, our differences of rank will nevertheless not be permitted to extend to painful extremes.

Are governments properly concerned with fostering **economic equality** — that is, with ensuring that every citizen has approximately the same amount of material goods? That controversial question is often sidestepped by arguing that government is responsible only to provide equality of opportunity in the economic domain — that the goal of economic equality is sufficiently served when government sees to it that opportunities to get the necessary training and education are equal and that there are enough jobs for everyone. After that, goes the argument, natural and acquired inequalities in ability should be allowed to have whatever effect they may in producing unequal economic rewards. Others argue that such an approach will never eliminate the suffering of the poor and that governments must assume a greater role by carrying out rigorous tax, land redistribution, or other policies designed to limit the growth of private fortunes.

Freedom

It is impossible to determine what government's role should be in ensuring any form of equality without confronting the concept of **freedom**. Any political measures taken to make us more equal are likely to make us both more and less free: more free to pursue some measure of happiness, less free to disregard the welfare of others while pursuing our happiness. But what is freedom? The Old English word *freo*, from which the word *freedom* comes, meant "not in bondage, noble, glad, illustrious." Even today the word carries a connotation of pride, of a sense of personal accomplishment in the fact of not being in bondage. Thus *freedom* means something more than *liberty*, which suggests simply the absence of constraint. In practice, however, the two terms are often used interchangeably.

There is general agreement today that it is the responsibility of all governments to keep their citizens free, in the sense of "out of bondage." At the same time, most people would agree that there are times when governments must limit individual liberty. The question is: Where shall the line be drawn? No one has argued more eloquently for maximizing individual freedom than John Stuart Mill, whose nineteenth-century essay *On Liberty* provides the classic defense of liberty as the guarantor of human progress. Only when men and women are free to explore and propound any idea they wish can there be a hope of discovering truth, said Mill, for only in the struggle against error can truth emerge. He went so far as to regret the "universal recognition" of any particular truth, because there is no better "aid to the intelligent and living apprehension of a truth [than] is afforded

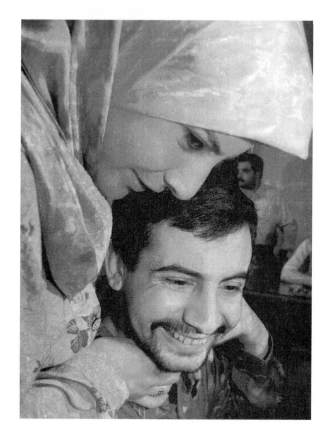

Free at last. A Lebanese woman, Layla Baalbaki, hugs her brother Issam, 20, of the Israeli-sponsored South Lebanon Army, who was a prisoner of Hezbollah (the extreme faction of the Islamic Republican Party) for three years. Issam was among militiamen of the SLA released in July 1996 in one of the biggest swaps of prisoners between Israel and Hezbollah. (AP Photos/Saleh Rifai/Wide World)

by the necessity of explaining it to, or defending it against, opponents."[23] Mill was also keenly aware of the threat posed to liberty by what seemed to him to be an excessive concern with political equality. If all are given an equal vote, politicians will simply comply with the will of the majority, however uninformed or misguided that will might be. There "ceases to be any social support for nonconformity."[24] According to Mill, "Eccentricity has always abounded when and where strength of character has abounded; and the amount of eccentricity in a society has generally been proportional to the amount of genius, mental vigor, and moral courage which it contained. That so few now dare to be eccentric, marks the chief danger of the time."[25]

Like equality, freedom comes in various forms. Political freedom means the freedom to dissent without fear of punishment. Social freedom means the freedom to behave as one wishes. Economic freedom means the freedom to acquire and dispose of one's personal wealth without hindrance. None of these freedoms is absolute in any land, but the extent to which each is protected varies enormously from nation to nation, and from time to time. It is an unending debate, one that often pits one kind of freedom against another, and different nations arrive at different resolutions. Governments in underdeveloped nations are sometimes so determined to maintain political stability that they use brutal means to stifle the free expression of ideas while encouraging a shift to greater economic freedom at the same time in order to stimulate the livelier competitiveness essential for joining a capitalistic global economy. In a series of military governments, contemporary Nigeria allowed crop prices to be determined by the market (abolishing price-fixing commodity boards), reduced the number of commodities requiring import licenses from seventy-four to sixteen, deregulated the banking system and foreign exchange market, and set up a privatization committee to sell off state-owned enterprises. But it also banned all political parties and any political assembly, severely restricted freedom of the press, and did nothing at all about the fact that women do not receive equal pay for equal work, are often denied commercial credit, and receive less than one-third the education given to men. Some European polities, on the other hand, prefer limiting economic freedoms to ensure that the gap between rich and poor does not become too great while taking freedom of expression, even for the most "dangerous" opinions, absolutely for granted.[26] How would you characterize your own nation in this regard?

Order

The problem of balancing government's responsibility to aid the needy with its responsibility to protect individual freedom is compounded by our need for order and stability. As we saw in Chapter 1, our life as a social, interacting species requires us to organize our relationships with one another, to create **order** out of chaos, and to develop some ability to predict what will happen next. Order is essential, yet it is often difficult to establish without sacrificing other desired conditions.

Consider, for example, the fact that one way order is achieved is through the division of labor; certain persons are authorized to perform certain functions. Inevitably, some functions prove more essential than others to the collective good, and it is likely that those functions will come to be better rewarded than others, which means the loss of whatever socioeconomic equality may have existed. A hierarchy of jobs evolves, including the job (usually at or near the top) of making decisions binding throughout the society — that is, the job of political leadership. Creating this job inevitably means creating institutions of government, which, aside from their more positive functions, provide the means by which those leaders, if left unchecked and so inclined, can suppress their subjects' most cherished personal freedoms. The quest for order seems inevitably to impede the quests for equality and freedom.

Progress

By now we begin to see why the design of the perfect human polity has so far proved beyond human abilities, given what appear to be the mutually exclusive goals of equality, freedom, and order. Nevertheless, most human beings remain convinced — sometimes despite the most appalling personal evidence to the contrary — that a better life is possible. Some eras have prompted greater certitude than others that progress for the entire species is not only possible but inevitable. The eighteenth, nineteenth, and early twentieth centuries appear to have been the high point of such confidence for north Atlantic populations. But overall, the history of humankind has been to a very large extent a history of change prompted by the expectation of improved conditions.

What is the role of the political process in fostering progress? However **progress** is defined, it must inevitably involve the reallocation of resources. The political process, as the means by which scarce resources are authoritatively allocated throughout a polity, is thus always likely to be part of any struggle to improve the human lot — or the lot of a particular group of humans. A regime that insists on maintaining the status quo no matter what conditions prevail, and that refuses to see signs of the need for change, stands in the path of progress. But how can even the most receptive and flexible political system be certain of distinguishing between positive input — which, if acted on, might lead to progress — and negative input, which might lead to disorder and decline? Furthermore, one group's progress might well be another group's regression. In such a case, how are those in political roles to judge that one is more important than the other?

These questions have no easy answers. Some nations state long-range goals in the preambles to their constitutions as guidelines to decision makers. Others adopt a body of religious precepts for the same purpose. An Islamic state, such as Saudi Arabia, is a state guided by the *Qu'ran*, and progress means progress in fulfilling the guidelines of that text. Still others, like the state of Israel, have opted for a combination of religious and secular guidelines.

Democratic systems provide for free elections, partly as a means to improve the chance that suggestions for change will reach those in positions of leadership, but elections do not solve the problem of distinguishing between good and bad suggestions. Indeed, they may simply produce a kind of knee-jerk responsiveness to the majority's will, regardless of the wrongheadedness of the policies thus adopted. Should the right to vote be limited to those who have a certain level of education, as some writers have suggested?[27] What happens then to the concept of political equality? And who would be so bold as to say that creative suggestions for progress come only from those with higher degrees?

As should be apparent by now, the thirteen concepts we have examined are strongly interconnected, and it is often difficult to discuss one without entering into a discussion of the others. These thirteen are, of course, only a fraction of the total number of concepts with which political scientists routinely deal. Here I have provided the beginning of an initiation into the language of political science. Throughout the rest of this book, other terms and concepts will be introduced as they are needed.

The language of political science is not difficult. Most of the terms are already familiar to you, so it is perfectly possible to discuss the subject matter of political science clearly. Still, political scientists — along with other social scientists — are often accused of taking deliberate delight in using unfamiliar jargon to conceal ideas and facts that are well known to anyone with a modicum of common sense. Is this accusation fair?

INSIGHT VERSUS JARGON IN THE STUDY
OF POLITICAL SCIENCE

> The word *free* still existed in Newspeak, but it could only be used in such statements as "This dog is free from lice" or "This field is free from weeds." It could not be used in its old sense of "politically free" or "intellectually free," since political and intellectual freedom no longer existed even as concepts, and were therefore of necessity nameless.[28]

The misuse and abuse of language is a serious and dangerous offense. Novelist George Orwell invented a world in which a new language, Newspeak, operated "not only to provide a medium of expression for the world-view and mental habits proper to devotees of [the new system], but to make all other modes of thought impossible."[29] Contemporary social scientists are sometimes accused of nearly equivalent abuses of the language. When the former United States ambassador to the United Nations, Jeane Kirkpatrick, urged Americans to distinguish between repressive totalitarian systems unfriendly to this nation and "moderately repressive" authoritarian systems that support us in the international arena, those who found the distinction semantically unsound as well as politically repugnant could (and did) point out that Ambassador Kirkpatrick was a former professor of political science.

Those offended by the language of social science usually complain less, however, of ideological manipulation than of simple obscurantism, jargon, and bad writing. Why should it be necessary to say, for example, "The responses of Italy and Mexico confirm the high incidence of output alienation in these countries. These people are alienated in their expectations of treatment at the hands of governmental authority and police" — when all one means is that Mexicans and Italians have a lower opinion of their governments and police than do citizens of other nations?[30] Or why say, "A polity marked by the proliferation of hereditary office-holding and the decline or disappearance of centrally controlled appointive staffs is paracephalous" if what one really means is that a chief characteristic of feudalism was the decentralization of power?[31]

Such complaints are often justified, and the language of the social sciences does sometimes become unnecessarily tortured and obscure. There is something of a contradiction, however, in the popular attitude toward the social sciences. On the one hand, the public accuses them of being unscientific and incapable of moving beyond common-sense descriptions of social relationships. On the other hand, as soon as political scientists (or sociologists, or economists, or historians) begin to develop a terminology that will permit them to describe such relationships more precisely and to make distinctions not immediately familiar to their audiences, they are told, "For heaven's sake, speak English!" Every effort is made to reduce their findings to well-known truisms, such as, "So Mexicans and Italians don't like cops — so what?" or "After all, it is common knowledge that a feudal lord was a law unto himself."

Such reductionism is not always justified. In both the examples cited here, the authors were in fact attempting to develop models for the analysis of whole political systems. The mention of hostility toward police and of well-known characteristics of feudalism are important not in themselves but as steps in building these models. In context, the language used is more helpful than quoting it out of context suggests. It certainly *could* be improved, but it does help the reader understand how these familiar facts, when examined in the framework of the authors' models, may contribute to an understanding of far more complex political phenomena.

Does this mean there is no such thing as jargon in political science? Of course not. All too frequently, sentences that seem to be taking a ridiculously long and difficult way to say one simple thing are doing exactly that. New words are invented to name things that have been named and understood for centuries. However, what I am suggesting here is that the judgment that this is the case should not be made too hastily. Stop and consider whether the words that seem merely to be retelling an old, familiar tale in a new version of gobbledygook are not, in fact, saying something new, interesting, and important. Do not be too eager to sift through complex material for one grain of timeworn "truth." You may well be able to find that same old grain if you pan for it, but in doing so you might be letting a fortune in new understanding slip through your fingers.

SUMMARY AND CONCLUSION

Political scientists commonly use three kinds of concepts in their work: those that name kinds of structures, those that name relationships of control, and those that name certain qualities of daily life that are subject to political determination.

Concepts that name structures include organizations, institutions, states, and systems. An organization is a body of persons working together in a structured way to achieve a specific purpose. An institution is a structure with established functions to perform, roles for carrying out those functions, and rules for how to do so. A state is a structure that has the legal right to make rules that are binding over a given population within a given territory. A system is a structure all of whose parts are interrelated, so that a change in one part means a change in all; a political system is a system that deals with political matters.

Concepts that name relationships of control include power, influence, authority, legitimacy and linkage. Power is a relationship in which control is achieved by threatening and sometimes carrying out severe sanctions for noncompliance with the power-holders' wishes. Influence is a broader form of control; it includes the exercise of power but it also includes persuasion without the threat of sanctions or the use of force; it includes all cases when one party's desires affect the behavior of another party. Authority is the right to exercise the power and influence of a given position that comes from having been placed in that position according to accepted procedures. Legitimacy is the condition of being regarded as correctly placed in a particular role and as carrying out the functions of that role correctly. Linkage is the act of connection within polities, whether between decisions made in different political systems (the most common usage in the study of international relations) or between citizens and the state (the most common usage in the study of domestic politics).

Political concepts regarding the quality of life including equality, freedom, order, and progress. Political equality means an equal right to participate in the political process and to be treated fairly by it. Political freedom means the freedom to dissent without fear of punishment. Political order is the organization of our relationships with one another within a polity. The quest for progress inspires most political change, but what constitutes true progress is always subject to dispute. The efforts made to achieve equality, freedom, order and progress often conflict with one another.

The language of political science — and of all the social sciences — can become unnecessarily obscure and jargonistic. Yet sometimes new words and new concepts are necessary to convey new understandings. Distinguishing between unnecessary jargon and important new terms is one of the most difficult and important skills of the political scientist.

Selected Readings

Beetham, David. *The Legitimation of Power* (New Jersey: Humanities Press, International, 1991). Provides an introductory discussion of the concept of legitimacy in contemporary politics.

Bourdieu, Pierre. *Language and Symbolic Power* (Boston: Harvard University Press, 1991). A collection of the writings of a noted French sociologist on politics, language, and discourse.

Connolly, William E. *The Terms of Political Discourse* (Princeton, N.J.: Princeton University Press, 1993). A study of political concepts such as freedom and interests.

Freeden, Michael. *Rights* (Minneapolis: University of Minnesota Press, 1995). Examines the evolution of the concept of rights in relation to politics.

Geis, Michael L. *The Language of Politics* (New York: Springer-Verlag, 1987). Examines the persuasive uses of language in politics. Areas of analysis include bias in journalism, the language of American presidencies, and press conferences.

Green, David. *The Language of Politics in America: Shaping Political Consciousness from McKinley to Reagan* (Ithaca: Cornell University Press, 1992). A historical study of the effects of political language on American politics.

Kedar, Leah, ed. *Power Through Discourse* (Norwood, N.J.: Ablex, 1987). A series of articles examining the relationship between language and power.

Laski, Harold J. *A Grammar of Politics* (London: George Allen and Unwin, 1925). A classic, dated but still informative, on the meaning and use of political terms.

Safire, William. *Safire's New Political Dictionary: The Definitive Guide to the New Language of Politics* (New York: Random House, 1993). A guide to the meaning and use of political words.

Sederberg, Peter C. *The Politics of Meaning* (Tucson, Ariz.: University of Arizona Press, 1984). An examination of the relationship of meaning and politics. Discusses different interpretations of political concepts such as leadership and freedom.

Shafritz, Jay M., Phil William and Ronald S. Calinger. *The Dictionary of 20th Century World Politics* (New York: Holt and Co., 1993). A useful reference for information on modern political terminology.

Sowell, Thomas. *A Conflict of Visions* (William Morrow, 1987). Concepts such as freedom and equality are viewed differently depending on whether one has a constrained vision (in which case one sees these rights in terms of *process*) or an unconstrained vision (in which case one looks for *results*).

Notes

1. In 1981, however, Ralph Goldman, Philip G. Schoner, and DeVere E. Pentony developed *The Political Science Concept Inventory* (Oxford: Clio Books, 1981), which lists 21,927 terms used in political science, of which 1,075 are considered terms that "undergraduate majors in political science should know well." Most of these 1,075 terms will be used in this book. Many (e.g., "Industrial Revolution," "American Bill of Rights," "veto") will already be familiar to most readers. For a more recent work on the concepts of our discipline, see Andrew Heywood, *Political Ideas and Concepts: An Introduction* (New York: St. Martin's Press, 1992).

2. When failure continues, the institution almost always falls: the members of the Argentine junta disbanded themselves in December 1983. *New York Times*, 11 Dec. 1983, 1.

3. Jan Woronoff, *Organizing African Unity* (Metuchen, N.J.: Scarecrow Press, 1970).

4. William Drozdiak, "French Parliament Votes Europe Changes," *Washington Post*, 24 June 1992, p. 23.

5. Gregory W. Gleason and Susan J. Buck, "Decolonization in the Former Soviet Borderlands: Politics in Search of Principles," *PS: Political Science and Politics* (Sept. 1993): 522–25.

6. The concept of *political system* has been most elaborately developed in David Easton, *A Systems Analysis of Political Life* (New York: John Wiley and Sons, 1965).

7. Robert A. Dahl, *Modern Political Analysis*, 4th ed. (Englewood Cliffs, N.J.: Prentice Hall, 1984), pp. 20–22.

8. Ibid., p. 41.

9. Harold Lasswell and Abraham Kaplan, *Power and Society: A Framework for Political Inquiry* (New Haven, Conn.: Yale University Press, 1950), p. 76; quoted in Dahl, *Analysis*, p. 47, n. 5.

10. For the argument regarding the Balkans, see *Wall Street Journal*, 28 July 1995, A1 and A4. For the return to violence in Ireland, see *New York Times*, 9 Mar. 1996, 3.

11. On the Indian political system, see Zoya Hasan, S. N. Jha, and Rasheeduddin Khan, *The State, Political Processes and Identity: Reflections on Modern India* (New Delhi: Sage, 1989).

12. Percy R. Luney, Jr. and Kazuyuki Takahashi, *Japanese Constitutional Law* (Tokyo: University of Tokyo Press, 1993).

13. M. J. Meggitt, "Indigenous Forms of Government

Among the Australian Aborigines," *Tot De Tall-, Land-en Volkenkunde* 6, no. 120 (1964): 163–80.

14. Mary L. Volcansek and Jacqueline Lucienne Lafon, *Judicial Selection: The Cross-Evolution of French and Amerian Practices* (New York: Greenwood Press, 1988), p. 110.

15. The European conquest of some African peoples was completed as late as 1911. See Robert I. Rotberg, *A Political History of Tropical Africa* (New York: Harcourt, Brace & World, 1965), p. 258. For an interesting fictionalized view of the relationship between authority and legitimacy, see Chinua Achebe, *A Man of the People* (Garden City, N.Y.: Anchor Books, 1967).

16. Robin Alison Remington examines the role played by rising nationalisms in contemporary Bosnia in "Bosnia, The Tangled Web," *Current History* (Nov. 1993): 364–69.

17. See, for example, John A. Hamilton, "To Link or Not to Link," *Foreign Policy* (Fall 1982): 62–81.

18. See, for example, V.O. Key, *Public Opinion and American Democracy* (New York: Knopf, 1964), pp. 409–558.

19. The forms of linkage discussed here are drawn from Kay Lawson, "Political Parties and Linkage," in Kay Lawson, ed., *Political Parties and Linkage, A Comparative Perspective* (New Haven, Conn.: Yale University Press, 1981), pp. 1–24.

20. Ayse Gunes-Ayata, "Roots and Trends of Clientelism in Turkey," in *Democracy, Clientelism, and Civil Society* (Boulder: Lynne Rienner, 1994), pp. 51–52, 58. For the shifting patterns of an enduring clientelism in Mexico, see Luis Roniger, *Hierar-chy and Trust in Modern Mexico and Brazil* (New York: Praeger, 1990), pp. 57–95.

21. Abraham A. Maslow identifies a "hierarchy of needs" in *Motivation and Personality* (New York: Harper & Row, 1954), pp. 35–58.

22. C. H. Firth, ed., *The Clarke Papers: Selections from Papers of William Clarke*, vol. 1 (Westminster, U.K.: Nicholos and Sons, 1891), p. 301.

23. John Stuart Mill, *On Liberty* (New York: Appleton-Century-Crofts, 1947), p. 43.

24. Ibid., p. 74.

25. Ibid., p. 67.

26. "Nigeria: Anybody Seen a Giant?" in "Nigeria Survey," *The Economist*, 21 Aug. 1993, 6–7, and Adrian Karatnycky, *Freedom in the World: The Annual Survey of Political Rights and Civil Liberties* (New York: Freedom House, 1994), pp. 434–37.

27. John Stuart Mill, "Considerations on Representative Government," in Millicent Garret Fawcett, ed., *On Liberty, Representative Government, the Subjection of Women: Three Essays by John Stuart Mill* (London: Oxford University Press, 1912), pp. 145–423.

28. George Orwell, *1984* (New York: New American Library, 1949), pp. 246–47.

29. Ibid., p. 246.

30. Gabriel A. Almond and Sidney Verba, *The Civic Culture: Political Attitudes and Democracy in Five Nations* (Boston: Little, Brown, 1963), p. 69.

31. Fred W. Riggs, "The Comparison of Whole Political Systems," in Holt and Turner, eds., *The Methodology of Comparative Research* (New York: The Free Press, 1970), p. 104.

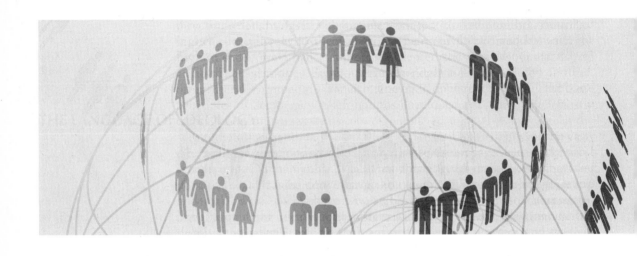

II THE CONTEXT OF POLITICS

3 Political Ideologies

SOMETIMES THE POLITICAL QUESTIONS we ask ourselves are explicit and specific. What is our government's role in providing free education? What domestic as well as foreign policy goals were served when the United States undertook to put the Aristide government back in power in Haiti in 1994? How did the victory of Jacques Chirac in the 1995 French presidential election affect the power relationships between Parliament and the presidency in the French system of government? Sometimes, however, we find ourselves thinking about politics in much broader terms, asking much more fundamental and far-reaching questions. Why has our political system taken the form it has? What would be the ideal political system? Would the ideal system be ideal for all peoples, or just for us? How could an ideal system be established?

When we try to find answers to these more fundamental questions, we are involved in an age-old quest, the search for a system of political beliefs. If we are concerned enough to do a little research, we will find a few well-formulated ideologies from which to choose, such as conservatism, liberalism, and socialism. If we are looking for something radically different from the status quo, we may explore the tenets of some of the more extreme ideologies, such as fascism or a branch of religious fundamentalism. Or perhaps the insights of contemporary feminism will seem to cover more of the problems we must deal with today — or the passions of ethnic nationalism will strike us as more relevant than any more comprehensive world view. Some of us will shop around, picking up an idea that makes sense here, another that seems exciting there, and gradually piece together a more or less coherent but still very personal view of political reality and possibilities. Not all of us will become *ideologues*.

WHAT IS AN IDEOLOGY?

Ideology is a word with almost as many definitions as there are people using the term. Most scholars would agree that an ideology attempts to offer answers to at least the first two questions just cited: How have our political systems taken the form they have, and what would be the ideal political system? Beyond this, there is little consensus. Some scholars argue that an ideology must be "accepted as fact or truth by some group," but others believe individuals can have personal ideologies, unshared and unadvertised.[1] Some think an ideology always claims "a monopoly of truth" and thus seeks to "explain everything and in so doing [will] refuse to tolerate rival views or opposing theories," whereas others believe most ideologies leave room for some opposition and point out that in fact a key component of liberalism is its insistence on the importance of the open competition of points of view.[2] Some think an ideology must be revolutionary to merit the name: "The ideologue is a revolutionary, dedicated to the overthrow of the existing system and concerned above all with the means by which this can be accomplished."[3] Others suggest that it is possible for an ideology to be simply a defense of the status quo (in which case its doctrine presumably suggests that the answers to the first and second questions are one and the same and that the other questions are without interest).

A little empirical work suggests that in each of these various controversies "others" are right. Individuals do develop personal, idiosyncratic ideologies; listen to any talk show for an hour or so if you are in doubt. Most ideologies are not entirely closed systems of thought, nor do their supporters claim they are — the very multiplicity of meanings we give to the words *conservative*, *liberal*, and *socialist* testifies to how far from closed these three dominant ideologies have been.

Similarly, not all ideologies preach revolution. Once a socialist system has been established, socialist ideologues can become strong defenders of the status quo — and of course the chief object of conservatism can be to make sure that nothing changes. (On the other hand, even conservatives can be change oriented when the present system appears unsatisfactory to them and their goal is to establish a more orderly or more libertarian political system.)

Saying that an ideology can be personal or shared with a group, open or closed, and revolutionary or defensive is all well and good, but it does not give us our own working definition; it simply tells us what to leave out of that definition. Let us approach the problem more assertively: an **ideology** is a comprehensive set of beliefs and attitudes about social and economic institutions and processes. It offers a critique of the existing system and a view of the ideal system. Where these differ, it suggests the means for moving from the existing to the ideal. It also presents a theory of human nature and, thereby, of human potentiality and of the need for particular modes of social control.

These various characteristics of all ideologies will become clearer as we discuss specific examples. But before we proceed, note the word that is missing from the preceding paragraph: *political.* All ideologies that merit the name deal extensively with political questions; all ideologies are, in some sense, political ideologies. But not all ideologies are predominantly political ideologies. Because they are comprehensive systems of beliefs and attitudes, they usually have as much to say about economic and social relationships as they do about matters purely political — or even more. When we talk about *political ideologies,* we usually mean that we are stressing the political aspects of ideologies. In the discussion that follows we will be looking at the political tenets of seven systems of belief. We will consider some economic and social factors taken up in each of these but will keep in mind that our focus is political and that the range of each ideology considered is far wider than the focus of this discussion permits us to show.

The most important ideas incorporated in the systems of belief that we will be examining are ideas that were conceived long ago. As we will show, most of them have been on the philosophic agenda ever since men and women first began to consider whether the system under which they lived was necessarily the best of all possible systems. On the other hand, political *ideologies* as we know them today did not fully emerge until relatively recent times. The major economic and social upheavals of the past three hundred years have both forced and enabled more of us to take the questions of ideology seriously and to seek new hope in the promise these systems of thought hold for creating a better world.

The ideologies that have evolved thus far in the course of human affairs have not all shown equal concern for the question that provides the theme of this book, global interdependence. Most of them have something to say, however, about what the relationship between polities should be. Indeed, their approaches to this problem reveal some of the most intriguing and significant differences among them, as I will try to make clear in what follows.

Conservatism

Conservatism is well named. The conservative believes first and foremost in conserving what exists, in the idea that "the accumulated wisdom and experience of the countless generations gone is more likely to be right than the passing fashion of the moment."[4] Thus, conservatives have a certain bias in favor of the existing political system. If change is needed, it should be approached very cautiously: "Man's hopes are high, but his vision is short. Efforts to remedy existing evils usually result in even greater ones."[5]

The conservative view of human nature is not entirely positive and is definitely nonegalitarian. Conservatives believe that some people contribute more than others to society and should therefore be more honored by society.[6] One such honor is the right to positions of political authority. If ordinary people are given the power to rule themselves, they are likely to be intolerant of anyone who does not fit the common mold and to sacrifice the protection of minority rights in order to ensure majority rule.[7]

Personal liberty is the individual right conservatives hold most dear, but this does not mean that everyone must be left to pursue his or her own interests with no restraint: "The result will be self-indulgence, anarchy, and a turn toward totalitarianism."[8] It makes sense to use the power of government to support traditional moral standards because "genuinely ordered freedom is the only sort of liberty worth having: freedom made possible by order within the soul and order within the state."[9] But the individual must not, in "the mindless assertion of appetite," depend on the state for security; to do so is to abdicate to the power of the state, to become part of a mass society, and to risk falling prey to tyranny. Self-determination means, on the contrary, "achieving the appropriate fit between personal character and the society's institutional requirements."[10]

Conservatives are divided on the question of international interdependence. Respect for the past and for established institutions, combined with the belief that each nation is an organic whole in which everyone has a place and function, leads naturally to a strong sense of patriotism, if not outright nationalism.[11] Some conservatives do tend to see other nations as threatening the values, confidence, or security of their own land and are likely to place greater trust in military might and action than in seemingly endless diplomatic negotiation.

At the same time, however, conservatives do not entirely deny the fact of interdependence. The staunch defense of imperialist ventures that European conservatives have advanced has traditionally been based on their assertion of the responsibility of the more advanced nations to bring the blessings of civilization to those less fortunate. Such a view emphasizes the dependence of others rather than interdependence, but most contemporary conservatives are willing to go a step further. The need to defend one's own system against external enemies makes it desirable to have external friends. It is important to give aid and comfort to allies, to keep them as allies, and to prevent them from becoming the friends of one's enemies.

Conservatives are sometimes viewed by others as unbending and incapable of compromise, but on many matters they show themselves to be far less dogmatic than supporters of other ideologies. They do not, for example, specify particular institutional forms of government as necessarily better than others, nor do they believe that those who rule must follow a

Conservatism. Conservatives maintain that "the accumulated wisdom and experience of the countless generations gone is more likely to be right than the passing fashion of the moment." Contemporary conservative leaders include German Chancellor Helmut Kohl, shown here recommending a plan to revive his nation's ailing economy by reducing welfare allocations (April, 1996). (AP Photos/Fritz Reiss/Wide World)

consistent program of domestic and foreign policy. For the conservative, it is far more important that the basic principles of conservatism (order, continuity, loyalty, protection of individual freedoms, piety, and nationalism) be maintained and that those who rule exercise practical wisdom in ensuring that they are. In that sense, conservatives are among the most pragmatic of political thinkers. Andrew Heywood goes so far as to say that "conservatism is the most intellectually modest of political ideologies . . . [it] has prospered because it has been unwilling to be tied down to a fixed system of ideas."[12]

The Development of Conservatism   Although conservatism must now contend with a multitude of other ideologies, it is fair to say that for centuries almost all significant thought on political affairs manifested these key characteristics of conservatism. The ideas of conservatism are found in some of the earliest recorded efforts to prescribe political order. Chinese philosophers decided over three thousand years ago that it "was the gentleman's duty to exercise benevolent rule over the small men," that they themselves had worked out "man's most perfect system of government and society," and that the beauties of peace could be "expressed through the word 'flat': no disturbances in the realm, the village, or the home."[13] Confucius (551–479 B.C.E.) gave even greater emphasis to the need for benevolence but never doubted that the superior man (*chun tzu*) must rule and the commoner (*hsiao-jen*) must bow before his authority: "The people [should be] like grass, the ruler like the wind."[14]

Similarly, conservative principles informed the thought of Plato (427–347 B.C.E.), who believed that in the ideal state authority rests in the hands of the philosopher-king, an enlightened despot assisted by almost equally enlightened "guardians." Both the Stoics (members of the dominant school of political thought in Greece and Rome as these city-states took on the attributes of empires) and the early Christians argued that human beings were basically equal but stressed nevertheless the duty of obedience to a divinely ordered government.[15] Augustine (C.E. 354–430) saw a firm government as the only possible earthly corrective to the sinful nature of humankind since its fall from grace; for Thomas Aquinas (1225–1274) the highest law was God's law, and a just king was one who ruled according to that law.[16] In the period of the Renaissance and Reformation, writers such as Bodin, Grotius, Machiavelli, Richard Hooker, and Thomas Hobbes all insisted that the state was sovereign and absolute.

However, by the time of Hooker (1553–1600) and Hobbes (1588–1679), new ideas were beginning to challenge even the most fundamental beliefs of conservatism. The Protestant Reformation seemed to threaten not only the Roman Catholic church but also the divine right of monarchs to absolute ascendancy in civil matters, a power given the blessings of that church. When theological radicals began to raise disturbing doubts, conservative appeals to order and obedience were used to defend royal authority against political dissidents as well as against those who wished to establish a new religion.

Nevertheless, the intellectual ferment continued into the seventeenth and eighteenth centuries and reached its climax in 1789, when the French Revolution brought about the collapse of an entire feudal, agrarian, and aristocratic order. British statesman and writer Edmund Burke (1729–1797) watched in horror as an established order crumbled and a new system emerged. This arch-conservative believed society is an organism to which everyone belongs and that institutions that have evolved within that organism, in response to national characteristics and conditions, could no more be casually cut away without jeopardy to the life of that organism than could the internal organs of any other creature.[17]

Across the Atlantic a new nation, the United States, was being forged after its own revolution. Yet many of the Americans who had accepted the idea that armed overthrow of an oppressive Britain was unavoidable nevertheless wrote in the conservative tradition. John Adams, Alexander Hamilton, and Fisher Ames all warned against carrying revolution to the dangerous point of establishing a mass democracy. As the nation did in fact slowly but inexorably democratize, leading conservatives like Daniel Webster feared that the extension of the right to vote would inevitably endanger the right to property. Southern conservatives had a different concern; in *Sociology for the South* (1854), George Fitzhugh saw the relationship between master and slave as one between natural leader and follower, a relationship "of mutual good will," in which the "whole life of the slaveholder" is spent in "providing for the minutest wants of others, taking care of them in sickness and in health." [18]

Defense of slavery was no more viable a stand than the effort to forestall democratic government had been, but toward the end of the nineteenth century, as the Western world became increasingly industrialized and great fortunes were amassed, conservative authors found a new and more popular cause, the glorification of the acquisition of wealth. An Englishman, Herbert Spencer, preached the doctrine of Social Darwinism — that is, that social and economic competition was natural, part of the process of ensuring that the fit should survive, and on the whole better for society even if it meant suffering for those less fit. The American clergyman Russell H. Conwell was more optimistic and believed that everyone could gain. "It is your duty to get rich," he told his countrymen. [19]

As should by now be clear, the substance of conservatism shifts with time and place. That which is to be protected varies according to the threats that are posed. In the early twentieth century, the welfare state became the favored target and conservatives fought for the rights of workers and employers to continue to make their own contracts, without risk of intervention by a state bent on protecting workers. U.S. President Herbert Hoover insisted even after the Great Depression of 1929 and his failure to win reelection in 1932 that "voluntary agencies" were the answer to the suffering caused by widespread unemployment. "I do not feel," he said, "that I should be charged with lack of human sympathy for those who suffer. . . . I am confident that our people have the resources, the initiative, the courage, the stamina, and the kindliness of spirit to meet this situation in the way they have met their problems over generations." [20]

At present, some of the most powerful parties in Europe and North America express the typical conservative concern for preserving traditional institutions (especially family, church, and nation-state) and traditional values (especially hard work, personal responsibility, and patriotism). [21] The U.S. Republican Party, the British Conservatives, and the French Neo-Gaullists are all examples of this kind of party. In many nations, the writings of neoconservative scholars and journalists are given close attention and neoconservative organizations and clubs have formed, sometimes to support such parties, sometimes to demand that conservative principles be carried further than the practical politicians are willing to do. [22]

Liberalism

The chief difference between conservatism and **liberalism** is the view each takes of human nature. Where the conservative is at best cautiously hopeful that the ordinary person will, in a well-ordered state, manifest the admirable characteristics of loyalty, patriotism, and piety, the liberal takes a much more egalitarian view. The liberal believes that human beings — all human beings — are capable of reason and rational action, but that they are often caught in difficult situations in real life. People are not born equal, but everyone has the capacity to live a satisfactory and productive life if given the chance. An essential role of government is to ensure that all citizens have the opportunity to develop their skills and abilities, whatever they may be.[23]

Such a view of human nature virtually guarantees that the liberal will be optimistic about the possibility of improving a particular political system and will expect the ordinary citizen to play an important role in bringing about such an improvement. The liberal is seldom a revolutionary, however, and never imagines that progress is inevitable. Given the positive attributes of human nature, it is worthwhile to try, but the outcome is uncertain.

Furthermore, progress cannot and should not be forced on an unwilling populace. The responsibility of people in power is to make it possible for all men and women to exercise reason, work for a better life, and make their own important choices. The liberal hopes that their choices will be wise, but individual liberty includes the right to make choices that work against one's own interests.

Liberalism, as may begin to be clear, is a difficult and sometimes ambiguous creed. It suggests that government should intervene to "help" but never to "curb freedom." In practice, it is often difficult to accomplish the one without the other. Liberalism says that ordinary men and women are entitled to satisfactory lives, but that individual liberties, including the right to prosper from one's efforts, should not be curtailed. This same ambivalence is apparent in the liberal approach to the question of interdependence, both among individuals and among nations. People and polities are interdependent and must show a humane concern for one another, but at the same time the individual person or state has the right to pursue individual interests. When these goals conflict, liberals (like conservatives) are content to look for pragmatic solutions according to the circumstances rather than to spell out one specific way to establish the ideal social system.

The Development of Liberalism   The liberal view of human nature also had its early proponents. At a mass funeral in 430 B.C.E. for warriors killed in the Peloponnesian War, Pericles asserted the Athenian belief that everyone is capable of free and rational deliberation. "If few of us are originators, we are all sound judges of a policy. The great impediment to action is, in our opinion, not discussion, but the want of that knowledge which is gained by discussion preparatory to action."[24] Some three hundred years later, the Stoic orator Marcus Tullius Cicero (106–43 B.C.E.) argued that "there is no difference in kind between man and man," that reason "is certainly common to us all," and that this quality not only "raises us above the level of the beast" but makes us capable of figuring out the "principles of right living" that have been implanted in us by "nature."[25] And in China in the fourth century B.C.E. the philosopher Mencius taught that "every human being can become a sage-king" — that is, that anyone can gain the wisdom needed to rule.[26]

The argument that everyone has the right to exercise independent judgment in at least some domains of life, and sufficient reason to do so adequately, was strongly advanced by the Protestant Reformation. Although the Judeo-Christian tradition had always stressed an element of free choice (virtue consists in willing and believing in the right, not simply giving in to force or custom), the Protestants went further. Believers could figure out for themselves how to achieve personal salvation by relying on the sacred writings of the church, so long as these scriptures were explicated by trained theologians. If they could manage that, argued such liberal Protestant philosophers as John Locke (1632–1704) and Jean Jacques Rousseau (1712–1778), then they could certainly judge for themselves as well in the matters of worldly affairs. In fact, both Locke and Rousseau were sure that they had done so in the past. Both believed that men and women had once lived in a "state of nature" and had decided to improve their lot by making a social contract, an agreement to create a political society and thus to order human affairs more satisfactorily.[27] They argued, however, that a contract is binding only as long as all parties adhere to its terms and only on condition that individual rights and liberties were maintained. If they were not, then the ones who governed had "put themselves into a state of war with the people, who are thereupon absolved from any further obedience."[28]

If the term *contract* strikes you as interestingly businesslike, you have picked up a clue to the reason the ideas of Locke and Rousseau and their various followers proved to have such wide appeal in the eighteenth and nineteenth centuries. The massive transformations in people's relationships that took place with the decline of feudalism, the birth of capitalism, and the onset of the Industrial Revolution stimulated the adherents of liberalism (as it had those of conservatism) to develop their arguments into a more formal ideology. What did these changes have to do with liberal thought? As Box 3.1 shows, they produced conditions that made the tenets of liberalism newly appealing — both to the worker seeking a freer and better life than could be found in agriculture and to the industrial employer seeking freedom of investment and a mobile labor force.

This era of new appreciation for liberal values produced its own crop of ideologues. David Hume (1711–1776), Adam Smith (1723–1790), Jeremy Bentham (1748–1832), and John Stuart Mill (1806–1873) spoke variously of "the greatest good for the greatest number," the benevolent guidance of

BOX 3.1   HOW THE DECLINE OF FEUDALISM STIMULATED THE RISE OF
                                          LIBERALISM

1. Evolving human technology and science, combined with the wealth accumulated from successful warfare, made it possible for Europeans to engage
   in global exploration and conquest.
2. Lands newly conquered, farmed by peoples newly conquered (often slaves),
   provided highly profitable crops.
3. The move into new environments stimulated human inventiveness.
4. High profits provided capital for investment in the development of new inventions to make new kinds of goods out of new kinds of raw materials.
5. The result was the large-scale development of machined goods — the Industrial Revolution — and of a new workplace, the factory.
6. Because factories tended to cluster where the import and export of goods
   was easiest, required workers, and paid workers more than they could earn
   in agriculture, more people moved to the city and urbanization accompanied industrialization.
7. As workers moved off the farm, old communal bonds loosened and broke;
   individual workers moved out on their own, seeking a freer and better life,
   but often found only long hours of labor in a confined and dangerous
   setting.
8. At the same time, a new freedom beckoned those with capital to invest. If
   government could be kept from interfering, there seemed to be no limits to
   capitalist entrepreneurship. Any human need might be met with a new
   product, and any amount of wealth might be acquired by meeting those
   needs.
9. The new era's promises of progress, freedom, and the redistribution of
   wealth appealed to almost everyone but were unequally kept. The tenets of
   liberalism addressed both the hopes and the disappointments that were so
   keenly felt.

"the unseen hand of the market" (or "laissez faire economics"), and "utilitarianism," but the underlying message was the same: pursuing individual
interests freely and rationally would lead to the best of all social systems.
The role of government was to protect the weak while leaving the strong
as free as possible to carry out their business.[29]

As we have already seen, the dual responsibility liberals assign to government is often difficult to fulfill, and as the Industrial Revolution went
forward the humming machinery set up by the strong seemed to drown
out the faint cries of the weak. Sweatshops, child labor, and intolerable
working conditions became the order of the day. But was all this really
liberalism in action? Some early twentieth-century liberals such as John

Dewey claimed that it was not, that the plight of the common citizen had been forgotten by those who were in power and made the subject of revolutionary rabble rousing by those who were not, whereas the true liberal stood resolutely for trust in reason, belief in progress, sympathy for the downtrodden, and protection of individual liberty. Others, such as sociologist Leonard Hobhouse and economist John Maynard Keynes, began to argue that under the new circumstances a more interventionist role for government in the economy was essential, that laissez faire economics could no longer ensure the conditions in which true liberal values could flourish. Still others clung to the belief that Smith was right, that the market, if not disturbed by wrong-headed reformism, would ultimately resolve all inequities, and that this was what liberalism most essentially meant.

By and large, the latter interpretation of liberalism has prevailed in Europe, but in the United States the problem of assigning a fixed meaning to the term has been yet further compounded over the past few decades. In the first half of the century, the Dewey-Hobhouse-Keynes interpretation of what it means to be a liberal clearly prevailed and won new adherents, particularly under the leadership of presidents Franklin Roosevelt, Harry Truman, and John Kennedy. Gradually, however, the word *liberal* has been slowly stripped of almost all its meanings except the idea of "sympathy for the downtrodden" and "government interventionism" — in short, the welfare state. In the increasingly market-oriented United States, *liberal* is now often used as a critical term to deplore the beliefs of those whom most Europeans would probably call "social democratic" — and the Americans who use it that way often have beliefs that most Europeans would say are "liberal" (but that they themselves call "conservative"). If you find this confusing, rest assured that so do Americans and Europeans who try to talk to each other about liberalism. Box 3.2 suggests that the problem has its amusing side; however, the inability of the world's most powerful and most consistently interdependent economic powers to develop a common usage of so vital a term no doubt does impede the ability of their citizens to understand one another and may not really be so laughable.

However, despite the present semantic confusion and oversimplification, the ideas of liberalism — *all* the ideas — still find their supporters in the closing decades of the twentieth century. Political parties and groups that accept existing economic and constitutional structures but nevertheless struggle to enhance minimum standards of living and individual rights, to foster popular participation in policymaking, or to fight for consumer protection are all examples of the contemporary staying power of liberalism. And as we have shown, those who are in favor of eliminating excessive government regulations are also really in the liberal tradition.

The leading conservative parties of today have brought Hume, Smith, Bentham, and Mill into their own pantheon. When European journalists

BOX 3.2

HOW THE WORD *LIBERAL* CAME TO HAVE OPPOSITE MEANINGS IN THE UNITED STATES AND EUROPE

Classical liberalism says government must "help" the unfortunate and yet must also "protect freedom."

Some early liberals placed the emphasis on the freedom of the market and gave less attention to helping the poor. Contemporary European liberals have followed this tradition.

Other early liberals placed the emphasis on helping, and saw protecting freedom more as a matter of protecting individual liberties of speech and association. Contemporary American liberals have followed this tradition.

Contemporary Americans who place great emphasis on the freedom of the market think of themselves as conservatives. Because they disagree with contemporary Americans who call themselves liberals, they never think of themselves as liberals at all. Nevertheless, Europeans call this kind of conservative a liberal. And Americans call the European kind of liberal a conservative.

Now is that perfectly clear?

refer to past U.S. Presidents George Bush and Ronald Reagan, or to House Speaker Newt Gingrich, as economic liberals, they are not confused — they are right.

Socialism

For socialists, the most important characteristic of human nature is each individual's natural sociability. Socialists believe that human beings readily engage in cooperative social activity when given a chance. Unfortunately, some individuals have selfishly established structures of control that make it impossible for this natural cooperative instinct to flourish. These structures have become progressively more oppressive, causing ever greater human suffering. The ideology of **socialism** evolved out of concern for the suffering caused by human exploitation of other humans.

Socialists have traditionally been critical of existing social systems, certain that better systems could be established and determined that an important characteristic of any new system would be the limitation, if not complete abolition, of private property. The possibility of acquiring unlimited private property, argues the socialist, has stimulated the greed that causes some people to exploit others and at the same time causes the people who are exploited to endure their lot, hoping thus to obtain a better share of the world's goods. The only solution is to enlarge the public domain dramatically, establishing a community in which the land, the factories, and perhaps all the means of production are owned by the state. The state itself should be controlled by the workers, who should use their new power to guarantee a job and a fair share of the national largesse to every citizen. Above all, human want and suffering must not be allowed to continue.

The word *socialism* covers a wide range of beliefs. Despite their agreement on the need to eliminate suffering by limiting private property, socialists disagree sharply on such matters as whether revolutionary methods will be required to set up the ideal system; whether a socialist revolution will necessarily be worldwide; what conditions make revolution possible; how extensive the limitations on private property should be; how large the ideal socialist community should be; and what roles, if any, government naive and the state should play.

The Development of Socialism   Although in most respects a conservative, Plato recommended the abolition of private property, at least among the ruling class (his guardians "will not rend the community asunder by applying that word *mine* to different things"). Similar themes can be found in the writings of such medieval philosophers as Tommaso Campanella and Sir Thomas More, and in the arguments of such early dissenters as Oliver Cromwell and Gerrard Winstanley.[30]

The actual practice of various forms of socialism was also widespread long before the doctrine was articulated by Western philosophers. The small community in which land and its produce are collectively owned is in fact the oldest form of social organization and continues even today among such indigenous peoples as the Quechua of Peru and the Paez of Colombia.[31]

Here again, the development of early musings and matter-of-fact practices into a well-articulated ideology begins with the Industrial Revolution. The same forces that compelled conservatives to formulate their ideas in defense of traditional ways, and liberals to express their belief that freedom and social justice could be combined, produced conditions that stimulated socialists to organize their thoughts and set forth manifestos of their widely ranging beliefs. Those who began the process have come to be known as *utopian socialists*. The French philosopher Henri Comte de Saint-Simon (1760–1825) argued that "the elementary needs of life are the most imperative" and that those "whose work is of positive utility to society" — specifically, scientists, artists, and artisans — should be placed in charge. His countryman Charles Fourier (1772–1837) stressed the importance of community and recommended the formation of small voluntary associations of producers. The Englishman Robert Owen (1771–1858) preached a similar sermon and furthermore practiced what he preached, providing the workers in his textile mills with inexpensive housing, food, and education and urging them to develop their moral and intellectual faculties and to work together for their common good in their own community. The utopian socialists believed the changes they recommended could be effected peacefully and cooperatively, through an evolutionary process.[32]

However, Karl Marx (1818–1883) found such recommendations naive

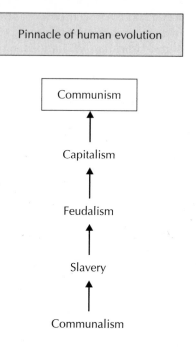

FIGURE 3.1   **Marx's Five Stages of Economic Organization**

and uninformed. He believed it was a waste of time to appeal to the con-
sciences of the capitalists who profited from the status quo. Marx and his
collaborator, Friedrich Engels (1820–1895), developed a much more complex and elaborate version of socialist ideology, which they termed **communism** and others have come to label Marxism.[33] (See Figure 3.1.)

To explain how the present system had developed, Marx took his cue
from the dialectical method of G. W. F. Hegel (1770–1831).[34] However,
where Hegel saw dialectical evolution taking place in the realm of ideas,
Marx found it in material conditions. Coining the term **dialectical materialism**, Marx asserted that human history was moving through five stages of
economic organization: communalism, slavery, feudalism, capitalism and,
finally, communism. Each stage was characterized by a different dominant
mode of production, and the social system was determined by who owned
the means of production. According to Marx, the fourth stage, capitalism,
would inevitably be replaced by a fifth, final, and climactic stage of human
evolution, *communism*, in which all the productive advantages of the earlier

stages would be retained but control over the means of production would be restored to the people who did the producing, the workers. At this point, Engels claimed, the state would "wither away" and government would consist of no more than "the mere administration of things." [35]

Marx argued that a chief feature of the three intermediate stages between primitive communalism and communism was that society was divided into two classes, those who owned the means of production and those who did not. The owners used their power not only for immediate economic gain but also to establish a political system that would endorse and defend their economic control over others. Class struggle was the inevitable by-product of noncommunal control of the means of production. The state and the dominant political ideology were merely the *superstructure* erected on a base of economic power: "The ruling ideas of each age have ever been the ideas of its ruling class." [36]

According to Marx, the final transition, from capitalism to communism, was inevitable. Capitalists would be certain to carry the exploitation of labor to the point where no one would be able to buy the goods produced, the market would shrink, the less aggressive capitalists would be forced into the ranks of the ever more exploited proletarian workers, and the workers would become aware that their only recourse was to abolish the system of private property. Because capitalism had become an international network of greed and exploitation (the Marxist viewpoint on the nature of interdependence in a capitalist world), the revolution would spread from nation to nation. The triumph of communism would be complete. "Let the ruling classes tremble. . . . The proletarians have nothing to lose but their chains. They have a world to win." [37]

Coming as it did at the height of the abuses of the Industrial Revolution, **Marxism** has had a powerful appeal from the start. Following its precepts, Vladimir Lenin (1878–1924) and his fellow Marxists worked to bring about the Russian Revolution of October 1917, adapting the Marxist prescription to fit the Russian reality. Lenin's major contributions to Marxist theory were the propositions that a communist revolution was possible even in a state that, like Russia, had only been partially industrialized; that imperialism extended the life of capitalism by developing supplementary markets and a new source of cheap labor and material; that the revolution would have to be the work of a small "vanguard" party of dedicated and informed revolutionaries who would take it upon themselves to act in the interests of the proletariat at first; and that the first stage of the revolution would produce a socialist system, in which the apparatus of the state would still be necessary, whereas true communism (and the withering away of the state) would appear only when it was finally possible to introduce the formula of "from each according to his ability — to each according to his needs." [38]

Lenin agreed with Marx that as soon as the spark of revolution was ignited in one country, the communist revolution would become international. But

The fall of Soviet-style communism in Romania. Here jubilant citizens in Bucharest celebrate their successful revolution against communist rule and the personal dictatorship of Nicolae Ceauşescu. (UPP/Photoreporters)

his successor, Joseph Stalin (1879–1953), countered that "socialism in one nation" was possible — a necessary adjustment given the tardiness of workers elsewhere to follow the Russian example.[39] Stalin also proceeded to establish one of the most ruthless dictatorships of the twentieth century, making imitation of the Soviet model less and less likely. His own successor, Nikita Khrushchev (1894–1971), attacked the "cult of the individual" that Stalin had set up and accepted the idea that communism could take different forms in different states.[40] The final attempt to adjust the meanings of communism in the Soviet Union proved to carry within it the seeds of the downfall of the entire political system. When Mikhail Gorbachev came to power on March 11, 1985, he introduced the idea of *perestroika* ("restructuring"), which included plans for economic reform, technological modernization, improved living standards, and, most significantly, the principle of *glasnost*. *Glasnost* means "openness," and by including it in *perestroika*, Gorbachev was saying that the Soviet version of communist ideology should henceforth include a much greater readiness to hear all points of view. The Soviet people responded with enthusiasm, and for a time it seemed the new leader's hopes that the deeply suffering Soviet economy could be brought back to life by strong injections of personal liberty might be well founded. But the medicine proved stronger than the system itself could bear, and the 1991–92 collapse of the Soviet Union, which we will discuss in later chapters, was the result.

At the same time that the cult of the individual was being repudiated in the Soviet Union under Khrushchev, the People's Republic of China was establishing its own experiment with communism under the ever more personal guidance of Mao Zedong (1893–1976). The need to build a strong military arm while raising the level of consciousness of vast numbers of illiterate and uneducated peasants prompted Mao to make his own contributions to communist dogma. It was Mao who explained how guerrilla warfare could be an instrument of political change as well as a tool of military takeover, how a "massline" of action could be developed by reconciling what the masses will support with what the party thinks they should support, and how economic backwardness could be overcome by encouraging the people to draw on their own common sense and experience rather than relying on foreign models.[41]

The years following Mao's death in 1976 were characterized less by ideological development than by a general relaxing of ideological rigor, combined with a repudiation of the worst forms of repression endured during Mao's reign. But relaxation was not to be overdone. In 1979, the party reminded the people that everyone must uphold the four fundamental principles of Chinese communism: socialism, single-party leadership, the dictatorship of the proletariat, and Marxism-Leninism as modified by Mao Zedong. And when mass demonstrations on behalf of democratic reform were held in Tianenmen Square in Beijing and elsewhere throughout the nation in 1989, the response was a brutal massacre that left hundreds of peaceful demonstrators dead and the watching world appalled. Post-Tiananmen developments in the Chinese political system will be discussed in later chapters; here we conclude this brief look at Chinese communism by noting that over 1 billion people — or approximately one out of every five presently living persons — are still living under this form of communist ideology.

At its height, communism was the official ideology of sixteen nations, ranging alphabetically from Albania to Yugoslavia, and geographically from Cuba to North Korea, and exerted a strong influence in the political systems of many other nations, where communist parties kept the dogma alive and constantly sought the means to take control.[42] However, as the number of communist nations and parties grew, so did the laments of those socialists who saw little if any similarity between the ideology they believed in and the practice of the so-called communist states. Calling themselves **democratic socialists** or just plain socialists (and called revisionists or rightwing counterrevolutionaries by Soviet communists), they developed a much more moderate form of socialist ideology.

One of the earliest and most effective democratic socialist movements was the Fabian Society, founded in 1888 in England by Beatrice Webb (1858–1943) and Sidney Webb (1859–1947). This group of concerned students and intellectuals rejected the idea of a desperate conflict that could only be ended by a workers' revolution but did believe that the owners of capital had become "merely the recipients of profits, interest and rent" always seeking to stifle competition and that they should be replaced by hired managers, permitting profits not needed for reinvestment to be used to address public needs. The Fabians' approach was to use reason and argument; their members wrote a series of essays that had considerable influence, and the society, which continues to the present day, played a key role in the formation of the British Labour Party.[43]

In other nations of western Europe, similar groups of intellectuals broke away from communist parties too closely aligned with the Soviets and formed their own labor or socialist parties. These more moderate socialists usually have the following beliefs in common:

1. Contemporary society is based on the class struggle.
2. The ideal society is one in which workers control the state.
3. Revolution is not essential to achieve that ideal.
4. The chief task is to organize the working class, develop its consciousness, and give it a voice in local and national government.

Such socialist parties have taken power in several European polities and shared in coalition governments in others. Their records of accomplishment are mixed, but they distinguish themselves from their former communist cousins in one important respect: They always make unambiguously clear their willingness to submit to the results of democratic elections, whatever those results may be.

Several more contemporary ideologies also fit unambiguously into the broad domain of socialist thought. *African socialism*, a body of thought developed by African writers and leaders in the postcolonial years, incorporates a desire to maintain the traditional communalism of small African polities with the more modern concern to wrest power from an oppressive class and restore it to the working class. In Tanzania this non-Marxist socialism is known as *ujamaa* ("familyhood") and has been written about extensively by that nation's former president, Julius Nyerere.[44] The Israeli *kibbutz*, a settlement in which all property is collectively owned and all labor collectively employed, is perhaps the closest modern version of the anarchist socialist's dream of self-sufficient community, despite the fact that each one operates within the context of a conservative deistic state.[45]

What, then, does socialism mean today? A 1989 conference of American professors attempted to formulate an answer. Socialism means, they

Socialism. Lionel Jospin, leader of the French Socialist Party, with supporters during his campaign for the presidency. Democratic socialists believe that if the working class is given a voice in government, socialist goals can be attained without revolution. (Harley/Bordas/Sipa Press)

said, that there will be "(1) no exploitation of man by man, (2) a comprehensive guarantee of social-economic rights, (3) concern for equality, (4) collective ownership, and (5) communal participation in the disposal of resources."[46] More recent developments have led some to argue that ideological demands for a fully socialist system are now out of the question — "there is no alternative to mixed economies, with ever-changing relations between public and private sectors, and with social minimums and safety nets," says Arno Mayer. Along these lines, John Roemer recommends a new form of mixed economy, one he calls "market socialism" in which money will be divided into two forms: "commodity money" to be used for ordinary consumer goods and "share money" that would be distributed equally and used only for buying ownership rights in firms.[47]

In any case, the socialist dream is far from dead, and as the dust of do-it-yourself democratization and marketization raised in the revolutions of 1989 slowly settles we are likely to see more and more systematic efforts to bring this ideology into keeping with contemporary reality. It is still too soon to say whether any of these efforts is likely to prove a sure and certain guide to the Moldavian mother, the Romanian mayor, or the Polish deputy who must meanwhile face the challenges of the present.

Fascism

Conservatism, liberalism, and socialism are all concerned with the problem of how a political system can best serve the needs of the citizens who compose it. They may all become distorted in practice into apologies for systems of exploitation, but all at least give lip service to the idea that what matters most is the lot of the citizen. Not so fascism. **Fascism** is predicated on the belief that what matters most is the nation itself. This ideology begins with the argument that citizens can prosper only when the nation prospers, but it carries this argument so far that the fate of the citizens becomes secondary to that of the nation they live in. Fascism is nationalism carried to the extreme.

Like conservatives, fascists think that some human beings are naturally better than others, but for fascists being better is not a matter of social class or circumstance but of race and nationality: If one person is better than others, it is because that person belongs to the "right" race or is a citizen of the "right" nation. There are, however, two qualities shared by all humankind. In the first place, all human beings are motivated by their emotions, not by their reason. According to the French historian Ernest Renan (1823–1892), later quoted approvingly by Benito Mussolini: "To expect reason directly from the people and through the people is a chimera."[48] Second, everyone is struggling to survive. The quest for self-preservation motivates us all. For the fascist, this fundamental human condition does not suggest the need for cooperative arrangements, acknowledging our interdependence and seeking the fairest possible distribution of the world's goods. On the contrary, the fascist agrees with Adolf Hitler that in such a world, "if men wish to live, then they are forced to kill others. . . . On earth and in the universe force alone is decisive. Whatever goal man has reached is due to his originality plus his brutality. . . . Struggle is the father of all things in this world."[49]

Given these characteristics of humanity, the greatest good that could be achieved would be for superior people to put themselves in the service of an organization that would permit them to engage in this perpetual struggle on the best possible terms. Such an organization is the fascist state, engaged in perpetual warfare. If the present system is such a state, there is no higher destiny than to commit oneself to its service. If it is not, the individual's task is to help bring that state into being. In serving their nation, fascists serve themselves, because only thus are they able to protect themselves from others, and only thus can they hope to impose their own dominion in a world where everyone is engaged in a ruthless battle to take the largest possible share of life's rewards, regardless of the needs of others.

The fascist state is characterized by absolute discipline ("No dogma! Discipline suffices," was Mussolini's slogan in the early days), by a ruling party, and above all by submission to the leader. Glorification of the leader is carried to the ultimate extreme: "Mussolini is always right," was one of the ten points in the Italian Fascists' Decalogue, and under Hitler the German National Socialist Party (the Nazis) stated that "the authority of the

Führer is complete and all-embracing; it unites in itself all the means of political direction, it extends into all fields of national life, it embraces the entire people, which is bound to the Führer in loyalty and obedience."[50]

In such a system all human interactions, including economic exchange, come under the sway of the state and the leader. Industry is nationalized or heavily regulated, not to benefit the workers but to benefit the nation (hence the German term *national socialism*). One Italian fascist wrote that "there cannot be any single economic interests which are above the general economic interests of the State." All industry is to be organized into "corporations" — guilds composed of employers and employees who work in the same branch of industry. "Through these corporations the State may at any time that it deems fit, or that the need requires, intervene within the economic life of the individual to let the supreme interests of the nation have precedence over his private, particular interests, even to the point where his work, his savings, his whole fortune may need to be pledged, and if absolutely necessary, sacrificed."[51]

The Development of Fascism   Although fascism has roots in the thinking of nineteenth-century nationalists and in the work of Friedrich Hegel, it did not come into its own until after World War I, when fascist movements emerged in both Italy and Germany. Although these nations had been on opposite sides in that struggle, both faced similar conditions afterward: high rates of inflation, high rates of unemployment, and large numbers of veterans returning from the war who had to be reassimilated into a peacetime economy. In fact, such conditions were endemic in western Europe at the time, but Italy and Germany had two further characteristics in common that other nations were fortunately spared: Neither had been a nation for very long (Italy was unified in 1861, Germany in 1871), and in each nation a young fanatic with the ability to move others with powerful oratory stood ready to capitalize on the situation and use it as a means of raising himself to power. Mussolini and Hitler were able to persuade both the angry workers and the industrialists frightened by that anger (and the talk of socialism that accompanied it) that the answer to the problems of Italians and Germans alike was a fascist state.

Although there are numerous historical parallels for fascist practice, the Italians and Germans were the first to elevate such practices to the heights of "philosophy." Since World War II, no nation has openly espoused fascism, but numerous groups and parties have openly or indirectly done so. Many of these organizations are found in the industrialized nations of Europe, in small far-right parties or groups whose leaders call for racial purity, fanatic nationalism, and undeviating loyalty to themselves. The appearance — and terrorist activities — of neo-Nazi groups in Germany itself has dismayed the world and the vast majority of German citizens (although German judges have been criticized for being unduly lenient with cases brought to court).[52] The National Front party in France, headed by far-right extremist Jean-Marie Le Pen, bases its appeal to voters on a stridently anti-immigrant campaign, claiming that most of France's economic problems are the result of the large number of Arab workers admitted during the full-employment era of the 1960s and early 1970s. Le Pen's blatant racism (which he constantly reiterates and just as constantly denies) brings him public condemnation; however, his party has become the new party of protest for disillusioned Frenchmen and women, and the vote for this modern version of an ugly past has climbed steadily in the past fifteen years, giving the National Front a current level of support that ranges from 10 to 14 percent. Highly disciplined rightwing terrorist movements seeking to undermine democratic states, secret paramilitary groups defending dictators from those who would assert constitutional rights, and religious cults insisting that the divinity of their leaders legitimizes their denial of basic individual rights and liberties to their followers are other sad reminders that fascist principles can still find expression.

WHEN IS AN IDEOLOGY NOT AN IDEOLOGY ?

Conservatism, liberalism, socialism, and fascism are all commonly accepted as ideologies. They meet the terms we set out at the beginning of this chapter: An ideology is a comprehensive set of beliefs and attitudes about social and economic institutions and processes. It offers a critique of the existing system and a view of the ideal system. Where these differ, it suggests the means for moving from the existing to the ideal. It also presents a theory of human nature, and, thereby, of human potentiality and of the need for particular modes of social control.

Today, however, political thought is moving in new directions — or moving with surprising passion in directions that are very, very old. Feminism, ethnic nationalism, and religious fundamentalism are three ways of thinking about politics that have achieved remarkable importance in the past few decades, often making our more conventional approaches seem out of date, perhaps irrelevant. To what extent are these new *isms* true ideologies? To what extent are they simply effective ways for groups to assert threatened or never-realized identities?[53] The only way to find out is to put them to the test, one by one, examining the beliefs and attitudes of each and determining whether these do in fact constitute "a comprehensive set of beliefs and attitudes about social and economic institutions and processes."

Of course, we know to begin with that whether or not they are full ideologies, each of these ways of thinking about politics has assumed enormous importance in recent years. For that reason alone, we need to know more about them all.

Feminism

To begin with, we may say that all feminists believe that women are at least the equals of men, that they deserve equal inclusion in society, and that they have been denied that status for centuries of human history.[54] Such a belief is, of course, profoundly political, if not in itself fully ideological. In fact, early feminists were not seeking to create a new ideology; they wanted to modify those that did exist, especially liberalism and Marxist socialism, in ways that would make them inclusive of women. Those who worked in the liberal tradition typically stressed the need for women as well as men to gain greater individual rights and equality of opportunity. One of the earliest liberal feminist tracts was *A Vindication of the Rights of Women* by Mary Wollstonecraft, published in 1779; another was Harriet Taylor's *The Enfranchisement of Women* on which her husband, John Stuart Mill, based his own *The Subjection of Women* (which, of course, things being as they were, became far better known).[55] In this century, Betty Friedan (*The Feminine Mystique*, 1963) and Alice S. Rossi ("Sentiment and Intellect," 1970) have been among those also identified as liberal revisionists.[56]

Others have approached the problem of the oppression of women from the perspective of Marxist socialism. In theory at least, Marxism also gave some attention to the oppression of women from the very beginning: Friedrich Engels, Karl Marx's collaborator (see above, p. 72) explained in 1884 how in a class society women were oppressed in the home just as the proletariat (presumably male) was outside the home, both by the ruling bourgeoisie.[57] More contemporary Marxist feminists include Claudia von Werlhof, interested in all workers who are either unpaid (mostly women) or earning only subsistence wages (men and women, mostly in the Third World); and Maria Mies, who has studied the impact of capitalist roles and technologies on poor rural women in India.[58]

If all feminists could be identified as revisionist liberals or Marxists, we could stop right here and say, sorry, this may be very important, but it is not a distinct ideology. But feminism has gone far beyond such revisionism. Often incorporating liberal and/or Marxist insights, contemporary feminists have placed more and more emphasis on themes all their own, particularly the idea of the **patriarchal** social system. The oppression of women by men precedes all other forms of oppression, they argue. "It is the hardest form of oppression to eradicate" and "causes the most suffering to its victims."[59] When we come to understand the oppression of women we will, suggests Shulamith Firestone in *The Dialectic of Sex*, be able to understand racism, classism, and all other forms of oppression. Thus, for example, Suzanne Pharr explains the oppression of gay men and lesbian women in feminist terms; she argues that by denying lesbians and gay men the fundamental civil rights that heterosexual women are allowed, heterosexual men ensure that most women will accept and depend on the patriarchal family structure.[60]

Other feminists have combined Marxist and patriarchal modes of interpretation, noting, for example, how patriarchy has for so long given men control of women's property, or pointing out how control over women's labor enhances men's control of all productive resources.[61]

Also not normally found in the more conventional ideologies (although not unknown in contemporary socialist thought) is the poststructural, deconstructionist approach of some feminists. As early as 1952, when she published *The Second Sex* in Paris, Simone de Beauvoir saw the importance of challenging not only current definitions of women and women's roles, but the very idea of the concept "woman" — "Are there women?" de Beauvoir asked.[62] Contemporary feminist poststructuralists are convinced that only by challenging (deconstructing) all established categories (structures) of social identity, including race, class, and gender, can we hope to break free of the confines of patriarchal language and practice.[63]

Insistence on the impossibility of separating oppression based on race and class from that based on gender is another poststructuralist feminist theme. Those who hope to understand and eradicate any form of oppression, feminists say, must pay attention to the structural factors that intersect to create sex, class, and race inequality.[64]

As the foregoing summary suggests, contemporary feminism has moved well beyond mere amendment of earlier modes of thought. Its critique of all existing political systems as profoundly patriarchal, its goal of species-wide egalitarianism, and its insistence on the interconnectedness of all forms of oppression summon up its own view of an ideal world.

Feminism also suggests how to effect change. Although most feminists seem to agree that the contemporary state is profoundly suspect, they emphasize that it is important nevertheless to change the policies of existing political systems. Joyce Gelb has examined how feminists in Britain, the United States, and Sweden have worked within their respective "political opportunity structures" to struggle for labor force equality, higher welfare benefits, better child care, and other specific policies relevant to women's condition.[65] Mary Hawkesworth has looked at feminist studies of substantive policy domains, commenting on the shift "from the critique of bias in existing programs to the formulation of proposals for alternative, equitable policies" in the areas of "health, housing, welfare, education, employment, equal protection, occupational safety, defense, foreign policy, development, abortion, reproductive rights, reproductive technology, rape prevention, sexual harassment, domestic violence, criminal justice, divorce, privacy, and pornography."[66]

Although many feminists thus seek specific short-range ameliorative reforms, all appear to agree that in the long run a more basic change must be made. For women and other oppressed persons to achieve equality, nothing less than a revolution is required. But it is a revolution of understanding, of consciousness, of meaning. Those who share these problems and these views must meet, discuss, write, and talk to others. International gatherings are particularly important so that no one will forget the many forms that patriarchy and related forms of oppression take across the globe. For most feminists, the concept of interdependence takes a negative form at the level of the state, as patriarchically dominated systems interact to maintain oppression, but a positive form at the level of the individual, as women meet from across the globe in forums such as the United Nations' periodic conferences on women, to share their histories and their insights and to move toward fundamental and global transformations in the way the human polity thinks about oppression.

Feminism thus clearly meets the criteria we have laid out to define what constitutes an ideology. Can the same be said for ethnic nationalism and religious fundamentalism?

Ethnic Nationalism

As the breakup of the former Soviet empire took place, we began to see the resurgence of another way of viewing politics: ethnic nationalism. We were forced to relearn something we really already knew — that modern *states* have often been formed out of many separate *nations*. And remembering this has compelled us to resharpen some of our definitions: A **nation** is "a relatively large group of people who feel they belong together by virtue of sharing one or more of such traits as a common race, a common language, a common culture, a common history, a common set of customs or traditions."[67] A **nation-state** is a polity in which sovereignty is coterminous with the sense of nationhood; everyone who lives within that political system feels he or she belongs with all the others nationally as well as politically. In fact, however, there is probably no nation-state in the world where certain pockets of **subnationalism** do not exist. **Ethnic nationalism** is subnationalism based on ethnicity. **Ethnicity** is a shared perception that one's own group is distinctive, usually based on "a sense of common experience . . . continuity through biological descent and the sharing of common social and cultural conditions . . . at the heart of ethnicity is the feeling of *being special*."[68]

Nationalism of any kind is the belief that the interests of one's own nation must take precedence over those of any individual, any group, any other nation, and — when they are in conflict — those of the state itself. The rise of nationalism tends to be strongly associated with those times when a people are reaching out collectively to maximize their collective power, either by extending their dominion over other peoples or by freeing themselves from domination by others. Imperialist conquest, sometimes termed *expansionist nationalism*, is an example of the former; rebellion against colonial domination established by imperialism is an example of the latter.[69]

In the case of ethnic nationalism, the domination that is resented may or may not have been originally established by imperial conquest, but it is always regarded as imposed by persons who are "not like us." The cases of the former republics of the Soviet Union and the warring nations of ex-Yugoslavia, so constantly before us in the news, have reminded us forcefully that peoples may accept common statehood with others for many long years without losing this sense of ethnic distinctiveness, without ceasing to dream of the day when the balance of power will shift and permit the establishment of a separate *nation-state*.[70]

Closer attention to other parts of the world shows us how widespread this sentiment has become of late. In recent years, militant and violent ethnic nationalism has raged in the Indian states of Punjab, Kashmir, and Assam; in Sri Lanka; in Nigeria; in Uganda; in Somalia and Rwanda. Ethnic subnationalism combines with religious subnationalism to fuel the continuing furies of the Middle East and of the United Kingdom. Pockets of ethnic nationalism pit the Basque people against the Spanish and the French, Native Americans against the U.S. government, and bastions of white supremacists against newly majoritarian South Africa. Many Canadians of French descent in francophone Quebec are firmly committed to the struggle to establish an independent state.

Ethnic nationalism has become a driving force for political change. Long-established states are breaking up, or appear on the point of doing so, and the magnitude of suffering and death caused by these struggles sometimes threatens to overwhelm our capacity to hope. If the world is becoming ever more interdependent, how can we be moving so passionately apart, at such enormous cost?

These are extremely important questions, questions to which we will often return in this book. But right now we have a simple (some might say, a colder) task; we need to decide if ethnic nationalism is an ideology. The definition we have adopted suggests that it is not. Nationalism is, as we have seen, one of the important "beliefs and attitudes" in both conservatism and fascism, and in the latter it has commonly taken the form of ethnic nationalism. But one conviction, no matter how passionately and desperately held, cannot be said to constitute an ideology. Look at the ethnic nationalists just listed. What common views do the anachronistic white supremacists of South Africa and the Native Americans of the United States share regarding human nature or social and economic institutions and processes? The Rwandan Tutus and the Quebecois autonomists? The Sri Lankan Tamils and the members of the Basque terrorist group known as the ETA? All have a keen sense of personal oppression, but we would be hard put, would we not, to find a common definition of "oppression" that would fit them all. All are caught in the grip of the same passion for control of their own destinies, but they have no agreement among themselves about what means to use to achieve that control or what form that ideal destiny would take.

Ethnic nationalism is a powerful force, and we must pay more attention to its causes.[71] We need to develop ways of assessing when the grievances so deeply felt merit the compassion of the human polity, when they are at any rate reasonable given the natural human need to possess and assert an identity, and when they bespeak nothing more than selfish unconcern for the rest of us. Above all, we need to find ways to put an end to the misery this passionate conviction so often leads human beings to inflict on themselves and others. But we don't need to call it an ideology. That doesn't make sense.

Religious Fundamentalism

For some authors, insistence on a religious identity has little to distinguish itself from insistence on ethnicity or race — it is simply one way of asserting rights, especially for members of a minority group.[72] But as we will see, religious fundamentalism is much more than the assertion of a religious identity. It is a complex body of thought, particularly difficult, as we will also see, to classify either as "an ideology" or "not an ideology."

Many religions — Christianity, Islam, Judaism, Sikhism, Hinduism — have lent themselves to the growth of fundamentalist thinking, although such thinking is never shared by all the followers of any of these religions. Furthermore, fundamentalists do appear to share a set of values across the lines of their religions. Do these shared values constitute an ideology? Let us take a closer look at what contemporary scholars of this phenomenon have found.

Neils C. Neilsen points out that fundamentalists everywhere believe that truth is to be found in the sacred texts of their religion, that in respecting that truth they live "in a well ordered world," but that "the tradition that guarantees them religious truth is threatened."[73] For Robert Frykenberg, other shared characteristics are the division of the world into true believers and unbelievers, the sense of being a specially chosen people, the belief in a preordained destiny that includes the creation of a new heaven on earth, the conviction that sinister opposition is at work (or will be soon) to attempt to prevent the inevitable millennium, and that conversion means an "altogether total transformation, a complete and drastic change."[74]

Such beliefs clearly have their implicit political connotations, as do the three traits John H. Garvey finds in all fundamentalist movements; they are all, claims this author, *conservative, popular* and *practical*. Protestant fundamentalists in the United States and Ulster; Muslim fundamentalists in Iran, Pakistan, Sudan, and Nigeria; and Orthodox *haredi* Jews all *conserve* long-established texts and traditions as guides to their behavior. All have interpreted these texts in a simple and nonhierarchical fashion, stressing the "fundamentals" and explaining them in ways everyone can understand, producing "a kind of stripped-down religion that travels light and fast" that gives them their potential for *popular* mass appeal. All, finally, offer a great deal of *practical* advice about how to conduct oneself in daily life, with detailed instructions regarding matters of "dress, diet, ritual, socialization and contact with modern culture."[75]

But fundamentalists share more explicitly political beliefs as well. If all truth can be found in the sacred texts, this includes, for the fundamentalist, truth about how to set up a government. Ann Mayer cites the Ayatollah Khomeini's insistence that "the entire system of government and administration, together with the necessary laws, lies ready for you. . . . There is no need for you, after establishing a government, to sit down and draw up laws, or [to] . . . run after others to borrow their laws. Everything is ready and waiting."[76] What waits for the fundamentalist Muslim is the Shari'a, drawn from the Qur'an and the Sunna; what waits for the fundamentalist Jew is the *halakha*, rabbinic interpretations of biblical law; what waits for Christian fundamentalists are the words of their god via the prophet Moses and the evangelists.[77]

Furthermore, although the political programs thus derived are not all the same, they do move in similar directions. All imagine and seek to establish a society in which the modern, secular division between public and private is abolished. In such a state, all behavior would be governed by religious precepts and further, within that state, by the *same* religious precepts. Freedom of religious choice is not a value for those who firmly believe their own contains all truth, nor are other individual liberties, such as the right to political dissent or the right to determine most of one's own behavior autonomously. The religious state will issue and enforce rules governing sexual behavior, family life, education, business affairs.[78] For the fundamentalist, "God shows concern for everyday matters, such as jobs, food, clothes, travel and repair of automobiles" and the religious state knows what that god requires, and sees to it that he is obeyed.[79]

The means of moving toward this ideal state vary, but such variance seems to depend on the circumstances in which different fundamentalist groups find themselves. Some, such as fundamentalist Sikhs mindful of the political autonomy that Southeast Asian Hindus find in Hindustan and Muslims in Pakistan, seek to be granted a separate state; others, such as the Amish or the original Mormons in the United States, seek an enclave of their own within the larger state; some, such as the New Christian Right in the United States or the *haredim* parties in Israel, seek to transform the dominant state so far as possible by making specific policy demands (for example, the teaching of creationism in U.S. public schools, the granting of greater powers to the rabbinic courts in Israel); and others seek nothing less than the takeover of entire existing states, whether by revolution, as in Iran, or via a combination of terrorist intimidation and participation in democratic elections, as in Algeria.[80] But none countenances the idea of permanent minority status. All believe a greater day is coming, and with it a greater state.

Thus, contemporary fundamentalism meets many of the terms of our definition of ideology. Today's fundamentalists share a common view of human nature: fallible but susceptible to correction by religious orthodoxy that is strictly maintained by an all powerful state. They share a belief in strict adherence to moral standards, with strong respect for family, personal honesty, and resistance to drugs and alcohol. They share the conviction that the modern state has lost its way, that social and economic

Fundamentalist Muslims hold aloft a banner reading "Our crisis is one of faith and morals" during a massive march on the presidential palace in Algiers. (UPI/Corbis-Bettmann)

institutions must be closely governed by religious precepts, and that a new day is coming when religious governance will prevail. They share a willingness to work by whatever means seem possible to move toward that end with passionate devotion.

Of course, even though fundamentalists share so many beliefs, *it does not seem so to them.* Any fundamentalists among the readers of this text must by now be thoroughly outraged at having been lumped together with those "others" whose views strike them as so patently erroneous. But the discomfort of the various adherents is not in itself sufficient reason to say fundamentalism is not an ideology. After all, today's democratic socialists do not enjoy being lumped in the same category as Chinese communists, nor are liberals who stress individual freedoms easy companions of those whose liberalism is confined to the marketplace. Yet the categories *socialist* and *liberal* have meaningful and separate paradigms, however great the diversity within them.

Which brings us back to conservatism. Fundamentalists clearly are, in the general sense of the term, very, very conservative. Is fundamentalism, then, merely an extremist subcategory of conservatism? One could perhaps say so, but then one would probably have to say the same for fascist ideology. However, both fascism and fundamentalism utterly reject, in their very different ways, a core value of conservatism: the importance of personal liberty. It is true that conservatism expects the ideal state to be compelled to place important restraints on that liberty in the interests of order and the maintenance of tradition. But where conservatism accepts and promotes such control by the state with regret and seeks as far as possible to achieve the ends of an ordered world by concentrating on the individual, cherishing "a spirit of character, marked by the virtue of thrift, hard work and prudence," fundamentalists turn joyously in the opposite direction, delighting in submitting their entire lives to the control of higher authorities who themselves are believed to be in touch with the highest of all.[81]

So the answer is yes. Religious fundamentalism is an ideology.

THE LANGUAGE OF IDEOLOGY

The political questions we term *ideological* are, as we have seen, of the most serious import to humanity. What are human beings really like? What kind of social organization do we have the natural ability and talent to set up and make work? Why have we established our present social systems? What would the ideal social system look like? These questions matter deeply, and when we figure out answers that seem correct and satisfactory, many of us find it difficult to accept the fact that not everyone else agrees with us. This discovery may lead us, if we are not careful, to seek to persuade by oversimplifying, and by labeling all systems of thought pernicious and false except the one we endorse — in short, by making irresponsible use of the language of ideology.[82] This all too common human failing causes others among us to turn away in disgust, making the very word *ideological* a pejorative term nearly synonymous with *fanatical*, and thereby depriving ourselves of the opportunity to consider matters of the most serious significance to our shared lives on this planet.

Is there any way to stop the human tendency either to preach intolerantly or to treat all such questions as socially "off limits?" Probably not. But we can make an effort in that direction by resolving to use the language of ideology with care and restraint, giving the key terms of ideological discourse their correct meaning and no other. It will help to keep in mind that terms such as *conservative, liberal, socialist, fascist, feminist,* and *fundamentalist* are all words with specific and often complex meanings, not just buzzwords suitable for the quick labeling of friends and foes. Before concluding, let us undertake a brief examination of five other terms that are often misused in ideological debate: *left, right, authoritarian, totalitarian,* and *democratic.*

Politically, *left* and *right* are comparative terms, used to locate ideological perspectives in relation to each other. Generally, **left** is used for ideologies that take a positive view of human nature and demonstrate a conviction that change and progress are necessary and possible to improve the human condition. **Right** usually means a more pessimistic view of human nature and a conviction that it is important to maintain tradition and order. It should be fairly obvious that liberalism and socialism and most forms of feminism are on the left, with socialism moving farther to the left as we talk about the more extreme versions, and that conservatism, fascism, and religious fundamentalism are on the right, the latter two on the far right. Figure 3.2 suggests how these spatial designations can be used to compare the six ideologies we have discussed in these pages.

There is nothing wrong with this exercise provided we do not give it more or less meaning than it has. Placing conservatism, fascism, and fundamentalism on the same side should not cause us to use the terms interchangeably, and the same is also true for liberalism, socialism, and feminism. It is also important to remember that this spatial arrangement refers only to certain characteristics of the ideologies *as ideologies*, not to the practices of political control adopted by people who assume power in the names of those ideologies. Some have argued, for example, that communism and fascism have much more in common than calling one *far left* and the other *far right* suggests. What these people are referring to, however, is not the content of the two ideologies but rather the authoritarian practices of rulers who call themselves communists or fascists. To lump the two together ignores the extremely different principles of leadership in the two ideologies — not to mention all the other significant differences.

Authoritarian and *totalitarian* are two other often misused terms. Neither refers to a belief system or to an ideology. Both refer to political systems in which political power is concentrated in the hands of a few. An **authoritarian system** is one in which the power of the authorities is virtually unlimited, although this power is not always exercised in all domains. A **totalitarian system** is one in which the authorities not only have unlimited power but attempt to exercise it over all domains of life — or simply authoritarianism carried to the ultimate extreme. You will often find, however, that the words are used — incorrectly — to distinguish between capitalist systems ruled by an authoritarian elite (called *authoritarian*) and socialist systems ruled by an authoritarian elite (called *totalitarian*). Both kinds of systems are in fact authoritarian, just as there are both capitalist and socialist democratic systems. Furthermore, capitalist authoritarian systems are not necessarily less concerned about controlling every aspect of their citizens' lives than are socialist authoritarian systems. The control exercised by a Hitler or a Mussolini was every bit as totalitarian as that of a Stalin or a Mao, and in underdeveloped nations that have fallen under dictatorial rule neither the socialist nor the capitalist tyrant is likely to find it physically possible to extend the power of government to every corner of the land.

	Communism	Socialism	Feminism	Liberalism	Conservatism	Religious Fundamentalism	Fascism
Preferred means of effecting change	Revolution — — — — — — — Persuasion and democratic elections — — — — — — — Coup d'etat
View of human nature	Predominantly unselfish and social — — — — — Somewhat selfish, yet social — — — — — Selfish, unsocial
Role of state	Ensure fair distribution of wealth — — — — Protect individual liberty — — — — — — Total control
Most important values	Economic equality — — — — Freedom and political equality — — — Freedom and order — — Order
Placement on political spectrum	Far left — — — Left — — — Center — — — Right — — — Far right

FIGURE 3.2   Key Characteristics of Major Political Ideologies

In this text I will use the term *authoritarian* to refer to all states that are elite controlled and drop the word *totalitarian* altogether. The fact that some authoritarian systems carry their tendencies to control the lives of their fellow citizens much farther than do others can be made clear as we proceed. (For that matter, so can the fact that some democracies carry their democratic tendencies much farther than do others.) When it becomes necessary to distinguish between economic systems, we will add such economic terms as *capitalist, socialist,* and *mixed economy* (see Chapter 4). This leaves us with the semantic problem that *socialism* is both an ideology and an economic system, but that conflation cannot be avoided. As we have seen in this chapter, the very essence of the ideology of socialism is the demand that a specific economic system be established.

This leaves one question that must surely be puzzling many readers: Why haven't I included democracy as one of the ideologies discussed in this chapter? The answer is that democracy, like authoritarianism and nationalism, is not a political ideology. It is a description of the relationship between citizens and their leaders. The conditions of personal freedom, free elections, and political equality are strongly associated with democracy and help make it possible, but the literal meaning of **democracy** is simply rule by the people. Such rule may be direct or, as is much more likely in today's crowded world, it may be effected through representatives elected by the people. But unless the citizens — and not just a few, but the people, a term that includes all adults not seriously disqualified by criminal behavior or mental incapacity — have the right and the means to exercise some form of genuine control over the government, democracy cannot be said to exist.

It is important to keep the true meaning of *democracy* in mind, if only because the term is used so loosely in today's world. The fall of Soviet communism is often attributed to the "triumph of democracy," and it is certainly true that the quest for the greater personal freedom associated with democratic processes played an important role in the determination of the nations and republics under Soviet control to seek autonomy. It should not be forgotten, however, that the major cause of the collapse of the Soviet empire was its own mismanagement, both at home and abroad.[83] The effort now to find ways to erect the structures of democratic capitalism on the ruins of this form of socialism is fraught with difficulty and peril, not least of which is the resurgence of unregenerate nationalism in polities that must be able to join the global economy in order to have a hope of independent survival.[84] Furthermore, many have begun to question how effectively the people can be said to rule in nations where voter turnout is so weak, other forms of political participation often ineffective, and special interest control of campaign finance so strong, questions we will return to in Chapters 6 and 7. Whether or not democracy will triumph under these conditions remains an open question, and one that requires our most sober attention.

SUMMARY AND CONCLUSION

An ideology is a comprehensive system of beliefs and attitudes about social and economic institutions and processes. It is an attempt to explain how an existing political system has come into being and to describe the ideal political system. It may be either strictly personal or shared with a group, open or closed, and revolutionary or defensive. An ideology offers a theory of human nature, and thereby of human potentiality and of the need for particular modes of social control. Five major ideologies are conservatism, liberalism, socialism, fascism, and feminism.

Conservatives believe in conserving what exists. They have a nonegalitarian view of human nature, believing that some people are born into a "natural aristocracy" and that those people can best protect the individual liberty of all. Personal liberty is extremely important to conservatives, which helps explain why they often wish to see the power of government reduced. On the other hand, they frequently propose that government power be used to ensure that traditional moral standards are maintained. Conservatives have traditionally believed that it is the responsibility of the more advanced nations to bring the blessings of civilization to those less fortunate and that it is necessary to maintain good relations with allies as a means of protecting one's own system against external enemies. Although conservatives are sometimes viewed by others as incapable of compromise, they take a pragmatic approach to many questions, provided that the end result will further the basic principles of conservatism (order, continuity, loyalty, protection of individual freedoms, piety, and nationalism).

Liberals believe that all human beings are capable of reason and rational action and should be helped by their governments to fulfill their potential. However, although governments should be ready to help, they must never force such assistance on unwilling citizens — it is also an important liberal value to maintain personal freedom. As much as liberals would like to create a more egalitarian society, they are unwilling to invade individual rights to do so. Thus, they hold two beliefs that are in practice extremely difficult to reconcile. Liberals commonly believe in some form of social contract — that is, in the idea that human beings consent to be ruled by others, but only on condition that individual rights and liberties are maintained. If the terms of this contract are not met, the consent to be ruled may be withdrawn. Liberals believe, however, that political change should be made by peaceful, not revolutionary, means.

Socialists believe human beings are naturally sociable and cooperative and that only the establishment of nonsocialist governments and exploitative work arrangements has interfered with these natural instincts. They believe that the solution is to limit or even abolish outright the institution of private property — which, they say, should be owned by a state that is in turn controlled by the workers.

The world has seen many varieties of socialism. The early socialists argued for the abolition of private property or simply acted out that belief by establishing communal ownership of land and other goods. Utopian socialists argued that human beings should and could work together for their common good in small communities. Marxist socialists follow the teachings of Karl Marx and believe that human history is moving inexorably through five stages of economic organization, each characterized by a different dominant mode of production and a different form of class struggle over ownership of the means of production. The final stage will be communism, in which control over the means of production will be restored to the workers, probably by means of a violent revolution. Soviet communists added to the ideas of Marx the teachings of Vladimir Lenin: that a communist revolution is possible even in a state that has been only partially industrialized, that only the emergence of imperialism has been able to extend the stage of capitalism, that the communist revolution is always the work of a small "vanguard" party of dedicated and informed revolutionaries, and that such a revolution leads at first only to a socialist system, in which the apparatus of the state will still be necessary, and only later to true communism. Later amendments to the doctrines of Soviet communism can be seen, from the vantage of hindsight, as the quest for philosophical arguments on behalf of political reforms whose ultimate result was to bring the experiment with the Soviet form of socialism to an end in most of the states in which it had been practiced. Other forms of socialism, as far apart as Chinese communism and democratic socialism, continue to attract adherents.

Fascism begins by arguing that the citizen can prosper only when the nation prospers and ends up placing the fate of the nation above that of its people. Like conservatives, fascists think that some human beings are naturally better than others, but for them being better means belonging to the "right" race or nationality. They think human beings are motivated by their emotions, not by their reason, and by the struggle for survival. Because this is so, citizens should accept the rule of the fascist state, which will permit them to engage in that struggle on the best possible terms. Under fascism, all human interactions — including economic exchange — are necessarily subject to the absolute discipline of the state and its leader.

Feminism is a relatively new ideology that began when women sought to modify liberalism and/or Marxist socialism to fit their needs and found it necessary to move on to formulate the concept of patriarchy and adapt the tools of poststructural deconstructionism. Feminists have a positive view of human nature, and argue for the right of all to share equally in the creation of our collective destiny, but they have a highly negative view of the state. They seek to move toward the ideal society by achieving a better understanding of the causes of all oppression, including that based on class and race as well as gender; they believe all forms of oppression are interconnected. While working for this understanding, often internationally, they also work for policy reform on questions of relevance and concern to women.

Ethnic nationalism is too narrow a concept and the values and hopes of those caught in its grip vary too widely for us to term this powerful motive for political behavior an ideology. Religious fundamentalism, on the other hand, meets the definition of an ideology, however profound the differences and the antipathies among its diverse adherents. Fundamentalism views human nature as flawed but susceptible to religious instruction, which can itself produce a heaven on earth when followed without question. It would give the religious state absolute power in all domains and expects true believers to move toward the establishment of such a state by whatever means possible.

In developing our personal systems of belief, we must not oversimplify or label every other ideology except the one we endorse false and pernicious. To be ideological is not the same thing as being fanatical, although ideologues do sometimes carry their convictions to that extreme and fanatics may believe they find confirmation in an organized system of thought. We frequently misuse such terms as *left, right authoritarian, totalitarian,* and *democratic* as well as the terms that name the ideologues we have studied. Left means taking a positive view of human nature and believing that change and progress are necessary and possible to improve the human condition. Right means taking a somewhat more pessimistic view of human nature and placing greater emphasis on the importance of maintaining order and continuity. Many variations are possible, however, within this simplistic dichotomy.

Authoritarian and *totalitarian* refer to political systems in which political power is concentrated in the hands of a few, the difference being that in a totalitarian system more effort is made to exercise that power in all domains of human existence. *Democracy,* like authoritarianism, is not a political ideology but rather a description of the relationship between citizens and their leaders. The conditions of personal freedom, free elections, and political equality are strongly associated with democracy and help make it possible, but the literal meaning of democracy is simply rule by the people.

We now have a shared language for speaking and writing about politics. We can turn next to the context of politics — that is, the economic and social settings in which politics must take place and the ways they affect the nature of politics. Many of the ideas we have touched on in Part I will assume new life when we consider the ways social and economic relationships really do shape our political lives together.

Selected Readings

Connolly, William E. *Political Theory and Modernity* (Oxford: Basil Blackwell, 1988). An analysis of the political ideas of classical theorists, such as Hobbes, Rousseau, and Nietzsche, within the context of the contemporary world.

Daniels, Robert V., ed. *A Documentary History of Com-*

munism and the World: From Revolution to Collapse (Hanover, NH: University Press of New England, 1994). A comprehensive study of communism worldwide, including the failure of communism in the Soviet Union.

Girvin, Brian. The Right in the Twentieth Century: Conservatism and Democracy. (London, New York: Pinter, 1994). An in-depth and historical overview of right-wing political movements worldwide.

Grey, John. Liberalism (Milton Keynes: Open University Press, 1986). Historical background and current significance of economic and political liberalism.

Heywood, Andrew. Political Ideologies: An Introduction (New York: St. Martin's, 1992). Covers a wide range of current political ideologies.

Honderich, Ted. Conservatism (Boulder: Westview Press, 1991). An introduction to conservative theory and opinion.

Kymlicka, Will. Contemporary Political Philosophy: An Introduction (Oxford: Clarendon Press, 1990). An examination of the major schools of modern political thought.

Rawls, John. Political Liberalism (New York: Columbia University Press, 1993). A collection of Rawls' lectures that provides an extensive study of liberalism.

Rejai, Mostafa. Political Ideologies: A Comparative Approach (Armonk, New York: M. E. Sharpe, 1995). Offers a framework for the comparative study of the major political ideologies.

Tong, Rosemarie. Feminist Thought: A Comprehensive Introduction (Boulder: Westview Press, 1989). A balanced overview and useful source for those seeking to learn more about feminist theory.

Notes

1. Lyman Tower Sargent, Contemporary Political Ideologies, 5th ed. (Homewood, Ill.: Dorsey, 1961), p. 3.
2. Andrew Heywood, Political Ideologies: An Introduction (New York: St. Martin's Press, 1992), pp. 7–8.
3. David E. Ingersoll, Communism, Fascism and Democracy (Columbus, Ohio: Charles E. Merrill, 1971), p. 8.
4. F. J. C. Hearnshaw, Conservatism in England (London and Basingstroke: Macmillan, 1933), p. 22.
5. Samuel P. Huntington, "Conservatism as an Ideology," American Political Science Review 51, no. 2 (June 1957): 456.
6. Sargent, Contemporary Political Ideologies, p. 67.
7. Alexander J. Groth, Major Ideologies (New York: John Wiley, 1971), p. 88.
8. Kenneth R. Hoover, Ideology and Political Life, 2nd ed. (Monterey, Calif.: Brooks/Cole, 1994), p. 41.
9. Russell Kirk, cited in Sargent, Contemporary Political Ideologies, p. 67.
10. Hoover, Ideology, p. 41.
11. Ibid., p. 40.
12. Heywood, Political Ideologies, p. 56.
13. Franz Schurmann and Orville Schell, eds., Imperial China (New York: Random House, 1967), pp. xv–xvi.
14. John K. Fairbank, "The Nature of Chinese Society," in Schurmann and Orville, eds., Imperial China, pp. 54–55.
15. See R. D. Hicks, Stoics and Epicureans (New York: Charles Scribner's Sons, 1910), and Henry Chadwick, The Pelican History of the Church: The Early Church (London: Hodder and Stoughton, York, 1967).
16. See Thomas Aquinas, Treatise on Law, Summa Theologica (Garden City, N.Y.: Tirage Books, 1969); and Augustine [St. Augustine of Hippo], City of God, trans. Henry Bettenson (London: Penguin, 1972).
17. For a commentary on Burke's use of the organic metaphor, see Gerald U. Chapman, Edmund Burke, The Practical Imagination (Cambridge: Harvard University Press, 1967), chap. 1.
18. George Fitzhugh, Sociology for the South (Richmond, Va.: A. Morris, 1854), excerpted in Jay A. Sigler, ed., The Conservative Tradition in American Thought (New York: Capricorn Books, 1969), p. 211.
19. Quoted in Sigler, Conservative Tradition, p. 24.
20. Herbert Hoover, a speech made 3 Feb. 1931, and reprinted as "Defense of Private Initiative," in Sigler, The Conservative Tradition, p. 323.
21. See Peter Steinfels, The Neo-Conservatives (New York: Simon & Schuster, 1959).
22. For an interesting discussion of some of the forms of neoconservatism, see Desmond S. King, The New Right: Politics, Markets and Citizenship (Chicago: Dorsey, 1987).

23. Heywood, *Political Ideologies*, pp. 21–22.

24. Thucydides, *The History of the Peloponnesian War*, trans. Henry Dale (New York: Harper, 1873), p. 114.

25. Marcus Tullius Cicero, *De Re Publica, De Legibus*, vol. 16, trans. by C. W. Keyes (London: William Heineman, 1977), p. 329.

26. *The Book of Mencius* (London: Penguin Classics, 1970), sec. 6b, 2.

27. For Rousseau, the original state of nature was an idyllic state and only its degeneration forced individuals to make an effort to return, through the use of reason, to the condition of freedom and harmony that had once been naturally theirs; for Locke, the social contract was an improvement on the earlier state.

28. John Locke, *The Second Treatise of Government* (New York: Liberal Arts Press, 1952), p. 124.

29. Adam Smith, *An Inquiry into the Nature and Causes of the Wealth of Nations* (London: Methuen, 1961); J. S. Mill, "Utilitarianism," in Mary Warnock, ed., *Utilitarianism and Other Writings* (New York: New American Library, 1974); J. Bowring, ed., *The Works of Jeremy Bentham* (Edinburgh: Wm. Tate, 1843); David Hume, *A Treatise of Human Nature* (New York: E. P. Dutton, 1920).

30. Plato, *The Republic*, translated by F. M. Cornford (London: Oxford University Press, 1941), p. 166.

31. Julian Sherword, ed., *Handbook of South American Indians*, vol. 2 (Washington, D.C.: U.S. Government Printing House, 1946).

32. For excerpts from the work of Henri Comte de Saint Simon's *New Christianity* (1825), Charles Fourier's *The Theory of Universal Unity* (1822) and Robert Owen's *An Address from the Association of All Classes of All Nations to the Governments and People of All Nations* (1837), see Carl Cohen, ed., *Communism, Fascism and Democracy* (New York: Random House, 1962), pp. 17–48. For a discussion of utopian socialism in general, see Gordon Graham, *Politics in Its Place: A Study of Six Ideologies* (Oxford: Clarendon Press, 1986), pp. 103–106.

33. For a good selection of the chief writings of Marx and his collaborator Friedrich Engels, see Robert C. Tucker, ed., *The Marx-Engels Reader* (New York: W. W. Norton, 1972).

34. See excerpts from G. W. F. Hegel, *Lectures on the Philosophy of History* (1861), in Cohen, *Communism, Fascism and Democracy*, pp. 57–66.

35. Friedrich Engels, *Anti-Duhring*, 3rd English ed. (Moscow: Foreign Languages Publishing House, 1962), p. 385.

36. Karl Marx and Friedrich Engels, *Manifesto of the Communist Party*, in Lewis S. Feuer, *Basic Writings on Politics and Philosophy of Karl Marx and Friedrich Engels* (Anchor Books: New York, 1959), p. 26.

37. Marx and Engels, *The Holy Family*, cited in Tucker, *Marx-Engels Reader*, p. 41.

38. V. I. Lenin, *State and Revolution* (New York: International Publications, 1932).

39. J. Stalin, *Dialectical and Historical Materialism* (New York: International Publishers, 1940).

40. Nikita Khrushchev, *Crimes of the Stalin Era, a Special Report to the 20th Congress of the Communist Party of the Soviet Union*, Closed Session, 25 Feb. 1956, reprinted in Cohen, *Communism, Fascism and Democracy*, pp. 248–54.

41. Michael Gasster, "The Rise of Chinese Communism," in Gary K. Bertsch and Thomas W. Ganschow, eds., *Comparative Communism: The Soviet, Chinese and Yugoslav Models* (San Francisco: W. H. Freeman, 1976), pp. 117–19. See also *Selected Works of Mao Tse-tung*, vol. 3 (Peking: Foreign Languages Press, 1965), pp. 264–67.

42. Of former communist nations, only Albania, China, Cuba, and North Korea can still be counted as unambiguously communist.

43. Charles Funderburk and Robert G. Thobaben, *Political Ideologies: Left, Center, Right*, 2nd ed. (New York: Harper Collins, 1994), pp. 85–86. For excerpts from the work of other leading social democrats, see "Part IV: Democratic Socialism" in H. B. McCullough, ed., *Political Ideologies and Political Philosophies* (Toronto: Wall and Thompson, 1989), pp. 150–71.

44. Barbara Stallings, "External Finance and the Transition to Socialism in Small Peripheral Societies," in Richard R. Fagen, Carmen Diana Deere, and José Luis Coraggio, eds., *Transition and Development* (New York: Monthly Review Press, 1980). pp. 65–66.

45. Paula Rayman, *The Kibbutz Community and Nation Building* (Princeton: Princeton University Press, 1981).

46. "Soviet Economic Reform: Socialism and Property," Report of the Thirtieth Strategy for Peace,

U.S. Foreign Policy Conference (Muscatine, Iowa: Stanley Foundation), 19–21 Oct. 1989.

47. Arno Mayer, "Past and Prologue," *The Nation*, 16 Sept. 1991, p. 290 and John E. Roemer, "A Future for Socialism," *Politics and Society*, 22, no. 4 (Dec. 1994), pp. 451–78. Under Roemer's scheme everyone would be given an equal share of coupons on reaching the age of majority, and on that person's death all shares and unspent coupons would revert to the state for redistribution. The market would otherwise function freely, but there would be a far more egalitarian distribution of property than under unrestrained capitalism.

48. See excerpts from Benito Mussolini, *The Doctrine of Fascism* (1932), in Cohen, *Communism, Fascism and Democracy*, p. 358.

49. From *Hitler's Words*, quoted in Cohen, *Communism, Fascism and Democracy*, pp. 409–10.

50. From Mussolini, *Doctrine of Fascism*, in Cohen, *Communism, Fascism and Democracy*, pp. 349–64, and excerpts from Ernst R. Huber, *Constitutional Law of the Greater German Reich* (1939), in Gould and Truitt, *Political Ideologies*, pp. 123–26.

51. See excerpts from Mario Palmieri, *The Philosophy of Fascism* (1936), in Cohen, *Communism, Fascism and Democracy*, pp. 369–90.

52. Charles Lane and Karen Breslau, "Germany's Furies," *Newsweek*, 7 Dec., 1992, 30–32, and *The Economist*, 5 Sept., 1992, 55.

53. See Valentine M. Moghadam, *Identity Politics and Women: Cultural Reassertions and Feminisms in International Perspective* (Boulder: Westview, 1994) for a variety of approaches to this possibility.

54. Jane C. Ollenburger and Helen Moore, *A Sociology of Women* (Englewood Cliffs, N.J.: Prentice Hall, 1992), p. 16. The following discussion draws heavily on Ollenburger and Moore, who note their own indebtedness to Alison M. Jagger and Paula S. Rothenberg, *Feminist Frameworks* (New York: McGraw-Hill, 1984) for their explanation of the different forms of feminist theory.

55. J. M. Todd, ed., *A Wollstonecraft Anthology* (Bloomington, Ind.: Indiana University Press, 1977); John Stuart Mill and Harriet Taylor Mill, *The Enfranchisement of Women and The Subjection of Women* (London: Virago, 1983).

56. Betty Friedan, *The Feminine Mystique* (New York: Norton, 1963) and Alice Rossi, ed., *Essays on Sex Equality by John Stuart Mill and Harriet Taylor Mill* (Chicago: University of Chicago Press, 1970).

57. Friedrich Engels, *The Origin of Family, Private Property and the State* (New York: International Publishers, 1884/1972).

58. Claudia von Werlhof, "Women's Work: The Blind Spot in the Critique of Political Economy," in Maria Mies et al., eds., *Women: The Last Colony* (London: Zed Books, 1988), pp. 13–26, and Maria Mies, "Capitalist Development and Subsistence Production: Rural Women in India," in Maria Mies et al., eds., *Women: The Last Colony*, pp. 27–50.

59. Jagger and Rothenberg 1984, p. 86.

60. Suzanne Pharr, *Homophobia: A Weapon of Sexism* (Inverness, Calif.: Chardon Press, 1988); Andrea Dworkin, *Women Hating* (New York: Dutton, 1974) and *Pornography: Men Possessing Women* (New York: Putnam, 1979); and Charlotte Bunch and S. Pollack, *Learning One Way: Essays in Feminist Education* (Trumansberg, N.Y.: Crossing Press, 1983). Dworkin and Bunch believe heterosexual women are too closely linked to their oppressors to be able to confront them.

61. Juliet Mitchell, *Woman's Estate* (New York: Pantheon, 1971) and *Psychoanalysis and Feminism* (New York: Pantheon, 1974); Heidi Hartmann, *Women and Revolution: The Unhappy Marriage of Marxism and Feminism* (London: Pluto Press, 1981).

62. Simone de Beauvoir, *The Second Sex* (New York: Knopf, 1952). De Beauvoir might well ask: she did far better than her fellow student (and lover), Jean Paul Sartre, when the two of them took an important philosophy exam, but their professors decided nevertheless to award the highest prize (and thereby significant financial aid for further study) to "the man."

63. S. Bordo, "Feminism, Postmodernism and Gender Skepticism," in L. J. Nicholson, ed., *Feminism/Postmodernism* (New York: Routledge, 1990) and R. Tong, *Feminist Thought: A Comprehensive Introduction* (Boulder: Westview, 1989).

64. M. B. Zinn, "Family, Feminism and Race in American Society," *Gender and Society*, vol. 4 (1990), pp. 68–83 and Ollenberger and Moore, *Sociology of Women*, pp.26–27.

65. Joyce Gelb, *Feminism and Politics* (Berkeley: University of California Press, 1989).

66. Mary Hawkesworth, "Policy Studies within a Feminist Frame," *Policy Sciences* 27, nos. 2–3 (1994): 99, 114–15. The entire issue of *Policy Sciences* is devoted to "Feminism and Public Policy," under the guest editorship of Hawkesworth. Other political scientists who have brought a feminist perspective to policy studies in recent years (dates following their names refer to years of publication of key works) include Ellen Boneparth and Emily Stoper (1988); Margaret Conway, David Ahern, and Gertrude Steuernagel (1994); Janet Flammang (1985); Jo Freeman (1989); Joyce Gelb and Marian Lief Palley (1987); Joni Lovenduski (1986); Barbara Nelson (1984); Sue Tolleson Rinehart (1992); Anne Schneider and Helen Ingram (1993); and Dorothy McBride Stetson (1991).

67. Reo M. Christenson, Alan S. Engel, Dan N. Jacobs, Mostafa Rejai, and Herbert Waltzer, *Ideologies and Modern Politics*, 3rd ed. (New York: Harper & Row, 1981), pp. 20–21.

68. Louis L. Snyder, *Encyclopedia of Nationalism* (New York: Paragon House, 1990), p. 94.

69. Ibid., p. 95.

70. For a comparative examination of the shifting meanings of several of these concepts, see Russell F. Farnen, ed., *Nationalism, Ethnicity, and Identity: Cross National and Comparative Perspectives* (New Brunswick, N.J.: Transaction Publishers, 1994), pp. 45–58.

71. Two examples of studies that seek to explain the factors that turn ethnicity into ethnic nationalism and thence into ethnic warfare are Ted Robert Gurr and Barbara Harff, *Ethnic Conflict in World Politics* (Boulder: Westview, 1994) and Subrata K. Mitra, "The Rational Politics of Cultural Nationalism: Subnational Movements of South Asia in Comparative Perspective," *British Journal of Political Science* 25, pt. 1 (Jan. 1995): 57–77.

72. Peter Janke, *Ethnic and Religious Conflicts: Europe and Asia* (Aldershot, Maine: Dartmouth, 1994), viii.

73. Niels C. Nielsen, Jr., *Fundamentalism, Mythos and World Religions* (New York: State University of New York Press, 1993), p. 8.

74. Robert Frykenberg is cited by both Nielsen and Garvey. See Robert Frykenberg and Pauline Kolenda, *Studies of South India* (New Delhi: American Institute of Indian Study, 1985).

75. John H. Garvey, "Introduction: Fundamentalism and Politics," in Martin E. Marty and R. Scott Appleby, *Fundamentalisms and the State* (Chicago: University of Chicago Press, 1991), pp. 15–17.

76. Ann Elizabeth Mayer, "The Fundamentalist Impact on Law, Politics and Constitutions," in Marty and Appleby, *Fundamentalisms and the State* pp. 110–151.

77. Garvey, "Introduction," p. 19.

78. Nielsen, *Fundamentalism*, p. 14.

79. Ibid., p. 10.

80. Garvey, "Introduction," pp. 23–24.

81. Comments on the importance of individual character were made by British Prime Minister Stanley Baldwin in 1924 and are quoted in Hearnshaw, *Conservatism in England*, pp. 30–31.

82. A particularly pronounced example today is found in the unfortunate proclivity of some in the Western world to assume that all followers of Islam are fundamentalists and that all Muslim fundamentalists believe in the use of the tactics of terrorism. This is untrue, unfair, and a sad example of how the language of ideology can be abused.

83. Michael Kinsley, "Just Why Did Communism Fail?" *Time*, 4 Nov. 1991, 98.

84. E. P. Thompson, et al., "What's Next?" *The Nation* 253, no. 9 (23 Sept. 1991), 323–40.

4 Political Economy

WHAT WAS A CENTRAL theme in the 1996 U.S. presidential election? Why are some Russians less than enthusiastic about the recent changes in their political system? Why did the Iranian government begin making conciliatory statements to the West condemning all terrorist activities? Why did Fidel Castro visit François Mitterrand in 1995, just at the end of the latter's tenure as president of France? What is the underlying subject matter of most of the bills that come before the Canadian National Assembly? What was one of the central motives for white South Africans to accept black majority rule at last?

These important yet seemingly unrelated questions all have the same answer: the state of the national economy. Economic values are primary in politics and have always been so. Look back at Chapter 1, and you will see that the need for government (and thus the introduction of politics) arose in the first place because human beings were developing more complex economic relationships and required a more orderly means of regulating their affairs. Try to think of a war that has been waged in which economic nationalism did not play a part. Indeed, try to think of any important political question that does not turn, at least in part, on economic considerations.

Trying to understand political processes without knowing about the economic interests that often guide them would be like trying to figure out the rules of a game of chess just by watching the players. You might eventually figure it out, but you would certainly waste a lot of time. Politics is a phenomenon that flows from the entire network of human relationships, and we cannot proceed without some direct attention to one of the most fundamental of those relationships, the quest for material well-being.

The theme of this chapter is **political economy** — that is, the relationship between economic conditions and the political choices we make.[1] We will look first at some of the more general relationships between these two forces that have existed almost from the beginnings of human society: how the basic quest to secure material goods, keep what one has gained, and — sometimes — to take such goods away from others has influenced the conduct of politics throughout human history. Next, we will take a closer look at some specific economic factors that shape our political choices: the size of a nation, the natural resources available to it, and its level of economic development. Then we will consider the more common modes of political response to economic imperatives — that is, the ways different political systems, based on different ideologies, have addressed the problems of providing material welfare by institutionalizing different economic systems: capitalism, mixed economy, socialism, corporatism (or neocorporatism), and colonialism (or neocolonialism). We will conclude by exploring the way the growing interdependence of the human polity has raised many of the issues of political economy to the global level, making these problems simultaneously more difficult and more urgent to resolve. In this final section we will focus in particular on the problems posed to the world at large by the environmental crisis, by increasingly interdependent international trade, by widespread stagflation and inflation, and by Third World debt.

Although the emphasis in this chapter will be on how economic factors help shape our politics, this should not be seen as suggesting that all political life is guided by material considerations. In previous chapters we have already given some thought to the power of political thought over political developments, and in succeeding chapters we will be examining how cultural and social factors and individual initiatives can also help to determine the course of political action. Economic motives do guide political choice, but they are only one force among many. Furthermore, as we note here and elsewhere, the pattern of cause and effect is always reciprocal. Our quest for material wealth influences our politics; our politics help determine the distribution of material wealth.

This chapter moves us briskly, perhaps even brusquely, into the present, a good place for political scientists to be. It carries us into considerations of how the present is changing and what the future may bring. But to begin with, we need to take a closer look at the history of the relationship between political and economic factors.

Home-building in the Peruvian highlands. An economic system, whatever its scale, is first and foremost designed to provide for the well-being of individual human beings. (Ira Kirschenbaum/Stock Boston)

THE EVOLVING RELATIONSHIP BETWEEN POLITICS AND ECONOMICS

An **economy** is a system of producing, distributing, and consuming wealth. The word comes from the Greek word *oikonomia*, which itself came from the word for "household" and for "managing." Although we now speak more commonly of the national economy and even the world economy, it is useful to keep in mind these more humble origins of the concept and to remember that any economic system, whatever its scale, is first and foremost designed to provide for the material well-being of individual human beings. It is designed in the hope of having enough food, shelter from the elements, medicine, means of transportation, knowledge, art, and other goods and services that make the human condition at least bearable and sometimes satisfying and happy. We live in a world in which such resources have never been adequate to meet all our needs, so the wealth distributed by most economic systems is limited and scarce. The successful economy is therefore likely to be one that is led by those who know how to *economize* — that is, how to avoid waste and eliminate needless expense.

The world's economies have taken many forms. In most parts of the world we began as hunters and gatherers, simply taking the materials provided by our habitats. When new supplies did not become available as rapidly as our appetites required, we moved on to richer supplies of berries, mushrooms, wild honey, grasshoppers, termites, birds' eggs, field mice, or the other delicacies we enjoyed. Gradually our hunting techniques grew more sophisticated, so we were able to take bigger game than we could trap with rapid hands; the use of knives, spears, and bows and arrows expanded our diet, as did the use of fire for cooking. We were a species always ready to be on our way, shifting camps as the need required.

As long as our economies were based on simply taking what was provided by the natural world, our forms of political organization were equally simple. The typical form of organization was the **band,** a group of families that moved together and determined together how goods should be shared, what individual behavior was permissible, and what ceremonies were necessary to propitiate the gods and satisfy the eternal longing that "there must be more to life than this." The group established the rules and customs that seemed likely to ensure the survival of its members, and every activity was in some way guided by the need to attain that single, all-important goal. This meant, for example, that when a village leader ordered a traditional ceremony for dividing the spoils of the hunt to be carried out, that person was simultaneously a political, economic, and religious leader — and no one saw anything strange in such a combination of roles.[2]

In such societies it was usually the women who gathered close to camp, and the men who hunted game as far afield as they dared to go. Thus it was women, or so some contemporary anthropologists now believe, who were responsible for shifting to a new and more secure mode of ensuring material survival: the cultivation of crops. Made less mobile by child-bearing and nursing, women stayed closer to camp (wherever camp was pitched) and had more opportunity to become familiar with the ways of the land, with its cycles of growth and decay, and with the production and planting of seeds. The reproductive functions of their own bodies no doubt helped them, however unconsciously, to understand what was going on in the natural world.[3]

These first efforts to raise our own food, rather than take what nature provided, were the beginning of agriculture. With the discovery of agriculture, it became possible to stay in one place and accumulate wealth, first in the form of land, and then, when grain crops were discovered, in the form of stored food. The development of granaries made animal husbandry possible and increased everyone's chances of surviving the winters, thereby leading to the rapid expansion of the population.[4]

As our early societies became more complex, so did the division of tasks among us. As different people performed different tasks, they quite naturally began to accumulate different amounts of material wealth. To keep the society functioning, it was necessary to develop new ways of governing the production and distribution of this wealth. Thus, as our economic relationships shifted, so did our forms of political order. In many parts of the globe we moved from the band to the **kinship system,** a means of ordering sociopolitical relationships in which each person's right to use a parcel of land and to own cattle or other property is determined by his or her place in the family lineage.

The patterns of relationship between political and economic factors evolved slowly and unevenly over time and around the globe, depending on natural resources, peaceful or warlike contacts between peoples, and a host of other factors. Many of us lived until well into the present century in conditions of such isolation and with access to such a limited range of raw materials that we continued to make our living by means of primitive agriculture, a few of us even continued to function as nomadic bands. Many of us, however, lived where it slowly became possible to change our ways of meeting our material needs and to make complementary changes in our political relationships. The development of mineral wealth meant the development not only of better tools for agriculture but also of better weapons for hunting. And weapons that could be used to hunt one's own game could also be used to take away the goods of others, inevitably an appealing if not a morally commendable way of meeting one's needs under the conditions of scarcity that prevailed. As a result, ever more elaborate weaponry evolved and hitherto peaceful communities were transformed into warrior states. In some polities the military barracks became as important a unit for political organization as the peasant farm.[5]

At the same time, the more goods we were able to produce and the greater their variety, the keener we were to enter into peaceful relationships of trade with one another. The development of trade — coupled with the evolution of more powerful weapons for gaining and guarding wealth — led in turn to the development, in widely distant parts of the globe (but not everywhere), of more specialized polities: market towns, headquarters, villages, cities, city-states, and eventually nation-states. Developed economies required states, institutions capable of maintaining order and security and engaging in large-scale public works such as the construction of roads and bridges.[6]

At first, political power was likely to be in the hands of those who could best combine great wealth with the intelligent or ruthless exercise of the skills of warfare and intrigue. In many places this concentrated power took the form of **feudalism,** a system in which the political leaders, the large landholders, and the serfs who worked the land were linked to one another by conditions of mutual political and economic dependency.[7]

As the goods of the world became ever more complex and varied, the work of those who produced them became ever more specialized. With specialization came independence from the land, and more and more people were now able to live by their craftsmanship. The growth of the crafts, and of commerce independent from the land, brought new forms of political organization. **Corporate guilds** were formed, led by **masters** who negotiated political as well as economic matters on behalf of the **journeymen** and **apprentices** who worked under them.[8]

Up to this point, the relationship between economic and political factors — and the speed with which changes in that relationship took place — varied greatly depending on where one lived on the planet. But in the fifteenth century a new era in the symbiotic evolution of economic and political systems began, one that was to have worldwide consequences. It was the century of overland and oversea journeys of discovery and conquest, undertaken on a scale never imagined before, in a quest for material resources not found at home.[9] Economically, the fifteenth-century voyages of discovery led to the wholesale takeover of others' land by the travelers and to a new mode of agricultural development — the large plantation.

Plantations were labor intensive, and when not enough workers were available locally the European conquerors brought in a fresh supply, African slaves. Exploitation of others' labor on so vast a scale soon meant a surplus of wealth for the owners, and this surplus became the base for the rapid advancement of **capitalism** and **industrialization** in the eighteenth century. On the political side, the desire to play for the largest possible stakes in the imperialistic contest led the dominant nations to adopt ever more centralized constitutional systems. Subjugated populations, on the other hand, were compelled to accept the political and economic dominion of others.[10]

By the nineteenth century, improved means of communication and transportation had increased the opportunities for economic exchange among nations, stimulated the formation of international trade agreements, and suggested the need for cooperative international organizations that went beyond the skeletal commissions established by economic and defense treaties.[11] Broader international political bodies did emerge in the following century — our own — but at the same time the competition among the more powerful polities for the right to exploit the less powerful and the invention of yet more powerful weaponry made the temptation to take what one needed by force of arms ever more irresistible — and its consequences ever more devastating.[12]

Within the nations on the losing end of these uneven struggles, some began to argue for the introduction of new systems for the production and distribution of wealth. Socialist systems of production and distribution — whether introduced by revolution or by election — required the introduction of still more centralized and more bureaucratized structures of government, capable of overseeing vast networks of economic exchange. Unable to meet the challenges posed by their own unwieldiness, internal corruption, international hostility, and the imperatives of an increasingly solidaristic capitalist world market, most of the world's unambiguously socialist systems have been drastically modified, and the subsequent (and consequent) expansion of world capitalism, and the imbalances inherent in that system, have forced remaining socialist or mixed economies to reevaluate their prospects and their plans as well (see Chapter 14).[13]

The current period is a time of fertile thought as well as pragmatic experimentation, as scholars and experts cast about for new economic forms. One idea receiving considerable attention as I write is a plan for a new form of mixed economy in which money would consist of *commodity money* to be used for ordinary consumer goods and *share money* that would be distributed equally and used only for buying ownership rights in firms. Under this scheme, everyone would be given an equal share of coupons on reaching the age of majority, and upon that person's death all shares and unspent coupons would revert to the state for redistribution. The market would otherwise function freely, but the state could ensure a far more egalitarian distribution of property than under unrestrained capitalism.[14]

This broad overview may help us see how closely economic and political change have always been connected. To gain a clearer understanding of the way the relationship works today, however, we must move from the general to the specific, from the historical to the contemporary, and from informed speculation to empirical investigation. The following section is an attempt to show how this task can be approached. It examines the characteristics of a nation's economy that are most likely to influence its political decisions, explores a few of the relationships that do in fact exist between political and economic factors, and gives some consideration to the methods that appear to work best in the study of political economy.

ECONOMIC FACTORS THAT COMMONLY INFLUENCE POLITICS

A nation's size, its supply of natural resources, and its level of economic development are three characteristics that help shape its internal politics as well as its political and economic relations with other nations.

The Size of a Nation   The size of a nation can be measured either as its territorial extent or as the number of citizens inhabiting its territory. Both these measures are influenced by geography as well as economics. Geographic conditions help determine how large a polity will be as well as how many people will seek their living within its boundaries. Climate, natural resources, and the likelihood of natural disasters (such as earthquakes, hurricanes, or floods) determine the suitability of any terrain for habitation. Such natural barriers as mountain ranges or bodies of water help to determine which people live and work together and which are considered "foreigners," with whom intercourse is infrequent and limited.

Once size is established, it inevitably becomes an economic factor. As such, size often has a profound impact on the course of political life. The territorial extent of a nation limits the number of people who can be fed and sheltered, given that society's particular level of development. If the resources within the polity's physical domain are inadequate to its population's needs, then the economic struggle for scarce resources may lead to political strife as well. Whether such economic and political strife is internal or directed outward often depends on another factor related to size, *jurisdictional integration* — that is, the extent to which all the units composing a state are legally integrated with one other. José M. Gonzalez-Eiras points out that the economic modernization and imperialistic ventures of Japan followed the Meiji Restoration of 1867–68, when that small nation's three hundred separate feudal domains were finally integrated and the entire nation turned toward foreign conquest as the way to secure the resources it lacked at home.[15]

The causal relationship between the economic consequences of size and the course of politics works both ways: the size of the system affects a nation's politics, and a nation's politics affects the size of the system. Political factors change territorial extent. Wars shift boundaries outward or inward, governments finance voyages of discovery and conquest, and legislatures grant free land to those who push into the wilderness and statehood or other formal recognition to distant territories. Political decisions also influence the number of citizens a state will have. Deciding to go to war can lead to enormous loss of life, offering government family allowances after such wars can lead to population growth, and pursuing government sterilization or contraceptive programs in nations where the supply of food is inadequate can reduce growth or even cause population to decline.

Despite the polite fictions of international law, which holds all sovereign states to be equal, small states *are* different from large states. When the Baltic states of Lithuania, Estonia, and Latvia first began to clamor for independence from the Soviet Union in 1991, even those most sympathetic to their concerns had to wonder how such tiny states could possibly expect to survive in the modern world (see Figure 4.1). The same concerns have been expressed as the nation of Yugoslavia, never economically strong at its most unified, has crumbled into ever smaller separate entities (see Figure 4.2). However, not all small states are weak: consider the size of Denmark — or Japan!

Natural Resources

One of the reasons small states are often at a disadvantage is inadequate natural resources. There is, of course, no direct relationship between size and natural wealth. Most nations' boundaries were established long before a full inventory of their resources could be taken. Furthermore, what constitutes a "resource" is constantly changing. Yesterday's frustratingly hard earth may have concealed today's uranium mine; today's thorny patch of scrub brush may turn out to be tomorrow's cure for cancer.

As new discoveries of hitherto hidden wealth are made, political forces shift and respond. The twentieth-century politics of oil offers us numerous

FIGURE 4.1   **The Baltic States**

examples. The discovery of oil in eastern Nigeria clearly played a major part in persuading the residents of that part of the nation that they might make a success of the independent state of Biafra — and in persuading so many other nations to provide weapons or other assistance to one side or the other in the civil war that ensued, in the hope of having access to that oil when peace was established.[16] The prolongation of the war in Vietnam may have had more to do with the discovery of offshore deposits of oil than is commonly recognized or acknowledged.[17] The oil-producing nations that have made common cause in OPEC (the Organization of Petroleum Exporting Countries) have done so for political as well as economic gain. Iraq invaded Kuwait in 1990 in order to take possession of oil deposits that would help restore her economy after a disastrous decade of war with Iran, and it would be foolish to imagine that the willingness of the United States and her allies to come to the rescue of Kuwait in 1991

**Commercial Energy Consumption, 1971–91
(in exajoules)**

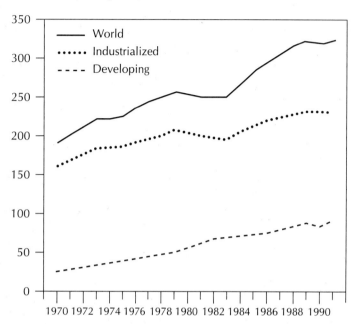

**World Share in Fossil Fuel
Consumption, Average 1986–90**

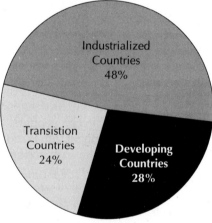

**Fossil Fuel ConsumptionTrends, 1961–90
Five–Year Averages (in petajoules)**

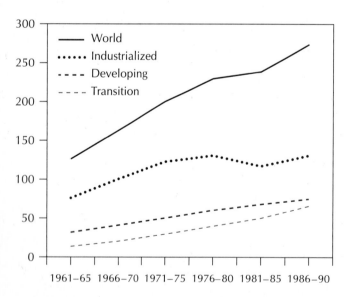

Source: *World Resources 1994–1995,* edited
by *The World Resources Institute.* Copyright
© 1994 by The World Resources Institute. Used
by permission of Oxford University Press, Inc.

FIGURE 4.2   **Trends in Energy Consumption**

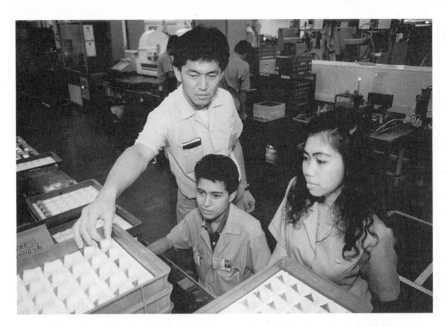

Technological interdependence stimulates economic development and political change. Here a Japanese technician aids his Malaysian counterparts in a joint economic venture. (Charlie Cole/Sipa Press)

was not owing in large part to the need to keep that tiny kingdom's oil flowing in the right directions (and the profits therefrom into the right pockets).

The question of the importance of natural resources to the economics and politics of a nation is not always unambiguous, however. The polities of Hong Kong and Singapore are only two examples of small polities, poor in natural resources, that have nevertheless become strong exporters of manufactured goods. Their ability to attract foreign investment permitting the import of others' raw materials and goods has allowed a degree of development that has little to do with what can be found above or below their own soil.[18] Furthermore, even abundant natural resources mean little so long as they remain entirely natural. If they are dramatic or beautiful to see, they may constitute important tourist attractions. They may even contribute to the psychic well-being of a citizenry, and thus indirectly to its productivity. But in most cases, resources, whether natural or imported, must be changed in some way if they are to bring economic rewards. Making those changes is the first step in economic *development*.

Level of Wealth Achieved

Economic development means acquiring the ability to transform natural resources (the nation's own or those imported from other nations as raw materials) into various more valuable processed goods, to provide valuable services, and to market those goods and services domestically and internationally in order to improve the material well-being of the nation's own people.

As this definition makes clear, the motivation spurring economic development is the desire to improve material well-being. (It need not be *greed*, which normally refers to a desire to get as much as possible of a desired entity without regard for the needs of others.) If natural resources can be processed in a way that makes them more useful or attractive, they are likely to bring greater profits, thus permitting the purchase of more goods from others. This economic fact of life spurs the **division of labor,** as we learn to process raw materials in different ways, and stimulates **technological development,** as we seek — and find — more interesting and more profitable ways to change the rocks, trees, water, and sunshine of our natu-

TABLE 4.1   **Technological Development and National Wealth**

Country	Gross National Product per Capita (1991)	Professional and Technical Workers as a Percentage of the Economically Active Population (1993)
Japan	27,300	11.5
Denmark	24,230	24.3[a]
United States	22,550	16.5
Canada	20,840	17.3
Kuwait	19,510	16.8
United Kingdom	17,400	11.5[a]
Mexico	3,051	9.5
Venezuela	2,609	11.9
South Africa	2,573	7.2
Chile	2,215	8.2
Syria	1,909	13.0
Philippines	694	5.7
Indonesia	577	3.4
Pakistan	369	4.5
India	303	2.9

[a]1991 figures (1993 figures not available).
Sources: *GNP:* U.S. Department of the Census, *Statistical Abstract of the United States: 1994,* 114th ed. (Washington, D.C.: 1994), p. 862. *Professional and Technical Workers:* Euromonitor, *International Marketing Data and Statistics 1995,* 19th ed. (London: 1995), pp. 283–85. *1993 Yearbook of Labour Statistics,* 52nd ed. (Geneva: International Labour Office, 1993), pp. 482–516.

ral habitat into useful goods and services. As work becomes more specialized and products more varied, a nation's ability to meet its own needs and
assume a competitive stance in the world market is likely to improve,
which usually leads in turn to a significant increase in national wealth.
Table 4.1 illustrates this point: the more workers employed in professional
and technological occupations, the greater a nation's overall wealth, as
measured by gross national product (GNP). The relationship is far from
perfect, but it clearly goes in the expected direction.

Once national wealth is achieved, those who achieve individual wealth
in that prosperous nation are more likely to receive respectful attention
when they offer advice on political affairs; the followers of billionaire Ross
Perot in the United States constitute only one recent example of this common phenomenon. Of course, in all nations the wealthy are likely to have
the means to influence the direction of politics behind the scenes (a practice we will explore further in Chapter 8), but it is safer to exercise that
influence openly as well when those less fortunate have quasirealistic hopes
of enlarging their own portion of a generous-sized national pie.

Furthermore, as international entities, wealthier nations are more influential in world politics than poor nations, often use that political strength
to further their economic dominance, and may do so in ways that make it
difficult for smaller and poorer nations to achieve the diversified labor force
so clearly related to economic development (a tendency we will discuss
further later in this chapter).

**Other Economic
Factors Likely to
Influence Politics**

A nation's size, supply of natural resources, and overall wealth are all unambiguously important in determining what political decisions can and
will be made and how successful that nation's leaders are likely to be in
meeting the material hopes and demands of their citizenry. We know that
individual leaders are often dismissed by democratic electorates when
these hopes and demands are not met. But we are less certain about the
relationship between such disappointment and open repudiation of a political system, and some of our findings in this area are surprising. We have
discovered, for example, that there is no direct relationship between the
number of incidents of political violence in a nation and that nation's gross
national product. Poor nations, like Syria, may go for many years with no
irregular changes of leadership and relatively few deaths from political
violence, or may, like India, experience constant and dramatically irregular changes of leadership and comparatively high numbers of violent
deaths. Similarly, richer nations, like France or the United States, may experience flareups of political violence and dramatically irregular changes
of leadership.[19]

Nor does the picture become any clearer when we consider the distribution of wealth within a nation. We all know perfectly well that no nation's wealth is shared equally by all its citizens; if in doubt, consider
Table 4–2. Most of a nation's wealth may well be concentrated in a few

hands, while the mass of the population lives at a near-subsistence level. But when we measure such maldistribution, we find no consistent association between political instability and the maldistribution of wealth.[20] And similarly puzzling results are likely to be found when we explore the idea that what leads to political instability is not so much the gap between rich and poor as the existence of worsening economic circumstances — rising rates of unemployment, say, or declining availability of low-income housing — or the more complex notion that these factors will be particularly provocative of political unrest when a heavy deficit in the balance of payments prompts a government to seek to increase domestic productivity and to curb the importation of foreign goods. Certainly, demands for increased labor productivity, coupled with the elimination of popular and inexpensive foreign goods, seldom increases political popularity and governments *have* fallen more than once in the course of making such demands — but they do not always do so.

As this example begins to suggest, the fact is that although economic forces shape our politics profoundly, they do not do so in isolation from

TABLE 4.2   **Internal Income Inequality in Selected Nations**

Country	Gini Score[a]	Percentage of National Income Going to those receiving least and most		
		Lowest 20%	Top 20%	Top 10%
Netherlands	.2664	8.3	36.2	21.5
Japan	.3002	8.7	37.5	22.4
United States	.3359	5.3	39.9	22.3
Canada	.3530	5.3	40.0	23.8
India	.4022	7.0	49.4	33.6
Venezuela	.4874	3.0	54.0	35.7
Senegal	.5031	5.5	60.9	45.4
Iran	.5489	3.4	62.7	47.4
Panama	.5642	2.0	61.8	44.2
Brazil	.5994	2.0	66.6	50.6
All nations	.4100	5.3	48.2	32.4

[a] The *Gini index,* a statistical measure developed by Corrado Gini, gives each nation what could be called an "inequality" score (a score of 0 would represent perfect economic equality).
Source: Denny Braun, *The Rich Get Richer: The Rise of Income Inequality in the United States and the World* (Chicago: Nelson-Hall, 1991), pp. 75–76. Reprinted by permission of the publisher.

each other or from other social forces. To understand the relationship between economic and political variables, we must do more than look for statistical relationships between single indicators of economic and political phenomena. The economic factors we have mentioned, and many others, may all be at work in a particular nation, but they will work in different ways in different places. Their effect will be mediated by a vast number of other factors: the nation's political, economic, and social history; the struggle among conflicting social groups; the level of political oppression within and between nations; cultural norms of political behavior, the strength and composition of political institutions — in short, nearly every topic we are exploring in this book.

More recent work in this subfield of political science shows respect for this complexity. Scholars have developed statistical methods that permit the inclusion of far more variables, and at the same time they attempt to explain more limited relationships.[21] On this new work — seemingly less ambitious, certainly more difficult — rests our present hope of assembling the body of knowledge on which we can build a broader and more realistic theory of the impact of economic factors on our political life.

POLITICAL DETERMINATION OF ECONOMIC SYSTEMS

Politics and economics are mutually causative. Economic conditions produce political responses, and political conditions produce economic responses. When we say (as in Chapter 2) that the political system authoritatively allocates values for a society, the word *values* is used to mean both *abstract norms* — the political system determines what norms the society (although not necessarily every individual within it) considers paramount — and *concrete goods* — the political system is the final arbiter of the distribution of wealth in a society. In this second meaning, the authoritative allocation of values includes political determination of economic conditions.

How do political decisions determine economic conditions? Stop for a moment and consider some of the powers the ordinary government has to shape a nation's economy. Even a few moments' reflection will give you a formidable list:

- The power to tax
- The power to spend revenue, including the power to subsidize particular sectors of the economy (by agricultural price supports, for example, or tax exemptions for religious institutions, or grants of support for the arts)
- The power to regulate the conduct of business (laws governing nationalized industry, for example, or the development of private business, or the formation of trade unions)

Political decisions determine economic conditions. Two Bosnian Serb refugees on a tractor loaded with furniture and personal effects flee Dobrinja, a Serb-controlled part of Sarjevo destined to be transferred to the Muslim-Croat Federation in early 1996. (AP Photo/Rikard Larma/Wide World)

- The power to issue and regulate currency
- The power to determine interest rates
- The power to make economic pacts with other nations
- The power to declare war and to make peace
- The power to levy fines
- The power to control the entry into and exit from the national territory of people and goods (including laborers, entrepreneurs, products, and currency)
- The power to make comprehensive long-range plans incorporating any of these specific powers

Each of these powers is an important means of shaping the direction of an economy and the distribution of its wealth. Consider, for example, the probable significance of the different allocations for military, education, health, and social security and welfare made by the nations included in Table 4.3.

The decisions each nation makes about exercising political control over its economic life will depend in large part on the nature of the economic system to which it is committed: capitalism, socialism, or some form of mixed economy. It can be argued, however, that the choice of economic system — and of whether to keep or change the existing system — is itself a political decision.

Capitalism

Do political systems govern the choice of economic systems? Govern is perhaps too strong a word, but they certainly play a major part in sustaining specific choices and in aiding transitions from one economic system to another. Consider the role of politics in the transition from feudalism to capitalism that took place in Europe in the sixteenth and seventeenth centuries.

Under feudalism the quantity and kind of economic production was determined by the contracting parties: serfs, lords, and — where he had

TABLE 4.3   **Selected Nations' Spending Priorities per Capital Expenditures (in percentages, 1992)**

	Defense	Education	Health	Social Security and Welfare
Australia	8.6	7.0	12.7	31.2
El Salvador	16.0	12.8	7.3	4.7
Israel	22.1	11.1	4.4	31.3
Kenya	9.2	20.1	5.4	3.4
Korea	22.1	16.2	1.2	12.5
Namibia	6.5	22.2	9.7	14.8
Nepal	5.9	10.9	4.7	6.8
Netherlands	4.6	10.8	13.9	40.9
Pakistan	27.9	1.6	1.0	3.4
Paraguay	13.3	12.7	4.3	14.8
Sweden	5.5	9.3	0.8	56.2
Thailand	17.2	21.1	8.1	6.7
Turkey	11.3	20.0	3.5	3.9
United States	20.6	1.8	16.0	31.1
Zimbabwe[a]	16.49	23.45	7.63	3.41

[a]1989 figures (1992 figures not available).
Source: *Government Finance Statistics Yearbook,* vol. 15 (New York: International Monetary Fund, 1991), pp. 58–61; and *World Development Report 1994: Infrastructure for Development* (New York: World Bank, 1994), pp. 180–81.

the power to make his will prevail — the king as the representative of the emerging national interest. The growth of centralized monarchies eventually caused the breakup of the feudal empires within the emerging nation-states. This collapse of the feudal system meant that goods could now be exchanged in a wider and freer market. The quest for yet broader markets and for expanded resources motivated another political development — the decision to finance foreign exploration and conquest. The spoils of imperialism made some goods cheaper to produce and more desirable than ever before. In response to increased demand, as well as to their new opportunity to conduct their enterprises free of feudal domination, the producers of such goods began plowing some of their profits back into their businesses in order to expand their productive capacity. This behavior — free entrepreneurs putting profits back into capital expenditures — is the essence of **capitalism**.[22]

Thus, political developments — the rise of the nation-state and the conquest of foreign territories — spurred the shift to a new economic system, capitalism. By the middle of the seventeenth century, the interaction between economic and political forces to make that system work was considerably more conscious and deliberate. It was then that the stronger nation-states adopted **mercantilism** as the surest means of maintaining the wealth and power of the state. The mercantilist theory of the relationship between the public and private spheres urges that the state use its powers openly to provide the best possible conditions for private entrepreneurs to carry on their business, thereby identifying the interest of the state with that of private business. Uniform monetary systems and legal codes were the positive achievements of mercantilism; permitting the often inhuman exploitation of laborers at home and abroad was the other side of the coin.[23]

The main point, of course, was that there should be plenty of coins, whichever side one looked at. And the mercantilist nations did prosper, so much so that the steady accumulation of capital provided the base for the eighteenth-century Industrial Revolution. As profits grew and the exploitation of labor worsened, however, the arguments in favor of having a supportive yet interfering partner — the state — began to seem less compelling to those who were developing great wealth. A new rationale was needed, one that would set business free to pursue the untrammeled growth that was to characterize the evolution of capitalism in the nineteenth century.

The answer was found by consulting and amending liberal political thought (see Chapter 3). "Let them do as they will," argued British theorist Adam Smith, asserting that if economic decisions were left to the free play of self-regulating market forces, the best of all possible systems for production and distribution of the world's goods would be found.[24] A **laissez-faire** economy is one in which government stays out of the world of business as much as possible. Laissez-faire economists believe that all government needs to do is ensure sound money (as when it backs the currency with gold deposits), balance its own budget (because a budget deficit represents an unfair incursion of government into the private economy), encourage free trade, and keep welfare expenditures to an absolute minimum.

By the beginning of the twentieth century, and especially after World War I, the world had changed. International markets were shrinking, colonized peoples were beginning the long trek to independence, and trade barriers were multiplying as individual nations sought to cushion their separate economies against the spreading Great Depression. The hope that capitalism would automatically provide plenty for all began to fade, and the people whose rewards had so far been limited to such hope began to lose their patience.

Alternatives to Capitalism: Socialism and the Mixed Economy

At this point, as we learned in Chapter 3, an alternative ideology, socialism, began to appeal to a wider audience. We have discussed socialism in sufficient depth in Chapter 3 that little more need be said here other than to point out the specifically economic components of this many-sided system of belief.

In its purest form, socialism carries the natural connection between the political and economic spheres to its logical conclusion. It calls for the absolute merger of the two. In the ideal socialist system, the state would control all the means of production and would itself be controlled by the workers. With absolute control, the state would in theory be able to establish and carry out long-range comprehensive plans of economic development. The socialist economy is a **planned economy**.

Furthermore, knowing that the state acted only in their own best interests, and that in working for the state they were working for themselves, the workers in the ideal socialist state would no longer be alienated from their jobs. They would therefore produce as well and as much as they possibly could. Either each would "give according to his ability and receive according to his need," or all would be paid equally regardless of the quality or usefulness of their work.

Efforts to put some form of socialist economic system into operation were undertaken in nearly every part of the world once the failings of unrestrained capitalism became apparent. Furthermore, even where the socialist prescriptions were consistently rejected, some form of a *mixed economy* — that is, an economy based on a mixture of public and private ownership of the means of production and on considerable public regulation of the private sector — was likely to be adopted. Soon there was no nation in the world in which every productive enterprise was in private hands, in which no effort was made by the state to consult workers' representatives in making economic policy, and in which the government never undertook to regulate prices or wages.

Why, once the inadequacies of unrestrained capitalism became clear, did some states choose socialism while other states were content simply to introduce certain socialistic practices into a capitalist system? No single definitive answer is possible, but once again it is important to consider the power of political decisions to guide our economic destinies. As a rough generalization, we can say that wherever political leaders were willing, for whatever mixture of self-serving and humanitarian motives, to permit the relatively free development of democratic political processes during the heyday of capitalism — by extending suffrage to ordinary men and women and by permitting the formation of competitive political parties — there it was possible to work out modifications of the capitalist system without abrupt political and economic change. By the end of the nineteenth century, and in many instances long before, the United States, Britain, and most of the nations of western Europe (Germany, Spain and Italy are important exceptions) had completely accepted the idea of popular sovereignty. Full rights of citizenship were extended to one group after another, often after determined resistance but never in open repudiation of the basic principles of democracy. Such nations developed and maintained mostly capitalistic economic systems.

On the other hand, in nations like the Soviet Union, many of the eastern European nations, and China as well as in the young African states and older Latin American political systems dominated by northern imperialist powers, the increasing concentration of economic power in the early capitalist period was accompanied by authoritarian leadership, either indigenous or imposed from without, that rigorously rejected all demands that political power be shared. In such political systems it was much more likely that political and economic revolution would take place, resulting, when successful, in the establishment of a socialist regime.

However, even as the more moderate aspects of socialism were being adopted in predominantly capitalist systems, and new more or less fully socialist experiments were being attempted in Central American and African states, the world's political-economic pendulum was starting its swing back in the opposite direction. Almost all of the states that had opted for the socialist solution in its purest form began to find it politically convenient to restore some characteristics of the much-maligned capitalist system, producing their own form of mixed economy. Significant advantages in wages and other material rewards were given to those with the greatest political power, new forms of social rank were allowed to evolve, and private enterprises began to flourish here and there, with or without the overt approval of the state.

But this was not all. As we have seen in the amazing changes of the past few years, this time the pendulum seemed to swing its way right out of the clock: the Soviet form of socialism has fallen apart, and the entire former eastern bloc has begun the shift to a capitalist economy. The continued existence of communist regimes in China, Cuba, and Albania and of strong (and sometimes ruling) social democratic parties in much of western Europe means that socialism is far from dead, but for now the capitalist system is clearly ascendant.

Has this sudden shift been caused primarily by economic or primarily by political factors? As we would expect in such truly momentous times, both kinds of forces have been strongly at work, and indeed the unraveling of the Soviet system has provided us with the strongest possible illustration of how closely intertwined political and economic forces can be. Before we proceed, write down the factor you think best explains the downfall of Soviet communism and ask yourself if it is a predominantly political or economic factor. Now take a look at reasons others have offered, singly and in combination, for the fall of the Soviet Union:

1. The American political decision to halt the spread of Communism by offering economic aid to nations tempted by communism immediately after World War II.
2. The American political decision to halt the spread of Communism, a pernicious ideology, by building an overwhelming military force and using it as necessary to that end.
3. The American economic decision to halt the spread of Soviet imperialism, a dangerous competitor for the world's natural resources, by building an overwhelming military force and using it as necessary to that end.
4. The Soviet political decision to advance the spread of communism, a noble ideology, by building a military force greater than the Soviet economy could sustain.
5. The Soviet economic decision to advance the spread of their own political power in order to gain access to the economic resources of other nations, and to do so by building a military force greater than the Soviet economy could sustain.
6. The economic decision of the people living under communism, in the Soviet Union and in the satellite states, to escape from an economic system that was unable to provide minimum comforts and was threatening to break down altogether, owing to excessive military expenditures, corruption, mismanagement, and general socialist ineptitude.
7. The political decision of the people living under communism, in the Soviet Union and in the satellite states, to break free from a repressive political system and enjoy the rights and privileges of a free people, no matter the cost.
8. The political (and cultural) decisions of the people living under communism, in the Soviet Union and in the satellite states, to break free from a foreign political system and reestablish the national identities that were theirs prior to Soviet takeover.
9. The political ineptitude of Mikhail Gorbachev, a leader farsighted and strong enough to lead his nation into a period of massive change, but incapable of keeping either right or leftwing forces under control once these forces were unleashed.
10. The political savvy and daring of Boris Yeltsin, who knew when and

how to jump on a tank in time for the evening news (and the similar savvy and daring of all the other revolutionaries, from the first person to chip away at the Berlin Wall through the thousands demonstrating in all the satellite nations and in the Baltic republics to those who rallied bravely around Yeltsin himself in Red Square during the attempted countercoup in August of 1991).

Whichever combination of answers seems most plausible to you, note how strongly intertwined are economic and political forces in causing the fall of the Soviet system.

Variations on the Mixed Economy: Corporatism and Colonialism

One of the interesting questions to keep in mind while watching the development of former communist systems in coming years will be to what extent they really do adopt pure market systems, and to what extent they maintain sufficient government regulations in place to qualify rather as mixed economies. There are many variations possible.[25] A **mixed economy** does not always mean such relatively simple combinations as nationalizing public utilities and imposing wage and price controls while leaving a large private sector in place (mostly capitalistic), or introducing wage incentives and permitting the market to set prices while maintaining public ownership of the means of production (mostly socialistic). Any economy based on a mixture of public and private control of the means of production may properly be termed a mixed economy. A brief look at two of the more distinctive variations, corporatism and colonialism, and their contemporary manifestations, neocorporatism and neocolonialism, will not only help to clarify this point but will also permit further demonstration of the close interrelationship between political and economic systems.

Corporatism and Neocorporatism   A **corporatist** economy is one in which formal ownership of the means of production remains in private hands but the state requires that all industries and other productive enterprises be grouped into units according to the function being performed. All enterprises devoted to metallurgy, for example, might constitute one *corporation* (the word is used in a broad and general sense), all farmers would belong to another, all seagoing merchants to yet another, and so forth. Even homemakers and students might be assigned to their own units. Under such a system, every corporation has its own ruling body to determine such matters as what goods and services shall be produced, what wages shall be paid, and what prices shall be charged. The state maintains close control over the selection of the leaders in the corporation, however, and is careful to see that the decisions reached are in accord with state policy. Further liaison between the political and economic spheres is provided by setting up a quasilegislative body to which the different corporations must send representatives. This economic-based senate takes the place of the more traditional parliament, which is based on geographic representation.

Although the corporatist ideal is clearly highly authoritarian in its classic guise and has been strongly discredited by the policies of the French, Italian, and Spanish regimes that experimented with it during the middle of the twentieth century, it continues to appeal as a mode of reducing the painful confrontations among workers, managers, and bureaucrats that we find in less rigidly regulated systems. It is not uncommon today for social scientists to urge a new, presumably enlightened **neocorporatism,** a system in which the state exercises its power much less dictatorially but does give official recognition to different interests by establishing boards of represen- tatives to advise the government. Under this version, the neocorporatist state closely controls who is appointed to the boards. It also guides their deliberations by such selective "encouragements" as government subsidies or other supportive legislation on behalf of those who are deemed properly cooperative.[26]

Colonialism and Neocolonialism. Colonialism is the imposition of a form of mixed economy by an external political system. Having won po- litical control of others' territory either by military conquest or by other means, the external polity sends in occupying forces to assert its dominion and to extend that dominion over the productive enterprises in which it has an economic interest. Normally both military and civilian personnel carry out the colonizing mission, and their economic tasks are usually lim- ited to taking over only certain specified enterprises, such as agriculture and the development of resources — at least in the early years. They may claim to have a "civilizing" or "religious" mission to perform as well — and, indeed, many of the missionaries and other colonizers may sincerely be- lieve that they have a duty to pass on the advantages of what they truly consider a "superior" culture. Any objective assessment of colonialism makes it abundantly clear, however, that the colonizing nation is motivated first and foremost by its interest in reaping economic advantage from oth- ers' labor, on others' land. This relatively simple economic system consti- tutes another variation on the idea of a mixed economy.

Colonialism is a mixed economy in two senses. First, there is a mixture of private (indigenous) and public (foreign) direction of the economy of the colonized nation. Second, the colonizing state itself maintains a home economic system that is entirely different, but not disconnected, from the one it maintains in the conquered territory. In fact, the ability to maintain the home economic system frequently depends on the material rewards gained from the distant colonized system. This is true whether the home system tends toward socialism or capitalism; imperialism is not a function of economic dogma.

As we have suggested, the colonized territory is seldom brought under total control. The state (that is to say, the occupying forces of the con- quering state) normally exercises absolute power only over those areas where the goods it is interested in are produced or processed. Furthermore, what state control means varies greatly from one colonized state to the next, and from one era to the next. It may mean direct state regulation — as when marketing boards are established to set production quotas for and prices paid to the producers of coffee, cocoa, groundnuts, and other crops, thereby assuring that any surplus value accrues directly to the colonizing state. Or it may be indirect — as when the occupying state authorizes its own people ("settlers") to take possession of native lands and enterprises.

Colonialism, like corporatism, is now widely recognized to be a system of unfair exploitation of others. Also like corporatism, it is more and more difficult to find in its pure form. Here, too, a successor form has emerged. As the world's attitude toward imperialist ventures has moved from admiring to disapproving, and as changing world conditions have made political subjugation more difficult to maintain, foreign control of other lands now more commonly takes a different form — that of neocolonialism.

Neocolonialism is a system for maintaining the economic dependency of colonialism while permitting political independence. As a disguised form of imperialism that avoids open military subjugation, it can either develop out of colonialism or be introduced by foreign powers in already independent nations. In the first type, the colonizing nation passes formal political control to native leaders of its own choosing, arranges for economic pacts highly advantageous to itself, and backs up the new leadership with military assistance when required. The new arrangements often take the form of "foreign aid," but as J. Barron Boyd has pointed out in the case of France and her former African colonies, such aid is "given for less than altruistic motives. It is used not only to support the export of French culture and education, but also to foster French investment, trade and, in some cases, even military involvement."[27]

The combination of neocolonial exploitation and internal corruption makes it extremely difficult for the people of the neocolonized nation to put their resources to work in their own interests. At the same time, the former colonizer is no longer seen by world opinion as responsible for levels of development in the dependent nation — any failures in that area are seen as signs the latter was "not ready for independence" — although in fact it has not yet achieved that hoped-for state in any meaningful sense of the term. Of course, not every state that has become formally independent has maintained this relationship of economic dependency to past political colonizers, but the pattern is a common one, particularly in Africa.

The second form of neocolonialism — a colonial-like takeover of an independent nation's economy — has been more common in Latin America. After a period of open colonization by Spain and Portugal, many formally independent Latin American nations have fallen under the economic domination of other nations, particularly the United States. Under this form of neocolonialism, major corporations of a foreign political system, working with the open or covert assistance of their government, make such vast development and trade agreements with the economic leaders of a nation as to place that nation's economy — or a significant portion of it — under foreign control. Although such arrangements are frequently described as beneficial to the general population of the neocolonized nation, they tend in practice to favor an already wealthy elite and to skew the development of the economy in directions that will meet the needs of the colonizing nation rather than domestic needs or those of other potentially better-paying foreign buyers.

Whatever form of neocolonialism is in place, a particularly unfortunate and common result is the failure of the dependent nation to make important adjustments to the changing international market, continuing instead to export the agricultural goods, minerals and other raw materials for which relative world demand is steadily declining. Thus developing nations in Latin America and Africa in particular have been steadily becoming less important players in the international market.[28]

Yet when neocolonial arrangements are threatened by internal political change that appears to foreshadow economic change, the answer has often been a preemptive military coup, carried out with the assistance of the outside power, in order to preserve the status quo. The histories of the regimes of João Goulart in Brazil, Salvador Allende in Chile, Pas Estenssoro in Bolivia, and Juan Bosch in the Dominican Republic — reformist leaders removed from power by coups d'état — illustrate this ultimate form of neocolonial intervention in other nations' economies. More currently, El Salvador and Nicaragua provide interesting variations on the theme. In El Salvador the neocolonizing nation (the United States) long sought to maintain a nonmilitary government in power, but one whose commitment to democratic procedures and principles seemed little stronger than that of the typical military junta. In Nicaragua, a leftwing coup overturned the preexisting neocolonial ties and the neocolonizing nation (again the United States) supplied rebel military forces with aid designed to enable such forces to restore by counterrevolution the *status quo ante* (that is, the status quo before the leftwing coup).[29]

The prevalence and variety of neocolonial relationships in today's world have led to the development of **dependency theory,** used to analyze the interaction between politics and economics in the international sphere. Unlike classic economic theory, dependency theory argues that the world market does not meet the conditions of a free market, that nations involved in that market are of different sizes and have different resources at their command, that they are caught in complicated, longstanding webs of power relationships with one another, and that even when past dependency relationships have been broken former colonies come into the world market with so many handicaps that in effect they have simply substituted one form of dependency (to a single nation) for another (to the world economy). Dependency theorists insist that understanding the international environment as well as domestic conditions is the key to understanding the development of national economies, and they recognize that the world market is regulated according to the political strength of the participants. "A basic hypothesis of dependency theories is that the more powerful benefit more from these rules and regulations than do the less powerful."[30]

The economic system a nation chooses to adopt is obviously of great significance to the people who must live within that system. In today's interdependent world, that choice — and indeed the ability to make that choice — has international ramifications. We find that our economic problems, like our political problems, are global in extent, yet our economies, like our politics, are based on widely varied ideologies and structures. As long as these conditions prevail, how can we hope to arrive at workable and mutually satisfactory solutions? In the final section of this chapter we will explore several issues of political economy that must be addressed cooperatively by the human polity as a whole. Later, in Chapter 13, we will examine some of the international institutions through which attempts are being made to rise above the ideological and institutional diversity we have described in these earlier chapters.

GLOBAL ISSUES OF POLITICAL ECONOMY

The interaction of political and economic factors is one of the most striking characteristics not only of individual polities but also of the human polity as a whole. The economic problems we encounter more and more frequently require at least some international political solutions, and political developments around the globe are more and more likely to have international economic repercussions. We are becoming increasingly dependent, around the globe, on one another's resources and levels of productivity — and consequently on the search for international agreements that will keep these economic factors in some kind of mutually satisfactory balance. In an era of environmental crisis, interdependent international trade, and outdated government economic policies, the human polity must somehow learn to manage its household.

Environmental Crisis: Resources and Population

In the past two decades, the human polity has been forced to recognize that the energy sources the more fortunate nations had grown accustomed to using lavishly to meet their needs of industrial development are limited, and that the date of their exhaustibility is closer than we once imagined. Early in 1981, reporter Leonard Silk put the problem for Americans in stark and simple terms: "This nation, long self-sufficient in energy and indeed a leading exporter of oil, woke with a shock in the mid-1970s to discover that its way of life — and the stability and growth of its economy — were dependent on millions of barrels of oil a day from the politically shaky Middle East and other Third World countries."[31]

The political results of this recognition have been profound, as the world's citizens have argued over whether the proper response is to cut back consumption — and if so, whose consumption — or to work harder

Plantu/Cartoonists & Writers Syndicate

to find alternative sources — and if so, what alternatives. This second choice has meant increased politicization of the issues of using nuclear reactors, strip mining for coal, and a host of other environmental concerns.

How serious *is* the problem? At current consumption levels we have enough petroleum for about twenty-six more years, enough natural gas for forty-seven years, and enough bituminous coal for about 170 years. Copper ores will be exhausted in about eighty years, meaning that copper must then be extracted from common rocks, a far more expensive process. The cheaper sources of gold, silver, tin, and lead will have been exhausted somewhat earlier.[32] Although commercial energy consumption appears to be leveling off somewhat, the overall trend continues upward (see Figure 4.3).

Thus, the resource crunch is a matter of serious concern. Even if we are granted a few years of oil "glut," as the profit-hungry oil-producing nations put more oil on the market than necessary to meet demand, we know that the long-term picture is one of steady decline.

Our need for the energy to run our machines is related to another, earlier change in our energy resource base — the shift away from animal and human labor to machines. The consequent surplus of such beasts of burden as horses, donkeys, and water buffalo was fairly easily dealt with, but we have a harder time thinking of *ourselves* as merely surplus labor.

Indeed, even as fewer and fewer persons are needed to run our machines,

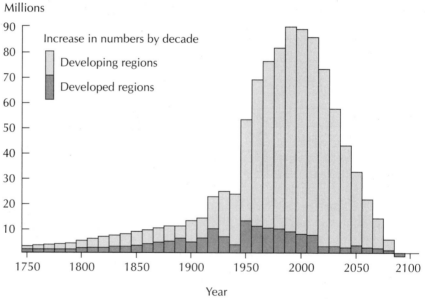

FIGURE 4.3   **World Population Growth: Developing and Developed Regions, 1750–2100**

Source: *World Resources 1987*, by the International Institute for Environment and Development and the World Resources Institute, p. 8. Copyright © 1987 by the International Institute
for Environment and Development and the World Resources Institute. Reprinted by permission
of Basic Books, a division of HarperCollins Publishers, Inc.

the world's population has been steadily growing because we are finding ways to reduce infant mortality rates, combat disease, and extend the lives of the elderly. As Table 4.4 and Figure 4.4 make clear, however, the population pattern is varied. Not all nations are moving in the same direction at the same pace. The world's population is increasing, but in some nations the number of citizens is either on the decline or growing so slowly as to be a serious cause of concern. All of the nations of western and eastern Europe except Albania are either growing at rates of less than 1 percent per year or are in fact registering a net decline for some years (net losses have occurred in recent years in Austria, Germany, Switzerland, and the United Kingdom; they are predicted in the near future for Denmark, Hungary, Luxembourg, and Sweden as well). The United States and Japan have been able to reduce their population growth rates, and other nations formerly plagued by runaway population growth have begun to get the problem under control.

The problem is severe in Asia, and very mixed. In newly industrialized South Korea the birth rate has dropped below the "fertility replacement

TABLE 4.4   **Selected Rates of Population Growth, in Thousands**

	Population	Growth Rate, in Percentage	Estimated Population
	1990	1990–2000	2000
Nigeria	86,551	3.2	118,620
Iraq	18,425	2.9	24,731
Kenya	24,229	2.9	32,479
Nicaragua	3,617	2.7	4,759
Mongolia	2,186	2.6	2,826
Ecuador	9,806	2.0	11,945
Venezuela	18,776	2.1	23,196
India	852,656	1.8	1,018,105
Albania	3,249	1.1	3,610
China	1,136,626	1.0	1,260,154
United States	249,924	1.0	275,327
Poland	38,112	0.4	39,531
France	56,720	0.5	59,354
Japan	123,540	0.3	127,554

Source: U.S. Bureau of the Census, *Statistical Abstract of the United States: 1994*, 114th ed. (Washington, D.C.: 1994), pp. 850–52.

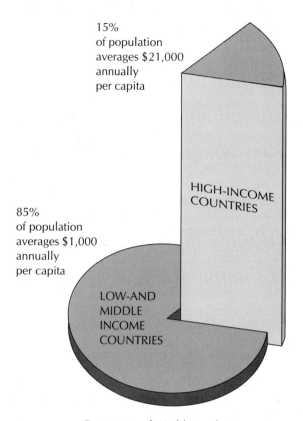

15%
of population
averages $21,000
annually
per capita

HIGH-INCOME
COUNTRIES

85%
of population
averages $1,000
annually
per capita

LOW-AND
MIDDLE
INCOME
COUNTRIES

Percentage of World Population

FIGURE 4.4   **Average Annual per Capita Earnings**

Source: Herman Daly, "The Perils of Free Trade," *Scientific American* (November 1993): 54.
Copyright © 1993 by Scientific American, Inc. All rights reserved.

level" — that is, less than two children born per woman — whereas in India fertility has leveled off at about four children per woman. There has
been a sharp decline in Bangladesh from its earlier rate of seven children
per woman, but the rate is still a high 4.7.[33] In China, officials hope that
the present population of over 1 billion (1,130,065,000 as of 1991) will
never increase to more than 1.2 billion, and will in fact drop to less than
700 million by the year 2080; some of the most stringent birth control
policies in the world (theoretically limiting each family to a single child)
have brought that nation down to below the replacement level sooner than
expected.[34] Overall, Asian families add some 57 million people to the
world's population every year.[35] And neither Latin America nor Africa is
expected to reach replacement level fertility rates until the middle of the
coming century.[36]

Thus it is in the poorest and most underdeveloped nations of the world — those least able to provide decent livelihoods for their citizens now living — that the rates of population growth remain worrisomely high, and are getting higher. A growing population means higher rates of unemployment, a greater demand for social services, and above all, more mouths to feed. The last problem causes the most severe human suffering. Despite a decrease in the absolute number of undernourished people in the world, our problems in this domain are far from resolved, particularly in Africa. The number of chronically undernourished on that continent increased from about 101 million in 1969–71 to 168 million in 1988–90.[37] And although the world's food distribution system has improved, political factors can still prevent relief from reaching those for whom it is intended. In 1991, southern Somalia suffered a prolonged drought and severe famine conditions at the same time that rival clans were fighting bitterly for political power. When international relief agencies attempted to respond, "an estimated 80 percent of food shipments were looted by armed groups affiliated with various clans."[38]

Even without such added impediments, meeting the global food demand is likely to become even more difficult in the future; by the year 2050, that demand is expected by some to be three times greater than today. Furthermore, the production growth rate for food is declining, and in 1991 there was actually a net decline for the first time in eight years. Again, the problem is most severe in Africa, where food production rates have fallen more severely than in the world at large and do not keep up with population growth.[39]

Interdependent International Trade

The environmental crisis can be said to be natural, economic, and political, in that order. Natural causes (human greed as well as resource decline) create the crisis, which in turn causes economic problems, which lend themselves, with greater or lesser ease, to political solutions. We turn now to a global issue that is economic, political, and *psychological* — and in which these three forces are impossible to order either chronologically or in relative importance, so intimately are they intertwined. That issue is international trade.

The Great Depression of 1929 set off a severe economic crisis that reverberated throughout the world. Those reverberations continued even after the worst effects of the depression had been overcome, as nation after nation maintained policies of economic nationalism and isolationism. Each nation sought to curb imports and strengthen exports, acting with only its own immediate benefits in mind. However, the spread of protectionist policies inevitably has the negative effects of increasing costs of production within societies (as other industries pay higher than world market prices for protected manufactured goods they need for their own production) and can seriously reduce productive efficiency as well.[40] This kind of response to the Great Depression may have had short-term benefits, but it also helped create the conditions of competition and hostility that played a key role in the outbreak of World War II.

In an effort to prevent the recurrence of such a response to domestic economic problems, the major Western nations created three important international institutions: the World Bank and the International Monetary Fund (IMF) in the Bretton Woods agreement of 1944 and the General Agreement on Tariffs and Trade (GATT) in 1947. All of these institutions have assumed new importance and new functions in recent years; to give a necessarily brief explanation of these developments, we begin with the last, GATT.

The purpose of GATT is to promote international trade that is as free as possible from protectionist limitations. This goal has been interpreted as meaning, in essence, mutual reduction of tariffs and equal treatment by each nation of all other nations in matters of trade (in accordance with the *most favored nation principle*, which means that no nation will be treated any less well than the nation with whom the most favorable conditions of trade are arranged).[41] As a result, tariffs have been significantly reduced across the globe, and, partly because of these reductions, world exports increased from $94 billion in 1955 to nearly $2 trillion in 1982, while global GNP grew from $1.1 trillion to $11.4 trillion. As of 1996, there were 131 signatories. The latest set of agreements, known as the Uruguay Round, will bring trade in agricultural and textile products into "regular GATT discipline," as well as establish the World Trade Organization (WTO), giving the GATT signatories a far more elaborate institutional structure (a secretariat, a director general, a staff) than it had in its first fifty years of existence.[42]

A key characteristic of GATT is its insistence on arriving at decisions by consensus among the participants in any set of agreements. Their relative strength naturally influences the outcome of those agreements, but within GATT itself there are no procedures for coercing consent. The World Bank and the IMF have not, however, proved so restrained. Decision-making power within these structures is not based on national sovereignty (one nation, one vote) but on level of participation; wealthy nations that contribute more have more power. And their influence determines which of the poorer nations will receive IMF funds for which projects.

To understand the new powers of the world's wealthiest nations via the World Bank and the IMF, we need to take a closer look at what has been happening to the world's poorest nations. The first thing to say is simple enough: they have been getting poorer. Overall expansion in world trade does not bring equal benefits to all nations, and poorer nations are not well placed to prosper from the world trade conditions fostered by GATT. The most favored nation principle makes it impossible to protect the less developed nations from the competition of more affluent nations, and their standing in the international economic arena has fallen rather than improved. Even among the more developed nations, the prosperity of some has come at the expense of others.

Partly in response to the conditions created by GATT, transnational corporations flourished in the postwar years, no longer so impeded by isolationist policies, and began moving enormous liquid assets from country to country, taking advantage of changing interest rates, currency fluctuations, and other marginal shifts in financial conditions that can mean production advantages that are anything but marginal. The rise of transnational corporations included multinational — or transnational — banks (TNBs). During the 1970s, loans made by such banks came to account for nearly 70 percent of all international finance, and the rate of return was impressive (Citibank, for example, earned 20% of its profits in the late 1970s from loans to a single nation, Brazil.[43])

The 1980s were, however, a time of reckoning. Many of the debtor nations, especially in Latin America, were unable to make their payments on these loans and defaulted. Defaults in Mexico (1982), Brazil (1983), Venezuela (1983), and Peru (1985) were serious enough to produce a massive international debt crisis. By the end of 1990, Western commercial banks were owed $350 billion by debtor countries in the developing world.[44] The response of the TNBs was to reduce and refinance foreign debts, providing lower interest rates and longer-term loans, in exchange for which the debtor nations have improved opportunities and conditions for foreign investments.[45] Such bargaining, aided by the IMF and World Bank policies discussed below, normally permits the delinquent nations to avoid default and even resume growth, but it also places yet more of the profits from such growth in foreign hands. According to one assessment, "households in Latin America were poorer in 1990 than they were in 1980, in Subsaharan Africa [poorer than in] 1960 . . . education and health budgets have been slashed in some debtor countries, further threatening the process of development that the loans were intended to support."[46] India, Russia, and most of the nations of eastern Europe are now major debtors as well. The problem of debt may be under a control of sorts, but it is far from resolved.

As the poverty of the poorest nations has increased rather than decreased over the past two decades, the IMF and the World Bank have moved in to offer their solution: Loans from these institutions for development projects would henceforth be made only after serious internal "structural adjustments" were made in the would-be borrower's internal economy. These "adjustments" normally are of a type to open up that economy to further foreign control. To show they are worthy of the funds, such states must now usually privatize a significant portion of the public sector, stop subsidizing inadequately profitable businesses, liberalize trade agreements with other nations, and pursue export development projects rather than focus on domestic consumption.[47] Such agreements will not only merit IMF funding but will also give foreign investors new incentives to move their businesses (and their jobs) abroad. The economies will prosper.

Or will they? Since the World Bank initiated these new lending practices in the early 1980s, the Third World's debt burden has risen from $785 billion to $1.5 trillion.[48] The IMF loans *have* helped bail out Western commercial banks; between 1984 and 1990 $178 billion flowed from the Third World to commercial banks through loan repayments.[49] And the World Bank is not losing money, as Herman Daly and John B. Cobb, Jr., explain:

> The fact is that the World Bank will almost always be repaid, even if the project or policy it finances produces only losses. This is because the Bank lends to sovereign governments that have the power to tax and print money. They cannot print foreign exchange, but they can buy it by printing more of their own money and accepting the consequences of inflation and devaluation — or they can tax their people honestly, rather than by inflation. In either case they can pay back the World Bank, and nearly always will do so rather than default and lose their credit rating. . . . [R]epayment flows on past loans are now so large that there is a 'negative net flow' of funds to the South from the Bank [that is, the Bank is receiving more than it is giving out].[50]

Furthermore, there is a growing body of evidence that the development projects financed by the World Bank seldom work out as planned. At the end of a soberly empirical assessment of efforts made under structural adjustment programs made in Ghana, Uganda, Tanzania, Kenya, Mozambique, and Zambia, Peter Gibbon, Kjell J. Havnevik, and Kenneth Hermele conclude "while there have been significant problems encountered in the implementation of adjustment programs, insofar as they have been implemented, the accompanying trends are not encouraging. Where it has occurred, growth has been generally low and/or temporary. In those few cases where it has been higher or more sustained, the results seem to have little to do with adjustment . . . a moratorium is probably merited, in which other options are explored."[51]

Finally, the massive shifting of assets from nation to nation, both for investment and for production purposes, is producing further shifts in the value of currencies on the world market and in interest rates, leading in turn to new decisions regarding where liquid assets might best be put to work. This new and potentially extreme volatility of the world's money markets is all but beyond political control and definitely beyond unilateral political control; no single nation can legislate stability under such conditions.

What, then, is the answer? On one hand, it appears that political action to ensure mutually acceptable international agreements providing a measure of stability is becoming ever more essential. On the other hand, how can we find a way to make such agreements work for the world's poorer peoples — and to keep the richer and more powerful nations from taking

BOX 4.1   **BEHIND THE BANK**

The World Bank, made up of 176 member countries, is controlled by those that contribute the most money. The largest contributors are the United States (17.9%), Japan (7.43%), Germany (5.74%), France and Britain (5.5% apiece). Each of these nations appoints its own "executive director," who has the responsibility of determining World Bank policies and approving loans. The remaining 171 countries must share 19 executive director positions. Traditionally, the Bank's president is nominated by the U.S. president and is a U.S. citizen. . . .

The Bank is primarily comprised of three lending agencies: the International Bank for Reconstruction and Development (IBRD), the International Development Association (IDA), and the International Finance Corporation (IFC).

The IBRD lends money to the governments of Third World countries. In 1993, the IBRD approved $16.9 billion in loans to 45 countries. Most IBRD funds come from bond sales, guaranteed by creditor governments.

Unlike the IBRD, the IDA lends money at below-market rates to the poorest countries. IDA loans are directed at infrastructure, such as roads, irrigation, agriculture and energy projects. In 1992, IDA loans totalled $6.5 billion. 100% of IDA funds comes from taxpayers' money.

The IFC lends money directly to the private sector to encourage the growth of private enterprise, and has no government guarantees. Although the IFC occasionally takes out loans from the Bank, the bulk of its funding comes from capital subscriptions (tax dollars) from member countries.

The World Bank and the International Monetary Fund are "sister" institutions; membership in the IMF is a prerequisite for membership in the Bank. The IMF was established to oversee currency exchange rates, and it offers short-term loans which require countries to follow its economic plan, known as structural adjustment. The same five countries that control the World Bank also control the IMF, between them accounting for 40% of voting power.

—*Shea Cunningham*

Source: *Dollars and Sense* 195 (Sept./Oct. 1994): 12. Reprinted by permission of *Dollars and Sense*, One Summer Street, Somerville, MA 02143.

control of the process and seeking to make it work in ways that simply improve their own advantage?[52]

Inflation, Lowered Growth, and Unemployment in Developed Economies

In addition, the problems resulting from environmental crisis; from the indeterminacy, complexity, and volatility of international trade; and from the disappointing results of intervention by international financial institutions are compounded by the efforts made *within* developed economies to maintain advanced standards of living despite declining rates of growth. The desire to keep profits and wages at levels that can be sustained only by continued growth has produced widespread **inflation,** or rise in price levels, in the world's more developed economies. The difficulty of selling goods to consumers with fewer jobs makes access to the world market all the more important, but goods that are too costly at home are even more overpriced for the world market, where other nations, paying their workers lower wages and/or relying heavily on automation to save on labor costs, are able to offer their goods at lower prices. And the poorly paid or under-employed workers of those nations are unable to serve as eager consumers of expensive foreign goods.

Lowered demand leads to still lower growth, to layoffs and the spread of unemployment, and to business failures. Efforts to curb inflation by set-ting higher interest rates and making money harder to attain may slow the rate of price increases, but they also put another brake on growth in many sectors of the economy, and they do not make the goods produced by the nations that attempt this solution significantly more competitive on the world market.

The governments of the world's industrialized nations have attempted to solve the problems posed by slowed growth, inflated prices, and unem-ployment with a range of solutions matching the range of their political and economic systems. Conservative capitalist systems such as the United States and Great Britain have experimented with raising and lowering in-terest rates, in the hope that the "supply side" of the free enterprise system will produce the necessary adjustments. Nations with more mixed econo-mies such as France, the Scandinavian nations, and most of southern Europe, try to stretch world-battered currencies sufficiently to make traditional welfare state responses to the problem, buying up major private businesses, pouring government funds into job-creating projects, and (sometimes) in-creasing the taxes of the wealthy. In the more authoritarian capitalist sys-tems of Asia and Latin America, the response to slowed growth is more likely to be a severe austerity program at home combined with improved conditions for investments from abroad. In 1995, Argentinian leaders de-manded of their citizens that they accept wage cuts, pay higher taxes, re-duce the consumption of imported goods, work harder, and even buy "patriotic" government bonds — and at the same time offered foreign com-panies sufficient inducements to maintain their investments.[53] And the world's few remaining communist systems, which have typically sought to keep everyone employed regardless of records of productivity, find them-selves either adopting ever more ruthless labor policies or moving in the opposite direction and adopting their own brand of mixed economy. The Chinese now claim to have a "socialist market economy" — whether or not that is a good name for it, laid-off "lifetime employees" are now discovering for themselves some of the more negative effects of free enterprise (see Box 4.2).

Although each of these approaches has brought about some change,

BOX 4.2

THE "IRON RICE BOWL" COMES UP EMPTY

Wang Xiujun is 38 years old, a mother of one tireless nine-year-old boy, and jobless. A former technician at Shanghai's China Record Factory, she was laid off during the summer of 1992. Her voice quakes with frustration from countless months of not finding new employment. "This is unfair," she insists. "I was supposed to be a lifetime employee."

She recalls when there were as many as 1,600 workers at the China Record Factory. Today, management wants to maintain a staff of 400 to 500. There are only two executives remaining in Wang's workshop.

"These managers are arrogant," she complains. "They're . . . sitting in their Mercedes-Benzes, and they don't care whether the workers . . . have jobs or not."

For Wang, and hundreds of thousands like her, the "iron rice bowl" has cracked apart in China's economic reform and enterprise restructuring. According to the Ministry of Labor, urban unemployment stands at 2.6 percent, or 4 million of the total urban work force. Although this number is low by Western standards, it conceals a statistical time bomb. At least 10 million of China's 74 million state-enterprise workers are now considered surplus.

The mammoth Wuhan Iron and Steel Corp. is in the midst of shedding two thirds of its employees, or 80,000 people. China's textile industry, which as of 1993 employed 7.5 million workers, is planning to "switch" 4 million employees to other sectors within the next three years. Meanwhile, the central government is cutting its own bloated work force by 25 percent, or 8.5 million employees.

The problem is how to take care of them. The socialist state enterprise has functioned as a social-welfare institution. It is the sole provider of housing, medical care, and retirement pensions for more than half of the urban labor force. "As things stand now, we can't let these insolvent factories just close down," one trade-union official says. In Shanghai, workers at insolvent state enterprises are being encouraged to retire early and find other work to supplement a reduced income.

Unemployment subsidies in Shanghai vary widely depending on the factory involved, but they seldom amount to more than 210 yuan ($24) a month, and are usually much lower. In a city where per-capita monthly income averages 324 yuan ($37), the difficulties faced by the unemployed are apparent to anyone who has tried to manage a household budget.

While those with technical training and manual skills have an easier time finding new or part-time employment, workers who are middle-aged and lack education must hit the streets and try their luck at parking bicycles, selling papers, or peddling fruit and clothing.

"I'm good at repairing houses," one laid-off machine operator says. "So I have been working for friends rather steadily. But others from my factory are out on the street selling eggs and spices."

—*T. S. Rosseau, "Eastern Express"*

Source: T. S. Rosseau, "Eastern Express" from *World Press Review* (July 1994): 12. Reprinted by permission of "Eastern Express," Hong Kong and *World Press Review* magazine, New York.

particularly in the reduction of inflation, growth rates in many nations have remained unimpressive and unemployment figures stubbornly unresponsive. Furthermore, since 1989 an entirely new set of global economic developments has emerged to compound these familiar and normally transient kinds of difficulties.

The Political Economics of Global Change

The approximately two-year interval between the demonstrations of East Germans around their side of the Berlin Wall in the summer of 1989 and the disintegration of the Soviet Union in the fall of 1991 was a period that brought more than the excitement of a sudden introduction of democratic and capitalist norms into nations that had seemed firmly committed to communism; it brought as well an array of new international economic opportunities, entanglements, and outright dilemmas to the global economy that are likely to take many years to resolve.

The ways in which this startling period in the history of the human polity has shifted the grounds and the dimensions of our global economic interdependency are far too numerous and too complex to be detailed in the last few pages of a single chapter of this book. All we can offer here are a few illustrations of the magnitude of the economic change that has taken place in the past few years.

- Reinforcing its economic and political unity, the European Union has grown to fifteen members (with the addition of Austria, Finland, and Sweden) and another nine (Poland, Hungary, Romania, Bulgaria, the Czech Republic, Slovakia, Latvia, Estonia, and Slovenia) are likely to join before the century's end. Others on the list of possible members include the newly independent former Yugoslavian states, the semiautonomous republics of the former Soviet Union, plus Malta and Cyprus.[54] Even Norway may yet reconsider its recent decision not to join. With this expansion, Europe is rapidly becoming the world's largest single market, with 370 million consumers and a combined GDP of more than 7 trillion dollars.[55] Although unemployment remains close to 11 percent and Europeans themselves are often pessimistic about the capacity of the Union to maintain growth (now about 3% per year), it is clear that Europe is steadily growing not only larger and more prosperous, but also more solidaristic. It is now a force with which other economies, large and small, must reckon on its own terms.
- The transition to capitalism in Russia has not been smooth, even if we look only at national figures and ignore (for the moment; we will come back to this question in later chapters) the vast upheaval in individual lives. The ruble has been in steady decline and the government must pay up to 18 percent interest on government bonds to keep itself afloat. Nevertheless, the transition proceeds: Russia now has about 2,500 licensed

commercial banks, 600 investment funds, and 40 million shareholders. Nearly 16,000 medium-sized and large enterprises were privatized in less than two years, and in 1994 the private sector produced 62 percent of the nation's officially recorded gross domestic product, a proportion higher than that in Italy. One close observer describes what is going on in these terms: "It's robber capitalism. It's lawless, but at the same time very vital and viable." But another is less optimistic, expecting those "robber barons" who are making their fortunes in these early stages to lobby the state for regulations to protect their gains, which will in turn "cause long-term stagnation . . . increase income inequality . . . cause social conflicts. Then you would have a serious danger of a radical, to-talitarian revolution."[56] Who is right? And what will be the impact of this still massive polity's transformation on the global economy?

- Poland and Hungary are, on the other hand, making the transition to capitalism much more cautiously, some might say much more partially. By the end of 1994, 60 percent of state-owned enterprises in Hungary were still state owned; in Poland the figure was closer to 64 percent. Furthermore, even when a public business is sold, it — or large shares of its stock — may be sold to another state agency. Or it may be sold to workers' cooperatives or simply allowed to fall into the hands of its own former state-employed managers (a practice even more common in Ro-mania). Extensive state support for favored private firms is another way these two nations have continued close connections between business and the state. Western economists believe such half-measures inevitably halt the growth a more aggressive capitalism would permit, but it is natu-ral for those raised in a socialist system to be unsure whether the profits possibly produced by unrestrained growth would be as equitably dis-tributed as the lesser gains their more mixed and gradualist approach may entail.[57]

- After World War II, Japan moved steadily forward to world economic leadership, based in large part on successful management techniques and careful long-range planning that produced startling technological achievements the rest of the world was willing to pay for. But the news of late has been less impressive. Shaken first by a sudden stock market slump and then by the high costs of the Kobe earthquake, the long-buoyant economy has run into serious trouble despite public expendi-tures designed to bail it out that have totaled over $546 billion since 1992.[58] Prices and profits have all been falling precipitously, as the yen has grown steadily stronger in the world market. A $127 billion trade surplus and currency that buys more per yen every day sounds fine, but not when it makes it more difficult to sell Japanese products abroad, not when it is more profitable to import cheaper foreign goods and sell them at home than produce your own (a practice severely limited by Japan's continuing protectionist tariffs), and not when more and more domestic

Japanese farmers protest U.S. policy on rice importation in a large demonstration at a central Tokyo park. Deteriorating trade relations between Japan and the United States compound difficult problems of global interdependence. (AP Photo/Wide World)

firms find that the only way to stay afloat is by cutting their work force, selling off assets, and reducing production.

If Japan's market-driven deflation continues unchecked, economists worry that this period of stagnation will turn into a period of prolonged recession for that country. For some, the agreement reached with the United States in 1995 to semideregulate trade in automobiles was a move in the right direction; only by opening up more thoroughly to the global market, they believe, can Japan force out its weaker players and give new stimulus to the strong.[59] Others fear the fresh winds of unfettered trade will assume hurricane force and do more harm than good.

Either way, what happens in an economy as important as Japan's happens in the world at large.

The immensity of these changes — and the burdens they have placed on more developed nations wrestling at home with ever more serious social and economic problems — has made the end of our century a time for deeply serious reflection. As noted in the previous chapter, ours is not an era in which simple remedies can be easily deduced from any single ideological approach. The satisfaction of seeing whole nations suddenly commit themselves to "our way" must necessarily be accompanied by sober thoughts of how to make "our way" work. Political scientists who know how to confront the complexity of the relationships between economic and political developments have an important role to play in this vital task.

SUMMARY AND CONCLUSION

In this chapter we have explored the relationship between politics and economics. Any economy is a system of producing, distributing, and consuming wealth. Whatever system is in operation strongly influences the course of politics — and political decisions, in turn, help shape the economic system. This was true when we lived and worked together in hunting bands, in primitive agricultural settlements, in kinship systems, in feudal estates, and in corporate guilds. It is equally true in today's more modern economic systems, be they capitalist, socialist, or mixed economies.

Some of the specific economic factors that shape a nation's political choices are its size, available natural resources, and level of economic development. A nation's size can be measured by either its territorial extent or the number of its citizens, but in either case small states function very differently from large states. Those differences include economic considerations, which influence political relationships. The nature and extent of a nation's natural resources also help shape its political decisions. Economic development means developing the ability to process and market raw materials in order to improve the material well-being of the nation's own people. The relationship between politics and economic development is complex and variable. Economic forces do shape politics, and profoundly, but they do not do so in isolation from one another or from other social forces.

Different political systems have led to the institutionalization of different economic systems: capitalism, socialism, mixed economies, corporatism (or neocorporatism), and colonialism (or neocolonialism). Capitalism is a system in which entrepreneurs are free to plow their profits back into capital expenditures. Unbridled capitalism can lead to such inequalities of wealth that a demand will arise for either socialism or some form of a mixed economy. Under socialism, the state controls all the means of production and is itself supposedly controlled by the workers. Nearly every nation in the world, however, has an economy based on a mixture of public and private ownership of the means of production and on considerable public regulation of the private sector.

The mixed economy comes in many forms. A corporatist economy is one in which ownership of the means of production remains in private hands but the state requires that all industries and other productive enterprises be grouped in units according to the function they perform. Colonialism is the imposition of a type of mixed economy by an external political system. Neocolonialism is a system for maintaining the economic dependency found under colonialism while granting the colonized nation political independence.

The growing interdependence of the human polity has raised many of the issues of political economy to the global level, making these problems simultaneously more difficult and more urgent to resolve. Particularly urgent are our shared problems of declining energy resources and increasing population — with population growth often most pronounced in nations that are already unable to meet the pressing needs of their people. Short-sighted government policies sometimes only deepen our economic dilemmas as we struggle separately and often ineffectually to cope with problems produced by interdependent international trade, widespread unemployment, unimpressive rates of growth, and the economic costs of a period of massive global political and economic change on a scale unseen since World War II.

In sum, the relationship between politics and economics is as close today as it was in our earliest efforts to establish a civilized life in common with our neighbors. In fact, our ever more elaborate political structures and our continued material development make that relationship constantly more complex — especially when we realize that for many purposes "our neighbors" are the nearly 6 billion people now living on the planet.[60]

Despite the immensity of the challenge, there is nevertheless reason to hope that we are finding new ways to address the present crisis in the world economy. Gone are the days of instant and dogmatic declarations of simplistic cures. When the needs are as urgent as they are at the present time, and when no nation, including our own, is exempt from the effects of global transformation, it is clearly time to extend our widest sympathies and to put our surest knowledge to work in the quest for solutions that reach far beyond the borders of a single state.

Selected Readings

Bulmer-Thomas, Victor. *The Political Economy of Central America Since 1920* (Cambridge, Cambridge University Press, 1987). An historical examination of economic and social development in Central America from the 1920s through the post-World War II period. A comparative approach is taken.

Caporaso, James A. and David P. Levine, *Theories of Political Economy* (Cambridge: Cambridge University Press, 1992). A useful framework for understanding the relationship between politics and economics.

Fardoust, Shahrokh and Ashok Dhareshwar, *A Long-Term Outlook for the World Economy: Issues and Projections for the 1990s* (Washington, D.C.: The World Bank, 1990). A comprehensive look at major indicators of growth and decline in the world economy.

Galbraith, John Kenneth. *A Journey Through Economic Time: A Firsthand View* (Boston: Houghton Mifflin, 1994). Considers the effects of war, revolutions, ideologies and government policies on the major economic and social events after World War I.

Griffith-Jones, Stephany and Osvaldo Sunkel. *Debt and Development Crises in Latin America: The End of an Illusion* (Oxford: Oxford University Press, 1986). An examination of the debt crisis that has developed in the 1980s in both Latin America and the industrialized nations.

Krueger, Anne O. *Political Economy of Policy Reform in Developing Countries* (Cambridge, MA: M.I.T. Press, 1993). Clearly explains the interaction between economic and political variables in economic development.

Malabre, Alfred L., Jr. *Understanding the New Economy* (Homewood, IL: Dow Jones-Irwin, 1989). Discusses the emerging global economy and the interdependency of nations in terms that make them personally relevant and easy to understand.

Pastor, Manuel, Jr. *The International Monetary Fund and Latin America: Economic Stabilization and Class Conflict* (Boulder, Col.: Westview Press, 1987). A discussion of the IMF in eighteen Latin American countries. IMF goals and the Latin American debt crisis are examined.

Raffer, Kunibert. *Unequal Exchange and the Evolution of the World System* (New York, St. Martin's Press, 1987). The Marxist economic idea of "unequal exchange" in the international economic system is discussed.

Reich, Robert B. *The Work of Nations: Preparing Ourselves for 21st Century Capitalism* (New York: Knopf, 1991). A call to Americans to learn to think of the economy in global terms, and to develop "a positive economic nationalism."

Singer, Hans Wolfgang and Sumit Roy. *Economic Progress and Prospects in the Third World: Lessons of Development Experience Since 1945* (Gloucester, England: E. Elgar Publishing, 1993). A balanced explanation of the economics of developing nations. Provides a detailed historical analysis and case studies in Nigeria and India.

Spero, Joan Edelman. *The Politics of International Economic Relations* (New York: St. Martin's Press, 1990). Provides a useful introduction to economic relations between the industrialized nations and between rich and poor nations. Includes a discussion of the economics and politics of money, trade, and foreign investment from 1945 to 1990.

Widner, Jennifer A., ed., *Economic Change and Political Liberalization in Sub-Saharan Africa* (Baltimore: Johns Hopkins, 1994). A discussion of the economic crisis in Africa in the 1980s. Analyses the effects of structural adjustment and economic reform programs.

Notes

1. For a good brief discussion of the various and shifting meanings of the term *political economy,* see Eileen R. Meehan, "Rethinking Political Economy: Change and Continuity," *Journal of Communication* 43, no. 4 (Autumn 1993): 105–109.

2. For an interesting discussion of the way of life of hunting bands, see Jacques Maquet, *Civilizations of Black Africa* (New York: Oxford University Press, 1972), pp. 33–67.

3. Rayna R. Reiter, *Toward an Anthropology of Women* (New York: Monthly Review, 1976). See also Rosalind Miles, *The Women's History of the World* (New York: Perennial Library, Harper & Row, 1990), pp. 5–8.

4. It is estimated that the population of Venezuela increased fifteenfold after the inhabitants made corn (which could be stored) rather than roots (which could not) the staple of their diet. *New York Times,* 27 Sept. 1981, p. 17.

5. Max Gluckman, "The Kingdom of the Zulu of South Africa," in M. Fortes and E. E. Evans-Pritchard, eds., *African Political Systems* (London: Oxford University Press, 1940), pp. 25–55.

6. "When we speak of *the* economy, we already assume the existence of a separable entity" but this "does not mean that the economy can, in fact, stand alone" nor the absence of "significant state involvement in economic life." James

Caporaso and David Levine, *Theories of Political Economy* (Cambridge: Cambridge University Press, 1992), pp. 28–29.

7. For a general study of the feudal era, see J. S. Citchley, *Feudalism* (London, Boston: G. Allen and Unwin, 1978). For the concept of feudalism and its importance in the transition to capitalism, see R. J. Holton, *The Transition from Feudalism to Capitalism* (New York: Macmillan, 1985), chaps. 1 and 6.

8. Steven A. Epstein, *Wage and Labor Guilds in Medieval Europe* (Chapel Hill, N.C.: University of North Carolina Press, 1991).

9. Two good studies of the age of discovery are Carlo M. Cipolla, *Guns, Sails, and Empires* (New York: Pantheon, 1966) and Fernand Braudel, *The Mediterranean* (New York: Harper & Row, 1973). See also chaps. 5 and 6 in Jan P. Nederveen Pieterse, *Empire and Emancipation* (Westport, Conn.: Praeger, 1989).

10. For latter-day imperialism, see Phillip Darby, *Three Faces to Imperialism: British and American Approaches to Asia and Africa 1870–1970* (New Haven: Yale University Press, 1987) and Michael W. Doyle, *Empires* (Ithaca, N.Y.: Cornell University Press, 1986).

11. See Joan Edelman Spero, *The Politics of International Economic Relations*, 4th ed. (New York: St. Martin's Press, 1990).

12. T. N. Dupuy offers a general overview in *The Evolution of Weapons and Warfare* (Indianapolis: Bobbs-Merrill, 1980); for more recent developments, see Eliot Brenner and William Harwood, *Desert Storm: The Weapons of War* (New York: Orion, 1991) and Patricia Axelrod's assessment of the cost in human lives, "Baghdad's Terrible Secret," *San Francisco Chronicle*, 20 Aug. 1995, D1.

13. Alec Nove, *The Economics of Feasible Socialism Revisited*, 2nd ed., (New York: HarperCollins, 1991).

14. John E. Roemer, "A Future for Socialism," *Politics and Society*, 22, no. 4 (Dec. 1994): 451–78.

15. José M. Gonzalez-Eiras, "International Trade and Economic Nationalism," in Antonio Jorge, editor, *Economic Development and Social Change: United States–Latin American Relations in the 1990s* (New Brunswick, N.J.: Transaction, 1992), p.3.

16. Olga Balgun, *The Tragic Years, Nigeria in Crisis, 1966–1970* (Benin City, Nigeria: Ethiope Publishing Corporation, 1973), pp. 101–107.

17. Fox Butterfield, "Now for Far East Oil Disputes," *New York Times*, 17 Feb. 1974, sec. 4, 3.

18. Gonzalez-Eiras, "International Trade and Economic Nationalism," p. 5.

19. U.S. Central Intelligence Agency, *Handbook of Economic Statistics, 1981* (Washington, D.C.: U.S. Government Printing Office, 1981); and Charles Lewis Taylor and Michael C. Hudson, *World Handbook of Political and Social Indicators*, 2nd ed. (New Haven, Conn.: Yale University Press, 1972), pp. 110–115 and 150–153.

20. Taylor and Hudson, *World Handbook*, p. 212.

21. See, for example, Sebastian Edwards, "The Political Economy of Inflation and Stabilization in Developing Countries," *Economic Development and Cultural Change*, 42:2 (Jan. 1994), pp. 235–66. Edwards focuses on whether inflationary financing results when governments develop financial policies they hope will control political instability (he believes it does). More broadly, he considers the general relationship between political and business cycles, but examines only one case in depth (Chile between 1952 and 1973).

22. The birth of capitalism is said to have occurred when sixteenth-century textile manufacturers in England began using profits to expand (rather than just to maintain) productive capacity. For a study of this era of development, see Immanuel M. Wallerstein, *The Modern World System: Capitalist Agriculture and the Origins of the European World Era in the Sixteenth Century* (New York: Academic Press, 1976).

23. Douglas A. Irwin, *Mercantilism as a Strategic Trade Policy* (Washington, D.C.: Federal Reserve System, 1990) and Immanuel M. Wallerstein, *The Modern World System II: Mercantilism and the Consolidation of the European World-Economy, 1600–1750* (New York: Academic Press, 1980).

24. Adam Smith, *Inquiry into the Nature and Causes of the Wealth of Nations* (New York: Modern Library, 1937).

25. Jon Elster and Karl Ove Moene, *Alternatives to Capitalism* (Cambridge/New York: Cambridge University Press, 1989).

26. Gerhard Lembruch and Phillipe Schmitter, *Patterns of Corporatist Policy-Making* (Beverly Hills, Calif.: Sage, 1982) and Frederick B. Pike and

Thomas Stritch, eds., *The New Corporatism* (South Bend, Ind.: University of Notre Dame Press, 1974).

27. J. Barron Boyd, Jr., "France and the Third World: The African Connection," in Phillip Taylor and Gregory A. Raymond, eds., *Third World Policies of Industrialized Nations* (Westport, Conn.: Greenwood Press, 1982), p. 48.

28. José M. Gonzales-Eiras, "International Trade and Economic Nationalism," pp. 12–13.

29. Jack Woddis, *Introduction to Neo-Colonialism* (New York: International Publishers, 1967), pp. 103–113.

30. Immanuel M. Wallerstein, *The Modern World System*, vols. 1 and 2 (New York: Academic Press, 1980); Immanuel Wallerstein, *The Politics of World Economy: The States, the Movements and the Civilizations* (Cambridge, MA: Cambridge University Press, 1984); Andre Gunder Frank, James D. Cockcroft, and Dale Johnson, *Dependence and Underdevelopment: Latin America's Political Economy* (Garden City, N.Y.: Anchor Books, 1972). Although dependency theory has lately been criticized for "not working," its critics have shown only that its proponents have not eliminated the inequalities in the world economy which they explain, not that the theory itself is wrong.

31. Leonard Silk, "A Growing Interdependence," *New York Times*, 8 Feb. 1981, sec. 12, 1.

32. International Institute for Environment and Development and the World Resources Institute, *World Resources 1987* (New York: Basic Books, 1987), 299.

33. World Resources Institute, *World Resources 1994–95* (New York: Oxford, 1994), p. 30.

34. *The World Almanac and Book of Facts 1991* (New York: Pharos Books, 1990), p. 479, and James C. F. Wang, *Contemporary Chinese Politics: An Introduction* (Englewood Cliffs, N.J.: Prentice Hall, 1992).

35. Lester R. Brown, "Nature's Limits," *State of the World 1995* (New York: W. W. Norton, 1995), pp. 3–20.

36. World Resources Institute, *World Resources 1994–95* (New York: Oxford, 1994), p. 30.

37. Food and Agriculture Organization of the United Nations, *The State of Food and Agriculture 1992* (Rome: FAO, 1992), pp. 16–20.

38. Helen Chapin Metz, ed., *Somalia: A Country Study* (Washington, D.C.: Federal Research Division, Library of Congress, 1993), p. 154.

39. World Resources Institute, *World Resources 1994–5* (New York: Oxford, 1994), pp. 107–108. See also Lester R. Brown, "Reassessing the Earth's Population," *Society* (May/June 1995): 7–10.

40. José M. Gonzalez-Eiras, "International Trade and Economic Nationalism," pp. 9–10.

41. David H. Blake and Robert S. Walters, *The Politics of Global Economic Relations*, 2nd ed. (Englewood Cliffs, N.J.: Prentice Hall, 1983), p. 12.

42. John H. Jackson, "The World Trade Organization, Dispute Settlement, and Codes of Conduct," in Susan M. Collins and Barry P. Bosworth, eds., *The New GATT: Implications for the United States* (Washington, D.C.: The Brookings Institution, 1994), pp. 63–83.

43. Stuart Corbridge, ed., *World Economy* (New York: Oxford, 1993), p. 27.

44. Ibid., p. 28.

45. See, for example, Kenneth N. Giepin, "Brazil in an Accord with Large Banks on Cutting Its Debt," *New York Times*, 16 Apr. 1994, A1.

46. Corbridge, *World Economy*, p. 29.

47. Herman E. Daly and John B. Cobb, Jr., *For the Common Good* (Boston: Beacon Press, 1994), p. 440.

48. Walden Bello and Shea Cunningham, "Reign of Error: The World Bank's Wrongs," *Dollars and Sense* 195 (Sept./Oct. 1994): 11.

49. Ibid., p. 11.

50. Daly and Cobb, *For the Common Good*, p. 440.

51. Peter Gibbon, Kjell J. Havnevik, and Kenneth Hermele, *A Blighted Harvest: The World Bank and African Agriculture in the 1980s* (Trenton, N.J.: Africa World Press, 1993), pp. 128–29.

52. Herman E. Daly and John B. Cobb, Jr. argue in *For the Common Good* that the task is so difficult the real answer is simply to return to national control of indigenous economies.

53. Matt Moffett and Jonathan Friedland, "Taking a Huge Risk, Argentina Intentionally Deflates Its Economy," *Wall Street Journal*, 21 Mar. 1995, A1, A17.

54. Dominique Moisi and Michael Mertes, "Europe's Map, Compass, and Horizon," *Foreign Affairs* (Jan./Feb. 1995): 122–34.

55. "European Union," *U. S. Global Trade Outlook: 1995–2000* (Mar. 1995): 31.

56. "Russia's Emerging Market," in "Survey on Russia," *The Economist*, 8 Apr. 1995, 3–5.

57. "Eastern Europe's Capitalism: Who's Boss Now?" *The Economist*, 10 May, 1995, 65–67.

58. "That Sinking Feeling in Japan," *Business Week*, 8 May, 1995, 52–54.

59. "OK, Mickey, Let's Say You Won," *The Economist*, 1 July, 1995, 65–66.

60. *The Statistical Abstract of the United States, 114th ed.* (Washington D.C.: U.S. Department of Commerce, 1994), p. 850 gives the world population as 5,643,290,000 persons as of 1994 and projects that it will be 6,165,079,000 as of the year 2000. Global rate of population growth is now 1.5 percent per year; there is an average of 112 persons per square mile on the planet's land mass.

5 Politics and Culture

THE POLITICAL CULTURE OF THE NATION-STATE

THE POLITICAL CULTURE OF SUBNATIONAL AND SUPRANATIONAL GROUPS
Ethnicity and Race
Religion

IMPACT OF CULTURAL DIVISIVENESS ON THE NATION-STATE

DISSEMINATING VALUES: POLITICAL SOCIALIZATION
Political Socialization by the Family
Political Socialization by the School
Political Socialization by Peers
Political Socialization by the News Media
Political Socialization by Political Events

SUMMARY AND CONCLUSION

ARE YOU A PATRIOTIC citizen? Do you get a lump in your throat when you see your country's flag waving in the breeze? Or do you feel rather cynical about what seems to you to be nothing more than nationalistic nonsense? Do you have stronger feelings of affiliation with a particular ethnic group than you do with the nation-state in which you live? Would you like to see the United Nations become a stronger body — or a weaker one? Do you think it might make sense to decriminalize the sale and use of drugs? What is your stand on the issue of abortion? How do you feel about welfare policies? Do you support the candidates of a particular political party? Which of the ideologies discussed in Chapter 3 made the most sense to you?

The point of all these questions is not to persuade you that you have political attitudes and opinions, but to get you ready for another question: Where did you get them? Why do you have these views about politics? And here's still another question: So what? Your beliefs may be important to you (let's hope they are), but does it make any difference to your political system that you hold the views you do? What about your counterparts in other political systems? Do the views of the Russian or Thai college students on matters of political significance have any impact on their nations' politics?

Perhaps your first instinct is to answer these questions more or less like this:

1. I have the opinions I have because I have given these matters rational thought and have made intelligent decisions.
2. My opinions matter when I vote, because I live in a modern democracy. Most of the time, however, no one besides my mother and my dog pays very much attention to what I think (and neither of them is really all that interested, either).
3. The political opinions of an ordinary citizen who lives in a nation that is not a modern democracy do not matter to anyone.

If these are your answers, then this chapter should give you grounds for rethinking them. First, the good news: Your political opinions (and those of your counterparts in other nations, whatever the nature of their political system) probably matter a great deal more than you think, especially if they are expressed by means other than merely voting. Then the not-so-good news: You may have worked out fine, logical reasons for holding the opinions you do, but chances are you got them in the first place because you were influenced by other forces in your life.

The subject of this chapter is the social and cultural context within which we make our political decisions, and the effect these have on politics. We will explore how different societies, and different groups within societies, develop and disseminate the values that shape political opinions, structures, and policy decisions. Our interest now is in **cultural values** — that is, values shared by a group of people in a given culture. (**Culture** is a word that has many meanings, as a quick trip to the dictionary will remind you; here I am using it to mean the ideas and customs shared by a given people in a given period of time.) Some cultural values are widely shared throughout a polity; others are shared less widely, by specific groups within that polity, or, sometimes, more widely, by groups whose boundaries are larger than that of specific states. In this chapter, we will consider first how cultural values are important at the level of the nation-state, and then consider their nature and impact at the subnational (or supranational) level. We will emphasize the cultural values of ethnicity, race, and religion, but we will also give attention to the values that groups share on the basis of shared class, language, gender, age, or region of residence. Finally, we will examine some of the more important findings in the subfield of political science known as *political socialization*, the study of the processes by which our political values are learned.

THE POLITICAL CULTURE OF THE NATION-STATE

Almost every polity has something that political scientists call a **political culture**, that is, a widely shared set of "cognitions, perceptions, evaluations, attitudes, and behavioral predispositions" that permit the members of that polity to "order and interpret political institutions and processes, and their own relationships with such institutions and processes."[1] Of course, the values that compose a culture may and normally do change over time. A recent study of American values finds, for example, that while acceptance of different ethnic groups and diverse lifestyles has increased in recent years, as has concern for the environment, there has, on the other hand, been a steady decline in the importance attached to obligations to others, to work for its own sake, and to following the conventions of the larger society.[2] But there are also continuities in the U.S. value system: Walter S. Jones points out that Americans continue to be much more concerned about how to protect political and religious liberty than about the capacity of a political system to ensure economic well-being and economic justice.[3]

The political cultures of other nations have also been analyzed and re-analyzed over time. In one study, German citizens were found to have a "detached, practical and almost cynical attitude toward politics," while Mexicans were said to reject bureaucratic authority as "corrupt and arbitrary," and the Italian political culture was described as one of "unrelieved political alienation and . . . social isolation and distrust."[4] These comments are all drawn from *The Civic Culture*, a large-scale comparative study of the political cultures of five nation-states, including the United States and Great Britain as well as Germany, Mexico, and Italy, made in the early 1960s. In this important study, authors Gabriel Almond and Sidney Verba set forth the ideal of a **civic culture**, one in which citizens combine a commitment to moderate political participation with a belief in the legitimacy of officialdom and a mild tendency toward **parochialism**, that is, toward withdrawing into the private sphere. Such an orientation, they argued, serves the citizen and the polity by keeping "politics, as it were, in its place," and ensuring the necessary "balance between governmental power and governmental responsiveness" necessary to maintain a stable democracy.[5]

The question of an ideal political culture is, of course, a normative one. Not everyone has agreed with Almond and Verba that their model of the civic culture is ideal. When belief in the duty and value of political participation is low, especially among the less advantaged groups in a society, the surface calm of the civic culture can be both deceptive and short lived. Great Britain was described by Almond and Verba as a "deferential civic culture" in 1963, but since that time has become subject to sporadic rioting by hitherto politically passive groups ("deferential" according to Almond and Verba). Such groups have now felt the impact of recent reductions in public spending on social welfare, health, and education as the British government has initiated an austerity program a more contemporary author describes as an outright "attack upon social citizenship rights."[6]

Dramatic changes have also taken place in the German political culture since *The Civic Culture* was published. In 1963, Almond and Verba found that only 7 percent of their German sample cited "governmental and political institutions" as "the things about this country that you are most proud of." A follow-up study done in 1978, after the memory of the institutions that nation had established during the Nazi regime had had fifteen more years to fade, found 31 percent of West Germans ready to give this answer to the same question.[7] Then came German reunification in 1990, posing immense new problems of national identity: "The new Republic has to . . . recover both the East German past and the past common to both states. . . . Unification entails the coupling, however uneven, of two ideological visions, two political and cultural projects, two different kinds of legitimacy and logic."[8] The evolving political culture of the new Germany includes such dangerous trends as increased hostility to the nation's large Turkish and gypsy populations and renewed emphasis on bonds of German kinship.

Italian political culture has also changed significantly in the past three decades. In assessing Italian political culture a key question has been the changing role of the family. In a book published about the same time as the Almond and Verba study, Edward Banfield argued that Italians always put the family and its interests first, regardless of the impact on community or national interests, an interpretation that seemed to explain why Almond and Verba found them so politically alienated and distrustful. In recent decades, however, the role of the family has greatly changed in Italy. Women have acquired more education, the birth rate has fallen, a feminist movement has emerged, and families often need more than one income to make ends meet, so that more and more women have moved into the workforce. At the same time, it has become more difficult for young adults to earn enough to live on their own. Staying at home unwillingly, they tend, says Donald Sassoon, to "challenge the very institution of the family, to develop an anti-familial ideology." Sassoon sees Italian youth as anti-authoritarian, often highly politicized, and having a strong sense of solidarity with their own age group, even across national borders.[9] Anna Emilia Berti agrees that Italian young people are not apolitical; her work demonstrates that by the age of 14 or 15 Italian schoolchildren tend to have a full understanding of the requisites of good governance, including political organization, community involvement in the making of laws, and the role of conflict.[10] In sum, Italian lack of respect for their own political system can no longer be explained as merely the by-product of an unusually strong sense of respect for the family, nor are the most alienated always simply uninformed and disinterested. As Mattei Dogan and Dominique Pelassy, among others, have pointed out, it is important to remember that sometimes negative evaluations of a system arise from historical and political fact rather than from dysfunctional cultural attitudes.[11]

Nevertheless, family values remain important in the study of national political cultures, as research unrelated to *The Civic Culture* has shown. According to Lucian Pye, the high value the citizens of Myanmar (Burma) place on obedience to parents is the basis for their apparent readiness to accept authoritarian leadership. To yield to the wishes of the parents is to act in an exemplary fashion. At a very early stage in life, the children in Myanmar are taught to be completely submissive before any form of authority and to expect that a passive and yielding attitude will be most likely to please those with power.[12] Pye has also stressed the importance of conformity in Chinese political culture: "The imperative of conformity fosters a make-believe world of politics, where . . . the emotional importance attached to maintaining 'face' produces a style of human relationships in which feigned compliancy is often the norm."[13] Note that Pye is not claiming that the Chinese always obey, but only that they usually pretend to be doing so: "Conformity and rebellion are the breath of Chinese politics," says Pye.[14]

Sometimes the most important value in a nation's political culture is simply pride in shared nationhood, a value we have already discussed in Chapter 3 as *nationalism*. This value is particularly likely to be stressed in the early years of a new nation or when a nation has been through a particularly harrowing period in its history. When France suffered humiliating defeats, both in World War II and in the loss of empire, the insistence by General and then-President Charles de Gaulle that French grandeur could yet make its mark in the world brought him strong support — especially as France struggled to keep from being overwhelmed by American wealth and power in the immediate postwar years — and a marked revival of French nationalistic spirit.

Of course, the task of creating a new sense of national unity is often complicated by the presence of groups whose tendency is to give their first loyalty to their own members. At such times, national leaders must find a way to balance the demands of such groups against the need for national solidarity. They cannot simply be ignored; precisely because a value is an opinion to which the holder attaches importance, acting without regard to values widely held in a society is one way to ensure a very brief tenure in office.

However, a wide repertoire of responses is available to those in authority, ranging from outright oppression to nationalistic exhortation to careful and pragmatic efforts to accommodate diversity without allowing it to tear the nation apart. Charles Tilly has suggested that when groups become sufficiently powerful to threaten the established leadership, more effort will be devoted to suppressing the group than to meeting its demands.[15] At such times, national leaders may engage in overt acts of repression, making it clear that to hold the contested value is to risk the wrath of the state and political punishment, as in China in June 1989 when then-Premier Li Peng ordered the troops to clear Tiananmen Square of student protesters seeking a democratic political system, killing and injuring hundreds, and later arresting thousands more.[16]

When leaders are more concerned about the survival of the nation-state than of their own power, they may rely more on exhortation than on represssion. When the new state of Zimbabwe was created after years of colonial domination by the British, the Ndebele and Shona peoples no longer had a common oppressor to hold them together and tribal conflict reemerged. In an effort to bring it to a halt, Joshua Nkomo, leader of the minority Ndebele, told his fellow tribesmen, "We are one people. You have got to accept that principle. We are one nation. There is no question of swallowing one another. Pick yourselves up, pull up your socks, and say we shall be one."[17]

But the most effective ways for nation-states to develop a shared sense of nationhood when significant differences exist within the polity is to find ways to accommodate those differences — ways that do not undermine the state. It may be possible to reach compromise positions on conflicting values, neither fully pleasing nor fully outraging any single set of sensibilities, as in recent Irish decisions to delay a referendum on permitting divorce while passing legislation to protect the property rights of persons divorced elsewhere.[18] Sometimes the nation-state seeks to ensure the trust and loyalty of diverse groups by enshrining such compromises in the nation's constitution. In multilingual India, for example, the constitution explicitly recognizes fourteen languages in addition to the principal one, Hindi (although in fact about 1,650 languages and dialects are spoken).[19] Federal systems, in which the constituent units (states, departments, provinces) have independent power over certain matters (as discussed in Chapter 13), permit different geographical regions to maintain different social norms on the matters under their jurisdiction. (Exactly which norms are protected in such systems is not always crystal clear: Canadians have recently battled over whether or not legislation forbidding businesses in the province of Quebec to use any language other than French on their outdoor signs really comes under the protection of that nation's federal constitution.[20])

Other important constitutional accommodations of conflicting values are clauses that ensure the protection of individual rights and liberties. The Bill of Rights in the U.S. Constitution, the French Declaration of the Rights of Man, the Indian Bill of Fundamental Rights, and the Venezuelan Bill of Rights are all examples of the ways polities attempt to ensure in their constitutions that citizens will be able to live according to their personal values as long as they do not interfere with the rights of others. Such clauses are usually addressed to individual values, but when they refer to matters of religion or language, or to the right of equal treatment under the laws regardless of gender, race, or ethnicity, then they are obviously of major significance for particular organized groups as well.

THE POLITICAL CULTURE OF SUBNATIONAL AND SUPRANATIONAL GROUPS

In the previous section, our focus has been on the shared culture of a nation-state, and the different ways such polities may seek to repress, limit, and/or accommodate subnational cultural differences that threaten national

BOX 5.1   **CLASS**

In most social systems, differences in level of income, level of education, and kind of occupation tend to cluster together and to produce, sometimes in combination with differences in the way we talk and dress and the kind of material goods we acquire, a class identity.[21]

Class identity can be a powerful force urging citizens to adopt distinctive political attitudes and beliefs. This is especially likely to be the case when two other conditions are met: First, the members of a class are conscious of that membership, and second, class membership is "bonded" with one or more other group identities.[22] To cite an example of the latter condition, trade unions have often been formed by people who have a sense of common destiny owing to shared social class, as well as by those seeking to improve conditions of employment. Class identity thus becomes bonded with union identity, and the possibility of acting on behalf of the two identities simultaneously gives added power to the members' political action. The Polish trade union Solidarnosc was formed by members of the Polish working *class* who were then able to use their years of experience working to defend the always embattled organization to engage in a political struggle of yet greater significance: helping to bring about the downfall of communism in their nation by forming a *party* and successfully campaigning to make their own leader, Lech Walesa, president of the new republic.[23]

Of course, the politicization of class interests is not always a working-class phenomenon. The social and business contacts of the more affluent with one another can also stimulate a sense of shared class, shared values, and shared responsibility to protect those values through political activism. Traditional middle class occupational groups who feel threatened as much by changing social mores as by automation and advanced technology sometimes seek political expression in new political movements, and rising class consciousness among peasant populations has played a key role in the growth of organized and sometimes successful rebel movements.[24]

unity. It is time now to look more directly at the nature and significance of subnational and supranational group cultures. What is the basis for their formation? Such a question, of course, has no single answer. Individuals within a polity may feel themselves separated from their compatriots — and closer to the citizens of other states — because of such personal characteristics as ethnicity (or race), religious affiliation, class identity (see Box 5.1), gender, age, language, or regional origins. This sense of difference may be present when the polity is first formed, in which case it may constitute one of the chief hurdles to the original establishment of the nation. Or it may develop during the lifetime of the polity, as wars shift national boundaries, as patterns of immigration and emigration change the mix of humanity contained within those boundaries, as the gap between rich and poor grows or declines, as values change regarding gender roles,

Politics and cultures collide. African and Arab immigrants, once welcome to carry out jobs not wanted by others but now blamed for high rates of unemployment, demonstrate near the Eiffel Tower to protest the French government's determination to send home all those whose papers or work permits have expired. (The photos carried by the demonstrators show fellow immigrants on hunger strikes.) (Reuters/Jacky Naegelen/Archive Photos)

or as the proportion and health of the aged change. The significance of group values for the political system can be better understood by looking briefly at two of the key variables — ethnicity and religion — in turn, and then considering two contemporary examples of the impact these forces have had in national and international politics.

Ethnicity and Race

Determining whether a given person belongs to a racial or an ethnic group or not is a highly subjective issue. This is particularly true of ethnic subdivisions within the same race. As Robert J. Thompson and Joseph R. Rudolph, Jr. have pointed out, "Ultimately, membership in an ethnic group is largely a matter of ascription. One belongs because one perceives oneself as a member of a group or because others so perceive one."[25]

Those who accept membership in a particular group, be it out of passionate conviction or passive acceptance, tend to share more than a single belief or value, and the values they share may well assume political significance. As Danuta Mostwin reminds us, "ethnic ties are among the strongest human feelings. They are the core of a person's self, the cornerstone of . . . identity."[26] The views of the group on such easily politicized issues as the content of schooling, employment services, welfare aid, the standards for promoting individuals to positions of responsibility, and procedures for adjudicating disputes may well run counter to the views of the larger society on the same kinds of issues. The consequences of such conflict can run the gamut from constant negotiation to open oppression to civil war.

The conditions of ethnic and racial distinctiveness, rivalry, struggle against oppression, and full or partial assimilation into the national ethos are not new, nor are they found with any greater frequency in one part of the world than in any other. It is useful to remember that the Chinese absorption of the Mongol and Tibetan peoples, the struggle of immigrants from former colonies for equal treatment in Great Britain, the determination of the Jewish people in Israel to build a state of their own, the rivalry between the Luo and Kikuyu groups in Kenya, the battle of African Americans in the United States for equality in the land their ancestors were brought to by force, and the treatment of indigenous populations throughout the Americas — different as they may be in other respects — are all manifestations of the conflict between group and national political cultures and the quest for a political resolution of that conflict, be it peaceful and accommodative or harsh and oppressive.

Yet the net result of such struggles is not always negative. The very process of politicizing group values and bringing them into a wider arena can serve as an important means of integrating the group into a larger world, blurring the distinctions between the political cultures of group and nation, or group and world community. Such a process can also serve to revitalize and strengthen the wider political culture, as everyone (or almost everyone) learns to incorporate some of the values of the newly assimilated group — perhaps adopting hitherto unfamiliar techniques for solving problems, perhaps gaining respect for a wider range of lifestyles and social values.

Religion

Many of the comments made about group distinctiveness based on ethnicity apply with equal force to groups based on religion. Indeed, ethnic and religious characteristics are often bonded, in the sense that the group identity is based on both, and the line between the two is difficult to distinguish. Catholicism is nearly as important as French ancestry in providing Canada's largest minority population with its sense of group identity. Judaism is a religion, but Jews share an ethnic as well as a religious heritage and constitute important minority populations in numerous countries. Significant Armenian-Christian populations exist in the predominantly Arab-Muslim nations of Iraq and Syria. The second largest ethnic group in the predominantly Malay-Muslim nation of Malaysia is Chinese Buddhist.

There are, however, societies that encompass separate group cultures

BOX 5.2   RACE AND ETHNICITY IN THE UNITED STATES

What racial or ethnic group do you belong to? U.S. citizens often refuse to play that game and proudly assert, "I am an American and that's that." Others are hard pressed to give an answer: "Well, my mother's mother was Welsh, and her father was a mixture of English, French, and Norwegian. My father's mother was half Cherokee, one-fourth African American and one-fourth Scottish and his father was part German, part Dutch, and part Indonesian. So you tell me: What ethnic group do I belong to?" But even in so large and heterogeneous a nation as the United States, there are many for whom racial or ethnic identity is a matter of great importance, and whose values and attitudes are shaped by this primary reference group.

TABLE 5.1   U.S. Population Percentages by Race, 1810–2050

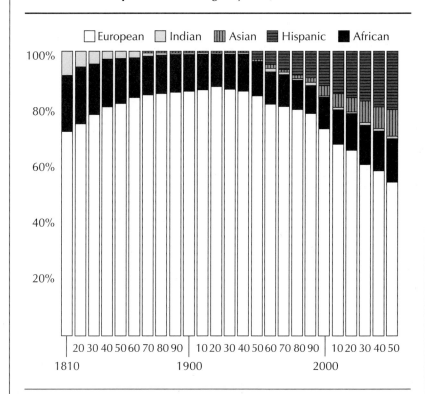

Source: Antonio McDaniel, "The Dynamic Racial Composition of the United States," in *An American Dilemma Revisited: Race Relations in a Changing World,* edited by Obie Clayton, Jr. © 1996 Russell Sage Foundation, New York.

based exclusively on religious differences. Muslim, Jewish, Buddhist, and Christian communities persist in cultures where the dominant religion is a different one and where the members of the religious minority are similar to the dominant populations in all other respects. In some cases, the religious distinction even arises within the same denomination as separatist sects develop among those who belong to the dominant religious group but practice their religion "with a difference." Members of both the Sunni and Shiite Islamic sects are Muslim, but the incompatibility between these two groups is severe; it played a major role in provoking war between Iraq and Iran and periodically produces armed clashes within nations like Pakistan in which both sects are found.[27]

In other cases, the distinction is not between religions or sects but simply between dramatically different interpretations of the same religion and the significance of its rulings for political affairs. Almost every Algerian is Muslim, but those who believe that the Qu'ran gives women full civil, social, and political rights and those who believe it says that women should remain invisible and in the home are presently in violent conflict. Over 30,000 persons have been killed over that issue in the past few years, including many women whose sole offense was to appear in public in Western clothes or wearing makeup.[28]

Religious values are, almost by definition, nonnegotiable, and the stakes are high. If I believe I will achieve eternal life and happiness by following a certain religious code, I will not be persuaded easily to give it up in the interests of such temporary comforts as peace on earth. Furthermore, the more my religious beliefs are challenged by the dominant culture, the more

TABLE 5.2   **Social Groups and the Presidential Vote in the United States: Percent Voting for Each Major Candidate, 1988 and 1992**

	1992			1988	
	Clinton	Bush	Perot	Dukakis	Bush
Race					
Blacks	82	11	7	86	12
Latino	62	25	14	69	30
Whites	39	41	20	40	59
Religion					
Protestant	33	46	21	33	66
Catholic	44	36	20	47	52
Jewish	78	12	10	64	35

Source: *New York Times,* 15 Nov. 1992, B9.

BOX 5.3   **RELIGION AND POLITICS IN THE UNITED STATES**

The relationship between religious identity and politics is strong and growing stronger in the United States. In 1988, it was considered something of an oddity that two ministers, Jesse Jackson and Pat Robertson, were among the serious early contenders for the presidential nomination of their respective parties, especially when the latter candidate campaigned almost exclusively on the moral issues associated with rightwing evangelicalism.[29] But by 1996, the Christian Right movement had become an even stronger force in U.S. politics, particularly within the Republican Party, and the growing power of this group forced candidates for that party's presidential nomination to demonstrate their good faith to them — in every sense of the word.[30] Although churches that enjoy tax exemptions are forbidden by law from endorsing or actively supporting candidates for public office, parishioners often do receive political guidance along with religious counsel.

likely I am to be persuaded that I am being tested. Do I really believe? Then I will endure any hardship rather than sacrifice one tenet of the faith I have chosen. The members of a minority religious group, scorned or perhaps actively oppressed by members of the dominant group, must either break away or develop a strong enough attachment to their religious values to be able to endure the insults and injuries that come their way. It is for these reasons that religious fanaticism is more common in minor sects. Of course, the fanaticism itself makes the group less and less acceptable to the dominant groups in the society. If the boundary between the religious sphere and the political sphere cannot be established and maintained, the result may well be a spiral of increased fanaticism on one hand and increased public condemnation on the other. (See Box 5.3)

IMPACT OF CULTURAL DIVISIVENESS ON THE NATION-STATE

The divisions created in societies by ethnicity and race, or by religion, are among the deepest we know. They can, of course, be a source not only of diversity but of important contributions to the strength and creativity of a polity. Furthermore, different peoples living harmoniously together in a single nation-state already know what it means to live in the human polity and are in that sense inevitably better equipped than more homogenous peoples to function effectively internationally.

In recent years, however, groups that formerly lived together in relative contentment (or resignation) within the same nation state have become determined to break apart, or establish new rules for living together. The end of the Cold War has meant the end of polarized conflict between blocs of nations each unified by a common goal of resisting the territorial and ideological encroachment of the other. Peoples whose struggle to maintain separate identities seemed long ago to have been forever submerged in this global battle have reemerged with seemingly undiminished needs to assert themselves and their nationhood. This has been particularly true of peoples whose cultural identity rests most heavily on ethnicity or race. The breakup of former Yugoslavia and of former Czechoslovakia as well as the efforts of the Baltic states and of the Chechnyans to establish independence from Russia are obvious examples of how the fall of the Soviet Union has permitted this kind of nationalism to reappear.

Not all ethnic intergroup struggles are clearly related to the end of the Cold War, however. The genocidal attacks of the warring peoples of Rwanda upon one another, the renewed insistence of some Canadians of French descent on the need for a separate state, and the complete transformation of legal and social relationships between white and black South Africans are examples of ethnic struggles that are only indirectly affected, if at all, by the fall of the Soviet Union. Their genesis is in more ancient battles: those of imperialist conquest and the resultant imposition of common nationhood on peoples who would have rather kept apart.

As merely mentioning these examples reminds us, the determination of different ethnic groups to redefine their legal and social relationships with other groups may be amply well motivated. They may also sometimes be peacefully pursued. Why do they sometimes lead to bloodshed and even civil war, and sometimes not? Looking more closely at two very different cases, that of ex-Yugoslavia and Canada, may help us find the answer to that question.

The background of the ethnic disputes in the territory of the former nation of Yugoslavia and in the present nation of Canada have a certain number of points in common. In both cases, national boundaries were determined by conquest and subsequent warfare, ultimately bringing together, not terribly long ago, people of different religions and different languages as well as different ethnic backgrounds. In both cases, the smoldering coals of old resentments have been periodically fanned by leaders seeking political gain, and these resentments have been deeply felt by many members of the general populace. Yet the struggle in Canada, while certainly intense and as yet unresolved, has for many years been waged within the confines of the democratic process, whereas in Yugoslavia it has now provoked open warfare and even attempted genocide.

To understand the differences, we must go beyond these superficial similarities and back in time — much farther back in the Yugoslavian case than in that of Canada. The early nations of Croatia and Serbia were two groups of Slav settlers in the Balkans. During the Middle Ages each practiced different forms of Christianity, the Croats becoming Roman Catholics within the Austro-Hungarian empire (beginning with the Treaty of Zagreb in 1102) and the Serbs following the tenets of Eastern Orthodoxy. The spread of the Ottoman empire in the 14th century meant the conversion of many in both groups to Islam. This third religion proved particularly strong in Bosnia-Hercegovina, a land in which both Croats and Serbs had settled and over which both ruled at different times. Some historians believe there is no separate Bosnian identity, pointing out that Bosnia had never been an independent state and that even "among Bosnian Muslims themselves . . . there are those who would argue that all Bosnian Muslims are simply Croats or Serbs who converted to Islam."[31] However, religious identity appears to be ascendant for Muslims, whereas ethnic identity as Serb or Croat is at least as important as religion for the self-identification of the Christian populations. Language is also a factor. Although all these peoples speak the same language, they use different scripts (Latin and Cyrillic) for writing it, and there are multiple dialects.[32] (See Figure 5.1.)

The first Yugoslav state bringing these peoples and others together was founded in 1918. In little more than a decade the more numerous Serbs imposed their rule over Croatia in the person of King Aleksander Karadjordjevic, who dissolved parliament and established a personal dictatorship. An underground Croatian resistance movement, Ustashe, led by Ante Pavelic, was formed and in 1934 the king was assassinated. As World War II began, the Yugoslav state was dissolved by Hitler, who gave the Croatian fascist movement, led by Pavelic, a free hand in the slaughter of somewhere between 350,000 and 750,000 Serbs, Jews, gypsies, and dissident Croats. To the extent they could, Serbs retaliated in their own resistance movement, the Yugoslav Army of the Fatherland (often referred to as the Chetniks) combining the pursuit of vengeance against the Croats with their battle against the Nazis. When Yugoslavia was recreated after the war its communist leader, Marshall Josip Broz Tito (and his successors after his death in 1980), sought to overcome this history, in part by suppressing it, in part by trying to substitute the ideals of communist egalitarianism for ethno-religious competition and in part by loosening ties with the Soviets and reforming the tenets of communist ideology to suit Yugoslav realities. But these efforts proved inadequate, especially as there continued to be different levels of economic development throughout the nation.

The fall of communism brought the Yugoslavs the opportunity to complete a process of separation from the Soviet bloc that was thus already well begun. Even more important, it brought them the chance to break away from each other, once and for all. Croatia and the more northern republic of Slovenia declared independence in July 1991. Each had maintained relatively cohesive religious, ethnic, and geographic identities, and these declarations were accepted by most of the international community. The Christian Serbs, however, were settled extensively throughout most of Yugoslavia and were determined to keep what remained of the nation intact, as well as to fight for the autonomy of Christian Serbian communi-

FIGURE 5.1   **The Present Boundaries of the Former Yugoslavia**

ties within the newly independent states. Muslim peoples, heavily concentrated in Bosnia but living throughout the region, were caught in the middle, whatever their lines of Slavic descent.

The difficulties of untangling this web have been tragically compounded by the readiness of demagogic leaders on both sides to stir up old memories that seemingly had begun to fade away, and to speak as if those guilty of crimes long past were in fact all the currently living members of the enemy group.[33] In addition, international forces such as the European Community, NATO, and the United Nations, as well as the world's strongest single power, the United States, all proved unable to work out timely, consistent, and realistic plans to avert the civil war that broke out in 1991.[34] It can be hoped that more recent diplomatic efforts to establish ceasefires, to redraw the map of Bosnia, and to create some form of confederal ar-

Nationalism is often at its strongest — and most irrational — when formerly united peoples decide to form separate polities. Here Serbians (above) and Croatians (opposite page) each raise their national flags in fervent demonstrations for separate nationhood, whatever the cost to their peoples and the land once known as Yugoslavia. (Above: AP/Wide World Photos; opposite: L. Delahaye/Sipa Press)

rangement (see Chapter 12) will succeed, but whether or not the peace they bring will endure is inevitably more dubious. This latest siege of geno-cidal slaughter and rape adds another not-to-be-forgotten chapter to a long history of conflict.[35] It is a history only too easy for leaders to sum-mon up whenever they believe it can be made to serve their own political ambition — and do not care how many additional lives are squandered to that end.

The conflict between the English-speaking and French-speaking popu-lations in Canada is very, very different. First, the history of both peoples in this part of the world goes back less than five hundred years, and large-scale settlement began only at the beginning of the seventeenth century. Second, both groups considered themselves colonists for the nations from which they had migrated, rather than independent peoples and states. Third, one group, the French settlers, came under the control of the other after only about 150 years of separate settlement and after only one relatively brief war; the so-called French and Indian wars ended with French defeat in 1759, and in 1763 the French ceded the colony to Britain.[36] A brief rebellion in 1837 was rapidly suppressed. Fourth, in combination, the British and French settlers soon outnumbered and outfought the indigenous residents of what later became the provinces of Quebec and Ontario, particularly the Iroquis and the Algonquins.

Fifth, from the beginning the nation of Canada, established in 1867 when the British granted nearly complete independence to their own compatriots, has been dominated by one contingent, the English-speaking citizens. Although relatively small indigenous Indian and Inuit populations combined with relatively large-scale immigration from other nations in Europe, Southeast Asia, and Latin America have meant that by the end of the twentieth century nearly half of all Canadians are of neither French nor British origin, the politics and government were nevertheless originally formed by and for those of English descent.[37] Newcomers have come as individuals, and although some settle in ethnic enclaves (e.g., the Ukrainians and the Dutch), they have accepted Canadian structures as they found them and most have learned to speak English.

Sixth, despite this continued dominance of the English-speaking population, those of French descent have always had a special status as the largest and most cohesive ethno-religious group, concentrated in a single region and present from the beginning of modern Canadian history. Canada thus has two official languages, English and French, and the province of Quebec, 80 percent French speaking, has numerous other special dispensations.

A seventh and final crucial difference between the Yugoslav and Canadian cases is that other nations have never attempted to play out their own struggles by waging warfare on Canadian soil (as did Hungary, Turkey, Germany, and the Soviet Union, in the case of Yugoslavia). Although the French have given their North American cousins strong moral support, they have never promised serious military aid for a battle for independence.

In combination, these factors have meant that Catholic French Canadians have really had no choice but to pursue their ends by peaceful means, and English-speaking Canadians no need to engage in violence to protect their ascendant position. The divisions between these two peoples are, compared to those between Croats and Serbs in ex-Yugoslavia, tidy and relatively peaceful. The absence of a history of repeated warfare between British and French-speaking Canadians means there are no memories of recent bloodshed and pillage by the other side that ambitious politicians can exploit to motivate new wars and build new careers. (The Indian and Inuit peoples who remain may have such histories, but they lack the power to form additional contingents in the current battle.)

But make no mistake. The struggle between French- and English-speaking Canadians is serious, ongoing, and very real. Today's French Canadians do not take their religion or their ethnicity less seriously than the embattled peoples of ex-Yugoslavia, and they have an extremely strong commitment to maintaining a different language from the majority population. They have often believed this heritage to be threatened by the policies of the national government. But they have been compelled by circumstance, not weakened by faint-heartedness, to wage their battle politically and constitutionally. This battle has not led them back to war, but it could yet lead them forward to secession. It provides ample fuel for occasional flareups of demagogic leadership.

The case of Quebec and the French Canadians is an interesting one that illustrates many other points we will make later in this book. We will return to them, and explain the current sources of their discontent as well as English-speaking Canadians' response, more fully later on. But for now, this example, contrasted with the Yugoslavian case, does help us understand some of the reasons why ethno-religious struggle sometimes leads to bloodshed and sometimes does not. It should help us as well to stifle the impulse to call for simple solutions, insisting that if one set of peoples can find peaceful ways to conduct their battles with one another, others "should" be able to do the same. History has worked for peace in eastern Canada, but for recurrent slaughter in southern Europe. The conditions present in the Yugoslav case cannot be transformed overnight. People raised in battle and the memories of battle cannot be expected suddenly to value peace over revenge and order over victory. An immense task of political resocialization lies before those who seek an end to religious-ethnic strife in this and similarly affected polities.

DISSEMINATING VALUES:
POLITICAL SOCIALIZATION

As we have already noted, not all cultural values endure, be they widely shared or subscribed to only by narrow groups. The lifetime of a value, however, is not determined by mere chance. Values endure when two conditions are met: (1) they continue to be relevant to objective needs, and (2) they are passed on clearly and persuasively by those who hold them to those who do not. Here we will focus on the second condition, the inculcation of values — a process known as **socialization**. Because we are interested in values that have political content, we will confine our study to **political socialization**.

Political socialization means the process by which we acquire our political opinions, beliefs, and values. Very shortly after my grandson Trevor came into the world, he lifted his head and looked around as if demanding to be told what this was all about. It was only with great restraint that I decided it was perhaps just a bit early to tell him he was now a citizen of the human polity. But only a little bit too soon. The world begins to teach us lessons about politics earlier than you might think. There is no better way to understand that truth — or to grasp what political socialization is all about in practice — than to explore your own memory. Take a moment to answer the following twelve questions:

1. What is your earliest political memory? What is the first political event you can recall? How did you learn about that event? What feelings did you have about it?
2. Was politics a subject for discussion in your home when you were a small child? If so, who talked about it? Did they talk to you about it directly? How would you characterize the general tone of such discussions? Interested or apathetic? Positive or negative? Factual or emotional?
3. Did the adults in your family vote? Did they tell you how they were voting? Did they themselves vote the same way?
4. Did anyone in your family take an active role in politics? What kind of role? Working for a political party or an interest group? Talking or writing to government officials about a problem requiring public ac-

tion? Running for elective office or helping in someone else's campaign? If so, were you yourself involved in any way in that effort?

5.   Do you know all the words to your country's national anthem? When and where did you first learn this song? Can you remember how you felt when you were first able to sing it?

6.   What are some of the subjects your teachers in elementary school and high school covered when they taught you about the government of your country? About its history?

7.   When did you get into your first political discussion? Who was it with? How did you feel about it?

8.   Did you ever find that you were a minority of one in a political discussion with fellow students? How did you feel about that situation? Have you ever joined with fellow students in trying to persuade someone else to adopt a particular political opinion?

9.   Do you watch the news on television, listen to it on the radio, or read it in the newspaper? If so, do you think you can tell how the newscaster or reporter feels about the political event he or she is reporting? If so, do you usually feel the same way?

10.   Do you pay attention to political campaigns? Do you try to figure out the character of political candidates as well as the content of their messages? Do you sometimes make up your mind how you will vote (or how you would vote) on the basis of such assessments?

11.   If you have a job (or have had one in the past), have you ever discussed politics with coworkers? How did it make you feel to find you were in agreement? In disagreement?

12.   How important do you think it is for people in love to have the same ideas about politics? If you are in love, do the two of you ever talk about politics? Do you tend to agree or disagree? Have you changed any of your political beliefs because of the ideas and arguments of the person you love?

If you have taken the time to probe for the answers to these questions, you have begun to get a good sense of how you personally were socialized to have the political beliefs you do. You can probably also see that political socialization is a complex, layered process. We do not learn about politics all at once, and no one receives only a single set of socialization messages from a single agent or institution. By looking at the most powerful agents of socialization — family, school, peers, media, and politics itself — we can learn a bit more about how political socialization really works.

Political Socialization by the Family

The family is almost always the most important agent of political socialization, even in homes where politics is never discussed. Adult family members (especially mothers and fathers, but aunts, uncles, and grandparents can also play important socialization roles if they live in the same household) guide children in the development of basic personality traits, atti-

BOX 5.4   TEACHING CHILDREN ABOUT WAR

1. Mother to 3-year-old son: "War is when many people are fighting. They fight all at the same time. War is not nice. We don't like the fighting." "Peace is when people everywhere like each other and get along. The people share. They don't hit each other nor hurt each other."

2. Father to 5-year-old son: "War is when two groups of people disagree so much that they are willing to kill other people to try to prove their point."

3. Mother to 6-year-old son: "[War is] when countries disagree and fight with each other. [Peace is] when countries are *not* fighting with each other."

4. Mother to 7-year-old daughter: "War is when two groups of people get mad at each other and stop trying to talk to one another. Then they start fighting each [other] and people on both side[s] get killed. The war isn't over until enough people on one side are killed and the other side can take over. When we think of peace we think of quiet, restful times. But I think peace is more than that. If two people are being noisy but they are having fun together and feel good about themselves — they are being peaceful. I think peace can be a lot of work to get — because peace is when people work hard to talk about their differences and work them out so that they can cooperate instead of fighting. If people are peaceful we don't waste time fighting and things are right so that good things can happen between people."

5. Mother to 10-year-old daughter: "[War is] fighting with words, attitudes and ammunition (guns, bombs, and knives). When you sisters fight and then refuse to speak to each other and fix your problem that is silent war. Peace is communication: [being] able to work, live and play together. Peace is restful and safe like our home. Peace is where love is: giving in to each other and preferring one another like Jesus taught us with his life."

6. Father to 12-year-old son: "War is armed aggression by one country on another. It is not abstract, one country fighting another. Real people are getting killed or maimed. War isn't fun or a contest: it's life and death and it should not be entered into lightly. Peace is the absence of war. It's toleration of others' opinions. Hopefully it's even cooperation and respect between different ways of life."

Source: Judith A. Myers-Walls, Karen S. Myers-Bowman, and Ann E. Pelo, "Parents as Educators about War and Peace," *Family Relations* 42 (January 1993): 66–73. Copyrighted 1993 by the National Council on Family Relations, 3989 Central Ave. NE, Suite 550, Minneapolis, MN 55421. Reprinted by permission. The war in question was the 1991 conflict in the Persian Gulf.

tudes, and values. Such guidance may be deliberate and benevolent or haphazard and even cruel, but because family members are in more or less constant contact with one another, and because the emotional ties between them are strong, the family inevitably plays the key role in the early socialization of the child.

Socialization within the family need not be "about politics" in order to include political socialization. It can be indirect as well as direct. As we are taught that certain general personality traits are desirable, we develop a personality that will have specific political as well as social proclivities. Tamar Liebes and Rivka Ribak found that different patterns of interpersonal communication within Israeli families were related to the political attitudes children developed and their level of commitment to political participation. Particularly important was the distinction between families that believed that conflicts should be minimized and even suppressed in the interests of harmony and those that believed they should be "resolved through clear representation and fair debate of diverse points of view."[38] Did your family emphasize obedience, responsibility, and orderliness? Or were you taught that discussion, independent thought and having the courage of your convictions were more important?[39]

Whether by direct or indirect means, the family has been shown to play an important role in one's choice of partisan affiliation. Children often have "strong positive or negative feelings concerning candidates as a result of parental suggestion" and in one study over fifty percent of American, British and German children chose the same party as their parents (American Democratic parents appeared to be the most influential; 70% of their children chose the Democratic party as their own, with 20% opting for "Independent" and only 10% choosing the Republican party).[40] In families where there is no conflict between the parents on that subject, parental influence is at its strongest, and the likelihood of such congruence is even greater in families where parents and their grown children have similar occupations, incomes, levels of education, and religion.[41]

Family influence on partisanship varies, however, as the social and political environment changes. The degree of similarity between parent and child partisan choices has been shown to have dropped considerably after World War II in Europe and Japan, and during the 1980's in the United States.[42]

Political Socialization by the School

Education is a second major force in political socialization. Political leaders in every part of the world have recognized the importance of the schools in developing loyal and productive citizens, and have worked to bring education under the control of the state. Thus, almost every school in the world, be it public or private, is required to function in accordance with an elaborate body of statutory law that prescribes (at least in part) the content of its curriculum, the training required for its instructors, and the standards established for admission and graduation. Is the course you are reading this book for meeting one of your requirements for graduation? Chances are good that the program making it so was reviewed at some level of your university's administration for its compliance with state educational policy.

This does not mean that the only purpose of the political socialization you receive in school is to ensure your loyalty to the system. Societies vary in the extent to which they insist that the schools perform such a function.

Saying the pledge of allegiance. Political socialization often takes place in the schoolroom. (Shirley Zeiberg/Photo Researchers Inc.)

In any case, numerous forces are at work in the average public school — curriculum, teachers, classroom rituals, extracurricular activities, and the attitudes of fellow students — and only the most rigorously authoritarian system is capable (or desirous) of ensuring that all these forces operate to inculcate the same set of political attitudes and values.

How do all these different forces influence a student's political choices? The curriculum is where we are most likely to find an emphasis on political indoctrination, or, more benignly, on civic training.[43] A person who is politically indoctrinated is simply given all the "right" answers, but a person who receives civic training learns the rules for playing the nation's political game, whatever that game might be. A citizen in an authoritarian regime is likely to find the emphasis on indoctrination; a citizen in a democracy normally receives a higher quotient of civic training.

Some of the tools of indoctrination in the schools include reciting a pledge of allegiance, raising and lowering the flag, working under the photograph of the smiling president or emperor, and singing patriotic songs.

Such rituals work to develop a sense of awe, devotion to the state, commitment to collective activity, and a feeling of belonging to a larger community. The Chinese school child is taught that the prodemocracy demonstrations in Tiananmen Square in 1989 were "the activities of hoodlums and counter-revolutionaries who attacked the army and killed many brave soldiers."[44] However, every political system includes some indoctrination of children, even the most democratic. Needless to say, such indoctrination does not always "work." Carol Seefeldt argues, for example, that the daily recitation of a pledge of allegiance in a democracy too easily becomes a meaningless ritual; she suggests it is more important for school children to be involved in the school community, taking part in setting rules as well as obeying them and seeking ways to change them democratically when they are not fair.[45]

In any case, the balance between the two forms of socialization in the schools is always subject to change, not only from nation to nation, but sometimes from community to community. There is some evidence, for example, that children in lower income settings in the United States are more likely to be taught that "politics is conducted by formal governmental institutions working in harmony for the benefit of citizens" (stress on indoctrination), while those in more affluent communities "encourage a belief in the citizen's ability to influence government action through political participation" (stress on civic training). Similarly, girls attending British private schools, including those from lower income families whose tuition is paid by scholarship, have higher levels of interest in politics, trust in the political process, belief in the stability of the political system, and knowledge of local politics than girls attending state schools. They are also more likely to anticipate being politically active in the future.[46]

Political Socialization by Peers

The study of political socialization has concentrated very heavily on what happens during childhood and adolescence, but more and more attention is now being paid to patterns of adult socialization. We do not spend our youth being taught how to think about politics and our adulthood acting out these acquired beliefs. We continue to be influenced by others, either to hold fast to our old points of view or to come to a different understanding of the world of politics.

Peers are a good example of a lifelong force for political socialization. We find them in the sandbox, at school, on the assembly line or in the office, in clubs, and eventually in retirement homes. They may be friends we have chosen, fellow students, or co-workers we do not particularly like but with whom we must perforce spend a great deal of our time. Sometimes they are peers only in the limited sense that we are all "grownups." Authority figures — the boss, the landlord, the military commander — may continue to shape our political choices for us in adult life as they did in childhood.[47]

How influential our peers will be depends in part on how we feel about them and in part on how much attention they give to political questions. It also depends on the nature of the times and the personal circumstances of those involved. If the society is in an era of change, as when a nation is recovering from a devastating war, or if our personal circumstances have changed significantly from what they were in the past, as when we gain or lose a fortune, we are more likely to be susceptible to the influence of our peers, seeking contemporary guidance in a strange new world. On the other hand, when we move with others like ourselves into new situations, these accompanying peers sometimes help us maintain the values we had in the past. A high-ranking New York City official riding on a bus filled with New York African-American leaders about to join the 1995 Million Man March on Washington, D.C. said, "All black men ought to be supporting this. We have a lot to overcome in this country. I'm here because I feel we ought to support each other." His words were directed to his peers — others like himself who had moved up economically and might be at risk of losing touch with the less fortunate members of their race.[48]

How much our political values are shaped by the values of our peers depends not only on the content of those values and the quality of those peers but also on the social context we live in. Peers may be the least or the greatest of the socializing forces in our lives.

Political Socialization by the News Media

The socializing forces we have discussed so far are what can be called **proximate forces** — that is, forces we encounter in person as we live with our family, go to school, or interact with others in a wide range of social settings. Human beings are also socialized by **nonproximate forces**, however — agents with whom we have no direct personal contact. One such force is the mass media.

We receive a constant flow of political messages from the media. The most obvious examples are reports of the political news. Today's transportation and communications technologies make it possible for the news media to cover almost any happening in the world with remarkable thoroughness. However, the commercial needs of the publishing and broadcasting companies, and the level of interest and comprehension of most audiences, combine to limit that coverage severely. As a result, we normally acquire only the most fragmentary understanding of local, national, and world events, and must rely on reporters and commentators to tell us what they "mean."

This is not to suggest that the news media are always in the business of handing out readymade political opinions. Indeed, in the United States and in many other Western nations there is a strong tradition of journalistic impartiality that prevents reporters from taking sides on controversial issues or introducing their own biases into straight news stories. A number of exceptions to this rule, however, are tacitly allowed. The news media in the United States, for example, seldom hesitate to show a strong bias in favor of national interests over the interests of other nations; they often present those who take action on behalf of unfamiliar or unpopular political opinions as eccentric, amusing, or contemptible; and they permit their reporters to use adjectives — or, in the case of television anchors, gestures — that help to convey the "correct" interpretation of the event being reported. The subtle and discreet nature of the commonly allowed exceptions to the rule of journalistic impartiality gives them all the greater power to shape our political opinions. We cannot resist what we normally do not even notice.

Furthermore, not all news is conveyed on news programs — much of it is now presented on talk shows on radio and television. Although such conversational shows normally discuss news that has already been presented in more conventional ways, in fact many citizens first learn of important events by listening to or watching their favorite talk show hosts and their guests. In these settings, the media escape most of the restrictions imposed on conventional news, and their hope of attracting viewers (and selling the products advertised on commercial breaks) stimulates them to stress entertainment values — which in turn inevitably means highlighting issues that arouse emotional response and discussing them emotionally. Yet nearly all of the questions discussed have a political component, and the net result is a powerful new form of political socialization. Is listening to and watching talk shows a good way to form opinions rationally, considering all the facts? If not, does it matter?

In any case, it is not hard to understand why the world's more authoritarian systems insist on absolute control over radio, television, and the press, and in some cases over all forms of the printed word. When the rulers of Myanmar refused to accept the result of democratic elections in 1990, they engaged in numerous killings, "disappearances," and acts of torture to suppress opposition — but they also took great care to maintain absolute control of all six newspapers published in the nation as well as all its radio and television networks.[49] Unfortunately, an almost endless number of similar examples could be cited from around the world.

Political Socialization by Political Events

Not all our political opinions are secondhand. We pay attention to what we are taught or advised to think about politics by our families, textbooks, teachers, peers, and the news media, but we are also directly influenced by the world of politics. We may get our information about a political issue or event from one of the socialization agents already cited and still adopt our own distinctive attitudes about the facts presented, regardless of what we are advised to believe. In some cases, we move out into the political world ourselves and form our opinions on the basis of direct experience.

In times of peace, children are rarely socialized directly by political reality but receive its impact indirectly through attention to other socializing agents: family, school, peers. But even though filtered through such a lens,

Algerian women wave pro-democracy banners and demonstrate against the Muslim fundamentalists seeking to keep all women in traditional roles. When the world of politics impinges directly on individuals, changing their destinies, powerful socializing forces are at work. (AP Photo/Wide World)

a major event like the assassination of a president may have as strong an effect on children as on adults. Studying schoolchildren's reactions to the death of President John F. Kennedy, Roberta Sigel found that they responded to the event with emotional reactions very similar to those of adults. They felt grief, sympathy for the family, shame (that "this could happen in our country"), and anger; they lost their appetites, had headaches, and had trouble going to sleep — and they reported all these reactions with just about the same frequency as adults.[50]

Long-term warfare, on the other hand, directly and painfully socializes all those in its path, including the children of the world. In the years between 1985 and 1995, between 4 and 5 million children were physically disabled by acts of war, more than 5 million were moved into refugee camps, and more than 12 million were made homeless. Children are themselves often drafted as combatants, sometimes as human minesweepers and sometimes even as spies. Not surprisingly, those who have been forced to play such roles are often unable to readapt to civilian life. Psychiatrist

Daya J. Somasundaram, who works at Jaffna General Hospital in Sri Lanka, a nation of continuing internal warfare in recent years, says that for such children "normal living becomes sort of dull." They develop, he says, a "tendency to sudden, aggressive outbursts — throwing things, assaulting people . . . these experiences go deep and become a permanent part of the personality."[51]

Other observers have noted the impact that political crises can have on the way young adults will later interpret political events and on the choices they are likely to make in the voting booth. Thus, American voters who came of age in the midst of the Great Depression are more likely than others to make political decisions on the basis of economic factors, whereas those who reached maturity during the height of the Vietnam War are more concerned with issues of war and peace. French citizens who came of age around the time of the massive student demonstrations of 1968 that brought the nation to a standstill and forced serious changes in its educational system are often referred to as *soixantehuitards* or "nineteensixty-eighters" — the term has come to mean not only those who took an active part in that year's massive and eventually nation-wide protest movement, but anyone of that age group who shows a tendency to reject the status quo and to insist on the need for reform. In Britain, the conservative beliefs of former Prime Minister Margaret Thatcher were more attractive to those who came of voting age in the relatively prosperous mid-1980s than to those who joined the political arena in the more difficult years just before.[52]

Of course, the world of politics sometimes impinges powerfully and directly on citizens of all ages, changing their views forever. The individual drafted to fight in wartime, or forced to donate the family's livestock to the cause of guerrilla insurgents, or arrested in a case of mistaken identity — or simply summoned to appear at the tax agency's office — may well have a different opinion of the political process after such a direct experience of "how it really works." The change may be a positive one. The military experience may produce a veteran more patriotic than the draftee; the guerrilla movement may succeed and introduce land reforms that give the farmer whose livestock was confiscated a sense of commitment to a glorious cause; judicial procedure may establish innocence with impressive speed and efficiency — and it is even possible that the tax agency will graciously acknowledge that the original payment was correct. But whether positive or negative, direct experience in politics and government does function as a force for political socialization.

The forces of family, school, peers, media and political events are not the only forces of political socialization, nor do they act separately on us. We can never be sure when the messages of one agency will be stronger than those of another in shaping how we respond to the political present.[53] But we *can* seek to be conscious of where we have learned our opinions and try to reevaluate them from time to time in the light of the best knowledge we may have gained since their original inculcation.

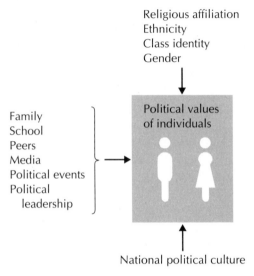

Religious affiliation
Ethnicity
Class identity
Gender

Political values
of individuals

Family
School
Peers
Media
Political events
Political
    leadership

National political culture

FIGURE 5.2   The Cultural Formation of Political Value

SUMMARY AND CONCLUSION

The culture that we live in powerfully shapes the political values we hold dear. Family, school, peers, media, and political events all exert a strong influence on our attitudes and opinions regarding the world of politics, and so do our religious, ethnic, class and other group identities — including that of national citizenship. When political values are bonded with cultural values, they have an added strength; we do not take lightly the efforts of any individuals or institutions to prevent us from living our lives according to those values. For this reason, our leaders, our institutions, and other nations interested in maintaining successful relations with us must give such values careful consideration and response, or risk the loss of legitimacy, political alienation, social unrest, and possibly even revolution or war. The formation of cultural values and their significance for the political process are summarized graphically in Figure 5.2.

Conflicting cultural values can trouble international relations in time of peace as well as in time of war. In some cases, problems develop because the parties involved do not even recognize that they are operating on different normative assumptions. In most African systems, great emphasis is placed on one's responsibility to take care of other members of one's extended family, if one is in a position to do so. In most European systems, great emphasis is placed on hiring the most qualified candidate for any job, regardless of that person's family ties. When African and European management teams attempt to work together on a development project, misunderstandings and recriminations over hiring practices are highly likely if both sides have not understood and resolved this fundamental difference in cultural values.

As the nations of the world grow more interdependent, will our cultural values grow more similar? Probably. After all, socialization can take place across national boundaries as well as across the livingroom table or the village well. The process is complex, as a simple personal example may serve to illustrate. When I am invited to a home in west Africa, I am unlikely to be offered kola nuts — but when my host passes the bowl to his other guests, he is now likely to be aware that I may find the omission disturbing and to take the trouble to explain to me that it is not the tradition to include women in this practice. I myself, aware of the many courtesies that have been extended to me, may be able to put my Western feminist instincts on hold, yet I feel compelled to make a point of including his wife in the political discussion we are having, whether she is interested or not. What is happening in such a case? Several persons whose cultural values are not the same are interacting. Although we disagree, we listen to each other and we are unavoidably socializing each other. It is unlikely that no change is taking place.

Then again, how desirable is it that the same values should be shared throughout the whole human polity? What if one of the values we come to share might be respect for each other's differences? Or might some values be called *requisite* values for humanity? Perhaps there really are values that must be universally held if there is to be any hope at all of harmonious resolution of the problems we confront — and share — in the human polity.

Selected Readings

Aaron, Henry J., Thomas E. Mann and Timothy Taylor, eds., *Values and Public Policy* (Washington, D.C.: Brookings, 1994). Essays discussing how values are formed and can mediate the effects of public policies.

Almond, Gabriel and Sidney Verba. *The Civic Culture* (Boston: Little, Brown, 1963). This is the classic study of political culture, focussing on political attitudes and democracy in Italy, Mexico, the United Kingdom, and West Germany. See also their edited volume, *The Civic Culture Revisited* (Newbury Park, Ca.: Sage, 1989).

Barner-Barry, Carol and Robert Rosenwein. *Psychological Perspectives on Politics* (Englewood Cliffs, N.J.: Prentice-Hall, 1985). An examination of political culture and socialization. Topics of discussion include the characteristics of politically active peo-ple and possible reasons as to why we hold the political beliefs we do.

Carment, David. "The Ethnic Dimension in World Politics: Theory, Policy and Early Warning, " *Third World Quarterly*, vol. 15, no. 4, 1994. An excellent summary of the different ways ethnic conflict may be studied, stressing the importance of developing ways to recognize "early warnings" of the imminent outbreak of such struggles.

Coyle, Dennis J. and Richard J. Ellis. *Politics, Policy and Culture* (Boulder: Westview Press, 1994). The authors argue that politics, policies and preferences cannot be understood without a consideration of culture.

Farah, Tawfic E., ed. *Pan-Arabism and Arab Nationalism* (Boulder, Col.: Westview Press, 1987). A series of articles on various aspects of Arab nationalism. Included are survey research studies, history and development of the movement, religious connections, current attitudes toward the movement, and its impact on the Arab/Israeli conflict.

Gellner, Ernest. *Culture, Identity, and Politics* (Cambridge, Cambridge University Press, 1987). Examines the relationships among the state, civil society, and culture in the context of political concepts such as nationalism and egalitarianism.

Hermann, Margaret G., ed. *Political Psychology* (San Francisco: Jossey-Bass Publishers, 1986). A reader on various psychological aspects of politics, including environmental beliefs, values, and areas of study such as the psychology of terrorism and the psychology of protest movements.

Howe, Carolyn. *Political Ideology and Class Formation: A Study of the Middle Class.* (Westport, CT: Praeger, 1992). An analysis of theories and opinion data on the political ideology of the middle class.

Michael Ryan, *Politics and Culture* (Basingstoke: Macmillan, 1989). An application of new modes of study derived from critical theory and post-structuralism, as well as more traditional marxist and psychoanalytic approaches, to questions of the relationship between culture and politics.

Sigel, Roberta, ed., *Political Learning in Adulthood: A Sourcebook of Theory and Research* (Chicago: University of Chicago Press, 1989). Eleven chapters by noted specialists in political socialization, with extensive reference guides to sources in this area of study.

Notes

1. This definition of political culture is used by Ann L. Craig and Wayne A. Cornelius, "Political Culture in Mexico: Continuities and Revisionist Interpretations," in Gabriel Almond and Sidney Verba, eds., *The Civic Culture Revisited* (Boston: Little, Brown, 1980), p. 340.
2. Henry J. Aaron, Thomas E. Mann, and Timothy Taylor, eds., *Values and Public Policy* (Washington, D.C.: The Brookings Institution, 1994), p. 5.
3. Walter S. Jones, *The Logic of International Relations*, 7th ed. (New York: HarperCollins, 1991), p. 53.
4. Gabriel Almond and Sidney Verba, *The Civic Culture* (Boston: Little, Brown, 1963), pp. 308–11.
5. Ibid., pp. 338–40.
6. Almond and Verba, *Civic Culture*, p. 315; Desmond S. King, *The New Right, Politics, Markets and Citizenship* (Chicago: Dorsey, 1987), pp. 121, 198; *New York Times*, 6 May 1985, 3, and 4 June 1985, 1.
7. David B. Conradt, "Changing German Political Culture," in *Civic Culture Revisited*, p. 230.
8. Anne-Marie Le Gloannec, "On German Identity," *Daedalus* 124, no. 2 (Winter 1994): 133–34.
9. Edward Banfield, *The Moral Basis of a Backward Society* (New York: Free Press, 1967) and Donald Sassoon, *Contemporary Italy: Politics, Economy and Society since 1945* (Essex, U.K.: Longman, 1986), pp. 102–103 and 114–16.
10. Anna Emilia Berti, "The Development of Political Understanding in Children Between 6–15 Years Old," *Human Relations* 41, no. 6 (1988): 437–46.
11. Mattei Dogan and Dominique Pelassy, *How to Compare Nations* (Chatham, N.J.: Chatham House, 1990), p. 74. Furthermore, as early as the late 1970s, Giacomo Sani found Italians "politically more aware and more inclined to get involved in political action" than they had been at the time of the Almond and Verba study. Giacomo Sani, "The Political Culture of Italy, Continuity and Change," in *Civic Culture Revisited*, p. 317.
12. Lucian W. Pye, *Politics, Personality and Nation Building* (New Haven: Yale University Press, 1962), pp. 183–84.
13. Lucian W. Pye, *The Mandarin and the Cadre: China's Political Cultures* (Ann Arbor: University of Michigan Press, 1988), p. 31.
14. Ibid.
15. Charles Tilly, *From Mobilization to Revolution* (Reading, Mass.: Addison-Wesley, 1978), p. 122.
16. *Los Angeles Times*, 9 June 1989, I1–I16; 13 June 1989, I8; 14 June 1989, I1, I7.
17. *Washington Post*, 17 Feb. 1988, A14.
18. *New York Times*, 8 Jan. 1995, 4.
19. *World Encyclopedia of the Nations: Asia and Oceania*, (New York: Worldmark Press, 1988), p. 92.
20. Barry Came, "A Grievance Upheld," *Maclean's* 106, no. 18 (3 May 1993): 26.
21. Standard works on the problem of class include Karl Marx, "Manifesto of the Communist Party," in Robert C. Tucker, ed. *The Marx-Engels Reader* (New York: Norton, 1978), pp. 469–500; "The Class Struggles in France," in ibid., pp. 586–93;

and "The Eighteenth Brumaire of Louis Napoleon," in ibid., pp. 594–617; Max Weber, "Class, Status, Party," in H. H. Gerth and C. Wright Mills, eds., *From Max Weber: Essays in Politics* (New York: Oxford University Press, 1946), pp. 180–95; and Thomas Humphrey Marshall, *Class, Citizenship and Social Development: Essays* (Garden City, N.Y.: Doubleday, 1964). For a contemporary summary and analysis, see Berch Berberoglu, *Class Structure and Social Transformation* (Westport, Conn.: Praeger, 1994).

22. On the question of class consciousness, see Clem Brooks, "Class Consciousness and Politics in Comparative Perspective," *Social Science Research* 23 (June 1994): 167–95.

23. Lawrence Goodwyn, *Breaking the Barrier: The Rise of Solidarity in Poland* (New York: Oxford University Press, 1991), pp. ix, xxvi–xxvii. Goodwyn argues that the shared experiences of the activist members of Solidarnosc were more important in bringing success than all the "documents of written exhortation — leaflets, pubic demands, organizing appeals, and the like" that others produced in their support (xxvii).

24. For an interesting study of peasant revolts, see Eric Wolf, *Peasant Wars of the Twentieth Century* (New York: Harper & Row, 1968). A recent example of a political party formed by both farm and working class interests in an effort to protect cherished values and defy "technocratic decrees" is the Hunt-Fish-Nature-Tradition party of France, whose members are as resistant to modern environmentalist values as they are to the automation of the traditional agricultural and artisan labor they represent. (*L'Express*, 5 Mar. 1992, 60–62.

25. Robert J. Thompson and Joseph R. Rudolph, Jr., "Ethnic Politics and Public Policy," in Dennis L. Thompson and Dov Ronen, eds., *Ethnicity, Politics and Development* (Boulder, Colo.: Lynne Rienner, 1986), p. 32.

26. Danuta Mostwin, "Ethnic Identity and the Polish Immigrant in America," *Migration World* 16, nos. 4–5 (June 1988): 25–31.

27. Akbar S. Ahmed, *Living Islam: From Samarkand to Stornoway* (New York: Facts on File, 1994), pp. 49–51.

28. Nora Boustany, "Targets of Opportunity," *Washington Post National Weekly Edition* (13–19, Mar. 1995), 17; "If Islamists rule Algeria," *The Economist* (25 Feb. 1995), 98. See also Karima Bennoune, "Algerian Women Confront Fundamentalism," *Monthly Review* 46 (Sept. 1994): 26–39.

29. For the Robertson campaign, see *New York Times*, 7 Sept. 1987, 7; 14 Sept. 1987, 1; 15 Sept. 1987, 19; 30 Sept. 1987, 20.

30. James A. Barnes, "Rightward March?" *National Journal* (6 Aug. 1994), 1847–51.

31. Robin Alison Remington, "Bosnia: The Tangled Web," *Current History* 92, no. 577 (Nov. 1993), 364–69. I have drawn extensively from this useful article; the quote comes from p. 366.

32. Ian D. Armour, "Nationalism vs. Yugoslavism," *History Today* 42 (Oct. 1992): 11–13.

33. Svetlana Slapsak, "Trains, Times Lost Forever," *The Nation* (31 May 1993), 740.

34. *Wall Street Journal*, 28 July 1995, A1–A4. For a discussion of the belief held by many Muslims that international reluctance to interfere effectively came from the fact that "[the West] does not want a viable Muslim nation in Europe," see Akbar S. Ahmed, "Ethnic Cleansing: A Metaphor for Our Time?" *Ethnic and Racial Studies* 18, no. 1 (Jan. 1995): 18.

35. The use of rape as a weapon of ethnic warfare, particularly against societies where illegitimate sexual acts dishonor entire families, is explained in Akbar S. Ahmed, "Ethnic Cleansing," pp. 19–20.

36. The French and Indian wars were actually a struggle between the British and the French for control of that part of North America which later became the Canadian provinces of Quebec and Ontario; the struggle began as the two European peoples sided with different Indian tribes engaged in battle — hence the name.

37. The word *Indian* is the official term used in Canada, although *Native American* would of course apply there as well as in the United States.

38. Tamar Liebes and Rivka Ribak, "The Contribution of Family Culture to Political Participation, Political Outlook and Its Reproduction," *Communication Research* 19, no. 5 (Oct. 1992): 618–41. The quote is on p. 620.

39. For another interesting study in this regard see Vesha V. Godena, "Hidden Tendencies and Unintentional Impacts in Family Socialization: The Example of Authoritarian vs. Non-Authoritarian

Family Socialization Type," Research Notes, *Journal of Comparative Family Studies*, XXII:3 (Autumn 1991), pp. 359–66.

40. Stanley W. Moore, James Lare, and Kenneth A. Wagner, *The Child's Political World: A Longitudinal Perspective* (New York: Praeger, 1985), p. 135 and Russell J. Dalton, *Citizen Politics*, second edition (Chatham, N.J.: Chatham House, 1996), p. 201.

41. Steven A. Peterson, *Political Behavior: Patterns in Everyday Life* (Newbury Park: Sage, 1990), p. 157. (Peterson offers an excellent general summary of socialization scholarship.)

42. Peterson, *Political Behavior*, 156; Jack Dennis and Donald J. McCrone, "Preadult Development of Political Party Identification in Western Democracies," *Comparative Political Studies*, 3, no. 2 (July 1970), 243–263; and Akira Kubota and Robert E. Ward, "Family Influence and Political Socialization in Japan," *Comparative Political Studies*, 3, no. 2 (July 1970), 140–175.

43. This distinction was first made by Richard Dawson and Kenneth Prewitt in 1969, in their book, *Political Socialization* (Boston: Little, Brown). They characterized the first as teaching "a specific political ideology which is intended to rationalize and justify a particular regime," and the second as teaching "how a good citizen participates in the political life of [the] nation." (pp. 147–148)

44. Clive Harber, "International Contexts for Political Education," *Educational Review*, 43:3 (1991), p. 247.

45. Carol Seefeldt, "The Pledge of Allegiance in Public Schools," *Education Digest*, 55, no. 1 (Sept. 1989), pp. 62–63.

46. For the British research, see Michael H. Banks and Debra Roker, "The Political Socialization of Youth: Exploring the Influence of School Experience," in *Journal of Adolescence*, vol. 17, no. 1 (Feb. 1994), pp. 3–15. The U.S. study is by Edgar Litt, "Civic Education, Community Norms, and Political Indoctrination," in Roberta S. Sigel, ed., *Learning About Politics: A Reader in Political Socialization* (New York: Random House, 1970), pp. 328–36. See also Michael H. Banks and Debra Roker, "The Political Socialization of Youth: Exploring the Influence of School Experience," *Journal of Adolescence*, 17 (1994), 3–15.

47. For an interesting study of political socialization in the West German military, see Roland Wakenhut, "Effects of Military Service on the Political Socialization of Draftees," *Armed Forces and Society*, 5, no. 4 (Summer 1979): 626–41.

48. See "Black Gentry Vows to Stay in Step," *New York Times*, 17 Oct. 1995, A13.

49. Charles Humana, *World Human Rights Guide*, 3rd ed. (New York: Oxford, 1992), pp. 55, 57.

50. Roberta Sigel, "An Exploration into Some Aspects of Political Socialization: School Children's Reactions to the Death of a President," in Sigel, *Learning About Politics*, pp. 152–72.

51. Molly Moore, "Victims in a Warring World: Millions of Children," *International Herald Tribune*, 18 Apr. 1995, A4.

52. A. T. Russell, R. J. Johnston, and C. J. Pattie, "Thatcher's Children: Exploring the Links between Age and Political Attitudes," *Political Studies* 40 (Dec. 1992): 742–56.

53. For two interesting illustrations of this fact, see Katharine Cutts Dougherty, Margaret Eisenhart, and Paul Webley, "The Role of Social Representations and National Identities in the Development of Territorial Knowledge: A Study of Political Socialization in Argentina and England," *American Education Research Journal*, 29, no. 4 (Winter 1992): 809–35 and Tamar Liebes, "Television, Parents, and the Political Socialization of Children," *Teachers College Record* 94, no. 1 (Fall 1992): 159–64.

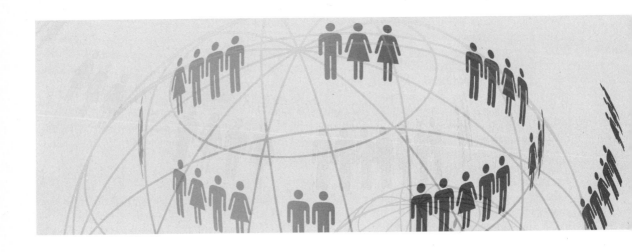

PART
III ACTING
IN POLITICS

6 The Individual in Politics

POWERFUL FORCES SHAPE OUR political life: institutions, ideologies, social pressure, and economic conditions. Even those of us who live in democratic systems often tend to assume that we have no way, as individuals, to influence the course of politics. We vote because we think we should, not because we believe our single vote can possibly change very much. If we want to bring about serious change, we usually try to do so in the company of others who agree with us; we join a group, a political party, or a social movement. We may try to prepare ourselves for a kind of employment that we hope will bring benefits to others, but usually we plan to do that work within an organization. We like to read about great men and women who have made a difference by following their dreams, but we imagine such exploits are unique, and perhaps no longer possible.

However, even in today's densely populated and increasingly complex world, the individual retains the capacity for meaningful political action. A Chinese student standing strong and firm against the advancement of a tank containing soldiers ordered to crush the demonstration he and his fellows have organized may attract the world's amazed respect and sympathy and thereby give courage to those who are determined to carry on the battle for democracy. A Latin American journalist may persist in telling the world of her government's repressive acts even after she herself is imprisoned and tortured, and thus force changes in that nation's way of dealing with political dissent. An African-American social worker who never misses a meeting of his city's board of supervisors nor an opportunity to speak on behalf of those he serves may influence the decisions of that body more than even he can tell.[1]

Individual political acts may be positive or negative — a dedicated artist may find the means to make the public newly aware of an endangered civil liberty or a raving maniac may shoot and kill a president — but the point is the same: individuals can make meaningful changes in the course of human history.

Sometimes the individual's act is meaningful only because other individuals are performing the same act simultaneously. Even then, however, if there is no organized cooperation, it is still individual political behavior that is influential. Individual voters, acting in unwitting concert, can change the composition of parliaments and the content of national policy. Individual citizens, each responding to specific internal promptings as well as to the exhortations of others, can form a jury that issues a verdict so patently unfair that riots break out, costing many lives and millions of dollars of damage. Individual persons, acting alone, sometimes *can* change the world.

Furthermore, even when individual actors are not interested in change, their political behavior can still be significant. The same kinds of personal action that we use to try to bring about change (voting, protesting, testifying) can be used with equal effectiveness to prevent change. The reelection of an incumbent president, a deluge of telegrams protesting a government's announced intention to send troops abroad, or the passionate testimony of a series of unacquainted and unorganized witnesses against a proposed new law or the appointment of a high official are all individual acts that can shape our collective destinies by preventing change rather than bringing it about.

Finally, even when individual political actions have no significant impact on the polity at large, they may still be very meaningful to the individual actor. Your grouchy grandfather might decide (as mine did) to send his Social Security check back to the government, muttering, "I've decided I don't believe in it." A Croatian tour director in Dubrovinik might decide, after the Serbs have leveled his apartment building, the hotel where he works, and a portion of the ancient city whose wonders provided him his livelihood, that the best thing to do is move his family and his skills to Italy. Or a soldier in the army of the Ivory Coast might opt not to reenlist because he is unhappy with the way the army is used for domestic chores (roadbuilding, peacekeeping), even though his fellows are all persuaded that the relatively good pay makes a second tour of duty attractive. In all these cases, individuals have made and acted on choices that are at least partly political but that are also atypical and attract very little attention.

Maggie Kuhn, founder of the Gray Panthers. The individual can make a difference in politics, sometimes by organizing others. (UPI/Corbis-Bettmann)

Such choices are unlikely to have any noticeable impact on the political system, but they can be very significant for the individual actors who make them. There are, then, at least three good reasons to study the individual political behavior of ordinary citizens: (1) It can change the course of government, (2) it can prevent the course of government from changing, and (3) it can have a profound significance in the lives of individual actors.

In this chapter we will consider, first, individuals' motives for behaving as they do in the political arena; second, the variety of political acts they perform; third, the most common act of political behavior, the vote; and fourth, factors that enhance or reduce a citizen's opportunity to take part in politics.

INDIVIDUAL MOTIVES FOR PARTICIPATION IN POLITICS

Did you vote in the last election, or do you know someone who did? Then ask yourself this question, "Why did I (or my friend Elmer Endicott) vote the way I (he) did?" Stop for a moment and give that question a brief answer — write it down.

Even if you wrote down something whimsical ("My mother told me to," or, "Elmer always votes for the loser"), your answer almost surely contains some information about your own or Elmer's motives for voting that particular way ("My mother's work as city manager has given her a lot of insight into political matters," or "Elmer has a strong sense of sympathy for political underdogs"). People may be motivated by their attitudes, beliefs, opinions, interests, or values. To understand behavior — to know how significant it is to the individual actor, to be able to predict how likely it is to change or remain constant, and to get a sense of the goals it is intended to achieve — we need to understand the motives behind that behavior. It makes a great deal of difference what blend of attitudes, beliefs, opinions, interests, and/or values guides the political actor, as the following discussion should make clear.[2]

Attitudes

Some of our acts are motivated by general, often unverbalized feelings about certain kinds of objects. Such feelings are **attitudes**, which are based on our *underlying* beliefs, opinions, interests, or values. If we sense, rightly or wrongly, that a candidate shares our ideas on matters we deem important, we may well vote for that candidate. When we act on this basis, we may be scarcely aware of the particular attitude in question or how it has guided us in making our choice. If we are asked to explain why we voted as we did, we may feel hard pressed to answer. Perhaps we will be able to bring the relevant underlying motive to the surface and say something like, "I voted that way because I think maintaining free enterprise is important," or, "I think it is more important to reduce crime than to pamper criminals; that's why I voted for candidate X." Or we may be unable to say anything more specific than, "I don't know; it just felt like the right thing to do."

Beliefs

The words *belief* and *believe* are commonly used in two senses. Sometimes we say we "believe in" something when what we really mean is that we value it ("I believe in the democratic system"). At other times we say we "believe that" something is true; what we mean then is that we think we have a good reason for being sure (or almost sure) that we are right. The word is used here in the second sense: **beliefs** motivate our political behavior when we think they represent truth. A belief is held more consciously than an attitude. To say that we believe something suggests that we have given the matter some serious, conscious consideration. We may, of course, be entirely wrong in our beliefs. A belief is not the same as knowledge. We do not *know* something unless it is in fact true, but we can believe all manner of strange and untrue things, and different people can have absolutely opposite beliefs. One person may firmly believe that allowing business corporations to pay lower taxes will increase capital investments, which will produce more jobs and more affluence for all. Someone else may believe just as firmly that the same procedure will simply increase profit margins for the rich and deprive the government of funds it needs for maintaining the national security and the general welfare. Whichever belief a citizen holds, and whichever (if either) proves to be correct, that belief itself can motivate that person to choose one candidate over another, to be supportive or hostile toward government policy, or to join a particular political group.

Opinions

There are two main differences between opinions and beliefs. First, the citizen who holds an opinion is less certain of its truth than the one who holds a belief (even a false belief), and furthermore is not *expected* to be as certain. This aspect of holding opinions is expressed clearly when we say, "Well, that's just my opinion," or, of someone else's ideas, "Well, I suppose you're entitled to your own opinion." We hold opinions when all the pertinent facts are not available, or at least not readily available to us, but the subject interests us, concerns us, and seems important enough to make us willing to venture a partially informed (or sometimes even totally uninformed) guess about it. When it comes to the political arena, where complete information is often extremely difficult and costly to acquire, most of us rely heavily on our opinions in deciding about our own behavior and in judging that of others.

A second difference between opinions and beliefs is that opinions are more likely to have a normative content. We can believe that something is true without regard to whether it is a good thing or a bad thing. A student of the law might believe that laws guaranteeing homosexuals equal rights to employment opportunities will not have the desired effect, without caring whether they do or not. But having an opinion almost always carries normative freight. Thus it is John's *opinion* that the United States should spend less on defense. This opinion is based in part on John's *belief* that if the United States were to spend less on defense, there would be more money available to meet social needs and in part on the *value* John places on the idea of collective responsibility for a nation's less fortunate citizens. Furthermore, John *believes* that the breakup of the Soviet Union has made a major defense establishment unnecessary; he *does not believe* that other threats to national security, present and potential, are serious enough to warrant maintaining the present level of defense expenditure; and he *values* peace so highly that it is difficult to get him even to listen to those who have different *beliefs* or different *opinions*.

The distinction between opinions and beliefs is not always observed as well as it might be, especially when we are not quite sure of our facts. John may say, "If the United States spends less on defense, the impact on the economy of states where armaments are produced will be insignificant" (a clear expression of belief), and then, confronted with strong arguments to the contrary, retreat to, "Well, that's just my opinion." John really should not be allowed to get by with that. One should know when to retract a statement of belief — "Excuse me while I go check the facts" — or how to avoid making simple opinions sound like firm beliefs in the first place.[3]

Interests

Another word with multiple meanings is **interest**. Here we are concerned with only one of those meanings, a clearly identifiable personal stake in a decision or the outcome of an event. If a proposed policy will clearly affect our personal fortunes, most of us respond to it differently from the way we would respond to a policy that will not impinge on our interests. Just consider, for example, how you — or your parents or your fellow students — respond when the news media report the introduction of a bill in the legislature that would change the terms for issuing government-sponsored student loans.

The government may follow several policies that affect our interests in conflicting ways — just as a candidate may make some promises we like and others we are not so sure about. When making up their minds, voters all over the world must find a way to distinguish between — and choose between — individual interests and the interests of larger groups to which they belong. When South Africa made its transition to democracy and President Nelson Mandela promised a peaceful, multiracial society in which there would be significant redistribution of wealth from the affluent white minority to the impoverished black majority, some whites recommended boycotting the first election in 1994 and a few went so far as to form militia movements and to engage in terrorist bombings. But the large majority of the minority group decided otherwise. Economic sanctions against South Africa had been lifted, and the nation was rapidly becoming a respected member of the international community. Furthermore, Mandela had promised to move in a cautious and conciliatory manner. Even if redistribution policies were followed, most members of the white minority reasoned that their own interests would now be better served by helping to make the transition as peaceful as possible. They opted to take part in the election, some of them voting for candidates of Mandela's own party, the African National Congress.[4]

Values

Values are yet another motive force in political decisionmaking. A **value** is a serious and deeply held normative principle with wide applicability. In the example just given, suppose you were a member of the white South African community. You might then have chosen to vote on the basis of your personal values, not your interests. In that case, you might have voted for Mandela's party because one of your highest values was racial equality, or majority rule, even though you believed that supporting such principles was in fact contrary to your own interests. Or you might have joined those who refused to vote altogether, on the grounds that whoever won, the election was arranged to ensure the defeat of white supremacy, your most cherished value, beside which questions of material gain seemed unimportant to you.

A Mix of Motives

Most of us base our political decisions (and indeed, all our decisions) on a complex blend of attitudes, beliefs, opinions, interests, and values. If asked, we usually claim that our choices are based on our beliefs and our values. We like to think we know the facts, or enough of them to warrant our having beliefs, and we also like to think that we have carefully chosen our values, know what they are, know how to resolve conflicts among them, and know how to act accordingly. It is not always so, however. Stop and consider your own views on a current issue of importance — for example, the advisability of relying on nuclear energy as an alternative source of power. When you express yourself on this topic, are you doing so on the basis of your attitudes, your beliefs, your opinions, your interests, or your values?

The Uses of Opinion

Political opinions, the most common motive force behind our political behavior, do not come to us out of the blue. As discussed in Chapter 5, we acquire our ideas about politics from a wide range of socializing agents. But why are some of us more responsive to these socializing agents than others? And why, when we receive conflicting messages, do we tend to listen to one set of messages rather than another? Some social scientists believe our choice of opinions is determined as much by psychological factors as by sociological factors.

In one of the first and most interesting studies of this type, M. Brewster Smith, Jerome Bruner, and Robert White pointed out that holding opinions can serve functions of which we are scarcely conscious. For example, applying our relevant opinions helps us to appraise objects — that is, to categorize new objects or events quickly and efficiently. Or we may adopt certain opinions for purposes of social adjustment. This can be a way of announcing our identification with a particular group whose members are known to hold that opinion — a way of saying, "I am like them." Finally, opinions can be a way of dealing with an inner difficulty — as when a shoplifter suffering from kleptomania (the compulsion to steal) becomes an ardent supporter of a political reform group fighting graft and corruption, thereby reducing internal guilt and fear.[5] This kind of motive for adopting particular opinions is, of course, extremely difficult to prove.

Public Opinion

We hear a great deal about public opinion these days. Is there any such thing? If so, what is it and what role does it play? In fact, when we speak of **public opinion**, we are usually referring to nothing more substantial

(Rob Rogers reprinted by permission of United Features Syndicate, Inc.)

than a more or less informed guess about the collective nature of a body of individual, more or less informed, guesses. But this does not mean that there is no such thing, nor that it is insignificant. On the contrary, public opinion — or at least what is taken, rightly or wrongly, to be public opinion — is one of the most powerful forces at work in any polity. Let us try to push our way a little bit further into this rather large conundrum.

The concept of public opinion is as old as the art of political inquiry. Aristotle, Plato, Machiavelli, Rousseau, Hobbes, and Marx all debated the proper relationship between the ruler's will and that of the general public — seldom if ever doubting that the latter might be conceived of as a singular entity. Yet when we give the subject a moment's thought, we realize that public opinion can only be the sum of private opinions, and further that in any polity, on any issue, private opinions will surely be found, on examination, to be varied and conflicting, held with different degrees of intensity by persons with very different degrees of access to political decision-making processes. Can we, then, really ever justify speaking of *public opinion*?

We can, but only if we keep the nature of the public in each case clearly in mind. For some observers the public means those citizens who really do take an active interest in politics and who take steps to make that interest known and felt. When the public is thus defined, the content of public opinion is usually determined impressionistically: the observer has witnessed a lively debate in the village square, listened to her concerned and influential friends at social and business events, followed the drift of letters and editorials in the newspapers, and — more and more likely — paid attention to talk show opinion on the subject at hand. This kind of public normally constitutes a very small percentage of the total population. For example, although 42 percent of the American public listens regularly to a talk show where public issues are discussed, only about 4 percent have had the experience of speaking on the air themselves.[6] Such "public opinion" may be very influential, but it may or may not be representative of the people who have not bothered to speak out.[7]

But for other commentators, the term *public opinion* indicates a very different public. For them, the public means a representative sample of the entire population, including those who have no opinion or who simply create one in a hurry in response to a pollster's inquiry. **Public opinion polls** are studies of the opinions of this public. Very rarely is any effort made to determine the intensity with which the opinion is held, or the effort any individual may have made (beyond voting) to convey that opinion to those who have the political power to act on it. On the other hand, such statistical reporting usually makes much clearer the fact that public opinion is divided and conflicting; we are told exactly what percentages of the population think what. (But for some of the limitations of polls, see Box 6.1.)

Between these two extremes, all manner of variations in defining, determining, and reporting public opinion can be found. Statistical polling may or may not break down the collective data over time, by income or occupational categories, or into various other subcategories. Impressionistic opinion sampling may or may not include "person-in-the-street" interviews. Writers may refer to both kinds of data in their analyses of what the public wants. Serious distortions can be introduced just in the way the question is asked: "When did you first start hating President Clinton?" Questions that interest the writer may be posed, questions that interest the respondent may never get asked. Journalists may try to find the answers to questions that require serious research and about which ordinary citizens have little or no information by taking a poll. (When we stop to think about it, we know perfectly well that asking a random sample of the population whether or not Bosnia should be a separate state, welfare recipients cheat, or O. J. Simpson was guilty of murder is a very poor way to seek the truth or decide what policy should be.)[8]

In any case, popular readiness to answer such inquisitive surveys varies from community to community, from nation to nation, and from time to time. Scots prefer to keep their opinions to themselves, and if pressed may find it amusing to mislead the self-important scholars who come their way. Americans used to feel offended if they had not been consulted, and when asked would try to answer as honestly as they could, but have lately been less forthcoming: the Gallup Organization reports that only 60 percent of those contacted will now cooperate, whereas the figure used to be 80 per-

BOX 6.1

CAN POLLS BE TRUSTED?

Not all polls are accurate measures of public opinion. Indeed, not everything called a poll really is one. Humphrey Taylor, president of a polling business, suggests some important points to keep in mind:

1. An unexpected poll finding is more surprising, and hence more "newsworthy," than one that confirms what other polls also report. Bad (i.e., inaccurate) polls are more likely to be surprising and therefore more likely to be reported.

2. Bad polls are cheaper than good polls. A survey of 600 people is less expensive than a survey of 1,250. A poll with very few questions is cheaper than one with more questions. High-quality sampling and interviewing cost more than poor-quality. And so on. If the media report findings regardless of their quality, why spend money on better polls?

3. One-day "instant" polls are much less accurate than polls conducted over three or four days because of all the people they miss. But, the media love them because they are the "first with the news" about public reactions to events.

4. 900-number straw polls are not polls. The people who are watching the TV shows and choose to phone in their answers are often very different from the population as a whole.

5. Poll results are the answers to questions and are therefore critically dependent on the wording and, sometimes, on the order of the questions. Never interpret the results without reading the questions carefully.

6. Opinion on most issues is more complicated than a yes/no to one or two questions. Polls inevitably simplify and categorize. To really understand public opinion on any issue—from abortion to economic policy—it is necessary to review the answers to a variety of questions addressing the issue in different ways.

7. A poll is valid only for the population surveyed and for the time of the survey. Surveys of adults, registered voters, or likely voters will all yield different answers.

8. Focus groups are not polls. Getting eight to ten people in a room to talk together has many uses, but it does not provide a measure of public opinion, as surveying a representative cross-section of people does.

9. Electronic town halls are not polls; they are not even a national version of the New England town-hall meeting. For that, tens of millions of people would have to participate, and there would have to be a comprehensive debate on each issue, with all major points of view discussed before a vote was taken.

10. Candidates' polls are often misleading. Polls are leaked not to inform but to influence the media and the public.

11. Polls really don't predict, they just measure. Good polls report what a representative cross-section of the public (or of likely voters) say when interviewed. The only reason that pre-election polls "predict" elections is that most people tell the interviewers how they think they will vote and then actually vote that way. But some people change their minds, and some of those who say they will vote don't. The difference between intentions and behavior, not sampling error, is the main reason why polls sometimes get it wrong.

Source: *National Review*, 19 Oct. 1992, 48. © 1992 by National Review, Inc., 150 East 35th Street, New York, NY 10016. Reprinted by permission.

cent.[9] And, of course, questions that make sense in one polity may make none at all in another. Daniel Lerner long ago discovered a classic case when he began an interview by asking a Turkish peasant what he would do if he were president: "'Me,' exclaimed the astonished man, 'How can I . . . I cannot . . . a poor villager . . . master of the whole world.'"[10]

Given all these difficulties in determining what public opinion really is and in using polls intelligently, why do we bother? In the first place, the system of representative democracy as presently practiced does not provide any systematic means for keeping those in power informed between elections of the will of those who have elected them. Political parties, pressure groups, and other political movements normally provide selective and limited input to elected representatives, who need to know public opinion at least in order to plan future campaign strategy, if not for the more noble goal of showing some respect for that opinion while in office. Parties and groups themselves need to know the public's views on the leaders and issues they support. Challengers to officeholders wonder if their alternative views or programs will find a receptive audience.

Public opinion polling is also proving to be extremely important as a tool for monitoring the impact on people's lives of the global shift away from communist rule to free market economies. Seeing this massive transformation as nothing more than the long-overdue introduction of democracy and personal freedom is clearly simplistic, and polls have helped the outside world understand the confusion and disillusionment of those who welcome their new liberty but not the sometimes desperate hardship that accompanies it. It may be disappointing to learn that five years after the revolution, 71 percent of Hungarians said they were either worse off or no better off today than in the communist era and that in Russia, 27 percent believe the takeover by Boris Yeltsin was "a tragic event with ruinous consequences for the country and its people," whereas, at the other extreme, only 7 percent say the coup was "a victory of the democratic revolution" — but it is important to have this kind of sobering evidence of how difficult it is to make such a massive change.[11]

In sum, however flawed our present definition of public opinion — and however unsophisticated our mode of discerning and evaluating its content — the human polity and the nation-states that compose it have many reasons for taking the aggregate of individuals' opinions seriously and using available means to discover its content.

MODES OF INDIVIDUAL PARTICIPATION

Individuals engage in politics more directly than just by giving answers to inquiring reporters and pollsters who are looking for that mythical beast, public opinion. They vote, they write letters or go to see those persons who have or appear to have political power, they donate money to groups working for causes they believe in, they demonstrate, they join community organizations or political movements. Sometimes a single issue can provoke every form of response; the debate over the 1991 nomination to the U.S. Supreme Court of a man accused by a respectable law professor of sexual harassment led to a wave of telegrams and letters addressed to U.S. senators, a march on the Senate, the formation of angry coalitions, and an apparent increased determination on the part of many women to use the vote in order to elect more members of their own sex to positions of power.[12]

Sometimes persons who disagree with each other on many other issues will find themselves making common cause and using common means to seek a particular political response. Thus advocates of free speech, "sex-positive" feminists, and persons openly engaged in producing pornographic materials have all sought to defend pornography, whereas feminists who believe pornography inflicts harm on individuals have been joined by those who attack all forms of what they call sexual "deviance," including homosexuality.[13] Such spontaneous coalitions of concerned individuals may bring together persons who would rather not be seen in each others' company — but can nevertheless have a powerful effect in stimulating new legislation or working to prevent its enactment.

Not all individual political activity is peaceful and law abiding. Some political activists are ready to engage in civil disobedience, breaking the law on behalf of causes they believe in. Such acts of defiance may be relatively limited in means and scope, as when American political activists deliberately violated U.S. immigration laws and helped illegal aliens fleeing political repression in Central America find sanctuary in American churches, or far more drastic and far reaching, as when the citizens of Poland, Hungary, Czechoslovakia, Bulgaria, Romania, and the former nation of East Germany carried disobedience to the point of revolutionary action and brought their repressive governments down. Civil disobedience does not always work, of course, and can bring yet greater repression; the demonstrations in favor of democracy in Tiananmen Square in the People's Republic of China in 1989 brought brutal repression to many of those known to have taken part.[14]

A useful way of categorizing individual political participation has been provided by Lester Milbrath and M. L. Goel. Using data collected by themselves and others, they propose seven common *modes of participation*:

1. *Apathetic Inactives*: no participatory activity, not even voting.
2. *Passive Supporters*: vote regularly, attend patriotic parades, pay all taxes, "love my country."
3. *Contact Specialists*: contact local, state, and national officials on particular problems.
4. *Communicators*: keep informed about politics, engage in political discussions, write letters to newspaper editors, send support or protest messages to political leaders.

5. *Party and Campaign Workers:* work for party or candidate, persuade others how to vote, attend meetings, give money to party or candidate, join and support a political party, serve as party candidate.

6. *Community Activists:* work with others on local problems, form a group to work on local problems, active membership in community organizations, contact officials on social issues.

7. *Protesters:* join in public street demonstrations, protest vigorously if government does something morally wrong, attend protest meetings, refuse to obey unjust laws.[15]

As Milbrath and Goel stress, it is possible to belong to one mode and still perform some of the activities of participants in other modes.[16] One belongs to a mode by virtue of one's most common style of political behavior. Dominant modes vary from nation to nation. Aside from voting, citizens in the United States and Great Britain are most likely to sign petitions (and so are the Germans and the French, but in lesser numbers — the French are also noteworthy for their readiness to take part in political demonstrations), the Dutch are most likely to contact a local official about a personal problem, Nigerians and Indians are most likely to take part in local community organizations, Austrians favor joining parties or other political organizations or attending political rallies, and the Japanese are most likely to attend a political rally than to take part in any other nonvoting political behavior.[17]

Participation By Voting In Elections

The most common act of individual participation in politics is to vote. It seems a simple act: just register, then walk in on election day and mark your choice. But it is not that simple at all. To understand participation by voting, we must look at voter turnout, of course, but also at the great variety of electoral systems throughout the human polity. Achieving effective participation by voting depends not only on whether or not citizens vote, but also on the nature of the institution that makes voting possible.

Voter Turnout   One of the most puzzling — and, for some, one of the most distressing — facts about voting is how very few citizens take part in this easiest form of political behavior in the United States. Voter turnout in the United States is low by any standards, and certainly low comparatively; in modern democracies, only Switzerland has a worse record for average turnout (see Table 6.1). Voter turnout in presidential elections in the United States has decreased steadily in recent years, with the exception of 1992, when the first candidacy of independent Ross Perot helped produce a temporary 4 percent boost in the figures (see Figure 6.1).[18] Voting in nonpresidential elections is marked by even lower turnout; in the 1994 congressional elections, only 36 percent of those eligible voted and the rate in municipal elections has at times fallen even lower.[19]

FIGURE 6.1   **U.S. Turnout Year by Year (in Percentage)**

Source: *New York Times,* November 5, 1992, p. B4. Copyright © 1992 by the New York Times Co. Reprinted by permission.

What explains this phenomenon? Not only is the answer hard to determine, but the question is one that has caused considerable dispute among political scientists. For some authors, social demographics tell us all we need to know. Having little education, being young, having a low income or being unemployed, belonging to a minority racial group, and living in the south are all demographic factors that have been associated with nonvoting in the United States. For others, psychological factors such as "civic attitudes" or political opinions such as "views of the parties" are more important (for all these factors, see Table 6.2).

TABLE 6.1   **Average Turnout in Twenty Democracies 1980–1989 (in Percentage)**

Country	Voting	Country	Voting
Belgium	94	Israel	79
Austria	92	Greece	78
Australia	90	Finland	74
New Zealand	89	United Kingdom	74
Sweden	88	Ireland	73
West Germany (pre-unification)	87	Canada	72
		France	70
Denmark	86	Japan	68
Italy	84	United States	53
Netherlands	84	Switzerland	49
Norway	83		

Source: Adapted from Ruy A. Teixeira, "Make Voting Easy, More Interesting," *Insight into the News* 10 (7 Feb. 1994): 28. Data are from national legislative elections, except in the United States, where they are from presidential elections.

TABLE 6.2   **Voters and Nonvoters in the United States, 1994 (in Percentage)**

	Voting Public	Nonvoting Public
DEMOGRAPHIC CHARACTERISTICS		
Percentage who...		
Are under 30 years of age	6	38
Have not attended college	51	66
Reported annual household income under $30,000	35	47
Are men	50	46
Are women	50	54
Are white	90	76
Are black	7	16
Have moved in the last two years	7	23
CIVIC ATTITUDES		
Percentage who . . .		
Say people like themselves do not have much say about what government does	64	70
Say government will not work better even if all new people are elected	59	50
Trust government to do what is right only some of the time or never	81	76
VIEWS OF THE PARTIES		
Percentage who . . .		
Have favorable view of Republican Party	56	52
Have favorable view of Democratic Party	45	43
Say country needs a new political party to compete with Democratic and Republican parties	50	61
Describe themselves as		
Democrat	36	33
Republican	36	29
Independent	24	31

Based on telephone interviews with 1,429 adults nationwide from 29 Oct.–1 Nov. The "voting public" and "nonvoting public" are identified by determining whether or not respondents are registered to vote and what their intentions of voting on Election Day are, as well as whether or not they say they voted in 1990.
Source: *New York Times,* 9 Nov. 1994, B2. *New York Times,* November 9, 1994, p. B2. Copyright © 1994 by The New York Times Co. Reprinted by permission.

But other authors reject the social-psychological approach altogether, arguing that political institutions and electoral law play a more important role. For Frances Fox Piven and Richard A. Cloward, the fact that in other nations social factors are not "so dramatically associated with high rates of nonvoting as they are in the United States" means we must look elsewhere.[20] They note that although Australia, Belgium and Italy legally require citizens to vote, inflicting minor penalties on those who do not, the significantly higher voting rates of almost all the other industrial democracies cannot be thus explained (see Table 6.2.) For them, the chief institutional culprit are U.S. registration laws, which they describe as "Byzantine compared with those that prevail in other democracies." They note that "the United States is the only major democracy where government assumes no responsibility for helping citizens cope with voter registration procedures," and argue this explains why, on the average, 40 percent of Americans eligible to register and vote are not registered — and so cannot vote. And indeed, when we look at voting rates of *registered* voters, we find the United States tied with the Netherlands and Germany for seventh place, rather than next to last (see Table 6.3).[21]

Passage of the so-called motor-voter bill in 1993, a law that requires states to permit registration when one applies for or renews a driver's license, to permit registration by mail, and to make forms available at certain

TABLE 6.3   **Turnout of Registered Population in Nineteen Industrial Democracies**[a]

Country	Percentage Voting	Country	Percentage Voting
Belgium	95	Denmark	83
Australia	94	Norway	82
Austria	92	Israel	78
Sweden	91	United Kingdom	76
Italy	90	Japan	74
New Zealand	89	Canada	69
Germany	87	Finland	64
Netherlands	87	Ireland	62
United States	87	Switzerland	48
France	86		

[a] Turnout in most recent major national election as of 1983; percentage of registered population who voted.

Source: "Harvard/ABC News Symposium" (1984:7), monograph *Voting for Democracy,* as adapted in Frances Fox Piven and Richard A. Cloward, *Why Americans Don't Vote* (New York: Pantheon Books, 1987), p. 19. Material from "Harvard/ABC News Symposium" reprinted by permission. Copyright ABC News 1984. All rights reserved.

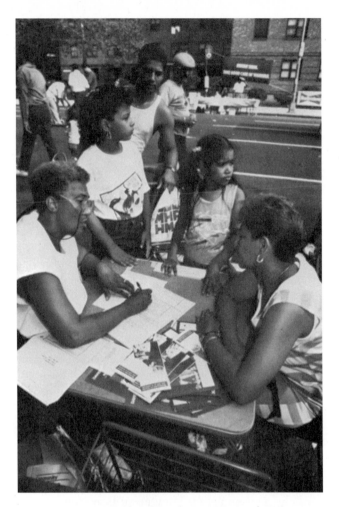

Voter registration in Spanish Harlem in New York City. Despite recent improvements, U.S. laws still make registration more difficult than in other major democracies. (Lisa Quinones/Black Star)

public assistance agencies, would seem to be a good step in the right direction, although it is too soon to be able to measure its effect.[22] However, not everyone is convinced that the problem can be solved simply with better registration procedures. Raymond Wolfinger and Steven Rosenstone have shown that even if all voters were allowed to register right up to election day, registration offices were kept open during regular working hours and in the evening or on Saturday, and absent civilians were permitted to register by mail (in ten states, only military absentee registration is permitted), U.S. turnout rates could be expected to increase by less than 10 percent.[23] Of course, 10 percent is in fact a rather good improvement, and significantly missing from this list of possible improvements is the idea of having the government itself take the responsibility to register voters (keeping track of all residents and sending them the necessary papers), as is done in Switzerland, Italy, Germany, Austria, France, Sweden, Great Britain, Belgium, and Canada.[24] Nor do they consider the possible impact of holding elections on weekends, as in Germany and France. Paying closer attention to the experience of other democracies and combining psychological attitudes, registration laws, and other institutional factors, including the party system, G. Bingham Powell, Jr. argues that the first (attitudes) actually give the United States a 5 percent advantage over other nations, whereas the second gives a 14 percent disadvantage and the last a 13 percent disadvantage.[25]

More recent analyses of the problem of low voter turnout in the United States suggest yet another cause: campaign targeting. We will discuss this technique more fully in Chapter 8, but its impact on turnout must be considered here. According to Marshall Ganz, the guiding principle of modern campaign management is "the allocation of each dollar to achieve maximum possible effect in the current election . . . precious campaign dollars should be invested in persuading more likely voters."[26] Targeting campaign resources means, says Ganz, ignoring those who have not voted and also those who have voted only occasionally. Furthermore, it makes to focus only on those whose electoral or personal histories suggest the possibility of a "swing" vote: Why bother with those who are always loyal to the same party? Taking all these factors into consideration, the "targeted" population for a modern campaign will be as little as 22 to 27 percent of the total potential electorate. Ganz adds that "these uncontacted voters are far more likely to be of lower socioeconomic status than those who are contacted. They never hear from a campaign and thus will likely stay at home on election day or vote the way they always have. The assumption that past voting behavior is predictive of future behavior becomes a self-fulfilling prophecy."[27]

The Electoral System   So far we have been stressing what makes individuals *want* to vote, which is a behavioral question. But it is also important to consider the *institution* that makes voting possible, which is a structural question (see Chapter 1). This institution is the *electoral system*, a structure that seldom receives the attention it deserves. We know that elections can be burdened with more issues than a legislative session, bring about judgments more far reaching than those of a court, attract more attention to qualities of leadership than a presidency, and sometimes stir up battle spirit as fiercely as any army. But we tend to act as if their existence and their characteristics were all preordained, immutable. We tend to forget that every election is the product of an electoral system, and further, that any electoral system is itself the entirely changeable product of fallible human beings, often guided at least in part by the desire to serve their own political fortunes.

What is an **electoral system**? The term is sometimes used simply to indicate how many offices are to be contested and how votes are to be cast and counted, but we will use it here in its broader sense to include all the rules and regulations governing the vote.

Every nation has some form of electoral system, but the opportunities for meaningful participation on the part of the would-be voter vary enormously according to the kind of system in effect. In a single-party dictatorship, elections may be held merely for ceremonial purposes, with no competition allowed. Or competition may be allowed within the party, as several candidates, all expressing their loyalty to the ruling party, are permitted to compete for a particular constituency's legislative seat.

It is not unusual for a nation to have two electoral systems — one dictated by law that calls for fair elections at specified times with full competition, and a second, determined by tradition and the actual distribution of political power, that allows for infrequent and irregular balloting, rigged in advance. The military coup makes a mockery of any electoral system, even one rigged to keep a single party in power, although some have argued that when coup follows upon coup, as has been the case in several African and Latin American nations, *that* is the electoral system.[28]

Furthermore, even where the electoral system is fair and scrupulously carried out, great variations are possible. There are, for example, important differences, worth taking a moment to understand, between the two ways the vote is translated into legislative seats in most Western democracies: the use of single-member districts or the adoption of a system of proportional representation.

Single-Member District System   The system most commonly used in the United States for state and congressional offices is the single-member district system. Under this system, the voters in each electoral district (also called a *constituency*) choose one person to fill a specific post, be it state legislator or representative to Congress. Whoever gets the most votes is elected. Several variations are possible. First, election may be by simple *plurality* (which means that whoever has the most votes wins, even if that number is less than 50 percent of the total). This system is used in Canada, India, Pakistan and Great Britain as well; using a racing metaphor, the British call it *first past the post* (or FPTP). It also produces the greatest discrepancies between the vote and the actual allocation of seats. In Great Britain the Alliance Party won one-fourth of the total votes cast in legislative elections in 1983, but gained only twenty-three seats in the House of Commons, less than one-twenty-fifth of the total.[29]

To avoid the drawbacks of the plurality system, some nations with single-member districts require the winner to have a majority. This may mean scheduling a runoff election if no candidate wins over 50 percent of the vote on the first ballot. In French legislative elections, any candidate with more than 12.5 percent of the vote may take part in the runoff, held two weeks later; in the race for the French presidency, only the top two candidates will be present at the second ballot. Such a system encourages minor parties to participate — one can never be certain which candidates will make it into the runoff — and thus provides individual voters with a wide choice, but at the same time it ensures strong support (usually an absolute majority) for the winner of the run-off.

A third variation designed to maximize the chances of majoritarian support while maintaining single-member districts is the *alternative vote* system, used in Australia for its lower house. In this system each voter *ranks* the candidates. When the votes are counted, if no candidate has a majority of first-choice rankings, then the candidate who is ranked first the least often is eliminated, and the votes of voters who preferred this candidate are assigned to the persons they ranked second. If this doesn't produce a majority for one candidate, the process is repeated; eventually, of course, the process of elimination means that one candidate *will* have a majority. Again, individual voters benefit by having a wide choice to begin with and by knowing that their votes (including, if need be, their second and third choices) have been thoroughly taken into consideration. Collectively, everyone benefits by knowing that the most preferred candidate has been selected. He or she may in fact be "everyone's second choice" but can never be a widely hated figure who has won only a slim plurality.

Proportional Representation   *Proportional representation* (often referred to by its initials as *PR*) requires multimember districts. Each district chooses several representatives, and each political party offers the voters a list of its candidates for those posts. In some nations, such as Belgium, the voter can vary the order of the candidates on the list; in others, as in Switzerland, the voters have multiple votes that they may spread around as they wish among the lists. In the simplest and most usual version, however, each voter casts one vote for one party list and the parties are then awarded seats according to the proportion of the vote they received. If a party gets 40 percent of the vote, the top 40 percent of its list is elected. But of course real life is seldom that tidy, and in practice it is necessary to have some kind of formula for determining how to assign the seats. The two most common formulas used are the *largest remainder* and the *highest average* systems (see Box 6.2). Whatever formula is used, the goal is to assign seats proportionately to the vote. Minor parties with very few votes may thus get a seat or two in the legislature and do not necessarily feel encouraged to drop out or to combine with other small parties just because they are not doing well. Although this gives voters the maximum amount of choice and ensures a parliament that is not only closely keyed to the actual vote but also one that is much more fully representative of all points of view, it can also

A Russion soldier posts electoral information at a military base in Lyubertsy, Russia, in preparation for the June 1996 presidential election. The new Russian electoral system makes it possible for a large number of candidates to compete for the presidency, and the outcome is no longer certain as it always was in the past. (Reuters/Dima Korotaye/Archive Photos)

have the effect of making it difficult to form majorities behind a government program. In the Netherlands, for example, where a party needs only .67 percent of the total vote to gain a seat in the 150-member parliament, it sometimes takes up to six months to organize a government after an election.[30] To avoid this effect, other nations using proportional representation normally require a party to obtain at least 5 percent of the vote in order to be entitled to such representation. Establishing such a threshhold has helped the new political systems in eastern Europe reduce the number of parties actually taking seats in their new parliaments, despite the amaz-

BOX 6.2

HOW PROPORTIONAL REPRESENTATION WORKS: THE "LARGEST REMAINDER" AND "HIGHEST AVERAGE" SYSTEMS:

The largest remainder system, common in Latin America, works like this: Say in a five-seat district 100 votes are cast: Blue 38, Red 32, White 17, Green 13. Each 20 votes (100 ÷ 5) get one seat. Any seats left go to whoever has the most votes remaining. Result: Blue (20 + 18) gets two; Red (20 + 12) one; White (0 + 17) one; Green (0 + 13) one. Hardly proportional. And see how small parties are favoured. Had White and Green merged, the joint "Lime" party's 30 votes would have earned only one seat.

Bigger districts are fairer. Say there are ten seats. Blue gets four; Red three; White two; Green one. And if White and Green had merged, "Lime" would still get three. Fair enough? In either case, "swings and roundabouts" even out the national result—but still with a bias to small parties.

The highest-average formula widely used in Europe allocates seats, one by one, to whichever party thereby shows the highest votes-per-seat. To do this, divide the party votes by 1, 2, 3 and so on, then pick out the highest five (or ten or whatever) figures from the resultant matrix, below. The winning figures are shown in **bold** for a five-seat district (the seat-number is indicated by a super-script figure), plus five more in *italics* for a ten-seat one:

	Blue	Red	White	Green
÷ by 1	**38**[1]	**32**[2]	**17**[4]	*13*
÷ by 2	**19**[3]	**16**[5]	*8.5*	*6.5*
÷ by 3	*12.7*	*10.7*	*5.7*	4.3
÷ by 4	9.5	8	4.2	3.2
Seats won:				
Five-seat	two	two	one	none
Ten-seat	four	three	two	one

Small parties suffer: were there only three seats, Blue would get two, Red one, White and Green none (where "Lime" would have got one). With eleven, even Red would get a fourth seat, Green still only one. But larger districts are usually fairer than small. The divisors can be varied: Scandinavian countries divide by 1.4, 3, 5 and 7, which aids medium-sized parties.

ing proliferation of parties in the first years of their transition to democracy: Eighty parties competed in the 1992 Czechoslovakian elections; that same year, there were 131 parties in Poland.[31]

It is possible to use both systems in the same polity. The Germans, for example, elect 664 deputies to their legislature, the Bundestag, by a dual procedure: Half are elected in direct balloting in their respective constitu-

BOX 6.3   AN UNUSUAL VARIATION: THE SINGLE TRANSFERABLE VOTE
(IRELAND)

A few countries use the single transferable vote, in multi-member districts.

Say there are five seats. The "quota" for election is then one-sixth (sic) of the total votes cast, plus 1. Voters number candidates in order of preference from 1 to 5.

First preferences are counted. Only Fergus O'Fail gets a quota. He is elected, and his "surplus" votes are shared out, in due proportion, among those candidates who were his backers' second choice. That brings Nuala O'Fail up to a quota. She is in, so share out her surplus votes.

No one gets a quota? Out goes the bottom name, Sean Gael, and *all* his votes are shared among those voters' second choices. Still no quota? Out too goes now-bottom Patrick Gael, and all his votes are shared. Now Liam Gael is over the top. Share out his *surplus* votes. And so on.

Result, say: two Fianna Fail, two Fine Gael and one Labour. But note: these are individuals—party people, but maybe not the ones the bosses most fancied.

Even with its districts of only 3–5 members, Ireland's STV produces quite proportional results nationally.

Source: "A Wide Choice of Ways to Choose," *The Economist* 327 (1 May 1993): 20.

encies, while the other half are selected proportionally from party lists of candidates in each of the *Länder* (states). Similarly, the Spanish senate is elected by simple plurality, but its lower house by the highest average version of proportional representation. Italy, long known for its most elaborately "fair" system of proportional representation, has recently switched to a system that is 75 percent plurality, 25 percent proportional representation.[32]

It is also possible to have multimember districts without using proportional representation, as is done in many polities at the local level; the candidates getting the most votes win the available seats on the city council or the county board. More unusual multimember districts without proportional representation have been used for the Irish legislature and the Japanese parliament (for the Irish case, see Box 6.3).

The range of choice is indeed wide and confusing, and there are no simple decision-making rules for nations wondering which method will work best.[33] Although some political scientists have customarily argued that proportional representation tends to produce fragmented and unstable government, they almost always cite the case of postwar Italy, where numerous other factors contributed to produce those conditions (and where a single party, the Christian Democrats, nevertheless stayed in power until 1994!), and do not look at the stable and effective coalition governments other nations, such as those in Scandinavia, have managed to produce using the same system. Similarly, single-member districts do not always close out minor parties altogether, although they do have a strong tendency to do so. Arguments that proportional representation works better for minority populations are shaky, unless such minorities form parties of their own, in which case they almost certainly limit their appeal. Expecting proportional representation to increase the number of women in office is also dubious. Although the parties can easily place women candidates on their lists, putting them at or near the top is less likely, says Karen Beckwith, unless other conditions are present such as "an active, visible feminist movement, and a climate of improved or improving status for women."[34]

Initiative and Referendum   So far we have been talking about ways the institution of an electoral system can offer citizens an opportunity to participate in the choice of representatives to lawmaking bodies. But elections can be devoted to other offices and to matters other than the choice of representatives. A polity's electoral system might include provisions for the **initiative**, enabling citizens to vote directly on specific proposals for new legislation. The only requirement is that a certain number of citizens (usually at least a specified percentage of the population that voted in the previous election) sign a petition within a specified number of days (frequently ninety days) proposing that a question be put on the ballot for everyone to vote on.

Somewhat more common is the **referendum**, a provision enabling a group of citizens, following procedures similar to those for an initiative, to "refer" a piece of legislation passed by the government to the voting public. Only if a majority approves does the legislation actually become binding. Some issues must automatically be made subject to such a procedure; state laws, for example, often require that school bonds be placed on a referendum ballot.

Another version of the referendum is found in systems that allow the executive branch of the government, under certain conditions, to rule by referendum — that is, to take a new proposal directly to the people. This kind of referendum is permitted in the French constitution and was a favorite device of former president Charles de Gaulle, who frequently staked his political life on a referendum vote, telling the French to vote for his proposal or accept the consequences — his own resignation. The inevitable result was that he won every single referendum vote except the last one he tried.[35]

It is often taken for granted that electoral systems allowing initiatives and referenda provide for more participation than those that do not, and there are many who urge the adoption of a national initiative system in the

United States. The matter is not quite as simple as it looks, however. It is no easy job to gather large numbers of signatures for a petition in a short period of time, and some observers have suggested that well-financed groups have an even greater advantage when this system of lawmaking is used than when laws are made by ordinary legislative processes. Such groups are far better able to hire the workers needed to gather the necessary number of signatures and to bombard the general public with the political advertising likely to persuade them to vote "correctly" than are less wealthy groups. It is also pointed out that debating complex issues in the public arena, without the benefit of careful deliberation by experienced representatives, makes the initiative and the referendum prime targets for demagogic politicking — that is, for appeals based on emotional sloganeering rather than on full and rational discussions of the issues.[36]

Other Electoral Opportunities to Participate   Other opportunities to participate by voting may include **recall elections**, held when a sufficient number of voters petition for a special election to vote on removing an official (usually an elected official) from office. The grounds for demanding a recall vary from genuine *malfeasance* — that is, acting contrary to law or failing to carry out the terms of office — to simple public discontent with the policies or style of the offending incumbent.[37] Other, more constructive options for participation include the election of such executive officers as attorney general and controller, the election of judicial officers, such as lower court judges in many states of the United States, and the political party primary election.

The **party primary** is a special form of election indeed, almost unique to the United States. (Belgium has a roughly comparable system, and in some nations with runoff elections the first election is referred to — not really correctly — as the primary election.) Although party primaries in the United States are set up and monitored by state governments, many of them are closed, which means that only the voters who have registered as supporters of the party are allowed to vote. This makes sense, because the supporters are not voting for a government official but simply for a candidate to run as the nominee of a private organization, the political party. On the other hand, the right to choose nominees for office has such far-reaching effects for all citizens that many states have adopted the institution of the *open* primary as a way to encourage greater individual participation in the political process. Still other states have continued to allow the party to control its own nominations (by internal party elections known as *caucuses*). This too makes sense: Why should persons who have taken no part in party affairs be allowed to tell the party which person it should run for office? As we will see in Chapter 8 it can also be argued that adoption of the primary, far from strengthening democracy, has served so to weaken political parties as agencies of linkage between citizen and the state that the net effect of this unique institution is actually antidemocratic.

Umberto Bossi, leader of Italy's Northern League party, declares independence for his self-styled state of "Padania" in northern Italy. Modern democracies permit all points of view to be expressed, confident that a sufficient number of voters will have the wisdom to resist the appeal of those that are unrealistic, racist, or otherwise contrary to the higher values of society. (Reuters/Vincenzo Pinto/Archive Photos)

ACCESS: HOW WELCOME IS INDIVIDUAL PARTICIPATION?

The factors we have considered so far do not exhaust all the ways individuals are stimulated to participate in politics — or to stay at home. We conclude by examining five other conditions that help determine how meaningful the concept of democratic citizenship is in actual practice.

Limiting the Electoral Option: Impersonal Restrictions

In every nation there will be electoral provisions or customs that have the effect, sometimes deliberate, of limiting individual opportunities for participation in politics. Some of these are impersonal — that is, they apply to everyone, with no apparent discrimination. Requiring citizens to have lived in their constituency for a certain period of time before registering and then again before voting can curb participation, as we have seen. Making absentee ballots difficult to acquire or placing polling stations in out-of-the-way locations will make participation harder for some persons than for others, but no particular person or group is openly targeted for discouragement. Purging the voting lists of the names of anyone who has not voted within a certain period of time makes it harder for chronic nonvoters to change their ways.[38] Calling political meetings without public notice or holding important political discussions in settings where women or minorities or persons of lower economic status are made to feel unwelcome is another way that access to politics is limited, although no one has posted a "No Trespassing" sign.

Indirect elections are another technically impersonal means of limiting the right to participate in elections. An election is indirect when only those who have already been elected to another post are entitled to vote. The ordinary citizens of a French village, for example, elect their municipal council, but only the council members can choose the mayor. And until 1916, U.S. senators were indirectly elected, by state legislatures.

Limiting the Electoral Option: Personal Restrictions

Other structured restrictions on the right to vote have been clearly directed at specific groups. Not all of these arouse our indignation. We normally tend to accept the idea that children, criminals convicted of serious crimes, the legally insane, and noncitizens should be kept off the electoral rolls. Yet even some of these restrictions are, in fact, debatable. The states of Maine, Massachusetts, and Vermont permit prison inmates to vote, as does the nation of Canada, but in thirty-five American states even persons who are not in prison but are on probation or parole are denied that right.[39] The question of whether or not to allow noncitizens to vote is also not always easily resolved. Is a nation that has encouraged large numbers of foreigners to cross its borders in order to assure the existence of a labor force willing to take the lowest-paying and most physically exhausting jobs really within its rights to deny this population the right to vote?[40] What about a refugee population, forced into that status by the takeover of their land by others? Are these people "aliens" in the ordinary sense? Should they have the right to vote?

One of the most consistently applied personal restrictions on the right to vote has been on the basis of race or ethnic origin. In the United States such electoral laws have been designed to keep African Americans from voting. Often thinly disguised as impersonal limitations — such as literacy laws, poll tax requirements, and the infamous *grandfather clause* (if your grandfather voted, you could vote without having to pass the literacy test, a stipulation impossible for former slaves to meet) — such devices were used in practice against only one group of citizens, African Americans, and consequently are properly classified as personal limitations.[41]

Today a changed climate of opinion and the Voting Rights Act of 1965 make it more difficult to devise such restrictions, but the practice has not been entirely eliminated, and important battles for minority voting rights are still being waged. The questions involved are not always simple to resolve. If, for example, a city draws voting district lines so as to dilute the strength of a racial minority, should members of that group have the right to insist they be redrawn to concentrate their strength and thereby assure them of representation on the elected governing body at issue? The Hispanic community of Los Angeles argued "yes" in 1991 and won their case in the courts.[42] But when President Bill Clinton proposed Professor Lani Guinier for the position of assistant attorney general for civil rights a mere two years later, the fact that Guinier had urged the adoption of other, milder electoral system reforms to ensure a modicum of representation for minority groups provoked such outraged opposition to her nomination that it was speedily withdrawn.[43] Should electoral systems be reformed to increase the importance of the vote of disadvantaged groups whose ballots may otherwise be entirely submerged in purely majoritarian polling systems? Why? Why not?

Freedom to Form Political Groups

Access to appropriate political groups depends partly on the willingness of citizens to form such groups and partly on the attitude of those in power toward their formation. The second question is not easily resolved, even in polities where the political culture includes respect for the constitutional principle of "freedom of association." Serious limitations on this right have been imposed at certain moments in U.S. history on groups seen as offering a dangerous threat to the democratic form of government, such as the American communist party.[44] Even today, requiring political parties to meet difficult tests of "significant support" — such as filing petitions signed by a number of people equal to a large percentage of the number that voted in the previous election — and setting early closing dates for such petitions to get candidates listed on the ballots is another way of limiting participation. Such restrictions are particularly hard on new parties trying to get organized for the first time.[45]

In other systems, constitutional or statutory limitations on individuals' rights to form and join political associations have been motivated more clearly by the simple determination of those in power to *stay* in power. President Alberto Fujimori of Peru stunned his nation and the international community by establishing "emergency" rule with military support, closing down Congress and the courts, and placing leaders of the opposition party APRA under house arrest.[46] In the nation of Georgia, a former Soviet republic, individuals who join groups loyal to ex-president Zviad Gamsakhurdia, ousted in 1991 by opposition forces, face repression and harassment and their demonstrations are brutally dispersed by government forces. The Moroccan goverment forbids the formation of any party seeking to contest elections under an Islamic banner.[47]

Freedom to Join Existing Groups

The right of individuals to participate in political groups is not simply a matter of such groups having the right to exist, nor even of the groups' right to conduct its activities without repression. There is also the question of whether or not individuals are allowed to join the groups of their own choice. Here two rights are likely to come into conflict: the right of private groups to determine their membership for themselves and the right of individuals to join whatever groups they wish. Americans have decided that political parties cannot deny membership on the basis of race but still allow private social groups, which frequently engage in influential political lobbying, to maintain discriminatory membership practices.[48] Membership in the communist party of China, which is a requirement for almost all the most desirable jobs in that nation, is viewed as a privilege, not a right, and is granted only to citizens who have met a long list of personal and performance criteria. Being denied membership in powerful political groups can obviously be more than personally offensive; it can mean the difference between a life of affluence and authority and one of the cruelest poverty and powerlessness.

Access to the Cultural Prerequisites for Political Participation

The ability to participate also depends in large measure on having access to the skills of participation and developing the confidence that one can engage in such activities effectively. The extent to which any person possesses such characteristics will vary enormously from individual to individual, no matter what the political system does. Nevertheless, political systems do enact laws that help determine their citizens' access to education and to political information. We looked at the social context of political action in Chapter 5, but it is worthwhile to point out here that governments play a powerful role in determining what that social context shall be. If the government ensures me a free education, at least to some minimal level; helps maintain an economy that increases my chance of gainful employment and thereby of a life of positive involvement in my community; and protects the news media's right to free expression and thereby my right to full political information, the likelihood of my being able to participate in my nation's politics is inevitably enhanced. Political structures — be they rules, institutions, or other means of imposing systematic patterns on our relationships with one another — have far-reaching effects, often beyond the intent of those who introduce them.

An interesting case in point here is the effect colonial powers have sometimes had in raising the political aspirations of their subjects for political freedom by introducing them to Western literature on the subject. The career of Mahatma Gandhi of India is a good example of this phenomenon — it was in the course of receiving a British education that Gandhi developed his passion for achieving Indian independence and thereby ensuring his compatriots the same rights and liberties his teachers had taught him existed elsewhere.

SUMMARY AND CONCLUSION

In this chapter we have considered individuals' motives for participating in politics; the variety of political acts they perform; different aspects of voting, and, in broader terms, the question of access: how welcome is individual participation in politics?

There are important but often misunderstood differences among attitudes, beliefs, opinions, interests and values. Holding specific political opinions may fulfill interesting functions for the psychological well-being of the individual. The concept of "public opinion" is old, yet still defined differently by different persons and under some circumstances the public opinion poll does not always measure what it claims to. Individuals adopt different modes of participation, depending on the opportunities open to them but also upon their own interests and propensities.

The mystery of low voter turnout in the United States is not such a mystery — not when we compare what other nations with higher turnout have done to facilitate and encourage voting. Achieving effective participation by voting also depends on the nature of the electoral system adopted. The two main types are the single-member district and proportional representation, but many variations are possible.

The right to participate in politics is limited in many ways in many lands: there are both personal and impersonal restrictions on the right to vote, as well as limitations on the right to form political groups, to join existing groups, and to acquire the cultural prerequisites for taking part in politics.

Although our emphasis throughout has been on conditions which enhance or obstruct participation, it is important that before quitting our subject we note that there is a whole other side to this coin, and that is the role individuals are *constrained* to play, whether or not they choose to participate. The laws governments make, with or without their citizens' consent, require a great deal of obedient responsiveness. Like it or not, we are all caught up in the world of politics in one way or another. We pay our taxes, obey traffic regulations, fulfill military obligations, conform to safety regulations, and otherwise comply with the rules imposed on us — or suffer the consequences, when our failure to do so is noted and the laws are fairly enforced. This other side of the individual's role in politics, the "subject" role, will receive more attention in Chapters 9 through 12, when we consider the national and local institutions that make the rules we are expected to obey. Our emphasis here has been on the part we as individuals can play in influencing the rules those institutions make. We turn now to the natural sequel to that topic — the part we can play as members of political organizations.

Selected Readings

Carstairs, Andrew McLaren. *A Short History of Electoral Systems in Western Europe* (London: Allen and Unwin, 1980). A historical study of Western European electoral systems in countries such as the Netherlands, Norway, Austria, Italy, and Finland.

Craig, Stephen C. *The Malevolent Leaders: Popular Dis-*

content in America (Boulder: Westview, 1993). Examines the rise and causes of political discontent in America since the 1960s.

Dalton, Russell J. *Citizen Politics*, second edition (Chatham, N.J.: Chatham House, 1996). Compares citizen participation, value orientations, and elections in the United States, Great Britain, West Germany, and France.

Dionne, E. J. Jr. *Why Americans Hate Politics* (New York: Simon and Schuster, 1991). The author argues that political apathy has increased because the choices offered by conservatives and liberals do not address the values and concerns of a majority of Americans.

Ginsberg, Benjamin and Alan Stone, eds., *Do Elections Matter?* (Armonk, New York: Sharpe, 1996). Questions the connection between the election choices of voters and policy decisions of politicians once they are elected.

Keith, Bruce E., et al. *The Myth of the Independent Voter* (Berkeley: University of California Press, 1992). The authors seek to counter the popular view that independent voters are a coherent third party force in American politics.

Lijphart, Arend. *Electoral Systems and Party Systems: A Study of Twenty-Seven Democracies* (Oxford: Oxford University Press, 1994). A comprehensive study of electoral systems, including how they influence election results and legislative representation.

Lipset, Seymour M. and Stein Rokkan, eds. *Party Systems and Voter Alignments: Cross-National Perspectives* (New York: Free Press, 1967). An early and still cited effort to compare voting behavior across nations.

Peterson, Steven A. *Political Behavior: Patterns in Everyday Life* (Newbury Park, Ca.: Sage, 1990). Argues that researchers need to focus more on how ordinary voters interpret their own political behavior and how their interpretations of what is political differ from those of the specialists.

Piven, Frances Fox and Richard A. Cloward. *Why Americans Don't Vote* (New York: Pantheon, 1988). The authors make a persuasive argument that the underlying cause of low voter turnout is that U.S. politics is primarily oriented toward the interests of economic elites, seriously compounded by difficult requirements for voter registration.

Smith, Eric R.A.N. *The Unchanging American Voter* (Berkeley: University of California Press, 1989).
Reviews the classic argument, first made by Angus Campbell et al. in *The American Voter* (1960) that Americans do not have much factual knowledge about politics and are ideologically unsophisticated. Finds that little has changed, despite rising education levels.

Notes

1. For some interesting examples of "dedicated community activists," see Janny Scott, "The Ultimate Volunteers," in *New York Times*, (4 Sept. 1994), 1QU.

2. Two general references for the subjects to be covered in this section are Carol Barner-Barry, *Psychological Perspectives on Politics* (Englewood Cliffs, N.J.: Prentice Hall, 1985), and David Horton Smith and Jacqueline Macauley and Associates, *Participation in Social and Political Activities* (San Francisco: Jossey-Bass, 1980). See especially pp. 76–167 in the latter.

3. For a similar set of distinctions see Barner-Barry, *Psychological Perspectives on Politics*, pp. 11–18.

4. Tom Maslund, "No News is Good News," *Newsweek* 125, no. 37 (15 May 1995): 37 and Richard Stengel, "White Right," *The New Republic* 212 (29 May 1995): 14, 16.

5. M. Brewster Smith, Jerome S. Bruner and Robert W. White, *Opinions and Personality* (New York: John Wiley and Sons, 1956), pp. 39–44.

6. Times Mirror Center for the People and the Press, *The Vocal Minority in American Politics* (Washington, D.C.: 1993), cited by Sidney Verba, "The 1993 James Madison Award Lecture: The Voice of the People," *P.S.: Political Science and Politics* 26, no. 4 (Dec. 1993): 679.

7. The early studies of public opinion did not go beyond the articulate few. See, for example, Walter Lippman's *Public Opinion* (New York: Harcourt, Brace, 1922). V. O. Key had a similar entity in mind when he spoke of the "political stratum" in *Politics, Parties and Pressure Groups*, 5th ed. (New York: Thomas Y. Crowell, 1965).

8. For other reasons poll data may be misleading, see "All Polls Are Not Created Equal," *U.S. News and World Report*, 28 Sept. 1992, 24–25 and chap. 3 "The Anatomy of a Public Opinion Poll," in Gary W. Selnow, *High-Tech Campaigns: Computer Technol-*

ogy in Political Communication (Westport, Conn.: Praeger, 1994), pp. 27–43. On the other hand, in Senlow chap. 4, pp. 45–66, "Technical Advances in Polling," shows how technology has revolutionized polling in recent years, improving its precision.

9. Daniel Schorr, "Washington Notebook," *The New Leader* 75 (4 May 1992): 3.

10. Daniel Lerner, *The Passing of Traditional Society, Modernizing the Middle East* (Glencoe, Ill.: The Free Press, 1958).

11. Robin Knight and Victoria Pope, "Back to the Future," *U. S News and World Report*, 23 May 1994, 40–43 and Lee Hoekstader, "Three Years Later, Russians Revising View of Coup Plotters," *Washington Post*, 21 Aug. 1994, A34.

12. *New York Times*, 9 Oct. 1991, A1 and 13 Oct. 1991, 34.

13. David Futrelle, "The Politics of Porn," *In These Times*, 7 Mar. 1994, 14–17.

14. *New York Times*, 4 June 1989, I1, I20, A2.

15. Lester W. Milbrath and M. L. Goel, *Political Participation*, 2nd ed. (Chicago: Rand McNally, 1977), pp. 18–19.

16. For example, most of those in modes 4 through 7 are also regular voters, and protestors may also be active in modes 4 through 6. One is assigned a mode by the distinctiveness of the package of activities in which one engages. Ibid., p. 20.

17. For these and other relevant data, see Sidney Verba and Norman H. Nie, "Political Participation," in Fred I. Greenstein and Nelson W. Polsby, eds., *Handbook of Political Science*, vol. 4 (Reading, Mass.: Addison-Wesley, 1975), pp. 24–25; Dennis Kavanagh, *Political Science and Political Behavior* (London: George Allen and Unwin, 1983), pp. 181–84; Russell J. Dalton, *Citizen Politics in Western Democracies* (Chatham, N.J.: Chatham House, 1988), pp. 47, 65.

18. According to Curtis Gans, director of the Committee for the Study of the American Electorate, nonmajor party voting increased by one-third in 1992, as compared to 1988, and most of that vote went to Ross Perot. (Interview, 9 Nov. 1992).

19. For a summary of recent trends in voter turnout in the United States and their effect on the parties, see Paul Allen Beck and Frank J. Sorauf, *Party Politics in America*, 7th ed. (Boston: Harper-Collins, 1992) pp. 212–25. For the 1994 results, see *Statistical Abstract of the United States 1995* (Washington, D.C.: U.S. Department of Commerce, 1995), 291.

20. Frances Fox Piven and Richard A. Cloward, *Why Americans Don't Vote* (New York: Pantheon Books, 1987), p. 15.

21. Ibid., pp. 17–19.

22. *World Almanac and Book of Facts* (New York: Funk and Wagnalls, 1995), p. 71.

23. Raymond Wolfinger and Steven Rosenstone, *Who Votes?* (New Haven: Yale University Press, 1980), p. 73. See also Steven J. Rosenstone and Raymond E. Wolfinger, "The Effect of Registration Laws on Voter Turnout," in Richard Niemi and Herbert Weisberg, eds., *Controversies in Voting Behavior*, 2nd ed. (Washington, D.C., Congressional Quarterly Press, 1984), pp. 66–67.

24. Russell B. Dalton, *Citizen Politics in Western Democracies* (Chatham, N.J., Chatham House, 1988), p. 39. See also William J. Keefe, *Parties, Politics and Public Policy in America*, 7th ed. (Washington, D.C.: Congressional Quarterly Press, 1994), p. 193.

25. G. Bingham Powell, Jr., "American Voter Turnout in Comparative Perspective," *American Political Science Review* 80, no. 1 (Mar. 1986): 17–41.

26. Marshall Ganz, "Voters in the Crosshairs: Elections and Voter Turnout," *The American Prospect* (Winter 1994): 4–10.

27. Ibid., p. 8. Ganz notes, "With both campaigns . . . using this kind of reasoning, it is not so surprising that, despite the city's troubles, less than 25 percent of the Los Angeles electorate turned out to vote" in that city's most recent mayoral election.

28. Walter Dean Burnham, "Parties and Political Modernization," in Richard L. McCormick, ed., *Political Parties and the Modern State* (New Brunswick, N.J.: Rutgers University Press, 1984), p. 123.

29. "Electoral Reform," *The Economist* 327 (1 May 1993), 19.

30. Kavanagh, *Political Science and Political Behavior*, p. 79.

31. *International Herald Tribune*, 5 June 1992, 7.

32. Martin Jacques, "The Godmother: Italy's Meltdown — and Ours: Crisis of Government Credibility," *The New Republic* (20 Sept. 1993), pp. 23–27.

33. For recent studies of the variety of electoral systems possible, see Arend Lijphart, *Electoral Systems and Party Systems: A Study of Twenty-Seven Democracies 1945–1990* (Oxford: Oxford University Press, 1994), and Joseph F. Zimmerman, "Alternative Voting Systems for Representative Democracy," *P.S.: Political Science and Politics* 27, no. 4 (Dec. 1994), 674–677.

34. Karen Beckwith, "Comparative Research and Electoral Systems: Lessons from France and Italy," *Women's Politics* 12, no. 1 (1992): 7.

35. Henry W. Ehrmann and Martin Schain, *Politics in France*, 5th ed. (New York: HarperCollins, 1992), pp. 213–219.

36. For a good discussion of the advantages and disadvantages of instituting a national initiative and referendum, see Thomas E. Cronin, *Direct Democracy: The Politics of Initiative, Referendum and Recall* (Cambridge, Mass.: Harvard University Press, 1989), pp. 157–95. See also Bruno S. Frey, "Direct Democracy: Politico-Economic Lessons from Swiss Experience," *American Economic Review*, 84, no. 2 (1994), 338–41

37. See Peter McCormick, "The Recall of Elected Members," *Canadian Parliamentary Review* (Summer 1994): 11–13 for an argument in defense of this institution and a recommendation that it be adopted in Canada.

38. George M. Anderson, "Voting Rights and the Poor," *America* (26 Sept. 1992), 180–96. In Arizona and New Mexico, states that purge every two years, those who vote only in presidential elections are sure to find their names removed from one such election to the next.

39. Andrew L. Shapiro, "Giving Cons and Ex-Cons the Vote," *The Nation* (20 Sept. 1993): 767.

40. This question was raised some time ago about Mexican farmworkers in the United States (see George C. Kiser and Martha Woody Kiser, eds., *Mexican Workers in the United States: Historical and Political Perspectives* [Albuquerque: University of New Mexico Press, 1979]), but at present majority opinion appears to be moving in the opposite direction. In 1992 the same question was raised by the European Economic Community, and it now appears likely that resident aliens will be given the right to vote in local elections in Europe long before a similar change is made in the United States.

41. Beck and Sorauf, *Party Politics in America*, pp. 208–12.

42. *Los Angeles Times*, 11 Dec. 1990, B1, B4 and 8 Jan. 1991, B1.

43. John L. Safford, "John C. Calhoun, Lani Guinier, and Minority Rights," *P.S.: Political Science and Politics* 28, no. 2 (June 1995), and Anthony Lewis, "Depriving the Nation," *New York Times*, 17 Sept. 1993, A17. For a general discussion of this issue as it affects Hispanics, see Linda Chavez, "Hispanics, Affirmative Action and Voting," *Annals of the American Academy of Political and Social Science* 523 (Sept. 1992): 75–87.

44. For a discussion of the limitations on the rights of American Communists contained in the Smith Act, see Edward S. Greenberg, *The American Political System: A Radical Approach* (Cambridge, Mass.: Winthrop, 1977), pp. 391, 410.

45. The best source for information on state laws limiting the rights of political parties, particularly the rights of new parties to get on the ballot and of minor parties to *stay* on the ballot is *Ballot Access News*, published privately by editor Richard Winger, Bx 47026, San Francisco, Ca., 94147.

46. *Los Angeles Times*, 7 Apr. 1992, A1, A14.

47. Adrian Karatnycky, *Freedom in the World: The Annual Survey of Political Rights and Civil Liberties 1994–1995* (New York: Freedom House, 1995), pp. 260, 415.

48. The "white primary" was a system that allowed Democratic Party organizations in the American south to deny African Americans the right to participate in their primary elections, on the grounds that parties were private organizations. This had the effect of disenfranchising African Americans altogether, since at the time the Democrats entirely dominated the south's electoral politics and whoever won the primary was sure of election to office. The Supreme Court ruled, in *Smith v. Allwright* (1944), that political parties played too important a role in the nation's political fortunes to be considered private organizations, and the "white primary" was accordingly ruled illegal.

7 Organizing for Politics: The Group

JOGGING CONTENTEDLY AROUND THE familiar track, a middle-aged American runner is startled to see a fellow jogger arrive with a poster: "Save Our Track. Sign the Petition." After completing her twenty laps, she trots over to see what is going on. The track is on the grounds of a school for the deaf and blind that is being sold to the local university. The school for the handicapped has always allowed the public to use the track; the university refuses to make any such promises. Fearful of being excluded, the alarmed joggers meet at the home of one of their number, choose a name (East Bay Community Track and Field Association), elect a president and a recording secretary, gather dues, distribute leaflets, write letters to city council members and state legislators, and arrange for a meeting in the mayor's office with representatives of the university. The smiling university attorney now assures them there will be "no problem." Continued public access to the track will be permitted. Three days later they have this promise in writing.

In this example of organizing for politics, the joggers form an interest group spontaneously as a way to use political means to meet nonpolitical needs.[1] This is a common beginning for interest groups, but not the only way to organize for political purposes. Let's look at another example.

Labor costs are seriously reducing profits, the chairman of a rapidly expanding Japanese electronics firm reports to his governing board. It is his view that government unemployment benefits are unrealistically generous, stimulating workers to hold out for higher wages. After heated discussion, the board resolves to attack the matter through the Unemployment Policy Committee of the Nikkeiren (Japanese Federation of Employers' Associations), to which the company has belonged since its formation in 1948. If the government expects to continue to receive the backing of Japanese business, declares the chairman, it must take steps to reward that loyal support. No one on the board appears to disagree.[2]

In this case, what is happening? A nonpolitical group (a business corporation) is itself a member of a political group (the employers' federation). When the members of the nonpolitical group decide to take political action, they may do so through the exterior group, drawing on the larger group's expertise and numerical strength to pressure the government for change. Their success in doing so will depend on their ability to persuade the other members in the federation that this is an appropriate path to pursue. Sometimes, however, belonging to an existing political group is not a satisfactory way to organize for one's own political purposes. Consider the next example.

Fascinated by politics and determined to devote his life to the struggle for his people's freedom, a student newly arrived in London from an African colony under British dominion soon assumes a leadership role in the activities of the West African Students' Union in London. His work in organizing international conferences brings him to the attention of the leaders of the United Gold Coast Convention, the strongest political party in his native land, and he responds to their request to come home and take the post of general secretary. Soon, however, he finds himself in disaccord with the other leaders of the party, who move too slowly and too cautiously for his taste. Quietly, he helps a friend form a Youth Study Group, which brings together young men and women eager to wage a more active struggle against colonialism. When this organization becomes strong enough, he aids in its transformation to the Convention People's party, breaks with the UGCC, and leads the new party to electoral victory — and the Gold Coast to independence as the new nation of Ghana.[3]

This third example is the true story of the early political career of Kwame Nkrumah, the former president of Ghana. So far we have looked at three ways individuals use political groups to accomplish their ends: They may form a group spontaneously, they may belong to a nonpolitical group that in turn belongs to a political group, or they may work within one political group to develop the strength to form another group more suitable to their purposes. But we have not yet considered the way most of us work through political organizations — that is, we simply join the one that suits us best, stay with it, and gradually come to accept its goals as our own. Those goals may vary from the most ordinary to the most extreme. Our last example falls into the extreme category.

The young Colombian university graduate, angry at her inability to find employment appropriate to her level of education despite apparent national prosperity and dismayed by large-scale corruption involving drug trafficking and criminal violence, joins others similarly situated to complain and argue over the causes of the nation's plight. She is gradually persuaded that the nation's turning point came on May 19, 1970, when General Gustavo Royas, a conservative reformist who had been in power in the early 1950s, was denied reelection (by voter fraud, her new friends insist). The only answer now, they say, is political revolution, and the only way to achieve that revolution is by violent means, such as those employed by M-19, a terrorist group named for the day of infamy. They decide to join, and in June 1985 they are among the M-19 members who take over the country's Palace of Justice, in which Colombia's Supreme Court is housed. The military fights back, and in the battle half of the Supreme Court justices and all of the M-19 participants are killed, including the angry young woman. In the aftermath, a few minor political reforms are enacted, but the problems of criminal dominance of the nation's politics are not resolved.[4]

The forms that political organizations take vary as greatly as the routes individuals follow to join them. The spontaneous, short-lived interest group, the permanent lobby, the political party, and the guerrilla movement mentioned in these examples only begin to suggest the range of political organizations found throughout the world. In fact, since a **political organization** is "any organization that is not itself a government agency but whose main purpose is to affect the operation of government," the subject is too vast to be covered in a single chapter.[5] Our solution is to discuss **interest groups** and **violent revolutionary groups** in this chapter and **political parties in** Chapter 8. All, of course, are political organizations, and the differences among them are not always easy to identify. But there are distinctions.

An **interest group** is an organization that seeks to affect the operation of government by using peaceful means to persuade key persons in government to act in accordance with the group's interests. The first two cases discussed in the opening pages of this chapter are examples of interest groups. A **violent revolutionary group** is an organization that seeks to achieve change in government policy — or to change the government altogether —by violent means; the fourth case tells of such a group. A **political party** is an organization that nominates and campaigns on behalf of candidates seeking office in an existent government through popular election; the third case describes the beginning of a new political party.

Although at any given moment in its life, a political organization is usually easily identified as an interest group, a political party, or a violent revolutionary organization, that same organization may well have begun as a different type, and may yet change again. Interest groups may become violent revolutionary groups when they despair of achieving their objectives by peaceful means; revolutionary groups, once successful or partially so, may change themselves into political parties; political parties may be forced underground by government repression and become violent revolutionary groups — or may lose so many elections at such great expense that they abandon the quest for office and become an ordinary interest group, exerting peaceful pressure on those who do win control of the government. Many other permutations are possible. Normally, it is the leaders of political organizations who choose the form (and when to change it), basing their choice on their values, their skills, their experience, and what they believe most likely to work for pursuit of the group's particular goals in its particular circumstances. Rank and file members — or potential members — may or may not be consulted.

INTEREST GROUPS

Most of this chapter will be devoted to the study of interest groups. We will consider the benefits they offer to those who join them, the nature of their organizational apparatus, the goals toward which they are directed, and the tactics they employ. We will also devote an entire section to an important problem posed by some interest groups today: their growing ability to substitute themselves for constitutional government.

Benefits to Joiners of Interest Groups

Individuals must be motivated to combine with others before group action can be effective in influencing government. No one joins a group without seeking some kind of reward. Robert Salisbury has suggested that individuals join groups seeking one of three kinds of benefits: material, solidary, or purposive.[6]

Material Benefits   Material benefits are goods and services made available to group members. Salisbury points out that members may join a group to improve their supply of these benefits either directly or indirectly. A group exercising political pressure to keep access to a jogging track is pursuing a material benefit directly. But a group trying to change government unemployment benefits so that businesses may employ workers at lower wages and thus retain greater profits for owners is pursuing such a reward indirectly.

Solidary Benefits   Others join groups less for what they can get materially than for the good feelings they get from joining. For some, these "good feelings" are **solidary benefits.** Joining the group gives these people a sense of belonging, a chance to socialize with others, or improved social status. Some of the men and women at the Gray Panthers' annual picnic may be there just to help raise funds for the lobbying efforts of this activist senior citizen group, but for most the opportunity to have a good time in congenial surroundings with others who share their interests may well be the

"You go on home without me, Irene. I'm going to join this man's cult."

(Drawing by Chas. Addams; © 1982 The New Yorker Magazine, Inc.)

primary motive for attendance. And the chance to go to the picnic may well have brought them into the Gray Panthers in the first place.

Purposive Benefits   Some groups offer their members another kind of "good feeling" reward: **purposive benefits**. Working on behalf of a value or cause they believe in can give some members so much satisfaction that they need seek no personal rewards. Groups fighting for such causes as human rights (the International League for the Rights of Man), environmental safeguards (Friends of the Earth), and consumer protection (the British Public Interest Research Centre) are likely to attract members in search of this kind of reward.

The categories are far from discrete. Individuals may join a group for a combination of motives, and groups may offer a combination of rewards. Suppose, for example, that one summer evening you are sitting at home watching the local news on television, after spending a hard, boring day at a temporary job as a word processor — a job you have taken just to earn some money for school expenses. Suddenly you see some familiar faces on the television screen. It is your good friend Angela and her boyfriend Jerry. Then suddenly Jerry is being knocked down by some very tough-looking characters, and Angela is being roughly shoved away. You sit up straight, pay close attention, and learn that your friends were peacefully marching in front of city hall for a cause they believe in — one that you yourself happen to think is worthwhile and important. The people who assaulted them do not agree, and furthermore seem to have little or no respect for other people's rights of free expression. Before you know it, you are on the phone to Angela and Jerry, offering your support. The next night you attend a meeting of their group, and for the rest of the summer you are one of its most ardent members, joining in all its activities. You scarcely mind that boring job anymore, you have so much to think about. Your coworkers are impressed when they see you being interviewed on television during the group's next major demonstration. The group itself likes your work so much that they offer you a paid staff position for the following summer.

What were your rewards? Were they material, solidary, or purposive?

Rewards also vary with intensity of membership. Many groups consist of a handful of activists, backed up by lists of supporters — who are merely all the people who have ever sent in a membership form, with or without a check attached. Active participation by the great majority of the members of interest groups is rare. Some groups deliberately limit the number of active members, either because they prefer a cohesive core to a larger and more heterogeneous group beset by factionalism or because by making membership a privilege and an honor they increase the readiness of those who belong to be generous in donations of time and money.[7] Presumably, those who take an active part in highly selective groups receive very significant solidary benefits, whereas those whose participation is limited to sending a check are more likely to be seeking and gaining only material or purposive rewards.

Finally, it is entirely possible for individuals to reap some of the rewards of interest group membership *without being a member*. **Collective benefits** are benefits that go to all the members of a polity whether they helped work for them or not. As a result, groups may find it difficult to recruit members even though the benefits their work eventually produces may be highly desirable to many. This is what is known as the *free rider* problem; the nonparticipants take a free ride on the hard work of a few. It is often the most difficult problem for a group that is determined to attract a mass membership.[8]

How Organized Is the Interest Group?

Interest groups vary not only in the kind of benefits they offer to their members but also in the degree to which there is a formal organization devoted to political action. Drawing on the work of others and observing groups in action today, we can identify seven levels of interest group organization.

Amorphous groups are groupings of individuals who share an interest and act on its behalf in a way that indirectly affects government policy, even though they do not see themselves as taking any action that might be called political.[9] *Spontaneous* groups are groups of unorganized individuals who act together politically and deliberately, but in unconventional and often violent fashion.[10] Student demonstrations in France, race riots in Great Britain, and wildcat strikes in the United States all fit into this category, as long as they begin without the participation of any formal organization. Only slightly more organized are the *nonassociational* groups, which make occasional representations to government officials on behalf of unorganized — or loosely organized — individuals who share a particular demographic characteristic. Mexican-Americans who testify in favor of bilingual education but do not organize an ongoing group around that issue or around their own ethnic identity provide an example of this level of group activity.

At a fourth level of organizational complexity are *institutional* groups. These are subgroups *within* such institutions as churches, business corporations, and armies. They take special responsibility for the institution's political interests by such tactics as lobbying individual government officials, testifying at hearings, and placing advertisements to arouse public support. When public agencies, officially part of the government, assume the guise of interest group, lobbying another part of government (the legislature or the chief executive), they may be seen as a particular kind of institutional group.

Fifth are *associational* groups, those fully organized groups that are formed specifically to represent the interests — political or other — of their members. These are the groups we most commonly think of when we speak of interest groups. Trade unions, business federations, professional associations, neighborhood associations, political action committees (PACs) and ethnic associations all fit here. Most of this chapter is devoted to their activities.

Sixth are *ad hoc coalitions*. An ad hoc coalition is a temporary organization created to allow several political organizations (which may be any combination of interest groups, parties, or other political organizations) to pool their resources in a joint effort in which all are temporarily interested. When various women's groups, such as the National Organization for Women, the National Council of Jewish Women, the League of Women Voters, and the General Federation of Women's Clubs, engage in *collective lobbying* on behalf of specific issues and then disband to pursue their more distinctive interests, they are creating ad hoc coalitions.[11] Antiwar sentiment may also produce ad hoc coalitions, as when the National Campaign for Peace in the Middle East, the Coalition for Democratic Values, the Coalition to Stop U. S. Intervention in the Middle East, and several Catholic and Protestant peace groups all united in an effort to rally public opinion against the Gulf War.[12] Such organizations are possible among enemies as well as among friends; this form of organization is purposive, pragmatic, and usually temporary.

Social movements may be called a seventh form of interest group, although they are in reality a kind of organization that is very difficult to classify. Such groups are interested in the reform of entire polities, normally on behalf of its least privileged members. If they employ — as many do — violent means, then they fall into the category of violent revolutionary groups; the Shining Path of Peru is an example. If they work primarily — as many do — via political parties, then they fall into that category; a principal example are the Green movements in many western European nations. But if they avoid the use of violence and enter partisan politics only intermittently and tangentially, then even though they may grow to dimensions that threaten to break its bounds, they still fit better in our present category, the interest group. Interest groups are often inspired by religious thought — the Christian Right in the United States, liberation theologists in Latin America — but not always, as we see in the examples of nonpartisan ecologist movements, the feminist movement at its height in the nineteen seventies, the Polish trade union movement Solidarity, and the U.S. civil rights movement.[13]

The Goals of Interest Groups

Interest groups may also be distinguished according to the purposes for which they work. Some work only on behalf of the immediate interests of their members, others on behalf of causes that their members believe will benefit all (or a significant portion of) humankind. Some work for a single purpose, others for a wide range of causes that seem to them to fit under a common rubric.

Special Interest Groups and Public Interest Groups   The most common goal of interest groups is to serve the "special interests" of their members. In almost every nation of the world, groups that focus exclusively on the interests of business, labor, or agriculture are among the best organized and most powerful of all. The Colombian National Association of Manufacturers (ANDI), the American Federation of Labor-Congress of Industrial Organizations (AFL-CIO), and the German Farmers League (*Deutscher Bauernveband*) all work for interests that are found worldwide and that tend to make strong representations to government wherever the most minimal freedom of assembly is protected. Other special interest groups, like the Quebec Teachers Federation, the Akhil Bharatiya Vidyarthi Parishad (India's largest student organization), and the Original Cherokee Community Organization, are also found around the globe; teachers, students, and members of oppressed minorities very often form groups to pursue their particular goals. Other kinds of groups, such as the Anti-Vivisection League or the Ku Klux Klan, are more truly "special."

In their efforts to influence government, special interests often struggle against each other. The Pacific Coast Federation of Fishermen's Association, a group representing west coast commercial fishermen, believed the livelihood of its members depended on maintaining the terms of the 1973 Endangered Species Act. However, the National Endangered Species Reform Coalition, an ad hoc coalition of 185 U.S. groups and companies, including major timber, mining, ranching, and utility interests, believed that same piece of legislation was seriously jeopardizing their ability to meet *their* economic needs. In 1995, both groups were actively lobbying Congress, the one to maintain and the other to remove major provisions of that act.[14]

Other groups organize for causes they claim are in the public's interest, not their own. The Sierra Club, the Consumer Federation of America, and Ralph Nader's Public Interest Research Group are American examples of groups that claim the identity of **public interest group**.[15]

Claiming such a status is clearly a good way to discourage opposition, but the question of when a group's goals are truly in the public interest is not always simple to resolve. The nineteenth-century British Union for the Abolition of Vivisection clearly worked for its members' special feelings about animal welfare and against research many others considered essential for human welfare. Contemporary animal protection leagues have also been accused of neglecting basic human needs — for example, the economic well-being of Inuit (Eskimo) families engaged in whaling — in their concern to protect other species. (Perhaps you have seen the bumper strip showing a picture of a concerned whale pleading, "Save the Humans.") Such cases require careful study and, finally, a normative choice to determine where the public interest truly lies.

Nor is it always certain that claiming that larger identity will improve a group's political effectiveness. The large and powerful American Association of Retired Persons sometimes remains quiet on major issues so as not to offend its diverse membership; when it does take action, it often aligns itself with congressional Democrats. In both cases, it risks the loss of partisan members who lean to the right and who have in response recently formed such frankly conservative and usually pro-Republican groups as the Seniors Coalition, the 60/Plus Association, and the United Seniors Association.[16]

Single-Issue Groups and Multiple-Issue Groups   Another distinction to be made between groups is the number of goals a group works toward. Some groups focus on single issues, others attack a broad range of political problems that they believe are linked to their members' interests. Large business federations, such as Italy's Confindistria or India's Chambers of Commerce and Industry; labor organizations, such as the Nigerian Trade Unions Congress or the American AFL-CIO; and some public interest groups, including Common Cause and the League of Women Voters, regularly undertake a program for government action that covers a wide range of topics. (Common Cause began in 1970 with a wide-ranging list of issue areas, including antiwar action, government reform, urban concerns, welfare, and the environment, but soon learned it would be more effective with a more limited agenda. Since then it has emphasized the reform of political procedures and institutions.)

Other groups, such as People for the Ethical Treatment of Animals (PETA) or the National Rifle Association (NRA), confine themselves to a single issue. Multiple-issue groups are sometimes accused of having too broad an agenda, but single-issue groups are often criticized for taking too little interest in the larger concerns of government, supporting or attacking government officials strictly according to the actions they take in their one area of concern. The conservative NRA has carried its battle against gun regulation to the point of targeting a Republican congressman whose only competition was a Socialist independent but who had dared to announce his support for a ban on assault weapons.[17] Another criticism of single-issue groups is that their members become so passionate about the single cause that they forget the importance of *aggregating* interests in a wide-ranging program for social change, with the result that those who might be political allies — be it on the left, right, or center — and thus helpful to one another, become competitors for public attention and resources, hurting each other's causes and accomplishing less for their own than cooperative tactics would permit.

The Tactics of Interest Groups

How *do* interest groups work to achieve their goals? To answer that question, we need to consider both *pressure methods*, the means groups use to exert pressure on government, and *pressure points*, the levels and branches of government that groups seek to influence.

Pressure Methods   The means of influencing government that is most often associated with interest groups is **lobbying**. In practice, however, groups have a large arsenal of methods at their command, and lobbying itself can take many forms. Waylaying the public official in the lobby of his or her workplace is still a lively art, and making personal offerings ranging from simple lunches to lavish gifts to outright bribes, another time-honored way of doing this kind of business, has by no means vanished from the globe.

The campaign contribution, whether made legally or illegally, is often a means of gaining access that smacks of bribery. Carol Greenwaid quotes one former Pennsylvania politician's very personal explanation of how it works: "I believe in a division of labor. . . . You send us to Congress, we pass laws . . . under which you make money . . . and out of your profits you further contribute to our campaign funds to send us back again to pass more laws to enable you to make more money."[18]

The *strike* is the time-honored tactic of labor unions. Here German public workers, including municipal theater employees, march to Frankfurt's city hall in a nation-wide strike that continued several weeks despite earnest negotiations between government and union leaders. (AP Photo/Wide World)

When successful candidates owe their election in significant part to financial assistance during the campaign, they usually know they are in debt, and know that such debts must be repaid with appropriate policy decisions or appointments. They themselves will normally deny that such is the case (former senator Boies Penrose, quoted earlier, is an exception), but the contributors themselves are often more forthcoming. Thus when asked whether he thought the $1.3 million worth of financial support his savings and loan firm had provided for various Democratic political campaigns had influenced the recipients to take up his cause, Charles H. Keating, Jr. answered candidly, "I want to say in the most forceful way I can: I certainly hope so."[19] Such contributions tend to flow to those already in power ($324,000 of Keating's contributions went to five incumbent Democratic senators), and when power changes hands, so does the flow of money. In the first half of 1995, the beleaguered tobacco industry gave the newly powerful national Republican Party over $1.5 million, and only $154,950 to national Democratic committees.[20]

Under campaign finance law in the United States, any group wishing to contribute money or services to a candidate must create a political action committee (PAC) and that committee must note detailed disclosure of expenditures both directly to candidates and independently on their behalf. PACs may not contribute more than $5,000 directly to any candidate, but there is no limit on independent expenditures — that is, on the amount of money that a PAC may spend directly on campaigning for a candidate. Furthermore, there is no limit on the amount that may be given to party committees (note the tobacco industry's contributions above), and although such monies are supposed to be spent on "party-building" purposes, the Federal Election Commission and the courts have been very liberal in their interpretation of what kind of activities may be covered by that term. The Federal Elections Commission requires elaborate reports of all receipts and disbursements by a candidate, but requires only the most simple accounting of itemized independent expenditures (See Box 7.1).

Independent expenditures have steadily risen in recent elections, accounting for an ever higher percentage of total expenditures. However, not every PAC was happy with the new freedom to make direct expenditures on behalf of favored candidates: "It's a lot more difficult than handing out a $5,000 check," said one PAC director. "It's expensive to get into. We spend a lot of money on polling. We do a lot of research. And if it's not handled correctly, it can cause a rift in your membership."[21] On the other hand, independent spending is often now viewed as the only way to be seen as a "serious player." According to the Director of the Auto Dealers and Drivers for Free Trade PAC, which spent approximately $1.5 million independently in 1988, the message is clear: "Auto dealers will back their friends no matter how much trouble they are in."[22]

In recent years, yet another means for funneling private money into political campaigns has emerged: the creation of tax-exempt foundations affiliated with elected officials or candidates for office. The most dubious version is the voter registration group or foundation. Such an association may accept unlimited sums without having to meet the Federal Elections Commission's disclosure requirements — and the contributions are tax deductible. However, such "nonpartisan" registration groups often focus their efforts on signing up only those persons likely to vote their way. Contributing to such groups was one way savings and loan officer Charles H. Keating, Jr. was able to contribute more than $1 million to the campaigns (or "causes") of several U.S. senators who attempted to save his failing company.

However, when the government official who has received PAC funding wishes to cooperate, be it out of innocent agreement or dishonest avarice, he or she will be more likely to be able to persuade their colleagues if a majority of the general public is on the same side as the donor. When they have the means, interest groups therefore do not confine themselves to contributions. The health and insurance industries that were opposed to the plans for health care reform by the Clinton administration were estimated to have spent over $40 million in campaign contributions, but also another $60 million in advertising, public relations, and lobbying, in their efforts to defeat that plan.[23]

Effective lobbying today usually means spending a great deal of time preparing the arguments and documentation that will help the cooperative official get the necessary agreement of other officials. Successful lobbyists seek to become such trusted sources of high-quality credible information that they create a dependency. Such dependency can be carried very far. In 1995, attorneys from a law firm representing numerous electric utilities were given the job (normally that of the appropriate congressional staff) of explaining to the Senate Judiciary Committee the latest version of a bill that would give such industries important new powers to challenge government regulations. It was unusual to see, commented one observer, "congressional staff members so openly and publicly embrace . . . legislative outsiders with extensive interests in the outcome."[24]

An old form of lobbying, writing letters, has taken a new form, as groups with the money to do so may now hire lobbying firms to generate what appears to be "grass roots lobbying." Thus in 1992 the Coalition to End Abusive Securities Suits hired the Wexler Group, a Washington lobbying firm, to ask companies and associations first to join the coalition and then to ask their members and employees to write to Congress, using packets of sample letters and computer disks supplied by the firm. Other such firms have used mass mailings of preprinted post cards and have even used phone banks to call potential supporters, transferring the calls to congressional offices when consent is secured.[25]

Interest groups with limited funds are particularly likely to employ means other than making financial contributions and lobbying to bring home their arguments. They hold demonstrations, organize boycotts, wage strikes, advertise, write books, stage various events to attract the attention of the news media, and use whatever means they can to call public and official attention to their cause. Student movements, from the Free Speech Movement of the 1960s in the United States to the Brazilian Youth Corps of Popular Action to the French students protesting educational reforms proposed by a rightwing government in early 1992, have moved into the streets with alacrity on behalf of a wide range of causes. Environmentalists have staged many kinds of theatrical events, from sailing into nuclear test zones to burying automobiles, in their efforts to arouse public interest and concern. Members of the AIDS Coalition to Unleash Power (ACT UP), who are middle-class professionals, have used "their clean-cut looks

BOX 7.1

RUNNING FOR CONGRESS—AND KEEPING THE BOOKS

Here are two pages from the Federal Elections Commission form to be filled out by a candidate for the United States Congress (the "summary page" and the "detailed summary page"), with illustrative entries. The marginal notes are FEC directions to the candidate, indicating where to find information about what is required for each entry.

SUMMARIZING CAMPAIGN FINANCE ACTIVITY

"Reporting Forms," page 26.

"When to Report," page 25.

"Terminating the Committee," page 34.

"Who Reports," page 24.

"Where to File Reports," page 24.

REPORT OF RECEIPTS AND DISBURSEMENTS
For An Authorized Committee
(Summary Page)

USE FEC MAILING LABEL OR TYPE OR PRINT

1. NAME OF COMMITTEE (in full)

   SAM JONES FOR CONGRESS

   ADDRESS (number and street) ☐ Check if different than previously reported.

   319 MAIN STREET

   CITY, STATE and ZIP CODE   STATE /DISTRICT

   CITY, STATE ZIP   ST/01

2. FEC IDENTIFICATION NUMBER

   000015551

   ☐ YES   ☒ NO

4. TYPE OF REPORT

☐ April 15 Quarterly Report   ☒ Twelfth day report preceding Primary (Type of Election)

☐ July 15 Quarterly Report   ☐ election on 9/13/94 in the State of (STATE)

☐ October 15 Quarterly Report   ☐ Thirtieth day report following the General Election on

☐ January 31 Year End Report   _____ in the State of _____

☐ July 31 Mid-Year Report (Non-election Year Only)   ☐ Termination Report

This report contains activity for   ☒ Primary Election   ☐ General Election   ☐ Special Election   ☐ Runoff Election

SUMMARY

	COLUMN A This Period	COLUMN B Calendar Year-to-Date
5. Covering Period 7-1-94 through 8-24-94		
6. Net Contributions (other than loans)		
(a) Total Contributions (other than loans)(from Line 11(e))	$20,802.67	$37,475.95
(b) Total Contribution Refunds (from Line 20(d))	$250.00	$640.93
(c) Net Contributions (other than loans)(subtract Line 6(b) from 6(a))	$20,552.67	$36,835.02
7. Net Operating Expenditures		
(a) Total Operating Expenditures (from Line 17)	$15,124.07	$27,785.67
(b) Total Offsets to Operating Expenditures (from Line 14)	$489.73	$724.15
(c) Net Operating Expenditures (subtract Line 7(b) from 7(a))	$14,634.34	$27,061.52
8. Cash on Hand at Close of Reporting Period (from Line 27)	$23,230.48	
9. Debts and Obligations Owed TO the Committee (Itemize all on Schedule C and/or Schedule D)	0	
10. Debts and Obligations Owed BY the Committee (Itemize all on Schedule C and/or Schedule D)	$14,432.39	

For further information contact: Federal Election Commission 999 E. Street, NW Washington, DC 20463 Toll Free 800-424-9530 Local 202-219-3420

I certify that I have examined this Report and to the best of my knowledge and belief it is true, correct and complete.

Type or Print Name of Treasurer
Joseph Dougherty

Signature of Treasurer   Date 8/31/94

NOTE: Submission of false, erroneous, or incomplete information may subject the person signing this Report to the penalties of 2 U.S.C. §437g.

FEC FORM 3 (revised 4/87)

"When to Itemize Receipts," page 27.

"Types of Contributions," page 5.

"Transfers," page 19.

"Loans," pages 5, 13, 29 and 50–53.

"Offsets to Operating Expenditures," pages 14 and 47.

"How to Itemize Disbursements" and "When to Itemize Disbursements," page 29.

"Contribution Refunds," pages 30 and 49.

"Contributions to Other Candidates," pages 29 and 49.

"Cash on Hand," page 26.

DETAILED SUMMARY PAGE
of Receipts and Disbursements
(Page 2, FEC FORM 3)

Name or Committee (In full) Sam Jones For Congress	Report Covering the Period: From: 7-1-94 To: 8-2-94	
I. RECEIPTS	COLUMN A Total This Period	COLUMN B Calendar Year-to-Date
11. CONTRIBUTIONS (other than loans) FROM:		
(a) Individuals/Persons Other Than Political Committees		
(i) Itemized (use Schedule A)	2,900.00		11(a)(i)
(ii) Unitemized	6,701.67		11(a)(ii)
(iii) Total contributions from individuals	9,601.67	22,496.12	11(a)(iii)
(b) Political Party Committees	2,000.00	3,000.00	11(b)
(c) Other Political Committees (such as PACs)	8,000.00	10,000.00	11(c)
(d) The Candidate	2,000.00	1,979.83	11(d)
(e) TOTAL CONTRIBUTIONS (other than loans)(add 11(a)(iii), (b), (c) and (d))..	20,801.67	37,475.95	11(e)
12. TRANSFERS FROM OTHER AUTHORIZED COMMITTEES	0	0	12
13. LOANS:		
(a) Made or Guaranteed by the Candidate	3,000.00	3,000.00	13(a)
(b) All Other Loans	3,000.00	13,000.00	13(b)
(c) TOTAL LOANS (add 13(a) and (b)	6,000.00	16,000.00	13(c)
14. OFFSETS TO OPERATING EXPENDITURES (Refunds, Rebates, etc.)	489.73	724.15	14
15. OTHER RECEIPTS (Dividends, Interest, etc.)	204.64	969.35	15
16. TOTAL RECEIPTS (add 11(e), 12, 13(c), 14 and 15)	27,496.04	55,169.45	16
II. DISBURSEMENTS		
17. OPERATING EXPENDITURES	15,124.07	27,785.67	17
18. TRANSFERS TO OTHER AUTHORIZED COMMITTEES	0	0	18
19. LOAN REPAYMENTS:		
(a) Made or Guaranteed by the Candidate	317.64	317.64	19(a)
(b) Of All Other Loans	882.80	2,378.37	19(b)
(c) TOTAL LOAN REPAYMENTS (add 19(a) and (b)	1,200.44	2,696.01	19(c)
20. REFUNDS OF CONTRIBUTIONS TO:		
(a) Individuals/Persons Other Than Political Committees	250.00	640.93	20(a)
(b) Political Party Committees	0	0	20(b)
(c) Other Political Committees (such as PACs)	0	0	20(c)
(d) TOTAL CONTRIBUTION REFUNDS (add 20(a), (b) and (c))	250.00	640.93	20(d)
21. OTHER DISBURSEMENTS	350.00	350.00	21
22. TOTAL DISBURSEMENTS (add 17, 18, 19(c), 20(d) and 21)	16,924.51	31,472.61	22
III. CASH SUMMARY		
23. CASH ON HAND AT BEGINNING OF REPORTING PERIOD	$	12,942.81	23
24. TOTAL RECEIPTS THIS PERIOD (Line 16)	$	27,496.04	24
25. SUBTOTAL (add Line 23 and Line 24)	$	40,438.85	25
26. TOTAL DISBURSEMENTS THIS PERIOD (from Line 22)	$	16,924.51	26
27. CASH ON HAND AT CLOSE OF THE REPORTING PERIOD (subtract Line 26 from 25)	$	23,514.34	27

An interest group at work. Here German members of Greenpeace have locked themselves in a cage outside the French embassy in Bonn to protest France's renewal of nuclear testing in the Pacific. The banner in the background reads: "You can stop our ships, but not our resistance." (Reuters/Ulli Michel/Archive Photos)

and natty attire [to] gain entry to the halls of government, finance and religion . . . halt the proceedings by shouting, playing dead, or handcuffing themselves to a fixture [in order] to force people to confront the AIDS crisis, and help get drugs for those dying of the affliction."[26]

Pressure Points   The choice of means is often closely linked to the second tactical question, the choice of whom or what to pressure. Interest groups seek to bring influence to bear on those capable of making a difference. In the U.S. presidential system, the separation of the legislative and executive branches and the increasing power of the executive, combined with the declining importance of political parties, means that groups must develop numerous points of access to be effective in promoting government actions they desire or in blocking actions they deplore. The successful group stays on good terms with the bureaucrats and congressional aides who draft legislation relevant to its interests, with the members of Congress who vote on it, with the members of the executive branch who counsel the president on such matters, and with the bureaucrats who see to the actual implementation of the policies adopted.[27]

In a parliamentary system, on the other hand, access to individual deputies and to members of the executive branch is very often through the political parties that play such strong roles in this form of government. In Great Britain, the close ties between the business interests of Great Britain and the Conservative Party, and between the labor unions and the Labour Party, mean that each kind of group has a vested interest in seeing the party it trusts take power. The business interests of Germany and the Christian Democratic Party have also always been close, as have business and the Rally for the Republic (the party whose leader, Jacques Chirac, was elected president in 1995) in France. French groups have also linked themselves to the strength of the presidency under the Fifth Republic by working with the Social and Economic Council, which includes in its membership more than 200 delegates from trade unions, agricultural associations, business organizations, and professional groups.[28]

In a highly centralized state such as France, bureaucratic ministries exercise great power and will also be the direct focus of industry efforts to influence policy.[29] In Japan, it is important for business to maintain good relations with the Japanese Ministry of International Trade and Industry (MITI), although the powers of that agency often prove limited in practice. Unrestrained by antitrust laws, Japanese firms are permitted to unite in massive holding companies, known as *zaibatsu* and typically consisting of a conglomeration of banks, insurance companies, and manufacturing concerns.[30] Such major business interests are able to offer strong incentives to high government officials and party leaders, incentives that may take the form of direct bribes or, more commonly, of the practice of *amakudari*, which means "descent from heaven" and refers to the fact that bureaucrats from the ministry often take comfortable positions with these firms when they leave the government. Thus their power has often proved more than a match for any efforts the MITI might make to direct their destinies. In 1991, it was revealed that several *zaibatsu* brokerage houses had compensated 187 of their larger clients for stock market losses "while maintaining ties with reputed gangsters," and that the MITI had known of the practice a full two years before the scandal broke but had done nothing whatsoever about it.

How Well Do Interest Groups Do Their Work?

What role do interest groups play in strengthening individual polities? Political scientists, like the general public, seem to be of two minds on this subject. Some have argued that all politics consists of the struggle among groups and the best system is the one that best protects the rights of free association and intergroup bargaining. Groups serve the interests of individuals far better than individuals are capable of serving themselves, say these political scientists, and those who find no suitable group should form one for themselves. Groups that are able to influence governments deserve to do so; they have shown the strength of their cause on the battleground of politics.[31] This theory of the relationship between groups and government is called **pluralism.**

Other political scientists, however, have been far less optimistic, and find the tenets of pluralism to be naive and unrealistic. Known as *elite theorists*, they trace their intellectual roots to the work of the late sociologist C. Wright Mills, whose book, *The Power Elite*, charged that effective control of power in the United States was in the hands of the wealthy and other powerful groups in society. Elite theorists point out the difficulties many underrepresented groups face in attempting to organize, given lack of time, energy, or political freedom (or all three), as well as the particular advantages the better-organized groups may have had in achieving that status.[32] Government oppression may be sustained by the more powerful segments of public opinion; in states where women, racial minorities, or immigrant workers are openly denied equal rights with other citizens, the control of the dominant groups over the shaping of public opinion can sometimes lead even the oppressed to believe their treatment is inevitable and just.

On the other hand, interest groups that seek support for "acceptable" causes may find that almost any tactics they use to gain their ends are tolerated, if not officially approved. Vigilante groups, whether composed of cowboys lynching horse rustlers in the Old West of the United States, armed guerrillas executing drug dealers in Medellín, Colombia, or revolutionary crusaders meting out summary justice to discredited leaders in postcommunist Romania, are an example of groups using illegal means to accomplish socially approved ends.[33] Even when the ends accomplished are not acceptable to a broader public, illegal means may be tolerated and even abetted by agencies officially responsible for their elimination. Under the ultraconservative leadership of J. Edgar Hoover, the U.S. Federal Bureau of Investigation not only failed to curb the known illegal activities of the Ku Klux Klan but even helped the Klan organize forty-one chapters in North Carolina.[34]

Finally, say some antipluralists, even people who are able to achieve significant roles in effective and well-established pressure groups are not necessarily adequately represented in the political process. After all, citizenship means a concern for national policy and practice that extends beyond the range of one's liveliest personal interests. Short-term personal interests may indeed be best served by joining specific groups, but for the broader concerns and responsibilities of true citizenship, a broader, more all-encompassing form of political organization, such as a social movement or a political party, is required.

A SPECIAL PROBLEM OF INTEREST GROUP BEHAVIOR: EXTRACONSTITUTIONALISM

Let us introduce the problem of extraconstitutional behavior by interest groups with an example or two, starting with one from Southeast Asia. When General Sukarno and his supporters ousted the Dutch in Indonesia after World War II, they had so much financial aid from Indonesian business interests that the new regime was considered to be "mortgaged" from the start. To this day the business community remains, according to Ulf Sundhausen, "relatively small and comparatively rich in a sea of poverty."[35]

Here's another example, from another continent, and about another interest. In Colombia, the Catholic church is one of the largest landowners and 90 percent of Colombians are Catholic. This makes the church a powerful force and ensures that its views on matters political are given close attention. The church has almost exclusive control of education, is a strong voice in determining social welfare policies, and has periodically influenced the government to engage in severe persecution of the minority Protestant population. There are reform-minded progressives within the Colombian Catholic hierarchy, but whether conservatives or progressives are dominant, the fact remains that state policy in such matters is determined by clerical rather than secular leadership.[36]

Finally, an international illustration. The agreement made among Sweden, the United States, and Liberia for the creation of the Liberian American Swedish Minerals Company (LAMCO) geared the marketing of Liberia's high-grade iron ore to an unrealistically low price that benefited a chief purchaser, Bethlehem Steel Corporation; ensured that abnormally low taxes would be paid to the Liberian government; and established several means of distributing profits to Swedish and American stockholders before allocating the remainder to the partner nations, including Liberia.[37]

As these three examples should suggest, sometimes certain groups grow so powerful that they usurp the power of constitutionally established governments. Extraconstitutional power is exercised when groups external to the government are able to exert *so much pressure* on the agents of government that the government has — or believes it has — *no choice but to comply*. In such cases the decision-making powers of government have been appropriated by powerful interests, and the government itself — that is, those persons who occupy all the constitutionally prescribed posts in government — no longer governs, or at least not exclusively. Now it often simply carries out the decisions made elsewhere. The two kinds of group that have most commonly assumed this degree of political power are business and organized religion.

Business as an Extraconstitutional Force

The power of business to set government policy varies according to the kind of political system, the kind of economic system, and the nature of the popular culture, but it is found throughout the world. This is not a new phenomenon, although it has accelerated a great deal in our own century, and particularly since World War II. Even before the outbreak of World War I, major German industrial and financial leaders who had established close ties with Kaiser Wilhelm II were able to persuade him of the importance of raising the level of German armaments to unprecedented heights. These industrialists included the armaments manufacturer Friedrich Alfred Krupp, who "made good use of Wilhelm's favorite idea that Germany needed a strong army."[38] A similar relationship between Japanese shipping interests and the Japanese imperial government during the 1870s helped account for the rise of the Mitsubishi Company, whose power to resist government regulation (see p. 000) has made it another borderline case of extraconstitutionality.[39]

Even fully socialized systems have not proved to be immune to extraconstitutional business influence. In such systems, *business*, in the sense of independent commercial interests, ceases to exist; the state assumes control of the means of production, and the business of business (like all economic planning) is done by employees of the state. The state-employed managers are expected to remain subordinate to the state. However, if they nevertheless manage somehow to make policy on their own, they are assuming an extraconstitutional role.

Does it ever happen? Of course it does. Until the fall of communism in most of the former Soviet bloc, the evidence was hard to find simply because political infighting in such systems received so little publicity.[40] However, once the old system began to crumble apart, it became apparent that in fact one of the main reasons for the fall of communist regimes was public disgust with the use party officials made of the system for their own personal aggrandizement. According to Pavel Voshchanov, a spokesperson for Russian President Boris Yeltsin, when party leaders realized a market economy was inevitable, they began setting up independent commercial ventures for themselves as early as 1988. Voshchanov claims that "the managing department of the Central Committee alone had control of more than sixty major facilities, with a total value of 1.3 billion rubles ($18.6 million). Much more belonged to those groups on the lower levels — the provincial, city and district party committees."[41] Furthermore, the corrupt practices of these new "robber barons" have apparently continued in the aftermath of the Yeltsin presidency. According to a U.S. observer, the Russian leader has issued decrees facilitating the process by which "yesterday's communist bureaucrats are simply converting themselves into the CEOs and owners of the Russia of tomorrow."[42]

Similar processes appear to be at work in China, where senior party and government officials who benefit from nepotism, favoritism, and corruption are known as "princelings" by a resentful population. As China seeks to encourage free enterprise within the context of the continuing authoritarian rule of the communist party, some efforts have been made to bring such corruption to an end, but other forms are ready to take their place. According to Walter L. Keats, the ancient system of *guanxi* (relationships) that has always controlled Chinese interpersonal relationships is experiencing a revival as party bureaucrats reveal confidential information to vendors with whom they have close relationships or allow them to ignore rules others must obey, all in exchange for favors that range from invitations to visit abroad to outright money bribes.[43] China has an unusually elaborate system for contending against such crimes (see Figure 7.1). But when the criminals are themselves members of the government, who will guard the guards?

Another way private business may have an undue influence on government policy is simply to refuse to play — that is, to take its money and its business elsewhere when the home government is not to its liking. When Britain's Labour Party took power in 1945, it stimulated a flight of British capital into other nations' economies. The party itself was later to estimate that between 1947 and 1949 over £645 million (approximately $2.4 billion) left Britain. Less than half of that was actually invested elsewhere; the remainder was simply "hot" money, the party stated, "quitting Britain because its owners disliked the Labour Government's policy . . . or were engaged in currency speculation."[44] When socialist regimes fight back by imposing heavy penalties for transferring money out of the nation, private business may refuse to make significant levels of investment altogether, preferring to wait for an expected change of command back to procapitalist hands. In either case, the expected high levels of unemployment are likely to impose strong pressures on the government to modify any policies the private sector finds repugnant.

In contemporary times, the capacity of modern business to withdraw its marbles from the national game is greatly heightened by the emergence and development of the **transnational corporation** (**TNC**, sometimes referred to as the **multinational corporation**, or **MNC**). The TNC is a cluster of businesses located in several different nations but owned and managed by the same people. Although they may have headquarters in a single nation (the United States and Japan are the first and second largest centers of transnational corporations), they carry out important management as well as production activities around the globe.[45]

TNCs are in some ways reminiscent of **cartels**, associations of businesses formed in the early twentieth century to establish national or international monopolies over particular raw materials or manufactured goods. However, despite their power, cartels depended in part on being able to maintain supportive economic and fiscal policies in the nations where they were headquartered. They were thus vulnerable to shifting political fortunes and the concomitant fluctuations in national policy. The modern TNC differs from the cartel in that it is more interested in expanding its profits than in establishing a monopoly, and it is a far more independent network of in-

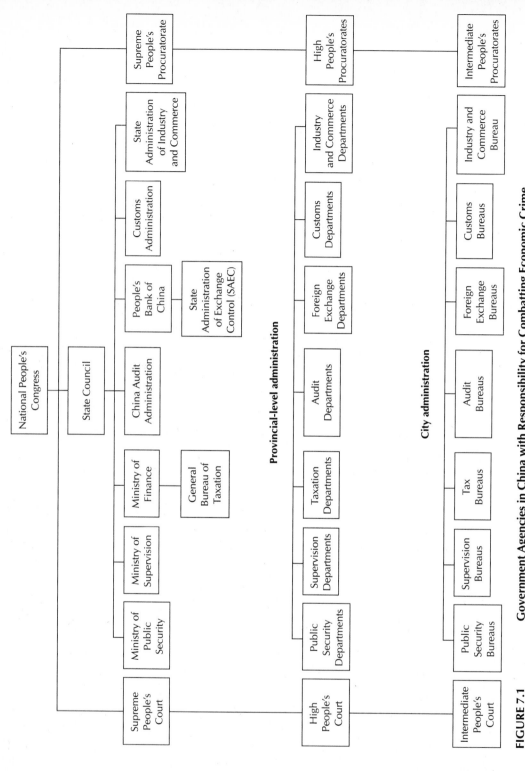

FIGURE 7.1 **Government Agencies in China with Responsibility for Combatting Economic Crime**

Source: Mitchell A. Silk, "Economic Crime in China," *China Business Review* (January/February 1988), p. 28. Reprinted with the permission of the *China Business Forum*, the U.S.–China Business Council, Washington, D.C.

vestment, research, productive, and distributive institutions. Some transnational corporations have become extremely large, with gross annual sales larger than the gross national products of many nations (see Table 7.1).[46] The ease with which TNCs can transfer monies and activities from nation to nation — and the fiscal pressures they can bring to bear on both national economies and the private bank accounts of all too human government officials — can make it almost impossible for individual governments to bring them under the effective control of national policy institutions, or for labor unions, normally functioning within a single nation and subject to its regulations, to bargain with them effectively.[47] As a consequence, TNCs sometimes engage "in a variety of injurious actions that would have been violations of criminal, regulatory, or civil law in their

TABLE 7.1 **Ranking of Countries and Corporations According to Size of Annual Product, 1993**

Rank	Economic Entity	$US (billions)
1	United States	6387.7
2	Japan	3926.7
3	Germany	1903
4	France	1289.2
5	Italy	1135
6	United Kingdom	1042.7
7	China	581.1
8	Canada	574.9
9	Brazil	472
10	Russia	348.4
11	Korea, South	338.1
12	Mexico	325
13	Netherlands	316.4
14	Australia	310
15	India	262.8
16	Switzerland	254.1
17	Argentina	244
18	Sweden	216.3
19	Belgium	213.4
20	Austria	183.5
21	Denmark	137.6

Continued

TABLE 7.1   *Continued*

Rank	Economic Entity	$US (billions)
22	Indonesia	137
23	**GENERAL MOTORS**	133.6
24	Saudi Arabia	128.4
25	Turkey	126.3
26	Thailand	120.2
27	South Africa	118.1
28	Norway	113.5
29	**FORD MOTOR CO.**	108.5
30	Hong Kong	104.7
31	**EXXON**	97.8
32	Finland	96.2
33	**ROYAL DUTCH/SHELL GROUP**	95.1
34	Poland	87.3
35	**TOYOTA MOTOR**	85.3
36	Portugal	77.7
37	Greece	76.7
38	Israel	72.6
39	**HITACHI**	68.6
40	**IBM**	62.7
41	**MATSUSHITA ELECTRIC INDUSTRIAL**	61.4
42	**GENERAL ELECTRIC**	60.8
43	Malaysia	60.1
44	**DAIMLER BENZ**	59.1
45	Venezuela	58.9
46	**MOBIL**	56.6
47	Singapore	55.4
48	Philippines	54.6
49	**NISSAN MOTOR**	53.8
50	Pakistan	53.3
51	**BRITISH PETROLEUM**	52.5
52	**SAMSUNG**	51.3
53	**PHILIP MORRIS**	50.6
54	**IRI**	50.5
55	**SIEMENS**	50.4
56	**VOLKSWAGEN**	46.3
57	Ireland	44.9
58	New Zealand	44.7
59	Algeria	44.3
60	**CHRYSLER**	43.6
61	**TOSHIBA**	42.9
62	Chile	42.5
63	**UNILEVER**	41.8
64	**NESTLE**	38.9

TABLE 7.1   *Continued*

Rank	Economic Entity	$US (billions)
65	United Arab Emirates	38.7
66	**ELF AQUITANE**	37
67	Egypt	36.7
68	**HONDA MOTOR**	35.8
69	**ENI**	34.8
70	**FIAT**	34.7
71	**SONY**	34.6
72	**TEXACO**	34.4
73	Hungary	34.3
74	Kuwait	34.1
75	Nigeria	34
76	Peru	34
77	**NEC**	33.2
78	**E.I. DUPONT DE NEMOURS**	32.6
79	**CHEVRON**	32.1
80	**PHILIPS ELECTRONICS**	31.7
81	**DAEWOO**	30.9
82	**PROCTOR & GAMBLE**	30.4
83	**RENAULT**	30
84	**FUJITSU**	29.1
85	**MITSUBISHI ELECTRIC**	28.8
86	**ABB ASEA BROWN BOVERI**	28.3
87	Czech Republic	28.2
88	**HOESCHST**	27.8
89	**ALCATEL ALSTHOM**	27.6
90	**MITSUBISHI MOTORS**	27.3
91	**PEMEX**	26.6
92	Libya	26.5
93	Bangledesh	25.9
94	**MITSUBISHI HEAVY INDUSTRIES**	25.8
95	**PEUGEOT**	25.7
96	**NIPPON STEEL**	25.5
97	Romania	25.4
98	**AMOCO**	25.3
99	Puerto Rico	25.3
100	**BOEING**	25.3

Sources: Country information is from Britannica 1996 Book of the Year (Chicago: Encyclopedia Britanica, Inc., 1996), pp. 792–796. Industry sales information is from Hoovers Handbook of World Business 1995–1996 (Austin, Tx: The Reference Press, 1995), pp. 28–29. Similar charts have been developed by many authors; to my knowledge the first one appeared in Abdul A. Said and Liuz R. Simmons, eds., *The New Sovereigns: Multinational Corporations as World Powers* (Englewood Cliffs, N.J.: Prentice-Hall, 1975), pp. 214–215.

home countries."[48] They have made illegal contributions to political parties, offered bribes to local officials, and refused to comply with the laws and regulations of the host nation. In one well-documented example, the International Telephone and Telegraph Company worked with the U.S. Central Intelligence Agency to try to prevent the election of Salvador Allende as president of Chile, and then, having failed in that endeavor, tried various means to remove him from power (a feat the CIA eventually accomplished on its own).[49]

Why should any polity allow so independent an entity to establish itself within its borders in the first place? The answer is that the advantages can be great, especially to less developed nations. TNCs bring in technology otherwise unavailable and involve the host nations in new levels of international trade, with profit to many. They often establish fairer standards of treatment for workers and promote desirable social, political, and economic change. They take economic risks that indigenous commercial interests could not afford, setting up in difficult conditions and forgoing profits for several years until the enterprise is well established.

But there are, of course, serious arguments against permitting the unchecked growth of TNCs. If they offer higher wages to skilled workers than the national average for comparable jobs, they may drive indigenous companies out of business. If they do not, they are perpetrating exploitation of cheap labor and often racist social patterns as well. The economic arrangements they make with the leaders of local governments often contribute to the evolution of a small wealthy elite, and so to growing class conflict within the host nation. They prevent the development of the more diversified economy needed by the local population by insisting on contracts ensuring their own supply of raw materials and the host nation's excessive use of imported technology. They hinder the development of local expertise by bringing in too many foreign experts. They impede the development of self-sufficiency by encouraging false dependencies on foreign imports. And, of course, they may simply insist on contracts that are harshly unfair to the host nation. (See the example of Bethelehem Steel, p. 237).

Whether good or bad, however, TNCs are a global fact of life. They are one of the clearest signs of the increasing interdependence of the human polity, and one of the most powerful forces helping to create that interdependence. Individual governments *do* have ways to curb their power, from driving hard bargains when original contracts are signed or must be renewed, to monitoring and screening investors and ownership, to rigorous taxation and investment policies, to outright nationalization.[50] But in the long run the only satisfactory solution for establishing sufficient controls over the extraconstitutional activities of transnational corporations may be the strengthening of transnational government — a topic we will return to toward the end of the book.

Organized Religion as an Extra-constitutional Force

It is important to be clear that when organized religion takes over — or plays a dominant role in — the functions of the state, its behavior as an interest group is not necessarily extraconstitutional. Many nations have decided either to establish outright *theocracies* or to give organized religion a strong constitutional role in governance. A **theocracy** is a state ruled by clergy, priests, or other religious leaders. The ancient kingdom of Tibet was a theocracy until it was compelled to become part of China in 1965. The Dalai Lama, a person chosen in accordance with religious traditions and ceremonies as the reincarnation of his predecessor, ruled with the assistance of two prime ministers, one a monk and the other a layman, plus a four-member Bka'-shag (Council of Ministers) to supervise home affairs, foreign affairs, defense, and economic affairs. The remaining structures of government, including a bicameral legislature, were similarly divided between religious leaders and lay persons. The Dalai Lama was the final authority in all matters. He decided what laws should be promulgated and what officials appointed to high office. (Today the Dalai Lama has many of the same powers, but these can only be exercised over the Tibetan refugee community in India, and only with the concurrence of the host nation.[51])

Although absolute theocracies are now hard to find, numerous contemporary states, including Israel and most Islamic polities, have decided to combine the religious and the secular in a more or less seamless web of regulation; here again, there is nothing unconstitutional in the role of organized religion. The Islamic religion, founded in the seventh century C.E., has consistently been closely associated with political governance. In the sixteenth century, when the Ottoman empire was at its peak and the rule of Islam extended from deep inside what is now Iran, across Asia Minor and north Africa, across the European Balkans, and up to what is now Austria, the sultan's power to rule was based entirely on his role as caliph, successor to the Prophet of God, overlord of all the Muslims. In contemporary Islamic states, which cover most of the same territory, excluding Israel and all southern European states except Turkey, but now including Iran, Pakistan, and Afghanistan, the tradition of combining the state and religion remains strong. Religious guides, known as *imams*, interpret the Koran and make sure Shari'a (Islamic law) is always given precedence. They are normally appointed, promoted, and paid their salaries by the state; there is no separate religious clergy.[52]

In other polities, however, the dominant tendency today is to insist on the complete or nearly complete separation of church and state, at least in constitutional theory. In some cases, the threat to this kind of constitution comes from its own internal contradictions: How can a polity which protects individual freedoms prohibit the political activities of religious political parties and movements whose goal is to change that constitution altogether? The repressive use of emergency law to restrict the activities of Islamic fundamentalists in Egypt may, some commentators argue, have done more to stimulate than to eliminate terrorist activity by such believers against the state.[53]

In other cases, the secular state has been a willing tool in the sacrifice of its own independence to religious leadership. In Latin America the leaders of the Roman Catholic hierarchy in each nation usually help direct the course of political events, whether the formal government is in civilian or military hands (see the Colombian example, p. 237). The relationship between church and state has been particularly interesting in Mexico. After that nation achieved independence from Spain in 1821, the Catholic church found itself both weakened and strengthened. The church was weaker because it was, after all, a Spanish institution, which meant not only that anticlericalism became in a sense patriotic, but also that many bishops, monks, and nuns returned to Spain. It was stronger because despite these difficulties it was an older and better established institution than the new government itself. By linking itself to conservative politicians, it managed to work out a modus vivendi (way of living) over the years, never entirely secure but far from powerless. A few examples make clear the extent of its extraconstitutional power.

- The Mexican constitution states that education is a function of the state, except when delegated to private schools with a nonreligious format. The church in fact administers an elaborate school system of its own without government interference.
- Seminarians are required, like everyone else, to fulfill a year of military service. In practice, these are weekend training sessions at the seminary.
- Officially, all church property belongs to the state. However, local communities are allowed to designate land for the construction of churches, and these arrangements are sanctioned by the government "even," notes Claude Pomerleau, "when the community has illegally seized government or private property." [54]

In addition, although in general the Mexican government does not allow "organized dissent that poses a realistic alternative to the regime," church leaders have been allowed to support opposition party calls for democratization with no significant repercussions.[55]

Even in states where the official exercise of religion is forbidden or socially frowned on, religious political activism has proved possible. Poland's Roman Catholic church was an interesting case in point in the years leading up to the overthrow of the communist regime. Antigovernment forces such as the trade union Solidarnosc and its supporters consistently used attendance at Catholic ceremonies — most dramatically during the 1979 visit of the first Polish pope, John Paul II, to his homeland — as a means of demonstrating their political convictions. The church in turn functioned as a mediator, strongly supporting Solidarnosc and the people's right to free assembly and freedom of expression but at the same time seeking to induce all the contending forces — authorities, workers, and peasants —

to settle their disputes without violence. The Polish church was the one agency the state would allow to speak on behalf of the dissenting population, a role that gave it definite but limited extraconstitutional power.[56] Since the revolution, the Polish parliament has attempted to curb the power of the church, and 60 percent of Polish citizens believe that the church's influence in public life is "excessive." However, the first postrevolution president, Lech Walesa (whose own rise to power from underground labor leader to chief executive owed much to the church), succeeded in blocking any legislation that would have that effect throughout his tenure in office.[57]

The Media as an Extraconstitutional Force

Another institution that now plays a very specialized role in extraconstitutional politics is the media. It is true that even in nations where freedom of expression is protected and the media are relatively free to publish and broadcast what they wish, they must still depend on the continued good will of either government or commercial advertisers, and there are usually some restrictions on their right to publish seditious, licentious, or libelous materials. Nevertheless, within these limitations, broadcast agencies and the press are often able to interpret events and structure public opinion so as to leave elected governments no effective choice but to make — either directly or indirectly — the recommended response. When Walter Cronkite, the most respected American television news anchor of the 1970s, saw wire service reports that persuaded him it was time for the United States to withdraw from Vietnam, he hosted a documentary in which he openly called for no further increase in U.S. involvement and for immediate negotiations with the enemy. His comments were widely regarded as creating the first major impetus for shifting opinion in Congress as well as among the general public. As other leaders of the media followed suit, the support for government policy fell away slowly but surely, and U.S. withdrawal became first possible, then inevitable.[58] A few years later, the double role of the media in revealing the Watergate scandal *and* guiding the formation of public opinion about the event was similarly apparent and dramatic.[59]

The media's influence is so great in the United States (and indeed, in most other developed nations) that those in positions of power must plan their statements and activities with it in mind. If they cannot win both publicity and editorial approval for their performance, their chances of success are poor. In such cases they may decide that their only alternative is to exercise firm control over the media, either by limiting its access to news of government actions or by engaging in direct censorship. The method of limiting access was followed by President Ronald Reagan during the 1983 invasion of the small nation of Grenada. No reporters were allowed on the island until the U.S. forces had the situation well in hand, and even then no one representing the daily newspapers was included among the fifteen reporters admitted — all of whom were kept under strict military supervision. Four reporters who managed to land on Grenada the day of the invasion were placed on board the U.S.S. *Guam* and held incommunicado for eighteen hours.[61]

The success of such rigorous censorship led to similar controls during the Gulf War in 1991. A significant difference in the latter case was the reporting of the Cable News Network (CNN), especially at the beginning, when the new and technologically advanced network seemed to have better intelligence than the military. During an early press conference, General Colin L. Powell, then chairman of the Joint Chiefs of Staff, "gave a plug to CNN that implied that the Pentagon itself was relying on its television set for military information."[61] However, it was not long before CNN was as carefully walled off as all the others from news the government did not wish to have revealed, and Powell's successor, Maj. Gen. John M. Shalikashvili, publicly deplored the "CNN effect," noting the dangers when, as in later operations in Somalia and Haiti, there were "bright lights on the beach of Magadishu as Marines [were] attempting a night amphibious landing [and] hundreds of reporters [were] waiting in Port-au-Prince the night of the [planned but canceled] airborne assault."[62]

The temptation to find some way to keep the media under wraps is often great and sometimes apparently irresistible. As a study of the role of the media in the United States has pointed out, "the evidence is indisputable and overwhelming. The media influence the decisions and actions of politicians and officials, change their priorities, and can reduce their ability to control events."[63] But here again, the case is interestingly ambiguous: Can an agency exercising a constitutional *right* (freedom of expression) do so in a way to exercise intolerable control over the ability of other agencies to carry out their constitutional *duties*?

Can you think of other examples of media power that you find more worrisome than the efforts of journalists to report the entire truth about military engagements?

In any case, although business, religion and the media appear to be the three kinds of interest groups which most commonly and most powerfully usurp roles assigned constitutionally to the structures of government, they are certainly not the only institutions that try to play that role. All powerful interest groups, including educational institutions, professional associations, trade unions, public agencies, or so-called public interest groups, may attempt to carry pressure politics to the point where it is in effect itself making policy within the domain that affects it, and may succeed. Furthermore, some agencies within the government itself may make so strong an effort to influence other government agencies (directly and via the public) that they themselves sometimes appear to be going beyond their appropriate constitutional limits. Consider, for example, the efforts (and expenses) of the Public Relations Division of the U.S. Department of Defense, which not only sends high-ranking officers to argue before legislative and other governmental bodies for its budgetary needs but also maintains a continuous flow of news releases, film clips and public exhibits to keep the American public supportive of those needs. To some this public relations effort appears an entirely appropriate exercise of the constitutional powers of the military; but others do not agree. What do you think?

VIOLENT REVOLUTIONARY ORGANIZATIONS

Not every group works peacefully to achieve its means. Some decide only violence will accomplish the ends they seek. But it is also true that not every revolutionary organization uses violence to pursue its goals. In politics, a **revolution** is any fundamental change in the political organization of a polity. An extremist political party, a fundamentalist religious organization, or a group of idealistic intellectuals seeking world government may all be bent on accomplishing such fundamental change, yet draw the line at the use of violence. However revolutionary their goals, such groups nevertheless fall into the category of interest group (see earlier) or political party (Chapter 8). Groups that are willing to use violence to achieve revolutionary change — perhaps by turning the clock backward, perhaps by inventing a "brave new world" — must be treated as a case apart. We will look at three subtypes: the terrorist group, the guerrilla organization, and the military mutiny.

Terrorist Groups

Terrorist groups are organizations that attempt to change the operation of government by using isolated and unpredictable acts of violence to induce fear of the consequences of *not* changing. Sometimes the attempt is made to instill fear in government officials, sometimes in ordinary citizens, and sometimes in both simultaneously (for example, by attacks on representatives of government in public places). If the focus is the ordinary citizen, the hope may be that the frightened populace will organize in more conventional ways to pressure the government to comply with the terrorists' demands. Leftwing terrorist groups sometimes operate on the principle that their activities will cause such widespread government repression of civil liberties in the course of efforts to end the terrorism as to arouse support for a popular revolution. Rightwing terrorists may entertain the hope that their activities will produce a military takeover, establishing a government more likely to function in accord with their values; many of the French rebels who launched terrorist attacks in the early 1960s in a vain attempt to prevent the granting of independence to Algeria were themselves military men.[65]

On the other hand, terrorist groups also often form around a political goal that is not identifiable as left or right: the goal of national autonomy. What the Irish Republican Army, the Basque Homeland and Liberty movement, and the Palestinian Liberation Organization all have had in common, as terrorist organizations, is the passionate desire to free themselves from what they consider to be intolerable foreign domination, to occupy

FIGURE 7.2   **International Terrorist Incidents over Time, 1975–1994**

Source: U.S. Department of State, *Patterns of Global Terrorism 1994* (Washington, D.C.: U.S. Government Printing Office, April 1995), p. 65. The graph does not include intra-Palestinian violence.

a homeland of their own, and to exercise popular sovereignty. Such a group may pursue its goals on behalf of an ungrateful populace that would much rather continue the present arrangements than use such means.[66]

Terrorism has been a mode of demanding change since time immemorial. But it has clearly experienced a resurgence in recent years, particularly in what is known as *international terrorism* — that is, terrorism directed by citizens of one nation against those of another in an effort to alter relations between political systems. Although terrorist groups seldom succeed in creating revolutionary change, they often push leaders weary of battle and people weary of fear long distances in the desired direction. Governments may try to distinguish between giving in to immediate demands (such as the release of political prisoners) and giving more thoughtful consideration to the issues of social justice that terrorists sometimes raise. Students of terrorist behavior seek to distinguish among the fanatical true believer, the simple criminal who conceals a desperate quest for personal gain in the rhetoric of a cause, and the paid employee of a nation-state that has adopted the sponsoring of terrorist acts as a means of achieving foreign policy goals.[66] New advances in the psychology of terrorism hold promise, as do improved security measures in airports, embassies, and other likely target sites. But as Figure 7.2 makes clear, we are very far from eliminating the quest for change by terrorist violence.

Guerrilla organizations use terrorist tactics but also set up institutions of alternative government and seek to take over altogether. Here Tupac Amaru Revolutionary Movement military chief Jaime Castillo Petruzzi shouts angrily as he is presented to the media by anti-terrorist agents in Lima, Peru. (Reuters/Marie Hippenmeyer/Archive Photos)

Guerrilla Warfare Organizations

We began to grow more conscious of the necessity for a definitive change in the life of the people. . . . The struggle shall be long and harsh, and its front shall be in the guerrillas' hide-out, in the cities, in the homes of the fighters . . . in the massacred rural population, in the villages and cities destroyed by the bombardments of the enemy. They are pushing us into this struggle; there is no alternative; we must prepare it and we must decide to undertake it."[67]

So spoke Che Guevara, the idealistic Latin American revolutionary who helped bring Fidel Castro to power in Cuba and then lost his life in revolutionary struggle against an oppressive dictatorship in Bolivia. Like Guevara, many guerrilla warfare leaders believe nonviolent means have proved to be inadequate to end the suffering of oppressed peoples. Violence becomes the necessary last resort. *Guerrilla warfare* is similar to the activity of terrorist groups in that it too seeks to inspire fear, and thereby change, and in that the perpetrators are highly unlikely to have either the personnel or the weaponry necessary for confronting an entire army openly. But there are important differences. Guerrilla warriors tend to establish headquarters away from urban centers and to set up institutions of alternative government, including those for education and health as well as military training. They are ready, they claim, to take over the established government altogether, not merely to compel change or to bring it down. They use standard military weapons as well as the equipment of the urban terrorist. They normally try to visit acts of violence only on those identified as the enemy or as persons who actively aid the enemy, and they are more likely to seek and even to expect (but not necessarily to get) widespead popular support for their activities. They make themselves easier to join.

The Military Mutiny   The *military mutiny* is a short-lived organization, usually led by high-ranking officers, who seek to accomplish a coup d'etat, the overthrow of the civilian government by force of arms. Such mutinous organizations within the military may be motivated by private or public goals, or a combination of the two. Private grievances may include dissatisfaction with levels of pay, promotion policies, or perceived inadequacies in state support for the military. The Ghanaian army's overthrow of Kwame Nkrumah was said to have been motivated in part by the fact that the president's "Own Guard Regiment" received better pay and equipment than the regular army. As one of the leaders of the coup wrote later, "One day [the regular soldiers] were to pay for their electricity; the next day they were to lose their training allowances; the following day they were to lose their travelling facilities. We all wondered what was happening to us."[68]

However, even when private complaints help motivate the takeover, the military always has public purposes as well. Military men live in a military culture and often come to hold nonmilitary ways in considerable contempt. Politicians may appear to them to be universally corrupt, demagogic, and inefficient. Personal qualities that can be tolerated in affluent, established nations become more difficult to endure in poor young nations, such as those of Africa after World War II, where coup succeeded coup with sometimes bewildering speed. In such a setting, the army often believes it has the training, the skills, and the values to set things right — that is, to establish stability and order, national unity, and rapid modernization. Yet once in power, its lack of institutionalized contact with the general population and its habit of resolving issues by force of arms often leads to a government more oppressive and more corrupt than any civilian government that may have preceded it. The abuse of human rights by the Haitian military junta after taking power in 1991 is a case in point.[69]

SUMMARY AND CONCLUSION

Political organization exists throughout the human polity. Even where participatory politics is banned or confined to state-sponsored directive structures, the human need to articulate and act on behalf of shared interests will find a way to make itself felt by those in power. Types of organization may be as rudimentary as the East Bay Community Track and Field Association or as complex as a transnational finance corporation, as supportive to government as the latest "Committee to Re-Elect the President" or as hostile as the Red Brigades; as long lasting as the American Democratic party (which traces its origins back to the original struggle over ratifying the Constitution) or as short lived as an ad hoc coalition to seek asylum for a poet who is a political refugee from his homeland; as close to the grassroots as the Potrero Neighborhood Merchants Association for Fairer Taxes or as remote from its membership as the Coalition on National Priorities and Military Policy, a group whose policy decisions are made, like those of most public interest groups, by a narrow leadership corps. Wherever human beings congregate, groups will form, and sometimes some of these groups will seek to affect the operation of whatever government exists.

Institutions other than the constitutionally mandated ones sometimes usurp the policymaking roles a nation's constitution prescribes for particular government institutions. The power of the business world to do so varies according to the kind of political system, the kind of economic system, and the size of the business in question. Transnational corporations, giant businesses that operate in several nations at once, may be able not only to control the relevant policymaking in those nations but also to substitute their own decision-making processes altogether. Religious interests sometimes control political processes constitutionally, but in states where the religious and the secular are constitutionally separate, churches are often permitted to carry out activities that any strict reading of the constitution and the statutory laws would show to be illegal. In socialist states organized religion may play a mediating role between the state and forces of dissent, thereby exercising an extraconstitutional influence on government policy.

Not every group works peacefully to achieve its means. Terrorist groups, guerrilla organizations, and the military mutiny are all different forms of violent revolutionary organization. Terrorist groups use violence to induce fear of the consequences of *not* changing. Guerrilla groups use it in an effort to take over the established government altogether and normally try to limit their attacks to those seen as the enemy or as persons who actively aid the enemy. The military mutiny is a short-lived organization, usually led by high-ranking officers, who seek to overthrow the civilian government by force of arms.

The forms of political organization we adopt inevitably influence the quality of life within individual nation-states and in the human polity at large. How well we are able to conduct our affairs, individually and collectively, depends to a large extent on how well our interests are articulated, compromised, and conveyed to those in power. When some interests are labeled out-of-bounds without fair hearing; when political organization takes the form of nontargeted rioting; when groups fall under the sway of leaders who use their resources for ends contrary to those of the membership; or when intragroup and intergroup compromises prove impossible to reach and maintain, the damage done will extend beyond those citizens whose interests are immediately affected. For unaccommodated interests, when they are seriously held, rarely dissipate, and the means used by the people who hold them to seek satisfaction are likely to grow progressively more disruptive to the entire political system. Nor do the disturbances that stem from failures of political organization necessarily stop at national borders. One of the chief causes of conflict in the human polity at large is the migration of unresolved internal disputes into the international arena, as representatives of the unaccommodated seek living space, material wealth, personal dignity, or whatever collective good they believe they cannot find in adequate supply at home.

Selected Readings

Alexander, Herbert E. and Rei Shiratori. *Comparative Political Finance Among Democracies.* Boulder: Westview Press, 1994. A comprehensive study of money in elections, with fourteen case studies from thirteen countries.

Berry, Jeffrey M. *The Interest Group Society,* 3rd ed. New York: Longman, 1997. The methods and influence of lobbyists in the United States, placed in the context of democratic theory, and including chapters on the rise of issue networks and on the relationship between corporate wealth and political advocacy.

Biggar, Nigel, Jamie S. Scott and William Schweiker. *Cities of Gods.* Westport: Greenwood Press, 1986. A discussion of Judaism, Christianity, and Islam and of political phenomena such as radicalism, human rights, and the state.

Allan J. Cigler and Burdett A. Loomis, eds. *Interest Group Politics,* 3rd ed. Washington, D.C.: Congressional Quarterly, 1991. An examination of the role played by such groups as labor unions, the American Agriculture Movement and Common Cause in the U.S. political process, with a consideration of how such groups are adjusting to increased competition for congressional attention.

Clawson, Dan, Alan Neustadt and Denise Scott. *Money Talks: Corporate PACS and Political Influence.* New York: Basic Books, 1992. How political action committees raise money and use political donations to influence public policy.

Gies, David L., J. Steven Ott and Jay M. Shafritz, eds.

The Nonprofit Organization: Essential Readings. Pacific Grove, CA.: Brooks/Cole, 1990. An in-depth look at the functions, roles, institutions, issues, traditions, and values that shape nonprofit organizations, intended for managers and board members as well as for students.

Ginsberg, Benjamin and Martin Shefter. *Politics by Other Means: The Declining Importance of Elections in America.* New York: Basic Books, 1990. An interesting look at paralysis in the U.S. government, which the authors suggest is due to the weakening of electoral politics.

Hiebert, Ray Eldon and Carol Reuss, eds. *The Impact of Mass Media.* New York and London: Longman, 1988. A series of essays debating the role of the mass media in modern political and social systems.

Manzetti, Luigi. *Institutions, Parties and Coalitions in Argentine Politics.* Pittsburg: Pittsburgh University Press, 1994. How special interests' competition for resources have prevented long-term political and economic stability in Argentina.

Petracca, Mark P. *The Politics of Interests: Interest Groups Transformed.* Boulder: Westview Press, 1992. A study of how and why people form interest groups and the role they play in the United States.

Poland, James M. *Understanding Terrorism: Groups, Strategies, and Responses.* New York: Simon and Schuster, 1988. Examines the structural organization of extremist and terrorist groups, including cases from the Middle East and Northern Ireland.

Villa-Vicensio, Charles. *Between Christ and Caesar: Clas-*

6 6

sic and Contemporary Texts on Church and State. Grand Rapids, MI: William B. Erdman, 1986. The relationship between church and state in doctrine and practice.

Walker, Jack L. Mobilizing Interest Groups in America: Patrons, Professions and Social Movements. Ann Arbor, MI: University of Michigan Press, 1991. A theory of interest group formation and maintenance emphasizing strategies and modes of mobilization.

Wilson, Graham K. Business and Politics, 2nd ed. Chatham, N.J.: Chatham House, 1985. A comparative examination of the relationship between business and politics in various countries, including the United States, the former West Germany and Japan. Discusses neocorporatist practices and the role of transnational corporations.

Notes

1. Such groups often decline almost as spontaneously as they form, once the crisis is past. The East Bay Community Track and Field Association never met again after its victory was won.

2. Jon Woronoff, *Japan as Anything but Number One* (Armont, N.Y.: M. E. Sharpe, 1991), p. 159.

3. Kwame Nkrumah, *The Autobiography of Kwame Nkrumah* (Edinburgh: Thomas Nelson, 1959), pp. 40–83.

4. Jonathan Hartlyn, "Colombia: The Politics of Violence and Accommodation," in Larry Diamond, Juan J. Linz, and Seymour Martin Lipset, eds., *Democracy in Developing Countries, vol. 4: Latin America* (Boulder, Colo.: Lynne Rienner, 1989), pp. 305–306, 319–20.

5. This is the definition adopted by the members of the organized section on Parties and Other Political Organizations of the American Political Science Association.

6. Robert Salisbury, "An Exchange Theory of Interest Groups," in Robert Salisbury, ed., *Interest Group Politics in America* (New York: Harper & Row, 1970), pp. 47–55. In this now classic work, Salisbury adopted a set of distinctions first made by Peter B. Clark and James Q. Wilson in "Incentive Systems: A Theory of Organizations," *Administrative Science Quarterly* 6 (Sept. 1961): 129–66.

7. Kay Lehman Schlozman and John T. Tierney, *Organized Interests and American Democracy* (New York: Harper & Row, 1986), p. 102.

8. Ronald J. Hrebenar and Ruth K. Scott, *Interest Group Politics in America* (Englewood Cliffs, N.J.: Prentice Hall, 1982), p. 18.

9. When Soviet consumers during the Stalinist years refused to spend their money on theatrical productions burdened with heavy political content and thereby forced the government to provide more entertaining fare, they were acting, claims David Lane, who invented the term, as an amorphous interest group. David Lane, *Politics and Society in the USSR* (New York: Random House, 1970), p. 251. We have already referred to this kind of individual action that inadvertently becomes group action in Chapter 6 (see p. 186).

10. This type and the following three are drawn from Gabriel Almond and G. Bingham Powell, Jr., *Comparative Politics: A Development Approach* (Boston: Little, Brown, 1966), pp. 75–76. These authors use the word *anomic* to describe the groups we have here termed *spontaneous*. Although they say such groups lack "any set of regulating values or norms" (which would justify calling them anomic), in fact many of the examples they cite are groups that might claim with considerable justification that they are simply fighting for the avowed values of the society — racial justice, equitable distribution of the nation's wealth, patriotism, and so on. In any case, such groups usually defend some values, and so are not normless, as the term *anomic* would imply. *Spontaneous* is a better term for this kind of organization.

11. Anne Costain and W. Douglas Costain, "The Women's Lobby: Impact of a Movement on Congress," in Allan J. Cigler and Burdett A. Loomis, eds., *Interest Group Politics* (Washington, D.C.: Congressional Quarterly Press, 1983), pp. 191–216.

12. *Washington Post*, 19 Jan. 1991, A5, and 26 Jan. 1991, A13–18.

13. The last two have, of course, been strongly infused with Christian thought, but cannot be said to have been inspired to form by it. For a study of social movements, see Cyrus Ernesto Zirak-

zedeh, *Social Movements in Politics: A Comparative Study* (Essex, U.K.: Addison Wesley Longman, 1997).

14. Timothy Egan, "Industries Affected by Endangered Species," *New York Times*, 13 April 1995, A7.

15. For a recent review of consumer group activities, see Ardith Maney and Loree Bykerk, *Consumer Politics: Protecting Public Interests on Capital Hill* (Westport, Conn.: Greenwood, 1994).

16. Marilyn Werber Serafini, "Senior Schism," *National Journal* 27, no. 18 (6 May 1995): 1089–93.

17. Andrew S. McFarland, Common Cause: Lobbying in the Public Interest (Chatham, N.J.: Chatham House, 1984), pp. 6–13; Carol Matlack, "Animal-Rights Furor," *National Journal* 23 (7 Sept. 1991): 2143–46; and Joan Biskupic, "NRA, Gun-Control Supporters Take Aim at Swing Votes," *Congressional Quarterly Weekly Report* 49, no. 10 (9 Mar. 1991): 604–607.

18. Senator Boies Penrose, quoted in Carol S. Greenwald, *Group Power, Lobbying and Public Policy* (New York: Praeger, 1977), p. 144.

19. Herbert E. Alexander and Rei Shiratori, eds., *Comparative Political Finance Among the Democracies* (Boulder, Colo.: Westview, 1994), p. 6. The connection between contributions and high appointments in the executive branch is even less hidden: U.S. Commerce Secretary Robert A. Mosbacher, who had been finance chairman of President Bush's campaign, did not hesitate to protest publicly when he felt that too few other postelection appointments were being given to those who had made major contributions to the Republican victory.

20. Jane Fritsch, "Tobacco Companies Pump Cash into Republican Party's Coffers," *New York Times*, 13 Sept. 1995, A1, A12.

21. Quoted by Chuck Alston, "PACs' Independent Expenditures Slow Down," *Congressional Quarterly Weekly Report* 46 (5 Nov. 1988), 3186. The title of this article is misleading; the expenditures have not slowed down; what has slowed down is the rapid growth in the number of PACs, which mushroomed from 608 in 1974 to 4,009 in 1984.

22. Quoted in Alston, "PACs' Independent Expenditures," p. 3186.

23. Sven Steinmo and Jon Watts, "It's the Institutions, Stupid! Why Comprehensive National Health Insurance Always Fails in America," *Journal of Health Politics, Policy and Law* 20, no. 2 (Summer 1995): 364.

24. Stephen Engelberg, "Business Leaves the Lobby and Sits at Congress's Table," *New York Times*, 31 Mar. 1995, A1.

25. Jane Fritsch, "The Grass Roots, Just a Free Phone Call Away," *New York Times*, 23 June 1995, A1, A11.

26. *Wall Street Journal*, 7 Dec. 1989, 1.

27. In a study with interesting implications for the focus of group efforts, Benjamin Ginsberg and Martin Shefter suggest that the focus of political battles in the United States has now shifted away from parties and elections to the media, congressional investigations, and judicial proceedings. See their *Politics by Other Means: The Declining Importance of Elections in America* (New York: Basic Books, 1990).

28. William Safran, *The French Polity*, 3rd ed. (New York: Longman, 1991), pp 110–24.

29. For an interesting recent study, see James A. Dunn, Jr., "The French Highway Lobby: A Case Study in State-Society Relations and Policymaking," *Comparative Politics* 27, no. 3 (April 1995): 275–95.

30. Alfred A. Marcus, *Business and Society: Ethics, Government, and the World Economy* (Homewood, Ill.: Irwin, 1993), pp. 256–57. The largest Japanese conglomerate, Mitsubishi, owns "significant" portions of Mitsubishi Trust Bank, Tokyo Marine, Mitsubishi Heavy Industries, Mitsubishi Corporation, Mitsubishi Electric, Asahi Glass, Kirin Beer, and Mitsubishi Chemical. Other important *zaibatsu*, according to Marcus, are Mitsui, Sumitomo, and the banks Fuji, Sanawa and Dai-ichi Kang.

31. Arthur F. Bentley, *The Process of Government: A Study of Social Pressures* (Chicago: University of Chicago Press, 1908); David Truman, *The Governmental Process* (New York: Knopf, 1951); and Robert A. Dahl, *A Preface to Democratic Theory* (Chicago: University of Chicago Press, 1956).

32. Michael Margolis, "Democracy: American Style," in Graeme Duncan, ed., *Democratic Theory and Practice* (Cambridge: Cambridge University Press, 1983), pp. 125–26. See also C. Wright Mills, *The Power Elite* (Oxford: Oxford University Press, 1957).

33. Douglas Farsh, "Vigilantes Retake Slums of Médillin," in *Washington Post* (7 Dec. 1991), A17.

34. Michael Parenti, *Democracy for the Few* (New York: St. Martin's, 1988), p. 144.

35. Ulf Sundhausen, "Indonesia: Past and Present Encounters with Democracy," in Larry Diamond, Juan J. Linz, and Seymour Martin Lipset, *Democracy in Developing Countries: Latin America* (Boulder, Colo.: Lynne Reiner, 1989), pp. 138–39.

36. Daniel H. Levine, *Religion and Politics in Latin America: The Catholic Church in Venezuela and Colombia* (Princeton, N.J.: Princeton University Press, 1981).

37. Stewart Smith, *U.S. Neocolonialism in Africa* (New York: International, 1974), pp. 68–69.

38. Hans Jaeger, "Business and Government in Imperial Germany, 1871–1918," Keiichiro Nakagawa, ed., *Government and Business* (Tokyo: University of Tokyo Press, 1980), p. 142.

39. Takeaki Teratani, "Japanese Business and Government in the Takeoff Stage," in Nakagawa, *Government and Business*, pp. 58–59.

40. In one of the few works by a disillusioned communist to reach a worldwide audience prior to 1989, *The New Class*, Milovan Djilas (a Yugoslavian official who defected to the West in the 1950's) asserted that all communist bureaucrats, including those in managerial roles in industry, were directing public policy in their own, not the nation's, interests. They were able to give themselves, said Djilas, "special privileges and economic preference because of the administrative monopoly" they held in various economic enterprises, in sports and humanitarian organizations, and in other branches of the government bureaucracy. Milovan Djilas, *The New Class* (New York: Praeger, 1957), pp. 39, 46.

41. Pavel Voshchanov, "The Secret Business of the Communist Party," *World Press Review* 38 (January 1992): p. 22.

42. *Los Angeles Times*, 1 Mar. 1992, A1, A12.

43. Walter L. Keats, "Corruption and the China Trade," *China Business Review* (January/February 1988): 30. For a case study of an effort to bring down one family of "princelings," see Steven Mufson, "Web of Intrigue in Chinese Steel Firm Probe," *Washington Post*, 16 Mar. 1995, A29.

44. "Challenge to Britain," Labour Party Policy Statement, 1953, p. 6, cited in A. A. Rogow, *The Labour Government and British Industry, 1945–1951* (Ithaca, N.Y.: Cornell University Press, 1955), p. 36. See also Sidney Pollard, *The Wasting of the British Economy* (New York: St. Martin's, 1982), p. 88.

45. The United States' share in the "outward stocks" of foreign investment has in fact been on the decline while that of Canada, Germany, Japan and Switzerland have been rising. Charles W. Kegley, Jr. and Eugene R. Wittkopf, *World Politics: Trend and Transformation*, 3rd ed. (New York: St. Martin's, 1989), p. 163.

46. Keith Cowling and Roger Sugden, *Transnational Monopoly Capitalism* (Sussex, U.K.: Wheat-sheaf Books, 1987), p. 2.

47. Robert Reich, *The Work of Nations: Preparing Ourselves for 21st-Century Capitalism* (New York: Knopf, 1991).

48. Raymond J. Michatowski and Ronald C. Kramer, "The Space Between Laws: The Problem of Corporate Crime in a Transnational Context," *Social Problems* 34, no. 1 (Feb. 1987): 34.

49. Kegley and Wittkopf, *World Politics: Trend and Transformation*, p. 170.

50. Kathryn Sikkink, "Codes of Conduct for Transnational Corporations, The Case of the WHO/UNICEF Code," *International Organization* 40, no. 4 (Autumn 1986): 815–40.

51. C. W. Cassinelli and Roben B. Ekvall, *A Tibetan Principality: The Political System Of Sa Skya* (Ithaca, N.Y.: Cornell University Press, 1969), p. 5 and Claude B. Levenson, *The Dalai Lama* (London: Unwin Hyman, 1988), p. 115. Small-scale Christian theocracies have often existed within nation-states. In the sixteenth century, the Swiss city of Zurich fell under the sway of Huldreich Zwingli, a Protestant reformer who regarded the population as a Christian congregation under the rule of God, entitled to defend itself even by aggressive warfare in order to prevent interference by nearby Catholic cantons. In the same century, John Calvin established his version of the perfect Protestant community in nearby Geneva, excommunicating and banishing all Catholics who did not submit to his regime. Two hundred years later, Count Nikolaus Ludwig von Zinzendorf set up Moravian communities throughout Europe and the United States, communities that

were expected to be entirely self-regulating and self-supporting, and in which individuals belonged to "choirs" strictly ordered according to age, sex, and marital status. And in 1849, in a territory that now makes up most of Utah, California, Arizona, Nevada, and Colorado, American Mormons set up the Provisional State of Deseret, ruled by a Council of Fifty that "set up law courts, established counties, and incorporated several cities" and further assumed responsibility for "taking defense precautions, investigating food reserves, regulating the making of roads and fences, and supervising the collection of taxes for all these purposes." P. A. M. Taylor, *Expectations Westward: The Mormons and the Emigration of Their British Converts in the Nineteenth Century* (Ithaca, N.Y.: Cornell University Press, 1966), p. 64. See also Leonard J. Arrington and Davis Bitton, *The Mormon Experience: A History of the Latter-Day Saints* (New York: Knopf, 1979), pp. 105, 114.

52. Ergun Ozbudun, "Turkey: Crises, Interruptions, and Reequilibrations," in Diamond, Linz and Lipset, *Democracy in Developing Countries*, 3, Asia, p. 190. There are two main Islamic sects, Sunnite and Shiite; members of the former are particularly attached to the letter of the Qu'ran and to tradition. According to Marvin Zonis, "Islam has never relinquished its essential political claim. . . . Islam cannot achieve justice by individuals living 'justly' but only through an Islamic community, that is, a community whose social and political relationships are organized according to Islamic beliefs. . . . An Islamic political order is as much a part of Islam as is an Islamic ethical system." Nigel Biggar, Jamie S. Scott, and William Schweiker, eds., *Cities Of Gods: Faith, Politics and Pluralism in Judaism, Christianity and Islam* (New York: Greenwood Press, 1986), p. 197.

The Islamic tradition is particularly strong in Iran and Iraq. In other states in which the Muslim religion is widely dominant, such as Turkey, Indonesia, and Pakistan (which was formed in 1947 *as* an Islamic state), internal subdivisions, both religious and social, have somewhat weakened the role of religion in politics. Larry Diamond, "Introduction: Persistence, Erosion, Breakdown, and Renewal," in Diamond, Linz

and Lipset, *Democracy in Developing Countries vol.* 3: *Asia*, pp. 16–17.

53. Mamoun Fandy, "In Egypt, Rising Fundamentalist Threat," *Christian Science Monitor*, 19 June 1992, 19. For the predicament faced by secular states with large militant Islamic minorities, see Charles P. Wallace, "Muslim Tide Rising in the East," *Los Angeles Times*, 8 Aug. 1992, A1.

54. Claude Pomerleau, "The Changing Church in Mexico and Its Challenge to the State," *The Review of Politics* 43, no. 4 (Oct. 1981): 540–559.

55. Daniel C. Levy, "Mexico: Sustained Civilian Rule Without Democracy," in Larry Diamond, Juan J. Linz, and Seymour Martin Lipset, *Democracy in Developing Countries, vol.* 4: *Latin America,* p. 467.

56. Jan Nowak, "The Church in Poland," *Problems of Communism* 31 (Jan./Feb. 1982): 1–16.

57. *Washington Post,* 7 June 1991, A18.

58. Robert M. Entman and David L. Paletz, "The War in Southeast Asia: Tunnel Vision on Television," in William C. Adams, ed., *Television Coverage of International Affairs* (Norwood, N.J.: Ablex, 1982), pp. 181–98.

59. Gladys Engel Lang and Kurt Lang, *The Battle for Public Opinion: The President, the Press and the Polls during Watergate* (New York: Columbia University Press, 1983).

60. *Facts on File,* 4 Nov. 1983, 830. See also Gerry O'Sullivan, "Against the Grain," *Humanist* 522, no. 3 (May 1991): 39–42.

61. *New York Times,* 17 Jan. 1991, A15. For further accounts of government control of the media during the Gulf War, see O'Sullivan, "Against the Grain" and *New York Times,* 18 Jan. 1991, A7.

62. Debra Gersh Hernandez, "The Media's Impact on the Military," *Editor & Publisher* no. 19 (13 May 1995): 14.

63. David L. Paletz and Robert M. Entman, *Media Power Politics* (New York: The Free Press, 1981), p. 249.

64. William Rosenaw and Linda Head Flanagan, "Blood of the Condor: The Genocidal Talons of Peru's Shining Path, " *Policy Review* 59 (Winter 1992): pp. 82–85; Marc Fisher, "Attacks by Skinheads on Asylum Seekers Unnerve Germans," *Washington Post,* 11 Oct. 1991, A22.

65. Of course, as we have already seen in the case of

Quebec, other separatist groups have found it possible to pursue their goals by peaceful means; not every group seeking national autonomy should be automatically classified as terrorist.

66. David E. Long, *The Anatomy of Terrorism* (New York: The Free Press, 1990). See especially chap. 2, "Understanding Terrorist Behavior," pp. 15–27.

67. Quoted in Andrew Sinclair, *Che Guevara* (New York: Viking, 1970), pp. 21, 94.

68. A. K. Ocran, *A Myth Is Broken* (Harlow, U.K.: Longman, 1969), p. 43, cited in Robert Pinkney, *Ghana Under Military Rule 1966–1969* (London: Methuen, 1972), p. 2.

69. Nancy Ely-Raphel, "Human Rights Situation in Haiti," *U.S. Department of State Dispatch* 5, no. 29 (July 18, 1994): 484. Unfortunately, the departure of the military does not always mean a reversal of patterns of abuse; see the story of the assassination of a prominent opposition figure several months after the U.S. overthrow of the junta in *New York Times*, 30 Mar. 1995, A3.

8 Political Parties

IN THE SUMMER OF 1948, a young political-scientist-to-be sat by the radio, holding her breath and listening to the third roll call of the Republican convention. On the first two ballots, Ohio senator Robert A. Taft and former Minnesota governor Harold E. Stassen had prevented New York governor Thomas E. Dewey from getting a majority of the votes. After the second ballot, the anti-Dewey forces had asked for a recess. Now they were back, ready to go. Had they worked out a coalition to stop the New Yorker, or were they giving up? As the voice of the leader of each state's delegation came over the airwaves calling out that state's vote, the avid listener wrote down the numbers for each candidate, adding them as she went along. When one of them suddenly shot past the magic number of 548, she was able to shout, loud and clear, "It's Dewey!" a whole millisecond before the roar of a cheering crowd came out of the little brown box on the table beside her. Her math was as fast as anyone's that summer afternoon, long before calculators and computers were in common usage. Undistracted by the sight of flashing electronic bulletins or frantic reporters and delegates milling about, her mind filled with images of what a convention ought to look like, she experienced a sense of instant participation in U.S. political party life, via the media. It was wonderful.

In the summer of 2000, a political scientist-to-be will sit by his combination television and home computer, holding his breath and watching the images on his screen, listening to the voices he hears, his hands poised above his keyboard. The images shift. Here are several men and women arguing animatedly around a table over which a sign reads, "Democratic Program Committee." Here is a convention hall of Democratic delegates watching, on more screens, the men and women arguing. Here is an attractive older woman, the well-known governor of a southern state, carefully explaining what is to happen next. Now a question appears on the screen about the important issue of public policy the committee has been discussing, followed by four possible replies. The governor's voice says, "You have one minute to type in your response, delegates and telepollsters." After only a moment's thought, our hero forthrightly types: c. At the end of 60 seconds, the screen shows the tally: how many and what percent of all American voters registered to vote prefer policy choice a, b, c, or d; how many delegates at the convention make each choice; and the totals for each, with the winning response outlined in bright red.

Now cut back to the Program Committee, so viewers can see its members looking at the results on their own large screen. Back to the governor: "Ladies and gentlemen, the Program Committee will now continue its deliberations. Thanks to you, the committee knows what the Democratic delegates prefer and what the nation at large prefers on this important issue. But the final decision is their own. As soon as we know what they have decided, we will let you know." Cut for the commercial. Our political scientist-to-be, one of those chosen to be part of the random sampling of the "nation at large" heaves a contented sigh and sits back in his chair. He has a feeling of instant participation in U.S. political party life, via the media. It is wonderful.

The 1948 example is a personal one, and I can tell you for a fact, it did indeed feel wonderful. And no doubt the 2000 version of participation via the media — or something similar — will also be filled with excitement and personal satisfaction. Yet although the media can and do give us such moments, their interaction with the U.S. political party system is fraught with controversy and, some would even say, with peril to democracy.

We will return to this matter later in this chapter. However, political parties have not yet been taken over entirely by the media, even in the United States, and other questions require our attention first. In this chapter we will consider the following topics: the difference between parties and interest groups, the functions parties are expected to perform, how parties begin, how they are organized, who their members are, how they choose their candidates, how they prepare their campaigns, how they use the media to carry out their campaigns (and how the media use them), how they try to carry out their programs once in government, the types of parties and party systems, and, finally, the role of political parties today.

POLITICAL PARTIES AS A UNIQUE FORM OF POLITICAL ORGANIZATION

In Chapter 7 we identified three kinds of political organizations: interest groups, political parties, and violent revolutionary organizations. Why do political parties deserve a category — and here, even a chapter — of their own? In particular, what makes them different from an interest group?

Three characteristics, two always present and a third commonly so, distinguish the **political party**:

1. The members of a political party, not content with trying to persuade the government to act in a particular way, instead always seek to *place representatives in the government.*
2. To accomplish this goal, *the party nominates candidates to stand for election* in its name.
3. The political party almost always claims that, if successful, it will *exercise power on behalf of the general public.*

Sometimes interest groups seek to place their representatives in the government (by appointment to advisory boards, for instance, or to other important offices), put up independent candidates for elective office, and claim to act on behalf of the general public. Unlike interest groups, however, political parties never fail to manifest the first two of these three characteristics. And when an interest group assumes all three features, it is no longer a separate organization interested in pressuring government. It is an organization interested in taking part in government; it is a *party* to the action.

Besides puzzling over the difference between interest groups and parties, political scientists have worried whether the **single party** — that is, a party that is the only party allowed in a political system — should be considered a party at all. Some have tried to write such parties out of their definitions: "[A party is] an organization of society's active political agents . . . who *compete* for popular support with another group or groups holding diverse views," says Sigmund Neumann, stressing that where there is no competition there can be no true political party.[1] Similarly, Joseph Schlesinger has offered this definition of party: "The political organization which actively and effectively engages in the competition for elective office."[2] The point is an interesting one but leaves the observer wondering — if a single party (which does, after all, meet the terms of the more standard definitions) is not a party, then what is it? Most writers are satisfied to count the single party as a type of party, and that will be my approach here as well.

THE FUNCTIONS OF POLITICAL PARTIES

What is a political party's job? In practice, political parties perform a surprisingly wide range of functions, ranging from providing holiday turkeys for the poor to making and carrying out a nation's foreign policy. Most commonly, however, parties are expected to conform to a somewhat more limited job description. Four functions appear on almost everyone's list of what a party does, or should do: leadership recruitment, interest aggregation, campaigning, and governing. We will treat each of these in greater detail later in the chapter; here we simply offer brief explanations of each.

Leadership Recruitment

Even in eras when parties are widely scorned and other groups and individuals perform many of the functions formerly ascribed to them, the political party is still likely to be the structure that identifies potential leaders, brings them to public attention, and secures them the support necessary for taking public office. As we shall see, this is not always the case in the United States.

Interest Aggregation

A second major function of parties is aggregating interests — that is, serving as mediator for a wide range of politicized demands. To do this, parties must set up internal party procedures that permit different points of view — different *interests* — to be presented, discussed, compromised, and *aggregated*. Study groups, issue-oriented clubs, backroom deals, and platform committees are some of the party structures that serve this function. The speeches of the parties' candidates, carefully addressing the various concerns of different groups whose support is being courted, are yet another instrument of interest aggregation.

Campaigning

Political parties normally play an important role in helping their candidates campaign for office. Even in today's world of mass media, political consultants, and direct mail advertising, the parties still play a part in ensuring that voters are registered, that they know the differences among the candidates, and that they know when and where to vote on election day. Where parties are strong, as in most western European nations, they may assume full responsibility for their candidates' campaigns, calling in media advisers, pollsters, and other professional experts only as they see fit.

Governing

Finally, the elected officials of victorious parties are usually expected to run the government, and in doing so to make an effort to translate the party's program into legislative bills, and thence into law.

Of course, parties do not always perform these four functions, and when they do, they do not always perform them to citizens' satisfaction. To understand the limitations on parties' ability to do the job we wish they would — and that they always promise to do — we need to go back to beginnings:

BOX 8.1   **THE TRANSITION FROM AUTOCRACY TO PARTY POLITICS**

- The king (or any autocrat) names a council of trusted advisers to assist him.
- The council becomes more and more powerful, perhaps because the king becomes more and more dependent on the resources it commands, perhaps because its members personally dominate a weak-willed monarch.
- The council bargains for and achieves a measure of power independent of the king's (to set taxes, say, or to raise armies), thus becoming a rulemaking legislature.
- Factions develop within the legislature, differing on how and for what purposes it should exercise its power.
- Members of these factions seek external support for their side.
- Motivated by the hope of finding more such external support, the monarch and the legislators agree to the principle of elected legislators.
- The right to vote for legislators is extended to more and more of the populace, for the same motives elections were begun in the first place.
- Specific groups within the legislature set up external organizations to assist them in persuading the electors that the public interest will be served by their reelection.
- Challengers set up counterorganizations to persuade electors that the public interest will be better served by substituting their candidates for the incumbents.
- The external organizations outlive the candidacies of the legislators they first support.
- The leaders of the external organizations begin to make their own decisions about which candidates the organization will support—that is, *political parties seek to place their representatives in government by nominating candidates to stand for election in their names, claiming that power so won will be exercised in the public interest.*

THE ORIGINS OF POLITICAL PARTIES

The earliest political parties found their genesis in the legislative branches of governments. Even today, some political scientists insist on the legislative connection of parties: A party is "any organization which nominates candidates for election to a legislature," says Fred Riggs.[3] It is, however, perhaps more exact to say that both legislatures and parties owe their existence to the decline of autocratic rule (see Box 8.1.)

What causes new parties to develop in modern times? Maurice Duverger prefers to keep the focus on the legislature. New parties, he says, form either inside or outside the legislature for the purpose of taking control (in part or entirely) of the legislature.[4] Access to the legislative arena will sooner or later be a central goal of almost any new party, but still

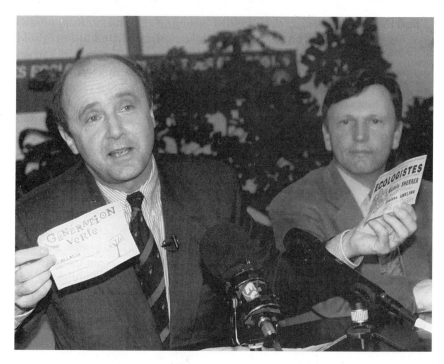

New parties may begin when old parties divide, especially in multiparty systems where it is not difficult to get a new party on the ballot. In French party politics Brian Lalonde (L), the leader of Génération Ecologie, competes with Antoine Waechter (R) who heads Les Verts ("The Greens") as well as with the major parties. (Reuters/ Christine Gunnet/Archive Photos)

Duverger's answer to our question may be a bit too simple. For one thing, it seems to suggest that parties are created out of whole cloth — "I think I'll form a party," said the disgruntled politician, and he did. In fact, most new parties evolve from other groups. The French Rally for the Republic, known in its early days as the Union for a New Republic, was formed out of a collection of groups and individuals who had very little in common other than the conviction that only Charles De Gaulle could save France from the crisis that its battle with Algerian rebels and rebelling French generals had produced.[5] Other parties began as trade unions (most of the socialist parties of Europe), as mutual aid associations (many African political parties began as ethnic societies), as farmers' cooperatives (the party that brought political independence to the Ivory Coast), as underground study groups (the communist party of the Soviet Union), as youth groups (the Guatemalan Revolutionary Party was founded by student activists), and as revolutionary movements (the Cuban communist party).

Sometimes a group sets up a party while maintaining its own separate identity. The Christian Democratic parties of Europe, heavily backed and guided by the Roman Catholic church, are prime examples. Often new parties begin when old parties divide, as in the cases of Italy's Socialist Party of Proletarian Unity and the short-lived "Bull Moose" (Progressive) Party in the United States, which broke away from the Republican Party in 1912.

At least as important as the setting for a new party's origins are the reasons for forming a new party. Some have suggested that new parties begin in times of systemwide crisis.[6] Not all important crises have produced new parties, however, and some parties have begun when no crisis was apparent, so such an explanation does not take us very far. An important factor seems to be the original organizers' belief that it will be useful to form a new party — that is, the conviction that the resources are available to achieve an acceptable degree of success and that success through this party is the best means to improve the status quo. Considering the motives of the leaders of any new party, as well as the conditions of the political system in which it is being formed, is a good way to figure out why a new party has been born.

PARTY ORGANIZATION: IS INTERNAL PARTY DEMOCRACY POSSIBLE?

The nature of parties, and the reasons for forming a new party, have much to do with the way parties are organized. A political party is formed by individuals who want to acquire or maintain power in government and who seek to gain that power by convincing large numbers of citizens that the organization's candidates will serve as their representatives if elected. Such a commitment puts the political party in a special predicament, which can be summarized in two questions: How can an organization represent "the people" unless it is open to the people and responsive to them? How can an organization subject itself to the fluctuating interests, fleeting passions, and unsophisticated methods of a constantly shifting band of uninformed enthusiasts and still get anything done? In a sense, the whole idea of a participatory organization is a contradiction in terms. The more participation, the less organization; the more organization, the less participation.

Is this conflict between the two goals to which all parties claim to be devoted unavoidable? Robert Michels thought it was, and furthermore was convinced that the battle was dramatically uneven, with participation always sacrificed to efficacy. The person "who says organization, says oligarchy," claimed Michels, and he documented this "iron law of oligarchy" with a convincing study of European parties, in which he depicted the members as apathetic, hero-worshiping, transient, and incompetent and the leaders as egotistically persuaded of their own indispensability — a set of characteristics many have claimed to find in parties in the United States as well.[7]

Other observers have agreed with Michels. Moisei Ostrogorski, who studied American parties of the early twentieth century, went so far as to claim that the pretense of mass participation in fact lessened the opportunities for true participation. By admitting the "mob," Ostrogorski said, parties set up conditions that made it impossible to arrive at decisions in party meetings. The true work of the party was thus always done by the "wire-pullers," usually "the ward secretary surrounded by his ring of associates concocting the business of the party behind the scenes."[8]

On the other hand, Maurice Duverger has provided grounds for a more positive view in his analysis of parties. If a party admits members freely but then requires their close affiliation, including payment of dues and attendance at meetings; if communication links are strong throughout the party structure; and if final decision-making powers are located at the top of the party in the hands of leaders chosen on the basis of their ability to perform important duties rather than on the basis of personal status, then, Duverger suggests, parties can hope to meet their dual obligation to be both representative and effective.[9] However, very few parties in the United States or elsewhere live up to these high standards.

Duverger's emphasis on centralized control is worth further consideration. At first we might imagine that decentralized organizations, where more decisions are made at or near the base, would be closer to the popular will. After all, authoritarian political systems are highly centralized, while the more democratic nations place greater stress on local government. The case of political parties makes clear, however, that decentralizing power is not always synonymous with democratizing power. The party bosses of city "machines," be they in New York or Marseilles or Singapore, have shown that local leaders can rule as autocratically as any national figure — if not more so — because they have fewer interests to accommodate and fewer potential rivals. Even where the boss can no longer rule singlehandedly, any power left to local parties has tended to fall into very few hands. The decentralized party is only one step away from oligarchy, says Samuel Eldersveld. It is a *stratarchy* — that is, an organization with many levels (strata), at each of which power rests in the hands of a few.[10]

Even Michels, however, recognized that the participatory impulse cannot be forever denied, that "the democratic currents . . . are ever renewed" even if they "break ever on the same shoal" of oligarchy.[11] Parties that allow power to become excessively concentrated inevitably face a falling away of support, especially if their followers become convinced that the power so concentrated is no longer being exercised in their interest. The German Green Party emerged to protect the environment, but its members insisted that improving the environment means improving the political environment as well — that is, ensuring more democracy at the base — and the new party introduced a number of rules in the effort to prevent the rise of oligarchy (for example, the principle of *leadership rotation* — that is, the rule that no one should stay in elected office more than a single term).[12] Yet more recently this same party has found it necessary to modify the rules intended to protect internal democracy in order to have greater continuity of leadership and program.[13]

Other parties have sometimes attempted to resolve the dilemma of effectiveness versus participation by offering a kind of sham participation. The classic example is the old Soviet party congress, where all decisions were made in advance but a gathering of disciplined party activists could somehow be motivated to meet periodically and give their enthusiastic and unanimous consent. A case could also be made that contemporary American or Canadian political conventions — or the annual meetings of the large central committees of European parties — provide very little more in the way of serious participatory input.[14] In many nations the average party militant simply works hard for candidates others have chosen, an observation that brings us to our next topic: the nature of party membership.

THE MEMBERS OF PARTIES

Ask a Chinese citizen if she belongs to a political party and she will be puzzled only by the suggestion that there might be more than one political party to join. She will know for a certainty whether or not she belongs to the party. But ask an American if he belongs to a political party and he is very likely to say, "Well, what exactly do you mean by *belong*, my friend?"

What does it mean to belong to a party? Closeness of affiliation is not always easy to measure across cultural boundaries. Attending discussion meetings, learning party history, contributing a fixed amount of one's earnings to the organization, and enrolling one's children in an affiliated youth club may constitute a remarkably high level of commitment to party in Great Britain but would reflect a simple regimen of self-interest in China. Duverger, as interested in this question as in forms of organization, named four levels of membership: sympathizers, adherents, militants, and propagandists.[15] A more common set of categories for membership in European parties today is simply supporters, adherents, and militants.

The *supporter* always (or almost always) votes for the party's candidates; the *adherent* joins the party formally, filling out a membership blank and paying dues; the *militant* can be counted on to work actively for the party, performing such mundane chores as stuffing envelopes and distributing leaflets as well as preaching the party's cause at every opportunity. "Talk to a Communist about anything, and in ten minutes you will know the Communist position on that matter," a member of a different party in France commented, sounding more than a little jealous.[16] But in the United States there are subtle cultural biases against open proselytizing on behalf of any party, and a "party card" is likely to be little more than a receipt for a contribution. Individuals can work militantly on behalf of particular candidates without concern for party affiliation (their own or the candidates'), and interest group members have been known to swamp party meetings, from local club to national convention, in order to win party support for their cause while making little or no promise of reciprocal loyalty to the party.

Party membership in the sense of becoming an adherent is generally in decline, even in the European nations where it has been strongest in the past (see Table 8.1) and even as the size of electorates (the number of qualified voters) has grown.[17] Jeremy Richardson argues that new interest groups and social movements are taking the place of parties now for citizens; that we have become *"consumers of participation and activism"* and that "a market," of participatory activities has now developed to meet our needs. There is now, he says, "a wide range of participatory organisations offering 'tailor made' opportunities for political activism. 'Brand loyalty' has decreased at the very time that new 'products' have arrived on the marketplace." Richardson points out that the breadth of coverage offered by parties may make them the less desirable choice for citizens determined to donate their time or money to support a single issue, even though democratic theory calls for citizenship that is concerned about the public good more generally.[18]

However, although the global tendency seems to be for lower levels of *adherence*, membership in the sense of offering *support* by voting consistently for the same party seems to have experienced a recent resurgence, according to Anders Westholm and Richard Niemi. They find "high levels of partisan transmission across generations" (that is, we still tend to vote as our parents did) as well as "high continuity of partisanship over time" (we tend to continue to vote the same from one election to the next).[19] On the other hand, high levels of party identification do not always mean electoral success, as the U.S. Democratic Party has discovered time and again, especially in presidential races (see Table 8.2).[20]

Related to the question of closeness of affiliation is the question of reason for affiliation. The distinctions used by Robert Salisbury to categorize the motives of those who join interest groups — material, solidary, or purposive (see pp. 222–224) — do not fit quite as well for the study of those who join political parties. Other motives are clearly at work, such as a sense of loyalty (be it to a particular candidate or to the organization itself), and the pursuit of power — that is, the pleasure some take simply in being in a position to control the action of others (which, of course, is something one does gain in winning a position of party leadership or, better yet, public office). For parties, a different list is required. There are motives that are purely *personal* (here we may include the material and solidary motives mentioned by Salisbury, but also the pure joy of exercising power over others); motives that have to do with one's *loyalty* to others; and, finally, the motive of *political conviction* (similar to the Salisbury notion of purposive motivation). As in the case of interest groups, it is of course possible and

TABLE 8.1   Party Membership as a Percentage of the National Electorate in Selected European Nations (Five-year Averages)

	1945–1949	1950–1954	1955–1959	1960–1964	1965–1969	1970–1974	1975–1979	1980–1984
Austria								
People's Party (ÖVP)					15.2		16.0	10.3
Socalist (SPÖ)	13.6	13.9	14.8	15.1	14.6	13.9	13.7	13.5
Belgium								
Christian (PSC/CVP)					2.4	2.4	2.8	2.7
Socialist		2.2	2.5		3.3	3.8	4.1	4.1
Volksunie					0.4	0.8	1.1	
Denmark								
Conservatives	3.3			3.8		3.2	1.7	1.2
Liberals	8.2			6.4		3.8	3.1	2.5
Social Democrats	12.0	10.9	9.6	8.1	5.9	4.4	3.4	2.8
Germany								
Christian Democrats	1.6				1.0	1.2	1.9	2.0
Free Democrats	0.4	0.2	0.2		0.2	0.1	0.2	0.2
Social Democrats	2.5	1.9	1.7	1.7	1.9	2.2	2.4	2.2
Italy								
Christian Democrats	2.7	3.4	4.2	4.4	4.8	4.9	3.4	3.1
Socialist (PSI)	2.2	2.4	1.8	1.4	1.7	1.4	1.2	1.2
Communists	6.1	7.0	5.9	4.9	4.3	4.2	4.3	4.0
Social Democrats (PSDI)				0.4		0.8	0.2	
Netherlands								
Catholic People's (KVP)	7.6	4.4	6.9	5.7	2.9		0.6	
Labor (PvdA)	2.1	1.9	2.2	2.1	1.7	1.2	1.1	1.1
Norway								
Liberal			1.2		0.8	0.4	0.3	0.4
Conservative	1.7	2.5	4.1	4.2	4.6	3.8	4.2	5.5
Center		2.2	2.8		2.5	2.1	2.0	1.7
Christian People's			1.3			1.6	2.1	2.2
Labor	9.7	8.1	7.3	7.0	6.3	5.5	5.4	5.4
Sweden								
Social Democratic	12.8	15.5	15.8	16.7	16.3	16.5	18.5	19.6
Conservative	2.4			4.0		2.3	2.1	2.1
Agrarian	3.1			3.5		3.2	3.6	2.2
Communist	1.1	0.7	0.6	0.5	0.5	0.3	0.3	0.3
United Kingdom								
Conservative	4.4	8.1		6.4		4.0		2.9
Liberal				0.7	0.7	0.5		
Labour[a]	1.9	2.7	2.4	2.2	2.1	1.7	1.6	1.4

[a] Individual members only.

Source: Richard S. Katz, "Party as Linkage: A Vestigal Function?" *European Journal of Political Research* 18 (1990): 148. Reprinted with kind permission from Klúwer Academic Publishers and Professor Richard S. Katz.

TABLE 8.2

The Poor Match Between Party Identification and Presidential Choice in the United States, 1972–1992 (Percent of Democrats and Republicans who voted for each candidate)

	Voting behavior										
	1972		1980		1984		1988		1992		
Party Identification	D	R	D	R	D	R	D	R	D	R	Perot
Democrat	67	33	69	26	79	21	85	15	77	10	13
Republican	5	95	8	86	4	96	7	93	10	73	17

Sources: William J. Keefe, *Parties, Politics and Public Policy in America,* 7th ed. (Washington, D. C.: CQ Press, 1994), p. 144 and (for 1992) *Vote by Party Identification (National Exit Poll)* (New York: Voter News Service, 1992).

indeed likely that a person will have more than one kind of motive for joining a political party.[21]

Some have suggested that a briefer list covers all the motives of party members: They are either *amateurs* (sometimes called purists), motivated by conviction, or *professionals* (sometimes called realists), motivated by the quest for some form of personal gain.[22] Those who make this simple distinction nearly always favor the professional, who keeps his eye on the doughnut of success rather than on the hole of ideological purity. Ordinary citizens, however, sometimes naively wonder if party politics really suffers more from the intrusion of idealistic newcomers than from the cynical tactics of battle-weary veterans. In any case, amateurs have a way of eventually becoming professionals, especially in parties that know how to welcome and use their energy and enthusiasm at the outset.

Besides asking how closely affiliated members are and studying their reasons for joining, it is also interesting to consider what kinds of people join particular parties. Is the membership of the party a heterogeneous microcosm of the nation itself? The Democratic Party of the United States, the Rally for the Republic in France, the Congress Party of India, and the Partido Revolucionario Institucional of Mexico are all examples of parties that have succeeded in attracting supporters from all their nation's major social categories. Or is the party composed predominantly of the members of a single ethnic group (such as the predominantly Kikuyu Kenyan African National Union), a single religious organization (the fundamentalist Sokkagakkai of Japan), a single language group (the Swedish People's Party in Finland), or a single class (the Peasant Party of Romania)? Richard Rose and Derek Urwin studied the social cohesiveness of seventy-six parties in seventeen Western nations and found that the more cohesive the party, the more limited and the more stable the party's share of the vote will be from election to election. At the same time, they found the presence of socially cohesive parties, especially those organized around religious or communal ties, likely to be associated with regime instability; the political issues generated by those deeply felt affiliations are difficult to compromise.[23]

The problem of communal parties has assumed new significance in recent years with the resurgence of ethnic nationalism in the new political systems of eastern Europe. Even when the overriding aim of an ethnic party is simply to protect its own peoples — as with the Hungarian Party in Romania, the German Minority Party of Poland, and the Movement for Rights and Freedoms (of ethnic Turks) in Bulgaria — the dangers of excessive fragmentation in newly forming democracies is very real.

THE SELECTION OF CANDIDATES

"Did he jump or was he pushed?" The question can be asked about individuals found at the top of party organizations as well as about murder mystery victims found at the bottom of cliffs. It is often unclear whether those who become candidates for office do so because of special characteristics that permitted them to make the jump or because they were pushed (or pulled) by others eager to recruit a winner. An extrovert personality possessed of a strong intelligence and an equally strong appetite for power may be able to build a personal organization capable of seizing the nomination. Control over a party's nominating processes may fall into the hands of a single autocrat (as Francisco Franco controlled the Spanish Falange) or a powerful lobby (as the railroad interests controlled California party politics at the turn of the twentieth century) — or simply remain the domain of its established leaders. In fact, in most cases the would-be candidate's personal traits and others' recruitment efforts interact so subtly that no one can be certain which is decisive. Here we will look at each aspect in turn, remembering that in practice no such separation can be made.

Certain personal characteristics do correlate strongly with political leadership. Leaders usually come from higher socioeconomic backgrounds than do their followers, although what constitutes higher socioeconomic status may vary from culture to culture. Having been a tribal leader was very important to someone seeking to lead an African party well into the latter half of the twentieth century, although such a qualification was usually combined with other, more modern indices of success, such as wealth, occupation, and education. Kwame Nkrumah took a chiefly title,

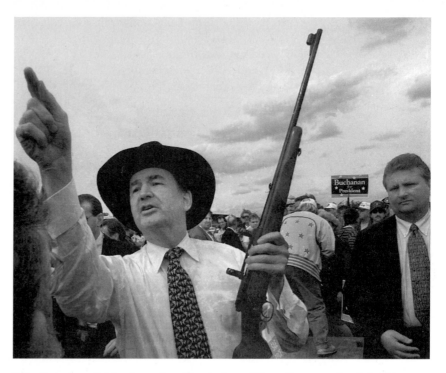

Selection of candidates for major office is done differently across the globe. Here Pat Buchanan seeks the primary votes of Arizona Republicans while waving a Winchester rifle at a gun show in Phoenix in February, 1996. (AP Photo/Eric Draper/ Wide World)

Osagyefo, on assuming political leadership in Ghana, but he had also nearly completed the course of study for a Ph.D.

Leaders also have usually grown up in more politicized homes than followers, have adopted a partisan identification at an earlier age, and are readier to adopt their parents' partisan affiliation. They have a stronger sense of political efficacy (more likely to be a result rather than a cause of assuming leadership roles), hold views more uniformly in accord with the party's positions, and possibly are more neurotic than followers. (Fortunately for the followers, the evidence is mixed on this final point.)[24]

Rising to the top ranks of a political party, however, has at least as much to do with factors external to the individual. If a nation is divided and the party wishes to reach beyond such divisions, it must seek a leader who is not strongly identified with a particular subgroup, or else set up a council of leaders drawn from all the important groups. If the electoral system offers a better chance to centrist candidates than to ideologues of either extreme, the parties are likely to choose their candidates accordingly.[25] On

(Oliphant/International Herald Tribune/Universal Press Syndicate)

the other hand, if standing as a candidate is personally risky, as it may be in unstable societies where electoral defeat can bring imprisonment or exile, the party may well seek out its most committed firebrands. If the party has no chance of winning, it is also more likely to urge the nomination of candidates of great ideological purity.

The presence or absence of major political issues also influences the kind of nominee a party seeks. If a particularly sensitive issue is at the forefront, the candidate's past and present pronouncements on that matter must be carefully reviewed. If the nation is in need of a drastic change in economic or foreign policy, the party may search for someone charismatic — that is, someone who has the gift of embodying the nation both at its traditional best and in its desired future state. The party formed to support French military hero Charles De Gaulle in 1958 was a dramatic case in point. More recent examples include Lech Walesa in Poland and Vaclav Havel in Czechoslovakia, two men who achieved prominence in the past in ways that lent them political legitimacy in a postcommunist world.

Finally, the kind of leader a party chooses rests to a large extent on the nature of the party's nominating procedures. In some nations, such as England and France, the top party leadership has the right to "parachute" candidates in — that is, to give the nomination to someone who does not even live in the electoral district where the contest is being waged. In single-party systems it is common practice for the national party leadership to form a national list of candidates without specifying districts at all.

(In such cases, being named to the list is tantamount to being elected.) Where local control is the rule, one must still ask whether final power rests in the hands of a small committee (as in Germany, Norway, and Sweden), is shared by all who pay dues (as in Belgium), or is distributed among all those who choose to attend the appropriate meeting and identify themselves as partisans (as in party caucuses in those U.S. states that do not choose delegates to the national convention by primary). Experience suggests that the lower the level of the party hierarchy involved in choosing the nominee, the more the candidate will represent local and special interests and the less he or she will adopt stances on national issues that attract wide popular support. Because candidates who cannot attract wide popular support are rarely winning candidates, we are back to the problem we encountered earlier: How can a party represent its followers and still do its job?

PREPARING THE CAMPAIGN

Preparing the campaign means more than finding the right candidates — or letting the candidates "find" the party. To do their job, parties also need money and a strategy. The latter includes a plan for developing a program, but also developing and deploying the technological expertise that constitutes so large a part of today's campaign.

Raising the Money   In the United States, most of the money collected for a political campaign is raised not by the parties but by the candidates, especially while they are seeking the nomination, and most of the funds so gathered come from individual contributions.[26] Once the nomination is in hand, most presidential candidates accept public funding (each major party candidate was entitled to $62.2 million for the general election campaign in 1996) and obey the requirement that they limit their spending to that amount. Independent expenditures (see Chapter 7) made by individuals and political action committees vastly increase the amounts of money spent in contemporary campaigns. Candidates who do not accept public funding (where that is available) are free to spend as much as they wish of their personal fortunes. Steve Forbes spent $16.5 million of his own fortune in 1995; although frontrunner Robert Dole raised and spent $21 million in the same time period, 2 million of that sum was spent on the costs of raising funds so as to qualify for matching funds under the terms of federal law.[27]

Despite the frenetic activities of the candidates, parties in the United States do still engage in fundraising themselves. Indeed, one of the key reasons for their continued importance regardless of voter disaffection is that they are able to raise and spend such monies legally and effectively. The Republican National Committee took the lead as early as 1962, when it first began making large-scale appeals by direct mail and collected

$700,000. The Democrats were not long to catch on but have never been able to match the Republicans; by 1990, the Republicans were able to raise $207.2 million (86% in individual contributions); the Democrats $86.7 million (64% in individual contributions). Herbert Alexander estimates that a total of $471.2 million was raised for campaign purposes in 1990 and since that time the parties' role has been far from negligible.[28] Fundraising efforts other than direct mail now include special dinners, special "clubs" such as the Republican Eagles and the Democratic Business Council (in both cases, the "dues" are $15,000 per year).[29]

A major fundraising advantage the parties have over the candidates' own organizations is that U.S. federal law permits state and local party committees to raise and spend unlimited amounts of what is known as *soft money* for voter registration, get-out-the-vote drives, and grassroots campaign materials (signs, buttons, party newspapers, bumper stickers), as well as for the printing and distribution of sample ballots telling voters how to vote.[30] The parties have thus become the recipients of very large contributions that individuals and political action committees could not legally make to the candidates but that are, of course, made to work for those candidates just as well as if they *had* been contributed to them.

The Republican and Democratic congressional committees, composed of those who have been elected to Congress on these two parties' labels, are powerful fundraisers and play a particularly significant role in financing the reelection campaigns of those of their colleagues whose resources are limited. They also make significant contributions to the campaigns of fellow partisans running for open seats but contribute less and less to those who are challenging incumbents of the opposing party. As Frank Sorauf points out, "legislative parties, as parties of incumbents, pursue their own narrow and well-defined goals for their segment of the party. Supporting almost certain losers, party label or no, is not one of them."[31]

In many nations, parties need not "raise" money; they merely have to figure out how to make good use of that which is given them by the state. In France a party receives up to 6 million francs (about $1.2 million) for its presidential candidate's campaign expenses, provided that candidate gains at least 5 percent of the vote on the first ballot. State funding is the most important source of funding for Norwegian parties and helps to make the parties roughly equal in resources. However, in Norway as in most nations where large-scale public financing is practiced, the party's share depends in part on how well it does in the vote, a practice that, as Alan Ware points out, "inevitably has a conservatizing effect in helping to protect currently large parties."[32] Germany has followed a path all its own. Having first decided that the direct financing of parties with public funds was unconstitutional, the German Supreme Court then ruled that it was acceptable for the state to reimburse the costs of campaigns for any party receiving 0.5 percent of the vote or more, a ruling particularly advantageous to smaller parties.[33] Later, the German legislature decided that parties which receive the least from private donations and membership fees should get proportionately more from the state.

Whether funds are raised or publicly given (or both), parties around the globe have sometimes engaged in fundraising practices that break the laws in their respective nations. Some of the most flagrant cases in recent years have included Italy, where the relevation of massive kickbacks to ruling parties in exchange for public works contracts resulted in an indignant public's voting to cancel all public funding to the parties; Japan, where the discovery of extremely large unreported "contributions" (i.e., bribes) to Liberal Democratic Party members of that country's parliament and cabinet ministers by individuals gaining illegal tax benefits brought about the fall of several prime ministers and eventually of the party itself; and Mexico, where in 1993 former president Carlos Salinas de Gortari asked thirty powerful business persons to donate $25 million each to the ruling Partido Revolucionario Institucional in exchange for special consideration during the negotiations of the North American Free Trade Agreement (NAFTA).[34]

Developing a Strategy

Of course, parties must also decide what to do with the money they raise. In addition, they need to plan the overall campaign. Determining the party's strategy depends on what role the party expects to play and what needs it expects to have. In nations where parties maintain control over their own nominations and are publicly funded and where paid advertising is kept to a minimum or forbidden, it is possible for parties to begin by formulating their programs. Individuals who hope to gain the nomination may work hard to influence the program, but technically the program comes first, candidate selection second. Where parties do not control the nomination, as in U.S. presidential elections, a party's own program-building activity will be much less meaningful; the program that counts will be that of the candidate who wins the nomination.

How do parties and candidates know what to put in their programs? The question itself is a sign of how much party politics have changed over the years — or at least how much our thinking about them has changed. In the past, it would have been assumed that they decided what they believed in and said so. But we are no longer so naive, and neither are the politicians (if they ever were). The art and science of figuring out what to say and where to say it is now highly dependent on a most sophisticated technology. According to David Selnow, the "twin engines" that "drive the political information machine" are public opinion polls and the database. But the engine that drives both of these, as Selnow also makes clear, is the modern computer.[36] Contemporary polling requires carefully crafted questionnaires, the selection of an appropriate sample of the population, and a complex process of data collection. Building a database means taking poll results and sorting out the electorate by almost every possible personal and political characteristic, including age, race, income, education, gender, partisanship and point of view on every conceivable question of the day — and, more and more important, proclivity to vote.

It is the computer that makes polling possible; it is the computer that creates the database out of the poll results. It is, of course, still a human being who tells the computer what to do. However, the guiding principle for that human being is now almost always the same: figure out how to maximize the chances of the candidate. The goals of the candidate and the party cannot credibly be changed beyond all recognition, but emphasis can certainly be placed on those positions that best fit the voters' current desires. Different positions — on different issues — can be emphasized in different communities, over different media. The point is to win. (For an application of this principle to voter registration, see Figure 8.1.)

Does this mean doing everything possible to attract as many votes as possible? The answer may seem obvious, but in fact, it is "no." As Paul Hernnson points out, "It makes more sense for candidates to allocate scarce campaign resources in the direction of large groups that vote in relatively large numbers than to direct those resources toward small groups that have low levels of voter turnout."[37] The tendency to ignore the habitual or probable nonvoter is now carried very far in the United States; according to Marshall Ganz, "As of election day, 63 percent of registered voters will not have been contacted by anyone. If, as is typical, only 60 percent of the eligible electorate [is] registered, 78 percent of the eligible voters in the district would never be contacted." Ganz does not accept this fact as calmly as other observers have; he believes that those who are not targeted to receive campaign messages are more likely to be of lower socioeconomic status than those for whom the message is designed and claims that "the introduction of the new political technologies has crippled the American attempt to combine equal voice in politics with unequal resources in economics."[38] Whether or not this is so, it seems unquestionable that the new technologies do not contribute to the democratic goal of rule by *all* the people.

Not every nation has gone as far as the United States in the direction of unrestrained targeting by computer science. Consultants and advertising agencies are widely employed, but in most nations the parties themselves and their leading candidates resist turning control fully over to such specialists. Parties in Austria incorporate outside consultants into internal decision-making structures in a formal and controlled fashion; parties in Germany and the Netherlands seek to develop in-house expertise — and some parties, such as the Swedish People's Party in Finland, the New Zealand National Party, the Austrian and German Green parties, and most Danish parties, are openly reluctant to use the new technologies at all, and try to do without them as much as possible.[39]

The modern technology does at least place a very high emphasis on listening and responding to the *voters*. In single-party systems the respon-

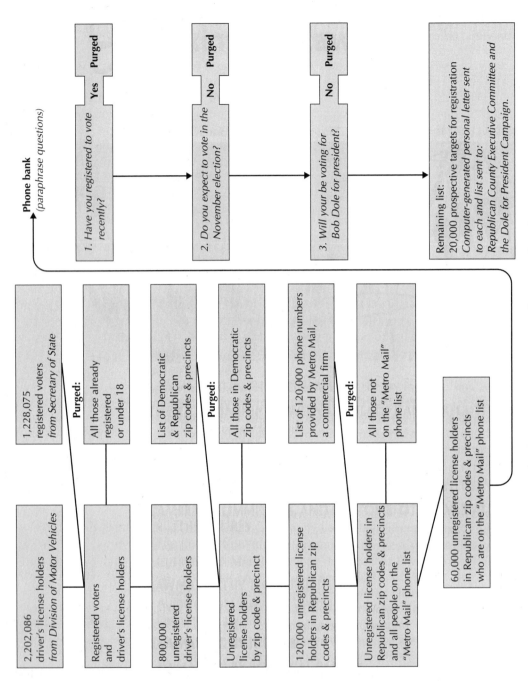

FIGURE 8.1   **How Computer Targeting Permits Focused Voter Registration.**

Copyright © *The Washington Post.*

sibility for formulating policy — and for educating the populace to understand the need for the policies espoused — is viewed as the organization's essential function, and little attempt is made to listen to the opinions of anyone else at all. The party must simply explain to the people how their interests will be best served, at least in the long run, by the proposed program. Lenin's theory of the vanguard party included this interpretation of the functions of party. Modern examples include the Iraqi Ba'th Party and the Cuban communist party.[40]

EXECUTING THE CAMPAIGN: PARTIES AND THE MEDIA

Once everything is in place, the next step is to get the messages of the party's candidates to the voters. The candidate, his or her *surrogates* (persons who are close enough to serve as personal representatives of the candidate, such as a husband or wife, a sister or brother, or a grown child), other known political figures who support the candidate and are not currently running for office, and selected volunteers all put in long, grueling days speaking to as many groups, visiting as many institutions as time and energy permit, and, especially in more local campaigns, going door to door.

Most important of all, however, and more important every year, is the campaign conducted via the media. Getting the media to cover the candidate's speech to the national meeting of the Businesswomen's Club or her visit to the workers in a garment factory is far more important than the immediate response of the businesswomen or the factory workers. However, the media have some very special characteristics that must be taken into account by the parties. To understand the special new relationship between these two powerful forces, we need to consider the evolution of the media over time as well as how parties and media use each other today and, finally, how citizens respond to media presentations of politics.[41] In the following pages we use the United States, where the new relationship is much more prevalent than in other nations, as our example. However, the same forces may be seen at work across the globe.

How Party Politics Became a National Entertainment

The main medium of communication in the early United States was the newspaper, and the first newspaper was entitled *Publick Occurances Both Forreign and Domestick*. It was published in Boston on September 25, 1690, with the announcement that it would reappear "once a month (or if any Glut of Occurrances happen, oftener)" — and then never appeared again.[42] But the precedent was set, and when other newspapers began to appear they too gave much of their space over to "Publick Occurances," including, of course, party politics. In fact, many of the early papers were published by political parties, some with the incumbent President's blessing.[43]

To achieve a large circulation and thereby attract sufficient advertising

BOX 8.2

MILESTONES IN THE DEVELOPMENT OF MODERN CAMPAIGN COMMUNICATION IN THE UNITED STATES, 1952–1994

1952 Richard Nixon's "Checkers" speech; first use by presidential candidates of televised spot advertisements.

1957 Supreme Court rules that broadcasters may not be held liable for content of campaign commercials.

1959 Enactment of exemptions to equal-opportunities provision of the Communications Act of 1934.

1960 First televised presidential debate; publication of the first *Making of the President* book, transforming press coverage of election campaigns; first use of election-night network news projections.

1961 First live televised presidential press conference.

1964 Redefinition of libel in *New York Times v. Sullivan;* first televised presidential adversary commercial; formation of News Election Service, permitting news organizations to acquire timely vote returns.

1968 First year of extensive coverage of national nominating conventions by networks; first use of exit polling by CBS.

1969 Publication of Theodore White's *The Selling of the President, 1968,* describing candidate control of campaign communication; attack by Spiro Agnew on the liberalism of the "northeastern establishment" press.

1972 Presidential primary process changed by Democratic Party reforms; Federal Elections Campaign Act takes effect.

1976 Federal Communications Commission reinterpretation of candidate debate regulation; spending limitations in effect during the presidential general election for the first time; network news offers regular primary-night news coverage.

1980 Exit polls used to project election results; extensive political advertising by political action committees.

1984 Networks reduce coverage of nominating conventions.

1988 Networks stop predicting the outcomes of elections before all polls have closed.

1992 Presidential candidates appear on talk shows and accept questions from callers. Independent candidate Ross Perot uses half-hour paid commercials to explain his program.

1994 Full Republican program reprinted in *TV Guide.*

Source: Adapted from Richard Joslyn, *Mass Media and Elections* (Addison-Wesley, 1984), p. 6, plus recent additions.

revenue to stay in business and make a profit, newspapers had to be interesting to the masses. This soon came to mean offering "stories" stressing the more sensational events of the day, a focus that carried into political reporting as well. Political scandals, violence, and corruption sold more newspapers than tame accounts of the debates in Congress or treaties

The first televised political debate. Senator John F. Kennedy and Vice President Richard Nixon debate the issues in the 1960 presidential campaign. Kennedy's superior use of the still-new medium was a key factor leading to his victory six weeks later. (UPI/The Bettmann Archive)

signed in Europe. In the twentieth century the invention and rapid spread of radio and then television suggested new ways the political news could be shaped to maximize audience, and thereby advertising revenue. Radio and television broadcasters made money by entertaining their listeners. Entertainment includes drama and excitement, and party politics could be made to fill the bill (see Box 8.2). In 1956, the National Broadcasting Corporation recognized the considerable entertainment value of the political convention and began giving both parties' nominations extensive coverage. In 1960, televised debates between Democratic candidate John Kennedy and Republican candidate Richard Nixon were credited with playing a major role in the victory of the former — but also with attracting unusually large audiences. The spread during the 1970s of the more colorful system of choosing convention delegates by primaries rather than by closed caucuses also played a role in stimulating television coverage of the parties.

Another turning point came in the early 1970s during Richard Nixon's tenure as U.S. president. The Watergate scandal (see Chapter 9) was the beginning, suggests Adam Gopnik, of the transformation of the American press to an "aggression culture." Since then, the media has seemed ever more determined to search out and report the most unpleasant aspects of every campaign, every candidate's personal life, every elected politician's tenure in office. It was not, says Gopnik, a matter of a free and independent media doing its job; the media "remained big, profit-seeking businesses, and journalists, whatever else they might be, were employees of those businesses . . . it was not ideological purity that was demanded so much as, simply, 'stories,' and those stories sounded better if they were tough."[44] Thomas Patterson agrees, pointing out that whereas in 1960 evaluative references to Kennedy and Nixon were only 25 percent unfavorable, by 1992 references to candidates Clinton and Bush were more than 60 percent negative.[45] (Historian Bernard A. Weisberger reminds us, however, that the present emphasis on aggressive reporting is not new, that George Washington was accused of "pusillanimous neglect" of the public welfare, Andrew Jackson was termed a murderer for having ordered several summary executions while a general, Mary Todd Lincoln was reported as having revealed military secrets to the Confederacy through indiscreet correspondence, Ulysses Grant was termed a "drunken Democrat . . . besmeared with the blood of his countrymen," and Franklin Roosevelt was routinely accused of "dragging the country down the road to socialism" — and all this in public print.[46])

How Parties Use the Media

But whether or not journalists are motivated to report the activities of parties and their candidates aggressively, the simple fact that most media are profit-making businesses seeking to entertain strongly influences the ability of parties and politicians to convey their messages to potential voters, and the ways they seek to do so. Four avenues are open to parties and their candidates seeking to reach the electorate via the media, although not all are open to all parties in all nations. First, they may take advantage of the free time specifically allocated to them in most nations of the world (but not in the United States). Second, they may pay the media to carry their messages, in the form of paid advertising, although this is carefully limited or prohibited altogether in most nations, and is nowhere else so widely practiced as in the United States. Third, they may seek to attract the media to give them free coverage. Fourth, they may use ever more available alternative media.

Free time   In many nations, the government requires the media to allocate free time to candidates for office, and these allocations go the parties, not to individual candidates. The media in Denmark and the Netherlands must give equal time to all parties, while those in Germany, France, and Israel must allocate time according to the proportion of the vote a party received in the past election (In Great Britain the two main parties are entitled to equal time and other criteria are used for allocating time to the smaller parties).[47] Since almost all nations except the United States limit the amount of time that can be purchased (France does not allow any political advertising whatsoever on the broadcast media), the provision of such time is an important determinant of the nature of the campaign.

The United States has never required the media to provide free time, although efforts to ensure fair access for a wide range of points of view have been made. Such regulations have included the **equal-time provision** (if a station gives or sells time to one candidate for a specific office, it must give or sell equal time to all of the candidates for the same office), the **fairness doctrine** ("reasonable time must be given for the expression of opposing views if a highly controversial public issue is discussed"), and the **right of rebuttal** (persons attacked on radio or television "in a way that damages their reputation" have the right to reply). None of these measures has been as effective as hoped by their proponents and the fairness doctrine was discontinued as a regulation in 1987. Instead of providing ample time to all candidates and points of view, U.S. broadcasters often try to stay within the rules by curbing the amount of time given to all.

Paid Political Advertising   Wherever it is allowed, paid political advertising consumes a very large share of candidates' and parties' budgets. Since 1976, major-party candidates in general U.S. elections have normally spent close to half their total campaign budgets on preparing and buying political ads for television.[48] The specific uses of ads have changed in recent campaigns, however. The strategists for candidate Bill Clinton actually spent a fairly low proportion of his budget on network television ads and focused their advertising dollars on thirty-two targeted states, placing no ads in the media of *top-end* states (states where they had about a 30 percent lead at the beginning of the campaign).[49]

The parties and their candidates have also become more sophisticated in the use of negative advertising. The first Clinton campaign used negative advertising to focus on President Bush's policies, not on his character — and to attack the press itself! In the latter case, the ad boasted of Clinton's abilities to stand up to the false attacks made against him by the media.[50] Bush made much freer use of negative advertising, as did Dole in 1996, forcing Clinton to develop rebuttal stories and ads; Clinton's strategists believed that "a charge left unrefuted is a charge the public will believe."[51] Meanwhile, Ross Perot has introduced the *infomercial*, buying 30-minute segments of time and using pie charts and diagrams to explain the specific details of his economic plan for the nation.[52]

Free coverage   A third way for parties and candidates to use the media is to attract free coverage. Government officials running for reelection or seeking to help those they wish to see win are at a great advantage, since they can often find ways to make campaigning look like the business of government. But even they, and certainly those who are not in office, will work hard to produce interesting political "stories" that can be told quickly and vividly. Of course, it is not enough for the candidate to offer a brilliant new solution to one of the nation's most pressing and complex problems. Such a solution would have to address the complexity of the problem, and that would probably be very time consuming and boring. Much more likely to gain the desired coverage is the well-designed *photo opportunity* combined with the well-prepared *sound bite*. A few seconds allowing the candidate to be filmed surrounded by adoring senior citizens at the annual picnic will bring out the television crews far more effectively than the preparation of a 200-page proposal to improve care for the elderly. The result, of course, is that very little substantive information is conveyed. According to Gary Selnow, the technology of the camera has "made it easy for news organizations and attractive for audiences to supplant abstract thought with concrete images. This highly visual and video-oriented society invests more in the illusion of television images than in the substance of reasoned analysis."[53] However true such an accusation may be (and indeed it is hard to deny), the parties have been willing to play along. Strategists for Clinton went so far as to establish a "Convention Satellite News Service," which provided prepackaged soundbites to local stations that could not afford to send reporters to the convention.[54]

Sometimes the second and third methods, paying and attracting the media, are actually combined. It is now more and more common in the United States for news broadcasts during election seasons to discuss political commercials as news. According to Kiku Adatto, 125 excerpts from such ads were shown on news broadcasts in 1988, but the question of whether or not the content of the ads was true was addressed less than 8 percent of the time: "Reporters became part of the campaign theater they covered — as producers, as performers, and as critics."[55]

Alternative Media   Given the limitations of the traditional media and the advances of technology, parties and candidates have begun to turn to other forms of communication. Cable television permits access to smaller but more homogeneous audiences, which in turn permits delivery of better targeted messages. Advertising on cable is far cheaper, which permits parties to use it more frequently and more repetitiously.[56]

Another form of alternative media is what Gary Selnow calls *direct-contact media*, media that allow the parties to go directly to the voters. Direct mail and the telephone are familiar forms of such contact, but use of electronic mail (e-mail) has been expanding by leaps and bounds in the past few years and the parties have not been slow to take advantage of its low cost and the possibility it offers for saying what they want to say how they want to say it.[57]

How the Media Use the Parties and the Candidates

Nevertheless, the main outlets for political news remain the traditional media, and their journalists and broadcasters continue to turn to the parties and the candidates for stories that will fit the entertainment values that

SENATOR

ROTHCO

"NEVER MIND MY CONSTITUENTS — HAVE YOU POLLED THE NETWORKS?"

(© Artemus Cole/Rothco Syndication)

govern their profession. They follow candidates for office everywhere they go, sponsor frequent polls in order to keep their readers up to date on who is ahead, and do their best to give the campaign all the qualities of a long and intensely exciting horse race.[58] Personal qualities and histories are explored for dramatic, even melodramatic, effect, and no aspect of a candidate's life is considered out of bounds. Family life is often given inordinate attention. As Ann Grimes has noted, "One of the bigger myths in Presidential politics is that because he has an adoring wife who is willing to function as an elbow ornament, [the candidate] has a viable family life and a good marriage," and, further, that such assets will make a difference in how successful he will be in office if elected.[59] "I always accuse him of marrying me to give himself a respectable image," said Betty Ford of former President Gerald Ford.[60]

However, other motives besides providing entertainment are at work in determining what political news the media will present and how they will offer it. "Freedom of the press belongs to the man who owns one," says the cliché, and in choosing what to present, media producers and reporters may well be guided by the very normal desire to please the boss. The "boss" is now likely to be both more difficult to argue with and more powerful. Most owners of media own more than one agency, controlling either several examples of the same type or different agencies of different types. The same person may own a community's only newspaper, only television station, and only radio station, thereby controlling all the important information sources. This is the case in France, where at one time the conservative publisher Robert Hersant controlled 29 percent of the newspaper distribution, a major television network, and his own advertising company.[61] In the United States, 80 percent of all newspapers are owned by corporate chains.[62] The "boss" may not even be in the same country as the media he or she owns; as of 1994, the Fox television network was more than 99 percent owned by Rupert Murdoch's News Corporation, based in Australia.[63] Even alternative forms of broadcasting are not exempt from the processes of media globalization; of the ninety cable franchises awarded in Britain by May 1990, more than 89 percent went to American corporations.[64]

Media owners and chief executives are the ones who hire media editors and producers, and they make a point of hiring capable men and women who agree with them. "I am the chief executive. I set policy, and I'm not going to surround myself with people who disagree with me," said Otis Chandler, publisher of the Los Angeles Times.[65] Although editors and journalists tend to have a spread of political affiliations comparable to those of the rest of the nation, owners are more likely to underrepresent the left and fall somewhere between centrist and arch-conservative. This political tendency, with some exceptions, is found from nation to nation and from the smallest to the largest media establishment.

Do journalists nevertheless find ways to introduce their own partisan biases into their reports? When and if they do, these biases are likely to be very similar to those of their audiences, at least in the United States. Although the average salaries for reporters, writers, and editors vary widely, journalism is a middle-class profession. In 1992, the median starting salary for newspaper reporters ranged from $24,700 to nearly $39,600 and "virtually all" experienced reporters earned more than $20,800.[66] The median annual salary for radio reporters was $16,000, for television reporters $21,825, with large differences depending on the size of the station.[67] Given their socioeconomic status, it is not surprising that, overall, journalists' political affiliations are similar to those of other Americans, with a somewhat greater number ready to state they are "independent."[68]

In any case, even when the presentation of partisan news is not biased, we should beware, say Dan Nimmo and James E. Combs, of imagining we can learn the truth about politics simply by following media reports. They suggest that the development of mass communication means the development of group fantasies about the nature of reality and argue that perhaps the required skills for citizenship are not those taught in civics texts —

BOX 8.3   **SURVIVAL TIPS FOR WATCHING POLITICAL ADS ON TELEVISION**

> **1.** Be aware that the ad is designed to create an emotional response. Think about what mood the ad is trying to create, particularly with music and images.
> **2.** Engage your intellect to examine the ad critically. Is there something that doesn't sound right? Does the ad raise more questions than answers?
> **3.** Don't assume the commercial's information is accurate. Misleading and just plain untruthful ads often get on the air.
> **4.** Don't figure that ads give you all the information you need. If you rely on political advertising to make a decision at the polls, you could be taken for a ride. Get more information from other sources: the *Voters' Pamphlet*, news coverage of the campaign, or knowledgeable friends whom you trust.
>
> Source: Jeff Mapes, "Do Campaign Ads Really Work?" *The Oregonian*, 30 Oct. 1994, A1. Reprinted with the permission of the publisher.

being interested and motivated to engage in political discussion and activity, acquiring political knowledge, being principled, and reaching choices by rational thinking — but rather learning how to assess dramatic performances, fantasy themes, rhetorical visions, and melodramatic rituals. Such skills might inspire us to demand more not only of parties, candidates, and journalists in the election melodrama but of ourselves as well.[69] (See Box 8.3 and, the next time you watch a political commercial, see if you can use some of the techniques recommended there.)

How Citizens Respond

How *do* citizens respond to the information about politics available via the media? Have we all become, as Roderick P. Hart suggests, "charmed" by television and ready to accept its cynical insistence ("cynicism . . . is television's most natural language") that "politics can be reduced to pictures," that it is interesting to "watch" but not really important, not really worthy of our involvement?[70] Or are we beginning to shake off the magic and look to other ways of getting political news as one step toward taking back control of our own destinies?

To begin to answer this difficult question, we first must recognize that access to the media and habits of usage vary across the world and over time. In the world at large, there are now more than 9,000 daily newspapers, selling in combination more than 600 million newspapers every day. There are over 2 billion radio receivers in the world and nearly 1 billion television receivers.[71] Of course, gross disparities in global access to modern means of communication still exist (see Table 8.3), but the new communications satellites now orbiting the globe make it possible "to provide reliable communications . . . to virtually every human community" and

TABLE 8.3   Global Media Distribution in Relationship to World Population (in percentages)

	World Population	Daily Newspapers (circulation)	Book Titles Published	Radio Receivers	Television Receivers	Long-film Production
Africa (excluding Arab states)	9.23	1.0	1.0	3.6	1.3	.1
North America	5.30	12.0	11.9	28.5	27.2	8.6
Latin America and Caribbean	8.47	6.4	5.9	7.6	8.7	5.1
Asia (excluding Arab states)	57.09	33.4	24.8	27.8	22.6	63.6
Arab states	4.18	1.2	.7	2.7	2.6	1.8
Europe (including former USSR)	15.23	45.0	54.0	28.3	36.4	19.9
Oceania	.05	1.5	1.7	1.3	1.3	.9

Source: Derived from *Statistical Yearbook 1991* (Paris: UNESCO, 1991), pp. 1–5 and 6–3. Reprinted by permission.

progress has been impressive in the past few years, especially in the provision of alternative media.[72] Cable television has shown remarkable growth (see Table 8.4) and diversity, ranging from extremist programming on the left or right to the unhurried, carefully balanced, and noninterventionist direct reporting of C-SPAN.[73] Fax machines, satellite television, computer modems, and radio talk shows have come to China and other nations where only a few years ago color television was a rarity.[74] The Pan African News Agency, located in Senegal on the west coast of Africa, has recently installed satellite and Internet communications systems to take the place of telegraph and radio links that were often incapacitated by desert dust storms or heavy rains.[75] The telecommunications industries of the European states are struggling to coordinate their information highways while Americans use the Internet for every conceivable political purpose, from ideological discourse to campaign fundraising.[76]

The tendency to use these alternative media for gathering and disseminating political news is a remarkable technological development, but it is also more than that. These are media that permit the presentation of programs that are more substantive, more opinionated, and more interactive than those offered by the traditional media, and their increasing use strongly suggests a growing discontent of the world's citizenry with the traditional media and its determination to treat politics — which after all, determines much of what happens in all our lives — merely as entertainment. In this regard, Christine Ridout makes a particularly interesting case

TABLE 8.4   **Growth of Cable Service in Selected Nations (in Percentages)**

Country	Cable Households as a Percent of TV Households	
	1985	1990
Austria	n.a.	23.7[a]
Belgium	78.3[c]	88.9[b]
Canada	63.5	73.6[d]
Denmark	n.a.	61.9
Finland	n.a.	42.3[a]
France	n.a.	1.5[b]
Germany	3.8[e]	32.3[e]
Ireland	30.0	30.9
Italy	n.a.	0.4[b]
Japan	1.1[f]	3.3[f]
Luxembourg	n.a.	64.3[b]
Netherlands	n.a.	79.5[b]
New Zealand	0	0
Norway	14.7[c]	31.8
Spain	n.a.	3.0
Sweden	5.4[h]	52.3[g]
Switzerland	n.a.	72.0
United Kingdom	0.6[h]	1.9
United States	35.2[c]	55.1[b]

[a] Data for 1991, calculated as percent of all households; source OECD (1992b).
[b] Data for 1989, calculated as percent of all households; source OECD (1992b).
[c] Calculated as percent of 1990 households; source OECD (1992a).
[d] Data for 1989.
[e] Data for former West Germany only.
[f] Includes broadband cable only, not community antenna systems.
[g] Data for 1991.
[h] Calculated as percent of 1991 households.
Source: Organization for Economic Cooperation and Development, *Competition Policy and a Changing Broadcast Industry* (Paris: OECD, 1993), p. 25. Reproduced by permission of the OECD.

BOX 8.4

THE TALK SHOW AS SOURCE OF POLITICAL INFORMATION

The *Today Show,* June 8, 1992

Viewer Questions	*Clinton's Answer*
Tax deductions for single income families	need a tax credit for children
Pro-choice/pro-life	strongly pro-choice
Plan to reduce deficit	line item veto; present a balanced budget; invest to create growth
U.S. nuclear weapons testing	supports test ban; part of effort to reduce nuclear weapons
Economic reform	must invest, control health care costs, create jobs, change tax code to encourage investment
Student college assistance	loans for everybody who needs them, pay back through public service
Gay rights	need a tolerant society that uses talents of all people
Veterans benefits	health care for veterans as part of a national program
Thoughts on Ross Perot	look at the candidates' records, need new approach, Perot is expression of frustration, we need action
What programs should be eliminated	reduce administrative costs, control health care costs, review all programs
Environment vs. the economy	no conflict between growth and environment; environmental technologies can create jobs
How campaign against Bush and a negative campaign	will talk about the issues and plans for future; answer charges
Gun control	support Brady bill, look at assault weapons
Women in your administration	wants administration to look like America, have hired women, need everyone
Restoration of democracy in Haiti	no military force, boycott, press for democracy, and not return refugees
Tax fairness	higher taxes on rich, taxes for investment, earned income tax credit, credit for children
Homelessness	home ownership, tenant management, housing rehabilitation for homeless, need a housing program
Changes in social security and Medicare	Medicare should include long-term care; control costs of entitlements with fees and taxes for high-income people
Government control of health care	government should control the *costs,* universal coverage with lower costs

Money to pay for your proposals	reduce defense and health care costs, higher taxes on wealthy and business, reduce costs of government; improve growth rates by investing
Policies toward Cuba	would continue the embargo, should keep pressure on Castro
Perot's record	Perot has no record, must look at his proposals; I will talk about my plans

Source: Christine F. Ridout, "News Coverage and Talk Shows in the 1992 Presidential Campaign," *PS: Political Science and Politics* (December 1993): 712–16. Reprinted by permission of the American Political Science Association and the author.

for talk shows in the United States. She credits them with turning the 1992 primary season around for candidate Bill Clinton at a time when the regular news media persisted in stressing the horse-race aspects of the campaign, made little reference to his or other candidates' substantive positions on the issues, and indeed kept insisting this candidate was "irrelevant," "practically invisible," and likely to end up in "an embarrassing third place." Clinton appeared on ten talk shows in June 1992 and used them to get his message across. By the end of the month, the percent of positive references to his chances in the regular media had risen from 33 to 71 percent. Ridout does not claim the talk shows did it all (indeed, it would make more sense to credit Clinton's string of victories in the primaries), but her analysis of the exchange between Clinton and viewer call-in questions on the *Today Show* on June 8, 1992 (see Box 8.4) certainly substantiates her claim that "talk shows provided an alternative form of communication which contributed to a substantive dialogue between candidates and voters."[77]

However we get the news about partisan politics, what does it mean to us? The question of media impact is a difficult one to study. Ask yourself what role the media played in your own choice in the last presidential election, and chances are you will be hard put to say. There is considerable evidence that U.S. citizens rely heavily on candidates' ads to "get some sense of what a candidate is like"; when asked, 62 percent either completely or mostly agree that "I often don't become aware of political candidates until I see their advertising on television." On the other hand, 74 percent say that news reports give them a better idea of where a candidate stands on the issues than do the ads, and 65 percent prefer news reports to ads for getting an "idea of what a candidate is like personally."[78] Canadians are somewhat less ambivalent: one-third of those polled would do away with ads altogether, and 77 percent believe there should at least be limits on party advertising; however, there seems to be, say André Blais and Elisabeth Gidengil, a majority conviction that ads "may sometimes play a useful role."[79]

Of course, we ourselves often do not know what role the various kinds of media play in helping us make distinctions between the parties or among the candidates, partly because the media seldom if ever reach us "unmediated." A medium is "an intervening thing through which a force acts or an effect is produced." The campaign news comes to us filtered not only through the commentaries of print and broadcast journalists but also through those of our friends and associates and, most important, through our own selective perceptions. We decide what we want to read or watch, and our choices are strongly conditioned by our desire to read or watch something that will confirm the beliefs we already hold; "good" news is news that tells us we were already right.

Furthermore, although those who pay attention to media coverage of campaigns tend to be better educated, more interested and active in politics, and more partisan, even they do not appear to remember much of what they watch, listen to, or read about. Studies in which television viewers have been interviewed show extremely limited recall. Two hours after a television network news show, viewers can normally remember only one of the twenty or so stories usually presented.[80]

At least in the United States, citizens do somewhat better at retaining personal information about candidates, including how well they are doing in the horse race. And they remember best of all favorable information about the candidates they prefer. Once the nominees are selected, over the course of the campaign Republicans become more and more favorable toward their candidate, Democrats toward theirs.

In any case, the parties themselves clearly believe in the power of the media. More and more, executing the campaign means taking it to the people via the media, and this in turn means accepting the profit-oriented demands of the media for stories that will attract viewers for their advertisers — or becoming paying advertisers themselves. Once the long electoral season is over, the parties claim it is they who will organize and conduct governments in our names, via their victorious candidates. We turn now to a consideration of whether or not this is so.

PARTIES IN GOVERNMENT

The idea that modern governments are run by political parties has been so widely accepted that the term *party government* has assumed the status of a concept, one that means government that is organized by the parties or, more specifically, the process whereby the leader of the party winning the most votes takes the top leadership role (be it president or prime minister), works with the advice of a cabinet formed of members of his own party or of other parties that have agreed to work with him, and sees his party's program translated into legislative bills, supported by party members or allies in the legislature, and made into the law of the land. But is party government really possible today?

In multiparty systems it is often necessary to form a ruling coalition by inviting leading members of different parties to take cabinet posts, thereby ensuring the support of their followers. When the parties take strongly different stands on major issues of the day, this can be a far from simple matter to resolve. No modern nation offers a better example of the intricacies of forming ruling coalitions than Italy, a nation in which the conservative Christian Democrats managed to remain in power for nearly forty years after World War II by the constant reshuffling of cabinet posts. In the late 1970s the party engineered the formation of a *minority government*, with cabinets composed of representatives of parties that had, altogether, only a minority of seats in the Chamber of Deputies — the communists, with 228 seats, could have brought the government down at any time but agreed to abstain in exchange for an unofficial but nevertheless significant say in all major issues. In 1981, as the communist vote was declining, the involvement of the Christian Democrats in a major political scandal forced them to share power with the small Radical Party to stay in power, and then, in 1983, it was the turn of the socialists to lay claim to a larger share of the pie, claiming and winning the prime ministership. In 1992, the legislative vote gave the four-party coalition that had been in power only 48 percent of the vote, and it was several weeks before the new cabinet could be formed.[81] Accumulating scandals and the ever more obvious and widespread power of the Mafia forced the Christian Democrats out of power altogether in 1994, when they won only 16 percent of the vote.[82] The new government was composed of three new center and center-right parties (Forza Italia, the Northern League, and the National Alliance), and it too was plagued by scandal and intercoalition squabbling, bringing it to an early demise. In 1996, the Italians formed their fifty-fifth government (cabinet) since the war, bringing in center-left as well as rightwing parties in the hope of having a strong enough majority to be able to move toward constitutional changes designed to end the chronic instability from which Italy has suffered so long.[83] The shifting division of power among Italian parties is shown in Figure 8.2.

The Italian example is an interesting one because it is so often cited as proof that multiparty systems inevitably produce excessive fragmentation and are likely to lead to corruption as well. In fact, however, almost all of the world's party systems are multiparty (even in "two-party" United States and Great Britain, minor parties do exist and do sometimes win office, especially at the local level), and of course not all governments are unstable and corrupt. Nor are two-party systems exempt from these deficiencies: in 1993, the elected members of the opposition party in one of the world's few genuine two-party systems, that of Jamaica, refused to attend the sessions of that country's parliament on the grounds that the election that year had been so marked by fraud and corruption as to be invalid.[84] As the Italians seem to recognize, and as we will consider further later in this book, government instability is likely to be a function of factors other than

Minority single-party government June 1976

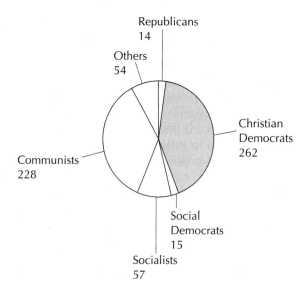

Republicans
14

Others
54

Christian Democrats
262

Communists
228

Social Democrats
15

Socialists
57

Coalition government June 1983

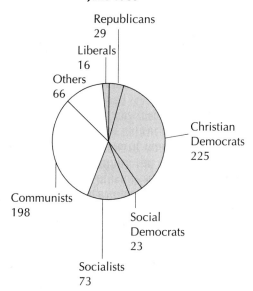

Republicans
29

Liberals
16

Others
66

Christian Democrats
225

Communists
198

Social Democrats
23

Socialists
73

Coalition government May 1992

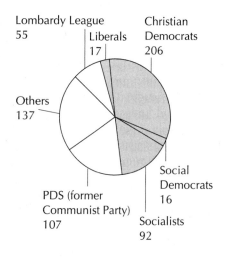

Lombardy League
55

Liberals
17

Christian Democrats
206

Others
137

PDS (former Communist Party)
107

Social Democrats
16

Socialists
92

Coalition government March 1994

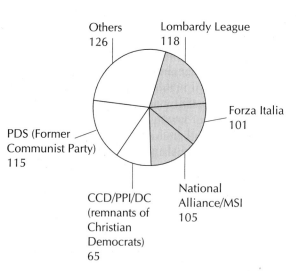

Others
126

Lombardy League
118

Forza Italia
101

PDS (Former Communist Party)
115

CCD/PPI/DC (remnants of Christian Democrats)
65

National Alliance/MSI
105

FIGURE 8.2   **Multiparty Coalitions in the Italian Chamber of Deputies 1976–1994**
The worldwide decline in Communist Party fortunes, the growth of anti-immigrant feeling (reflected in the strength of the new Lombardy League), and the fall of the scandal-ridden Christian Democrats have changed the nature of Italian coalition politics.

the number of parties — indeed, some argue that the absence of significant choice in a party system is more likely to produce discontent and instability than the difficulties of forming a government representative of a wide range of perspectives.

Even in different constitutional systems, however, effective party government is far from easy to establish. If the system allows for the separation of powers — and if electoral results sometimes place the legislative and executive branches of the government in the hands of different parties, as in the United States — then party government is possible only if each branch is run by well-disciplined party loyalists, with policy outcomes the result of interparty as well as interbranch compromise. On the other hand, systems that allow only one political party do not guarantee that that party will actually govern. As power shifts in today's more centralized governments from legislative to executive hands, the leaders of political parties are hard pressed for means to assert control over their one elected representative in the executive branch (the president or prime minister), his or her numerous appointees, and the army of bureaucrats who remain in government regardless of the changing winds of politics. Single-party nations are not immune from this shift to executive power; if anything, the tendency to concentrate power is stronger in nations with long histories of authoritarian rule. The very forces that impel such a nation toward a single party in its early political struggles will serve to demote that party to a lesser role once an independent government takes hold.[85]

Types of Parties

Is it possible, after considering all the different characteristics of political parties, to discern distinct types of parties? In the interests of organizing the knowledge we have and making it easier to use in the effort to acquire further knowledge — the fundamental reason for setting up any typology — several authors have tried to do so. Some have striven to combine organizational, membership, and leadership variables, classifying parties according to the nature of internal power relationships among leaders, activists, and followers. Thus, Maurice Duverger identified two types: **mass parties** with large, dues-paying memberships, centralized, bureaucratic leadership, and strong communication links running throughout the organization and **cadre parties** with small, loosely affiliated memberships, a coopted elite leadership with limited control over the base, and weak

---

Sources: Giacomo Sani, "The Italian Electorate in the Mid-1970s: Beyond Tradition?" in H. R. Tenniman, *Italy at the Polls, 1976* (Washington, D.C.: American Enterprise Institute, 1977), p. 90; Giacomo Sani, "Italian Voters, 1976–1979," in H. R. Tenniman, *Italy at the Polls, 1979* (Washington, D.C.: American Enterprise Institute, 1981), p. 44; Alberto Marradi, "Italy: From 'Centrism' to Crisis of the Center-Left Coalitions," in Eric C. Browne and John Dreijmanis, eds., *Government Coalitions in Western Democracies* (New York: Longman, 1982), pp. 33–70; *Le Monde,* April 9, 1992, p. 4; *International Herald Tribune,* April 7, 1992, pp. 2 and 4; Mark Donovan, "The Politics of Electoral Reform in Italy," in Pippa Norris, ed., *The Politics of Electoral Reform,* special issue of *International Political Science Review* 16, no. 1 (Jan. 1995): 47–64.

communication links.[86] A similar distinction was made by both Thomas Hodgkin and Ruth Schachter Morgenthau in their division of early African parties into mass parties and parties of notables.[87]

Another way of classifying parties that attempts to combine organizational, membership, and leadership variables is linkage theory. In *Political Parties and Linkage: A Comparative Perspective,* I distinguished among **participatory, policy-responsive, clientelistic,** and **directive** parties. Participatory parties aid their members to participate directly in policymaking processes; the candidates and the program are chosen by the militants and any elected representatives of the party take the program militants seriously and make every effort to turn it into the law of the land.[88] **Policy-responsive parties** work to ensure that policy is made in the interests of their supporters but are not directly guided by their own members.[89] **Clientelistic parties** make sure their followers receive certain material benefits for their support but do not encourage them to express opinions on matters of policy.[90] Finally, **directive parties** link voters to government by helping the government maintain coercive control over its subjects.[91]

For other authors, the most important determinant of party type has been the way the party performs the function of aggregating interests. Seymour Martin Lipset and Stein Rokkan identified four important political cleavages in modern times: church versus state, center versus periphery (that is, the nation versus component units), workers versus employers, and rural versus urban. They argued that twentieth-century political parties had been formed around those cleavages and that these earlier origins created enduring party systems.[92] In a simpler typology related less to the question of those interests a party aggregates than to how it does this task, Gabriel Almond and James Coleman divided parties into three types: pragmatic-bargaining, ideological, and particularistic. The **pragmatic-bargaining party** aggregates interests through negotiations, which reach unconcernedly across conflicting values. The **ideological party** is a party of true believers who gradually rally others to their cause; such parties do not aggregate interests so much as pursue a single set of values. The **particularistic party** also minimizes interest aggregation, identifying as it does completely with the interests of a specific social group.[93]

A party type (in this case not placed in a larger typology) that seems particularly relevant to many today is the **catchall party,** identified by Otto Kirchheimer as a party that makes concrete, pragmatic short-range promises to fulfill the immediate interests of as many voters as possible.[94] More recently, Jean Charlot has written of the **party of electors,** which places great emphasis on finding out what voters want and attempting to carry out their wishes — a combination, perhaps, of the policy-responsive party and the catchall.[95] But Peter Mair and Richard Katz do not think parties are very interested any more in catching all of us. They see a new kind of party emerging, which they call the **cartel party** and which they say consists of leaders who collude with other parties simply to ensure the survival of them all.[96]

Types of Party Systems

The term **party system** is really just a short way of saying "political system defined by the number of parties that operate within it." Studying the type of party system a nation has usually means trying to see how the number of parties a nation has influences the kind of political system it has.

Does it matter how many parties a nation has? In looking at the question of the possibility of party government earlier (see pp. 294–297), we have already suggested that little relationship seems to exist between the number of parties and the capacity of parties to organize government effectively. Here we turn to other possible relationships. For example, it is almost always assumed that the existence of a single-party system inevitably means authoritarian politics, sometimes defended on the grounds of the need for concerted struggle against the twin forces of oppression and underdevelopment, as in Vladimir Lenin's passionate defense of the single party in prerevolutionary Russia.[97] Other, more recent founders of single-party systems, such as former African presidents Julius Nyerere of Tanzania, Sékou Touré of Guinea, and Kwame Nkrumah of Ghana, have argued that the resources of new nations are too limited to permit the luxury of multiple parties. In such states, they claimed, all those trained in the skills of leadership must be put to work, not divided into active victors and inactive and contentious losers. They carried the argument to the point of insisting that only the single party permits true democracy, since only it provides a structure that allows all interested and able participants to take part in government.[98]

In recent years, arguments in favor of single-partyism are rarely heard, particularly as the International Monetary Fund has made the adoption of a multiparty system one of its conditions for "structural adjustment" prior to the receipt of large-scale loans and aids. Such artificially induced multipartism may, however, take strange and not particularly democratic new forms, as in the Ivory Coast, where the ruling party stays in power after having permitted the creation of a tame opposition fragmented into forty different parties, a pattern some of the remaining single-party states (such as Kenya, Uganda, Tanzania, Malawi, Zambia, Zaire, Guinea-Bissau, Mozambique, and Angola) are also expected to adopt.[99]

The Ivory Coast example is an extreme case of what some have labeled the **hegemonic party system,** a system in which more than a single party exists but one party has established hegemony — that is, pronounced and continuing dominance — over all the others. In China, small parties that are scarcely distinguishable from special interest groups are tolerated but rigidly excluded from sharing power with the ruling Communist Party. The Partido Revolucionario Institucional of Mexico offers another example. In that nation, such smaller parties as the Partido de Acción Nacional are sometimes able to win local office but have much less strength at the national level.[100] In contemporary South Africa, the African National Congress has been described as "dominant but not monolithic" and its opposition as "fragmented, regionally based, and coopted at the center" — clearly a hegemonic party in the making.[101] Hegemonic parties do not last forever, although it sometimes seems as if they will. The example of the Italian Christian Democrats, discussed earlier, is a case in point; the long but finally terminated tenure of the Liberal Democratic Party of Japan is another (although that party has recently returned to power).[102]

Another useful distinction is that made by Giovanni Sartori between party systems of **moderate pluralism,** in which numerous parties are only moderately differentiated from one another ideologically, and **polarized pluralism,** in which parties are ideologically separated by vast distances. Sartori cites Belgium, Iceland, and Switzerland as examples of the first; Chile before 1973 and contemporary Israel as examples of the second.[103] (The fact that the Labor and Likud parties of Israel were able to enter into coalition government in the mid-1980s would seem to suggest that Sartori's classification of the last was unsound; on the other hand, the two parties found their ideological differences so great as to make joint rule extremely difficult no matter how pragmatic politically.)

On the whole, the party systems that appear to function most equitably are the ones in which political power is neither so concentrated as to make authoritarian rule all but inevitable nor so dispersed as to make any government at all difficult to establish and maintain — that is, a party system consisting of a moderate number of parties that are moderately antagonistic toward one another. Despite a strong American bias to the contrary, there is no evidence to suggest that having only two parties is necessarily better than having several, nor is there any guarantee that a moderately multiple party system (say, two to six "significant" parties) will in fact produce an equitable system. Certainly, multiparty systems can establish governments as exclusionary as any single-party system — witness the case of South Africa during the years of apartheid — and "two-party" systems can be as incapable of effective rule as any other — witness the United States at the outbreak of the Civil War or during the height of the Watergate era or, some would say, at the end of the twentieth century. The fairness, stability, and efficacy of any political system clearly depends on far more than the number of political parties active in its electoral arena.

THE ROLE OF PARTIES TODAY

Political parties are held in low esteem in most nations today. Americans tend to rank parties near the bottom of any list of public institutions. Asked to give a letter grade to the performance of the two parties in the 1988 presidential campaign, a national sample gave both parties an average grade of C, and by 1991 41 percent of Americans saw no difference between the parties in their ability to handle "the nation's most important problem" (whatever the respondent deemed that problem to be).[104] The citizens of other nations seldom show their parties more respect, and sometimes show them less. Parties are viewed as selfish, dishonest, biased, and incapable of recruiting leadership of the quality citizens feel they deserve. Leftists imagine that parties work only for the elite members of society; elitists are certain they are the ignorant instruments of mobocracy.

The fact is that parties have almost always been held in contempt, and yet they continue to exist, be formed, and be reformed. If we dislike them so, why do we keep them? James Madison faced part of the answer squarely in Federalist Paper no. 10, when he recognized that the one thing worse than factionalism was a state that denied its citizens freedom of assembly.[105] The late shah of Iran acknowledged another aspect of the power of party when he formed a state-run party, the Rastakhiz, in a belated attempt to create a structure for rallying supporters. Charles De Gaulle discovered twice in his life that the forces of party could be stronger and more enduring than those of personal charisma. Both his retirements — in 1953 and in 1969 — were hastened by the machinations of party. In 1980, independent candidate John Anderson found how little enthusiastic public response counted for in the United States without the multiplier effect of a major party's nomination; in 1992, independent Ross Perot, supported by millions of Americans but not by an organized party, lost heart for the battle and dropped out early in the race, only to announce in 1995 that he would try again, this time with a real political party of his own (despite the fact that to place a single candidate on the ballot in all states, a new party in the United States must collect over 750,000 signatures).[106]

Fully understanding why we keep forming institutions in which we place so little faith, however, requires sorting out two matters that are commonly confused. First, we do *need* political parties. We have already reviewed the reasons parties are formed in the first place and the many functions they traditionally perform. Second, we are not satisfied with the *kind* of parties we get. Few observers of political parties deny that they are guilty, at least on occasion, of all the sins of which they have been accused.

For some, the answer to this dilemma is simple: Reform the parties. Efforts at reform, however, often either place the powers of party in the hands of the reformers, who soon begin to perpetrate the very abuses they swore to eradicate, or else rob the parties of much of their capacity to perform their appropriate functions. The latter problem has been particularly pronounced in the United States, the Western nation in which political parties are the most severely regulated.[107]

Why is it so difficult to devise reforms that work? Part of the answer lies in the connection between parties and power. Party militants want to win elections in order to obtain specific rewards. Obviously, not all the men and women who seek such rewards do so at unreasonable cost to others. But then again, what seems reasonable to me may well strike you as self-serving and exploitative. As long as we have no universal agreement on the rightful distribution of power and the resources it commands, and as long as mere human beings stay in charge of political parties, we must expect that their performance will continue to be disappointing to many.

However, another part of the answer may lie in the fact that we may have been too quick to assume we know the procedures that make democracy work, including how best to organize and regulate our parties. Is it true that parties are impossible to reform, or have we simply not yet given the problem sufficient attention? Despite the fact that political parties are capable — at least in theory — of providing wide-ranging programs and popularly selected candidates and thereby giving citizens a serious link to all the work of their governments, our general dissatisfaction with their performance may soon reach the point of no return. But when we seek to organize in a way to reach our governments on behalf of more than a single cause, what alternatives do we have?

SUMMARY AND CONCLUSION

Political parties are a unique form of political organization, characterized by their effort to place representatives from their own membership in office, which they do by nominating candidates to stand for election in their name. Their principal functions are leadership recruitment, interest aggregation, campaigning, and governing.

Parties began inside legislatures as factions developed among those elected to office but did not reach full development until organizations outside the legislature were created to persuade electors to vote for the members of a particular group. New parties often begin in a time of crisis, but there must always be individuals who believe that it will be useful and possible to form a new party (even if they are wrong!).

Internal democracy is extremely difficult to establish within a political party because of the typical characteristics of members, leaders, and organizations themselves. Decentralizing power does not mean eliminating oligarchic control; it can even make it easier for local oligarchs. Nevertheless, the effort to democratize parties seems to be an unending one, most recently epitomized by the new Green parties of Europe.

Party members may be supporters, adherents, or militants. The motives for joining parties may be summarized as personal objectives, loyalty, and political conviction; as in the case of interest groups, individuals may have more than one kind of motive. Some parties attract members from every sector of society, whereas others focus on the members of a particular ethnic group, religion, or language group. Candidates are chosen by a very wide range of methods throughout the world, and different qualifications are sought according to the conditions of the campaign to come.

Preparing the campaign requires raising funds and developing a strategy; in both cases, modern technologies play an ever more important part. Carrying out the campaign is more and more likely to be done via the media. To understand the role of the media in modern politics, it is important to understand the history of the media as a business enterprise, their consequent dependency on attracting as large an audience for their advertisers as possible, and the effect this need has had on their presentation of political news, including political campaigns. Parties and candidates gain access to the media via legally required free time, paid advertising, free coverage, and alternative media such as cable television, direct mail, the telephone, and electronic mail. Media reporters and editors use political news to attract as large an audience as possible and also to meet the demands of the owners, who may have specific political agendas of their own. Citizens have lately shown increasing interest in alternative media, including talk shows, but still tend to gather a large portion of what information they have about politics from paid ads, especially in the United States.

Once in government, the elected representatives of parties do not necessarily rule. They may be hampered by divided government, by their inability to form a governing coalition, by their own corrupt behavior, and/or by the excessive power of the civil service.

There are different types of parties as well as different types of party systems, but no consistent relationships exist between the kind or number of parties and their honesty or effectiveness. The fairness, stability, and efficacy of any political system depends on many other factors. Parties themselves are inevitably disappointing; we need them to make democracy possible, yet they are formed to gain power, and those who seek power have their own motives for doing so. Perhaps the only answer is to learn to accept our need for these puzzling and annoying organizations and give more serious attention to how to make them work for us and our democracies.

Selected Readings

Beck, Paul Allen. *Party Politics in America*, 8th ed. New York: Longman, 1996. This basic text provides careful and readable coverage of the key topics in the study of U.S. parties.

Coggins, John and D. S. Lewis. *Political Parties of the Americas and the Caribbean: A Reference Guide.* Essex, England: Longman Current Affairs, 1992. Provides detailed information on parties in the Americas and the Caribbean, including background information on the constitutional structures and electoral systems of the countries discussed.

Duverger, Maurice. *Political Parties. Their Organization and Activity in the Modern State.* Translated by Barbara and Robert North. New York: John Wiley and Sons, 1954. One of the first comprehensive, comparative studies of political parties, with chapters on organization, membership, leadership and the nature of party systems.

Gaffney, John, ed. *Political Parties and the European*

Union. London: Routledge, 1996. Fifteen case studies and four general discussions regarding the relationships between individual European parties and the institutions of the European Union.

Hoftstadter, Richard. *The Idea of A Party System: The Rise of Legitimate Opposition in the United States, 1780–1840.* Berkeley: University of California Press, 1972. One of the most interesting analyses of U.S. party history, tracing the slow legitimization of the idea of a competitive party system, as it reached fruition during the presidency of Martin Van Buren.

Katz, Richard S. and Peter Mair, eds. *How Parties Organize: Change and Adaptation in Party Organizations in Western Democracies.* London: Sage Publications, 1994. Case studies of political party organization drawn from the United States and eleven European nations.

Lawson, Kay, ed. *How Political Parties Work: Perspectives*

from Within. Westport, Conn.: Praeger, 1994. A collection of case studies illustrating the difficulties of achieving internal party democracy, the relationship between leadership and organization, the ways internal organization affects parties' performance and how external events can cause change in their internal organization.

Michels, Robert. *Political Parties.* New York: Dover Publications, 1915. The classical study of the rise of elite control (oligarchy) in all political organizations, even in those political parties most strongly dedicated to democratic procedures.

Schattschneider, Elmer E. *Party Government.* New York: Holt, Rinehart and Winston, 1942. Another classic in the literature, defending political parties as superior to interest groups as agencies of linkage in modern democracies.

Selnow, Gary W. *High Tech Campaigns: Computer Technology in Political Communication.* Westport, Conn.: Praeger, 1994. An explanation of targeted communication and of the universal trend in political campaigning to focus on ever narrower audiences, with a concluding discussion of the effects of these technologies on American voters, the press, and the political system.

Ware, Alan. *Political Parties and Party Systems.* Oxford: Oxford University Press, 1996. A comparative introduction to the study of parties and party systems, with an emphasis on the parties of Great Britain, France, Germany, Japan and the United States.

Notes

1. Sigmund Neumann, ed., *Modern Political Parties* (Chicago, University of Chicago Press, 1956), p. 395.
2. Joseph Schlesinger, "Party Units," *International Encyclopedia of the Social Sciences* (New York: Macmillan, 1968), p. 428. Italics added.
3. Fred Riggs, "Comparative Politics and Political Parties," in William J. Crotty, ed., *Approaches to the Study of Party Organization* (Boston: Allyn & Bacon, 1968), p. 51.
4. Maurice Duverger, *Political Parties,* trans. Barbara and Robert North, 2nd ed. (London: Methuen, 1959), xxiii–xxxvii.
5. Jean Charlot, *L'U.N.R.* (Paris: Armand Colin, 1967), pp. 37–38.

6. Joseph La Palombara and Myron Weiner, *Political Parties and Political Development* (Princeton, N.J.: Princeton University Press, 1966), pp. 7–21.
7. "These former believers, these sometime altruists, whose fervent hearts aspired only to give themselves freely, have been transformed into sceptics and egoists whose actions are guided solely by cold calculation." Robert Michels, *Political Parties,* trans. Eden and Cedar Paul (New York: Dover, 1959), p. 209. The quotation comes from page 401.
8. Moisei Ostrogorski, *Democracy and the Organization of Political Parties,* vol. 1 (New York: Anchor, 1964), p. 177.
9. Duverger, *Political Parties,* pp. 4–202.
10. Samuel Eldersveld, *Political Parties, A Behavioral Analysis* (Chicago: Rand McNally, 1964), pp. 98–117.
11. Michels, *Political Parties,* p. 408.
12. Donald Schoonmaker, "The Challenge of the Greens to the West German Party System," in Kay Lawson and Peter Merkl, eds., *When Parties Fail: Emerging Alternative Organizations* (Princeton: Princeton University Press, 1988), pp. 41–75.
13. Thomas Poguntke, "Goodbye to Movement Politics? Organisational Adaptation of the German Green Party," *Environmental Politics* 2, no. 3 (Autumn 1993): 379–404.
14. For a study of this question in Canada, see John C. Courtney, *Do Conventions Matter? Choosing National Party Leaders in Canada* (Montreal and Kingston: McGill-Queen's University Press, 1995).
15. Duverger, *Political Parties,* p. 82.
16. From a personal interview with a party militant, June 1978.
17. Richard S. Katz, "Party as Linkage: A Vestigial Function?" *European Journal of Political Research* 18 (1990):143–61, and Richard Katz et al., "The Membership of Political Parties in European Democracies, 1960–1990," *European Journal of Political Research* 22 (1992): 329–45.
18. Jeremy Richardson, "The Market for Political Activism: Interest Groups as a Challenge to Political Parties," *West European Politics* 18, no. 1 (Jan. 1995): 116–39. See also Kay Lawson and Peter Merkl, eds., *When Parties Fail: Emerging Alternative Organizations* (Princeton: Princeton University Press, 1988).
19. Anders Westholm and Richard G. Niemi, "Po-

litical Institutions and Political Socialization: A Cross-National Study," *Comparative Politics*, 15, no. 1 (Oct. 1992): 25–41.

20. William J. Keefe, *Parties, Politics and Public Policy in America*, 7th ed. (Washington, D.C.: Congressional Quarterly Press, 1994), p. 144.

21. This reformulation of Salisbury's list is based on Kay Lawson, "Toward a Theory of How Political Parties Work," in Kay Lawson, ed., *How Political Parties Work: Perspectives from Within* (Westport, Conn.: Praeger, 1994), pp. 288–91.

22. A distinction made by James Q. Wilson in *The Amateur Democrat* (Chicago: University of Chicago Press, 1963), passim.

23. Richard Rose and Derek Urwin, "Social Cohesion, Political Parties, and Strains in Regimes," *Comparative Political Studies* 2 (April 1969): 7–67.

24. Useful studies include Barbara Kellerman, *Political Leadership* (Pittsburgh, Pa.: University of Pittsburgh, 1986); Bryan D. Jones, ed., *Leadership and Politics: New Perspectives in Political Science* (Lawrence, Kansas: University Press of Kansas, 1989); and John W. Gardner, *On Leadership* (New York: The Free Press, 1990). See especially chapter 14 in Gardner.

25. See Chapter 6 for a discussion of electoral systems.

26. Herbert Alexander, *Financing Politics: Money, Elections and Political Reform*, 4th ed. (Washington, D.C.: Congressional Quarterly Press, 1992), p. 50.

27. Stephen J. Wayne, *Road to the White House 1996* (New York: St. Martins Press, 1996), p. 45; *International Herald Tribune*, 7 Feb. 1996, p. 3.

28. Alexander, *Financing Politics*, p. 63.

29. Ibid., pp. 53–54.

30. Federal Election Commission, *Campaign Guide for Corporations and Labor Organizations* (Washington, D.C.: Federal Election Commission, 1994), pp. 45–51; Alexander, *Financing Politics*, pp. 65–366. FEC publications are available free of charge and may be obtained by dialing 800-424-9530 or (for immediate fax delivery) 202-501-3413.

31. Frank Sorauf, *Inside Campaign Finance: Myths and Realities* (New Haven: Yale University Press), p. 116.

32. David P. Conradt, *The German Polity*, 4th ed. (White Plains, N.Y.: Longman, 1989), pp. 123–4.

33. Alan Ware, ed., *Political Parties: Electoral Change and Structural Response* (Oxford: Basil Blackwell, 1987), p. 18.

34. Werner Kaltefleiter, unpublished paper presented to the Fifteenth World Congress of the International Political Science Association, Buenos Aires, Argentina, 1991.

35. Herbert E. Alexander and Rei Shiratori, *Comparative Political Finance Among the Democracies* (Boulder, Colo.: Westview, 1994), pp. 3–5.

36. David Selnow, *High-Tech Campaigns: Computer Technology in Political Communication* (Westport, Conn.: Praeger, 1994), pp. 13–14.

37. Paul S. Hernnson, "Field Work, Political Parties, and Volunteerism," in James A. Thurber and Candice J. Nelson, eds., *Campaigns and Elections American Style* (Boulder, Colo.: Westview, 1995), p. 154.

38. Marshall Ganz, "Voters in the Crosshairs: Elections and Voter Turnout," *Current* (May 1994): 4–10.

39. Shaun Bowler and David M. Farrell, eds., *Electoral Strategies and Political Marketing* (New York: St. Martin's Press, 1992), pp. 226–28.

40. See Marion Farouk-Sluglett and Peter Sluglett, "The Iraqi Ba'th Party," in Vicky Randall, ed., *Political Parties in the Third World* (Beverly Hills, Calif.: Sage, 1988), pp. 57–74 and John Griffiths, "The Cuban Communist Party," in ibid., pp. 155–73.

41. Semantic note: *Media* is the plural form of *medium*. When we say "the media," we normally mean the **communications media**, referring in particular to newspapers, magazines, radio, and television, but also to films and recordings, and many of the newer uses of the telephone, radio, and television (jointly referred to as *telecommunications*).

42. Bernard Rochco, "The Evolution of News Content in the American Press," in Doris A. Graber, ed., *Media Power in Politics* (Washington, D.C.: Congressional Quarterly Press, 1984), p. 8.

43. "Jefferson and Jackson sponsored party newspapers that, without pretense of impartiality, gave readers the view from the White House." Bernard A. Weisberg, "The Press and the Presidents," *American Heritage* 45 (October 1994): 24.

44. Adam Gopnik, "Read All About It," *The New Yorker* 70 (12 Dec. 1994): 86, 92. Some of the recent works cited by Gopnik include John

Anthony Maltese, *Spin Control: The White House Office of Communications and the Management of Presidential News* (Chapel Hill: North Carolina University Press, 1994); David L. Protess et al., *The Journalism of Outrage: Investigative Reporting and Agenda Building in America* (New York: Guildford, 1991); and Mark Wahlgren Summers, *The Press Gang: Newspapers and Politics, 1865–1878* (Chapel Hill: North Carolina University Press, 1994).

45. Thomas E. Patterson, *Out of Order* (New York: Knopf, 1993). See also William Glaberson, "The New Press Criticism: News as the Enemy of Hope," *New York Times*, 9 Sept. 1994, sec. 4, 1.

46. Weisberg, "Press and the Presidents," p. 22–24.

47. Lynda Lee Kaid and Christina Holtz-Bacha, eds., *Political Advertising in Western Democracies: Parties and Candidates on Television* (Thousand Oaks, Calif.: Sage, 1995), pp. 14–15.

48. Thomas E. Patterson, "Television and Presidential Politics, A Proposal to Restructure Television Communication in Election Campaigns," in Alexander Heard and Michael Nelson, eds., *Presidential Selection* (Durham: Duke University Press, 1987), p. 303.

49. Bruce I. Newman, *The Marketing of the President: Political Marketing as Campaign Strategy* (Thousand Oaks, Calif.: Sage, 1994), pp. 114–115.

50. Ibid., p. 113.

51. Gerald M. Pomper et al. *The Election of 1992: Reports and Interpretations* (Chatham, N.J.: Chatham House, 1993), p. 85.

52. Newman, *Marketing*, p. 83.

53. Selnow, *High-Tech Campaigns*, p. 143.

54. Newman, *Marketing*, p. 112.

55. Kiku Adatto, "The Incredible Shrinking Sound Bite," *The New Republic* 202, no. 22 (May 1990): 20–23.

56. Selnow, *High-Tech Campaigns*, p. 140.

57. Ibid.

58. For a case study of the horse-race phenomenon in the coverage of American campaigns, see Henry E. Brady and Richard Johnston, "What's the Primary Message: Horse Race or Issue Journalism?" in Gary R. Orren and Nelson W. Polsby, eds., *Media and Momentum: The New Hampshire Primary and Nomination Politics* (Chatham, N.J.: Chatham House, 1987), pp. 127–86.

59. Ann Grimes, "The Making of a Bachelor President," *New York Times* 6 Oct. 1991, sec. 4, 17.

60. Ibid.

61. *Le Monde*, 18 Feb. 1987, p. 10. In other cases, large corporations control numerous media enterprises along with several other types of businesses. The General Electric corporation media holdings are large enough and successful enough to make it fourth in a 1990 list of "100 leading media companies." R. Craig Endicott, "100 Leading Media Companies," *Advertising Age* 61, no. 26 (25 June, 1990): 51–58.

The tendency toward concentrated ownership of the media by large-scale holding companies whose chief interest is the profit margin has been spurred by the growing profitability of the media. The hundred leading media companies in the United States took in combined revenues of $71.2 billion in 1989, up 8 percent from the year before. Magazine and cable companies are particularly strong moneymakers. Newspapers, although still generating the greatest revenue, are steadily falling behind as advertisers switch to other, more popular media. Fewer than 4 percent of American cities now have competing newspapers under separate ownership. Ibid. and Parenti, *Inventing Reality*, pp. 27–28.

62. Foreign Policy Association, "Media's Role in Shaping Foreign Policy," *Great Decisions* (New York: Foreign Policy Association, 1991), p. 90.

63. *New York Times*, 30 Nov. 1994, 1.

64. Ralph Negrine, "The Media and the Public Interest: Questions of Access and Control," in Meryl Aldridge and Nicholas Hewitt, *Controlling Broadcasting: Access Policy and Practice in North America and Europe* (Manchester: Manchester University Press, 1994), p. 58. For a general review of legislation designed to maintain diversity and competition in European broadcasting industries, see chap. 10, "Competition Policy and the Broadcast Industry in Member Countries" in Organization for Economic Cooperation and Development, *Competition Policy and a Changing Broadcast Industry* (Paris: OECD, 1993).

65. Quoted by David L. Paletz and Robert M. Entman, in *Media Power Politics* (New York: Free Press, 1981), p. 15, from a paper prepared by Diana Tillinghast for the 1980 meetings of the Western Political Science Association.

66. John W. Wright, *The American Almanac of Jobs and Salaries* (New York: Avon, 1993), p. 434.

67. U.S. Department of Labor, *Occupational Outlook*

Handbook, 1994–95 Edition Lincolnwood, Ill.: NTC, 1994), pp. 186–87.

68. David H. Weaver, *The American Journalist* (Bloomington: Indiana University Press, 1986), p. 83. According to Weaver, women reporters average $5,500 per year less than men, women supervisors $5,000 less. However, these differences by gender are much less pronounced for beginners.

69. Dan Nimmo and James E. Combs, *Mediated Political Realities* (New York: Longmans, 1983), p. 69.

70. Roderick P. Hart, *Seducing America: How Television Charms the Modern Voter* (New York: Oxford University Press, 1994). According to Hart, "television's greatest danger is the license it gives to citizen inaction" (p. 98).

71. *Statistical Yearbook 1994* (Paris: UNESCO, 1994), pp. 6.2, 6.8, and 6.9.

72. Heather Hudson, "New Communications Technologies: Policy Issues for the Developing World," *International Political Science Review* 7, no. 3 (1986): 332. These satellites are used for data communications and teleconferencing as well as for broadcasting. Although very few of the thirty-four nations classified as low income have bought into the INTEL-SAT system for international communications or into one of the regional systems such as ARABSAT or PALAPAB, India, Brazil, and Mexico have created their own domestic satellite systems, and other low-income nations have announced plans to do so.

73. On C-SPAN, see Lou Prato, "Politics in the Raw," *Washington Journalism Review* (September 1992): 35–38.

74. Xiao-huang Yin, "China's Gilded Age," *Atlantic Monthly* (April 1994): 42.

75. *New York Times*, (1 Oct. 1994), A2.

76. Bruce Barnard, "A Revolution in the Making," *Europe* (Oct. 1994): 20–22.

77. Christine F. Ridout, "News Coverage and Talk Shows in the 1992 Presidential Campaign," *PS: Political Science and Politics* (Dec. 1993), pp. 712–16. Quote on p. 715. For two other perspectives on talk shows in politics, see Kenneth S. Stern, "Hate on Talk Radio," *USA Today Magazine* (July 1992): 58–61, and Howard Fineman, "The Power of Talk," *Newsweek* (8 Feb. 1993), 14–29.

78. *The People, the Press and Politics 1990* (Washington, D.C.: Times Mirror Center for the People and the Press, 1990), p. 133, cited by William J. Keefe, *Parties, Politics and Public Policy in America*, 7th edition, (Washington, D.C.: Congressional Quarterly Press, 1994), p. 142.

79. André Blais and Elisabeth Gidengil, *Making Representative Democracy Work: The Views of Canadians* (Toronto and Oxford: Dundurn Press, 1991), pp. 113–26.

80. Richard Joslyn, *Mass Media and Elections* (Reading, Mass.: Addison-Wesley, 1984). p. 176.

81. *International Herald Tribune*, 7 April 1992, 1.

82. For the 1994 shift, see Mark Donovan, "The Politics of Electoral Reform in Italy," in Pippa Norris, ed., *The Politics of Electoral Reform*, special issue of *International Political Science Review*, 16, no. 1 (Jan. 1995): 47–64; David Henderson, "Little Joy for the Italian Left," *New Statesman and Society* (1 April 1994): 10; David I. Kertzer, "Italy Produces a Ballot-Box Revolution," *Baltimore Sun*, (3 April 1994), 1E+; and Mario Sznajder, "Heirs of Fascism? Italy's Right-Wing Government: Legitimacy and Criticism," *International Affairs* 71, no. 1 (Jan. 1995): 83–102.

83. *International Herald Tribune*, 1 Feb. 1996, 5 and 2 Feb. 1996, 1, 11.

84. Basil Wilson, "Fifty Years of Party Politics in Jamaica," *Everybody's* (July 1993): 15–18. Jamaica has had only two parties for over fifty years but has also had frequent periods of instability, particularly during the 1970s.

85. For an example, see Yahya M. Sadowski, "Cadres, Guns and Money: The Eighth Regional Congress of the Syrian Ba'th," in M.E.R.I.P. *Middle East Report* 134 (July-Aug. 1985): 3–8.

86. Duverger, *Political Parties*, pp. 4–202.

87. Ruth Schachter Morgenthau, *Political Parties in French-Speaking Africa* (London: Oxford University Press, 1964), pp. 336–41; Thomas Hodgkin, *African Political Parties* (London: Penguin, 1961), pp. 68–75, 81–124.

88. For an example, see Tom Truman, "The Australian Labor Party and the Trade Unions: Linkage as Penetration and Reaction," in Lawson, ed., *Political Parties and Linkage*, pp. 154–82.

89. Samuel Elderweld has given a good example of such parties in a study of the ways Dutch legislators manage to establish positive working relationships with Dutch bureaucrats. "Political Elite Linkages in the Dutch Consociational

System," in Lawson, *Political Parties and Linkage*, pp. 154–82.

90. The Italian Christian Democratic party's distribution of jobs in both the private and the public sector during its long reign in power provides an example, as do the relationships established in many Latin American communities where the local boss helps only those who vote as instructed. See Robert Leonardi, "Political Power Linkages in Italy: The Nature of the Christian Democratic Party Organization," and Steffen Schmidt, "Patrons, Brokers and Clients: Party Linkages in the Colombian System," both in Lawson, *Political Parties and Linkage*, pp. 243–88.

91. For example, by giving traditional authorities (chiefs) some of the lesser posts in the party, the Popular Revolutionary Movement of Zaire was long able to control these authorities in a way that worked to suppress popular participation in that nation. See Thomas Turner, "Chiefs, Bureaucrats, and the M.P.R. of Zaire," in Lawson, *Political Parties and Linkage*, pp. 370–91.

92. Seymour Martin Lipset and Stein Rokkan, *Party Systems and Voter Alignments: Cross-National Perspectives* (New York: Free Press, 1967. See also Stein Rokkan, *Citizens, Elections, Parties* (Oslo: Universitets Forlaget, 1970) and, for a more recent and more elaborate typology based on the Lipset-Rokkan version, Daniel-Louis Seiler, *De la comparaison des partis politiques* (Paris: Economica, 1986). Although all this work is based on types of cleavages rather than types of parties, it clearly has relevance here.

93. Almond and Coleman, *Politics of the Developing Areas*, pp. 43–45.

94. Kirchheimer, "Transformation," in La Palombara and Weiner, *Political Parties and Political Development*, pp. 177–200.

95. Jean Charlot, "Catch-allism revisited," paper presented at "Party Politics in the Year 2000," Manchester, January, 1995.

96. Richard S. Katz and Peter Mair, "Changing Models of Party Organization and Party Democracy: The Emergence of the Cartel Party," *Party Politics* 1, no. 1 (1995): 5–28.

97. V. I. Lenin, *What Is to Be Done?* (New York: International, 1929).

98. Sékou Touré, *L'Action Politique du Parti Démocratique de Guinée* (Conakry, Guinea: Imprimerie Nationale, n.d.); Julius Nyerere, *Freedom and Unity* (London: Oxford University Press, 1967); and Kwame Nkrumah, *Consciencism* (London: Heinemann, 1964).

99. Victoria Brittain, "Democracy Takes a Few Steps," *World Press Review* (Aug. 1991): 14–16.

100. Martin C. Needler, *An Introduction to Latin American Politics: The Structure of Conflict*, 2nd ed. (Englewood Cliffs, N.J.: Prentice Hall, 1983), pp. 21–25. For recent signs that the PRI may be beginning to lose its grip, see Paul B. Carroll and Craig Torres, "As Elections Approach, the Uprising in Mexico is Shaking up Politics," *Wall Street Journal*, 7 Feb. 1994, A1.

101. Alexander Johnston, "South Africa: The Election and the Emerging Party System," *International Affairs* 70, no. 4 (October 1994): 721–36.

102. For interesting studies of several hegemonic parties, see T. J. Pempel, ed., *Uncommon Democracies: The One-Party Dominant Regimes*, (Ithaca: Cornell University Press, 1990).

103. Giovanni Sartori, *Parties and Party Systems: A Framework for Analysis* (Cambridge, England: Cambridge University Press, 1976), pp. 127 and 179.

104. *The People, the Press and Politics 1990* (Los Angeles: Times-Mirror Center for the People and the Press), 16 Nov. 1990, and *Gallup Poll Monthly* 300 (September 1990): 32 and 308 (May 1991): 36.

105. Alexander Hamilton, James Madison, and John Jay, *The Federalist Papers* (New York: Mentor Books, 1961), pp. 77–84.

106. *New York Times*, 28 Sept. 1995, A11.

107. For details of state regulation of parties in the United States, see Kay Lawson, "How State Laws Undermine Parties," in A. James Reichley, *Elections American Style* (Washington, D.C.: Brookings, 1987), pp. 240–60.

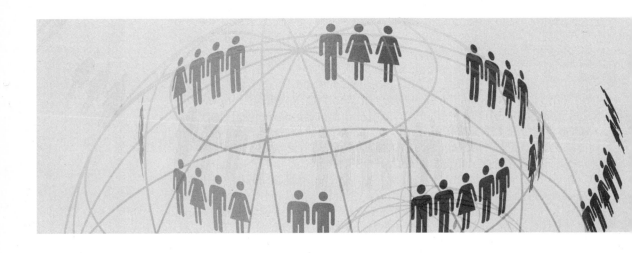

IV THE WORK OF GOVERNMENT: LEGISLATIVE, EXECUTIVE, AND JUDICIAL FUNCTIONS

9 Making the Laws

D O YOU REMEMBER YOUR first day in college? Chances are you spent most of that day trying to figure out the rules. All kinds of rules presented themselves to you: rules about which pieces of paper you had to have, where to exchange them for other pieces of paper, where to put your things, where to put yourself. Some rules were more compelling than others: If you are a young man receiving a government-backed loan for your education, you may have been required to demonstrate that you had registered for the draft in order to receive that aid. Other rules were given quietly and following them was clearly optional: You learned without being told that there was or was not a specific way to dress, to talk, perhaps even to sit and look about. In any case, there you were, an independent human being with the ability to decide for yourself which rules to follow and which to reject. Once you had sorted it all out, made your decisions, followed some rules to completion ("Here is the check for my tuition"), adopted others as a pattern for your behavior ("I will be in my botany class by 8:10 every Monday, Wednesday, and Friday morning"), and rejected others ("I don't care what the others do, I'm going to wear the clothes I have and that's that"), chances are life began to seem a little bit easier. You knew what you were doing.

What you went through in those first few days tells you a great deal about the role of rules in our lives — including the role of those rules we call laws. A rule is a guide to behavior. It may be a regulation established by persons in authority, a principle of conduct that one sets for oneself, or simply something that normally happens ("As a general rule, Americans eat three meals a day"). A law is a rule of the first category: a regulation established by persons in authority. But not all such regulations are laws. A **law** is a regulation established by *public* authorities and backed by the collective power of the polity to which it applies. It is, in effect, a *plan* — a decision to handle a particular problem in a particular way — and a *commitment*, made by the entire polity when they acquiesce in the authority of those making the plan, that the plan will in fact be carried out. Because it is so strongly backed, it is the most powerful kind of rule. We have the power to act contrary to the law, but we do so at our peril.

The polity for which a particular law is made may range from the smallest village to the nation-state. (The uncertainty of enforcement of international law places it in a special category. See Chapter 13.) At the lowest level are local **ordinances,** sometimes referred to collectively as **municipal law.** "The charge to the university for providing police protection at university events shall be $35 per hour per officer" is a rule set by officeholders (perhaps a council, a board, a mayor, or a sheriff) who have been granted the authority to make such rules throughout a governmental domain (a village, township, city, or county), either by other officeholders or by statute.

Laws are made at all levels of government, and rules with the force of law can be made by any branch of government. We think of the legislative branch as the lawmaking branch of national government, and quite rightly so; thus, the work of legislatures will be the central topic of this chapter. However, legislators are not our only national lawmakers; rules issued by executives also have the force of law, although they may be called by a different name. "I have ordered the National Guard to remain on twenty-four-hour duty at all campuses of the university where disturbances have been reported" is a rule set by a chief executive. Such a rule is often called a **decree** but may also be called an ordinance, an executive order, or a decree law.

The pronouncements of judges are more likely to be rulings than rules, but these too can have the force of law. "The right of students to use notes in university examinations is not protected by the First Amendment; there was, therefore, no violation of the Constitution in the university's decision to withhold the degree" is a **ruling,** which is to say, an interpretation of a rule (such as a clause in a constitution, law, ordinance, decree, or executive order) that affects the applicability of the rule. A nation's constitution is a set of rules that has precedence over all other rules. The constitution and judicial rulings about the meaning of the constitution are together called **constitutional law.**

Some rules have the force of law even when made outside government.

"Henceforth the party's policy is that only those veterans with three or more years' membership in the party are eligible for educational benefits" is a rule that may have the force of law if the party in question has unrestrained power to tell the legislature what laws to write and pass.

Finally, some rules are written to be laws from the very beginning. In 1976, the U.S. Congress ruled: "Institutions of higher education receiving financial assistance whether directly or indirectly [shall not] undertake any study or project or fulfill the terms of any contract containing an express or implied provision that any person or persons of a particular race, religion, sex, or national origin be barred from performing such study, project, or contract."[1] That rule, once entrenched in the U.S. code, became part of the law of the land. Such laws can only be reversed by other, subsequent laws, or by ruling of the U.S. Supreme Court that they are in some way contrary to the U.S. Constitution.[2]

This chapter is about the making of those rules that are called laws or that have the force of law. Our primary emphasis will be on how laws are made in legislatures, but our functional approach (see Chapter 1) helps us recognize that other governmental and even extragovernmental bodies also make rules or rulings that have the force of law. Thus, we will also consider how executive and judicial agencies make law and will end with a few words about how laws are sometimes shaped by extragovernmental bodies.

LAWMAKING IN THE LEGISLATURE

A **legislature** is an institution in which individuals gather with the primary purpose of making laws. It need not be an elected body, although it often is. It need not be a permanent body convened periodically; sometimes it is, sometimes it is not. A legislature is established every time a tribal chief, king, military commander, or the highest potentate in a theocracy summons some of the elders, nobles, senior officers, or higher clergy (respectively) to help work out policy on a matter of politywide concern. When the governor of a colonial territory appoints a few trusted individuals to form a legislative council, as was the British practice in the heyday of empire, that too is a legislature.[3]

The more familiar form of a modern legislature, however, is a permanent, periodically convened institution composed of officials elected for a limited term for the express purpose of making laws, such as the German Bundestag, the British House of Commons, the Japanese Diet, the French National Assembly, the Mexican National Congress, and the U.S. Congress. Even in this category there are numerous variations. The legislature's relationship to the executive branch and the individual legislators' relationships with their constituents vary significantly from polity to polity. Other differences include the number and nature of the individual houses of the legislature, the power of committees, and the customs and mores of the particular legislature.

THE RELATIONSHIP BETWEEN LEGISLATIVE AND EXECUTIVE POWER

Legislative power need not be separate from executive power. Indeed, it seldom is. Just how closely connected they are, and what the balance between them may be, depends on a nation's constitution and whether it prescribes a parliamentary system, a presidential system, or a blend of the two. The simplest way to make this distinction clear is to describe each of these three systems in turn. The diagrams illustrate how each establishes a different relationship between legislative and executive power.

The Parliamentary System

In a **parliamentary system**, the legislature maintains extremely close bonds with the system's executive leadership and has significant power of its own. Because this system works very differently from the one you probably know best, it may help you to refer to Figure 9.1 while reading the next few pages. In the diagram, a solid arrow shows the direction of effective control of one body over another and a broken arrow indicates some degree of control, often varying according to political circumstances.

In a parliamentary system the same executive leadership directs the work of the legislature, called *parliament* and consisting of an upper house and a lower house, and the work of the *bureaucracy*. The bureaucracy includes all the departments or ministries of government; it is sometimes called the *administration*. That executive leadership is the *cabinet*, which is composed of the heads of the departments of government, usually called *ministers*, occupants of important appointive posts, such as the head of the national security agency, the top leader in the military forces, or an important prelate in a system where church and state are closely intertwined; and the chief executive, usually called the *prime minister*. The cabinet in a parliamentary system is often called the *government*, not because it is in fact the entire government but in recognition of the key role it does play.

Where do parliamentary cabinets come from, and what do they do? In the most typical form, the individual members of the cabinet are chosen by the prime minister but must be approved by the lower house (see pp. 333–334 for the difference between the lower and upper houses of legislatures). To become prime minister, one must be a leader (usually the top leader) of a political party. If that party wins a majority of the seats in the lower house of the legislature, its senior leader will be asked to try to "form a government." If he or she can win the approval of the lower house of parliament for the cabinet proposed (and if the party has won the majority of seats in the legislature, such approval is virtually assured), then the new

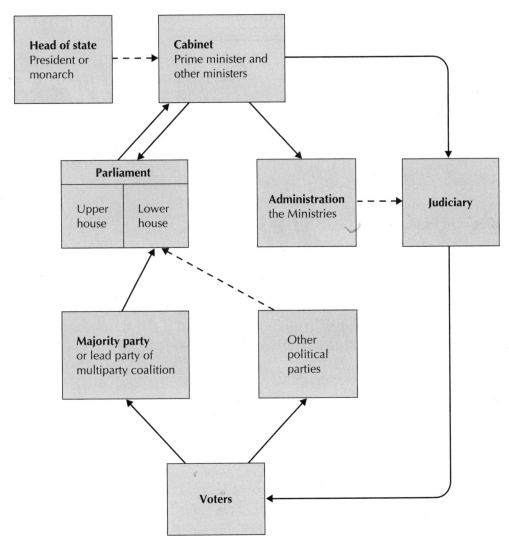

FIGURE 9.1   A Parliamentary System

government is established and the party leader in question becomes the prime minister. The cabinet may be formed exclusively of members of parliament (who may or may not be allowed to keep their seats in that body), or it may include some persons who have not been elected to any office whatsoever; the more common pattern is for cabinet members to be members of parliament as well.

In a parliamentary system, the person who asks the party leader to try to form a government is the nation's monarch or president (often referred

The first meeting of the newly reunited German parliament at the opening session of the assembly in Berlin's Reichstag in October of 1990. (AP Photo/Wide World)

to as the **head of state**). This is the most important role — or at least the most politically powerful role — that a monarch or a president can play in a parliamentary system; the other functions of the head of state are all purely ceremonial. Even in this case, if the party leader leads a party that has indeed won a majority of seats in the lower house, the head of state can only follow a script written by others. Everyone knows that the majority party's leader must be asked to form a government and will succeed in doing so.

In **multiparty parliamentary systems**, however, where it often happens that no party wins a majority of the seats, the ceremonial leader may have an opportunity to exercise a very real influence on the course of events. In such a case it is usually still expected that the leader of the party winning a plurality of seats will be given the first chance to form a government, often by asking leading members of various other parties to take posts in the cabinet in order to form a *coalition* government. If that cabinet cannot win the approval of the lower house, the same person may be asked to try again with a different cabinet, or the leader of another party may be asked to try. Sometimes a nation's politics are so fragmented that no single leader is considered dominant over all the others in a particular party; in that case, the job of trying to form an acceptable cabinet may be passed on to someone else in the same party. As a general rule, the more difficult it is to form a government (cabinet) that the lower house will accept, the more power will be exercised by the monarch or president in a parliamentary system, at least during this difficult period. However, even in cases where it is very difficult indeed to form a new government, the ceremonial leader customarily takes the advice of the nation's most astute and most powerful politicians in deciding whom to ask next.

Once formed, the new cabinet becomes the center of the entire governmental process in a parliamentary system. It assumes primary responsibility for the formulation of new legislation and accounts for the initiation of most new bills. Government bills (bills proposed by the cabinet) typically have precedence over bills proposed by individual members of parliament. In some systems, individual members are not allowed to introduce certain kinds of bills — for example, those that would require additional expense with no provision for additional revenue. At the same time, it is also the duty of cabinet members to see to it that the bills are properly carried out by the appropriate departments or ministries once they become law.

So far it may appear that once the legislature has approved a cabinet and a government is formed, the ordinary members of parliament will find themselves playing an insignificant role in the making of laws. Such an impression is not correct. Although most bills are initiated by the cabinet and all laws must be carried out through the administrative apparatus the cabinet controls, the members of parliament still have an important role to play in shaping the content of legislation. (We will come back to this in discussing the role of committees.) No bill becomes law without the consent of at least the lower house of the legislature; more commonly, both houses must approve. Furthermore, it is usually possible for the legislature to put an end to the life of any cabinet. The most forthright way of doing so is by calling for a motion of censure or by voting negatively when the government itself calls for a vote of confidence. If a majority of the lower house votes for the motion (or against the government), the government is dismissed — or, in the term more often used, *dissolved*. However, this procedure normally means not only that the cabinet must resign but also that the members of the lower house will themselves have to face new elections. Since this is not always politically convenient, members of parliament often prefer to accept partial changes to the cabinet, engineered by the majority party's leadership (see Box 9.1).

However, if it proves impossible to form a new cabinet that can command a majority, then elections must be held. In parliamentary theory, the

BOX 9.1

A PRIME MINISTER RESIGNS IN GREAT BRITAIN; A PARTY STAYS IN POWER

In November 1990, the prime minister of Great Britain, Margaret Thatcher, resigned. The end of her reign was as dramatic and unusual as had been her rise to power and her style in office. She was the first woman to lead the Conservative Party (one of the two major parties of Britain), the first woman prime minister, the prime minister who stayed in power the longest (twelve years) in British history, and the only prime minister in the twentieth century to lead her party to victory in three consecutive elections.

Thatcher did not achieve such a record by being nice. She was hard fighting, confrontational, and ruthless, and she earned her nickname "Iron Lady" many times over. She led Great Britain into a period of privatization and austerity that, while bringing benefits to a portion of the middle class, increased the gap between rich and poor, increased the number of the latter, and did little to improve the nation's declining fortunes in the world economy. She maintained a fiercely constrained view of the proper role for the European Community, fighting with particular vigor against any expansion of its powers that would compel the maintenance of social benefits she believed Great Britain's economy could no longer afford to provide. She led her nation to battle for the maintenance of British supremacy in the Falklands, a distant set of islands off the coast of Argentina, despite the fact that their possession brought no real advantage and that their defense came at high cost in British lives and equipment.

Throughout this period, however, she maintained just sufficient popularity — for the benefits she provided to many and convincingly promised to others, for her dramatic style, for the psychic boost a successful battle gives a nation in decline — to keep her party in power, and thus herself in its leadership. Thatcher's downfall came in large part owing to her effort to pass a flat tax (a *poll tax* that would have been added onto other more standard taxes) and, more immediately, her ever-hardening stand against the economic integration of Europe. But the clincher was the declining strength of her party in the polls and the fear of its other leaders and *back-benchers* (ordinary members of parliament) that only a change in leadership would permit them to win the elections that had to be held within the next year and a half. The party did not re-elect her as its leader, which, under the parliamentary system, meant she was thereby required to resign as prime minister as well. The Conservatives were free to pick another leader (and did: John Major, former Chancellor of the Exchequer), who then automatically became the new prime minister. When the next elections were held, the gamble proved to have worked: Once again, the party gained a majority of seats in the House of Commons, and once again its leader assumed the nation's highest post, prime minister.

vote of the electorate may resolve the dispute on which the government foundered, but this does not always work: postwar crises in Italian parliamentary government have come about in part because the vote has consistently failed to produce a clear majority for any party or ideologically workable coalition of parties. By 1996, fifty-four different cabinets had been installed since the end of World War II and in that year the government "fell" again. Italian President Oscar Luigi Scalfaro, unable to find a parliamentary leader capable of putting together an acceptable new cabinet, was forced to call for new elections. Scalfaro's failure had been more or less expected but was not seen as inevitable, since time and again Italian presidents have managed to engineer a change of cabinet without the need for new elections; there have been only about one-fourth as many legislative elections as cabinet collapses in the same fifty-one years since World War II. However, since the fall of the Christian Democratic Party in 1994 after successive revelations of criminal behavior by its leadership, the balance of power among the new Italian parties has made the formation of governing coalitions yet more difficult, with power split among the increasingly popular Democratic Party of the Left (successor to the former communist party), the Forza Italia (the right-leaning party of entrepreneur and former prime minister Silvio Berlusconi, also accused of criminal activity), the hard-right National Alliance (successor to the prewar fascist movement of Benito Mussolini), and the almost equally rightwing Northern League, as well as numerous smaller parties (see Chapter 8, p. 295).[4]

A parliamentary system is the very antithesis of a system based on the separation of powers. Even the judicial branch, made up of judges (often, at the highest level, appointed by the prime minister without need for ratification by parliament) and other court officers, is closely linked to the other two branches of government, and sometimes considered part of the administration. In Great Britain, the highest court in the land is a committee of the House of Lords (the "Lords of Appeal in Ordinary"), and even its rulings can be — and have been — overruled by legislation passed by the two houses of Parliament. Since the British House of Lords has the power only to delay legislation, not to veto it and since the majority in the lower house, the House of Commons, commonly votes as directed by the cabinet (unless so unhappy with that body that it helps bring about a dissolution) ultimate power over the judiciary resides in the cabinet in Great Britain as in most other parliamentary systems.[5]

The parliamentary system is, in fact, predicated on keeping the functions of government tightly interwoven. The link between legislative and executive functions is considered so important that one author has referred to it as the "buckle" that holds everything together and makes the system work.[6]

The Presidential System

The **presidential system** is characterized by weak ties between the legislative and executive branches and a shifting balance of power. The presiden-

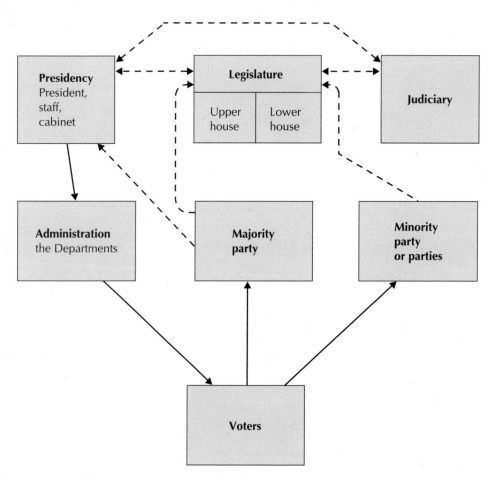

FIGURE 9.2   A Presidential System

tial system (illustrated in Figure 9.2) functions quite differently from the parliamentary system. It rests on the assumption that placing too much power in the hands of too few is dangerous to the liberty of citizens. The government is therefore divided, on the principle of the **separation of powers**, into three branches: legislative, executive, and judicial. Each branch is given a separate domain, a separate source of power (the chief executive and the legislators are elected independently, the highest judges are appointed), and the power to correct the abuses of the others. Under such a system the relationship between the executive and legislative branches, which may and often do come under the control of members of opposing parties, is likely to be contentious and fraught with difficulty. (See Box 9.2) Defenders of this system argue that such conflict is a small price to pay to protect the nation against the tyranny that might arise with more concentrated power.[7] But those who prefer parliamentary government point out that that system permits stronger parties, more frequent elections (when deemed necessary) and, most importantly, more cohesive government.

Whatever side one takes in such a debate, it is important to understand four crucial differences between presidential systems and parliamentary systems: The different sources of executive power, the different roles of the executive in the initiation of legislation, the presence or absence of ceremonial leadership, and the different roles of political parties. Exact procedures vary, but the more usual patterns are as follows.

Source of Executive Power   In a parliamentary system, the prime minister is chosen first by a party (as party leader), second by the voters in a particular constituency (as their representative to the lower house of the legislature), third by the ceremonial leader (as a possible head of government), and fourth by the lower house of the legislature (as prime minister in fact). The other members of parliament are chosen by the voters within their constituencies. National legislative elections are always important: they determine the balance of power in both the legislative and executive offices.

In a presidential system, on the other hand, the president is chosen first by a party (as nominee), and second by the voters of the entire nation (as president).[9] The members of the legislature are also chosen first by the parties (as nominees) and second by the voters (as representatives) in elections that may or may not be held at the same time as the presidential election. In any case, the members of the legislature in a presidential system have terms of office different from that of the president and play no part in his or her selection. Presidential elections are normally considered far more important than legislative elections in a presidential system.

Initiation of Legislation   In a parliamentary system, the prime minister and the cabinet can and do initiate legislation. In a presidential system, the president and the members of the administration may initiate new legislation, but only indirectly, working through individual members of the legislature who agree to sponsor such bills. Those bills have no special priority over other bills proposed by the same or other individual members. However, we should not exaggerate the importance of this difference, since in practice the legislative leaders in a presidential system are usually extremely well aware which bills have the backing of the president, and such bills will almost always receive greater and more favorable attention than bills sponsored by ordinary members.

Ceremonial Leadership   In a parliamentary system, the ceremonial leader plays a role in establishing the link between executive and legislative powers by calling upon the party leader most likely to gain the approval of the lower house to form a government. The ceremonial leader takes power either by right of birth or by election (but in either case, the

choice of that official is far less important than the choices made in legislative elections). In a presidential system, the president is also the ceremonial leader.

Role of Political Parties   In a parliamentary system, the political parties
choose the candidates for the legislature and choose their own leader in
the knowledge that if enough of their legislative candidates are successful,
that leader will become the prime minister. They also know that the leader
will count on the votes of the successful candidates of the party not only
to take office but also to carry out the party's program. This means that the
party plays a far more critical role in parliamentary systems than in presidential systems. Furthermore, the constitutional link between executive
and legislative power in parliamentary government forces a link between
the party's candidates for executive and legislative power. This means a
more unified party, better able to maintain party discipline in the legislature, and thus better able to combine legislative and executive power in
implementing its program. In a presidential system, the political parties
choose legislative and executive candidates separately, receive little encouragement from the constitutional system to operate in harmony, and
are thus more likely to permit undisciplined voting in the legislature. The
end result is that although the voters in a presidential system directly elect
the president as well as the legislators, choosing between competing candidates from different parties, they do not have the advantage of knowing
that strong and well-disciplined parties will hold their successful candidates responsible to the program on which they campaigned (hence the
broken lines in Figure 9.2 from the parties to the presidency and the
legislature).

The combined effect of these four differences between a presidential
system and a parliamentary system is to make the ties between executive
and legislative power much looser in a presidential system. Looser ties in
turn tend to leave the determination of which branch is more powerful to
other, nonconstitutional factors, which vary from time to time and from
nation to nation. The degree of the nation's need for rapid and forceful
decision making from its executive, and/or for personal strength or popularity from the occupants of its different offices, thus assume much greater
significance in determining the distribution of power in presidential systems than in parliamentary systems. In times like the present, presidential
systems lead to greatly strengthened executive branches, yet the legislative
branch may retain enough power to block and frustrate the most powerful
president while lacking the internal unity and constitutional authority to
take power on its own (see Box 9.2).

**The Presidential-
Parliamentary
System**

The **presidential-parliamentary system** is characterized by strong ties between the legislature and the executive and a weak legislature. A constitutional system that has become increasingly common in recent years not
only in Europe but in several of the new African states, it is a blend of the

BOX 9.2

U.S. PRESIDENT VERSUS CONGRESS: THE SEPARATION OR STALEMATE OF POWER?

For several years, the United States has been experiencing the downside of the principle of separation of powers: the possibility of stalemate between its executive and legislative branches. For years the problem took the form of Republican presidents versus Democratic majorities in Congress. Then in 1994 the tables were reversed, as Democratic President Bill Clinton found himself faced with Republican majorities and, in particular, a resolute band of budget-trimming freshmen under the leadership of House Speaker Newt Gingrich. Determined to carry out the unambiguous "Republican Contract" on which they had campaigned and won in the mid-term elections, the House Republicans passed bill after bill — on such questions as reforms to the welfare system and the legal system, the weakening of environmental regulations, the battle on crime, and the use of American troops in United Nations operations — which the president, equally determined, promised to veto.

The president had already responded to the rightward shift of the 1990s by abandoning his plans for reforming the health care system as well as stressing his own interest in trimming the deficit and in reforming the welfare system ("We all know what we need," he said on the last subject, disappointing many of his own supporters with some of his ideas, "we need time limits for welfare recipients, we need strict work requirements, we need very tough child support enforcement, we need more flexibility for states"). By the end of 1995, however, Clinton had reached, at least for the moment, the limit of his own flexibility, and refused to sign a Republican budget bill that included many of the kind of provisions he had earlier announced were unacceptable. The result was that funding for many government services ran out and "the government closed down." (In fact, most offices remained open; the impact was most severe on certain limited groups — and on the public servants who could not be sure when and if lost pay would be made up to them.) Continued negotiations at the White House between the president and congressional leaders produced continued stalemate, as neither side was ready to compromise. When the Republican leadership was ready to agree, the adamant freshmen refused, producing a minivictory for the Democrats, who could then claim the stalemate was the fault of their opponents, unable to agree among themselves. Meanwhile, of course, the problems that the disputed legislation was supposed to resolve remained largely unaddressed. Power was so well distributed it had almost ceased to exist.[8]

presidential and parliamentary systems, as illustrated in Figure 9.3. At first glance, this system looks very much like a parliamentary system. A president chooses a prime minister, who must win the approval of the legislature's lower house for a cabinet. However, several key differences weaken the power of the legislature while maintaining a strong bond between the two kinds of power. The net result is a much stronger executive. (See

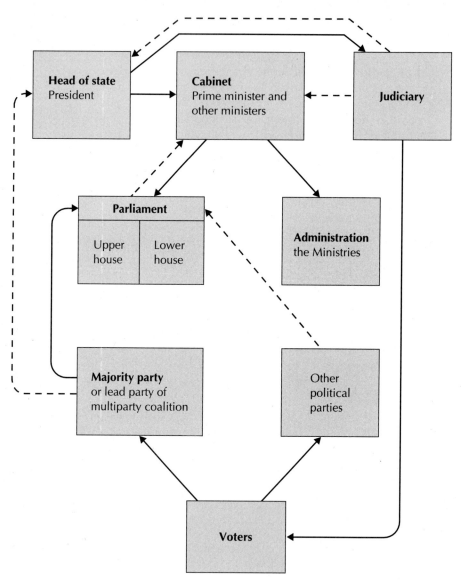

FIGURE 9.3   *A Presidential-Parliamentary System*

Box 9.3 for a description of a critical moment in the life of the French Fifth Republic, a good example of a presidential-parliamentary system.)

The first essential difference between a parliamentary system and a presidential-parliamentary system (sometimes referred to as a **quasipresidential system**) is that the president has the power to appoint anyone at all as prime minister and to remove that person at will. The prime minister

BOX 9.3

CHALLENGING PRESIDENTIAL POWER IN FRANCE

In 1968, students in France became increasingly disenchanted with the policies of President Charles De Gaulle. Some of them wanted an education that would prepare them better for the technocratic age, others resented altogether the Gaullist shift to technocracy, and many were dissatisfied with the government's policies both at home and abroad. Their anger led to open protest. What began simply, as a protest demonstration over the entirely collegiate issue of visiting rights between men's and women's dormitories, escalated rapidly to a full-scale protest against government policies. Although peaceful at first, the demonstrations brought a heavily repressive police response, which led in turn to increased student militancy. Large-scale demonstrations and sit-ins in university auditoriums and classrooms became the order of the day, interspersed with scuffles with the police, which usually ended in arrests.

President De Gaulle's first inclination was to leave the matter to the police and not dignify it with presidential attention. Then the workers joined the students, staging their own strikes and demonstrations. France appeared on the edge of a general strike, if not a coup d'état. When his ministers urged him to take action, the president said he would hold a referendum, offering the French the chance to change their constitution to make the Senate a place where students and workers could be directly represented. But Prime Minister Georges Pompidou, knowing that this gesture would be repudiated as useless and beside the point, persuaded De Gaulle to let him try his hand at resolving the crisis.

The prime minister was a great success. He restrained the police in their dealings with the students, negotiated wage settlements with the workers, and convinced De Gaulle to dissolve parliament and call for new elections, which gave the Gaullists a stronger majority than ever before in the National Assembly. De Gaulle appeared on television during the election campaign looking old, tired, and finished. Was power passing to the prime minister?

Not in France, birthplace of the presidential-parliamentary system. De Gaulle had the means to reassert his power, and he used them. Only a few short weeks after the crisis he calmly arranged for Pompidou to "resign." His able servant had proved too able for his own good. (The following year De Gaulle offered the French his referendum on the Senate and it went down to defeat. De Gaulle thereupon resigned, opening the path for Pompidou to take the presidency.[11])

need not be a member of parliament, need not be a leader of a major party, and in fact need not even be a member of a political party. The prime minister forms a cabinet, which must be approved by the legislature, but again, cabinet members need not be members of parliament or leaders or members of political parties. It is normal in such a system for the president to be elected directly by the people; the prime minister and cabinet members need not have been elected at all. Such a system permits the president to become a very active player in the game of ministerial musical chairs that takes place when parliamentary cabinets falter and political support declines. When the French people became particularly discontented in the spring of 1992 over continuing problems of unemployment and the high cost of living, and manifested that discontent by voting heavily against the ruling socialist party in regional elections, Socialist President François Mitterrand replaced Prime Minister Edith Cresson with Pierre Beregovoy. This action, combined with several other important cabinet changes, temporarily calmed the troubled waters.[10]

The constitution of a quasipresidential system may also give the president the right to name the highest judges, rule the nation directly during states of emergency, and declare when such a state of emergency exists. These supplementary powers may or may not require the signature of the prime minister; because that official's tenure in office is subject to the will of the president, little restraint on the president's power is implied by such a stipulation in any case. Clearly, in such a system the president is not a ceremonial leader but rather the most powerful figure in the government. But the chief executive's power is not unlimited. The prime minister retains the important powers of setting the government's daily agenda and overseeing both the formulation and the execution of policy — it is the prime minister who plays the most active role, but that role must be played in a way that is satisfactory to the president, to whom the prime minister reports and who has the power to remove him or her from power.

A more serious potential check on the powers of the president rests in the political parties and their elected representatives, particularly if a party other than the president's party gains control of the legislature. In that case, a united and determined majority, following party discipline, may refuse to approve the cabinet (including the president's choice for prime minister) until one is appointed that will act in accordance with its will.

Nevertheless, the trumps are all held by the president in such a system, backed by that officer's ability to remind the others that only the president is elected by all the voters. Thus, the flow of power in a presidential-parliamentary system is almost always that indicated by the arrows in Figure 9.3. The bonds between executive and legislative powers remain strong, but they now serve to hold together the unequal partners of a greatly strengthened executive and a greatly weakened legislature.

REPRESENTATION: LEGISLATORS AND THEIR CONSTITUENTS

We have just examined three versions of the legislature's relationship to the executive branch. Another key difference in legislatures around the world is seen in the relationship that legislators maintain with their constituents. One question all legislators must resolve is whether to act independently on the basis of what they personally believe to be correct principles or to attempt to carry out the will of constituents even when it runs contrary to those principles.

Any attempt to answer the fundamental question is likely to lead to a host of other problems. It is often difficult to know the will of constituents with certainty. It is not easy to treat all constituents as equals — some will be better informed and more articulate than others, some will be major contributors to the legislator's campaign fund, and some will be other powerful political leaders who helped the representative secure the nomination in the first place. Sometimes nonconstituents have a claim to legislative attention on the grounds of past favors, promises of future help, or the national importance of the causes they represent. Even if a legislator wishes to be loyal to his or her own constituents, it is often very difficult for that legislator to be sure that the will of the voters truly reflects their own interests. Furthermore, these interests may be extremely varied and not easily compromised. The interests of the whole (the community) are not always in accord with the sum of the interests of the parts (the individual citizens and groups), and both may be in conflict with the interests of the larger polity (the nation) of which they form a part.

Even when legislator inclination, constituency will, and national interests conveniently match, problems remain. These problems are related to the theme of interdependence we are pursuing throughout this book: How do international developments impinge on the proposed legislation, and what is the responsibility of the individual legislator to add "best interests of the human polity" to the list of objectives to be served?

Consider, for example, the problems the U.S. Congress had to wrestle with after the brutal repression of student demonstrations took place in China in June 1989. Many members of Congress believed that global protection of human rights required that the United States impose economic sanctions on China as well as issue strong statements of disapproval, whereas others believed such a move would do more damage to U.S. business interests in China than good to the cause of fostering democracy. In the final analysis, the latter camp prevailed. The United States severely criticized the Chinese government but limited more substantive response to a temporary ban on diplomatic visits between the two nations and on new loans to China by the World Bank and other international development banks. When the new Clinton administration put the question of human rights back on the agenda for discussion with the Chinese, it did not stay there long; by the end of 1994, the policy of linking trade benefits to human rights had again been openly abandoned.[12]

Every representative, and every political scientist writing about the problem of representation, has a slightly different way of trying to resolve such dilemmas of representation. Edmund Burke, the eighteenth-century British statesman and philosopher, wrote at length on this question, and his words are still cited with approbation or contempt, depending on the citer's own views on this important question. Burke believed that the representative should act independently but should remain reasonably aware of his constituents' major interests. He defined interests very narrowly. For him they meant simply that the district one represented might be characterized by a dominant mode of making its livelihood — for example, fishing, raising corn, or mining precious minerals.[13] Burke told his own constituents they could expect no more than this from him; his constituents told him, by way of the vote that removed him from office, that they had a rather different definition in mind.

Hannah Pitkin, a twentieth-century commentator on this problem, has offered a different resolution. She would leave representatives considerable latitude but would insist that their job is to find the best possible way to combine the interests of constituents (which are, for Pitkin, all the individual concerns that are or might be affected by government policy) with those of the nation. When this cannot be done and representatives find it necessary to act contrary to their constituents' will, it is their responsibility to make every effort to explain why and to persuade their followers that the national interest is in fact also their own interest — in short, to attempt to change the will of constituents whenever they cannot follow it. For Pitkin, political representation is never a matter of a single action but rather "the patterns emerging from the multiple activities of many people."[14] She stresses the importance of facilitating representation by having the appropriate institutional framework. The right to vote, sufficiently powerful elected officials, a significant opposition, and a multiple-member lawmaking body are all essential ingredients of representative government, according to Pitkin.

Those of us who have observed representative politics in recent years would probably want to add still further institutional guarantees. In Pitkin's world, representatives are men and women of principle. They must wrestle with difficult questions, and they do not always resolve them wisely or in the best interests of their constituents, but they never stop trying to do so. Unfortunately, such leadership is not always characteristic of those who take on the tasks of representation. Special interests can and often do pay the bulk of campaign expenses and control the votes of particular representatives, and such interests may operate from outside the legislator's constituency altogether. Nor is a strong opposition always a sufficient safeguard against misbehavior in office. Individuals waiting their turn to take power may be eager to do so on behalf of those same special interest groups rather than on behalf of a wider public. They may well be willing to join those in power in return for a piece of the pie — a tendency Italians call *trasformismo*, meaning a readiness to transform oneself (or, in the British phrase, "cross the carpet"), providing only that the price is right.

A further problem in securing fair representation is the inability of certain groups to elect persons like themselves to serve in their nation's legislative bodies. Sometimes this is simply a matter of voting rights; for example, it is only very recently that the majority black population of South Africa has achieved full voting rights, but that transition was swiftly followed by the transformation of that nation's legislature as well. Often, however, the problem is social and political rather than constitutional. Take a moment to read Table 9.1: In how many nations have women had the right to vote and to be elected for more than thirty years yet still not gained more than 15 percent of the seats in the legislature? What accounts for the slow progress of women in gaining full representation?

TABLE 9.1   **Women in National Legislative Office**

Selected Countries	Date of Right to Vote	Date of Right to Be Elected	Percent of Women in Parliament 1991
Algeria	1962	1962	2.4
Argentina	1947	1947	4.7
Australia	1901/1967[a]	1901/1967[a]	6.7
Bangladesh	1947	1947	10.3
Brazil	1934	1934	6.0
Bulgaria	1944	1944	8.5
Cameroon	1946	1946	14.4
Canada	1917/1918/1950[a]	1920/1960/1969[a]	13.2
Chile	1931/1949[a]	1931/1949[a]	5.8
China	1949	1949	21.3
Cuba	1934	1934	33.9
Czechoslovakia	1920	1920	8.7
Denmark	1915	1915	33.0
Ecuador	1946	1946	5.5
Egypt	1956	1956	2.2
El Salvador	1961	1961	8.3
Equatorial Guinea	1963	1963	0.0
Finland	1906	1906	38.5
France	1944	1944	5.7
Gabon	1956	1956	4.2
Germany	1918	1918	20.4
Greece	1952	1952	5.3
Hungary	1945	1945	7.0
Iceland	1915	1915	23.8
India	1950	1950	7.1
Indonesia	1945	1945	12.4
Iraq	1980	1980	10.8
Iran	1963	1963	1.5
Ireland	1918	1918	7.8
Israel	1948	1948	6.7
Italy	1945	1945	12.8
Ivory Coast	1952	1952	4.6
Jamaica	1944	1944	5.0
Japan	1945/1947[a]	1945/1947[a]	2.3

Continued

TABLE 9.1   *Continued*

Selected Countries	Date of Right to Vote	Date of Right to Be Elected	Percent of Women in Parliament 1991
Jordan	1974	1974	0.0
Kenya	1963	1963	1.1
Korea (North)	1946	1946	20.1
Korea (South)	1948	1948	2.0
Laos	1958	1958	8.9
Kuwait	not yet	not yet	0.0
Luxembourg	1919	1919	13.3
Madagascar	1959	1959	6.5
Malaysia	1957	1957	5.0
Mexico	1947	1953	12.4
Mongolia	1923/1924[a]	1923/1924[a]	2.1
Morocco	1963	1963	0.0
Mozambique	1975	1975	15.7
Nepal	1951	1951	3.4
New Zealand	1893	1919	16.5
Nicaragua	1955	1955	16.3
Norway	1907/1913[a]	1907/1913[a]	35.8
Pakistan	1937	1937	0.9
Papua New Guinea	1975	1975	0.0
Peru	1950	1956	5.5
Philippines	1937	1937	9.0
Poland	1918	1918	13.5
Portugal	1931/1976[a]	1931/1976[a]	7.6
Romania	1929/1946[a]	1929/1946[a]	3.6
Rwanda	1961	1961	17.1
South Africa	1930/1984[a]	1930/1984[a]	2.6
Spain	1931	1931	14.6
Sweden	1918/1921[a]	1918/1921[a]	38.1
Switzerland	1971	1971	14.0
Syria	1949	1953	8.4
Thailand	1932	1932	3.8
Togo	1956	1956	3.9
Tonga	1960	1960	0.0
Tunisia	1959	1959	4.2
Turkey	1930/1934[a]	1930/1934[a]	1.3
United Arab Emirates	not yet	not yet	0.0
United Kingdom	1918/1928[a]	1918/1928[a]	6.3
United States	1920	1788	6.4
Venezuela	1947	1947	9.9
Vietnam	1946	1946	17.7
Zambia	1962	1964	5.1
Zimbabwe	1957	1978	12.0

[a]Where several dates are shown, full suffrage for all adult women came in several stages.
Source: Irene Franck and David Brownstone, *The Women's Desk Reference* (New York: Viking, 1993), pp. 806–807. Reprinted by permission of the authors.

There is no easy cure for skewed representation where all have the vote, but remedies for corrupted representative leadership are even more difficult to devise. Two practices that offer some hope of protection are by no means foolproof. One is the establishment of independent watchdog agencies, such as the office of ombudsman in Sweden. It is the task of the ombudsman to expose (and presumably end) the more heinous abuses of the privileges of office.[15] Of course, such agencies do not always work as intended. The laws governing the U.S. Federal Elections Commission, established to weaken the control of large monied interests over individual candidates, have, as we discussed in Chapters 7 and 8, left loopholes permitting more private money to be funneled into American campaigns than ever before.

Because such watchdog agencies are themselves part of the government they are expected to monitor and control, a stronger institutional safeguard against corruption rests in the existence of a wide range of political organizations outside government. Ironically, however, such organizations often contribute to the problem. Political action committees and other special interest groups are a case in point, even if some groups (and some parties) may provide elected representatives with helpful reminders of the scope of their responsibilities and the possibility of their removal from office. Furthermore, protecting the right of free assembly that ensures the existence of a pluralistic political system is a task that inevitably devolves on government — that is, on the very officials whose actions we hope to guide and control. Institutions can take us only so far. There comes a time when we must rely on the quality of the men and women inside them.

CAMERAS, COMMITTEES, AND CUSTOMS: OTHER VARIATIONS IN LEGISLATURES

The term *camera* originally referred to a chamber or a room and only later came to mean a device for taking photographs. Thus, when we say that a legislature is *unicameral* or *bicameral*, we are referring to the number of houses (chambers) it has. A **unicameral legislature** has one house, a **bicameral legislature** has two.[16]

Most legislatures have two houses to ensure that different interests — and different principles of representation — will have appropriate arenas of action. Normally the lower house is elected directly by the people, with each representative serving approximately the same number of constituents. Upper houses vary from system to system, but they are usually made up of elder statesmen, elected indirectly (for example, French senators are elected by local and regional government officials) and in office for a longer term than their counterparts in the lower house. In some nations the upper house consists entirely of appointed members and in Great Britain it is composed of "lords," most of whom have little claim to glory beyond the fact that they have inherited titles of nobility. In *corporatist* states, one or both houses (if there are two houses) will be composed of representatives from different occupations and branches of industry, not from different regions (for example, the Corporazione of Italy under the rule of Benito Mussolini before and during World War II).

In most nations with bicameral legislatures, the lower house is far more powerful than the upper house; the upper chamber deliberates on all bills, but it is easily overridden by the lower house in the event of disagreement. There are, however, exceptions. The U.S. Senate — directly elected by the people since 1913 — has always been at least coequal with the House of Representatives in the exercise of power.

Another exception was the Supreme Soviet of the former Soviet Union — a bicameral body consisting of the Council of the Union, in which each delegate represented 300,000 inhabitants, and the Council of Nationalities, in which the union and the autonomous republics were represented. The two Soviet houses had equal power, but it would be more accurate to say they were equally powerless, because their activity was normally limited to giving unanimous approval to legislation or decrees that originated in the top councils of the Communist Party.[17] Under former Soviet president Mikhail Gorbachev, the lower house of the national legislature became the Congress of People's Deputies, but once he was seriously weakened by the attempted coup in August of 1991 Gorbachev decided to abolish the Congress and replace it with a unicameral–appointed Legislative Council consisting of twenty deputies from each republic. When this and his other efforts did not succeed in stopping the hemorraging of power at the top, Gorbachev was forced to resign and Russian President Boris Yeltsin, elected in June 1991, declared, "The Union of Soviet Socialist Republics, as a subject of international law and a geopolitical reality, is ceasing its existence." The new Commonwealth of Independent States left routine lawmaking to the individual republics; for the time being, policies affecting the entire commonwealth would be made "cooperatively" by consultations among ministers from the member republics, meeting in a "Council of Heads of State." For the former USSR, a quasi-representative legislature with two extremely weak houses had been replaced by none at all.[18]

Such a situation could not, of course, endure. By the end of 1991, the former superpower had become fifteen sovereign states. Russia, by far the largest and most powerful state, was still technically governed by the shards of the Soviet constitution but was in fact torn apart by internal wrangling over the division of power. In September 1993, President Yeltsin dissolved the parliament, which promptly rejected this act as unconstitutional (it was) and convened itself in the White House (the name of the parliament building). In October, militant defenders of the legislators launched an armed struggle against the pro-Yeltsin forces, giving the president the excuse to take back parliament by armed force. Several hundred lives were lost.

A new constitution, giving the president vast powers (including direct responsibility for television and radio and for the foreign, defense, and interior ministries), was ratified by a slim majority in December elections at which the voters (only about half of the registered electorate) also chose a new bicameral parliament with a majority of anti-Yeltsin representatives, including the openly anti-Semite and dangerously nationalistic Vladimir Zhirinovsky. By now, the number of houses of parliament was of little concern to anyone; the question was whether even a semblance of power would be left to that body.[19]

The Role of Committees

Even in systems where the decision-making power of the legislature is weak or nonexistent, the actual work of turning bills into laws can be onerous and timeconsuming. The concerns of modern government range far beyond the expertise any single man or woman can acquire, yet legislators are expected to exercise an informed judgment about each piece of legislation that comes before them. This problem has no real solution, but the work of modern legislatures is made somewhat easier by the use of the **committee system.**

There are basically two kinds of committee systems. In some legislatures, such as the U.S. Congress, each committee has a specialized function, and only bills having to do with that specialization may be referred to it.[20] The Merchant Marine and Fisheries Committee of the House of Representatives deals with the merchant marine and fisheries, and nothing else. This system of **specialized committees** permits legislators to develop more expertise on particular subjects, since they will consistently be concerned with bills relevant to the same subject matter.[21]

In other legislatures, such as the British Parliament, a composite committee system exists. Specialized committees are established for some purposes, such as the British Specialist Select Committee for Agriculture, but other committees are general **standing committees** to which different questions may be referred. There are no permanent memberships on the standing committees, which are labeled simply by the letters of the alphabet: "When a bill is sent to committee, the Committee on Selection appoints sixteen to thirty members to serve on that committee to deal with that bill only. Thus although standing committee A may deal with several bills — totally unrelated to each other — during a given session of Parliament, the membership of the committee will change completely from one bill to the next."[22]

In a detailed study of the committee systems of eight nations, Malcolm Shaw has ranked the relative importance of these bodies to the work of their legislatures as follows (from most to least important): the United States, Italy (pre-1994), Germany (pre-reunification), Philippines (pre-1972), Canada, Britain, India, and Japan (pre-1993). On the basis of these eight cases, he demonstrates that committees are strongest in political systems where parties are weakest, where presidents are strongest (presidential or quasipresidential systems), and where bills are debated in committee before being given full debate on the floor of the house.[23] Shaw's findings suggest that committees, if given the chance to formulate the terms of debate in the absence of strong party leadership, can be effective ways for legislatures to reestablish some of the power otherwise lost to chief executives.

In any case, it is clear that committee systems are one way to free legislators from having to consider every piece of legislation in depth. Even so, the workload of the individual committee member can be very great. In many legislatures each committee has a paid staff to help the legislators who serve on it. In addition, individual legislators usually have some help from a staff of their own in determining what position to take on any bill that comes before the committees on which they serve or before the full house. Where no such aid is given, or where it is given in inadequate amounts, the individual legislator is inevitably more dependent on others' opinions about the merits of all bills presented. Because they need help in sifting through the masses of materials presented to them, poorly staffed legislators are likely to be more open to lobbying efforts by private groups or by representatives of other branches of the government than are those with adequate help. Lobbyists are always ready to offer interpretations of pending legislation, with supporting documentation, but their interpretations are likely to be anything but objective.

Customs and Mores

There are also significant differences in the customs and mores of the world's legislative bodies. Differences in style may seem to be of little importance, but they can in fact have a strong influence on the course of government. Most African legislators are still influenced by the traditions of palaver (discussing each topic as fully as possible), consensus (doing everything possible to reach a unanimous decision rather than simply abiding by majority rule), and respect (especially for those elders who have achieved the status of "leaders of thought") that were likely to prevail in the decision-making processes of earlier, smaller communities. In some Western legislatures occasional raucous outbursts by opposition deputies protesting government policy are considered acceptable behavior. The British House of Commons is particularly notorious for these spectacles, especially since its proceedings have been televised, a practice that seems to have heightened the intensity of opposing MPs verbal assaults on one another rather than lowering it. The new Russian parliament seems to have fallen into the same kind of behavior (see Box 9.4). At the same time, of course, losing one's temper is regarded as unseemly and counterproductive in many other parts of the world. In some legislatures a certain amount of friendly accommodation, even across party lines ("We'll vote with you on X, if you will help us out on Y"), is seen as essential to good government; in others a tradition of strong party discipline ensures strict partisan voting on even the most minor matters.

BOX 9.4 **RUSSIA'S DUMA ADOPTS WESTERN WAYS**

Ultranationalist leader Vladimir Zhirinovsky battling with Russian lawmaker Yevgeniya Tishkovskaya in session of the *Duma,* the lower house of the Russian Parliament. (AP Photo/Misha Japaridze/Wide World)

In September 1995 the Russian parliament debated the nation's position on the use of force by NATO in former Yugoslavia and the maintenance of sanctions against Serbia. The position of Andrei Kozyrev, foreign minister, supporting both the use of NATO force and sanctions, was supported by a few deputies. However, the followers of ultranationalist Vladimir Zhirinovsky were speedily able to turn the issue into a patriotic test case, stressing the strong cultural and religious ties between the Serbs and the Russians. Passions ran high — so high that a nationalist deputy assaulted a radical Orthodox priest, tearing a crucifix from his neck, after which Zhirinovsky picked a fight with a woman deputy who opposed his position, calling her "scum." Far from discrediting the nationalists, such behavior seemed only to serve their cause; the legislature voted 258 to 2 that their country should unilaterally lift United Nations sanctions against Serbia and impose them against Croatia, at the same time calling for an end in Russia's participation in NATO's "Partnership for Peace" program. Given the strength of presidential powers in the domain of foreign affairs, the vote was not binding, but the pressure on Yeltsin was obviously increased, especially with parliamentary elections due at the end of the year.[24]

Source: *Financial Times,* 11 Sept. 95, A1. Adapted by permission from the *Financial Times.*

Autocratic lawmaking. Iraqi President Saddam Hussein makes all major policy decisions for his nation, despite the fact that his is an *executive,* not a *legislative,* office. (AP Photos/Wide World)

LAWMAKING BY THE EXECUTIVE

The lawmaking powers of formal legislatures have been progressively eroded in many polities. In some cases legislatures have been devised from the outset to serve only as rubber stamps for decisions made by the nation's leader or leaders. In others, the shift to executive lawmaking has been more subtle, more gradual, and less complete.

Autocratic or Oligarchic Lawmaking

Where legislatures serve merely to formalize decisions made elsewhere about the laws that will govern the citizens of the polity, it is important to find out where laws are really being made and exactly what procedures are being followed. In some polities it is very clear that laws are effectively being made by the chief executive. It is almost part of the definition of charisma that the charismatic leader will have the final word (and sometimes the first and only word as well) on all matters of importance. Hereditary rulers have traditionally felt free to issue new and binding commandments in the form of law, with or without the advice of others. But even modern constitutions may be written to give a particular executive carte blanche in the making of laws. Thus, Kwame Nkrumah was made president for life in Ghana and explicitly given extensive powers in the legislative, judicial, and executive domains.[25] Other chief executives have not always gone through the niceties of seeking constitutional ratification of their usurpation of legislative power. In April 1992, Peru's President Alberto Fujimori, who had already issued some 126 decree laws in his first twenty months in office and was in constant battle with the Chamber of Deputies, simply suspended the nation's democratic constitution, closed down the legislature, dismantled the judiciary, and assumed dictatorial rule. It was an *autogolpe*, which is to say (in Spanish), "a self-coup."[26]

More often, however, executive usurpation of the lawmaking function is a collective enterprise, not the act of a single person. Even Fujimori could succeed only because he had the support of a majority of military officials, business elites, and even of the general population (although 75 percent said they preferred democracy to dictatorship, the same percentage approved the takeover, apparently owing to a conviction that only autocratic rule would be able to address the nation's declining living standards and increased political violence).[27] In other systems, dictatorial takeover has often been the result of the military acting on its own to stage a coup and set up a ruling junta (team of leaders), which then makes all policy decisions by authoritarian means. When the army took power in Thailand in a military coup in 1991 and placed Prime Minister Chatichai Choonhavan under arrest, the military immediately wrote a new constitution and promised new elections but made it clear that in the meantime legislative powers — and all others — would remain in its own hands.[28] When the first round of legislative elections in Algeria in December 1991 gave victory to Muslim fundamentalists, the military took power immediately, forced President Chadli Benjedid first to dissolve parliament and then to resign himself, and set up a seven-person Constitutional Council to rule by decree.[29]

In other nations, the military has been effective in aborting or reversing coups d'etat that threaten legislative control of the lawmaking process. Although the military at first supported the suspension of the Guatemalan constitution by President Jorge Serrano in 1993, its high command changed its mind after noting the resistance of the National Forum for Consensus, an ad hoc coalition of businesspeople, moderate politicians, media representatives, and distinguished celebrities, and the support given to the Forum by the Constitutional Council. Surprising many, the military forced Serrano from power, convened Congress to elect a successor, and gave its support to their choice, the government's human rights ombudsman, Ramiro de Leon Carpio.[30]

Delegated Lawmaking

Legislatures do not always lose to executive dominion, but neither do they always maintain their powers even when they may appear to do so. In some polities, a pretense may be maintained that lawmaking is the job of the legislature, but in practice that body has progressively allowed the executive branch a larger and larger role in the exercise of that function. Such delegation of the lawmaking power may be overt and deliberate, taking place through formal processes and at a specified point in time. The U.S Congress, for example, has formally established independent regulatory commissions and given them the right to issue rulings with the force of law.

In other cases, the delegation of power may take place slowly, almost accidentally, emerging in response to changing circumstances and the strength or weakness of particular leaders and particular institutional constraints. Here, too, the United States provides an example. As Harold Hongju Koh has shown in his analysis of the "national security constitution," the American president's right to issue executive orders with the force of law in matters affecting national security has grown out of the practice of delegating such powers to the chief executive in time of war, a practice never successfully challenged by Congress or the judiciary in peacetime.[31]

However, legislators do sometimes have second thoughts about the wisdom of giving so much of their own function over to officials formally responsible for carrying out, not making, the nation's laws. This kind of hindsight has been apparent in the United States regarding the powers the president has been given in the name of national security. The War Powers Act of 1973 required that the president report to Congress any involvement of the United States in hostilities within forty-eight hours and terminate such involvement within sixty days if Congress should so direct by concurrent resolution. Even this weak effort to retake some control was challenged as "allowing Congress to tie the president's hands" by the strongest defenders of presidential supremacy, and in 1991 President George Bush made it clear that he was asking for congressional *support*, not authorization, when he asked for its vote on whether or not to begin the Gulf War, a precedent President Bill Clinton followed when sending troops to Bosnia in 1995.

Do legislators best serve those who elected them by handing over their powers to presumably more efficient executives in times of national danger? Certainly the practice is fraught with peril; it was, after all, the German parliament that gave Adolf Hitler his unlimited powers. Of course it is true that legislative kowtowing has seldom been so extensive or had such dire results, but still it is important to remember that a nation's legislature is the one arena where representatives of all interests can be expected to meet as equals, struggle to find compromises, and formulate policy acceptable to all. The damage done to the political process by casual self-abnegation of those rights can never be deemed inconsequential.

LAWMAKING BY JUDGES

When rueful legislators do attempt to repossess the powers they have allowed others to usurp, they may well find it necessary to turn to a third

BOX 9.5

LAWMAKING BY JUDGES: THE CASE OF *MARBURY v. MADISON*

When President John Adams lost his bid for reelection to Thomas Jefferson in 1800, he did what he could to fill the offices of government with members of the Federalist Party before leaving the presidency. But not all of the new appointments could be made official before he left office. One undelivered commission was the one that made William Marbury justice of the peace for Washington, D.C. Marbury asked Jefferson's new secretary of state, James Madison — whose job it was — to deliver the commission. Madison refused, saying the new government had the right to name its own appointee to fill the post. Marbury went to court, asking for a writ of *mandamus* (a court order forcing delivery of the commission), as was his right under the Federal Judiciary Act of 1789, and counting on the partisan sympathy of Chief Justice John Marshall, also a Federalist. But Marshall ruled for Madison, on the grounds that the Federal Judiciary Act of 1789 was itself an unconstitutional invasion of the appointment rights of the executive branch by the legislative branch.

Well satisfied, the new government accepted the ruling and in doing so helped Marshall establish the precedent for judicial review — the right of the courts to review the nation's laws to ensure that they are in accordance with the Constitution. Marshall thereby took for himself and the Court a power far more important than control of the minor office of justice of the peace for Washington, D.C. And he established two great principles with a single blow: one of government (judicial review), the second of politics (be willing to lose a small battle if in doing so you can win a larger one).

branch of government, the judiciary, to adjudicate disputes that arise when they attempt to rectify what now appear to them to have been mistaken delegations of their powers. Similarly, embattled executives may seek judicial endorsement for maintaining powers they have become accustomed to exercising or to keep legislatures from invading what appear to them to be constitutionally protected executive functions.

Whichever side is the plaintiff, the ironic effect is likely to be that the judiciary itself becomes seriously involved in the making of laws. In no other nation is the judiciary so heavily implicated in the lawmaking process as in the United States. In that nation, justices routinely take it upon themselves to decide whether or not legislation conforms to the Constitution, a process known as **judicial review**. As most students of American history will recall, this power was not explicitly given to the courts by the Constitution but was effectively asserted by the first Chief Justice, John Marshall, in the 1803 case of *Marbury v. Madison*. It was a classic case of executive-legislative struggle in which the winner was the judiciary (see Box 9.5).

The power of judicial review is one that the United States judicial system has continued to develop. The current controversy over abortion illustrates the significance the process has assumed in great national debates. When the Supreme Court decided in the case of *Roe v. Wade* in 1973 that there was "a privacy right to abortion" in the Fourteenth Amendment's due process guarantee of personal liberty, state legislatures and lower courts throughout the nation found themselves faced with some very tough questions, defended pro and con by some very tough advocates: May and should a state legislature write laws either making abortion illegal under certain circumstances or reinforcing abortion rights? May and should a court find a particular state law relative to abortion unconstitutional? Should the opinions on this matter of candidates for judicial posts enter into the decisions of those charged with their appointment? The controversy has become one of the most bitter in the nation's history, and the form it takes is shaped by the right of judicial review.[32]

In more recent constitutions, the power of judicial review is explicitly included. The Japanese constitution, for example, gives the Supreme Court of Japan the "power to determine the constitutionality of any law, order, regulation or offical act."[33] But in other nations, judges have no place at all in lawmaking. They are expected to assume that all legislation is constitutionally correct and then simply to adjudicate disputes that arise under existing law. Other nations allow a modified form of judicial review, as in France, where the leaders of the government (the prime minister, the president, and the presidents of the two houses of parliament) all have the right to ask a nine-person Constitutional Council to rule on the constitutionality of an act of parliament. Unlike the U.S. Supreme Court, the French Constitutional Council is not the highest appellate court (see Chapter 11); it has only limited functions, and it can review the constitutionality of legislation only on substantive, not on procedural, grounds. On the other hand, the Constitutional Council has the right to review acts of parliament before they become law, and its powers are carefully spelled out in the French constitution — two advantages denied the U.S. court.[34]

Assuming the power to scrutinize the work of the legislature is not the only way judges become involved in the making of laws. Under the terms of many nations' constitutions, the chief executive has the power to appoint the highest-ranking judges. Not infrequently, when the right of such an executive to issue a particular decree is challenged, the matter will end up in court. Judges who owe their appointments to powerful executives are unlikely to be fully impartial in their rulings at such times.

LAWMAKING BY POLITICAL PARTIES

In nations where legislators meet infrequently, conduct their work in remarkable harmony or even in unanimity, and are themselves not well-known public figures (or are far better known for their performance in other roles in the political system), it is likely that laws are being written, but not made, in the legislature.

In such cases, where the legislature is obviously merely rubber-stamping decisions made elsewhere, the problem is to find out where the lawmaking power truly resides. The first place to look, as already noted, is in the executive offices and often enough the search can end right there. Sometimes, however, the chief executives themselves are simply carrying out the wishes of another powerful body, the ruling political party.

At first glance, it may seem inappropriate and even *extraconstitutional* (see Chapter 7) for a party to be the source of a nation's legislative agenda. But in fact a strong defense for *party government* (see Chapter 8) can be made. Suppose you lived in a system where political parties awarded their nominations only to candidates who were pledged to support the party program. You would have the advantage of knowing not only exactly what the candidates running in your constituency stood for but also what it would mean if the various candidates of a particular party won a majority of the seats in the legislature. It would mean that the program of that party would be carried out and that the business of government could be carried forward relatively smoothly, with a minimum of intraparliamentary squabbling and rancor. Furthermore, it would mean that if the program did not work to your satisfaction you could hold the elected representatives of that party, and the party itself, accountable, and you could vote for the candidates of a different party next time. What is wrong with that?

But party government *is*, at least in part, extraconstitutional government. It means that the decisions on new laws are made outside the legislature, in the conferences of the party as it decides on the content of its program. If the party itself is open and democratically organized, party government can mean the broadest possible democratic participation in the work of government — with citizens joining the local branches of the party they prefer and taking meaningful part in the formulation of issues and the nomination of loyal candidates. But if the party is closed and elitist, party government can make a mockery of any representative pretenses in a nation's constitutional system. Effective power will be exercised by an unelected few behind closed doors at party headquarters rather than by the elected many in the open forum of a legislative body. It all depends on the nature of the party itself.

The danger of nonrepresentative and nonaccountable party government is clearly greatest in single-party systems. In such systems, still found in the remaining communist states (e.g., China, Cuba), key decisions on new legislation are made in the top ruling body of the party. Although the members of that body are formally elected by the second-highest party body, the Central Committee, the elections are normally controlled by a narrow elite and the flow of power is definitely from the top down. Lower-level organisms of the party serve to educate party members about the necessity and desirability of the new policies, not to discover and reflect popular opinion, and the members in turn play the same educational role in the population at large.[35] The laws thus made may or may not be made in the interests of the people governed, but they are certainly not made *by* those people.

SUMMARY AND CONCLUSION

Oliver Wendell Holmes once said, "When I think of the law, I see a princess mightier than she who once wrought at Bayeux, eternally weaving into her web dim figures of the ever-lengthening past — figures too dim to be noticed by the idle, too symbolic to be interpreted except by her pupils, but to the discerning eye disclosing every painful step and every world-shaking contest by which mankind has worked and fought its way from savage isolation to organic social life."[36]

As Justice Holmes's compelling imagery suggests, the law never exists *ab ovo* (a useful Latin term meaning "from the egg" — that is, as if with no other beginning) but is made — and remade — in all kinds of places, for all kinds of purposes. Furthermore, contrary to Holmes (who was, after all, making an address to a bar association dinner and was not above flattering his auditors), we have seen that it is not always made by those with the grace and authority of mighty princesses, nor by those who are constitutionally responsible, nor even by those who are responsive to the needs of ordinary citizens.

We have also seen that even when the lawmaking function is exercised predominantly in representative legislatures designed for that purpose, the exact division of labor is likely to vary. There may be one or two houses, specialized or nonspecialized committees, and a host of customs and mores unique to each nation to determine what laws can be made, how, and by whom.

In all probability, however, the right to make a nation's laws will not be held exclusively by the legislature but will be shared — to a greater or lesser extent — with others outside that body. The executive almost always plays a role in making as well as executing the law, and judges, party leaders, religious authorities, corporation heads, and military chiefs of staff may also feel obliged to join the work of lawmaking when the circumstances make it possible for them to do so.

Furthermore, when legislative power is shared with the executive, the balance of power between the two branches differs according to whether it is a democratic or a nondemocratic system. In a democratic system, it makes a great deal of difference whether we are talking about a parliamentary system, where power may be shared fairly equally; a presidential system, where power is likely to shift back and forth between the two; or a presidential-parliamentary system, where the executive tends to take and keep the upper hand. In all three such systems the question of who shall make the law is decided in part permanently and deliberately, mandated by constitutional provision, and in part temporarily and almost accidentally, as legislators delegate others to perform tasks that were originally theirs — or simply allow such powers to drift into others' hands. In nondemocratic systems, on the other hand, legislators may share the right to make a nation's laws reluctantly and resignedly — or even give up such rights altogether — when an autocratic or oligarchic executive forcibly usurps powers that do not constitutionally belong to that branch.

In pointing out how active a role the executive plays in the making of laws, we have already had quite a bit to say about the executive powers of governments. It is time now to focus directly on that subject. Laws mean little or nothing until someone carries them out. What does it mean to execute the law? The next chapter will be an attempt to answer that question.

Selected Readings

Congressional Quarterly. *Congress, A to Z: A Ready Reference Encyclopedia.* Washington, D.C.: Congressional Quarterly, 1993. A useful reference book describing the organizational structure of Congress, the legislative process, important members and issues.

Franks, C. E. S. *The Parliament of Canada.* Toronto: University of Toronto Press, 1987. A detailed study of the Canadian legislature, including such topics as political parties, workload, procedure, debate, accountability, and reform.

George, Stephen, ed. *Britain and the European Community: The Politics of Semi-detachment.* A collection of writings examining the domestic policy conflicts faced by the British government since Britain joined the European Community.

Hickock, Eugene W., Jr. and Gary L. McDowell. *Justice vs Law: Courts and Politics in American Society.* New York: Free Press, 1993. The authors argue that controversial policy issues that should be addressed by Congress are being left to the U.S. Supreme Court to decide.

McWhinney, Edward. *Supreme Courts and Judicial Lawmaking: Constitutional Tribunals and Constitutional Review.* Dordrecht, the Netherlands: Martinus Nijhoff, 1986. A comparative jurisprudential study of supreme courts and their lawmaking role in France, Canada, Japan, Germany and the United States.

Rhodes, R. A. W. and Patrick Dunleavy. *Prime Minis-*
ter, Cabinet and Core Executive. New York: St. Martin's Press, 1995. An introduction to the roles of the prime minister and the cabinet in British government.

Spitzer, Robert J. *President and Congress: Executive Hegemony at the Crossroads of American Government.* New York: McGraw Hill 1993. A historical study of the relationship between presidents and Congress with a focus on the formation of policy and legislation.

Thaysen, Uwe, Roger H. Davidson, and Robert Gerald Livingston, eds. *The U.S. Congress and the German Bundestag.* Boulder: Westview Press, 1990. A long (nearly 600 pages) comparative study of two of the world's most important legislative bodies.

Westlake, Martin. *A Modern Guide to the European Parliament.* London: Pinter Publishers, 1994. An in-depth study of the European Parliament and the changes it has undergone as a result of the ratification of the Maastricht Treaty.

Notes

1. U.S. Code, 1976 ed., title XX, sec. 1145b.
2. Efforts to change affirmative action laws in fact began in the mid-1990s. The Board of Regents of the University of California voted to stop giving women and minorities preference in college admissions, the U.S. District Court of Appeal

for the District of Columbia Circuit barred the plans of the Federal Communications Commission to give companies owned by women or minorities a series of financial preferences in their planned auctioning of nearly 500 licenses for new wireless telephone and data services, and the backers of the California Civil Rights Initiative began gathering signatures to put that anti-affirmative action law on the books. Edmund L. Andrews, *New York Times*, 16 Mar. 1995, A 22; Ramesh Ponnuru, *National Review* 47, no. 15 (14 Aug. 1995): 23.

3. Michael Crowder, *West Africa: An Introduction to Its History* (London: Longmans, 1977), p. 155.

4. *International Herald Tribune*, 1 Feb. 1996, 3 and 2 Feb. 1996, 1, 11; 12 Feb. 1996, A3; 16 Feb. 1996, 5.

5. Richard Rose, *Politics in England: Change and Persistence*, 5th ed. (Basingstoke, U.K.: Macmillan, 1989).

6. "A cabinet is a combining committee, a *hyphen* which joins, a *buckle* which fastens, the legislative part of the state to the executive part of the state." Walter Bagehot, *The English Constitution* (London: Oxford University Press, 1867), p. 12. Italics in original.

7. In a comparative study of several presidential and quasi-presidential systems, Matthew Soberg Shugart has shown that the president's party's share of legislative seats tends to be reduced after midterm elections and in systems where electoral laws permit legislative candidates to function independently of their parties (that is, are "localizing rather than nationalizing"). "The Electoral Cycle and Institutional Sources of Divided Presidential Government," *American Political Science Review* 89, no. 2 (June 1995): 327–44.

8. "Political Leaders Make no Progress on a Budget Deal," 1, *New York Times*, December 18, 1995.

9. The U.S. presidential system has an intermediate step: the Electoral College. Originally each state's voters chose electors, who met and chose the president. Technically, the system remains the same today, except that it is now understood (and in many states, mandated by law) that the electors will all vote for the candidate who won the majority of that state's popular vote.

10. *Le Monde*, 4 April 1992, 1–9. The pacification no doubt worked in part because Cresson, the first woman prime minister in the history of France, was intensely unpopular. The French argue to this day how much that unpopularity was simply the result of her gender; this observer had no trouble at all in being sure the answer was, "A lot."

11. For an excellent review of the French crisis, see Bernard Brown, *Protest in Paris* (Morristown, N.J.: General Learning Press, 1974).

12. John Felton, "A Policy Confrontation on China?" *Congressional Quarterly Weekly* 14 June 1989, 1564 and *New York Times*, 12 Nov. 1994, 6. In mid-1995, James B. Steinberg, director of the Policy Planning Staff of the U.S. Department of State, confirmed the new policy: "Russia and China are no longer our ideological or strategic adversaries" he said, adding, "While we feel deep frustration at our limited progress in securing human rights in China . . . we must make sure the response we adopt will help achieve our goal." *U.S. Department of State Dispatch*, 6, no. 19 (8 May 1995): 392.

13. For a good discussion of Burke's interpretation of interests, see "Representing Unattached Interests: Burke," chap. 8 in Hannah Pitkin, *The Concept of Representation* (Berkeley: University of California Press, 1967), pp. 168–89.

14. Ibid., p. 221.

15. Ulf Lundvik, "Sweden," in Gerald E. Caiden, ed., *International Handbook of the Ombudsman* (Westport, Conn.: Greenwood Press, 1983), pp. 179–81.

16. This is also the sense of the word behind the phrase *in camera*, referring to proceedings of legislative or judicial bodies held in secrecy.

17. Frederick C. Barghoorn and Thomas F. Remington, *Politics in the USSR* (Boston: Little, Brown, 1986), p. 314.

18. *Time*, 23 Dec. 1991, 19–22; *Current Digest of the Soviet Press* 43, no. 51 (22 Jan. 1992): pp. 2–6.

19. Thomas E. Weisskopf, "Yeltsin's Russia: Bleak Prospects for Democracy and Prosperity," *Dollars and Sense* (March–April 1994): 22–25 and Vladimir Orlov, "Government Makeover Boosts Chernomyrdin's Role," *Current Digest of the Post-Soviet Press* 46, no. 2 (9 Feb. 1994): 16.

20. For the work of committees in the American Congress, see Malcolm Shaw, "Committees in Legislatures," in Philip Norton, *Legislatures* (Oxford: Oxford University Press, 1990), especially pp. 258–59.

21. For an interesting recent discussion of a similar

system, see Austin Mitchell, "The New Zealand Way of Committee Power," *Parliamentary Affairs* 46, no. 1 (Jan. 1993): 9–19.

22. Alex N. Dragnich and Jorgen Rasmussen, *Major European Governments*, 7th ed. (Homewood, Ill.: Dorsey, 1986), p. 133.
23. Shaw, "Committees in Legislatures," pp. 237–67.
24. John Thornhill, "NATO Force Debate Sparks Duma Fight," *Financial Times*, 11 Sept. 1995, A1, 18.
25. Henry L. Bretton, *The Rise and Fall of Kwame Nkrumah* (New York: Praeger, 1966), pp. 50–51, 107. Nkrumah's powers in other domains included the right to detain anyone he suspected of disloyalty without trial or appeal; the right to appoint and remove all judges of the superior courts; and the right to appoint, promote, dismiss, and discipline members of the civil service.
26. Cynthia McClintock, "Peru's Fujimori: A Caudillo Derails Democracy," *Current History* (March 1993): 112–19.
27. Ibid.
28. *New York Times*, 2 March 1991, A3.
29. *Washington Post*, 14 Jan. 1992, A16.
30. Richard L. Millett, "Central America's Enduring Conflicts," *Current History* (March 1994): 124–28.
31. Harold Hongju Koh, *The National Security Constitution: Sharing Power After the Iran-Contra Affair* (New Haven: Yale University Press, 1990); see especially chap. 2, "Recognizing the Pattern of History," pp. 38–64.
32. Steven Pressman, "Abortion Politics," *California*

Journal 20, (Oct. 1989): 395–97; Joan Biskupic, "Pennsylvania Case Portends New Attack on Abortion," *Congressional Quarterly Weekly Report* 50, no. 4 (25 Jan. 1992): 169–71. Note also the entry of the courts into the latest battles over affirmative action law: see the decision of the U.S. District Court of Appeal for the District of Columbia Circuit to prevent the Federal Communications Commission from giving companies owned by women or minorities special advantages in the acquisition of licenses for new wireless telephone and data services, mentioned in note 2 above. Edmund L. Andrews, *New York Times*, 16 Mar. 1995, sec. A, 22.
33. Nishi, *Unconditional Democracy*, p. 125.
34. For a good discussion of the Constitutional Council, see William Safran, *The French Polity*, 4th ed. (White Plains, N.Y.: Longman, 1995), pp. 216–220.
35. In the Chinese case, party is supreme in theory, but in practice its role appears to vary considerably; power is in fact often in the hands of a few key leaders, although they themselves are normally members of the highest party committees. Gary K. Bertsch, Robert P. Clark, and David M. Wood, *Comparing Political Systems: Power and Policy in Three Worlds*, 3rd ed. (New York and London: Macmillan, 1986), p. 295.
36. Oliver Wendell Holmes, "The Law," an address before the Suffolk Bar Association Dinner, 5 Feb. 1885. Reprinted in *Collected Legal Papers* (New York: Peter Smith, 1952), p. 27. "She who once wrought at Bayeux" refers to Joan of Arc.

10 Running the Government: Executives and Bureaucrats

HERE YOU ARE, READING this book, trying to get caught up on your homework. Suddenly it occurs to you (and not for the first time, either): I'd like to stop all this studying and start doing. I'd like to be active in politics and get into government. And I'd like to be a real leader, too, not just one of those bureaucrats.

Well, why not? But let's be practical. Let's think this thing through. So take a piece of paper. First, jot down the steps you might take to get into a position of political leadership. Once you have arrived at the top, what will your duties be? Then write down a few ideas about what a good leader should be like, including some thoughts about the relationship between leader and follower. Then think how you will feel about leaving power when the time comes, and under what conditions you are likely to do so. All done? Good.

Now let's give a little more thought to those poor despised bureaucrats. After all, it could just happen that you might never make it to the presidency, might even find yourself in a bureaucratic job. Isn't that a terrible thought? After all, what did any bureaucrat ever do for you?

Better turn that piece of paper over and add a few more notes. First, get it out of your system: Write down ten bad things that never would have happened to you (or a friend or a relative) if it hadn't been for "one of those bureaucrats." Now for the hard part: Write down ten good things that

(Drawing by Anthony; © 1988 The New Yorker Magazine, Inc.)

never would have happened *for* you (or a friend or a relative) if it hadn't been for "one of those bureaucrats." And, finally, the *really* hard part: can you think of anything good — for a *polity* — about having a bureaucracy?

Put that piece of paper in a safe place, please. And then do me one more favor—read this chapter before you hit the campaign trail.

BECOMING A LEADER

There are four main ways to become a leader: by ascription, by appointment, by election, and by force. Although they may be combined in actual practice, we will look at each separately.

Ascription

In some societies the route to power is open only to those who possess certain characteristics. If they are believed to have those characteristics (that is, if those characteristics are *ascribed* to them), they may become leaders; if not, they cannot. In the most extreme case, the characteristic is something one — and only one — person has by birth. The system of hereditary monarchy, which ensures that only one person can be "next in line," is the most obvious example; there are still over thirty reigning monarchs in the world (see Table 10.1). Of course, the word *reigning* must not be taken literally for those in Western parliamentary democracies (see

Chapter 9), and indeed the marital shenanigans of the British heir apparent and his spouse have provoked many in that nation to question whether an ascriptive monarchy really is appropriate in lands where the important decisions are all made by elected representatives.[1]

A slightly different definition of **ascription** is offered by Talcott Parsons and Edward Shils, who say it means assigning people to leadership positions (as well as giving them other forms of differential treatment) on the basis of their attributes (including the groups they belong to and the wealth they possess) rather than on the basis of anything they have accomplished or might accomplish in the future.[2]

If this is confusing, then let's try again. What Parsons and Shils mean by ascription is simply that in some systems in order to be chosen for a leadership role you have to be the "right" sort of person, belong to the "right"

TABLE 10.1   **Ascriptive Power: Monarchs in the Modern World***

Bahrain:	Sheikh Isa bin Sulman al-Khalifa (emir since 1971)
Belgium:	King Baudouin Albert Charles Leopold Axel Marie Gustave (1951)
Bhutan:	The Druk Gyalpo Jigme Singhye Wangchuk, King of Bhutan (1972)
Brunei:	H. M. Sultan Haji Hassanal Bolkiah (1968)
Denmark:	Queen Margrethe II (1972)
Great Britain:	Queen Elizabeth II (1952)
Japan:	Emperor Akihito (1989)
Jordan:	King Hussein ibn Talal (1953)
Kuwait:	Sheikh Jaber al-Ahmad al-Jaber al-Sabah (1977)
Leichtenstein:	Hans-Adam II (1989)
Lesotho:	King Letsie III (1990)
Luxembourg:	Grand Duke Jean (1964)
Monaco:	Prince Rainier III (1949)
Morocco:	King Hassan II (1961)
Nepal:	King Birendra Bir Bikram Sha Dev (1975)
Netherlands:	Queen Beatrix Wilhemina Armgard (1980)
Norway:	King Harald (1991)
Oman:	Sultan Qaboos bin Said (1970)
Qatar:	Sheikh Khalifa bin Hamad al-Thani (1972)
Saudi Arabia:	King Fahd ibn Abdul Aziz (1982)
Spain:	King Juan Carlos I (1975)
Swaziland:	King Mswati III (1986)
Sweden:	King Carl XVI Gustav (1973)
Thailand:	King Bhumibol Adulyadej (1946)
Tonga:	King Taufa'Ahau Tupou IV (1965)

*As of 1993. There are also seven sheikdoms in the United Arab Emirates, whose rulers were installed between 1948 and 1990.
Source: Derived from Geoffrey Smith, "Must Royals Take a Back Seat?" *World Monitor* (March 1993): 36–41.

group (ethnic group, kinship group, social club, geographic community, or other type of "collectivity") or have the "right" kind and quantity of belongings. In such societies, you belong to the pool from which leaders are chosen if you meet the appropriate ascriptive standards; if you do not, nothing you can do to show your ability to perform the job will make any difference.[3]

As Parsons and Shils point out, all polities — even the most democratic — specify and abide by some measure of ascription. Age is the obvious example. Despite biblical injunction and the occasional coronation of an infant, no people really allows a little child to lead them.[4] Criteria of race, ethnicity, sex, and geographic community are also very common, even in systems that claim otherwise. Write to me when the United States chooses an Asian woman from the small state of Delaware as its president and I will happily eat my words.

As all this suggests, ascriptive criteria in most cases simply narrow the pool of possible leaders. Moving into a leadership role is still likely to depend on being appointed, being elected, or exercising force.

Appointment

Although some form of election, however rigged or manipulated it may be, is employed in choosing the top leadership of almost every nation, nearly every system fills a large number of its lesser leadership positions by appointment. When this happens, some of the interesting questions are: What kinds of positions are filled by appointment? Who gets to do the appointing? What motivates the appointing party to appoint one person rather than another?

Kinds of Positions Filled by Appointment   A great deal of variation is found from one polity to the next on the kinds of positions that are filled by appointed officials, but as a rule of thumb we may say that the more specialized the position — that is, the more the job in question requires a high degree of a limited kind of expertise — the more likely it will be filled by appointment rather than by election. The voters of the German state of Hesse may be competent enough to choose their chief executive, the Ministerpräsident, but the Hessian minister of finance must be chosen — or so the reasoning goes in the selection of specialists across the globe — far from the heat of electoral competition, and as much as possible on the basis of expertise rather than personal attractiveness or other characteristics.[5]

There is another rule for determining which positions will be filled by appointment: The more autocratic the regime, the greater the use of the appointment power. The reason for this is obvious; one of the best ways to stay in power is to control who works for you and to make sure they understand to whom they owe their jobs. It is thus not surprising that Jerry Rawlings, who has twice taken over the government of Ghana by military coup, keeps the right to appoint high-ranking members of the civil and police services for himself. Nor are leaders of ostensibly democratic regimes immune to the temptation to enhance their power by using the power of appointment to the utmost. When Vladimir Meciar, head of the Movement for a Democratic Slovakia, managed to return to the position of prime minister in Slovakia in 1994 after having been removed earlier in the year, he quickly made sure his own supporters were put in charge of all the major appointive offices (including the Supreme and Constitutional Courts).[6]

Who Appoints?   The simple answer to this question is that appointments are made by those already in leadership positions. As usual, the simple answer is a little bit too simple. In the first place, sometimes the appointment is preordained by law and need not be made by anyone. This is the case when the law states that people who occupy one position are *ex officio* (that is, owing to the office) entitled to occupy another position. The governor of the state of California is always a member of the Board of Regents of the University of California. The voters elect the governor; the fact of being governor secures the incumbent appointment to the Board of Regents.

And even when appointments are made by other leaders rather than by force of law, the answer to the question "Who appoints?" is not always an easy one. It is often the case that more than one leader will be involved in the making — or the blocking — of a major appointment. Watching our own presidents anxiously awaiting senatorial confirmation of their choices for their cabinet or for Supreme Court vacancies gives us a recurrent example of appointments that require the concurrence of many individuals beyond the person whose job it is to suggest a nominee. Never was this clearer than in the 1991 confirmation of Clarence Thomas as Justice of the United States Supreme Court by a vote of 52 to 48 in the U.S. Senate, after days of nationally televised debate over the testimony of law professor Anita F. Hill that Thomas had subjected her to continued sexual harassment when she was his employee.[7]

Motives Guiding Appointments   Suppose you have just been elected governor of your state and you have several important appointments to make when you assume office. While the world waits, an inquiring reporter asks you what motives will guide you in your choices. Having just won an election, you are probably smart enough to answer, "I am simply looking for the most capable man or woman to fill every single post." But both you and the reporter know full well there is more to it than that.

This is not to say, however, that finding qualified persons is of no concern to the leader with the power to appoint other leaders. Most elected or appointed officials have agendas they believe in and want the best possible people to help them carry them out. Furthermore, how well or how badly one's appointees perform inevitably reflects on one's own record in office.

But other motives are also at work. We have already considered (see pp. 352–353) the motive of enhancing one's own control by filling appointive posts with as many supporters as possible. Appointing a particular person to high position may also send a special signal regarding what the executive intends to have happen next. When Russian President Boris Yeltsin appointed Yegor T. Gaidar as acting prime minister in June 1992, his doing so was interpreted internationally as a signal of commitment to serious and rapid reform because Gaidar had been the chief architect of the nation's new economic reform program.[8] The appointment by the British of Chris Patten, a "political heavyweight" with the personal backing of Prime Minister John Major, to be Governor of Hong Kong shortly before the 1997 deadline for the return of that colony to Chinese control, was seen as a way to send a strong message to the Chinese government regarding the British determination to protect its own interests. As one journalist put it, "Patten's resumé includes something the Chinese recognize as *guanxi*, or connections."[9]

The power to appoint is also the power to reward. Appointments frequently go to those who have worked hard (or contributed heavily) to secure the election of the officeholder. For many years the office of postmaster general in the United States traditionally went to the chairman of the party whose nominee won the presidency. Ambassadorships are often meted out to the close friends and associates of the chief executive — or to *their* friends and associates. When Pamela Harriman was appointed ambassador to France in 1993, the widow of Governor Averell Harriman of New York owed the honor partly to her reputation as someone who "knew and understood the inner workings of government," but her principal qualification was clearly her status as "the doyenne of Democratic politics and [as] a leading fund-raiser and donor."[10] Lower-level posts are also open to loyal supporters of party politics. Among Western democracies, the bureaucracies of Italy and Israel have been particularly open to political appointment, but the practice has not been unknown in the United States. It is said that Abraham Lincoln, on taking office in 1860, found it necessary to give 1,457 of the 1,639 available posts to party loyalists.[11]

Today the idea of using an appointment to reward a supporter evokes a mixed response. Having witnessed a series of scandals (ranging from Watergate to Whitewatergate) in the United States, we are only too well aware that the appointment of "cronies" can lead to corruption and inefficiency. Nevertheless, a strong argument can be made that rewarding a supporter with an appointment can lead to good government, *provided that* the appointee meets certain minimal standards of qualification. To test the soundness of this argument, put yourself in the position of the committed supporter. Suppose you have worked long and hard for a candidate and a cause that you believe in with all your heart. You know your work has been good and could be even better in the future. Your candidate wins, and there is an opening that fits your capabilities perfectly. But it does not go to you, it goes to someone from out of state, with more years of education and related experience than you have, but whom you know to be totally uninterested in either the cause or the candidate — someone who is merely looking for the best-paying job. Now who do you suppose would really do better work?

In fact, the answer to that question — even when one is personally involved — may still be uncertain. The point is simply that supporters *may* have qualities of loyalty, trust, and commitment that will make their on-the-job performance more impressive than that of the otherwise better qualified stranger, and that giving patronage appointments for those reasons to people who have proved their devotion should not be deplored automatically by people who do not know the circumstances of the case. As Leon Epstein has noted, an argument can be made that "distribution of many government jobs [is] essential for parties in a democratic society." [12]

Finally, an appointment may well be motivated by the desire to **coopt** someone whose support one seeks but does not yet have. Cooptation is sometimes used on erstwhile enemies, as when newly elected Mexican President Ernesto Zedillo appointed a member of the opposition Partido Acción Nacional (PAN) as the new attorney general in 1995. [13] Others may use appointments to coopt those who are not yet either friends or enemies but who would be useful to have as the former. Newly elected President Bill Clinton and his choice for Secretary of State, Warren Christopher, had little past history in common, but the appointment of the experienced diplomat put a strong player, known for his capacity to conduct long and cautious negotiations on the nation's behalf, on the Clinton team, and offered reassurance to those fearful of the young president's "sky-high expectations." [14]

One of the advantages — for the appointing officer, not for the appointee — of placing someone in office by appointment is that the process often works both ways: the person appointed can also be removed. When José Lutzenberger, an outspoken spokesperson for environmental causes in Brazil, became a liability — "his outspokenness enraged conservatives and his distaste for administration alienated environmentalists" — he was dismissed from his post as Secretary of the Environment by President Fernando Collor de Mello just a few weeks before the United Nations Conference on Environment and Development held in Rio de Janeiro in June 1992. [15]

Election to Office

We have already given some consideration in Chapter 6 to the different rules and regulations that govern voting throughout the world, but our focus then was on what these differences meant to individual participation in the political life of a nation. In Chapter 8 we looked at elections again, this time focusing on political parties and the media. Here our concern is with election as a means of achieving a position of leadership and with how the nature of different electoral systems influence the quality of leadership as well as the quality of citizenship throughout the human polity.

The best way to understand how the circumstances surrounding elections influence the quality of leadership is to imagine yourself a candidate in various systems. Getting elected is not just a matter of getting the most votes. Write-in candidacies are seldom allowed, and where permitted they are seldom successful. You must get on the ballot to have a good chance of becoming a leader through the electoral process. This usually means that you must meet certain personal standards of age and residency. It may very well mean that you must have been nominated by an officially recognized political party — and not all parties find it easy to win and keep that recognition. In single-party systems the would-be candidate has only one place to turn.

In any case, winning a party's nomination means going through a completely separate battle for leadership status before you can even think about competing for government office. If who gets the nomination is controlled by a primary election, your job is to win votes at the polls. But if the party itself decides who its candidate will be — as is the case in most political systems, the American primary election being an exception — then winning the nomination usually means building a record of loyalty to the party and of hard work on its behalf. The party may expect you to have shown you can muster an adequate campaign fund and a personal organization of devoted followers — or perhaps such assets will be seen as liabilities, suggestive of excessive pride and independence. Then there are personal characteristics to consider. Winning the nomination is very likely to mean being a member of the gender, the religious group, and the ethnic group your party is looking for this year. It may mean having the right kind of family life as well as being a good speaker and reasonably attractive to look at. Not to mention being smart enough, educated enough, tough enough, nice enough — and well balanced enough — to endure the ordeals of candidacy without having a nervous breakdown.

Or perhaps you are seeking a nonpartisan post. More than 50 percent of elected officials in the United States have gained their posts through nonpartisan elections — that is, elections in which parties are not allowed to participate.[16] Such elections are particularly common at the local level. In such a case you may still have to show support by presenting a petition signed by a minimum number of your fellow citizens who are willing to assert that the world (or at least Fairview City) will be a better place if you are allowed to run for office. To become a candidate, you must be able to get those signatures. In most countries you must also be able to pay a filing fee, which may or may not be refundable if you win a certain percentage of the vote.

The question of money is, of course, another major consideration. Campaigns are always costly, no matter where they take place. In some systems those costs are covered, wholly or in part, by the government. In others, the parties are able to cover a major portion of their candidates' expenses.

Private interests may fill a candidate's coffers, but as we have seen, they are likely to expect something in return.

As should be clear by now, the preliminary stages of the electoral struggle are likely to eliminate vast numbers of able potential leaders from waging, much less winning, the battle for votes. But let us say that you have nonetheless managed to get on the ballot and amass the funds to run an adequate campaign. At this point, the features of the electoral system we discussed in Chapter 6 are likely to make themselves felt. If you are campaigning in a system in which extensive personal and impersonal restrictions are placed on the right to vote, you will have to be able to fit your appeal to the relatively narrow interests of the voting population. During the years of white supremacy, the comparatively liberal candidates of the United Party of South Africa could not count on support from the majority whose disenfranchisement they protested to bring them to office — they needed a way to appeal to those who did have the right to vote. On the other hand, if you are campaigning in a large and heterogeneous system in which nearly every adult has the right to register and vote, you must be the kind of candidate who can find and take positions with a broad appeal and who is willing to let more divisive issues fall by the wayside.

Similarly, it makes a difference whether you are running in a single member constituency or under a system of proportional representation (see Chapter 6). If you are one of several representatives to be chosen in your district and the candidate of one party among many, you will be busy calculating what percentage of the vote you or your party will have to win for you to gain office. Perhaps the number will be sufficiently low to permit you to wage an issue-oriented campaign that does not appeal to a sizable majority in your constituency but that earns the complete loyalty of a big enough minority. If you are running in a single-member district, you will want to know if there are provisions for a runoff, and if so, what it will take for you to get into that runoff.

Another feature of the electoral system will have an impact on the quality of elected leaders: its honesty. Candidates who are willing to enter a campaign knowing that the election is very likely to be rigged — either for or against them — are bound to be different from those who anticipate a fair contest.

In short, the nature of the electoral system influences the calculations the candidate will make, the kind of campaign he or she will wage, and — given varying abilities to run the necessary kind of campaign — the quality of the leaders who are ultimately chosen.

Force

The reasons that have been given for taking power by force — or for trying to do so — are many and varied; but prime among them, even though rarely mentioned, is likely to be the belief that other routes to leadership are closed. Political systems that pose excessively narrow ascriptive criteria for the pool of potential leaders, that fail to use the powers of appointment to maintain and broaden support, that keep large numbers of voting-age adults off the electoral rolls, or that manipulate election results to suit the purposes of incumbent leaders are clearly more likely than others to be considered illegitimate and thus deserving of overthrow by force.

Often, of course, those who exercise force do so only in order to take (or repossess) power with little concern for moral justification. A time of rapid change often gives the advantage to those with the greatest armed might, as several of the former states of the Soviet Union have discovered in recent years: The governments of Tajikistan, Turkmenistan, Uzbekistan, Kazakhstan, and the Ukraine were all accused of using force to oppress dissent in the early 1990s.[17] At other times the decision to substitute force for other forms of power is more surprising: we have already noted (see Chapter 9) the case of President Alberto Fujimori, who, not satisfied with being elected to office, staged a coup against his own government.[18]

But not all assassinations, coups d'état, and revolutions have been motivated solely by the ambitions of those who ended up taking power. Sometimes the new leader does not take part in the act of force at all but simply finds a way to turn a complex situation to his or her advantage and then, once in power, shows little sign of sharing the values of those who accomplished the forceful overthrow of the previous government. Shakespeare's characterization of Mark Antony—as a bystander who publicly laments the murder of Julius Caesar by others while calculating how to turn it to his own advantage — has had more than one real-life parallel in the twentieth century.[19]

Indeed, assassinating a leader is often just one way to ensure that one's own life will be forfeit and that the dead leader's successor will be someone ready to carry out the existing program. U.S. President Lyndon Johnson, Egyptian President Hosni Mubarak, and Nigerian Supreme Military Commander Olusegun Obasanjo all came to power as a result of the murderous acts of others, and all made every effort to carry on the plans of the leaders they replaced. Any innocent successor who shows signs of doing otherwise is likely to be in serious trouble — remember that Andrew Johnson, who came to power when Abraham Lincoln was assassinated and who then began to take a softer line with the defeated South than Lincoln's supporters believed their fallen hero would have done, was the only president ever to be impeached by the U.S. House of Representatives.[20] The principle applies to leaders in the other branches of government as well. When the Mafia crime syndicate had a well-known Sicilian judge assassinated in 1992 for his unrelenting efforts to bring its leaders to trial and imprisonment, the result was to catalyze anti-Mafia sentiment among the general population of that beleaguered Italian island as never before.[21]

A successful coup d'état or revolution (revolution provokes a far more extensive change than a coup, which is largely confined to changing the top leadership of a regime) is a more effective means of ensuring that leadership will be transferred into sympathetic hands, if not into those that held the gun. Political coups are led by politicians of all political persuasions: Fidel Castro of Cuba, the Ayatollah Ruhollah Khomeini of Iran, and Vaclav Havel of the Czech Republic all came to power as the result of successful coups d'état or revolutions. In 1992, the Algerian military backed a coup designed to prevent a Muslim fundamentalist takeover of the democratic government — but that takeover would have been via democratic elections! [22]

However, coups d'etat do not always produce the expected results. One of the most remarkable stories of achieving power by force can be found in the career of Boris Yeltsin, president of the Russian Federated Republic in the new Commonwealth of Independent States. The force that brought Yeltsin to power was not his; it was, in fact, exercised by persons in deep opposition to everything he stood for. But when Yeltsin and his supporters succeeded in rousing sufficient public support to doom the efforts of rightwing plotters to overthrow the government of then Soviet President Mikhail S. Gorbachev, it was he who proved the hero of the day and the ultimate winner of power, not the visibly shaken Gorbachev, whose inability to predict and prevent his own arrest by the rebels led to the further diminishment of his already shaky reputation. In the unraveling of the coup, the government *did* fall, but not into the hands of those who had instigated it. [23]

Wars are seldom fought simply to place certain people in power, but it is not unusual for them to be waged to remove an existing leadership, as the first step to ensuring a more favorable policy toward the invading nation. Iran invaded Iraq in the summer of 1982 with the avowed purpose of "liberating" that nation from the "infidel" rule of President Saddam Hussein, and many believed — erroneously, as it proved — that the United States would not end its intervention in Arab politics during the Gulf War of 1991 until it had finished what Iran had left undone. [24]

The tiny nation of Haiti has seen more than its share of the transfer of power by force since 1991. Coup d'état has been followed by armed invasion to remove the military, succeeded in turn by an increase in "common criminality." It all began when the duly elected president, Jean-Bertrand Aristide, made it clear during his inaugural address in February 1991 that as the country's first democratically elected leader he intended to bring the military under control; the response nine months later was his arrest by army officers in a rebellion that claimed at least twenty-six lives. The subsequent three years of military rule under Lt. General Raoul Cedras brought massive human rights violations, at least 3,000 more deaths, and, finally, invasion by 20,000 U.S. troops in September 1994 to restore Aristide to power. However, the restored president lacked the resources to establish an adequate police force, and outside observers now comment on "a marked increase in banditry and criminality," directed largely against the elite who formerly benefited from military protection. [25]

In some situations the threat of force is sufficient to change the occupants of leadership roles. A minimum of force was exercised in the ouster of Ferdinand Marcos from the presidency of the Philippines in 1986; the knowledge that the U.S. government expected him to leave and was ready to add its military might to the limited arms of his local opposition if necessary was quite sufficient to persuade the corrupt and unpopular Marcos to depart. The departure of the communist leaders of eastern Europe was also accomplished in most cases by the threat rather than the exercise of violence against their persons, the 1989 Christmas Day execution of Romanian President Nicolae Ceausesçu providing the noteworthy exception.

WHAT CHIEF EXECUTIVES DO

We take it more or less for granted that the most important person in any political system is that nation's chief executive officer, be it president or prime minister or head of the military junta. However, when you stop and think about it, isn't it a little bit strange — at least in democratic systems — that so much emphasis should be placed on that one leader? After all, in democratic systems the chief executive is simply supposed to see to the carrying out of laws that others have made, right?

Wrong. We have already seen that in nation after nation the chief executive plays an important role in initiating and formulating the bills that the legislature will eventually enact into law and in rallying public support for the policies that are explicit or implicit in those laws. The chief executive's role as chief executor of the laws is almost always less significant than his or her role as partner in the making of those laws. And it is the combination of those roles — a combination normally found only in chief executives and their immediate staffs — that gives these leaders the power they have.

It is, however, the second aspect, the literal "executing" role of chief executives, that concerns us here. And having said that the executing role is less significant than the legislating role, I must immediately make clear that it is nevertheless a far from negligible task. The three principal *executive* tasks of the chief executive are to make appointments, oversee the bureaucracy, and guide public opinion. We have already covered the first (pp. 352 – 355); we turn now to the other two.

Overseeing the Bureaucracy

Once they have made their appointments, chief executives are responsible for keeping a constant eye on the activities and accomplishments of the people they have appointed. Overseeing that bureaucracy — the public employees whose job it is to carry out the laws of the land — is a task normally shared (not always easily and cooperatively) by the chief executive and the legislative committee responsible for the particular laws being carried out. Carrying his or her share of the surveillance burden is one of the most difficult and thankless tasks any president, prime minister, or other chief executive must face. Contrary to what might at first be expected, the problem is not just making sure that enough work gets done; it is also trying to keep too much useless work from being done. Bureaucrats are very much like other workers; some simply want to get through the day with as little effort as possible, but others — perhaps the majority — want to do their work well, so well that they will be praised, promoted, and put in charge of other bureaucrats. Hardworking bureaucrats do not want to be overseen, they want to be encouraged to do more of what they think they do best.

These very natural human tendencies are found in nearly every workplace but cause special problems when the workplace is a government office. In government, one important aspect of the normal relationship between management and the workforce is reversed. In private business, the managers have usually been around a lot longer than most of the people they manage; in government, the newcomers are more often found in management and the oldtimers in the workforce.[26] The new executives are imposed on the bureaucratic workforce by a powerful outside body that usually has little expertise in the actual business of government — that is, by the voters or the leaders of a coup d'état.

Having the right to bring in new management — which is what voters do every time they elect a new president or change the balance of power in a parliament and thereby force the selection of a new prime minister — is an essential element of the democratic process. Even when the new management is brought in by force, it can sometimes produce salutary results if the ousted government was more authoritarian and more remote from the people's will than its successors are. In any system, new managers may be more up to date in their area of specialization, more politically sophisticated, and more in touch with the popular will than the managers they replace. On the other hand, the imposition of new management by nonexperts can also mean that inexperienced and temporary top managers will be unable to exercise full control over an experienced and self-aggrandizing workforce.

Chief executives cannot oversee every department personally. There were, for example, 2,971,357 people employed in the U.S. federal government in 1994.[27] Their natural inclination is to establish some sort of administrative office to help with the task, or to ask the legislature to set up such an agency. This is especially true when new problems must be solved: Consider the proliferation of environmental agencies at the state and federal level when the seriousness of environmental hazards to the planet's and our own well-being began to be recognized. Or consider the creation of the *Treuhandanstalt* ("trustee agency") in Germany at the time of that nation's reunification, an agency whose sole mission was to oversee the transfer to private ownership of the more than 8,000 state-owned enterprises in eastern Germany.[28]

Leadership by persuasion. U.S. president Bill Clinton explains his point of view to construction worker Dexter Holmes during a visit to a road improvement project in Washington, D.C. Listening are Mayor Sharon Pratt Kelly (L) and congressional representative Eleanor Holmes Norton. (Reuters/Corbis-Bettmann)

Guiding Public Opinion

Another chore that falls to chief executives is one for which they are often far better qualified: rallying the public in support of the decisions they or other government leaders make. Making one's way to any nation's top executive post almost always means mastering the arts of persuasion. Richard Neustadt has pointed out the importance of this role for presidents of the United States; an American president must, he says, "be effective as a teacher to the public." Neustadt identifies four ways presidential teaching is different from classroom teaching. First, there is no captive audience; most of the "students" live far away and are preoccupied with their own lives. Second, these students pay attention only when they are already concerned about the matters the president wants to teach them about. Third, the president teaches more by doing (or not doing) than by talking. Fourth, the public's evaluation of the president's past performance always influences how susceptible they will be to the efforts of the chief executive to teach them anything new.[29] Neustadt could have added a fifth difference, one that perhaps seemed too obvious to mention: The position of the presidency gives its occupant a unique combination of prestige, power, and visibility, advantages that go far to overcome the disadvantages suggested in the first four points.

Although Neustadt is probably right that presidents teach more effectively by doing than by talking, chief executives around the world do offer a good deal of direct explanation to the voters, openly explaining the virtues of the policy in question and asking for support. Thus, when Great Britain was about to join the effort to force Iraq from Kuwait in the 1991 Gulf War, Prime Minister John Major personally explained why he believed this to be necessary; the cost of war, he said, would be "less than that of failing to defend principle."[30] When Jean Chrétien, Prime Minister of Canada, decided it was time to take steps to reduce that nation's mounting public debt, he spoke first through his finance minister, Paul Martin, who said the debt must be brought down "come hell or high water" and then went himself on a morning television news show, *Canada A.M.*, to prepare his listeners for the cuts he believed were essential, telling them bluntly, "Too many people have become too dependent on government."[31] Executives may also seek to prevent the development of unrealistic expectations. When former president Jimmy Carter visited North and South Korea seeking to facilitate their reunification, South Korean President Kim Young Sam spoke through his press secretary Park Chin, "On the surface, what Mr. Carter [said] looks positive. Of course, we have heard many of these things before. Still, it seems momentum has been created."[32]

Sometimes the message the chief executive tries to get across has less to do with future policies for which he seeks public support than with an effort to place the effects of past policies in the best possible light. This tactic, popularly known as "spin control," depends heavily on creating spectacles that both attract the media (see Chapter 8) and carry the "right" message. It isn't easy to do, since the media is just as likely to make news out of the effort to spin as to carry the message itself — John Anthony Maltese tells how in his early months in office Bill Clinton was castigated as a "tax and spin" president, despite his carefully nonpartisan appointment of Republican commentator David Gergen as his "Communications Director."[33]

Refusals to Execute   In one of those paradoxes that make governments work better while confusing the people who observe them, it is common constitutional practice to give the government officials whose duty is to carry out the laws the power to refuse to do so. Chief executives very often have the right to refuse to sign — that is, to **veto** — the acts of legislatures as well as to interfere with the carrying out of judicial decisions by pardoning men and women who have been found guilty and sentenced to imprisonment or capital punishment.

Sometimes the **executive veto** is absolute, but more commonly it can be overridden if the legislature can muster the votes to pass it again by a large enough majority. According to Richard Watson, U.S. presidents have traditionally used the veto to protect the executive against legislative encroachment on its powers, to protect the constitution, or to prevent the introduction of new laws that appear administratively unworkable, fiscally unsound, or simply unwise. He points out that the U.S. Congress has not been reluctant to overrule the president. The record was set during the tenure of Harry Truman, when 37 percent of that president's vetoes were overturned by a second vote.[34]

Vetoing a bill checks the power of legislatures; a **pardon** issued to someone convicted of a crime checks the power of the judiciary. The executive right to pardon is normally extensive in theory but quite limited in practice. Pardons can be granted to those convicted of ordinary crimes when new and unusual circumstances are uncovered after the sentencing, but under such circumstances it is much more likely that the convict's lawyers will simply seek a new trial. Pardons are more commonly granted for political reasons — either to bring the governmental process into closer accord with public opinion or to curry political favor openly with particular individuals or groups. Although the latter motive is never openly acknowledged, it is often very clear, as when Argentinian President Carlos Saul Menem signed presidential pardons in late 1990 for seven of the men who had been leading protagonists of that nation's "dirty war" of internal repression in the mid-1970s. Menem was under such heavy pressure from the military to free the men that he did so despite the fact that their activities had led to the loss of over 9,000 lives and despite the anger he knew the pardons would provoke at home and abroad.[35]

LEADERSHIP AND FOLLOWERSHIP

Thus far in our study of leadership in government, we have been proceeding as if all it takes to become a leader is to occupy one of the positions of power — to become, in one way or another, a high government official. However, leadership does not mean merely exercising power. The other side of leadership is **followership**. Some leaders attract support by honest means, while others rely on manipulation. And whether openly or deviously, leaders relate to followers in four distinctly different ways: charismatic, dictatorial, representative, and egalitarian.

Shared Motives and Trust versus Manipulation

James MacGregor Burns believes that "leadership over human beings is exercised when persons with certain motives and purposes mobilize, in competition or conflict with others, institutional, political, psychological and other resources so as to arouse, engage and satisfy the motives of followers." A central point for Burns is that true leaders do not wield power without paying attention to the goals of their followers — that leadership is in fact "inseparable from followers' needs and goals." To lead, one must induce followers "to act for certain goals that represent the values and the motivations . . . *of both leaders and followers.*" However, followers do not always know their own goals, much less their values and motivations, and rulers may "arouse" motives that followers never knew they had. Burns suggests that rulers who appeal to lower or artificially induced needs ought to be termed manipulators. True leaders are the ones who can arouse the higher and more noble aspirations of their followers once lesser needs are met.[36]

Other writers have also tackled the problem of distinguishing between mere manipulation and the arousal of higher motives, perhaps by manipulative means. Plato believed that leaders must devote themselves to the highest possible goals and argued that the greatest good was the pursuit of wisdom — not happiness, not imperial domination, not unlimited wealth. Only philosophers, therefore, were worthy to assume the highest leadership posts. Even the philosopher-king, however, might find it necessary to lie to his followers: "If anyone, then, is to practice deception, either on the country's enemies or on its citizens, it must be the rulers of the commonwealth acting for its benefit; no one else may meddle with this privilege." [37]

Another philosopher, whose work made his own name synonymous with devious tactics for assuming and maintaining power, was less concerned that leaders work for the highest motives than that they appear to do so. Niccolò Machiavelli openly advised sixteenth-century potentates to concentrate on their own goal of staying in power, and to do so by appearing to be that which they were not: "Having [qualities of goodness] and always practicing them is harmful, while seeming to have them is useful . . . let a prince then concern himself with the acquisition or the maintenance of a state; the means employed will always be considered honorable and praised by all, for the mass of mankind is always swayed by appearances and by the outcome of an enterprise." [38]

Contemporary authors like Burns normally take a somewhat more positive approach. For Charles Joiner, leadership is "the silent force that brings the whole together, forming one living entity," and James Kouzes and Barry Posner are confident that "over time, those who would be followers will determine whether [a] person should be — and will be — recognized as a leader. Leadership is in the eye of the follower." [39] For a recent example of how changeable the views taken by followers may be, see Box 10.1.

Modes of Leadership   Once we accept someone as a leader, how much trust should we place in that person? In some polities we find that trust in leaders is absolute, in others that it is carefully measured, in still others that it is strong but ephemeral (see Box 10.1 for an example). In our discussion of fascism (Chapter 3) we noted that one of the central features of that ideology was the belief that the leader can do no wrong and must be trusted and obeyed without reservation. At various times, nonfascist societies have taken a similar attitude toward their leaders. France under Napoleon (and, to some

BOX 10.1

LEADERS AND FOLLOWERS: THE VOLATILE AMERICAN ELECTORATE

The 1991 war in the Persian Gulf brought President George Bush extraordinary levels of support from the American people. His overall "job approval rating" surged to 90 percent by the end of the war and 84 percent of the respondents in a national poll answered "yes" when asked, "Do you think Bush is able to deal with the big issues facing this country?" These high scores were found in almost all demographic groups, including 85 percent of self-described liberals, 84 percent of Democrats, and 77 percent of African-Americans. "I didn't vote for him but I would now," said one life-long Democrat. "He was always so positive. He wasn't going to take no for an answer. He was always very serious and determined, and always made you feel he was so full of confidence."

But by November 1991, only nine months later, President Bush's overall job approval rating had dropped back down to 51 percent, just two points higher than it had been a year earlier, before the war began. As the nation turned away from war and back to ever worsening domestic problems, a sober re-evaluation of the president's abilities was clearly being made. As the end of the year approached, 74 percent believed the condition of the economy was either "fairly bad" or "very bad." Two groups especially likely to rank the president lower than before were voters from the ages of 30 to 44 and middle-income earners ($30,000 to $50,000). Only 40 percent of liberals, 34 percent of Democrats, and 45 percent of African-Americans still thought the president was doing a good job. Two months later, the news was even worse for the president: now only 46 percent approved of his conduct of foreign policy, 73 percent thought the country was in worse shape than five years earlier, 78 percent thought the economy was "in bad shape" and his overall approval rating had dropped to 43 percent.

Sources: *The People, the Press and Politics* (Los Angeles: Times Mirror Center, 16 Nov. 1990), p. 7; *New York Times,* 27 Feb. 1991, A1, B10; *Washington Post,* 6 March 1991, A1, A4; *New York Times,* 26 Nov. 1991, A1, A18; *New York Times,* 10 Jan. 1991, A1, A14; *New York Times,* 28 Jan. 1992, A1, A16.

extent, under Charles De Gaulle), Ghana during the later years of the regime of Kwame Nkrumah, and China under Mao Zedong are some of the examples that come easily to mind. But other polities, among them the representative democracies of the world, have been less trusting and more determined to protect the right of citizens to choose their own leaders and to replace them periodically. Still others attempt to involve the citizens themselves in the work of government to the greatest extent possible, leaving only a greatly diminished role for leadership of any kind.

These variations in our willingness to trust our fortunes to our political leaders are associated with four modes of leadership: charismatic, dictatorial, representative, and minimal leadership (the last being the form of leadership in a participatory democracy). Various combinations of these four types are possible, and I treat them separately here only for convenience.

Charismatic Leadership   **Charisma** is one of the much-abused terms of the social sciences. It has its origins in the Greek word *kharis,* meaning "gift," and was developed as a sociological concept by Rudolf Sohn and Max Weber to refer to individuals who have the "gift of grace" that raises them above ordinary mortals and makes others willing to accept them as great leaders.[40] The gift is a gift in two senses: It is a gift to have the necessary qualities, and it is also a gift from one's followers to be recognized as having those qualities.

The gift of recognition is most commonly granted when nations are in a state of turmoil and change and the natural inclination is to seek out the extraordinary person and even to endow more ordinary mortals with the qualities we would like them to have. Commonly, we look for those who seem to embody both the past and the hoped-for future, who can help us make the transition demanded of us not only by their skills in effecting it but also by appearing to carry forward in their persons the best of what has gone before. Such a leader fully deserves the label **charismatic.**[41]

Thus the term *charisma* has a very specific meaning, although in practice we use it very casually and often apply it before the person so labeled has even had the opportunity to demonstrate whether circumstances will permit the promise to be fulfilled. Sometimes, however, these seemingly premature pronouncements prove well-founded. Almost as soon as Nelson Mandela was released from twenty-seven years of imprisonment in South Africa, reporters were ready to label him "blessed with a double helping of charisma." The remarkable qualities of the even-tempered but unrelenting opponent of South African apartheid were very evident. As Ahmed Kathrada, the man who shared the long years in jail and then served as his publicity director, said, "Mr. Mandela is a type of man one doesn't get very often." And as time went by, Mandela made it clear that he met even the more demanding criteria for true charisma; he personally symbolized both the past — a long history of racial oppression — and the future — an unwavering demand for political equality.[42]

In any case, no matter how beloved and successful the person, once charismatic leadership is in place, the problem often becomes knowing when to stop. Once a people has become accustomed to hero worship, they often find it difficult to withdraw the absolute trust they have placed in their leader. Yet true charismatic leadership never endures for long. Either the required change is accomplished or the leader's efforts to bring it about become clearly hopeless — it cannot be done.[43]

What happens next varies greatly from system to system and from era to era. Sometimes all that happens is a return to the previous political system. The reestablished institutions may be monarchical or military, collec-

South African President Nelson Mandela has been described as "blessed with a
double-helping of charisma." Here he speaks in London in July 1996, seeking to
promote British business interest in investing in his nation. (AP Photo/Jacqueline
Arzt/Wide World)

tivist or democratic, but in any case the source of political power will once
again be the strength of an institution, not the personal magnetism of a
single individual.

Dictatorial Leadership   Unfortunately, one of the most common after-
maths of charisma is the rise of dictatorship. Under a **dictatorship**, power
remains concentrated in the hands of a single individual, but the authority
of that person's rule rests on the exercise of raw power, frequently supported by the deliberate and mechanistic encouragement of a personality

cult. The easy and joyous support followers once gave to the charismatic leader can be transmuted to the bitter burden of enduring tyranny and corruption. Joseph Stalin assumed the charismatic mantle of Vladimir Lenin on Lenin's death in 1924 and completed the Russian Revolution, but the tactics he chose to maintain himself in absolute power were tyrannical in the extreme. Similarly, Indira Gandhi took over the prime ministership of India in 1966, seeming at first to follow in the footsteps of her widely respected father Jawaharlal Nehru but soon adopting methods of exercising power that combined corruption with tyranny.[44]

Representative Leadership   Representative leadership is not easily established — whether it comes about as a sequel to charismatic rule, is imposed by foreign conquest (as in Germany and Japan after World War II), or emerges more gradually over the years (as in the slow evolution of the constitutional monarchies of western Europe). In the first place, there is no guarantee that the shift to representative rule, once made, will really take hold. The first U.S. constitution proved unequal to the task of institutionalizing representative government, in large part because of its failure to give adequate protection to the more powerful interests in the new nation; thus, the Articles of Confederation were replaced by our present constitution.[45] The new constitutions of the formerly communist nations of eastern Europe have all the usual trappings of democracies, but the revival of ethnic nationalism, the suffering caused by drastic and rapid economic change, and the ambitious pursuit of political power by an unprecedented number of parties and groups have thus far prevented these nations from achieving the degree of stability required for effective representative rule, and many fear they may yet return to authoritarian dictatorship or "post-communist" rule.

In the second place, we have never really resolved what we mean by **representative leadership**. We generally agree that it means that the people will be able to choose certain individuals to attend to matters of state on their behalf. But such a formulation, while simple enough on its face, covers a multitude of possibilities and a wide range of unanswered questions. Who are the people who may choose? How do they choose? Are there limits on the kind of people who may be chosen? What are properly "matters of state?" And, perhaps most difficult of all, what does it mean "to act on behalf of the people" (a question we have considered briefly in the previous chapter)?

Although the answers to these questions vary from system to system, the basic idea of representative leadership is one of the world's most compelling philosophical inventions. Charisma is inevitably short lived and dictatorship is always oppressive, yet few of us are keen to assume the burdens of true self-government (for reasons we will examine in the following section). Choosing a responsible delegate to attend to public affairs seems the ideal solution, especially where those affairs grow constantly more complex and demanding.

Minimal Leadership   Suppose you received a telephone call inviting you to a neighborhood meeting to discuss priorities for next year's national budget. Suppose you went to the meeting, listened to others, spoke your own mind, voted on resolutions, and were then yourself elected to carry the resolutions to a countywide meeting on the same topic. Suppose you went through the same procedure at this county meeting and there helped elect someone else to go on to a statewide meeting, where the process was repeated again and delegates were sent to a national meeting. Suppose, finally, that the national meeting was the legitimate rulemaking body for the nation and that the resolutions finally adopted there were in fact the law of the land.

If such a procedure were open to you, you would be participating in a government in which the people rule themselves as far as is possible and leadership is minimized. **Minimal leadership** is at least theoretically possible in what is commonly called **participatory democracy**. Such a government is government immediately by the people — not by their representatives, not by charismatic or dictatorial autocrats, not by anyone other than the citizens themselves. However, an entirely participatory democracy is physically impossible in large polities; we cannot all go to Washington, D.C., or any other capital of a large nation-state.

On the other hand, suppose the purpose of that telephone call was to inform you of the next meeting at town hall, and suppose that at that meeting you were able to vote on the ordinances that would be governing your municipality. In that case, you would *almost* be engaging in participatory democracy and certainly leadership would be minimized. However, to the extent that your decisions at town hall could be overruled by a higher body (for example, the federal Supreme Court), there would still be some discrepancy between theory and practice.

Minimal leadership may seem to you, quite reasonably, to be the very antithesis of charismatic rule. Yet one of the recurrent paradoxes of human political development is the emergence of charismatic leadership at the head of a revolutionary movement dedicated to the introduction of participatory democracy. Men and women passionately devoted to the idea of eliminating not only the present government but the need for elite leadership altogether are often amazingly ready to submit themselves to the guidance of a single master as they pursue their dream.

That dream seems never to fade entirely away — and never to be fully realized in any community for long. Sometimes the revolution that has been waged on its behalf leads to personal dictatorship, as the cases of the Soviet Union under Stalin and the People's Republic of China under Mao Zedong suggest. In other cases, the results are more mixed. A genuine effort may be made to set up communal decision making, people's courts, worker control of the factories, or other institutions associated with participatory democracy, yet somehow effective control remains at the top. As Robert Michels has pointed out, whenever human beings get organized they display a natural tendency to divide into those who lead and those who follow, partly because of the skills and ambitions of the leaders, partly because of the absence of these qualities (along with a tendency toward hero worship) in the followers, and partly because the nature of an organization itself seems to require someone "in charge."[46]

Yet as Michels himself foretold, the dream of reducing our need for leadership does not die easily. For some, the way to get there is through more traditional leadership; the leaders of today must find the will to work selflessly and incessantly to "raise the intellectual level of ever-widening strata of the people," said Antonio Gramsci.[47] Franz Fanon agreed: "To educate the masses politically does not mean, cannot mean, making a political speech. What it means is to try, relentlessly and passionately, to teach the masses that everything depends on them . . . that there is no famous man who will take the responsibility for everything."[48]

So far, however, we human beings do not seem to have developed the capacity for either such disinterested leadership or such attentive followership. Leaders of parties ostensibly devoted to carrying forward a popular revolution continue to convert their organizations into instruments of manipulation and control. Indonesia gives an extreme but not entirely unique example: Shortly after gaining independence from the Dutch in 1949, its leader Sukarno converted his National Indonesian Party into the tool of "Guided Democracy" — democracy so thoroughly "guided" that Sukarno was declared president for life. Although Sukarno was removed by coup d'état in 1965, his successor General Suharto created a new party, Sekber-Golkar, which, strongly controlled by the military, continued to give its undivided support to the new dictator (reelected president unopposed in 1993) and to the doctrine of *Pancasilla*, one of the five principles of which is — guess what? — "democracy."[49]

Humanity is, however, still fairly new at the tasks of social organization, and just beginning to develop some understanding of the psychological needs political leadership may fill. Perhaps in the future we will find a way to minimize our dependency on others to tell us what to do. Perhaps it is not inevitable that there should be, in the words of Gaetano Mosca, a "chosen minority to which the lot of every country is entrusted."[50] Perhaps we will become as skilled at the arts of participatory citizenship as many of us presently are in other complex but widely practiced arts, such as driving automobiles, cooking gourmet meals, or figuring our income tax. As the human polity grows ever more complex, its individual polities ever more interdependent, and our combined capacity to self-destruct ever more ominous, we may decide that knowing how to participate in politics, like knowing how to drive, is so necessary to our well-being that everyone will be required at last to learn how it is done.

FROM LEADER TO LEADER: THE PROBLEM OF SUCCESSION

When Calvin Coolidge told the reporters gathered for one of his rare press conferences, "I do not choose to run for president in 1928. There will be nothing more from this office today,"[51] he was not only setting a record for brevity of communication. He was also demonstrating that he was one of the very few people with a natural immunity to the dread disease of Caesarism, otherwise known as addiction to power.

Most men and women who achieve positions of great power find it difficult to relinquish that power. No one ever found it harder than Napoleon Bonaparte, who managed somehow to return from defeat and exile on the island of Elba to resume control of his empire; vanquished a second time at the Battle of Waterloo in 1815, he spent his remaining years on the yet more remote island of St. Helena plotting a third conquest of power; some say only murder (by a close associate in the pay of the new French government) was able to call a final halt to his fierce ambition.[52]

Even when leaders accept the necessity of passing on the duties of office to others, they still often seek to determine who their successors will be and to exercise continued control. The Mexican constitution limits the presidency to a single term, but custom requires that the outgoing president have a significant say in who will succeed him. In 1994, outgoing president Carlos Salinas chose Luis Donaldo Colosio; when Colosio was assassinated during the campaign, Salinas immediately gave the *dedazo* (the "big fingerpoint") to Ernesto Zedillo, who made it into office without further drama.[53]

Of course, sometimes even a designated successor proves disappointing; in that case the former leader may try to find a way to return to power. Theodore Roosevelt, dismayed by the protectionist stance taken by his hand-picked successor, William Howard Taft, vainly sought to take back the presidency four years after leaving it by running as the candidate of the Progressive (Bull Moose) Party in the 1912 election.[54]

Once out of office, it is common for former leaders to expect to be consulted as elder statesmen and to work hard at their memoirs, hoping to influence the history that will be written of their regimes and thereby to maximize the continued power of the ideas they stood for, the laws they made, and the pacts they negotiated with the leaders of other nations. In an extreme case, former president Richard Nixon, discredited, disgraced, and ultimately forced from office by acts so heinous that only his successor's pardon prevented his being charged with criminal behavior, was able to maintain a posture of some importance in the United States and international political arena after his resignation from the presidency.

This reluctance to relinquish power is perhaps the most difficult problem facing the human polity. How can we tell our leaders when we have had enough? For chief executives, there are three common solutions to the problem, which we may call the democratic, autocratic, and oligarchic solutions. The **democratic solution** is to insist on limited terms with succession determined by free elections. Table 10.2 gives a representative list of nations that have adopted this means of determining succession to leadership. (As noted elsewhere, whether elections are truly open and free is always a matter for empirical confirmation.)

The **autocratic solution** is based on the principle of holding office for life with succession determined by heredity. This method leaves the question of succession to the ascriptive criterion of lineage; custom or law decrees who in the current occupant's family shall be next in line, and the occupant is expected to stay in office until removed by disability or death. The solution is autocratic because only one person can possibly qualify to replace the existing leader, and no other individual or group need be involved in determining who that should be. This form of succession for major leadership roles is now far less common than heretofore, but is still used in Morocco, Oman, and Saudi Arabia.[55]

In the **oligarchic solution**, the length of term and succession are determined by a narrow elite. A common way of resolving the problem of succession, it allows the present occupant to stay in power until others, each individually less powerful than the occupant but collectively capable of removing him or her from office, decide to bring down the curtain. A number of variations on this theme are possible. The normal expectation may be that the holder of power will keep it for life and those charged with finding a successor will act only on his or her death, a system we saw at

TABLE 10.2   **Limited Terms with Succession Determined by Free Elections**

Nation	Most Important Office	Term
Canada	prime minister	up to 5 years
Denmark	prime minister	up to 4 years
France	president	7 years
Greece	prime minister	up to 4 years
India	prime minister	up to 6 years
Israel	prime minister	up to 4 years
Japan	prime minister	up to 4 years
New Zealand	prime minister	up to 3 years
United Kingdom	prime minister	up to 5 years
United States	president	4 years
Venezuela	president	4 years

Source: *The Europa World Yearbook, 1995* (London: Europa Publications Limited, 1995). Reprinted by permission.

work throughout the history of the Soviet Union (the last time was on the death of Konstantin Chernenko in 1985, when the Politburo convened to choose Mikhail Gorbachev as his successor), and we see it in the Vatican every time a pope dies and the College of Cardinals meets to choose a new prelate. The actual mode of succession may vary greatly. The elite group may vote on the matter, may talk it over and make the choice by appointment, or may exercise force to place its nominee in office — and combinations of all three methods are entirely possible. Table 10.3 offers some examples of polities where a version of the oligarchic solution is used to find successors when leaders fall from power.

Modes of Succession: What Difference Does It Make?

It makes a great deal of difference which system of succession is used. Only the first system — limited terms with free elections — is compatible with democratic government. The second — succession determined by heredity — is often an effective means for maintaining the stability of a system, though whether or not the system in question ought to be maintained is a normative question. The third — succession determined by a narrow elite — is by definition most compatible with authoritarian rule. That rule may or may not be tyrannical in practice, but where it is not, the effective restraints lie outside the system of choosing the leadership. The oligarchic solution is also the system most conducive to instability, espe-

TABLE 10.3

Succession Determined by a Narrow Elite

Nation	Name of Office	Nature of Elite with Power to Determine Successor
Brazil[a]	president	political/military
China	premier	political
Iran	velayat faghih[b]	religious/political
North Korea	president	political
Turkey	president	military/political
Vatican	pope	religious
Zaire	president	political

[a] In 1988 Brazil shifted to a nonrenewable five-year term for the presidency, with the provision that in 1993 a referendum would be held to determine whether to remain a presidential system or shift to a parliamentary or monarchical form of government.
[b] *Velayat faghih* means "religious leader." Under the new Iranian constitution, when it is time to choose a successor to this leader, a council of experts will have the choice of selecting a single leader or a council composed of three or five persons, to be called the Council of Leadership.
Sources: Arthur S. Banks, ed., *Political Handbook of the World* (New York: CSA Publications, 1991), p. 82, and *The Europa World Yearbook, 1995* (London: Europa Publications Limited, 1995). Reprinted with permission.

BOX 10.2

A DANGEROUS MOMENT FOR DEMOCRATIC SUCCESSION IN THE UNITED STATES

Even the commitment of the United States to democratic succession has had its shaky moments. In the early years of the Repubic, Federalists and Antifederalists tended to view each others' policies as intolerable dangers to the new nation's survival. There was a real possibility that either side would, in the event of the other's electoral victory, actively revert to the tactics that had secured power in the recent past: armed revolt. As it happened, the Federalists were able to swallow the advent of Antifederalist leadership in 1800, thereby setting the precedent for the peaceful and law-abiding relinquishing of power, but they were helped to do so by a most unusual set of circumstances. When the Electoral College vote was counted, it was discovered that two Antifederalists, Aaron Burr and Thomas Jefferson, had tied for first place. This meant that the election would be decided in the House of Representatives, where the Federalists held the majority. The result was a great deal of secret negotiating, each candidate promising the defeated party as much as he dared in order to appear the lesser of two evils, before Jefferson was finally given the nod by his political enemies. Allowing the "ins" to choose between two or more nominees put forward by the "outs" may not be a practicable or desirable fourth system of resolving the problem of succession, but it worked remarkably well in that case.[57]

cially if the question of who may be a member of the elite depends on nothing more than who happens to be most powerful and most prompt to act when the moment to choose a successor arises. A better recipe for producing an intraelite struggle for power leading either to leaderless deadlock or to civil war can scarcely be imagined.

It is important to ask not only which system a polity has formally adopted but also how leaders are really replaced, whatever the constitution may say. More than once a leader in power has flatly refused to accept an electoral decision. In 1993, Nigerian military leader General Ibrahim Babangida created two political parties and imposed platforms on each, but then suspended the elections held in June when early unofficial results showed that the "wrong" man was winning and appointed a businessman, Ernest Shonekan, as head of state. Even that step proved unsatisfactory to General Sani Abacha, the nation's defense minister, who forced Shonekan out in November and gave Nigeria, once again, an entirely military government.[56] And such reluctance to accept the outcome of democratic elections is by no means limited to the Third World. (see Box 10.2)

This may be a good time to take a second look at the notes you made at the beginning of this chapter. How do the answers you gave about political leadership look to you now? Do they hold up pretty well? Which of them would you change, and how? Were you surprised to find that it wasn't, after all, all that hard to find a few good things to say about bureaucrats — if only because, once you think about it, you know so many of them? Perhaps you even began to give the idea of joining the ranks of the bureaucrats some consideration yourself. We turn now to a fuller consideration of the world of bureaucracy.

THE BUREAUCRACY

If you are attending a community college, a state college, or a state university, you deal with bureaucrats every time you pay your school fees. Regardless of what kind of college you are attending, you may be paying those fees at least in part with a government loan or with financial aid from the government. You may have been to see government bureaucrats recently to arrange your transportation: to get a driver's license, a student bus ticket, or a license for your bicycle. Many of you have registered to vote. Probably all of you have Social Security numbers. Some of you are paying income taxes. Some are married, some are divorced, and some have had to register the births of their children. In every case it was necessary to fill out the proper papers with the government.

The same or similar experiences are common to the lives of everyone in the human polity. A young Paraguayan decides to pursue his studies at the National University of Paraguay and fills out the necessary papers. An Indian mother decides to take the rewards offered by her government for joining its sterilization program and signs the appropriate form. A Canadian veteran decides to buy a larger house in Moosejaw, Saskatchewan, and applies for the government loan her military service has entitled her to seek. An Albanian alcoholic agrees to work on his problem and signs himself into the government hospital for treatment.

Not all bureaucratic experiences are initiated by citizens. Some of us get arrested for crimes we may or may not have committed, get drafted into armies we would prefer not to serve in, or have our paychecks garnished for taxes we failed to pay. If we live under a heavily authoritarian government and dare to express dissent, we may find agents of government taking over our property, getting us fired from our jobs, and even subjecting our bodies to confinement and torture.

But even if our experiences have been much less traumatic, almost all of us resent having to go through the normal bureaucratic procedures: standing in lines, submitting to interviews, filling out forms, identifying ourselves by numbers, signing everything in triplicate. *Bureaucracy* means, first and foremost, "administration of government," but it also means "governmental officialism," and the adjective *bureaucratic* is usually interpreted to mean "following an inflexible routine." When pressed, we will probably

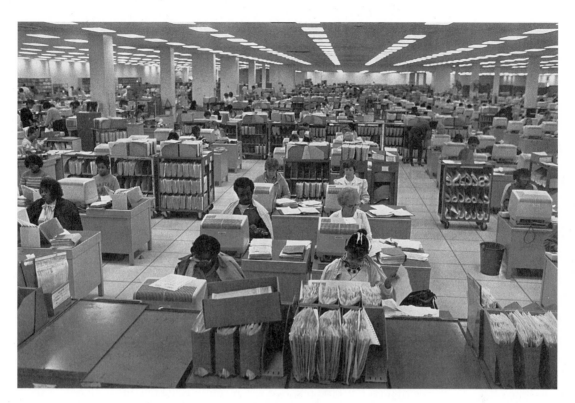

The work of bureaucracy is never done. Here hundreds of Internal Revenue Service workers check through tax returns at the IRS Service Center in Philadelphia. (UPI/ Corbis-Bettmann)

agree that we need government to help us solve some of our individual and collective problems (although we will disagree among ourselves about how much help we need) and also that we believe in "equal protection under the law" — that is, in having the laws applied to all of us in the same way. But shouldn't there be a better way than "inflexible routine" and "governmental officialism" to accomplish these goals?

Before we can consider how the world's bureaucracies might be improved, we need to know more about how they operate now. We need to look at the work of the bureaucrats, considering who they are and how they do their jobs in various nations, before we can properly consider the interesting question of whether or not there is any way to have "administration of government" without "inflexible routine."

The Work of Bureaucracy

As the work of governments grows ever more complex, the world's bureaucratic work forces grow ever more elaborate and specialized. Special agents are required for everything from inspecting nuclear power plants to supervising the artificial insemination of prize heifers on ranches receiving government subsidies. Books must be kept on expenditures of all kinds, for political campaigns in Iowa's First Congressional District, for laying transcontinental gas pipelines in Russia, for shipping kangaroos from Australia to the world's zoos. Of course, not all bureaucratic activity is domestic; a vast array of bureaucratic officialdom is devoted to foreign affairs. In our increasingly interdependent world, some nations, such as Japan, even maintain a special bureaucratic corps to help foreigners develop international trade.[58]

The activities of bureaucrats, however diverse, have in common the fact that they all involve the efforts of bureaucrats to *implement* government policy. To accomplish this broader goal, it is not enough, however, simply to do the job called for by policy. Bureaucrats must also gather the funds to pay for the work of government, disburse those funds to the other bureaucrats or private sector entrepreneurs who do that work, and see to it that no laws or rules are broken in the process. These three more specialized tasks of bureaucrats are worth a closer look.

Collecting Revenue   Bureaucrats collect the revenue necessary to do the work of government. They write up the tax forms and instruction booklets for all kind of taxes, personal income taxes, corporate income taxes, import and export duties, license fees, inheritance taxes, and taxes on purchased goods are a few of the more common ones. Taxes are levied even on illegal activities; until the practice was recently ruled unconstitutional by the Supreme Court as a form of double punishment, farmers convicted of marijuana farming in Montana were taxed "$100 an ounce or 10 percent of market value, whichever is greater."[59] Bureaucrats not only levy taxes, they also process the penalties, settle disputes (although, as in the Montana case, final appeal may be made to the judicial branch of the government), and help prepare legislation to change the laws governing the collection of taxes and other revenues.

Disbursing Government Funds   Bureaucrats also disburse government monies. They prepare the government's budget, and once it has acquired any necessary ratification from other branches or offices of the nation's government, they carry it out. They are the ones who purchase raw materials and finished goods (including all those necessary for the nation's defense establishment); pay bills; meet payrolls; process applications for government loans; pay interest on government bonds; give political parties and their candidates whatever help with campaign expenses they are entitled to by law; pay price supports to farmers; pay a wide range of social benefits, from welfare to family allowances to full medical coverage; support the United Nations and its affiliated agencies; and send foreign aid to other nations. They even manufacture the nation's money in the first place. Sometimes, of course, goods rather than money are disbursed. The United

States sends surplus food abroad, but the bureaucrats of poorer nations also distribute (and redistribute) goods, especially land; the bureaucrats in the Ministries of Agriculture and Construction in Ethiopia have been major (and sometimes conflicting) actors in the massive distribution of new lands to thousands of peasants suffering from drought and famine in the Wollo and Tigraye regions of that nation.[60]

Preventing or Punishing Infractions of the Law   Bureaucrats are also expected to see to it that the rules a government sets for the personal behavior of its citizens are obeyed — or at least that infractions meet with the prescribed sanctions. Some of these rules, such as laws determining what acts constitute criminal behavior, apply to everyone; others apply only to those entering into particular relationships with government.

Whether the rule is intended to prevent crime, to protect the environment, or to meet some other social goal, if it is a rule made by government it will be the work of some bureaucrat to see that it is obeyed or to call the malefactor to account. Police officers, prosecuting attorneys, and prison administrators are bureaucrats who try to enforce laws against criminal activity; health inspectors, welfare "snoops," and government safety commissioners are bureaucrats who try to enforce laws concerning other forms of activity that policymakers have decided are desirable or undesirable. The line between the two kinds of policing is not always easily drawn; serious infringement of rules set to accomplish social goals can lead to prosecution for criminal behavior.

Subdividing the Work of Bureaucracy   Max Weber, one of the first serious students of bureaucracy, believed that in the ideal bureaucracy all tasks would be assigned carefully on the basis of *specialization* and *hierarchy*. Everyone would do the job for which he or she was best suited, every job would be specific and limited, and every bureaucrat would occupy a clear-cut place in the chain of command, with no confusion as to who had authority over whom.[61]

Even Weber might be surprised if he could see how seriously modern bureaucracies have taken his advice regarding specialization. Consider, for example, the fine distinctions made between the jobs of Oven-Press Tender I and Oven-Press Tender II in the U.S. government (see Box 10.3). States that take direct control of industrial development must make an even broader range of distinctions; consider the posts assigned in the cabinet of the Chinese government and imagine the vast responsibility of each minister in this nation of over 1 billion citizens (see Box 10.4).

Obviously, overspecialization can hinder effective performance by individuals who dare not step past the limits of their own job description. It can also make meeting Weber's second recommendation — keep the lines of authority clear — very difficult. States with highly specialized bureaucratic structures almost always find it hard to maintain clear lines of au-

BOX 10.3

IS TOO MUCH BUREAUCRACY SLOWING US DOWN?

573.685-042   OVEN-PRESS TENDER (asbestos prod.) I

Tends hot press and related equipment that hardens asbestos disc pads for use as brake linings; Positions metal die plate on roller-type conveyor, picks up stack of asbestos disc pads from table, and places individual pads into wells of die plate. Discards broken or defective pads. Pushes filled die plates onto racks of hot press. Starts machine that automatically closes press to heat-treat pads for specified time and opens press at end of press cycle. Pulls die plates from press onto conveyor. Removes cured disc pads from die plates, using knockout device that forces pads from plates. Loosens stuck pads with rubber mallet and tosses pads into storage container. Sprays empty die plates with silicone solution, using spray gun, to prevent pads from sticking to plates during heat-treating process. GOE 06.04.19 PD M 08 09 15 17 EC 07 M1 L1 SVP 4 SOC 7675

573.685-046   OVEN-PRESS TENDER (asbestos prod.) II

Tends hot press that hardens asbestos disc pads for use as brake linings; Pushes metal die plates filled with asbestos disc pads onto feed elevator of machine. Presses buttons to open press, move die plates from elevator into press, and closes press. Observes timer lights, dials, and pressure gauges on control panel of machine to determine end of press cycle. Presses buttons at end of cycle to simultaneously open press and move cured disc pads from press onto discharge elevator. Pushes die plates from elevator onto roller-type conveyor, using metal rake. GOE 06.04.19 PD M 08 09 15 EC 07 M1 L1 SVP 4 SOC 7675

Source: U.S. Department of Labor, Employment and Training Administration, *Dictionary of Occupational Titles,* 4th edition supplement (Washington, D.C.: U.S. Government Printing Office, 1986), p. 38.

thority. The very principle of specialization suggests that the person doing the job knows best how it should be done — better than any alleged superior. As Weber himself noted, "The trained permanent official is more likely to get his way in the long run than his nominal superior [when the latter] is not a specialist." [62] Furthermore, specialization and hierarchy are difficult to combine because those who specialize do not always respond well to proposals that they coordinate their work with that of other specialists. Specialization is thus likely to lead to the proliferation of bureaucratic units with overlapping jurisdictions. Resentful of competition, the person in charge of each unit may well become extremely jealous of his or her own authority, insisting on control of everything that happens within that unit and refusing to cooperate with other units in any way that might impair that authority.

BOX 10.4

MINISTRIES IN THE CHINESE CABINET

Agriculture	Public Health
Chemical Industry	Public Security
Civil Affairs	Radio, Film and Television
Coal Industry	Railways
Communications	State Commission for Economic
Construction	Restructuring
Culture	State Commission for Economic
Electronics Industry	Trade
Finance	State Commission for Education
Foreign Affairs	State Commission for Family
Foreign Economic Relations	Planning
and Trade	State Commission for Nationalities
Forestry	Affairs
Geology and Mineral Resources	State Commission for Physical
Internal Trade	Culture and Sports
Justice	State Commission for Planning
Labor	State Commission for Science
Light Industry	and Technology
Machine Building Industry	State Commission for Science,
Metallurgical Industry	Technology and Industry for
National Defense	National Defense
Personnel	State Security
Posts and Telecommunications	Supervision
Power Industry	Water Resources

Source: Arthur S. Banks, ed., *Political Handbook of the World: 1993*, Binghamton, N.Y.: CSA Publications, 1993), p. 167. Reprinted by permission of the publisher.

Who Are the Bureaucrats?

Although we often think of bureaucrats as white-collar workers standing behind a counter with a grill or seated behind a desk, in fact any employee of a large organization is a bureaucrat, and any employee of government can therefore be called a *government bureaucrat*, including the engineers, teachers, janitors, and other specialized employees who work on the government's payroll. In practice, however, it is more useful to say that a **bureaucrat** is someone who does the administrative work of government — that is, who has responsibility for interpreting and implementing government policy, whether as the cop on the beat or the highest-ranking minister.

Taking on the role of bureaucrat also means taking on the *bureaucratic style*. To do their work, bureaucrats have developed a set of norms to guide them. The important principle here is *fairness* — or *the appearance thereof*.

Whether or not the concept is enshrined in the constitution, as in the case of the United States (see the Fourteenth Amendment), every nation at least gives lip service to the ideal that the laws must be applied with equal force to every citizen; this is the *sine qua non*, the minimal requirement, of bureaucratic fairness. To accomplish this goal, bureaucrats attempt to follow the law to the letter — that is, to carry it out exactly and explicitly. Because most laws are written in language open to a wide range of interpretations, the bureaucratic solution is to write a set of rules detailing exactly how each law is to be carried out, and then to attempt to follow these rules without exception. This can lead to an appearance (and in some cases a practice) of rigid, inhuman, and even ridiculous behavior on the part of some bureaucrats — the kind of behavior that leads us to use the word *bureaucratic* as a pejorative. When we ordinary citizens want something perfectly reasonable from a government office and are told by a clerk, "I'm sorry, but according to the rules it simply cannot be done," our normal response is to feel angry and frustrated, and to storm out muttering "Bureaucratic!" as if it were one of the worst terms of opprobrium. But the next time you are tempted to do that, you might stop to consider that this determination to stick to the rules *does* have its positive side, *does* mean that the clerk has been taught to adhere loyally to the principle of equal protection under the laws. There certainly may be better ways to protect that principle, but most of us would agree that protecting it is worth a few inconveniences.

How to Become a Bureaucrat

There are basically two routes to a bureaucratic position: You may be given a political appointment, or you may be hired on the basis of merit. We have discussed political appointments at length (see p. 352). When bureaucrats are hired on the *basis of merit*, a number of different methods may be employed to determine the most meritorious applicant for the job. Years of experience in related tasks, years of education in relevant fields of study, and level of performance on tests designed for the job in question are some of the criteria most commonly employed.

The use of tests was common practice long before the emergence of modern bureaucracy. Passing rigorous examinations was the most honorable path to advancement for administrators in ancient China.[63] Under the Russian czar Alexander I, the law required candidates to pass examinations in Russian, mathematics, Latin, and modern languages before they could be promoted to "collegiate assessor, the eighth rank, or state councillor, the fifth rank."[64]

Specialized training for government work has become more and more important in the modern age, and without such training the elected official is likely to find it more and more difficult to hold his own with the bureaucrats he is expected to guide. Some polities have established special schools to train those who aspire to high bureaucratic position. France has an entire system of *grandes écoles* (literally, "great schools") for educating its public servants, and those who are able to pass the rigorous entrance examinations for the National School of Administration (ENA) are almost always assured of a high government post upon graduation. Such training has become important for those who seek high elective posts in France as well; almost all French presidents, prime ministers and major cabinet ministers in recent years have been either "Enarques" (the popular term for ENA graduates) or graduates of other *grandes écoles*.[65]

Success in Third World bureaucracies is also likely to depend on suitable expertise, in particular a background in global economic affairs. Nicephore Soglo, the president of Benin, was himself an official of the World Bank, and, as Victoria Brittain points out, the presidents of Cameroon, Congo, Gabon, Ivory Coast, Senegal, and Zaire have all tended to seek out "techno-politicians" with "years of experience in multi-lateral agencies" for senior appointive positions.[66]

Of course appointment by political patronage is still widely practiced in every nation in the world. However, it is rare that the executive making the appointment fails to consider the actual capabilities of the would-be bureaucrat. A new British prime minister is expected to appoint only parliamentary members of his own party to all the paid positions associated with the Cabinet, but M.P.'s who lack administrative competence for the post in question are as unlikely to be chosen as those who are deficient in personal loyalty.[67]

TOO MUCH GOVERNMENT? OR TOO LITTLE?

We human beings are difficult to please when it comes to the operation of our governments. We don't like it when the garbage is not collected, when our roads develop potholes, or when our unemployment benefits run out. We are deeply dismayed when government aid in times of natural catastrophe is slow to arrive, when "nothing is done" about inflation, or when our armies are defeated in foreign wars. On the other hand, we resent seeing our paychecks whittled away by taxes, we don't like to stand in line, we hate to fill out forms, and we detest having to answer the questions of bureaucratic busybodies. And some of us are sure that government benefits are going to all the wrong people — to "welfare cheats" or "exploiting capitalists."

Even when we admit that a bureaucratic system is a necessary part of any modern government, that after all it makes no sense to elect officials to make government policy if no one is in place to ensure that the policy is carried out, still we tend to hold the very idea of bureaucracy in contempt. Is this because we have too much bureaucracy in our lives? Or because the job of bureaucracy is poorly done? Or is it because our expectations of what can and should be done by government bureaucrats are simply unrealistic?

"ON THIS PROJECT, I WANT YOU TO FORGET THE FEDERAL, STATE, AND LOCAL GUIDELINES—JUST FOLLOW THE HOCHFELDER GUIDELINES!"

(Singer/Singer Media Corporation)

As you probably expect, the answer is a combination of all three, and the exact proportions in that combination vary from polity to polity.

Too Much Government

Duplication and waste are found in every domain of human effort. We need only take a critical look around our own homes to find embarrassing examples of waste — food we allowed to spoil, magazines we bought and never read, notes we made and then forgot to consult. And all of us have been known to engage in overkill — making three copies where one would do, checking ten books out of the library when we knew perfectly well only three of them were likely to be useful for that missing section in the term paper we had to write, or reminding a good friend over and over not to forget an important appointment.

What accounts for such behavior? Without troubling our fellow social scientists the psychologists for an answer, we can speculate that such behavior will be most pronounced when four conditions prevail: relative affluence (we can afford a little waste), a strong desire to reach relatively limited and particular goals (so we give tasks pertinent to those goals excessive energy and attention), nonaccountability (no one else pays much attention to these useless and wasteful activities), and failure to use common sense (we "just didn't think").

All four conditions are all too likely to prevail in the normal bureaucratic setting. First, bureaucrats find themselves in the happy position of spending other people's money — a circumstance that can easily bring a sense of relative affluence. Citing instances of rank extravagance in the Agency for International Development, Sheila Kaplan suggests the ruling motto appeared to be, "Why Pay Less?".[68]

Second, most bureaucrats occupy highly specialized roles. If they are ambitious, their hopes for promotion are likely to rest on demonstrating superior performance of specific tasks. Their jobs seldom require them — or permit them — to consider means of accomplishing overall policy goals that might entail shifting energies and expenditures away from their own narrow domains. Like specialists in any large organization, they seek to use every possible means to create a praiseworthy record of accomplishment, even at the cost of duplication and waste.

Third, bureaucrats are very difficult to hold accountable. Their claims of expertise are often well founded, and their ultimate bosses — temporary elected officials — cannot always deal with them in terms that command their respect. Furthermore, any efforts to improve accountability may simply stimulate greater waste, as reports fly back and forth and efforts are made to meet — or to give the appearance of meeting — standards of efficiency set by those too remote from the tasks being performed (see Figure 10.1)

Finally, it often seems especially difficult for even the best-intentioned bureaucrats to operate according to the dictates of common sense. This difficulty flows in part from two other problems in the bureaucratic world that we have already mentioned: the need to succeed within a narrowly defined domain and the absence of true accountability. Under these circumstances, the typical bureaucrat tends to operate strictly according to the rules, regardless of how patently ridiculous or unproductive the consequences of doing so may be. If in doubt, take another look at Figure 10.1.

Too Little Government

It is no paradox to say that we can have both too much and too little bureaucracy. For at the same time that bureaucrats are busily duplicating their activities and wasting their energies, they may also be failing to do what really needs to be done — that is, putting the laws and rules that are supposed to govern the nation into actual practice. Probably more social problems persist because of a failure to implement laws already on the books than because of an absence of such legislation. Yet sometimes the failures of implementation are owing to the nature of the laws themselves. As we saw at the beginning of Chapter 10, laws are merely plans, and, like

```
Department of the Treasury

Internal Revenue Service


PAPERWORK REDUCTION ACT NOTICE


The Paperwork Reduction Act of 1980 says we must tell you why
we are collecting this information, how we will use it, and whether
you have to give it to us. We ask for the information to carry out the
Internal Revenue laws of the United States. We need it to ensure
that taxpayers are complying with these laws and to allow us to fig-
ure and collect the right amount of tax. You are required to give us
this information.


Notice 610 (22-81)
```

FIGURE 10.1   **One Result of the Paperwork Reduction Act of 1980**

all plans, they can never be entirely complete, can never foresee all contin-
gencies, and need elaboration and modification when it comes time to
carry them out. What we so easily label "bureaucratic inefficiency" may
result simply because agency officials are being asked to carry out tasks so
large under conditions so difficult that normal standards of efficiency are
simply impossible to meet.[69] The failure of the U.S. Food and Drug Administration to take steps to implement serious regulation of the tobacco industry prior to the appointment of David Kessler as its new commissioner
in 1990 has been an interesting case in point. "We just didn't want to fool
with tobacco," said a former official of the agency, stressing the power of
two forces: the smoking habit and the industry itself.[70]

It would be naive, however, to deny that bureaucratic misimplementation — or nonimplementation — can also be deliberate. To understand
why this is so, it is important to realize that the more power shifts to the
executive branch, the more those affected by public policy shift their lobbying efforts to that branch. Bureaucrats are subject to a wide range of
temptations to abandon the rules of strict neutrality that supposedly govern their work. They may be bribed to carry out their roles in ways the
groups they are supposed to be regulating desire. Or they may simply find
that it is suddenly remarkably easy to gain membership to distinguished
private clubs or to book good seats for the theater. Perhaps they will be
offered a chance of lucrative employment in the private sector when they
leave government, if they have done their job "well" in the meantime.

But the most common means lobbyists employ in dealing with bureaucrats is one that is entirely legal and, on the face of it, merely supportive and useful. As already noted in Chapter 7 (p. 231), they simply provide the bureaucrats with information. The information they offer will not be effective if it is too blatantly biased or inaccurate, but inevitably it will be one sided and partial. Nevertheless, bureaucrats all over the world welcome the help and often depend on it. Close ties develop between the regulator and the regulated; the lobbyists become the "clients" of the regulators, exchanging information and services for a form of policy implementation that is sympathetic to their needs.[71] And like all good merchandisers, the bureaucrats take care of their clients, subtly (and sometimes not so subtly) shaping their interpretations of the law in such a way as to minimize inconvenience to those they oversee, even when the net result is a clear violation of legislative intent. Some have gone so far as to lobby Congress on behalf of those whose behavior they are supposed to regulate, as when U.S. Interior Secretary Manuel Lujan asked Congress to waive a key requirement of the proposed Endangered Species Act in order to save the lumber industry (instead of the spotted owl).[72] When such a pattern of misimplementation evolves, ordinary citizens suffer from both too much and too little bureaucracy. Too much is done for a privileged few, and too little is done to carry out laws originally intended to apply with equal force to all.

The widespread prevalence of this problem of **bureaucratic drift**—drift away from control by elected representatives of the people they serve and drift toward control by the very persons and organizations they are expected to guide and supervise — has led to a number of attempted reforms. In the United States, the General Accounting Office (GAO) audits the spending of other bureaus, and the Office of Management and Budget (OMB) has a management section that continually reviews the leadership, organization, and overall effectiveness of all programs submitting requests for funding. Such offices are, however, themselves part of the bureaucratic apparatus and thus are inevitably susceptible to the same viruses that sometimes infect their fellow bureaucrats. More promising means of holding bureaucrats responsible to the general public must come from the public itself. When well informed by responsible news media, well socialized to accept and carry out the duties of citizenship, and well equipped with a strong party system capable of keeping elected representatives aware and accountable to their interests, the people themselves are the surest means of ensuring bureaucratic responsiveness to the public will, as expressed in the law of the land.

SUMMARY AND CONCLUSION

This brief introduction to the many questions involved in the study of executive and bureaucratic government may have given you some further ideas about the questions we raised at the beginning of the chapter. You know now that when you are trying to persuade others to accept you as their leader, it would be helpful to have at least some of the ascriptive criteria commonly looked for in those chosen for positions of power, although chances are you are more interested in figuring out how to earn the approval of those who choose leaders on the basis of their proven abilities. But what kind of abilities? Will you try to develop the specialized expertise more commonly associated with taking office by appointment, or will you work instead to master a wide range of information, to make friends with all kinds of people, and to exhibit the mixture of personal stability and charm that are the essential attributes of the elected officeholder? You are probably not giving serious thought to the idea of taking power by force. Besides the fact that it is likely to be contrary to your moral principles, such a tactic has a very poor record of success in recent years.

What would you now expect your relationship be to your followers to be? Charismatic? When I was first teaching, I was also quite obviously preparing to add to our family. One of my students kindly wrote at the end of her final examination, "I hope you have a very charismatic baby!" It turned out to be a very nice baby, but as we have seen, whether or not she developed charisma was likely to depend as much on her circumstances as on her innate characteristics. Still, not everyone is ready for the "charismatic situation" when it develops. What about you? Chances are you are more realistically asking yourself how you would solve the conundrums of representative leadership. If you are chosen to represent, how closely will you follow the will of your constituents? How much will you trust your own judgment? How will you react when the two conflict? Will you seek followers who trust you implicitly, or will you have the strength to prefer those who are moderately skeptical, whose trust must be earned? Perhaps you may even go so far as to hope that a greater measure of popular participation in the tasks of leadership might be introduced in your own political system and are wondering how you might help bring this about.

As you no doubt knew before you opened this book, the jobs of chief executives go well beyond carrying out the law. Indeed, one of their most important roles is to appoint and supervise others who will do the actual job of implementation. Another important task is to find ways to guide the formation of public opinion, using the prestige and visibility of your office to rally support for policies you believe in. You may be wondering how you would use the powers of the veto and the pardon, powers that can be used to prevent decisions made by others from being enacted.

Perhaps you have given some additional thought to how you will step down from power when the time comes. You may occupy an elective post with a limited term. If so, there may be a chance that you can serve more than one term. Or perhaps you will hold an appointive post. If so, the successor to the person who appointed you may have the right to appoint someone to take your place, or it may be a post from which you can be removed only by your own incapacity or death. Perhaps your tenure in office will depend on maintaining the good will of a narrow elite. When it is no longer possible to maintain that good will, or when the power to fill your office has shifted to another group, you may need to give serious consideration to ways to move out of office not only gracefully but with adequate protection of your personal well-being.

Or perhaps you will never be a top executive but will instead become a bureaucrat, a public servant with direct responsibility for interpreting and implementing government policy. As we have seen, the chores of the much-maligned bureaucrats are many and varied. Not only must they take the necessary steps to carry out policies made by others, but they must also take responsibility for collecting and disbursing the revenue that makes the government's work possible and for preventing or punishing infractions of the law. So complex is the work of bureaucracy that it must be subdivided and parceled out into the hands of specialists. However, the greater the specialization, the more difficult it is to maintain clear lines of authority, because those who specialize accept the guidance of nonexperts only reluctantly.

It is possible to have too much government, but it is also possible to have too little. Duplication and waste prevail under conditions of relative affluence, intense need to reach relatively limited and particular goals, relative nonaccountability, and refusal to follow the dictates of common sense. However, poor implementation of policy can also be the result of procedures that produce conflicting results, pervert the intention of the policymakers, or regulate the activity in question right out of existence. It can be caused by inappropriate response to lobbying by an agency's "clients," by plain inefficiency, or by the overwhelming difficulty of the task.

The numerous problems associated with executive and bureaucratic government make public administration one of today's most challenging professions. Nowhere is there more need for well-qualified, well-motivated, and *persistent* men and women. Nowhere are there greater opportunities to bring about change that will have an important and salutary impact on the lives of millions. The fact that the hurdles to doing this are so many and so high only makes the challenge that much greater.

Perhaps the real question to ask today is where we will find the men and women ready and able to meet that challenge. You may simply be more certain than ever that political leadership is not for you. But please do not be too quick to dismiss the idea. After all, those who do lead have not yet shown us remarkable success in solving all the problems of the human polity. Leadership is one of the developing arts and sciences, not a fixed craft. You may have more to offer than you imagine, and an ability to acquire the skills and knowledge you currently lack. After all, you *are* a student of the science of politics.

In any case, even though not all of you will join the ranks of government, all of you have reason to hope for the best possible performance by those who do. When executives and bureaucrats fail to implement policy in accordance with the laws we have set, we do have another place to turn. The function of judicial bodies is to adjudicate the disputes that arise under the implementation of the law. We will examine these bodies and their work in the next chapter.

Selected Readings

Bass, Bernard M. *Stogdill's Handbook of Leadership,* 3rd ed. New York: Free Press, 1990. A comprehensive study of styles of leadership, their applications, and implications.

Casamayou, Maureen Hogan. *Bureaucracy in Crisis: Three Mile Island, the Shuttle Challenger, and Risk Assessment.* Boulder: Westview Press, 1993. Personal interviews and public testimony are used to illustrate how bureaucratic failures contributed to these two catastrophes.

Foley, Michael. *The Rise of the British Presidency.* Manchester, England: Manchester University Press, 1993. The author argues that personal political leadership has become more important to the role of prime minister in Great Britain. The British prime ministership is compared to the U.S. presidency.

Gardner, John W. *On Leadership.* New York: The Free Press, 1990. A study of how leadership skills are developed and what it means to be a leader.

Hart, John. *The Presidential Branch.* New York: Pergamon Press, 1987. An examination of the presidential staff, including historical origins, functions, and power, as well as a discussion of the difficulties of maintaining congressional oversight of presidential staff activities.

Kingdom, J. E., ed. *The Civil Service in Liberal Democracies.* London and New York: Routledge, 1990. A comparison of the civil service in six European nations and the United States.

Glentz, Harris. *Heads of State and Governments: A Worldwide Encyclopedia of Over 2300 Leaders, 1945 through 1992.* New York: McFarland, 1994. A useful source for detailed biographical information on heads of government worldwide.

Kerbel, Matthew Robert. *Beyond Persuasion: Organizational Efficiency and Presidential Power.* New York: State University of New York Press, 1991. An in-depth look at the components of presidential power in the United States.

Machiavelli, Niccolo. *The Prince.* New York: Appleton-Century-Crofts, 1947. Writing in the early sixteenth century, Machiavelli laid out pragmatic rules for taking and maintaining power without regard for the rights of others or for any other principles of moral behavior.

Mezly, Michael L. *Congress, the President and Public Policy.* Boulder: Westview Press, 1989. Author argues that the current relationship between the president and Congress has adversely affected the ability of the U.S. political system to produce good public policy.

Neustadt, Richard E. *Presidential Power.* New York: John Wiley, 1960. The classic study of the American presidency, with insights still applicable today.

Watson, Richard. *Presidential Vetoes and Public Policy.* Lawrence, Kansas: University Press of Kansas, 1993. Provides a historical view of how presidents have used the veto to influence policy. Includes examples from recent presidencies.

Notes

1. Michael Elliott, "Why the Monarchy Must Go," *Newsweek,* international edition, 11 Mar. 1996, 24. Not only in the West — and not only in the interests of democracy — have the powers of the monarch been limited: in Cambodia the kingship has traditionally been elective, although the new constitution now says the monarch must be "a member of the Khmer Royal Family, aged at least 30 years, coming from the bloodline of the King Ang Duong, Norodom or Sisowath." William Shawcross, *Cambodia's New Deal,* (New York: Carnegie Endowment for International Peace, 1994), p. 53.

2. Talcott Parsons and Edward Shils, "Orientation and Organization of Action," in Talcott Parsons and Edward Shils, eds., *Toward a General Theory of Action* (New York: Harper & Row, 1951), p. 82. Their exact definition of ascription is "the normative pattern which prescribes that an actor in a given type of situation should, in his selections

for differential treatment of social objects, give priority to certain attributes that they possess (including collectivity memberships and possessions) over any specific performances (past, present, or prospective) of the objects." This is a good example of the use of unnecessary jargon in the social sciences ("social objects" means people!), and I have taken the liberty of providing a translation.

3. The opposite of ascription, according to Parsons and Shils, is "achievement: the normative pattern which prescribes that an actor in a given type of situation should, in his selection and differential treatment of social objects, give priority to their specific performances (past, present or prospective) over their given attributes (including memberships and possessions), insofar as the latter are not significant as direct conditions of the relevant performances." Ibid., pp. 82–83.

4. See Isaiah 11:6, *The Holy Bible* (Boston; Massachusetts Bible Society, 1965), p. 655.

5. For the Hessian example, see David P. Conradt, *The German Polity*, 4th ed. (New York: Longman, 1989), p. 217.

6. Samuel Abraham, "Early Elections in Slovakia: A State of Deadlock," *Government and Opposition* 30, no. 1 (1995): 86–100. In this century no one has understood and used the powers of appointment for the purposes of autocracy better than Generalissimo Francisco Franco during the thirty-nine years he ruled Spain. Franco selected, appointed, and dismissed the prime minister and all ministers at will and saw to it that the occupants of other significant offices were appointed by his own appointees. Any official who had significant power to exercise did so only so long as he remained in the favor of the Generalissimo. Since Franco's death in 1975, Spain has adopted a much more democratic constitution, in which appointive offices such as the president's cabinet, high judicial offices, and the Constitutional Court are carefully specified and regulated.

7. *Congressional Quarterly Weekly Report*, 49, no. 42 (19 Oct. 1991): 3026–33.

8. *International Herald Tribune*, 16 June 1992, 1.

9. Benedict Brogan, "Heavyweight in Hong Kong Ring," *The Herald* (Glasgow): 25 April, 1992, p. 9; Anthony Blass, "Burke's Heir," *Far Eastern Economic Review*, October 22, 1992, pp. 25–26.

10. *New York Times*, 24 March 1993, A7.

11. Eva Etzioni-Halevy, *Bureaucracy and Democracy* (London: Routledge and Kegan Paul, 1983), p. 164.

12. Leon Epstein, *Political Parties in the American Mold* (Madison, Wisc.: University of Wisconsin Press, 1986), p. 137.

13. *Wall Street Journal*, 8 Sept. 1995, A11. For the widespread use of cooptation in Mexico, see also César Cansino, "Mexico: The Challenge of Democracy," *Government and Opposition* 30, no. 1, pp. 60–73.

14. Christopher Muhlemann, "Clinton's America and Clinton's World," *Swiss Review of World Affairs* (March 1993): 2–3.

15. *New York Times*, 11 Mar. 1992, A7.

16. Xandra Kayden and Eddie Mahe, *The Party Goes On* (New York: Basic Books, 1985), p. 43.

17. Adrian Karatnycky, "The Comparative Survey of Freedom: 1994 — Freedom in Retreat," *Freedom Review* (Jan./Feb. 1994): 4–9.

18. *Los Angeles Times*, 7 April 1992, A1.

19. "Here comes his body, mourned by Mark Antony: who, though he had no hand in his death, shall receive the benefit of his dying . . ." William Shakespeare, *Julius Caesar*, act 3, sc. 2–ll. 45–47.

20. Murray Clark Havens, Carl Leiden, and Karl M. Schmitt, *The Politics of Assassination* (Englewood Cliffs, N.J.: Prentice Hall, 1970). Johnson was impeached by the House but not found guilty by the Senate and so stayed in office.

21. Judge Giovanni Falcone was assassinated in Sicily on May 23, 1992. For the response of the Italian public, see *Le Monde*, 26 May 1992, 3, and *New York Times*, 26 May 1992, A3.

22. Edward Gonzalez, *Cuba Under Castro, The Limits of Charisma* (Boston: Houghton Mifflin, 1974); Amin Saikal, *The Rise and Fall of the Shah* (Princeton, N.J.: Princeton University Press, 1980), and Kim Murphy, "Algeria Struggles to Retain Democracy — But Can It Survive After Being Voted Out?" *Denver Post*, 1 Feb. 1992, 19A.

23. *Los Angeles Times*, 21 Aug. 1991, 1, A8–A16, 22 Aug. 1991, 1, A7; *The Current Digest of the Soviet Press*, 43, no. 51 (22 January 1992): 1–6.

24. "A Quest for Vengeance: Khomeini's Legions Invade Iraq and Threaten the Whole Arab World," *Time*, 26 July 1991, 18–25.

25. *New York Times*, 2 Oct. 1991, A6; Jean-Bertrand

Aristide, "Stronger than the Gun," *Sojourners* (July 1992): 24–27; *Los Angeles Times*, 18 Sept. 1994, A1; *Washington Post*, 30 Mar. 1995, A1; *Miami Herald*, 6 Feb. 1995, p. 305. Another example of the difficulties of effecting desired change by bringing in external force is the case of Panama: although the removal of General Manuel Noriega from power in 1989 was explained as a necessary step in the battle against the flow of drugs into the United States, as late as March 1992 the U.S. State Department reported that "narcotics trafficking and money laundering continue to be serious threats to democracy in Panama" and that the nation remained "a major transhipment point for cocaine destined for the U.S. and Europe." *New York Times*, 11 April 1992, A1, A12.

26. To be sure, private business does hire new executives from time to time and does not always promote from within. But in such cases the new executives are hired by those already in place and can be expected to have similar values and priorities. In government, however, the new executives periodically taking over the top positions are not hired by those already hard at work.

27. U.S. Bureau of the Census, *Statistical Abstract of the United States*, 115th edition (Washington, D. C.: 1995), p. 350.

28. *The Europa World Year Book*, vol. 1 (London: Europa Publishers Limited, 1992), p. 1177.

29. Richard E. Neustadt, *Presidential Power* (New York: John Wiley, 1961), p. 100.

30. *The Times* (London), 16 Jan. 1991, 5.

31. Craig Turner, "Canada's Leader Takes Aim at National Debt," *Los Angeles Times*, 22 Oct. 1994, A2.

32. T. R. Reid, "Two Koreas' Leaders Seek First Summit," *Washington Post*, 19 June 1994, A1.

33. John Anthony Maltese, *Spin Control: The White Office of Communications and the Management of Presidential News* (Chapel Hill: University of North Carolina Press, 1994), pp. 232–39.

34. Richard A. Watson, *Presidential Vetoes and Public Policies* (Lawrence: University Press of Kansas, 1993), pp. 133–51. For a comparative study of the veto power, see George Tsebelis, "Decision Making in Political Systems: Veto Players in Presidentialism, Parliamentarism, Multicameralism and Multipartyism," *British Journal of Political Science* 25, no. 3 (July 1995): 289–25.

35. *New York Times*, 30 Dec. 1990, A9. "This is the saddest day in Argentine history," said former President Raul Alfonsin, under whose administration the men had been brought to trial and sentenced a mere five years earlier.

36. James MacGregor Burns, *Leadership* (New York: Harper & Row, 1978), pp. 18, 19, 457–460.

37. Plato, *The Republic* (New York: Oxford University Press, 1945), p. 78.

38. Niccolò Machiavelli, *The Prince* (New York: Appleton-Century-Crofts, 1947), p. 51.

39. Charles W. Joiner, *Leadership for Change* (Cambridge, Mass.: Ballinger, 1987), p. 160; and James M. Kouzes and Barry Z. Posner, *The Leadership Challenge* (San Francisco: Jossey-Bass, 1987), p. 15.

40. Rudolf Sohn, *Kirchenrecht*, vol. 1 (Munich: 1923), as cited by Jean Lacouture, *The Demigods, Charismatic Leadership in the Third World* (New York: Knopf, 1970), p. 14; and Max Weber, *The Theory of Social and Economic Organization* (New York: Glencoe Press, 1957).

41. Daniel Lev has gone so far as to say that "there is no such thing as charismatic power, only charismatic situations." The same point was made by the Indian socialist leader Jayaprakash Narayan: "It is not so much the hero who shapes the times as the times that shape the hero." Both Lev and Narayan are quoted by Lacouture, *Demigods*, p. 16.

42. Roger Thurow, "Mandela Legend Grows to Superhuman Proportions," *Wall Street Journal*, 19 June 1990, A21.

43. Weber referred to this stage as the "routinization of charisma." With all due respect, it has to be pointed out that the term is not apt. What Weber really meant is the routinization of power holding as charisma fades away. And in one passage Weber does distinguish routinized charisma from "genuine charisma." In H. H. Gerth and C. Wright Mills, eds., *From Max Weber* (New York: Oxford University Press, 1958), p. 262.

44. Isaac Deutscher, *Stalin, A Political Biography* (New York: Oxford University Press, 1977); Albert Marrin, *Stalin* (New York: Viking, 1988); Pranay Gupte, *Vengeance, India after the Assassination of Indira Gandhi* (New York: Norton, 1985).

45. For the argument that our present constitution was written in large part to give greater representation and security to the more monied interests than they had under the Articles, see Charles A. Beard, *An Economic Interpretation of the*

Constitution of the United States (New York: Macmillan, 1913).

46. Robert Michels, *Political Parties* (New York: Dover, 1959).

47. Antonio Gramsci, *The Modern Prince and Other Writings* (New York: International Publishers, 1957), p. 73.

48. Frantz Fanon, *The Wretched of the Earth* (New York: Grove Press, 1963), p. 197.

49. Paul Brooker, *Twentieth-Century Dictatorships: The Ideological One-Party States* (New York: New York University Press, 1995), pp. 181–193.

50. Gaetano Mosca, *The Ruling Class*, trans. Hannah D. Kahn (New York: McGraw-Hill, 1939), p. 493.

51. William Miller, *A New History of the United States* (New York: Dell, 1968), p. 354.

52. Ben Weider and David Hapgood, *The Murder of Napoleon* (New York: Congdon and Lattes, 1982.)

53. John Ross, "Mexico: Historic Turning Point," *Global Exchanges* (Summer 1994): 1–6.

54. Miller, *New History*, pp. 312–313.

55. *The Europa Year Book, 1982: A World Survey*, vols. 1, 2 (London: Europa, 1982).

56. John Mukum Mbaku, "Military Coups as Rent-Seeking Behavior," *Journal of Political and Military Sociology* 22, no. 2 (Winter 1994): 241–84.

57. "The defeat of the Federalists in the elections of 1800 represented *the first occasion in modern politics in which an incumbent political party suffered an electoral defeat and simply turned over power to its opponents*," says Seymour Martin Lipset in *The First New Nation* (New York: Basic Books, 1963), p. 44. Italics in original.

58. Ku Tashiro, "Japan," in Donald C. Rowat, ed., *Public Administration in Developed Democracies* (New York: Marcel Dekker, 1988), pp. 380–382.

59. *Washington Post*, 7 June 1994, A6.

60. Alemneh Dejene, *Environment, Famine and Politics in Ethiopia: A View from the Village* (Boulder, Colo.: Lynne Rienner, 1990), pp. 95–109.

61. Weber also believed that the rules of bureaucratic behavior should be clearly set, should be impersonal — that is, apply to all without favoritism — should be based on written documents, and should apply only at work; the private and public spheres should be clearly distinct. Max Weber, *Essays in Sociology*, trans. and ed. H. H. Gerth and C. Wright Mills (New York: Oxford University Press, 1958), pp. 196–97.

62. Max Weber, *The Theory of Social and Economic Organization*, translated by A. M. Henderson and Talcott Parsons (Glencoe, Ill.: The Free Press, 1947), p. 338.

63. Pao Chao Hsieh, *The Government of China* (Baltimore: Johns Hopkins Press, 1925), p. 143; E. A. Kracke, Jr., "Region, Family and Individual in the Chinese Examination System," in John K. Fairbank, ed., *Chinese Thought and Institutions* (Chicago: University of Chicago Press, 1959), pp. 251–68.

64. Edward C. Thaden, *Russia Since 1801: The Making of a New Society* (New York: Wiley, 1971), p. 51.

65. William Safran, *The French Polity*, 4th ed. (New York: Longman, 1995), pp. 243–45.

66. Victoria Brittain, "Democracy Takes a Few Steps: The Charismatic Populists are Gone," *World Press Review* (August 1991): 14–16.

67. Dennis Kavanagh, *British Politics: Continuities and Chance*, second edition (Oxford, England: Oxford University Press, 1990), 203.

68. Sheila Kaplan, "Porkbarrel Politics at U.S. Aid," *Multinational Monitor* (Sept. 1993): 10–15. According to Kaplan, this U.S. agency not only authorizes the payment of excessively high fees for expertise and materials but also the hiring of "advisers" who are in fact "on the lookout for overseas business" in the nations where they are doling out advice.

69. For general discussions of the problems of implementation, see Cathy Marie Johnson, *The Dynamics of Conflict Between Bureaucrats and Legislators* (Armonk, N.Y.: M. E. Sharpe, 1992) and Edward C. Page, *Political Authority and Bureaucratic Power* (London: Wheat-sheaf Books, 1985). For a detailed study of the implementation of a single law, see Michael C. LeMay, *Anatomy of a Public Policy: The Reform of Contemporary American Immigration Law* (Westport, Conn.: Praeger, 1994).

70. *Wall Street Journal*, 22 Aug. 1995, A1, A5.

71. Joseph La Palombara first explained this form of clientelism in *Interest Groups in Italian Politics* (Princeton, N.J.: Princeton University Press, 1964), chap. 8.

72. *New York Times*, 21 Feb. 1992, A12.

11 Justice Under the Law

I N EVERY SYSTEM OF government, three tasks must be performed: Laws must be made, laws must be carried out, and some effort must be made to see that justice is done in the process.

Few qualities of human existence are more deeply valued than justice, although we are not always aware how much it means to us. Ask your friends to list eight or ten great goods of human existence in order of importance (give them *love* and *friendship* as examples if they need help getting started), and chances are that most of them will not even mention *justice*.

However, this may simply be a sign that people you know have never felt that they have been treated unjustly by the legal system. Suppose, however, that one of your friends was Cuban poet Maria Elena Cruz Varela, who was forced to eat copies of her dissident poetry, then dragged by the hair down four flights of stairs and into the street, arrested, and later sentenced to two years in prison for her membership in the opposition group known as Criterio Alternativo.[1] Or perhaps the good friend you ask is Fauzi Saado, a Lebanese refugee in the German town of Huxene, just after he has sat in court listening to Judge Walter Stoy reduce the charges against the three neo-Nazi skinheads who set his home afire, declaring they were "youthful offenders" (the youngest was 18, the others were 19) who had been drunk and had not intended to kill anyone, and sentencing them to a maximum of five years' imprisonment despite the fact the result of their rampage was serious injury to two of the Saado children, leaving one of them deformed for life.[2] Or suppose you asked your question of 27-year-old Jerry Dewayne Williams, who was sentenced in 1995 to twenty-five years to life imprisonment for having stolen a slice of pepperoni pizza from a group of children. The sentence was mandatory under California's new "three strikes" law, which applies to any person with two previous convictions (of which one was for a serious or violent felony) who then commits a third crime — Williams the pizza thief "qualified."[3] Might we not expect Ms. Varela, Mr. Saado, and Mr. Williams to be more likely to include *justice* on *their* lists? We sometimes learn how much we cherish fair treatment under the law only when we encounter what appears to us to be its very opposite.

WHAT IS JUSTICE?

Most of us are likely to say that an injustice has been done when we believe that we ourselves or those for whom we feel compassion have not been treated fairly *by people in positions of authority*. Not all acts of fair treatment are acts of justice, just as not all rules are laws. **Justice** is a possible result of decisions made by those who have been granted authority to determine what constitutes fair treatment. In the case of governments, justice means *fair treatment under the law*. These five simple words contain a wealth of meaning. Treating people — that is, meting out rewards and punishments — *under the law* means showing respect for the most fundamental principle of human rights: the rule of law. Only by establishing laws that apply equally to all do those in power gain legitimacy in the minds of those over whom they rule. There can be no belief in the possibility of justice without the prior establishment of the principle of the rule of law. There can be no justice without a body of law to guide the judges.

However, the mere existence of a body of law and of properly credentialed judges in no way guarantees that justice will prevail. No one who has studied the 1857 Dred Scott decision of the U.S. Supreme Court can doubt that those who have been given the authority to determine what is just may make errors of judgment.[4] All we have said so far is that just government is a product that *may* result from the decisions of those who are formally authorized to determine how the laws shall be applied.

What, then, do we mean by *just*? The answer is not easy. What seems just to me may seem highly unjust to you. The California State Attorney General saw nothing wrong with sending someone to jail for a minimum of twenty-five years for stealing a slice of pizza: "We at least can think our children can sit down in peace in broad daylight, without a 6-foot 4-inch, 220 pound ex-con threatening them and taking away food from them," said Daniel E. Lungren, and presumably there were other Californians who agreed.[5] Justice is a relative term. A decision is considered *just* if it meets a society's current standards of what constitutes fair treatment under the law.[6] Such standards evolve from tradition, from religious belief, from moral codes, and sometimes from simple pragmatic need. It may be just to hang a man for stealing a horse when the community's very survival depends — or seems to depend — on the government's ability to protect cattle ranching.

Are we treading dangerous ground here? Yes, indeed; but then, nobody promised you easy solutions to tough ethical questions when you took up the study of politics — at least I hope nobody did. Most of us do not want to manifest the cultural arrogance of the British colonial authorities who ruled that African chiefs could mete out justice on the basis of native law and custom as long as their decisions were not "repugnant to humanity" — we know that no one people or race has an innate right to determine what is or is not to be considered moral by another. Most of us accept the principle of **cultural relativism** — the idea that each society sets its own standards in accordance with its own culture, and that what is correct in one society may be repugnant in another. But when we apply that principle to our considerations of justice, we may get the uncomfortable feeling that our own values are slipping away as guides to reality. Are we obliged to call laws that sanction slavery just as long as most people in a slave-owning society find them so? Must we agree that torture is an acceptable punishment for political dissent if we know that those so punished would use the same means if they themselves could acquire power? Should we accept as a mere statement of fact the information that in some Arab societies women may be divorced by the simple word of the husband but have no equivalent right themselves — and that there is little or no evidence the women themselves find this practice unjust?

This problem of cultural relativism in the determination of what is just is one of the most difficult problems in the human polity. There is no simple solution to the ethical dilemmas it poses for us, but observing certain precautions can help us find our way. First, we must be careful not to assume that the standards of justice of ordinary men and women around the globe are actually as different as the laws made by the powerful sometimes suggest. Has anyone, for example, really studied the beliefs of ordinary citizens in a slave-owning society, of divorced women in an Arab state, or of the men and women who have been tortured for their political beliefs?

Second, it is important to distinguish between making an evaluation of a given practice and assuming the right to impose change. Surely I have the right to my negative opinion of public whipping as a punishment for adultery, say, whether or not I have the right (or the power) to move in and take the whip away. Third, let us remember that as the world shrinks we may be evolving toward an international code of justice. It may be that your own great-grandchildren, finding this book in the attic and thumbing through it idly, will find this discussion old-fashioned and unnecessary, having grown up in a world in which there are no longer significant differences in what different people find just or unjust throughout the human polity. We ourselves may hasten that day by working with other peoples to create a shared vision of a just world toward which all (ourselves very much included) might resolve to strive. Acknowledging cultural relativism need not mean abandoning hope for a better world.[7]

In the meantime, different conceptions of justice do exist, and different systems have been developed for the administration of justice. Yet even now there are certain similarities across the globe in the way the job is done. Whatever the standards of justice, in every polity there are people whose job it is to make certain that the laws of the land are just, and that they are justly administered. To some extent, this is a job shared by everyone in government. Lawmakers (legislators) and law implementers (executives) are expected to carry out their functions in a manner consistent with those standards. But human nature being what it is, those who make and execute the laws may not always themselves be just. For this reason, most polities have established an institution of government, the **judiciary**, whose particular function it is to see to it that the citizens receive fair treatment under the law. The job of *assuring* justice is first and foremost the work of judges — not legislators, not executives.

In this chapter we will explore the judicial function. There can be no judiciary without a body of trained, authorized judges, so we will begin with a consideration of the ways judges are chosen throughout the human polity. Then we will explore the question of judicial independence. How free are judges from political intervention, and what are the consequences for the political systems within which they carry out their functions? Then we will review and explain the principal systems of law used in the administration of justice. We will conclude with an overview of regional variations in the rule of law.

CHOOSING CREDIBLE JUDGES

Implicit in the very idea of a judicial system is the conviction that there must be some place where final decisions on political and governmental matters can be made, and made so as to command respect and obedience. For this condition to be fulfilled, the people who make such decisions must know and respect their society's system of law and standards of justice. But it is not enough for them to have this knowledge and respect. They must be believed to have it; they must have legitimacy in the eyes of the public. Such legitimacy is traditionally achieved by three means — by appointing only those whose past careers seem likely to have given them that knowledge and respect, by giving the right of appointment to government officials who are themselves respected because of the importance of the offices they occupy, and by surrounding the judicial role with the physical accoutrements of dignity and stature.

Experienced Judges

In some nations, no one can become a judge who has not followed a clearly defined educational and career path. In others, those who have the power to appoint judges can appoint whomever they please but are expected to choose only those with obviously relevant experience. In Germany, law students must choose at the end of their studies whether to become a judge, prosecutor, civil servant, notary public, or private lawyer. Those who decide to become judges must go through a three-year probationary period, but after completing that successfully they are given a judgeship with lifetime tenure and security. Once made, the decision is fixed — German lawyers do not later become judges, and German judges do not decide to leave the bench and take up lawyering. By the time the German judge achieves appointment to one of the high federal courts, he or she is likely to have acquired a wealth of experience.[8]

In Great Britain, the young man or woman bent on a legal career does not have to decide between being a lawyer and being a judge but rather between being a *barrister* — a lawyer qualified to appear as an advocate in court — and being a *solicitor* — a lawyer qualified to do the paperwork in law offices. Most of those who become barristers have solidly middle-class or upper-class origins and have attended private schools for their secondary education and then the more prestigious universities and law schools (such as Oxford, Cambridge, and the Inns of Court in London). British judges are chosen from the ranks of practicing barristers.[9]

In other nations, however, it is legally possible to become a judge with no formal training or experience whatsoever. This is the case in the federal court system in the United States, where it is not even necessary to be a lawyer to become a federal judge. And in Denmark two ordinary citizens serve alongside one professional jurist as judges in municipal courts and rule on lesser, but still criminal cases; in appeals from municipal court cases to a high court, three citizen judges participate with three jurists.[10]

Respectably Chosen Judges

Who is to say who is to say? Never is it more important to find the right answer to this question than in determining who will choose the men and women who are to say what is just. The answer varies a great deal from polity to polity. Nearly all German judges are appointed by the state ministers of justice and are considered civil servants, and thus part of the bureaucratic hierarchy, promoted on the basis of recommendations from superiors. They have middle-class or upper-middle-class backgrounds; only 6 percent come from working-class families. German reunification has played a part in recent judicial recruitment: many of the judges in former East Germany were considered "poorly prepared for Western styles of judicial and legal practice or . . . compromised by past political connections" and have been replaced by judges from former West Germany.[11]

In other systems, all but the highest judges are appointed by the judges themselves. In Mexico, the Supreme Court judges appoint all the judges for the lower courts and elect their own chief justice.[12] In Canada, the federal government controls the appointment, salary, and tenure of judges.[13]

BOX 11.1

TWO JUSTICES FOR THE U.S. SUPREME COURT: SOUTER AND THOMAS

In October 1990 David H. Souter was confirmed as the 105th justice of the U.S. Supreme Court. The Senate voted 90 to 9 in favor of the new justice, who was praised for having "a reasoned approach and sound understanding" of the Constitution. Several of the nine senators who opposed the confirmation worried about Souter's refusal to state his position on privacy and abortion rights, but the whole matter was quickly and quietly resolved and the new justice took his seat immediately on the bench.

In October 1991 Clarence Thomas was a new nominee. From the beginning, Thomas was under serious attack for his relative inexperience, his failure to reveal his position on many issues during the confirmation hearings, and his known conservative stance on many other issues. Still, everyone expected the black nominee to be appointed; the recent retirement of the Court's only other black justice, Thurgood Marshall, dictated a replacement based in part on color, and Thomas's liabilities — viewed as assets by some — seemed unlikely to keep him from the post.

But then an Oklahoma law professor, Anita Hill, decided to speak out. Hill asserted that the judge had sexually harassed her when she was a young employee in his office at the Education Department and at the Equal Employment Opportunity Commission. The professor was black, professional, dignified, and very, very serious. Her testimony was detailed, explicit, and absolutely convincing, not only to many of the senators but also to many who watched her on television.

The hearings continued for several days, with new charges of harassment and new testimony that the judge could not possibly be capable of such behavior. Whom to believe? What to do if one believed the charges? On October 15, 1991, the Senate voted 52 to 48 to confirm the nomination.[16]

In Zambia, Kenya, Malawi, Senegal, and the Ivory Coast, judicial commissions composed of the nation's chief justice, representatives of the bar association, and officials from the executive branch advise the president in the appointment of judges. Malawi, however, actually has two judicial systems: traditional and magisterial. Certain criminal cases are heard in the traditional courts and are judged on the basis of traditional law by judges who are also traditional chiefs.[14] In Israel, appointments are made by a highly prestigious nine-member appointments committee; tradition requires that at least one religious leader serve on the high court and that women be well represented.[15]

Legislators often play an important role in the appointment of judges. American presidents must get senatorial ratification of all appointments they make to the federal judiciary. When such appointments become controversial, not only the senators but the general public may well become involved (see Box 11.1).

"Lights! Camera! Justice!"

(Drawing by Dana Fradon; © 1992 The New Yorker Magazine, Inc.)

Dignified Judges   Making sure that judges have appropriate qualifications and are appointed through time-honored official procedures is clearly a reasonable way of ensuring their credibility. A third method seems less logically defensible yet may be even more effective. It is common practice to surround the judicial office with all possible material attributes of seriousness and high purpose. Almost everywhere, judges are expected to wear special somber apparel, to speak carefully, and to refrain from laughter or other signs of lightheartedness (no matter how humorous or even laughable the proceedings in the courtroom may occasionally be). A sergeant-at-arms or bailiff reminds everyone in the courtroom to rise when the judge enters and to maintain appropriate behavior. In Britain and several other nations in the British Commonwealth, it is still the custom for judges and the barristers who plead cases before them to wear powdered wigs.

Although such practices still prevail, the dignity of the court has nevertheless suffered in recent years from a more modern phenonemon: the invasion of the camera. The difficulty of maintaining a sober atmosphere when a trial is receiving constant publicity and can be followed minute by minute on the screen was made all too amply apparent in the O. J. Simpson case in the United States, when a black sports hero was accused of killing his wife and another man. The knowledge that they were being watched clearly influenced the behavior of everyone in the courtroom. Typical comments were, "There is no question that both the prosecution and defense . . . overtly played to the gallery," and "The judge and the lawyers on both sides seem unable to curb their appetite for attention."[17] The media, often accused of covering trials irresponsibly and biasing the jurors (whose isolation from their coverage is never likely to be complete), defend themselves on the vague grounds of the "people's right to know" and, in the United States, on the basis of the First Amendment. News media cameras and microphones are now permitted in forty-seven states in the United States. The same kind of coverage is possible in Canada, with one important exception: The judge always has the right to order a news blackout if he or she believes the case will be too sensational, and this is often done. Even a Canadian editor who favors changing the law acknowledges the damage done to the dignity of the courts by the presence of the camera eye: "The circus aspect to some trials is disturbing," he says, and adds, "To see evidence related to a trial on *Eyewitness News* is, shall we say, inelegant."[18]

AN INDEPENDENT JUDICIARY: THEORY AND PRACTICE

An important set of questions for constitutional experts derives from the problem of deciding what the relationship between the judiciary and the other branches of government should be. Should the judiciary be fully independent? How independent should it be? By what means should that independence be secured? If it should not be independent, what effect will this have on the right of citizens to be free from excessive government intervention in their lives?

How Independent Should Judges Be?

There is no liberty, if the judiciary power be not separated from the legislative and executive. Were it joined with the legislative, the life and liberty of the subject would be exposed to arbitrary control; for the judge would be then the legislator. Were it joined to the executive power, the judge might behave with violence and oppression. There would be an end of everything were the same man or the same body, whether of the nobles or of the people, to exercise those three powers, that of enacting laws, that of executing the public resolutions, and that of trying the causes of individuals.[19]

French political philosopher Charles Montesquieu's eloquent statement is usually taken as the basis for the principle of separation of powers that is embedded in the U.S. Constitution. But his arguments on behalf of separating the judicial branch from executive and legislative functions have a special cogency. **Judicial independence** means that the judiciary is protected — usually by constitutional guarantees — from interference by the other branches of government in the conduct of its work.

As we saw in Chapter 10, even in parliamentary systems — in which

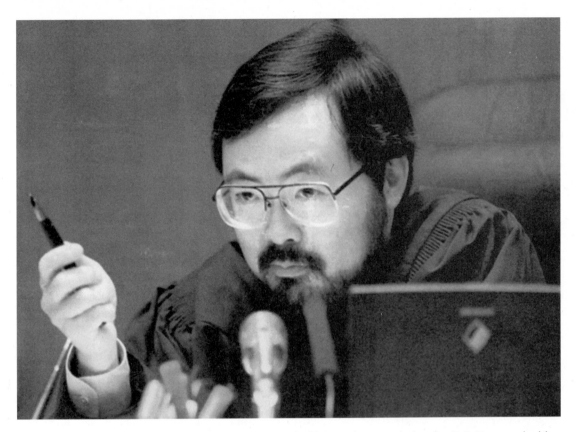

Superior Court Judge Lance Ito addresses the court during the O. J. Simpson double-murder trial in 1995. Judge Ito sometimes found it difficult to maintain the dignity of the proceedings given the constant presence of the media. (AP Photo/Mark J. Terrill, Pool/Wide World)

the executive and legislative functions are closely joined — the judiciary often maintains a significant measure of independence. The constitution of the Federal Republic of Germany declares without equivocation, "The judges shall be independent and subject only to the law" and are perceived as simply "neutral administrators of the law."[20] Even where such independence has been violated in practice — as in India, when prime minister Indira Gandhi was accused of making openly political appointments to the highest courts — the principle of judicial independence is accepted as legitimate.[21] Only openly authoritarian systems fail to offer the judicial process at least a semblance of protection from interference by others in power.

The arguments for an independent judiciary come easily to mind. If judges can be removed from office for unpopular decisions, they are likely to try harder to please the people who have that power of removal than to determine what constitutes the fair application of the law. If judges' decisions can easily be set aside or overthrown, the painstaking, expensive, and time-consuming judicial process becomes an empty exercise. If judges must always rule as instructed by those in high executive office, regardless of the clear meaning of existing law or the principles of fair practice, they will be helpless to foster respect for the law, for those principles, or for the political system itself.

However, there are also some interesting arguments against the establishment of an entirely independent judiciary, even in democratic systems of government. Judges are almost always appointed rather than elected, so it can be argued that they should not be able to set aside the will of the people by selective interpretation of the laws written by the people's elected representatives. The argument against judicial review of laws regulating abortion largely revolved around this question, with some going so far as to claim that in this matter the U.S. Supreme Court had perpetrated "an unconstitutional abridgment of . . . fundamental rights."[22] Such arguments have become less common with the emergence of a more conservative court and consequent uncertainty about which way the court will "jump" on a particular abortion-related statute; however, this very uncertainty has complicated the lawmaking process, helping to make legislative debate on the issue "more varied and more contentious than any in recent memory."[23]

A second argument against absolute judicial independence is that the powers this gives to judges are difficult to limit by law and are consequently likely to be extended ever further. Such *judicialization* or *judicial activism* is most likely in liberal democracies, argues C. Neal Tate, who shows how the process is now well underway in the recently democratized Philippines.[24] Although such a trend may have been originally inspired by an effort to extend the protection of individual rights, there is no guarantee that judges who overstep traditional bounds will always be on the side of the common man, or even on the side of the highest law of the land. In the United States, for example, federal appeals courts have long taken for granted their authority to review juries' decisions to make "excessive" awards of damages, but some attorneys argue that the reexamination clause of the Seventh Amendment to the U.S. Constitution actually forbids judicial review of any lower case decision in which a jury has ruled (except under conditions which do not apply to this kind of case).[25]

A third argument is made on the simple grounds that beneath their impressive robes judges are, after all, mere human beings. There is always the chance that they will begin to manifest the various frailties of the species yet be impossible to remove from power. Some observers of the U.S. court system have suggested a constitutional amendment limiting federal judgeships to a single ten-year term, and indeed in most other nations such limitations do exist.

Challenging the legal system. Dr. Jack Kevorkian (C), flanked by his attorneys, faces criminal charges in his determination to establish the right of individuals to medically assisted suicide and of doctors like himself to provide that assistance. Is the judicial system out of touch with the public on the issue of euthanasia? (Reuters/Corbis-Bettmann)

Finally, we have said that what is considered just depends on each polity's particular standards. When those standards change, the society's judges — often socially isolated by virtue of their lofty and engrossing occupations — may be among the last to recognize what has happened. If it is impossible to remove judges who are out of touch with the evolution in the thinking of ordinary men and women, it may be equally impossible to ensure that justice will be done.

The arguments against unlimited judicial independence have inspired some polities to choose judges by election, particularly those at the lower levels of the court system. Although the general public usually approves of judicial elections, the judges themselves would almost always prefer to reach office by appointment, pointing out the difficulties of maintaining accountability to two masters: the voters and the law.[26]

How Judicial Independence Is Maintained

Given the arguments for and against judicial independence, it should not be surprising that great variety can be found in the degree of independence actually accorded to that branch of government and its functionaries in various nations. And where judges *are* granted a measure of independence, a wide variety of means is used to achieve that end.

One means of protecting judges from political or other interference while maintaining some control over their activities is to give only other judges the power to exercise that control. Italian judges cannot be transferred without their own consent or a special decision by their own Superior Judicial Council, which also determines who will and will not be promoted.[27] Lawyers and judges also often set up self-regulating agencies of their own creation. For example, the Judicial Conference of the United States has established a Committee on the Judicial Bench to examine all aspects of federal judicial service.

As pointed out earlier, another way to encourage judicial independence is to make the process of removing judges extremely difficult and complex. U.S. Supreme Court justices can be removed only by impeachment (the House of Representatives brings the charges, the Senate tries the case). Japanese Supreme Court judges are secure in office for only ten years: at the end of every decade in office they must be reelected by the people or relinquish office.

Giving judges the right of **judicial review** (the right to review a nation's laws to ensure that they are in accordance with the constitution; see Box 9.5 on p. 341) is often cited as a particularly powerful means of maintaining judicial independence. If judges can rule legislation or executive decrees unconstitutional, they have (it is argued) a powerful means of warning other officers of government to keep within their proper bounds. But there is a leap in logic here. The right of judicial review is next to meaningless in practice unless other means are used to secure the independence of the judges who exercise that power. Even constitutional protections may be changed; under Idi Amin's rule in Uganda, the constitution was amended to provide that judicial review was subject to "executive suspension."[28]

Furthermore, when judicial review is exercised with impunity, it may be more sensible to see it as a way of weakening legislative and executive independence from the judiciary than as a way of strengthening judicial independence. Such weakening of the other branches may sometimes be the only way to achieve fair government — but it can also be a way to permit judicial activism to extend to dangerous usurpation of the powers of those directly elected by the people.[29] Which point of view we adopt all too often depends on what rulings are being made, and how they impinge on our own fortunes or those of persons we care about.

In any case, however established and however evaluated, the continuing independence of the judiciary inevitably depends on the judges themselves, and on the support they receive from the public. The continuing struggle of Italian judges to fight political corruption in their nation is an interesting case in point. The story begins in 1982, when Sicilian judge Giovanni Falcone, undertook what proved to be a ten-year crusade against the Mafia, bringing many to trial and some to conviction, all the time well aware that many in the government were cooperating with the organized crime syndicate. In May 1992, Falcone, his wife, and three bodyguards were assassinated. When an outraged public called for stronger measures against the Mafia, acting Prime Minister Giulio Andreotti replied, "We do not intend in any way to deflect from the line that we have pursued until now."[30] At this point, the Italian people had clearly had enough. Andreotti fell from power and was himself indicted "on charges that he acted as a protector for the Mafia during his many years in power."[31] When his businessman successor, Silvio Berlusconi, was charged with tax evasion and bribery of tax inspectors, his response was to launch an attack on the prosecutors, claiming they were abusing their powers for political purposes: "If you cut off the right hand of everyone who has paid the Guardia di Finanza [the national tax agency], you would have a country of left-handed people," claimed one Berlusconi supporter.[32] But Berlusconi himself went down to defeat shortly thereafter, and a new center-left government came to power in April 1996. Whether it will prove less corrupt — or merely less subject to the careful scrutiny of Italy's newly empowered judiciary — is anybody's guess.

The Problem of Enforcement

What happened in Italy demonstrates that even in states where judicial independence has legal and ethical status, the final judicial word is not always, in fact, the final word. If legal rulings are not respected by the chief executives of a state, judges have no independent means to insist on their enforcement. When Germany's Constitutional Court ruled that the state of Bavaria had no right to insist that crucifixes be hung in all classrooms that state's education minister said, "The crosses are hanging and will remain hanging."[33] Since 58 percent of all Germans rejected the ruling, only 37 percent supported it, and Chancellor Helmut Kohl also criticized it openly, the chances the crosses would come under the rule of law seemed dim.

In openly autocratic regimes, all pretense of honoring the rulings of the regular court system may be set aside, as the autocrat calls for the creation of special courts to do his will. During the period of Joseph Stalin's rule in the Soviet Union, political trials were conducted by the office of the People's Commissar of Internal Affairs. Stalin personally appointed the commissar, and when one proved "too slow" in ordering executions, Stalin replaced him with another, Nikolai Ivanovitch Yezhov, who dutifully inaugurated a period of "tremendous growth in mass repression."[34] In contemporary Iraq a system of "revolutionary courts" has been set up to try political offenses, narcotics trafficking, and "crimes against God." In these courts the accused are charged with such behavior as "moral corruption," "antirevolutionary behavior," and "siding with global arrogance." There are "virtually no procedural or substantive safeguards," and trials often last less than five minutes.[35]

But it is not only autocratic executives who sometimes make it difficult to achieve justice in the courts. In China the problem is, says Fu Xiangtao, "draconian officialdom." Xiangtao acknowledges that "with such an immense population to take care of the state genuinely needs a large and reasonably strong body of administrators," but says that the problem has been the excessive capacity of government officials to interrupt and influence the daily work of the courts. Although reforms have been introduced, including the introduction of the Administrative Procedural Law permitting common people to file suit against officials, judicial independence from the administration remains uncertain in China.[36]

In other nations, the exercise of justice under any form may be difficult to maintain, a condition particularly likely in regimes caught in the grip of civil war. Political violence in El Salvador all but crippled that nation's judicial system throughout the 1970s and 1980s; "the homicide conviction rate . . . dropped as low as 4 percent in rural areas [and] citizens had little confidence in obtaining redress of grievances through the courts."[37]

As the world moves gradually toward establishing international institutions consistent with the spread of interdependence, yet another form of restriction on the power of a single nation's judicial rulings is making its appearance: the supranational court. However, these courts also face the problem of enforcement. Thus when the European Court of Human Rights ruled in 1995 that the British Army had illegally killed three members of the Irish Republican Army (who were, ruled the court, clearly trying to surrender) and ordered Britain to pay legal costs to the victims' families, the response of the British deputy prime minister was that that nation would simply ignore the verdict.[38]

Finally, it is important to note that enforcing court rulings and carrying out accepted principles of justice do not always fully coincide: the rulings of the courts may themselves be, as we saw at the beginning of this chapter, inconsistent with basic notions of justice. One issue of considerable controversy in this regard is the practice of *plea negotiations*, in which attorneys, judges, and defendants arrive at pretrial decisions that permit the defendant to enter an "appropriate" guilty plea to reduced charges, eliminating the need for a trial — and, of course, the due process protections that are contained in the more normal legal proceeding.[39] Other departures from accepted principles of justice lack even the cover of pragmatism and may be based simply on racism or sexism. Certainly no legal code in a modern democracy overtly states that persons of color accused of crime should be treated differently from whites, nor that women victims of crime should receive less protection than men, but in fact there continue to be constant signs that practice contradicts principle. Great Britain seems to go in the opposite direction — judges are allowed to increase a punishment if they detect racist motivation behind the criminal act — yet it is also true that in that nation blacks frequently receive harsher sentences than whites for the same crime.[40] In the United States, a nation with an incarceration rate four times that of Canada, five times that of England and Wales, and fourteen times that of Japan, the rate of imprisonment for blacks is more than seven times as high as that for whites.[41] Similarly, women's advocates in the United States are still able to cite convincing evidence of judges who

Kinds Number 1: Laws are based on:	**Natural Law** Discovered truth	**Positive Law** Common sense pragmatism
Kinds Number 2: Laws are made by:	**Codified Law** Designated lawmakers writing statutes and devising constitutions	**Common Law** Cumulative judicial decisions regarding the meaning and applicability of other laws and general principles of fairness
Kinds Number 3: Laws govern:	**Criminal Law** Criminal behavior	**Civil Law** Disputes between law-abiding citizens
Kinds Number 4: Laws apply to:	**Domestic Law** Relationships within states	**International Law** Relationships between states

FIGURE 11.1   **The Kinds of Kinds of Law**

refuse to take seriously cases of women assaulted by men, despite a new awareness of the problem since the Simpson case and a new Violence Against Women Act passed in 1995.[42]

GUIDELINES FOR ADJUDICATION: THE KINDS OF KINDS OF LAW

As we noted earlier, normative standards of what is just vary from culture to culture. So do the kinds of law in which those standards are given legal expression — laws that guide the rulings of jurists whose job it is to determine what constitutes fair treatment. We will consider first the different kinds of law that have emerged in human history and then the kinds of law that are dominant in the various "legal cultures" presently found throughout the human polity (see Figure 11.1).

Before we begin, however, a word of caution is in order. Trying to understand the different kinds of law can be difficult until we grasp that there are "kinds of kinds" — which is to say, there is more than one way to categorize the kinds of law we human beings have devised. We find out about these different "kinds of kinds" when we ask different questions. If we ask the question, "Are laws based on discovered truth or on commonsense pragmatism?" then we are likely to hear about the difference between *natural law* and *positive law*. But if we ask, "Are laws always written and codified by officially designated lawmakers, or do they emerge more gradually over time, as judges decide thorny questions in the courtroom?" then someone will be ready to explain to us the difference between *statutory law* and codes of law on one hand, and *common* (or "judge-made") *law* on the other. Or perhaps we wonder, "Is there a difference between laws that determine what punishments fit what crimes and laws that are designed simply to settle disputes and provide retribution?" In that case we will be told: Yes, there is *criminal law* and *civil law*. Finally, it may occur to us to ask, "Is there a body of law that governs the relationships between nations, separate from the law that governs relationships within them?" — thereby stimulating someone to tell us all about the difference between *domestic law* and *international law*.

The task for beginners would be considerably easier if there were well-known names for these kinds of kinds of law, and if scholars would always make clear exactly what kinds they are talking about. Unfortunately, commentators tend to jump about from one kind to the other without raising any signals, and even to use the same terms to identify quite different distinctions. We will try to avoid that pitfall here. To help you find your way, we will take up each kind of kind of law in turn, give them names that signal (even if somewhat roughly) what each is about, and keep our usage of these terms consistent throughout.

Law's Relationship to Truth: Natural Law versus Positive Law

Life on this planet is sometimes extremely perplexing. How did we get here? Are we here for a reason or just by accident? How should we spend our time here? And what, if anything, happens next? These questions all fall within the domain of philosophy and theology — that is, the domain of metaphysics. However, the third question, "How should we spend our time here?" is also partly the domain of law, which determines what conduct is not permitted as well as what acts must be performed.

This overlapping of the worlds of law and metaphysics has led some philosophers to believe that philosophy should instruct law. If philosophy or religion can tell us in general how we should spend our time on earth, then we ought to be able to deduce the particular rules we should follow — or so say those who believe there is such a thing as **natural law**. We ought to be able to discover the laws that already exist in nature, which have been, some would add, implanted there by a divine creator. The idea of natural law can be traced back to the Greek and Roman Stoic philosophers, and particularly to the ideas of Marcus Tullius Cicero, who argued that there was a universal law of nature, discoverable by "right reason" and binding on all.[43] Islamic law is still largely based on the philosophy of natural law. The *qadi* (judge) is expected to reach a decision by considering first "the claims of God" — the rulelike statements of law" contained in the Qur'an — and second the Traditions, statements about what the prophet Mohammed actually said or did in determining justice. The judge then seeks to discover how the present case is analogous to a situation cited in these basic texts and rules accordingly.[44]

Those who have argued for positive law, or law made by humans, usually have not denied the various precepts of their society's dominant religion or philosophy. What they *have* denied is the possibility of discovering laws in that way. They argue instead that laws are and must be made pragmatically, to meet given ends. Laws should be clearly *promulgated* (announced), as should the punishments or other sanctions applied to those who transgress them. Such laws should be in accord with the society's moral principles, but they should not be seen as having the weight and authority of absolute truth. They should be recognized, say the positivists, as the instruments of mortal, fallible humans who are simply attempting to establish order on the basis of their empirical experience.[45]

In recent times, the positivist view of law has been dominant. But the idea that natural law exists and can be discovered has had great appeal in the past. If it can be argued that the law represents absolute truth of divine origin, then who dares to challenge any law as unjust? Throughout much of human history, the principles of natural law were used to bolster the authority of autocrats. Kings succeeded to power, it was argued, only because it was the will of a divine being that they do so. Thus, their decrees had divine sanction and had to be accepted without question. Even when the "divine right of kings," as this theory is called, led to patently outrageous abuses of power, uncompromising believers in natural law argued that the edicts of kings must be obeyed.

However, such abuses inevitably led other political thinkers to look for arguments that would permit the dethroning of tyrants without denying the existence of natural law. In the seventeenth century, John Locke found such an argument. Natural law was given, said Locke, for the preservation of humankind and to ensure the public good of society. Its commands were binding on sovereigns and legislators as well as on ordinary men and women; when those in power acted in a manner contrary to those purposes, it was a sign that they themselves were contravening natural law. In such a case, it was the right and indeed the duty of the people to replace their rulers with those who would act more in accord with the strictures of natural law.[46]

How Law Is Formalized: Common Law and Codified Law

Many of those who puzzle about the nature of law are content to leave the question of its relationship to truth unresolved and do not feel the need to categorize law as either natural or positive. For them, a more important question is how the law was established. The categories that matter to

412 Chapter 11 Justice Under the Law

them are common law, and codified law. Other variations in how law is formalized include equity law, statutory law, and constitutional law.

When the Roman empire grew to include vast numbers of peoples, each with its own established laws, problems developed in maintaining peaceful relationships throughout the land. What was normal practice in one province might be a serious crime in another. Simply imposing Roman law on everyone could have created as many problems as it solved. The Roman answer was to establish special courts to hear cases involving disputes between inhabitants of different territories. The judge (known as a *praetor peregrinus*, or judge for foreigners) would then consider the legal principles of both lands, look for common ground between them, and — failing that — propose a solution based on *equity*, that is, a solution based on an abstract notion of fairness. These decisions frequently served as precedents for succeeding cases. Eventually, in the sixth century C.E., Emperor Justinian ordered Roman jurists to codify the body of law that was emerging in this way. The result, known as the "law of the peoples" (*jus gentium*), was the "first comprehensive compilation of the rules of any legal culture."[47]

The Roman solution offers good illustrations of several of the ways laws can be established. When the judges for foreigners took it upon themselves to declare what was just, then took note of one anothers' decisions and treated them as **precedents** — that is, as examples to be followed in succeeding cases — they were building a body of "judge-made law," a kind of law that would later be known as *case law* or **common law**. Common law has both the virtue and the flaw of flexibility. In most systems it is only as fixed as the judges want it to be, which means that unfair decisions can be set aside relatively easily — but so can those that are fair. None of the participants can be certain when the judge's ruling will be *stare decisis* ("let the [previous] decision stand") or when he or she will decide that previous decisions do not really apply to the case at hand.

Today common law is particularly "common" in northern Europe and the United States. The evolution of the legal system of the Republic of Ireland offers an interesting example of the twists and turns possible over the centuries. Some Irish law finds its roots as far back as the customs of the seventh century, when Ireland was composed of separate kingdoms and fiefdoms and the law and its application were in the hands of a small group of teachers and judges. Conquest by the English led, especially after 1800, to a body of English-Irish common law, much of which remained operative after independence was granted in 1922. Beginning with the 1924 Courts of Justice Act, the newly free republic revised its laws to suit itself but often used English law as its model nonetheless. Since 1973, judges have been influenced by European Community law, but Irish courts continue to be required to follow precedents, so long as the earlier decisions "meet the requirements of aptness and similarity."[48]

Not surprisingly, a body of common law often emerges — or is extended — when a nation must deal with remarkably new and challenging circumstances, circumstances that existing laws simply fail to cover.[49] When, during the Watergate scandal of 1972 to 1974, the U.S. Congress became persuaded that something had to be done about the infusion of large sums of private money into political campaigns, it passed the Federal Election Campaign Act of 1974. This act imposed rigorous requirements for the disclosure of the sources of all political funds and imposed strict limits on both contributions and expenditures for campaigns. It also raised almost as many questions as it answered, such as, When does a contribution become an expenditure? How can spending and contribution limits be reconciled with rights of free speech? The result was a series of court cases, usually brought by people who had been affected by the Federal Election Commission's interpretation of the act. These cases have in turn produced an interesting contemporary example of the building of common law.

Another development in common law is taking place right now, as cases are being brought before the courts of several modern nations that involve the new problem of computer theft. Ingenious *hackers* (computer hobbyists) can now crack code after code and enter the secret systems of governments and business corporations, and the courts are under heavy pressure to interpret existing laws in such a way as to halt such practices. As they do so, they will be further extending the reach of the common law, although whether the precedents thus established will be codified in the future remains to be seen.[50]

Codified law is a body of law that has been set down in writing, as Justinian directed his jurists to do in the sixth century. It may draw on many sources; edicts, treaties, decrees, legislative enactments, and the substance of common law decisions are all grist for the mill of the codifiers, who may themselves write new law to eliminate contradictions or to fill gaps in the material before them. Codified law need not be permanently fixed, but changes in a code of law are usually made more formally than are changes in common law. The Roman code was modified again and again over the centuries until, early in the nineteenth century, Napoleon ordered a new systematization of law throughout the empire he had built for France. The Napoleonic code was built on the Roman code, as were subsequent modifications of that code, such as the code of the German Empire of 1900 and the Swiss code of 1907.[51]

Equity law is a form of law that developed as a way of compensating for another difficulty that arises from common law. Common law can usually be applied only after a crime or a damaging act has occurred. In a typical example of equity law, a judge might decide that waiting for an anticipated act to occur before deciding whether it is legal would do irreparable harm and might therefore issue an order forbidding the intended act. The act in question might be one performed by a private party (for example, your landlord may plan to install insulation materials to which you are violently allergic) or by government (for example, the Highway Department's bulldozers are bearing down on your cherished elm tree because they want to widen your street). The most frequent modern legal action invoking equity comes in the form of an **injunction** issued to suspend proceedings until one party or the other has time to prepare a fuller case.[52]

Statutory law includes all legislation, treaties, executive orders, and decrees as well as codes of law. As we noted, law codes usually incorporate whatever statutory law exists at the time of codification. But the other forms of statutory law continue to be written, day after day, year after year. New statutes may or may not be incorporated into an existing code. In some nations, such as Norway, judges have at their command a rich tradition of common law, supplemented by a wide-ranging and ever-changing body of uncodified statutory law. Special forms of statutory law, such as **administrative law** (the rules and decisions of administrative agencies) and **admiralty** and **maritime law** (for cases having to do with shipping and waterborne commerce), are sometimes considered to be altogether separate forms of law.[53]

A **constitution** is itself a special form of law, often referred to as the "highest law in the land." **Constitutional law** is law that has evolved in cases that require independent judicial interpretation of the provisions of a constitution (such as all cases of judicial review). As such, constitutional law can be seen as a form of common law.[54]

Different Law for Different Acts: Criminal Law and Civil Law

Another way to subdivide the kinds of law is to consider the acts of the parties in the case — or rather, the alleged acts. Is someone claiming that a crime against the public order has been committed and must be punished by society? Then the judge must decide the applicability of the appropriate **criminal law** to the case. Or is someone alleging that one individual has acted unfairly toward another in a way that damages only that individual — not the society at large — and that some form of retribution must be made to the individual who suffered the damage? In that case, the judge will turn to **civil law**.

Civil law covers cases dealing with such matters as divorce, child custody, inheritances, and contracts. Criminal law covers any act that is considered an offense against society, from the most serious cases of rape, arson, or murder to the most petty infraction of parking regulations. The line between civil law and criminal law is not always clear; some acts can be considered simultaneously offenses against society, requiring punishment, and offenses against individuals, requiring restitution. One way to decide which form of law applies is to consider the circumstances. An act that was intentional or reckless may be deemed criminal, while the same act may be subject only to civil law if it results from negligence or accident.[55]

A separate but related distinction is made between crimes with victims and such victimless crimes as gambling and possession of marijuana. It is sometimes argued that "victimless" crimes should be subject to neither criminal penalty nor civil retribution because there is no nonconsenting

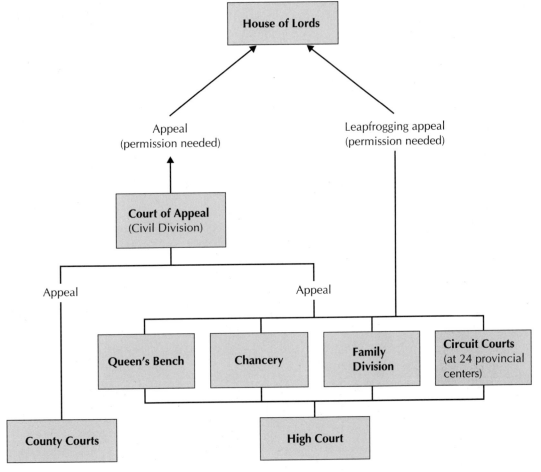

FIGURE 11.2   **The British Judicial System: Courts Exercising *Civil* Jurisdiction**

Source: Philip Norton, *The British Polity,* 2nd ed. (New York and London: Longman, 1991), p. 346. Reprinted by permission of Cambridge University Press.

victim in such cases. However, most polities have decided that at least some of these activities do constitute offenses against the society at large and should be punished as such — that is, under criminal law.[56]

Ordinary citizens who have occasion to deal with the courts are likely to find the distinction between civil law and criminal law more important than any other. The rules of proceeding and the range of possible outcomes vary radically according to whether a civil or a criminal case is under consideration, so much so that it is common to establish two entirely separate systems of courts to deal with each. (For the two separate systems in Great Britain, see Figures 11.2 and 11.3.)

FIGURE 11.3   **The British Judicial System: Courts Exercising *Criminal* Jurisdiction**

Source: Philip Norton, *The British Polity,* 2nd ed. (New York and London: Longman, 1991), p. 346. Reprinted by permission of Cambridge University Press.

The Scope of Law: Domestic Law and International Law

A final categorization of kinds of law derives from the territorial scope of any law. The most obvious distinction here is between **domestic law**, the body of laws that nations apply only within their territories, and **international law**, the law that applies in relationships between nations, or between the citizens of one nation and either the government or individual citizens of another nation.

We will examine the provisions of international law more carefully in Chapter 13, but here we will consider two essential differences between domestic law and international law. First, domestic law has much greater legitimacy than international law. Domestic law evolves from the beliefs and the culture of a particular society and is therefore likely to be accepted as reasonable and understandable by most of the members of that society. But international law is not based on the culture of those to whom it applies, and its dictates may draw on notions of fairness that are puzzling, unfamiliar, and even repugnant to those to whom they are supposed to apply.

Second, domestic law is much easier to enforce than international law. The weapons and armies of the world are under national, not international control, even when they are temporarily on loan for the peacekeeping missions of international organizations. Furthermore, the strength of nationalistic sentiment is such that any effort at armed enforcement of an unpopular settlement is always likely to deteriorate into simple warfare between nation-states. The Korean conflict in the 1950s makes an excellent case in point.[57]

Nevertheless, both the body of international law and the machinery for arriving at settlements under that law do exist, and they do "work" more often than might at first be expected. Karl Deutsch has suggested that international law prevails (when it does) because "it serves the nations to coordinate their mutual expectations and behavior *in their own interest.*"[58] It is in every nation's interests, for example, for all diplomats to receive special attention and privileges, as outlined in the Vienna Convention of 1961. This often includes immunity from arrest except in the most serious cases. In recent years, however, there have been incidents suggesting to some that such privileges are being abused beyond endurance. In one case, shots fired from the Libyan embassy in London on a crowd of demonstrators killed a British policewoman. The response to this kind of case has been not to change the law regarding diplomatic immunity but to insist on its more careful and more measured observance. Diplomats *"are not immune from the laws of the country where they are accredited,"* Grant V. McLanahan reminds us, "but only from the usual methods of enforcement." Host nations are now more likely to "institute preventive measures, issue systematic warnings, and announce possible penalties to diplomats"; those who go too far may now well find themselves expelled altogether.[59]

The slow but steady strengthening of the European Economic Community has brought new considerations regarding the scope of international law to its member states. The EEC writes laws to which these states are expected to conform, even when their domestic laws may conflict. The Maastricht Treaty (see Chapter 13) brought the dilemma home to the French in 1992. Although committed to endorsement of the treaty, the logical French had to admit it required commitments from them that were expressly forbidden not merely by domestic law but by their national constitution. What to do? The answer was clear: The French revised their constitution to make it possible to approve the treaty.[60]

Even when a nation is opposed to some provision of international law, and has the strength to be able to flout it with seeming impunity, responsible leaders are usually aware that the situation may be drastically changed at some later date. "Most nations do well," says Deutsch, "to consider the possibility, and indeed the probability, of role reversal in the future."[61]

There are, of course, also differences in the scope of law *within* nation-states. Municipal ordinances, county rules, state or provincial law, and national legislation all vary in the territorial extent of their coverage. However, local law within nations, a topic we will return to in the next chapter, must always be consistent with national law and, except in rare instances, can always be overturned at the national level. The difference between domestic and international law is in that respect a different kind of difference (a different kind of kind).

REGIONAL VARIATIONS IN THE RULE OF LAW: LEGAL CULTURES

In any given polity we will find aspects of nearly all the kinds of law we have been discussing. Some legal principles will appear to be based on unquestionable truth even in the most pragmatic of cultures. Every society has some form of statutory law, yet every society also has judges who occasionally take it upon themselves to assert a little courtroom inventiveness — and whose decisions earn the flattery of imitation by other judges. Every polity has a way of settling disputes between individuals that is different from the way it punishes crimes against society. And in no part of the world is international law as binding as is domestic law.

Despite this overriding similarity in diversity, however, several distinctive **legal cultures** can be found as we examine how the human polity goes about providing for fair treatment under the law.[62]

The Romano-Germanic Legal Culture

The pattern most widely adopted is the one Henry Ehrmann called the **Romano-Germanic legal culture**, by which he meant those nations (or in some cases, those subunits within nations) in which judicial decisions are based on codes of law based on the Roman tradition.[63] This system prevails in most of Europe, all of Latin America, the nations in west and central Africa that were formerly under French imperial control, and to some ex-

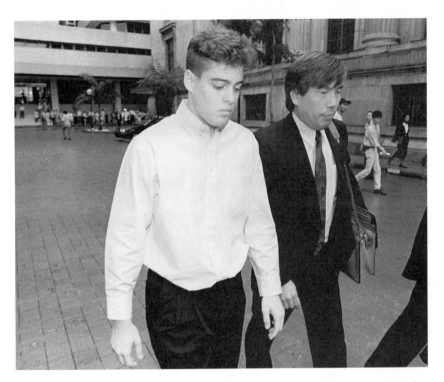

Not all legal cultures are the same. Here U.S. teenager Michael Peter Fay, 18, enters Singapore's high court to appeal his caning sentence for vandalism. Fay's sentence of six strokes of the cane, four months imprisonment and a fine was upheld by the court. (Reuters/Jonathan Drake/Archive Photos)

tent in the Canadian province of Quebec and the American state of Louisiana. (Both Quebec and Louisiana have strong ethnic and cultural links to France, and thus to the Napoleonic code.) In such cultures, judges are expected not to make law but to exercise the greatest possible care in determining if and exactly how a given law applies to a given case. They are not expected to consult other judges' decisions in similar cases; each case is taken up *ab ovo*.[64]

Although the basis of law in the Romano-Germanic legal culture is codified law, not all law is found in the codes. In the Federal Republic of Germany, for example, "any legal rule that has been enacted and promulgated by those state authorities which are constitutionally entitled to enact and promulgate laws" is considered part of *Gesetz*, that is, statutory law. German law also relies on *Gewohnheitsrecht*, or custom, defined as "the regular and general public practice of law." However, appeals to *Gewohnheitsrecht* are usually made in order to supplement the statutory rules, not contradict them.[65]

In other European nations, the mixture of codified law and common law is so balanced that it is difficult to say to which legal culture the system should properly be assigned. The Danish king Valdemar Victorious ordered a royal committee to draft the Jutland code in the mid-thirteenth century, but that code has since been supplanted not only by a more modern code but also by very heavy reliance on judicial custom and precedent. Norway has followed a similar path, gradually repealing much of its code of 1688 and replacing it with a mixture of "fragmentary codifications," other statutes, and customary law.[66]

The heavy reliance on codified law in the Romano-Germanic legal culture has the advantages — and the disadvantages — of codification in any sphere of human endeavor. Codification makes it easier to know what should be done but harder to adapt to changes that occur after the code has been established. As a general rule, we can say that nations that adopt this legal culture tend to lose in flexibility what they gain in precision.

The Common Law Legal Culture

The **common law legal culture** exists wherever judges are given wide latitude to interpret existing law and their decisions themselves become part of the law to be interpreted by their successors. The roots of the common law tradition are found in England during the Norman Conquest, when the king's judges traveled throughout the land settling disputes by drawing on local custom, their own often quite rudimentary legal training, and any innate wisdom they might happen to have regarding the tenets of justice. Over the years there slowly emerged what the judges were pleased to refer to as "general immemorial custom of the realm." As Ehrmann points out, a jurisprudence based on (or at any rate seeming to be based on) the people's own habits, and built up slowly over the years, is "an excellent means of nation-building."[67] In the English case, it was also a useful way to protect the powerful; the early English judges were closely tied to landowning interests, and in acting as the people's defenders against executive power they were at the same time protecting themselves and other members of their class from incursions by the sovereign on their own wealth and power.

The common law tradition spread throughout the British empire and is still dominant throughout the British Commonwealth, in the United States, and in other former British colonies. Although it had its beginnings in the days when all law was judge-made law, common law today is everywhere combined with law written by legislatures. The extent to which statutory law has come to supplant custom and judicial precedent as the basis for court decisions varies from nation to nation within the common law legal culture.

English resistance to codification is particularly strong, and in that system the greatest possible respect is paid to the principle of *stare decisis* — that is, to the obligation to abide by preceding decisions: "A lower court is absolutely bound to follow the law as laid down by a higher court. The lower judge has no right to construe a statute independently or to disregard an established rule of case law once the upper court has ruled on the point. Every court, even the highest, must follow its own established rulings so that there may be no fluctuation in the law and so that its certainty may be maintained."[68] African nations, on the other hand, have woven a large measure of respect for their own traditional law, heavily based on custom, into their legal systems, but at the same time they regularly augment and amend that law as the needs of modernization require and the force of public opinion permits.

The American Legal Culture

The extent to which custom and precedent guide American jurists varies considerably, from era to era, and from state to state. A New Hampshire judge once scorned codes of law as "devices of ignorance." California, by contrast, is considered "the leading code state. . . . Extensive codification of private law was undertaken there, not only because common-law traditions were thin, but also because it seemed necessary to end once and for all the lingering influence of Mexican law."[69] In general, the American system is a hybrid mixture of codified law and common law, with heavy emphasis on the latter, especially at the national level of the judiciary.

The mixed nature of the American legal culture is apparent when we follow the course of adjudication on a specific topic, such as relations between the races. The shifting course of race relations in the United States has been matched by a shifting course of judicial decisions, each interpreting the Constitution and statutory law in a manner to suit the sentiments of the judges and the times. In 1896, in the case of *Plessy v. Ferguson*, the Supreme Court declared that racial segregation did not constitute discrimination and that states could require the separation of races as long as equal accommodations were provided for all.[70] This decision was considered progressive at the time because it did establish at least the principle of equal facilities for black and white. However, only two years later the Court ruled in *Cumming v. County Board of Education* that equal protection under the law was not denied when a county provided a high school for white children but none for black children.

Throughout the first half of the twentieth century, the Court continued to rely on the *Plessy v. Ferguson* precedent, interpreting each allegation by black citizens that they had been denied equal protection of the law in light of its "separate but equal" doctrine — sometimes ruling in their favor, sometimes not, but always reaffirming that segregation itself was not illegal. But the U.S. Supreme Court is never absolutely bound by precedent, no matter how many times it has conveniently chosen to pretend to be so. In 1954, the Court abandoned *Plessy v. Ferguson* and ruled, in the case of *Brown v. Board of Education*, that segregation in the public schools was unconstitutional. This new case now became the precedent on which others were to be decided, and in case after case the Court reaffirmed and extended its newfound conviction that segregation was unconstitutional and must not be practiced in any public facility in the United States.

During this period, the U.S. Congress passed the Civil Rights acts of 1957, 1960, and 1964, and the Voting Rights Act of 1965, giving the Court a new body of statutory law to enforce or cite in decisions designed to extend equal protection of the law to all Americans. Working together, the legislature, the executive, and the judiciary gradually pushed back the barriers that had been erected against the nation's black citizens. By the late 1970s, however, resistance was forming against two practices the U.S. government had widely endorsed as a means of equalizing opportunities for all: affirmative action and busing to achieve school integration. Once again, the Court shifted ground, ruling in *Board of Regents v. Bakke* that programs designed to take affirmative action in improving conditions for blacks or other minorities may not include specific quotas, and declaring in *Milliken v. Bradley* that busing pupils from one neighborhood to another in order to achieve racial integration in the schools could be required only if school authorities had in the past intentionally discriminated against minority students: "Absent an interdistrict violation, there is no basis for an interdistrict remedy." Similarly, in the 1990 case of *Wards Cove Packing v. Antonio*, the Court reversed an earlier decision (*Griggs v. Duke Power Company*, 1971) and ruled that it was up to the plaintiffs to show that an employee's practices were discriminatory rather than the responsibility of the employer to demonstrate that they were not. Although the Court continues to uphold the principles of racial equality, in recent years it has been markedly more conservative in adjudicating disputes that arise over how this goal is to be achieved.[71]

The pattern revealed by this very brief review of major judicial decisions in the area of race relations is repeated again and again in the American legal culture. Sometimes judicial decisions adhere closely to the letter of the law as codified in Constitution or statute — a practice known as **strict construction**. Sometimes judges treat their own or their predecessors' past decisions as inviolable common law precedent. And sometimes they use their right of judicial review to overrule both legislative statute and court decision (including their own) — a practice known as **judicial activism**. This shifting blend of judicial styles has often produced contradictory and inconsistent decisions, but the net result is a system of justice as heterogeneous and as volatile as the people it serves.

The Socialist Legal Culture

The primary sources of law in Russia under the czars were statutes and codes, supplemented by the personal decrees of the emperor.[72] The revolution of 1917 extended into the courts: from that time forward, all reference to the law of the czars was forbidden. At first the Soviets attempted to settle disputes with no formal law whatsoever, believing that commitment to the principles of socialism would be sufficient to ensure justice. This naive hope was quickly dashed, and the next step was to go to the opposite extreme, establishing an elaborate law code that was intended to embody the principles of the **socialist legal culture**.

The law code of the USSR was not the same as the law code of the Romano-Germanic legal culture, but it showed many affinities with that earlier culture. The Soviet code varied from the Romano-Germanic code because it had to deal with the different socioeconomic conditions that emerged when all the means of industrial production were under state control, and because it was kept unambiguously subordinate to political purposes. As Ehrmann reminds us, "Everywhere legal institutions have a political purpose," but the Soviet system differed in "making this explicit and reminding its public of it on every occasion."[73]

Although Soviet law was heavily codified and much lip service was given to the principle of codification (as opposed to permitting bourgeois judges to interpret and misinterpret the law as they saw fit), the legislators often left considerable scope for judicial activism in practice, especially in criminal cases, where the code leaves the judges wide latitude to determine which articles should be applied in particular cases.[74]

None of the nations of eastern Europe that joined the socialist legal culture — such as Poland, Czechoslovakia, or Hungary — followed the Russian example of jettisoning, even temporarily, all existing law. New codes were adopted when communist parties took over, but they were intended to supplement or supplant existing law only when necessary. As long as judges interpreted the older body of law (itself largely based on the Romano-Germanic model) so as to ensure adequate response to "the imperatives of the new social and political order," that body of law was allowed to remain on the books.[75]

Since the fall of the Soviet Union, the transformation of its component parts and of the political systems under its sway has included numerous changes in the nature of law. The Russian republics appear to be evolving toward "a novel hybrid system with [coded] law and [common] law coexisting together with remnants of socialist laws." Among the nations of eastern and central Europe seeking to establish constitutional democracy, only the two separate Czech and Slovak republics are able to draw on fully democratic pasts, and even there the experience was of brief duration (between the two world wars). Two fundamental legal reforms in most of these nations is the extension of constitutional protection to the private realm and the institution of judicial review.[76]

In remaining communist states such as China and Cuba, socialist-coded law is still in effect and remains subordinated to political purposes. In China the rulings of the Communist Party prevail at every level of government despite the "lack of any clear constitutional or statutory authority for [its] omnipotence." The party controls the National People's Congress, which in turn has the authority to amend the constitution and enact "basic laws" (*jiben falu*).[77] As basic policies shift — "from 'continuing revolution' and class struggle to economic development and modernization, from intractable opposition to the West to active cooperation and promotion of foreign investment" — the law can be and is freely adjusted. When Beijing was made the locus for the United Nations Women's Convention of 1995, the government went speedily to work to adopt a new "Law on the Protection of Rights and Interests of Women." Although the law clearly represented a step forward in a nation notorious for the suppression of women's rights, its mechanisms for implementation and enforcement have been termed "singularly weak," and many see its main function as little more than that of raising the consciousness of Chinese women — one-fifth of the women in the world.[78]

Similarly easy to change, Cuban law was codified in the penal code of 1971 and then thoroughly revised in the penal code of 1987 to bring it more closely in accord with new socialist principles emphasizing reeducation. The new code was written in the belief that "antisocial actions . . . considered [to be] crimes resulted from a lack of civic or political education and from the scarcity of consumer goods due to the economic embargo and blockade imposed on our country by powerful foreign enemies of the revolution." However, shortly after this reform Cuba witnessed an upsurge in criminality, prompting many to seek "repenalization" of acts for which the penalties had been sharply reduced.[79]

The Natural Law Legal Culture

In a **natural law legal culture**, the system of law rests in large part on the precepts of religious and philosophical thought.[80] The Confucian system, which has now largely been replaced by more modern codes in the Asian nations where it once held sway, was until recently one of the clearest examples of a natural law legal culture. Confucianism assigned an elaborate set of rights, responsibilities, and attitudes to each level of society, and this code of ethics provided the basis for Chinese jurisprudence. According to Confucius, "heaven's mandate" was bestowed on the ruling family, and each emperor's task was to make that mandate "manifest . . . in strict accordance with the ideal order of nature."[81] Every citizen was to live in accord with *li*, "a maze of social rules, moral principles, etiquette requirements, references to natural correspondences, and taboos that supplied directives for each person's life in strict accord with his birth, sex, family status, profession, [and] guild membership."[82] *Li* was given to humankind by "the Will of Heaven and the structure of the Universe"; legal rules (*fa*) might be necessary to control disorder, but they were never more than a temporary expedient.[83]

Both China and Japan have attempted to move away from the rigid social stratification of Confucianism — the former by adopting a socialist legal culture, the latter moving in the direction of Romano-Germanic coded law — and to deemphasize the role of religion as the basis of law.[84] However, something of the old religious culture lingers in both systems, not only in the normative content of modern codes of law but also in the continuing tendency to place a heavy emphasis on social pressure and persuasion to ensure compliance with the new norms of behavior.[85]

Natural law legal cultures coexist with — and sometimes conflict with — more modern legal cultures throughout much of the developing world, especially at the local level. Thus, many contemporary Indian villages continue to apply ancient Hindu law, in which the dominant legal axiom is to conform to the duties incumbent on one's station in life (such station being determined by the divine forces that govern one's birth), no matter how egalitarian the national constitution or the laws made in the capital city of New Delhi have become. Traditional African law, derived from indigenous religions, lives on similarly in the otherwise modernized legal cultures of that continent.

The strongest infusions of natural law in contemporary legal systems are found in Muslim nations. Islamic law (Shari'a) has been defined as "the knowledge of the rights and duties whereby man is enabled to observe right conduct in the world, and prepare himself for the future life."[86] Even in the branches of Islamic law that have been heavily westernized, such as contract law, Muslim codes often urge judges to have recourse to the Qur'an (the Muslim holy book) in difficult cases.[87] But as is the case in all religions, the same religious texts do not always receive the same interpretations. For the Ayatollah Ruhollah Khomeini of Iran, the Shari'a made it clear that Salman Rushdie, the author of the novel *The Satanic Verses*, and his publishers must be sentenced to death because the book blasphemously employed Islamic myths and Qur'anic motifs in contemporary and futuristic settings.[88] In Iraq, Saddam Hussein has defended punishing criminals by amputating hands, feet, or ears as consistent with Islamic law.[89] In contemporary Egypt, on the other hand, there is far less agreement "regarding what Shari'a means or what form its application should take." Some would pursue the example of more conservative Islamic states, but "liberal and secularist" Egyptian intellectuals argue that Islamic texts and legal opinions can and should be used "to establish reason as the guiding force in modern society." For them, the true aim of the Shari'a is to build an honest and just society in which freedom and dignity are enhanced.[90]

CONVERGENCE OF LEGAL SYSTEMS

As you have no doubt noticed, the distinctions among legal cultures are by no means precise and fixed. As globalization proceeds and nation-states become ever more interdependent, it is natural that such distinctions should become even more blurred, a process legal scholars refer to as *convergence*. Peter de Cruz describes the tendency of common law systems like England to rely more on regulations "as a means of speedy implementing of legal reforms rather than [allowing] the courts to develop the law as they have been doing for several hundred years." At the same time, German constitutional courts and French administrative courts — that is, judiciaries in coded law systems — are more and more likely to make their decisions on the basis of case law. According to de Cruz, three important developments contributing to convergence are the spread of American business law to the rest of the world, especially Europe but also in the Far

East; the fall of the Soviet Union and the consequent westernization of the legal systems formerly under its control; and the proliferation of international and regional agreements such as the European Human Rights Convention, the UN Convention on the Rights of the Child, and similar treaties of wide extent.[91]

SUMMARY AND CONCLUSION

As we have seen, the meanings and means of justice vary throughout the human polity. In general, we may agree that justice means "fair treatment under the law," but in practical terms justice is whatever a particular society believes it is. Still, it is important not to exaggerate the differences among various systems' notions of justice; the ordinary men and women of the world may have more shared beliefs about what is just than their systems of law would suggest. Even when we do not agree with one another, our new interdependence forces us to understand and accommodate one another's conception of justice — if only to permit us to do business with one another. Nevertheless, we can reserve the right to apply our own standards in evaluating other systems, once we have made a serious effort to understand why and how other polities have developed their own values about law and justice, acknowledged their right to do so, and firmly rejected the ethnocentric assumption that we ourselves know all the answers and therefore have the right to impose our views on others.

The means of establishing just government also vary. Every nation tries to choose credible judges by appointing only experienced people to that post, by giving the right of appointment to people who are themselves respected by virtue of the office they occupy, and by surrounding the judicial office with the physical accoutrements of dignity and stature — but each nation determines for itself what constitutes appropriate experience, respectable officeholding, and sufficiently impressive judicial insignia. Similarly, despite the obvious connection between keeping judges free from political restraint and protecting individual rights, there is no widespread agreement that the judiciary should be independent of the other branches of the government, or if so, how independent it should be. Where judicial independence is deemed desirable, various means are used to secure that independence — from giving only other judges the power to discipline judges to making the process of removing judges extremely difficult and complex. Giving the courts the power of judicial review is not, however, a dependable means of ensuring judicial independence.

Enforcing justice is often as difficult as ensuring fair adjudication. Executives have a number of motives and means for failing to carry out the will of the courts, political circumstances may make it impossible to conduct normal peaceful judicial processes, international or regional bodies may have the power to contradict rulings made within a single state, and the judges themselves, too eager to reduce the workload on an overburdened system or too guided by their own racial or gender biases, may sometimes be guilty of setting aside their own nation's principles of justice.

In carrying out their work, the judges of the world draw on several kinds of kinds of law. Sometimes law is categorized according to how close it is believed to be to absolute truth, sometimes according to the process by which it is created and formalized, sometimes by the kind of act to which it applies, and sometimes by the territorial extent of its coverage. Some aspect of every kind of law is likely to be present in any given polity, but most systems tend to have a dominant legal culture. The Romano-Germanic legal culture relies heavily on codified law, the common law legal culture on "judge-made" law, the socialist legal culture on statutory law made to fit the particular exigencies of state control of the economy, and the natural law legal culture on the guidance of religious precept, more or less formally enshrined in written law.

Despite these differences, however, there is a contemporary trend toward *convergence* of the world's legal systems, a process consistent with our growing interdependence and speeded on by the downfall of the Soviet Union, the spread of American business law, and the proliferation of international treaties.

In every nation, the application of the law is inevitably uneven, whether by deliberate intent (more common in hierarchical systems) or by the accidents of interpretation (more common in democratic states). The application of the law becomes more personal, as well as more arbitrary, the closer we move to the local level. Indeed, most people have direct experience of government of any type only at that level. To broaden our understanding of the nature of that experience, we turn our attention now to local and regional government.

Selected Readings

Belliotti, Raymond. *Justifying the Law: the Debate Over Foundations, Goals, and Methods*. Philadelphia: Temple University Press, 1992. A critical survey of the works of leading legal minds and of the different schools of legal thought.

Beloff, Max and Gillian Peele. *The Government of the United Kingdom: Political Authority in a Changing Society*. London: Weidenfeld and Nicolson, 1985. A comprehensive study of the British political system with a strong section on the citizen and the legal system.

Christenson, Ron. *Political Trials: Gordian Knots in the Law*. New Brunswick, N.J.: Transaction Books, 1986. A study of political trials that attempts to answer some of the questions of justice that such trials raise, such as responsibility and representation.

de Cruz, Peter. *A Modern Approach to Comparative Law*. Boston: Kluwer, 1993. Provides an introduction to the comparative study of law and legal systems.

Edelman, Martin. *Courts, Politics and Culture in Israel*. Virginia: University Press of Virginia, 1994. The author examines Israel's many legal systems and the difficulties such multiplicity causes for the development of a modern democracy, and urges their reconciliation in a written constitution that includes a bill of rights.

Katz, Alan M., ed. *Legal Traditions and Systems: An International Handbook*. Westport, Conn.: Greenwood Press, 1986. Includes chapters on legal systems around the world ranging from Italy to Bangladesh.

Litan, Robert E., ed. *Verdict: Assessing the Civil Jury System*. Washington: Brookings, 1993. Essays on the civil jury system in the United States, providing historical background as well as a thorough analysis of the contemporary system.

Lobban, Michael. *The Common Law and English Jurisprudence 1780–1850*. Oxford: Clarendon Press, 1991. Discusses the intellectual history of law and the formation of the legal framework in Britain in the late eighteenth and early nineteenth centuries.

Lynn, Naomi B., ed. *Women, Politics and the Constitution*. Binghamton, N.Y.: The Haworth Press, 1990. The authors contributing to this volume discuss the role the U.S. constitution has played in women's history and in the development of women's rights.

Smith, Christopher E. *Courts and Public Policy*. Chicago: Nelson-Hall, 1993. Synthesizes scholarly arguments and findings on judicial policy-making. Discusses the constitutional scope of judicial authority and practical questions about the policy-making capabilities of the court.

Tate, C. Neal and Torbjorn Vallinder. *The Global Expansion of Judicial Power*. New York: New York University Press, 1995. A study of the increasing power of the judiciary throughout the world.

Weinreb, Lloyd L. *Natural Law and Justice*. Cambridge, Mass.: Harvard University Press, 1987. An examination of concepts such as justice, liberty and equality in the tradition of natural law.

Notes

1. *New York Times*, 8 Dec. 1991, 3.
2. Tamara Jones, "Germany's Troubles," *Los Angeles Times*, 7 March 1993, 14.
3. *New York Times*, 5 March 1995, 21.
4. In 1857 the Supreme Court ruled that Dred Scott, a slave who had claimed freedom after being taken to a free state, was nevertheless still a slave and furthermore said that "Congress could not deprive persons of any kind of property anywhere in the United States [and] that the old Missouri Compromise itself, which had set boundaries to slavery, had been unconstitutional all along." William Miller, *A New History of the United States* (New York: Dell, 1968), p. 196.
5. Just for the record, let it be noted that Mr. Williams was in fact 6 feet 5 inches tall and weighed 185 pounds. *New York Times*, 5 March 1995, 21.
6. See John Rawls, *A Theory of Justice* (Cambridge: Belknap Press of Harvard University Press, 1971), pp. 1–16.
7. For an interesting contemporary discussion of this age-old problem, see Christina M. Cerna, "Universality of Human Rights and Cultural Diversity: Implementation of Human Rights in Different Socio-Cultural Contexts." *Human Rights Quarterly* 16, no. 4 (November 1994): 740–52. Cerna concludes that "international norms dealing with rights that affect the private sphere of human activity will take the longest time to achieve universal acceptance" (p. 752).
8. David P. Conradt, *The German Polity*, 5th ed. (New York and London: Longman, 1993), p. 179.
9. "Judicial System," in F. M. Leventhal, ed., *Twentieth-Century Britain: An Encyclopedia* (New York: Garland Publishing, 1995), p. 417.
10. Stanley Anderson, "Lay Judges and Jurors in Denmark," *American Journal of Comparative Law* 38, no. 4 (Fall 1990): 839–864.
11. Conradt, *The German Polity*, p. 179 and Thomas Reynolds and Arturo Flores, "Germany" in *Current Sources of Basic Codes and Legislation in Jurisdictions of the World: Western and Eastern Europe*, vol. 2 (Littleton, Conn.: Rothman AALL publications series No. 33, May, 1995), pp.3–4.
12. Scott B. MacDonald, "Latin America," in Alan M. Katz, ed., *Legal Traditions and Systems: An International Handbook* (Westport, Conn.: Greenwood Press, 1986), p. 207.
13. Gregory S. Mahler, *Comparative Politics* (Cambridge, Mass.: Schenkman, 1983), p. 99.
14. Harvey M. Feinberg, "Africa," in Katz, *Legal Traditions and Systems*, p. 14 and Bureau of Public Affairs, U.S. State Department, "Malawi," *Background Notes* (Feb. 1989), 1–5.
15. Asher Arian, *Politics in Israel: The Second Generation* (Chatham, N.J.: Chatham House, 1985), p. 182.
16. *Congressional Quarterly Weekly Report* 48, no. 40 (6 Oct. 1990): 3228 and 49, no. 42 (19 Oct. 1991): 3026–33.
17. Charles S. Clark, "Courts and the Media," *C.Q. Researcher* (23 Sept. 1994), 819–35 and Marc Fisher, "Simpson Ad Nauseam? Tell It to the

Judge," *International Herald Tribune*, 23 May 1995), 1, 3.

18. Clark, "Courts and the Media," p. 831.

19. Charles Secondat Montesquieu, *Spirit of the Laws*, ed. Franz Neumann, trans. Thomas Nugent (New York: Hafner, 1949), pp. 151–52.

20. Conradt, *German Polity*, pp. 179. On the other hand, the Constitutional Court, which has the power of judicial review, is seen by Conradt as having an "explicitly political character" since "both state and party/political factors" play an important role in the selection of its members (p. 183).

21. Robert L. Hardgrave, Jr., *India: Government and Politics in a Developing Nation*, 3rd ed. (New York: Harcourt Brace Jovanovich, 1980), pp. 78–79.

22. "Introduction to This Issue," *Judicature* 65 (Oct. 1981): 177.

23. Thomas P. Carr, Karen J. Lewis, and Michael J. Matheron, "Waiting for Roe II," *Congressional Research Service Review* (Sept. 1991): 5–6.

24. C. Neal Tate, "The Judicialization of Politics in the Philippines and Southeast Asia," *International Political Science Review* 15, no. 2 (1994): 187–97.

25. Jonathan S. Massey and Kennth J. Chesebro, "Challenging Federal Appellate Review of Damage Awards: Lawyers Should Cite the Forgotten Second Clause of the Seventh Amendment," *Trial* 31, no. 5 (May 1995): 52.

26. *New York Times*, 12 Feb. 1992, A1.

27. Frederic Spotts and Theodor Wieser, *Italy: A Difficult Democracy* (Cambridge: Cambridge University Press, 1986), pp. 150–51.

28. Fletcher N. Baldwin, Jr., "A Constitutional Comparison: Mexico, the United States and Uganda," *California Western Law Review* 10, no. 1 (Fall 1973): 97–98.

29. For two conflicting arguments on the point, see Lino A. Graglia, "Judicial Activism: Even on the Right, It's Wrong," *Public Interest* 95 (Spring 1989): 57–74 and David Schultz and Stephen E. Gottlieb, "Legal Functionalism and Social Change: A Reassessment of Rosenberg's *The Hollow Hope: Can Courts Bring About Social Change?*" *The Journal of Law and Politics* 12, no. 1 (Winter 1996): 63–91.

30. *New York Times*, 26 May 1992, A3; *Le Monde*, 26 May 1992, 3.

31. *New York Times*, 3 March 1995, A1.

32. *New York Times*, 15 June 1995, 3.

33. *New York Times*, 8 Sept. 1995, A10.

34. Samuel Kucherov, *The Organs of Soviet Administration and Justice: Their History and Operation* (Leiden: E. J. Bull, 1970), p. 691.

35. "Iran" in House Committee on Foreign Affairs, *Country Reports on Human Rights Practices for 1993* (Washington, D.C.: U.S. Congress, 1994), pp. 1176–83.

36. Fu Xiangtao, "Battling Bureaucracy Through the Ages," *China Today* (April 1993): 41–43.

37. Richard A. Haggerty, *El Salvador: A Country Study* (Washington, D.C.: Department of the Army, 1990), pp. 251–52.

38. *New York Times*, 28 Sept. 1995, A7.

39. Aogán Mulcahy, "The Justifications of 'Justice': Legal Practitioners' Accounts of Negotiated Case Settlements in Magistrates' Courts," *The British Journal of Criminology* 34, no. 4 (Autumn 1994): 411–30. Mulcahy believes those who favor plea bargaining in fact favor "crime control" over "due process" (p. 427).

40. *The Economist*, (18 June 1994): 62–63.

41. *New York Times*, 28 Oct. 1994, 1, A9. As of the end of 1993, 2,432 blacks out of every 100,000 blacks in the country were in prison; the number of whites per 100,000 was 203.

42. Ted Gest with Betsy Streisand, "Still Failing Women?" *U.S. News and World Report*, (19 June 1995): 54–55.

43. *de Re Publica, de Legibus* by Marcus Tullius Cicero, with an English translation by Clinton Walker Keyes (Cambridge, Mass.: Harvard University Press, 1966), *passim*.

44. Lawrence Rosen, *The Anthropology of Justice* (Cambridge: Cambridge University Press, 1990), pp. 41–42. Rosen notes, however, that the *qadi's* decision must also have "the general agreement or consensus of the community" since the prophet is believed to have said, "my community will not agree in error."

45. One of the earliest proponents of positive law was John Austin, in his *Lectures on Jurisprudence* (London: J. Murray, 1869). This view of the law emerged simultaneously with a more positive approach to all social phenomena — using the word *positive* with its dictionary meaning of "concerned only with real things and experience; empirical; practical." In this regard, see the work

of the nineteenth-century philosopher Auguste Comte, in Gertrud Lenzer, ed., *Auguste Comte and Positivism* (New York: Harper & Row, 1975).

46. See John Locke, *Two Treatises of Government* (New York: Hafner, 1947), pp. 188–94; and Richard Hooker, *Of the Laws of Ecclesiastical Polity* (New York: Dutton, 1958), pp. 187–201. For an interesting discussion of these questions, see Lloyd L. Weinreb, *Natural Law and Justice* (Cambridge, Mass.: Harvard University Press, 1987).

47. Henry Ehrmann, *Comparative Legal Cultures* (Englewood Cliffs, N.J.: Prentice Hall, 1976), p. 14. See also W. W. Buckland, *The Main Institutions of Roman Private Law* (Cambridge: Cambridge University Press, 1931), pp. 1–24; and H. F. Jolowicz, *Roman Foundations of Modern Law* (Oxford: Clarendon Press, 1957), pp. 6–21.

48. Reynolds and Flores, "Ireland" in *Current Sources of Basic Codes and Legislation in Jurisdictions of the World: Western and Eastern Europe*, vol. 2 (Littleton, Conn.: Rothman AALL publications series no. 33, May, 1995), pp. 1–5.

49. Theodore F. T. Plucknett, *A Concise History of Common Law* (Boston: Little, Brown, 1956), p. 83.

50. Of course, existing criminal law amply covers those who use such tactics to obtain other persons' credit card numbers and personal security codes for automated bank teller machines, a new form of fraud now costing credit card corporations hundreds of millions of dollars per year. *New York Times*, 9 April 1992, A25.

51. Ehrmann, *Comparative Legal Cultures*, p. 14. Codified law is sometimes also referred to as *civil law*, although that term is commonly used to identify law developed to settle disputes (as distinguished from criminal law). To avoid confusion, I will use *civil law* only in its most common meaning. I have drawn heavily from Ehrmann's excellent work in this chapter, but I think his use of *civil law* to refer to "the codified systems of continental Europe" is unfortunate and confusing to novice legal scholars.

52. Plucknett, *Concise History of Common Law*, p. 675.

53. C. John Colombos, *International Law of the Sea*, 6th ed. (New York: David McKay, 1967), sections 47–50; Richard B. Stewart, "The Reformation of American Administrative Law," in Howard Ball, ed., *Federal Administrative Agencies* (Englewood Cliffs, N.J.: Prentice Hall, 1984), pp. 30–37.

54. E. C. S. Wade and A. W. Bradley, *Constitutional Law*, 5th ed. (London: Longmans, 1955), p. 7.

55. David M. Walker, *The Oxford Companion to Law* (Oxford: Clarendon Press, 1980), pp. 316–17. Political scientists, following the work of Gabriel Almond, sometimes refer to the judicial function as the "adjudication of disputes." A moment's careful consideration of the kind of cases that fall under criminal law, however, should make it obvious that such a definition trivializes the work of the courts.

56. Joel Feinberg, *Harm to Others* (New York: Oxford University Press, 1984), pp. 12–13.

57. Bruce Cummings, *The Origins of the Korean War* (Princeton, N.J.: Princeton University Press, 1981), pp. 101–29.

58. Karl Deutsch, *The Analysis of International Relations* (Englewood Cliffs, N.J.: Prentice Hall, 1968), p. 162.

59. Grant V. McClanahan, *Diplomatic Immunity* (New York: St. Martin's Press, 1989), p. 16.

60. *Le Monde*, 16 June 1992, 1 and 11; *International Herald Tribune*, 20–21 June 1991, 4. The amendment authorizes transfers of sovereignty for the purpose of establishing a single European currency and a common foreign, security and visa policy, and to permit EC citizens residing in France to vote in local elections.

61. Deutsch, *Analysis of International Relations*, p. 163.

62. Ehrmann, *Comparative Legal Cultures*, pp. 11–19.

63. Ibid., pp. 13–15.

64. *Ab ovo* (introduced in Chapter 9) means "from the beginning."

65. E. J. Cohn, *Manual of German Law*, 2nd ed., vol. 1 (London: Oceana Publications, 1968), p. 4.

66. Lester Bernhardt Orfield, *The Growth of Scandinavian Law* (Philadelphia: University of Pennsylvania Press, 1953), pp. 14–15, 170–171.

67. Ehrmann, *Comparative Legal Cultures*, pp. 22–23.

68. Phanor J. Eder, *A Comparative Survey of Anglo-American and Latin-American Law* (New York: New York University Press, 1950), p. 14.

69. Ehrmann, *Comparative Legal Cultures*, pp. 23, 25.

70. Elder Witt, ed., *The Supreme Court and Individual Rights* (Washington, D.C.: Congressional Quarterly, 1980), pp. 217–218.

71. *New York Times*, 8 July 1984, 1 and 12; Opoku Agyeman, "The Supreme Court and Enforcement of African American Rights: Myth and Re-

ality," *The Black Scholar* 21, no. 3 (Summer 1990): 22–28.

72. John N. Hazard, Isaac Shapiro, and Peter B. Maggs, *The Soviet Legal System* (New York: Oceana Publications, 1969), p. 39.

73. Ehrmann, *Comparative Legal Cultures*, p. 17.

74. Hazard, Shapiro, and Maggs, *Soviet Legal System*, p. 40; Ehrmann, *Comparative Legal Cultures*, p. 44.

75. Ehrmann, *Comparative Legal Cultures*, p. 17.

76. Peter de Cruz, *A Modern Approach to Comparative Law* (Deventer, The Netherlands: Kluwer, 1993), pp. 328, 333–334.

77. James V. Feinerman, "Economic and Legal Reform in China," *Problems of Communism* 40, no. 5 (Sept.-Oct. 1991): 62–75.

78. Lisa Stearns, "The New Chinese Women's Law," 19, no. 1, *WIN News* [a publication of the Women's International Network] (Winter 1993): 54.

79. Raul Gomez Treto, "Thirty Years of Cuban Revolutionary Penal Law, *Latin American Perspectives* 18, no. 2 (Spring 1991): 114–25.

80. Ehrmann calls his fourth type *non-Western* but was unhappy (and I would say rightly so) with the "patently Western-ethnocentric" bias of the label (p. 13). Because almost all of the legal systems he treats under this category rely heavily on religious precepts, I have taken the liberty of renaming this final category *natural law*, to suggest its primary difference from the three other kinds of legal culture.

81. Adda B. Bozeman, *The Future of Law in a Multicultural World* (Princeton, N.J.: Princeton University Press, 1971), p. 140.

82. Ibid., p. 144.

83. Ehrmann, *Comparative Legal Cultures*, pp. 45–46.

84. Bureau of Public Affairs, "Japan," in *Background Notes* (Washington, D.C.: U.S. State Department, 1990), pp. 1–8.

85. Ibid., p. 94.

86. Bozeman, *Future of Law in a Multicultural World*, p. 62.

87. Ehrmann, *Comparative Legal Cultures*, p. 18.

88. "The 'Satanic' Furor," *Maclean's* 102, no. 9, 27 Feb. 1989: 16–19, 22, *New York Times*, 15 Feb. 1989, A1, A10 and 23 Feb. 1989, A15.

89. *Time* (6 Feb. 1995): 46.

90. Fauzi M. Najjar, "The Application of Shari'a Laws in Egypt," *Middle East Policy* 1, no. 3 (1992): 62–73.

91. de Cruz, *Modern Approach to Comparative Law*, pp. 332–37.

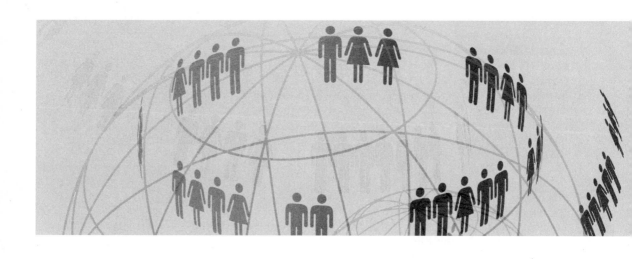

ALTERNATIVE ARENAS
OF GOVERNMENT

12 Accessible Government: Local and Provincial Politics

THE NATURE OF SUBNATIONAL GOVERNMENT

UNITARY, FEDERAL, AND CONFEDERAL POLITICAL SYSTEMS

INTERMEDIATE LEVELS OF GOVERNMENT
Provincial Government
Regional Government

LOCAL GOVERNMENT
Rule Making at the Base
Rule Application at the Base
Rule Adjudication at the Base
Submunicipal Government

CENTER VERSUS PERIPHERY: DILEMMAS OF CENTRALIZATION
Development, Resettlement, and the Environment in India
Fishermen as Politicians in Puerto Rico
Drawing the Lessons

SUMMARY AND CONCLUSION

T̲AKE ME TO YOUR leader," says the charming but obviously well-armed extraterrestrial visitor. Assuming you decide to comply, what do you do next?

Take her home to meet Mother?
Take her to the chief of police, the mayor, or the county commissioner?
Take her to the governor?
Take her to the president?
Take her to the United Nations Secretary General?

Of course you would like to take her to the president, but chances are you will decide to settle for a local government official. When we need government in a hurry, for a particularly urgent problem, we turn to local government. Ask yourself what level of government you would turn to in the following slightly more realistic emergencies:

You see the sky filling with black smoke a few blocks from your home.
You see a stranger taking valuables from your absent neighbor's home.
Your rural county's only doctor has collapsed of a heart attack on your doorstep.
You find a lost child.

If you think these examples are too carefully chosen, try this exercise: Make your own list of the first twenty emergencies, common to the human condition, that come to mind. Cross out the ones you would try to deal with without contacting any government agency (but be careful — hospitals are often city or county owned and operated). Then figure out in what percentage of the remainder you would be likely to turn to *local* government agencies. Even in this day of vastly expanded federal power, I will bet you a subway token that in well over 50 percent of the emergencies that require government assistance your first move will be to contact a local government body.

THE NATURE OF SUBNATIONAL GOVERNMENT

Subnational government is any government less broad in its extent and applicability than an entire nation. Only in the twentieth century has the distinction between national and subnational government become worldwide, or nearly so. When human beings lived in small communities, all government was local, and those who led the government were likely to be leaders in other domains as well, such as religion and hunting. Even today many nation-states have populations no larger than those of cities — and rather small cities at that (see Table 12.1).

Most nations, however, are too large to be served by a single level of government. Some problems cannot be solved the same way throughout the realm. Some problems do not manifest themselves everywhere. And above all, some problems require attention from people on the scene who are well acquainted with the local community.

TABLE 12.1   **World's Largest Cities and Smallest Nation-States, by Population**

Largest Cities	Population	Smallest Nations	Population
Tokyo-Yokohama	27,245,000	Nauru	10,000
Mexico City	20,899,000	Tuvalu	10,000
São Paulo	18,701,000	San Marino	24,000
Seoul	16,792,000	Liechtenstein	30,000
New York	14,625,000	Monaco	31,000
Osaka-Kobe-Kyoto	13,872,000	Saint Kitts and Nevis	41,000
Bombay	12,101,000	Marshall Islands	54,000
Calcutta	11,898,000	Andorra	64,000
Rio de Janeiro	11,688,000	Antigua and Barbuda	65,000
Buenos Aires	11,657,000	Seychelles	72,000

Source: *The World Almanac and Book of Facts 1995.* Copyright © 1994 by K-III Reference Corporation, Mahwah, NJ 07495.

All this is simply common sense. But these obvious and noncontroversial statements inevitably raise questions that may lead to debate and confusion. First, what specific kinds of problems require the attention of subnational units of government? Second, what should be the division of power among the various levels of government in a nation-state? Third, what kind of intermediate levels of government are required to meet a society's needs for governance? Fourth, what kind of institutional structures are appropriate to local government? Fifth, how can the quest for grassroots citizen involvement, most easily accommodated where local government structures are strong, be balanced against the need for centralized planning and allocation of resources, a function that must fall to the national government?

Different nations have given different answers to these questions, and individual nations do not always give the same answers in every era — or region. One way to address the first two questions — what kinds of problems to refer to subnational governments and how much power to give these governments to handle those problems — is to adopt a unitary, federal, or confederal system of government. In the next section we will examine the difference between these three ways of dividing the work of government. In the two following sections we will examine some of the answers that have been given to the third question — what kind of intermediate structures are needed — and the fourth — what institutional structures are appropriate for local governments. The problem of how to establish the right relationship between national and subnational governments will be discussed in a final section.

Before we begin, however, let us clear up two matters of terminology. Political scientists sometimes use the word *local* to refer to any subnational government body and sometimes to refer only to the governments of cities or still smaller units. We will follow the latter practice here and label *intermediate* or *provincial* any government body that is narrower than an entire nation yet wider than a city in the scope of its coverage — such as the American state, the French *departement*, or the Swiss canton. The term **subnational** will refer to both intermediate and local units of government.

The use of the word *federal* can also be confusing, since Americans often refer to the federal government when what they really mean is the national (or central) government. We will try to avoid that common yet understandable error. Here, *federal* will have only the meanings assigned to it in the next section.

UNITARY, FEDERAL, AND CONFEDERAL POLITICAL SYSTEMS

We may agree that it is necessary to have more than one level of government to meet our immediate national and international needs for the exercise of collective power, but we still have to decide which tasks to assign to each level and how much power to give them. In a **unitary system** all the powers of government are reserved to the central government. That government may delegate the exercise of those powers to such subunits as counties or departments, but any such delegation can be revoked at any time. In a **federal system** of government, on the other hand, certain powers are reserved to the central government, but others are constitutionally reserved to the governments of the nation's constituent parts — that is, to the states, provinces, or cantons. Finally, in a **confederal system**, the units are actually independent states that have decided to join together in a formal alliance, acting as a single unit for some limited purposes but not for others.

All three systems have clear advantages and disadvantages. In a federal system, the national government is, at least in theory, freer to deal with national issues. Citizen participation is made easier by the existence of several levels of government, some close at hand. Governmental experiments (primary elections, welfare aid, and abolition of the death penalty are examples in the United States) can be tried out and modified in a limited setting. And when new groups seek statehood or cantonhood, additional units can be added with no disruption of the system.[1]

In a unitary system, on the other hand, laws are much more likely to be uniform throughout the nation and representation is more likely to be equal throughout the nation (with no "federal" provisions for equal representation of every constituent unit regardless of the number of its inhabitants, as in the case of the U.S. Senate, for example). It is less likely that some parts of the nation will have greater tax revenues than others. Finally, in a unitary system, no sphere of independent power is capable of blocking the execution of national policy, and there is no difficulty keeping the lines of authority clear.

A confederal system lacks most of the advantages of either federal or unitary government. It does, however, provide a structure for harmonious interaction on a limited number of matters for peoples for whom single nationhood is not yet — or is no longer — tolerable. It is often a transient system, for systems on the way to greater unity or greater independence, but as such can provide an extremely useful set of institutions.

However, which system a nation adopts is likely to depend far less on the careful weighing of such pros and cons than on the conditions prevalent at the time the new nation comes into existence. If the demands for unified action in the face of a hostile world are extreme and if authoritarian leadership is accepted as the norm — two conditions prevailing when most of the older nations of Europe and Asia were formed — a unitary system is likely even when the peoples joining together have very different backgrounds and customs. When a number of Gallic tribes united under the bold leadership of Vercingetorix in an effort — vain, as it proved — to resist the advance of Julius Caesar and his armies in 52 B.C.E., that was the beginning of modern France. The forceful imposition of nearly forty years of communist rule on most of eastern Europe was maintained by creating unitary states, with power strongly concentrated at the top. China is another example of a unitary state created by force in which all power is exercised at the center. According to that nation's constitution, each province's government is the administrative arm of the central government; whatever powers it has may be revoked at any time. National bodies have the power to annul "those local regulations or decisions of the . . . provinces, autonomous regions and municipalities . . . that contravene the Constitution, the statutes or the administrative rules and regulations" of the central government, as well as "to exercise unified leadership over the work of local organs at different levels throughout the country."[2]

This is not to say, however, that all unitary states have come into being as the result of the exercise of force — either by others who threaten from outside or by homegrown tyrants who seize control — over disparate peoples who would otherwise prefer to remain apart. Most of the nations of the world are unitary, and many have formed their governments out of a sense of shared identity and geographical common sense. And even when originally compelled to unite out of fear, most modern unitary states have evolved a strongly shared sense of identity and nationhood.

If a nation-state is to be created out of what have been largely independent units, each with a separate political culture and separate bases of economic and military power, if the motive to join together is strong but no unit or individual has the force to impose unity against the will of the others, and, finally, if not everyone is sure that a single polity is possible or desirable, federalism may be the answer. Federalism is a complex form of government, but that very complexity may be what it takes to make government work in a complex situation. Consider the proposals made to resolve the problems in ex-Yugoslavia (see Box 12.1).

In any case, once the decision is made to adopt a federal system, some powers must be allocated to the national government and others to the constituent units, and this must be spelled out carefully in a written constitution. In some federal systems, specific powers are assigned the national government and all other powers are reserved to the constituent units — a solution adopted by the United States, Australia, and Switzerland, for example. The Swiss constitution says, "The cantons are sovereign as far as their sovereignty is not restricted by the Federal Constitution, and as sovereign cantons they exercise all those rights which are not transferred to the federal power."[4] The result is that the Swiss cantons are responsible for law and order, education, culture, and public works, whereas the central government's domain covers defense, foreign affairs, the postal service, and most of the railway system. In other federal systems, such as Canada's, the powers of both units are specified in separate lists.

Whatever the formal distribution of power, however, in most federal systems the trend has been for the central government to take on ever

BOX 12.1

CAN FEDERALISM BRING PEACE TO FORMER YUGOSLAVIA?

The effort to bring peace between Bosnia-Herzegovina and Serbia has focused heavily on the search for a federal solution. Plans accepted by both sides in November 1995 call for a federated Bosnia, divided into two separate territories. One territory is to be a Serbian "republic" in the northeast, occupying 49 percent of the territory of the new federation, while the other is to be a Muslim-Croatian federation controlling 51 percent of the nation. Each territory is to have the right to "develop special ties to neighboring countries." The presidency will be a collective body, with two-thirds of its members from the Bosnian-Croat federation and one-third from the Serbian "republic."

Can there be a "republic" within a federation? For that matter, can there be a federation within a federation? Will the Serbian republic simply become, de facto, a state of neighboring Serbia, especially after it has developed its "special ties to neighboring countries?" Is there any reason a federal solution, however fine-tuned, should work any better now than it did in the former Yugoslavia, itself a federal state? None of these questions can be answered yet; all we can say is that the efforts to achieve peace in this beleaguered land involve some of the most complex federal proposals yet devised within the human polity.[3]

greater responsibilities. Population growth, the development of large cities, nationwide and worldwide communication and transportation systems, and the emergence of multinational corporations have contributed to the growth in the powers of central governments, even in federal systems. Such developments produce problems that are at least national in scope and often beyond the capabilities of constituent units to solve, whatever the constitution may say.

The problem of adjusting to a shifting balance of power between central and provincial powers is apparent in Canada. When first formed in 1867, the Canadian federal system allowed the provincial governments considerable autonomy, but it is now much more common for the national and provincial governments to cooperate in development schemes, particularly in the areas of health, welfare, and transportation. When a new airport is built, for example, the nearest city, the province, and the central government all have carefully specified roles to carry out. When originally established, the intent of these development schemes was to give the provincial governments the power to select the programs, to initiate plans for projects, and to administer them once adopted. However, it soon became normal for the national government to take the lead role, in the interests of improved efficiency. Recognizing the drift toward centralization, Canadian provinces have recently begun to make serious efforts to regain lost powers.[5] In Quebec, as we have seen (see p. 000), this concern has led a very large minority to seek total separation.

Although they cover nearly half of the world's land surface, only about

Unpopular federalism. Here Quebec separatists demand that their province be set free from Canadian federalism by marching in a giant "Yes" parade in Montreal in October of 1995. Although the separatists lost in the subsequent referendum, it was by a very narrow margin. (Reuters/Archive Photos)

one-tenth of the world's nations have federal governments.[6] Table 12.2 lists ten major federal systems and their constituent units.

The **confederation** is a form of limited unification which is now in the process of being reinvented. Until the recent astonishing transformations in the map of the world — especially in Europe — the standard example of a confederation was drawn from history. The thirteen American colonies were far from certain they wanted to be even as closely allied as federalism requires, and the first U.S. constitution, the Articles of Confederation, called only for a partnership among nearly independent equals. The earliest U.S. political parties were named, significantly, the Federalists and the Antifederalists — those who argued for and against a "more perfect union." The Swiss provided another historic example, having joined together in the thirteenth century as a loose confederation of cantons, but they too eventually decided to form a federation, in 1848.[7]

Lately, however, we have witnessed the emergence of new confederations. Europe itself seems to be assuming, under the Maastricht Treaty, the

TABLE 12.2   **Ten Major Federal Systems**

Nation	Number and Name of Units
Australia	6 states, 2 territories
Brazil	26 states, 1 federal district
Canada	10 provinces, 2 territories
Germany	16 states
India	25 states, 7 union territories
Mexico	31 states, 1 federal district
Nigeria	30 states, 1 federal capital territory
Russia	21 autonomous republics, 49 oblasts, 6 krays
South Africa	9 provinces
Switzerland	20 cantons, 6 half cantons
United States	50 states, 1 federal district

Source: *The World Almanac and Book of Facts, 1996* (Mahwah, New Jersey: Funk and Wagnalls, 1996), pp. 740–831, passim.

form of a confederation, perhaps on some not-too-distant day to become a true federation, a United States of Europe. The breakup of the Soviet Union brought movement from the opposite direction: A nation was a federation, the Soviet Union of Socialist Republics — consisting of fifteen union republics, twenty autonomous republics, six krays, 120 oblasts and eight autonomous oblasts — that sought to turn itself into a confederation, the Commonwealth of Independent States (CIS), consisting of Armenia, Azerbaidzan, Belarus, Georgia, Kazakhstan, Kyrgystan, Moldova, Russia, Tajikstan, Turkmeinistan, Ukraine, and Uzbekistan. The nation of Czechoslovakia provided a third kind of transformation, from a unitary state into a loose confederation consisting of just two states.

In fact, however, neither of these latter two efforts proved successful: The CIS is simply an extremely loose association of separate nations. It has no capital, no independent budget, and in effect no government. The hopes for coordinated activity among its members have not been met, except to a slight extent in the realm of banking.[8] Similarly, the pretense of confederalism in Czechoslovakia very rapidly gave way to the creation of two separate states, the Czech Republic and Slovakia.

We should not, however, be too quick to dismiss these efforts at confederation building. The move to confederalism was no doubt a good way to ease the process of separation. Consider the comments of the Slovak leader Vladimir Merciar at the time of the transition: "We are not going to fight, we are not going to dispute. We will try to understand each other. There was a great risk of not understanding each other, leading to destruction. We drew nearer together. We are satisfied we have arrived at a means of negotiation."[9] These careful words reveal how complex it is to change the

Federalism is not an easy system of government to establish. Here a Russian cheerfully explains the traffic jam: "We have pluralism! One light is for the city, one for the region, and one for the country!" (SovFoto/EastFoto)

relations between whole peoples, and how a seemingly weak and indecisive form of union, the confederation, can provide exactly the structure needed in difficult times, however briefly it may endure.

Before leaving this topic, we must note that not every contemporary state fits clearly into one of the three categories of unitary, federal, or confederal. The new Russia is an interesting example in that regard. Theoretically, Russia contains twenty-one "autonomous" republics, designated as "independent participants in international and foreign economic connections," a status that comes very close to suggesting a confederation. In practice, however, it has become clear that these republics (which account for 29 percent of the nation's territory and 15 percent of its population) are not at all autonomous. Neither Tartarstan nor Chechnya has ever opted to be part of Russia, and the oppressive military response to the efforts of the latter to break away and form a genuinely independent state has made clear how little independence has actually been granted to these units. Since 1991 President Boris Yeltsin has seesawed on the question of regional powers, attempting to curry the favor of regional leaders in his struggle with the Russian parliament and other opponents in Moscow.[10] But his ability to take away at will what has been given makes it clear that in many respects Russia more closely fits the definition of a unitary state.

INTERMEDIATE LEVELS OF GOVERNMENT

What kind of intermediate levels of government are required to meet a society's needs for governance? The answers given have been many and varied. Choosing between a federal and a unitary system is only the first step. Both federal and unitary states require subnational units. True, only in federal systems do such units have complete responsibility in certain domains, and in actual practice national governments are increasingly exercising broader control over subnational units even in federal systems. Nevertheless, there remains a significant scope for the exercise of state (or cantonal or provincial) power in every federal system. Furthermore, even though the policymaking powers granted subnational units in unitary systems can readily be revoked, in practice such units typically have a considerable measure of independence as long as they operate within national guidelines. And in both federal and unitary systems, subnational governments bear the heavy burdens of administering policies made either by themselves or at the national level.

Provincial Government

Much of the real work of government is carried on at intermediate levels. All but the world's smallest nations have some level of intermediate government between the central government and municipal government. In federal systems they are usually called states, provinces, or cantons. In unitary systems the more common name is department. Be careful, however — the name itself is not a sure guide to the kind of system under study. The French, for example, whose government is strictly unitary, use the word *canton* to refer to the constituency from which are elected representatives to the *departmental* level of government (there is no cantonal level of government any more than there is a congressional district level of government in the United States), and when they talk about life in "the provinces," they do not mean "in the *departements*" but rather anywhere in France that is not Paris. And of course, the word *state* is often used to refer to the nation-state, as is the word *republic* (but the latter was also the name for the subdivisions of the Soviet Union). To keep confusion down to a minimum, here I will use the term *provinces* to mean all intermediate governments that are directly above the local level yet still below the level of the national government, trusting you to remember that this includes American states, Canadian provinces, Israeli administrative departments, Swiss cantons, French *departements*, British counties, and numerous other units.

Whatever its name and whatever its powers, the provincial government occupies a difficult position in any nation's hierarchy of governmental bodies. Normally it has come into being because its inhabitants have some qualities or needs in common that are not shared by the rest of the nation. The provincial government must strive to protect its inhabitants' interests, whether the system is federal or unitary. The government of the Canadian province of Quebec seeks to maintain a fair balance between its majority population, which is of French extraction, and the British-descended minority, while at the same time ensuring that the rights of its French-speaking people are protected within Canada at large. Even where the boundaries have been drawn by imperialistic conquest, breaking up formerly united peoples, as in Africa, or by nature, following rivers or mountain ranges, or by ruler-wielding bureaucrats (look at the straight-edge boundaries of the American state of Colorado), a sense of common identity often builds within the unit. With that identity comes a shared set of goals requiring purposeful government action.

At the same time, the provincial government often lacks both the powers and the resources to meet those goals. It must struggle with both central and local governments to recruit the leadership, acquire and keep the rights of taxation, and rally the degree of popular support that will permit it to meet the demands placed on it by those governments as well as by its own inhabitants. Its struggle with national government is likely to be particularly difficult and frustrating, as that body becomes ever more powerful and uses its powers of taxation to redistribute a nation's wealth in accordance with national policy.

On the other hand, provinces seldom accept the yoke of central control without a struggle. If the situation becomes intolerable, and circumstances suggest the plan is plausible, a province may even seek to set itself up as a separate nation, as has been the case with the Republic of Chechnya in the new Russian Federation.[11] More commonly, when a provincial government, or one of its agencies, is particularly dissatisfied, it seeks to gain the support of one branch of the national government in curbing what it views as the excesses of another. In the United States, the courts often play a particularly important role in this regard, adjudicating disputes between the levels of government. Another approach that may work is to rally public opinion against national policy. For example, when a local environmental protection agency in Siberia opposed the Russian government's agreement to give Weyerhaeuser Corporation, a U.S. timber company, access to some 1 million hectares of Siberian forest land, it was able to gain sufficient international publicity for its cause to slow the project down. Still, when the province is up against international business as well as its own national government, as in this case, the scales may seem unfairly weighed against it. Weyerhaeuser has undertaken its own extensive public relations campaign and is now providing funding for a local research institute that was originally one of the strong opponents of the logging plan. The company is expected to "go into Siberia towards the end of the century."[12]

Provincial governments also struggle with each other in their incessant quest for a greater resource base. This aspect of the problem is further complicated by the fact that needs, goals, and even political identity patterns are constantly shifting among constituent units. States that were on opposing sides in a historic civil war may find themselves embattled partners in the struggle to get a fair share of revenue allocation from a burgeoning oil industry now developing in other states — states that may themselves have been enemies but are now united in their efforts to protect a new source of wealth.

Regional Government

One answer to the shifting dilemmas of provincial government is to establish yet another intermediate level of government: the *region*. A region is usually formed by grouping provincial units. It is intermediate government just below the level of the national government and above the level of the province. Occasionally a region is formed *within* a single province, but even then it usually is responsible only to the national government. There are two kinds of regional government, distinguished by the scope of their coverage and also to some extent by how permanently each appears to be embedded in the nation's political system.

Structural Regionalism   In the first kind, **structural regionalism**, provincial units are grouped in regions by constitutional fiat. Regional assemblies, normally composed of elected representatives from the provincial level, meet to deal with matters of regional significance and concern. This kind of regionalism is normally established by constitutional amendment, and the regions thus created are expected to be permanent additions to the body politic. As an example, under the Fifth Republic, France has been divided into twenty-two regions, most of which are made up of several of the republic's ninety-six departments. Each region has its own council, charged with "assuming the burden and receiving the benefits of [the region's] share in the national economic plan."[13] Established by the followers of Charles De Gaulle when the Fifth Republic was created in 1959, the new regions were considerably strengthened by the socialists when they came to power in 1981. The socialist government quickly moved to establish direct elections to the regional councils and to eliminate the requirement that they submit all their deliberations to a regional prefect for approval. These changes have been maintained as the Gaullists have regained control of the French parliament (from 1986 to 1988 and again in 1993).

Structural regionalism has also been used to permit minority nationalities living in compact communities to exercise some degree of autonomous power. China has five autonomous regions: Guangxi Zhuang, Nei Menggu (Inner Mongolia), Nijgxia Hui, Xinjiang Weiwuer (Uighur), and Xizang (Tibet). Although power is still rigorously controlled from Beijing, regional identity permits symbolic remnants of cultural-historical distinctiveness — such as the "Nine Leagues and Forty-Seven Banners" of Inner Mongolia — to be retained (see Figure 12.1).[14]

Functional Regionalism   The second kind of regional government, **functional regionalism**, is more limited in scope. It is usually not a permanent

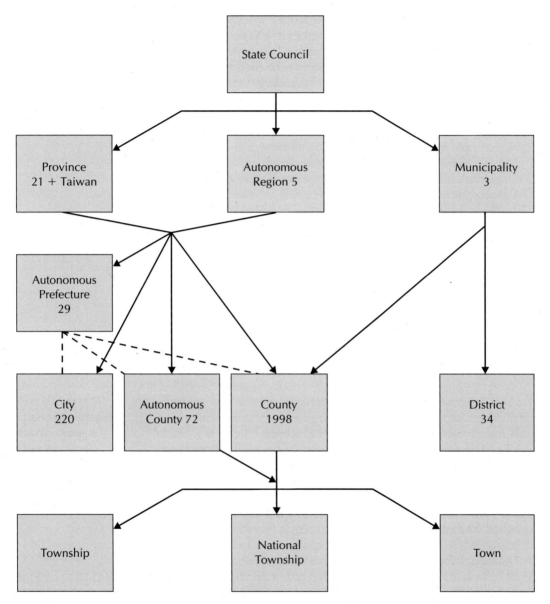

FIGURE 12.1   **China's Governmental Structure**

Source: Eileen Martin Harloff and Cuivi Wei, "Present Day Local Government in China," *Planning and Administration,* vol. 16, 1989–92, p. 115. Reprinted by permission of the International Union of Local Authorities.

structure established constitutionally but rather a short-term statutory solution to current problems that may or may not endure. Such regional governments are normally established to deal with only a single problem, such
as the development of electricity, the conservation of water resources, or
other specific policy areas not easily accommodated by municipal, provincial, or national centers of government. The Bay Area Air Quality Management District (BAAQMD), established to limit air pollution and offensive
odors in the San Francisco Bay Area, is an example of such particularized
regionalism. The district maintains a professional and effective staff, and
investigates some 7,000 pollution complaints per year. It maintains a toll-
free complaint hot line and investigates all complaints, if possible within
45 minutes of the call.[15]

Particularized regionalism develops within provinces as well as above the
provincial level. Beginning as early as 1910, the U.S. Census Bureau recognized the need to identify urban regions, a need that quickly became particularly pronounced in the domain of transportation, since both goods and
people move regularly across municipal and provincial borders. The answer
was to create Regional Transportation Authorities, ranging from New York's
Metropolitan Transportation Authority (MTA) to the Metropolitan Atlanta
Rapid Transit Authority (MARTA) to the San Francisco Bay Area Rapid
Transit District (BART). All are government bodies empowered to deal
with transportation problems within their special jurisdictions.[16]

One of the problems with functional regional governments, however, is
the difficulty citizens (and sometimes even other government officials) may
have in remembering that they exist. Suppose you were annoyed by one
of the following problems:

- a bad taste in the water
- the subway is *always* late
- there are never enough picnic tables available in the park
- traffic control on the bridge you drive across is poorly designed and is
  costing you precious study minutes every day
- your local library never gets the books you order on interlibrary loan in
  time for the papers you have to write

In all these cases, it might well be that the best way to draw attention to
the problem — especially if you live in a large metropolitan area — would
be to register a complaint with the appropriate functional regional government. Would you know which one to call? Take a look at the list in
Box 12.2. Pick one of the problems just listed and imagine yourself living
in Oakland, California. Which agency would you call?

The reasonable answer, regardless of which problem you selected, is
probably, "None of them." Your first call should almost certainly be to your
own local city hall, in order to find out whom to call next. However, functional regionalism is definitely on the rise. One of your questions to city
hall should be: "Is there a regional agency that handles matters like this?"

BOX 12.2

REGIONAL GOVERNMENT IN THE SAN FRANCISCO BAY AREA: AGENCIES AND PURPOSES

Alameda–Contra Costa Transit District (AC Transit). Purpose: Public bus transit

Association of Bay Area Governments (ABAG). Purpose: Areawide comprehensive planning; cooperative action among Bay Area governments

Bay Area Air Quality Management District (BAAQMD). Purpose: Air pollution control

Bay Area Dischargers Authority (BADA). Purpose: To collect data on aquatic wildlife and quality of water; to assess the effect of pollution on San Francisco Bay

Bay Area Rapid Transit District (BART). Purpose: Rail rapid transit system

Bay Conservation and Development Commission (BCDC). Purpose: Regulate filling, dredging, and changes in existing uses of the Bay and shoreline

East Bay Dischargers Authority (EBDA). Purpose: Wastewater disposal

East Bay Municipal Utility District (EBMUD). Purpose: Water supply, wastewater treatment, management of public use lands

East Bay Regional Park District (EBRPD). Purpose: To provide open space, regional parks, trails, recreational opportunities and environmental education for the public

Golden Gate Bridge, Highway and Transportation District (GGBHTD). Purpose: To operate and maintain Golden Gate Bridge, bus and ferry systems

Metropolitan Transportation Commission (MTC). Purpose: Comprehensive regional transporation planning; allocation of state and federal transportation funds

Midpeninsula Regional Open Space District (MSORD). Purpose: Acquisition and preservation of open space lands for low-intensity recreation and greenbelt

Regional Water Quality Control Board (RWQCB). Purpose: To protect the quality of surface and ground-water

Source: Jane Bergen, League of Women Voters of the Bay Area *Decision Makers: Directory of Regional and Inter-County Agencies 1995–1997*, 15th ed. (Lafayette, Calif.: League of Women Voters of the Bay Area Education Fund, 1995). Reprinted by permission of League of Women Voters of the Bay Area.

LOCAL GOVERNMENT

The structures of local government are, if anything, even more varied than those of intermediate or national government. Human beings live in all kinds of aggregations, from isolated hermitages to small farms, from compounds or small villages to suburban settlements, from towns to medium-sized cities to major metropolises of several million inhabitants. With such immense variety, what does it take for government to be "local?" Is a nearby city hall serving millions more local than a distant county seat serving a mere handful of ranchers?

Here we shall interpret **local government** to mean any government that can be physically known to each and every citizen. Local government is government that citizens can quite literally get in touch with — and vice versa. It may be a hard day's drive away, but the ordinary citizen can achieve some degree of personal access to local government, if only to hand over his or her tax payment to a bored bureaucrat. It may be possible for some citizens to acquire the same degree of access to other levels of government, but local government is close and accessible to everyone. (That being the case, you may find it useful to take a break in your reading and go visit some unit of local government yourself. Attending a town meeting, interviewing a mayor or city manager, or just watching your local board of education in action is an excellent way to learn how meaningful this level of government can be to citizens affected by its action.)

Local governments, like provincial and national governments, have rule-making, rule-applying, and rule-adjudicating functions to carry out. However, local government is typically under the control of provincial government — even in federal systems, since the federal principle is never extended to the grassroots. Consequently, mayors, chiefs, councils, and boards all carry out these functions only at the sufferance of higher authorities.

Rule-Making at the Base

The form local government takes is usually determined by the national or provincial governments. The most common rule-making body at the local level is the **elected board** or **council**. Each French commune has its *conseil municipal*. Each Chinese county has a County People's Congress. Each of the main islands of the Cook Islands has an elected Island Council.[17]

These local legislative bodies normally make rules (commonly referred to as *ordinances*) that apply to the local matters over which the central government has delegated them the authority to rule. When national matters assume deep importance locally, a local council may well be tempted to overstep these bounds. A number of American city councils, for example, have taken it upon themselves to declare their cities "nuclear-free." Is nuclear policy always a matter for national policymaking only? Not necessarily, says Albert Donnay, director of Nuclear Free America: "Cities do have a right to regulate what goes on within their border for their own self-interest." The federal government, in sharp disagreement, has taken the matter to court.[18]

However, the more common problem facing local legislative bodies is not how to acquire more or broader rule-making power but rather how to acquire greater resources to finance the programs they would like to carry out under the powers they already have. The tax base of local governments is always limited, the demands of citizens for local government response

A neighborhood meeting in Austin, Texas. The most common problem facing neighborhood groups with specific demands and their local legislative bodies is how to acquire the resources they need to finance the programs they would like to carry out. (Bob Daemmrich/Stock Boston)

to their daily needs are not. Local communes constantly seek new sources of revenue to finance programs that higher levels of government have assigned to their domain (see Box 12.3).

In Norway, for example, local government is responsible for providing day care centers, basic education and primary health care for the elderly. However, the local authorities rely on grants from the central government and income taxes for almost all their revenue, and it is the national government which determines what the income tax rate shall be. Property taxes provide 10 percent of total revenue, but these too are limited by national law. Thus when national growth rates in the overall economy decline or stagnate, the tax base is weakened and central government grants are reduced. At such times, local governments in Norway find it difficult to meet their obligations; they bear the responsibilities for key aspects of social welfare but lack the resources to carry out their functions well.[20]

Even Orange County, California, one of the wealthier communities in

BOX 12.3

LOCAL GOVERNMENT RULE MAKING IN NORTHERN CALIFORNIA

The problem to be resolved at the November 1994 meeting of the Point Arena City Council seemed a simple one: whether or not to buy the "intrinsically safe" radio (a radio that does not spark and can be used at incidents invovling hazardous materials) requested by Fire Chief Nyal Thomas. But Public Safety Commissioner Judy Beier, whose approval was required, was opposed, because, she said, the Fire Chief had not gone through the proper channels. Harbormaster and Director of Emergency Services Bill Pettigrew was so incensed he offered to resign his position, saying he "could not work with a commissioner who was uninformed about firefighting and public safety issues and was unwilling to listen to those who were." Beier replied, "I resent the fact that you say I'm uninformed and untrained. I don't think you're giving me credit for my talent and skills." Councilmember Richie Wasserman urged the parties to get over personality conflicts and work together: "You are all irreplaceable." Fire Chief Thomas wondered if they weren't "burnt out" trying to solve the fire protection problem. Beier offered another reason for holding back on the radio purchase: The California Department of Forestry and Fire Protection would soon be inventorying the city's firefighting equipment and giving the Council a list of the items the City should buy. "Under our contract with CDF," said Beier, "we are obligated to meet this cost." Mayor Raven Earlygrow did not take part in the discussion; he was listening to local election returns on his pocket radio. The matter unresolved, the council moved on to the next item on the agenda.[19]

the world, found itself desperately low on cash at the end of 1994 when several Wall Street brokerage houses refused to renew short-term loans of $12 billion that the county had borrowed in order to develop an investment portfolio worth $20 billion. Unable to repay the loans, the suddenly impoverished government declared bankruptcy.[21] Although it may be hard to work up much sympathy for Orange County, the problem exists throughout the human polity, with more painful results in the poorer nations of the world. In Mexico, says Daniel C. Levy, "muncipalities depend on states and the national government regarding leadership and funds, and funds are very unevenly disbursed; most municipalities lack income beyond very small appropriations and fees from licenses and fines."[22]

Rule-Application at the Base

There is great variation in how local rules are carried out and by whom. The chief executive at the local level may be a traditional *chief* entitled to his post by his place in the kinship system, a *mayor* elected by the people or by the rule-making council, a *city manager* hired by that council, or a *civilian* or *military administrator* appointed by the national government or by the government of a conquering nation. The powers of each of these leaders may be extensive or merely ceremonial. In earlier times, African chiefs sometimes ruled autocratically, but they were more often limited by the knowledge that they could be removed from power if they went too far beyond the will of those they governed. Ashanti chiefs, for example, always knew they could be "destooled" — that is, have the symbol of power, typically a three-legged stool on which no one ever actually sat, taken from them. In contemporary Africa, the chief has often become a merely ceremonial figure, although that status in itself may help him achieve appointment as a modern paid administrator.

The bureaucratic apparatus available for carrying out local rule is similarly varied. City hall may be an elaborate edifice such as the Hotel de Ville in Paris or the kitchen table of a part-time mayor in an Appalachian town. Public service may be more or less personal, more or less efficient, and more or less humanitarian, but in all cases the problems of limited funds, limited powers, and unlimited demands are likely to make themselves felt.

On the other hand, not all local communities have the same response to limited funds, not even within the same nation. Robert Putnam argues that it makes a great deal of difference whether or not the community has strong traditions of civic engagement of any kind. According to Putnam, when citizens routinely take part in their community life — such as reading the local newspapers, joining music or literary societies, or taking part in a soccer club — local government is likely to work well. Civic engagement produces social capital, a reservoir of trust, and makes it possible to get things done even when resources are limited. Anticipating an argument, Putnam insists such communities "did not become civic simply because they were rich. . . . They have become rich because they were civic."[23] He seems to suggest that solutions to the problems of local communities lie in their own hands, regardless of national or provincial funding, regardless of levels of affluence within the community, and regardless of any history of political oppression. (For some interesting figures on the second point — levels of affluence within the community — see Table 12.3.)

A more promising approach to improving the effectiveness of local government may be contemporary efforts that combine local and provincial or national government resources and expertise to combat a local problem experienced in numerous communities throughout a nation. Violence by and against young people became that kind of problem in the United States in the early 1990s, a time when the adolescent homicide rate doubled, when gunfire became a leading cause of teenage death, and when more than 60 percent of persons arrested and charged with crimes were between the ages of 13 and 29.[24]

The sense of crisis that such conditions reasonably produced has been met with a variety of responses attempting to draw on all possible resources. In crime-beleaguered Las Vegas, local and state officials work together to provide counseling, social services, dispute mediation, and other services in local centers, some of which are in buildings provided by private persons. The state of Missouri has set up an Intensive Case Monitoring program that assigns (and pays) college students to tutor, counsel, and "keep a close watch" over juvenile delinquents. The state of Washington has fourteen violence-prevention projects funded with a combination of federal, state and local resources. Such efforts have yet to be evaluated for long-term results, but recent statistics suggest that nationwide the problem remains severe: even as the crime rate among adults is falling, that for those below the age of 25 has been on the rise.[25] It should come as no surprise that those who work in juvenile justice at the local level continue to clamor for more state funds.[26]

TABLE 12.3   **Differences in Income in the Ten Largest U.S. Cities**[a]

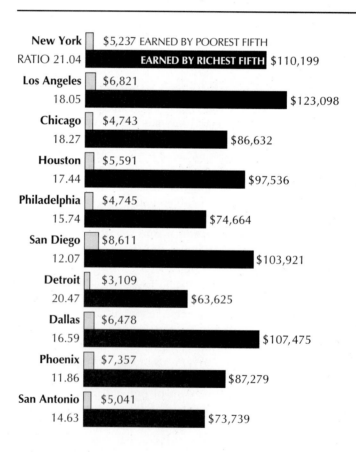

City	Earned by Poorest Fifth	Earned by Richest Fifth
New York (RATIO 21.04)	$5,237	$110,199
Los Angeles (18.05)	$6,821	$123,098
Chicago (18.27)	$4,743	$86,632
Houston (17.44)	$5,591	$97,536
Philadelphia (15.74)	$4,745	$74,664
San Diego (12.07)	$8,611	$103,921
Detroit (20.47)	$3,109	$63,625
Dallas (16.59)	$6,478	$107,475
Phoenix (11.86)	$7,357	$87,279
San Antonio (14.63)	$5,041	$73,739

[a] Median annual incomes of the poorest fifth and richest fifth, with difference expressed as a ratio.
Source: *New York Times,* 26 Dec. 1994, A20.

Rule-Adjudication at the Base

No question of local government is more sensitive than the resolution of disputes. When crimes are committed, reputations are besmirched, or contracts are violated, tempers flare and the human heart reaches out for help — social help. Whether or not that help will be available depends in large part on the local judicial apparatus.

Technically, the local police are not part of that apparatus; their job is simply to carry out the rules. In practice, however, the police are often both the first and the last agency of local justice with which the citizen comes into contact. Typically, police officers arrive on the scene, attempt to calm tempers and impose order, and suggest solutions. Although most police are careful to carry out these duties within the limits of the law, some are not; police racism, brutality and corruption are widespread evils. Comments made during and after the 1992 riots in Los Angeles following the jury's verdict in the case of Rodney King suggest that the massive and costly explosion of anger was caused not merely by the patent unfairness of that one decision but also by the sense of despair so many felt to think that police brutality against persons of minority race was somehow acceptable to white Americans.[27] When "justice is done" on the spot, by a uniformed and armed agent of the executive branch of government, it must be perceived as truly just by all concerned.

Of course, the police do not always have the final judicial word, and it matters a great deal what other, more formally juridical bodies are available at the local level. In many villages, especially those more remote from large centers of population, the lowest level of the judicial branch is a local notable with minimal training and credentials who has been assigned to "keep the peace" by settling minor disputes. In American small towns this may be the justice of the peace; the Nuer people of the Upper Nile River valley used to assign one of their members to be the "leopard skin chief"; and in China, neighborhood committees deal with first-time offenders who have committed minor crimes, seeking to reeducate them, and turn offenders over to public security units only if the deviant act is repeated.[28]

What if the matter is too weighty for such relatively informal adjudication, or the decision seems unsatisfactory and unfair to one of the parties? At this point almost every government provides some way of linking local judicial functions to the national court system. Whether the dispute goes to a municipal criminal court, a small claims court, or a nearby national appeals court, a line is being crossed — away from relatively autonomous local justice and into a national network of courts, appeals, higher courts, and "courts of last resort" (which may not be courts at all; chief executives sometimes personally fulfill that function).[29] Nations that cannot establish such links from local to national systems of justice are not, finally, sovereign states. They are little more than loose confederations — otherwise they would not leave final authority in such an important domain in the hands of local fiefdoms. The effort in the United States to eliminate "vigilante justice" — that is, justice administered by bands of armed men self-appointed to hold others accountable to what they conceived society's norms of righteous conduct to be — was thus a key step in nineteenth-century nation building. Similarly, the Constitutional Council of Nigeria had to find a way to persuade northern Nigerian authorities that citizens in their region had the right to appeal decisions of the Islamic local courts to the secular national court system. Making such links is no easy matter. American vigilantes often had to be treated as criminals themselves before the authority of the national system could be established; in Nigeria the Constitutional Council had to agree that the national courts would include judges well versed in Islamic law, and even then consent was tacit and grudging during that nation's most recent experiment with civilian rule.

Submunicipal Government

Not all local government is at the level of the municipality. When the municipality in question is extremely large (see Table 12.1), smaller ruling bodies are sometimes formed. Most common is a system in which the city is subdivided into *wards*. In such systems each subunit has its own offices, complete with bureaucratic functionaries and executive authority, but operates strictly within the limits set by higher levels of government. These offices are where citizens go to register births, get married, sign children up for school, pay taxes, request and receive social benefits, and register deaths. In a normal, law-abiding, and uncontentious lifetime, a citizen may never come into contact with any higher level of government.

Such decentralization often works well for the citizen as subject, but what about the citizen as participant? To meet the need for citizen participation in local government in large metropolises, still other structures have been devised. One of the most common is the *neighborhood council*, often established in response to national government restrictions that permit such groups to appeal for and employ national funds, or to be consulted when such funds are secured by others for local purposes. Since the councils must normally meet certain standards of institutionalization (for example, having elected officers and regular meetings) to qualify for this kind of involvement in the work of government, they quite naturally develop a permanent identity and become a rallying place for other, more political forms of local activism.[30]

Another form of submunicipal government is the *workers' council*, located in the factory, office, agribusiness, or other large-scale economic enterprise. In France, all the larger corporations are required by law to set up workers' councils, which have the right to help determine such matters as working conditions and fringe benefits problems that are frequently the subject of national government policy.[31] Is this local government? As is often the case, the line between private and public domains is blurred. The businesses in question may be in either the private or the public sector (a large share of French economic enterprise is under state control), and the matters being resolved by the workers' councils are matters that might otherwise be resolved by private employers without government interference or advice. Does the fact that the state requires the formation of the councils make them government bodies? The answer is not clear.

In other, more defined socialist systems, the role of workers' councils as official submunicipal units of government is considerably more obvious. In Cuba, *consejos de trabajo*, composed only of workers, were set up in 1965 and given the power to rule on problems of discipline and violations of labor law. Although these councils originally had a significant degree of power, it was power that the government had given and thus could take away, which is exactly what it did in 1980 with Law 32, a law that transferred most of the workers' power back to management. Since then, not surprisingly, "an overwhelming atmosphere of weariness" characterizes the work of the councils, according to one sympathetic observer.[32]

CENTER VERSUS PERIPHERY: DILEMMAS OF DECENTRALIZATION

As you are no doubt well aware by now, there are no easy answers to the problems posed by the modern state's need for several layers of government. One of the most severe of these problems is the question of the proper relationship between the national government and subnational units. This problem is frequently posed as a struggle in which the "center" (the national government) tries to achieve power over the "periphery" (provincial and local governments), and the periphery fights to maintain its right to exercise power independently. The language itself has a touch of bias. Why should the national government be the center rather than the local city hall, where we achieve our most immediate and often most significant contact with the world of government? Indeed, from the citizen's point of view the national government often rests on the periphery of consciousness, not quite real until it is time to pay taxes or go to war. The terminology used contains an unfortunate hint that it is somehow always better to have expanded central control. However, rather than making up equally awkward and biased substitutes here, we will use the standard language, with the caveat that it must be separately determined in each case whether greater national (central) control over local and provincial (peripheral) arenas of political power is desirable.

Let us pursue the point a little further before turning to examples drawn from reality. Presumably any national government has come into being at least partly in response to a felt need for cooperative endeavor across a wider expanse than the municipality or province can encompass (ministates such as Monaco always excepted). How can these ends be met unless there are national agencies able to engage in centralized planning and allocation of resources? On the other hand, if everything is decided at the center, how can local needs be adequately understood and addressed, and how can the local populace have any sense of involvement and citizenship? Does periodic voting for representatives to a centralized government provide the average citizen with all the "involvement" he or she can handle, and all that is needed to give the actions of that government sufficient legitimacy? Or do the imperatives of local circumstances and individual citizenship require more substantive participation on the local level?

Whatever the answers may be, the tension between the center and the periphery is one of the key characteristics of today's human polity. Two contemporary examples may give us a better understanding of the rewards and perils of centralizing — or decentralizing — the functions of government.

Development, Resettlement, and the Environment in India

The $4 billion Sardar Sarovar Dam planned for the Narmada River in the state of Gaharat in India released a flood of controversy in the early 1990s. Central government planners argued that large dams like this one are "the best answer for drought-plagued and power-short areas," able to transform deserts into "lush agricultural lands" and making jobs for the needy.[33] Others were less certain, noting that the dam would flood tens of thousands of acres, eliminate forests, and submerge many frequently visited religious shrines. Furthermore, the project would force the resettlement of 70,000 persons, relocating many in the state of Madhya Pradesh, and experts and affected citizens alike worried that the resources of the national government and the new state would not be sufficient to compensate those relocated for the losses they would incur. "I don't trust the government," said one threatened citizen, "It makes promises and then goes back on them." A social worker concurred, noting that the losses would be more than economic because those who moved were likely to "be considered inferior, their language is different, and their daughters couldn't be married."[34]

Fishermen as Politicians in Puerto Rico

In La Parguera, a small rural *barrio* on the southwest coast of Puerto Rico, small-scale fishermen felt threatened by plans to develop a marine sanctuary. As the island shifted away from traditional agriculture to a leisure-oriented economy, demand for coastal space had increased and was threatening their existence. In self-defense, they organized to object to industrial pollution of coastal lagoons and estuaries, coastal gentrification, and practices of sand extraction to improve beaches for tourists. The Department of Natural Resources of the Commonwealth of Puerto Rico (DNR) proposed to set aside 68.27 square nautical miles in and near La Parguera as a marine sanctuary. The goal, said the government, was to protect the environment and provide recreational facilities for visitors, but also to "enhance the long-term ability of the resources to sustain the local fishing industry." The fishermen did not believe the DNR, having found several regulations and prohibitions in the proposal which they believed would seriously affect their livelihood. Their two leading associations met together, enlisted the help of Puerto Rican Legal Aid services, and registered their complaints: lack of consultation, U.S. government interference, and fear that a private fishing company would move in once their own independent fishing had been destroyed. They interested the media and roused public opinion, and finally the central government was forced to abandon the project. When the DNR decided, five years later, to present a "management plan for the Special Planning Area of La Parguera," their first step was to set up a consulting program ensuring the full participation of the fishermen. The new plan was accepted by the community and by the fishermen.[35]

Drawing the Lessons   Three of the principal causes for friction between central and local governments when they attempt to interact are illustrated by these two examples. The first is poor communication. The Puerto Rican and U.S. government agencies failed at first to involve the fishermen of La Parguera in planning for a sanctuary that did, in fact, have "several potential benefits for the fishermen and for the community at large."[36] Given its past performance, the word of the Indian government was not enough for those threatened by the Sardar Sarovar Dam. Successful interaction between center and periphery requires mutually respectful communication and consultation.

A second cause is political imbalance. In India, citizens, environmentalists, scientists, and social activists opposed to the Sardar Sarovar Dam united to stage a protest rally but lacked the political organization of state and central governments, which were in turn responding to pressure by the World Bank to speed up the resettlement process. Small-scale producers in the Third World may find it difficult to develop political strategies and actions. The fishermen of La Parguera showed an unusual ability to use and manipulate political resources, the media, and public opinion.[37] Equitable and well-balanced interaction between center and periphery requires that each side be able to rally a constituency of supporters to defend its fair claims and that each be aware of and responsive to the constituency of the other.

A third cause of tension between center and periphery is the struggle for economic gain. Puerto Rican fishermen and leaders of the island's tourist industry battled over the proposed marine sanctuary because the outcome was seen as likely to have an important impact on their respective profits. Builders of the Sardar Sarovar Dam and businesses whose services were needed for the massive resettlement of the citizens involved would profit from the project; those who were being asked to accept the move did not believe they would personally benefit from the new jobs and improved lands the government promised them. Realistic interaction between center and periphery can take place only when both sides recognize such interests, find the means to discriminate between those that are legitimate and those that are not, and arrive at some means of distributing the rewards of their cooperative endeavors fairly among the former.

SUMMARY AND CONCLUSION

Subnational government is government we cannot do without, even if it is also government we cannot always make work in comfortable tandem with national politics. Most polities are simply too large and too complex to be served adequately by a single level of government. It always helps, and is often essential, to have local authorities who understand and can respond to purely local needs, even if the resources must be obtained from higher levels of government.

In a unitary system, all the powers of government are reserved to the central government but may be temporarily delegated to such subunits as states. In a federal system, certain powers are constitutionally reserved to the government of the nation's constituent parts, although the tendency in recent years has been for the national government to assume an ever stronger role. In a confederal system, largely sovereign states maintain a loose association that permits coordinated action on a limited number of matters.

A federal system can free the national government to deal with the more important national issues, allow citizens more meaningful participation at a lower and more immediate level of government, permit governmental experimentation on a limited basis, and allow for the addition and subtraction of constituent units with relatively little turmoil. A unitary system often provides its citizens with more uniform laws, provides for more equal representation and disbursement of government monies, has clearer lines of authority, and avoids the development of independent spheres of power. A confederal system sometimes offers a useful transitional structure as peoples move closer together or further apart.

Whichever kind of larger system they belong to, intermediate levels of government are often caught between the devil of national power and the deep blue sea of local needs and demands. One answer is to establish an additional layer of intermediate government, the region, either as a permanent constitutionally prescribed body of government or as a more particular and possibly less enduring functional agency.

Local government is government that can be physically known to each and every citizen. Its rulemaking functions are normally carried out by elected bodies acting within the constraints imposed by higher levels of government — particularly the economic restraints of a severely limited power to tax or otherwise raise revenues adequate for the services their constituents demand. Local justice is often rendered by an executive agency, the police, and that agency may be responsible to national rather than local authorities, further complicating the relationship between the two. Once the more formal local judicial system is brought into a dispute, the crucial question becomes the nature of the link between that system and the national judiciary. Establishing some such link is essential for maintaining the sovereignty of the state at large.

In larger municipalities the more accessible local government may be submunicipal. Wards, neighborhood councils, and workers' councils are some of the more common examples.

The question of the proper relationship between the national (central) government and local (peripheral) government is difficult to resolve in theory and often impossible to implement in practice. Three key impediments to their successful interaction are failures of communication and consultation, unequal and/or unacknowledged political strength, and the tendency of both to battle with each other and with other, nongovernmental forces over the economic profits to be gained from the resources they control.

As we have seen, subnational governments are essential components of the human polity. Indeed, because they are the governments we have most immediate access to, they are the governments we would most like to see assume a truly human face. But local and provincial government officials occupy a difficult terrain, caught between the multitudinous hopes and aspirations of the citizens they live among and the distant centers of national power whose purposes they must serve to serve their own. If they do not always respond as we might wish, there is nothing to stop us from scorning them in private, and those of us living in systems with free elections may do so openly — blithely throwing the rascals out from time to time. However, before grasping the momentary satisfactions of democratic empowerment, we might sometimes do well to consider the limitations under which they labor, and ponder whether those we propose to send to city hall or to the provincial capital in their stead will be any better able to overcome the restraints inherent in the very principle of divided government power. In the next chapter we turn to yet another set of constraints operating on government officials — at local, provincial, but especially at national levels — the nature of relationships among all the nations of the world.

Selected Readings

Beer, Samuel Hutchison. *To Make a Nation: The Rediscovery of American Federalism.* Cambridge, Mass.: Belknap Press, 1993. A readable study of the origins of federalism in the United States.

Bennett, Robert J. *Local Government in the New Europe.* New York: Halstead Press, 1996. Examines local government systems and the process of political decentralization throughout Europe.

Berry, Jeffrey M., Kent E. Potney and Ken Thomson. *The Rebirth of Urban Democracy.* Washington, D.C.: Brookings, 1993. How citizens in five major U.S. cities collaborated with their governments to bring about positive change in their communities.

Burgess, Michael, ed. *Canadian Federalism: Past, Present and Future.* New York: Leicester University Press, 1991. Essays on the evolution of Canadian federalism.

Cairns, Alan C. *Charter versus Federalism: The Dilemmas of Constitutional Reform.* Montreal and Kingston: McGill-Queen's University Press, 1992. The role of the constitution in Canadian society, with an emphasis on how the Charter of Rights and Freedoms introduced in 1982 has affected the relationships between the national government and the provinces.

Duchacek, Ivo D. *The Territorial Dimensions of Politics Within, Among and Across Nations.* Boulder, Colo.: Westview Press, 1986. Examines the relationships of local, regional, national and international territories, as well as federalism and the degree of centralization.

Levy, Gary and Graham White, eds. *Provincial and Territorial Legislatures in Canada.* Toronto: Toronto University Press, 1989. A series of studies on local government with particularly good chapters on Saskatchewan, Quebec and Alberta.

Lewis, Norman. *Inner City Regeneration. The Demise of Regional and Local Governments.* Buckingham, Pa.: Open University Press, 1992. Argues that local governments in the U.S. suffer from a "legitimation deficit" and lack of the power and resources to cope with the socioeconomic decline of older cities.

Mabileau, Albert, et al. *Local Politics and Participation in Britain and France*. Cambridge: Cambridge University Press, 1990. A collection of essays exploring the ways in which reforms in local government and administration have changed opportunities for the French and British citizen to participate in government.

Michelmann, Hans J. and Panayotis Soldatos, eds. *Federalism and International Relations: The Role of Subnational Units*. Oxford: Clarendon Press, 1990. Essays on the performance of federal systems as actors in international relations. Cases include Australia, Austria, Belgium, Canada, Germany and Switzerland.

Schumaker, Paul. *Critical Pluralism, Democratic Performance and Community Power*. Lawrence, Kansas: University Press of Kansas, 1991. Focuses on the policy-making process at the community level of government and examines how decisions about the distribution of public resources are made.

Notes

1. The Brazilian federal constitution allows the states of that nation to divide or join with others freely, a right that is quite frequently exercised — as recently as 1988 a former Brazilian territory, Fernando de Noronha, became part of the state of Pernambuco. See "Brazil," in Arthur S. Banks, ed., *Political Handbook of the World* (New York: CSA Publications, 1991), p. 82.

2. Article 67, sec. 8, and Article 89, sec. 4, General Principles of the Constitution of December 1982 adopted by the Fifth Session of the Fifth National People's Congress. From "The People's Republic of China," *The Europa World Year Book*, vol. 1 (London: Europa Publications Ltd, 1994), pp. 781, 783.

3. *New York Times*, 1 Nov. 1995, A9, and *San Francisco Examiner*, 1 Nov. 1995, A16.

4. Ulrich Kloti and Kurt Nussli, "Constitutional Reform in Switzerland: Task-Distribution, Political Ideals and Financial Interests," in Michael Burgess, ed., *Federalism and Federation in Western Europe* (London: Croom Helm, 1986), p. 187. The Tenth Amendment was added to the U.S. Constitution to make it completely clear that "the powers not delegated to the United States by the Constitution, nor prohibited by it to the States are reserved to the States respectively, or to the people." Martin Shapiro, ed., *The Constitution of the United States and Related Documents* (New York: Appleton-Century-Crofts, 1966), p. 22.

5. T. N. Brewis, *Regional Economic Policies in Canada* (Toronto: Macmillan, 1969), p. 107; Anthony G. S. Careless, *Initiative and Response: The Adaptation of Canadian Federalism to Regional Economic Development* (Montreal, McGill-Queen's University Press, 1977), p. 205; Ivo D. Duchacek, *The Territorial Dimension of Politics Within, Among, and Across Nations* (Boulder, Colo.: Westview, 1986), pp. 94–95, 149–50, 169–70, 236.

6. Duchacek, *Territorial Dimension of Politics*, p. 68.

7. Kloti and Nussli, "Constitutional Reform in Switzerland," p. 187. Ivo D. Duchacek distinguishes among *polyethnic federations*, in which each constituent unit has a clear ethnic identity of its own, such as in Myanmar; *mixed federations*, in which some units are ethnically defined and some are not (e.g., Canada, India, Switzerland, and Nigeria) and *monoethnic federations*, in which, no matter how great the ethnic diversity of the nation at large, none of the constituent units is based on the ethnic identity of its inhabitants (the United States and Australia). See *Territorial Dimension of Politics*, pp. 107–108.

8. Colin Campbell, Harvey Feigenbaum, Ronald Linden, and Helmut Norpoth, *Politics and Government in Europe Today*, 2nd ed. (Boston: Houghton Mifflin, 1995), p. 430.

9. *Le Monde*, 21–22 June 1992, p. 3. See also *The Economist* 323, no. 7765 (June 27, 1992): 55.

10. Campbell et al., *Politics and Government in Europe Today*, pp. 496–99.

11. Andrei Shoumikhin, "The Chechen Crisis and The Future of Russia," *Comparative Strategy*, 5:1, 1996, 1–10.

12. Divish Petrof, "Siberian Forests Under Threat," *Ecologist* (Nov./Dec. 1992): 167–70.

13. Henry W. Ehrmann and Martin A. Schain, *Politics in France*, 5th ed. (New York: HarperCollins, 1992), pp. 370–84.

14. Eileen Martin Harloff and Cuiyi Wei, "Present Day Local Government in China," *Planning and Administration* 16 (1989): 115.

15. Noga Morag Levine, "Between Choice and Sacrifice: Constructions of Community Consent in Reactive Air Pollution Regulation," *Law and Society Review* 28, no. 5 (1994): pp. 1051–53.

16. For an argument that new regional agencies in transportation and other areas of government are needed now, see *Los Angeles Times*, 19 Jan. 1990, A24.

17. Except the island of Rarotonga, which is divided into three tribal districts (*vaka*). *The Europa World Yearbook, 1991*, vols. 1 and 2, 32d ed. (London: Europa, 1991).

18. *New York Times*, 8 Sept. 1989, A10 and 22 Dec. 1989, B6. In April 1990, a federal district judge ruled that a 1988 ordinance proclaiming Oakland, California a nuclear free zone "interfered with the Federal Government's constitutional authority over national defense and atomic energy." *New York Times*, 18 April 1990, A11.

19. Lisa Walker, "City Council Tackles Dispute Among Safety Officials," *Independent Coast Observer* 16, no. 33 (11 Nov. 1994), 1, 10.

20. Rune J. Sørensen and Arild Underdal, "Coping with Poverty: The Impact of Fiscal Austerity on the Local Budgetary Process in Norway," *Scandinavian Political Studies* 16, no. 1 (1993): 58 and 59. See also Gunnar Rongen, "Efficiency in the Provision of Local Public Goods in Norway," *European Journal of Political Economy* 11 (1995): 253–64.

21. *New York Times*, 7 Dec. 1994, 1, C5.

22. Daniel C. Levy, "Mexico: Sustained Civilian Rule Without Democracy," in Larry Diamond, Juan J. Linz, and Seymour Martin Lipset, eds., *Democracy in Developing Countries: Latin America*, vol. 4 (Boulder, Colo.: Lynne Rienner, 1989), p. 470.

23. Robert D. Putnam, "The Prosperous Community: Social Capital and Economic Growth," *Current* (October 1993): 4–9.

24. Carla Nielsen et al., "Youth Violence," *State Government News* (August 1994): 20–35. In 1991, 27 out of every 100,000 persons in Calhoun County, Florida were children killed by gunfire. Other cities have lower rates, but it is hardly reassuring that the figure was "only" 3.9 per 100,000 in Cook County, Illinois, 5.6 in Baltimore, 2.6 in Las Vegas, 6.6 in the Bronx, 4.7 in Dallas, and 4.8 in Los Angeles.

25. *New York Times*, 6 May 1966, A1.

26. Nielsen, "Youth Violence," p. 23.

27. "Don't white folks . . . believe in justice?" wondered one African-American commentator. "After all, they're the ones who created the Constitution and the Bill of Rights." *New York Times*, 1 May 1992, A12; see also *Los Angeles Times*, 2 May 1992, A2, A20, and 3 May 1992, A1, A14. For a general study of the role of the police as mediators in neighborhood disputes, see Wayne A. Kerstetter, "Who Disciplines the Police? Who Should?" in William A. Geller, ed., *Police Leadership in America* (Chicago: American Bar Association, 1985), pp. 149–82. Of course, police brutality is not only an American problem. For stories regarding abusive behavior by police in Japan, Canada, and Mexico, see *Washington Post*, 30 April 1990, A13, A19; *Christian Science Monitor*, 31 July 1991, 4; and *New York Times*, 1 April 1992, A3.

28. See E. E. Evans-Pritchard, "The Nuer of the Southern Sudan," in M. Fortes and E. E. Evans-Pritchard, *African Political Systems* (London: Oxford University Press, 1940), pp. 291–94 and James C. F. Wang, *Contemporary Chinese Politics: An Introduction*, 2nd ed. (Englewood Cliffs, N.J.: Prentice Hall, 1985), p. 123.

29. For a contemporary example of vigilantism, this time in Venezuela, see Diana Jean Schemo, "Lynch-Mob Justice Growing in Poor Sections of Caracas," *New York Times*, 12 May 1996, A4.

30. Jeffrey Berry, Kent E. Portnoy, and Ken Thompson, *The Rebirth of Urban Democracy* (Washington, D.C.: The Brookings Institution, 1993), 65.

31. William Safran, *The French Policy*, 4th ed. (New York: Longman, 1995), p. 30.

32. Janette Habel, *Cuba: The Revolution in Peril* (London and New York: Verso, 1991), pp. 81–85.

33. *Christian Science Monitor*, 11 Oct. 1990, p. 6.

34. Ibid.

35. Manuel Valdes-Pizzini, "Fishermen Associations in Puerto Rico: Praxis and Discourse in the Politics of Fishing," *Human Organization* 49, no. 2 (Summer 1990): 164–72.

36. Valdes-Pizzini, "Fishermen Associations in Puerto Rico," 172.

37. Ibid., 164.

13 International Relations

CONTEMPORARY ISSUES OF INTERNATIONAL POLITICS
Proliferation of Arms
Protection of Human Rights
International Impact of Ethnic Nationalism
Protection of the Environment

THE ACTORS IN INTERNATIONAL POLITICS
Changing Rules of the Diplomatic Game
Intelligence Versus Espionage

ORGANIZING INTERNATIONAL POLITICS
Treaties: Functionally Limited Pacts
Regional Organizations
The United Nations

THE CONDUCT OF INTERNATIONAL POLITICS: LAW VERSUS FORCE
International Law
Warfare: The Politics of Force

SUMMARY AND CONCLUSION

ONCE UPON A TIME, when we were young and not so foolish, my husband, our small son, and I spent a year living on a boat moored on the Seine, in the heart of Paris. The boat was one of several small but livable craft rented out to an international community of young people like ourselves, newly arrived in Paris, ready for adventure and unwilling to move into any of the dingy apartments we could otherwise afford. In the midst of this enthusiastic group lived one middle-aged woman, the mother of a young Englishman, who had come along to "keep boat" for him. She, unlike the rest of us, was less than thrilled with her accommodations. She didn't mind the low ceilings, the butane heaters, or even the way the dishes rattled in the galley every time a barge went by. But she was sure she would never be able to bring this nautical home up to her own standards of cleanliness. "Because you know, my dear," she told me in her haughtiest British tones, there in the middle of Paris, "foreigners are always so dirty."

Some of us are never foreigners, at least not in our own eyes. Either we never travel, or when we do we move through the world so immersed in our own sense of nationhood that we never really see the world at all. Such uncompromising chauvinists go beyond patriotism. They believe not only that their nation is the best nation, but that it is the only one that really matters. In some cases, they suffer from **xenophobia**, the fear or hatred of anything foreign or strange.

This book is dedicated to the principle that all nations, and all their citizens, matter. The human polity is the composite of all the world's polities. But is there really such a thing as "the human polity?" Is there a whole that is greater than — or at least different from — the sum of the parts? Throughout this book we have discovered a number of similarities in the politics and government of the world's nations, and a number of signs of their interdependence. But by and large we have continued to treat different nations as distinct and separate entities. Now we will look more closely at the interrelationship among polities, the *inter-nation*, or *international*, relationships. Although these relationships almost always stem from the efforts of individual nations to expand or defend their territorial, material, and cultural goods, they have inevitably produced a vast web of global interdependence. It is this web of interdependence that gives substantive content to the idea of a human polity.

In this chapter we will consider some of the more important contemporary issues of international politics and the ways such politics are conducted: the nature of the principal actors, the organizations and treaties that give international relations structure and coherence and the rules of law and force that govern behavior in the world arena. By chapter's end we should be in a better position to assess the extent to which the citizens of the world may be starting to conceive of themselves as global compatriots — rather than just themselves, the good guys, versus the others, the dirty (or primitive, or pagan, or warmongering, or fanatical, or oppressive) *foreigners*. We should have a clearer notion of whether the human polity really exists or is just the figment of one former foreigner's imagination.

CONTEMPORARY ISSUES OF INTERNATIONAL POLITICS

Many of the contemporary crises of international politics have been deliberately provoked by nations exercising force against other nations in order to pursue what they perceive to be their own best interests. When Iraq invaded Kuwait in 1990 and when the United States led a concerted retaliatory attack on Iraq in 1991, the participants knew they were making trouble for other polities. When arms were taken up in 1992 by Russians against Chechnyans (and vice versa) and by Serbs against Croats (and vice versa), everyone knew the effect on international relations would be painful and direct.

Other international controversies grow out of policies that apply directly only to domestic matters but are intended to have an indirect effect on other nations. The proposal that American cars be required to contain a certain proportion of "domestic content" raw materials was intended to curb foreign takeover of the U.S. market for steel. The limit the British place on the amount of cash their citizens can take abroad is designed to improve that nation's balance of payments vis-à-vis other nations.

Still other crises in world affairs evolve from decisions policymakers make largely out of domestic concerns. When the Clinton administration placed a 100 percent tariff on thirteen Japanese luxury cars in 1995 to force Japan to open its market to American cars and car parts, the American president was clearly more interested in pleasing U.S. labor unions and voters whose jobs were threatened than in improving relations with Japan.[1] And even policies that seem not to be related to international relations at all — such as those that govern labor-management relationships, redistribute land, break up monopolies, or seek to stimulate small business — can have a lasting influence on the role a nation plays in the world economy, and thus on the fortunes of other nations that depend on the global marketplace.

But whether a nation's policies are focused on foreign or domestic affairs, whether they are openly belligerent or only indirectly influential on other nations' destinies, the growing interdependence of individual polities has so extended the scope of international politics that almost *any* course of action undertaken by a single nation will have some influence on the well-being of one or more other nations. To illustrate the impact of our increasing interdependence in international relations, we turn now to some of the key issues of great concern in global politics today, beginning with the proliferation of arms.

Proliferation of Arms

The principle of *national sovereignty* suggests that each nation has the right to decide whether to protect itself by armed force, and if so, what kind of arsenal and how large a one to develop. Yet no single national decision has more far-reaching effects on citizens throughout the world.

For most of the second half of the twentieth century, the problem of arms control was above all the problem of avoiding nuclear war between the Soviet Union and the United States. In this time period, beginning with the year when the United States developed and deployed its first operational atomic bomb, the two nations spent approximately $15 trillion in the effort to stay ahead of each other in the arms race. By the 1960s, the massive financial drain on the two economies, along with the growing awareness of the impossibility of finding satisfactory solutions for the disposal of hazardous waste produced in the process, provoked recurring efforts to arrive at international agreements to limit the proliferation of such weapons, and the two nations began slowly moving — much too slowly, many believed — toward disarmament. Considerable progress had been made by the time of the breakup of the Soviet Union in 1991, and in June 1992 the United States and Russia agreed to eliminate within eleven years all multihead intercontinental ballistic missiles and to reduce by two-thirds the number of nuclear warheads each possessed.[2] The world was free to turn its attention — and its fearfulness — away from the threat of superpower apocalypse to the more mundane but equally dangerous problem of massive global proliferation of weaponry, nuclear and conventional. Although only the United States, Russia, Britain, France, and China were "full

The dangerous work of arms control. A United Nations Special Commission inspection team consisting of 50 persons representing fifteen nationalities carries out an investigation of Iraq's largest chemical weapon production facility. Here an inspector from the Netherlands measures the volume of nerve agent in a container. (United Nations Photo 158837)

nuclear weapon countries," at least ten other nations were known to be capable of manufacturing such weapons, and there was a strong belief that four others — Israel, India, South Africa, and Pakistan — had in fact done so. Nine more had built or were capable of building nuclear bombs but were so far "refraining" as signatories to the 1968 Nuclear Nonproliferation Treaty. Some wondered how long Iran, Libya, Egypt, Syria, and North Korea could be kept out of the "nuclear club," and almost everyone worried about Iraq (also a treaty signatory), whose purchase of a "research" reactor from France in 1976 was revealed during and after the Gulf War to have been merely the first step in a massive hidden program for the development of the bomb, a program that no one was certain had been fully crushed by the war.[3]

    At the same time, proliferation of conventional arms seems to be moving ahead unchecked. By 1990, the United States had become the biggest supplier of weapons to the Third World and to the Middle East; in that year

American sales reached a record of $18.5 billion, up 42 percent from the year before. In second place was the Soviet Union, with $12.1 billion sales, and distant but still awesome third and fourth places were taken by China, with $2.6 billion, and France, with $2.3 billion worth of arms sales agreements (see Figure. 13.1). Soviet sales had been falling, but in the fall of 1991 they rose again as the disintegrating federation began selling off some of its own arsenal in an effort to help its ailing economy. All told, Third World purchases reached a total of $301.7 billion in the period 1983 to 1990, with Saudi Arabia buying about 19 percent of the total (78 percent of all American arms sales), and Iraq another 10 percent.[4]

What can be done about such dangerous proliferation? Many believe the United Nations International Atomic Energy Agency (IAEA), the body charged with policing the Nonproliferation Treaty, could and should be given the power to engage in "radically more intrusive inspection" and to extend its domain to chemical and biological weaponry as well. Acting on the recommendations of its Committee on Disarmament and International Security, the UN General Assembly has passed numerous resolutions stressing the need to bring about the complete elimination of nuclear weapons, to initiate a moratorium on the export of landmines, and to "curb the illicit transfer and use of conventional arms," but the closest it has come to taking action in this domain seems to be its recent request to the International Court of Justice for an advisory opinion on whether the "threat or use of nuclear weapons in any circumstance" was permitted under international law.[5] The difficulty the international community has in moving beyond pious talk is clearly compounded by the fact that First World economies, struggling to overcome high rates of unemployment and negative balances of payment, show little sign of imposing voluntary curbs on one of their most profitable exports: the instruments of death (see Figure 13.1)

Protection of Human Rights

Another major issue in contemporary international politics is the violation of human rights by governments who imprison, torture, and execute their own citizens. Often these citizens' only offense is political dissent. The military weapons and methods now available to control domestic populations have made tyranny more fearsome than ever before; even the most determined band of dissidents is a poor match for the strength of the modern police state. When dictatorships are ruthless in the execution of policies designed to eliminate protest, the only hope of their oppressed citizenry is likely to be appeal to more powerful external forces — that is, to other nations and to world opinion.

The Universal Declaration of Human Rights, adopted in Helsinki, Finland in 1975, states that "everyone has the right to life, liberty and security of person." The exercise of political power to deny these basic rights is certainly not a new phenomenon in human history, but the scale of punishments meted out to those who attempt to exercise such rights has

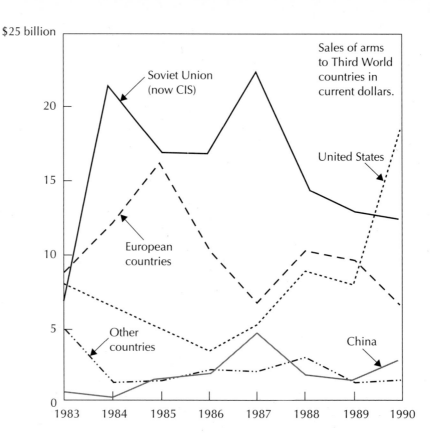

FIGURE 13.1   ***Third World Arms: The Sellers***

Source: *The New York Times,* August 11, 1991, p. 10. Copyright © 1991 by The New York Times Co. Reprinted by permission.

reached truly horrifying proportions as twentieth-century technological efficiency is exhibited in the instruments and strategies of oppression. China's swift and bloody suppression of the student-led democracy movement in 1989 deeply dismayed a watching world, as did the revelations that in the Philippines Fernando Marcos had ordered some 50,000 persons to be arrested, detained, and, in many cases, tortured and killed.[6] Elsewhere — out of camera range, as it were — other appalling events have been taking place in the past quarter of a century. Over 500,000 people were killed by the Indonesian army, assisted by gangs of youths belonging to a fundamentalist Muslim party, in the nine months following the attempt of dissidents to overthrow the government in 1965. In Cambodia under Khmer Rouge rule (1975–1979), between 1 and 3 million people were killed in a series of purges that began with the highest officers of the preceding government and worked steadily downward through lower officials, intellectuals, teachers, students, members of ethnic minorities, and finally even members of the current government who were considered less than 100 percent loyal to the leadership. The numbing statistics go on: Up to half a million killed in Uganda during the eight-year rule of President Idi Amin (1971–1979); 5,000 political opponents killed in a single Ethiopian city in a three-month period (November 1977–February 1978); more than 80,000 killed in Burundi in the spring of 1972; 11,712 noncombatants killed in El Salvador during 1981; as many as 20,000 persons described as "the disappeared" in Argentina between 1976 and 1984; about 20,000 Hindu Tamils killed in Sri Lanka since 1983; and over 25,000 persons killed from 1980 to 1992 in the fighting between members of the Sendero Luminoso (Shining Path) guerrilla movement and three successive Peruvian governments.[7]

Every one of these numbers is made up of a series of individuals — of human lives. A man or woman or child woke up, considered the day ahead, got dressed, ate whatever breakfast was available, and sallied forth to death. Such assassinations and massacres are not only committed outside anything that can be called the law, they are for the most part entirely unwarranted even on grounds of fear of opposition. Whole ethnic groups or social classes are labeled undesirable. Their most innocent and nonpolitical members are killed indiscriminately along with the dissenters — and of course those who have dissented have frequently done so only by means that would be considered legitimate and fair in polities that respect human rights. Furthermore, these figures — far from complete — say nothing of the even greater numbers of people who are imprisoned and tortured by such governments. Nearly half of the 184 nations that make up the United Nations are believed to be holding in prison people whose only offense is their beliefs or origins. Since 1979, 60 nations have been accused of practicing torture.[8]

Such wholesale contempt for human life and liberty is a major issue in international relations today, and a wide range of international remedies has been sought. Declarations and covenants abound: the Nuremberg Charter, the Geneva Conventions, the International Covenant on Civil and Political Rights, the American Convention on Human Rights, the African Charter on Human Rights, and the European Convention on Human Rights are the six most widely cited. Although their high-sounding language may seem a weak defense against ruthlessness on the scale we have just reviewed, these covenants provide the necessary definitions and distinctions on which to base more substantive intervention. (For example, they set standards for fair trials, for legal use of the death penalty where serious crimes have been committed, and for "acceptable" killings during times of war and other armed conflicts.) The UN Human Rights Commission is devoted to the protection of human rights, and regional organizations such as the European Parliament, the Inter-American Commission on Human Rights, and the African Commission on Human and Peoples' Rights have also sent fact-finding missions and published reports identifying abuses of human rights.[9]

One of the most powerful international agencies in the struggle to protect human rights is a private group, Amnesty International. Founded in 1961 and awarded the Nobel Peace Prize in 1977, this organization has emphasized wide publicity for human rights violations and has organized international visits and letter-writing campaigns as a way of bringing pressure to bear on governments responsible for human rights violations (see Box 13.1).

The problems posed by arms proliferation and human rights violations are the result of national policies that have had the effect of endangering the safety or outraging the sensibilities of the larger human polity. But some of the issues that have acquired international significance are caused as much by the activities of particular groups, companies, or individuals as by globally unacceptable national policies. Two examples here are ethnic nationalism and devastation of the global environment. We have considered both problems earlier (see Chapters 1, 4, 5); our purpose now is simply to say a few words about how the international community tries to act, collectively, to resolve such issues, and the difficulties it inevitably encounters in doing so.

International Impact of Ethnic Nationalism

Among the 184 independent nations represented at the United Nations today, there are over 8,000 distinct ethnic cultures. Some ethnic groups are, of course, perfectly content to live within existent national boundaries, but others — or subcommunities of others — are not. They may insist they need a separate nation of their own — that is, they wish to *secede* — or they may seek to add territory not presently included in their own nation state. The latter desire is known as *irredentism*, a word that means, literally, "unredeemed-ism" and, in practice, refers to the conviction that there exists a territory outside a state that properly belongs to that state and thus need to be "redeemed."[10] The collapse of the Soviet Union brought a quantum leap in the number of groups certain the time had come to satisfy their urge for secession or irredentist expansion (see Table 13.1).

As news reports have made amply clear to us all, efforts to achieve such desires have led to massive slaughter and destruction and to spillover effects of increased ethnic violence in neighboring countries, yet the countervailing efforts of the international community have often been disappointingly ineffectual. According to Karin von Hippel, this failure has been owing in part to the fact that there are so many unanswerable questions arising out of every case, such as whether or not the new state will be economically viable, how minorities within it will be treated, and what

BOX 13.1

AMNESTY INTERNATIONAL: FIGHTING FOR HUMAN RIGHTS WITH PRIVATE MEANS

Amnesty International, a private organization based in New York City, describes itself as "a worldwide movement working impartially for the release of all prisoners of conscience, fair and prompt trials for political prisoners, and an end to torture and executions." One way the organization works is to send its members a monthly "Freedom Writers" newsletter, telling of two or three cases of human rights violations that the organization has investigated. Members are asked to write protest letters to the authorities responsible for the unfair trials, imprisonment, and/or torture being endured, and to send short postcards of encouragement to the victims as well. Addresses are provided, as well as sample letters that can be used. Here is a typical case, reported in the July 1996 newsletter:

> **Zhao Lei** and her husband **Bai Weiji** are serving prison sentences of 6 and 10 years respectively for "illegally providing national secrets to a foreigner." The information they reportedly provided — news articles and reports on economic and foreign policy — would not be considered secret in many other countries. Bai Weiji had worked for the Foreign Ministry but lost his job when he organized workers to support the pro-democracy demonstrators in Tiananmen Square in 1989. Zaho Lei is also a former employee of the Foreign Ministry. She and her husband have a five-year-old daughter. Please send cards [addresses of Zhao Lei and Bai Weiji are given].

Usually the newsletter has some good news to report as well, although not every case has a happy ending. Here are some "Case Updates" from the same issue of the newsletter:

- **Kelthoum Ahmed Labid El-Ouanat** of Morocco/Western Sahara (May 1996 *Freedom Writer's Bulletin*) — Released from prison along with five co-defendants.
- **Wafa' Wasfi Ahmad** of Kuwait (October 1994 *Freedom Writer's Bulletin*) — Released from prison.
- **Jose Luis Grave de Peralta Morell** of Cuba (February 1994 *Freedom Writer's Bulletin*) — Released from prison.
- **Zikrayat Mahmud Harb** of Kuwait (August 1993 *Freedom Writer's Bulletin*) — Released from prison.
- **Thomas Wainggai** of Indonesia (May 1991 *Freedom Writer's Bulletin*) — Died on March 12, 1996, while being transferred from prison to a hospital.

Amnesty International also holds annual regional conferences throughout the world; works on special problems (for example, a worldwide campaign to help refugees in 1997); sends its representatives to meet with government officials; publishes an annual report and *Amnesty Action,* a quarterly newspaper, in addition to the newsletter; and raises private funds to pay for its actions. It limits itself to "state-backed human rights violations" and does not focus on abuses perpetrated by individuals.

Sources: *Freedom Writers* (July 1996), *Amnesty Action* 19, no. 1 (Winter 1996) and New York Times, 16 July 1995, A10.

TABLE 13.1

Countries and Claims Deriving from the Collapse of Communism and the Former Soviet Union

States	Other Claimant States, Disputed Subregions, or Persecuted Minorities
Albania	Greece[a]
Bulgaria	Ethnic Turks
Hungary[b]	
Bosnia-Herzegovina	Muslims, Croats, Serbs[c]
Croatia	
Slovenia	
Yugoslavia (Serbia & Montenegro)	Kosovo,[d] Vojvodina, Novi Pazar Sanjak
Macedonia (FYROM)[e]	Greece[f]
Czech Republic	
Slovakia	
Estonia	Ethnic Russians
Latvia	Ethnic Russians
Lithuania	Ethnic Russians
Armenia	
Azerbaijan	Nagorno-Karabakh[g]
Belarus	
Kazakhstan	
Kyrgyzstan	
Moldova	Dniester and Gagauzia[h]
Romania	Ethnic Hungarians, Transylvania region[i]
Russia	Chechen-Ingushetia, Kaliningrad, North Ossetia,[j] Siberia, Tatarstan, Volga region
Tajikistan	Kulyab, Leninabad oblasts
Turkmenistan	
Ukraine	Crimea, Northern Bukovina, Serpents' Is., Transcarpathia
Uzbekistan	
Georgia	Abkhazia, South Ossetia Karelia and Petsamo[k]

[a] Ethnic Greeks in southern Albania are worried about their treatment by the government of Albania, and some want to federate with Greece.

[b] There are approximately 3,160,000 ethnic Hungarians living outside Hungary, and they fear persecution in the countries where they now reside. Of that total, 2 million are in Romania, 600,000 in Slovakia, 400,000 in Serbia, and 160,000 in Ukraine. The Hungarians claim a slightly higher total of 3.5 million.

[c] All three groups claim persecution.

TABLE 13.1   *Continued*

---

^dEthnic Albanians make up a minority in Kosovo and are worried about ethnic cleansing by Serbs.

^eMost states recognize it as the Former Yugoslav Republic of Macedonia (FYROM).

^fGreece recognizes the region as a separate state, but not the use of the name "Macedonia" for this part of the former Yugoslavia. Greece fears that such recognition will generate irredentist claims on the people living in the Macedonian area of northeastern Greece who also speak the Macedonian language.

^gNagorno-Karabakh wishes to join Armenia, and likewise, Armenia claims it.

^hDniester and Gagauzia oppose any Moldovan attempt to join with Romania.

ⁱDisputed between Hungary and Romania.

^jThe Christian North Ossetians are fighting the Muslim Ingushetians.

^kDisputed between Russia and Finland.

Source: Karin von Hippel, "The Resurgence of Nationalism and Its International Implications," *Washington Quarterly* 17, no. 4 (Autumn 1994): 194. © 1994 by the Center for Strategic and International Studies (CSIS) and the Massachusetts Institute of Technology. Reprinted by permission of MIT Press Journals.

constitutes a legitimate base for a secessionist or irredentist claim ("does the fact that the Arabs and the Moors inhabited Spain for almost 800 years between C.E. 711 and 1492 entitle Morocco to lay claim to present-day Spain?").[11] Others have stressed the dangerous tendency to take sides when such conflicts erupt rather than focusing on peacemaking activities that recognize that in most cases no group or state has all the justice and honor — nor all the guilt and blame — on its side alone.[12] Most seem to agree that the earlier the international community recognizes and responds to the problem the better. Ted Gurr and Barbara Harff urge a steadily escalating involvement, beginning with fact-finding missions and widespread publicity early on, followed by the offer of "political and material incentives to encourage contenders to reach agreements," but going as far, when and if the situation worsens, as the use of collective military intervention.[13] The real world is not, however, always that neat: and it is sometimes only after collective military intervention has failed to bring peace that exhausted contenders can be brought to the bargaining table. The case of Bosnia and Herzegovina, Croatia, and Serbia and Montenegro is a case in point (see Box 13.2).

Protection of the Environment

One reason the whole world must pay attention to the problem of environmental degradation is that the whole world seems to be guilty of creating the problem. Pollution and consumerism have resulted in the destruction of 90 percent of the coral reefs in the Philippines; the total fish catch off the northwest coast of the United States has fallen 32 percent since the 1970s; the giant panda of China is on the endangered species list; the

BOX 13.2

TEXT OF THE AGREED BASIC PRINCIPLES ENDORSED BY THE FOREIGN MINISTERS OF BOSNIA AND HERZEGOVINA, CROATIA, AND SERBIA AND MONTENEGRO, SEPTEMBER 8, 1995.

1. Bosnia and Herzegovina will continue its legal existence with its present borders and continuing international recognition.

2. Bosnia and Herzegovina will consist of two entities, the Federation of Bosnia and Herzegovina as established by the Washington Agreements, and the Republica Srpska (RS.)

2.1 The 51 : 49 parameter of the territorial proposal of the Contact Group is the basis for a settlement. This territorial proposal is open for adjustment by mutual agreement.

2.2 Each entity will continue to exist under its present constitution (amended to accommodate these basic principles).

2.3 Both entities will have the right to establish parallel special relationships with neighboring countries, consistent with the sovereignty and territorial integrity of Bosnia and Herzegovina.

2.4 The two entities will enter into reciprocal commitments (a) to hold complete elections under international auspices; (b) to adopt and adhere to normal international human rights standards and obligations, including the obligation to allow freedom of movement and enable displaced persons to repossess their homes or receive just compensation; (c) to engage in binding arbitration to resolve disputes between them.

3. The entities have agreed in principle to the following.

3.1 The appointment of a Commission for Displaced Persons authorized to enforce (with assistance from international entities) the obligations of both entities to enable displaced persons to repossess their homes or receive just compensation.

3.2 The establishment of a Bosnia and Herzegovina Human Rights Commission, to enforce the entities' human rights obligations. The two entities will bide by the Commission's decisions.

3.3 The establishment of joint Bosnia and Herzegovina public corporations, financed by the two entities, to own and operate transportation and other facilities for the benefit of both entities.

3.4 The appointment of a Commission to Preserve National Monuments.

3.5 The design and implementation of a system of arbitration for the solution of disputes between the two entities.

Source: *U. S. Department of State Dispatch* 6, no. 37 (11 Sept. 1995): 679–80.

birthrate in Uganda (and in many other nations) is more than seven children per woman; and every year 5,335 square miles of forest is destroyed in Brazil.[14] The problems are severe almost everywhere. Among the industrialized nations they appear to be worst of all in eastern and central Europe, where, according to Ronald A. Taylor, four decades of ignoring even the most minimal requirements for clean air and water have produced a nightmare of environmental pollution, ranging from contaminated drinking water in Bulgaria to apples and lettuce laced with lead in Poland.[15]

Although such problems must receive the attention of individual nation-states, the international community has been taking an ever more active collective role in addressing the issue. The United Nations conducts research and fact-finding missions, tries to raise global consciousness of the importance of these problems, and works to bring its members together in international meetings where common ground can be found and agreements reached on the remedies required. Its Conference on Environment and Development (UNCED), popularly known as the Earth summit, was one such meeting, held June 13–14, 1992 in Rio de Janeiro, Brazil. The meeting brought together 178 national delegations (including 117 heads of state) to study the key problems of the environment: global warming, overpopulation, pollution, and endangered species. The conference produced an "Earth Summit" treaty with twenty-seven non-binding "principles" for the good management of the resources of the planet; Agenda 21, a program of action containing 800 measures from which each country could choose its own priorities; and three considerably more specific agreements concerning the exploitation of forestlands, maintaining biodiversity, and reducing atmospheric pollution. The United States was the only nation to refuse to sign the biodiversity agreement, claiming it imposed unacceptable restraints on U.S. biotech industries. The agreement on reducing atmospheric pollution had neither a calendar nor a rigorous set of standards. But on the whole the conference was considered a success.[16] Other United Nations activities in the domain of the environment have included its establishment of a Convention on the Law of the Sea and a Global Environmental Monitoring System.[17] Outside the UN, the World Commission on Environment and Development is another worldwide organization that has worked to accomplish the same ends.

THE ACTORS IN INTERNATIONAL POLITICS

Who participates in international politics? The answer that first comes to mind is a simple one: individual nations. But it is more and more common for private groups as well as nation states to work actively in the international sphere, and even nations must act through individuals. Who, then, are the key actors in international politics? In a certain sense, all of us are. We may act openly, taking part, for example, in a letter-writing campaign denouncing the continued imprisonment of a Chinese dissident or telephoning the office of a chief executive to say how deeply we approve or disapprove of a particular treaty or (more likely) act of war. But even our private acts help influence the course of world events. The decisions an individual consumer makes about whether to take her vacations by air, train or car have their impact, however small, on whether or not the United States will decide to upgrade its railway system to European standards by importing a rapid train system from France, Japan, or Germany (presently the three leaders in this industry). The unwillingness of a Japanese farm community to sacrifice its land for the building of a new international airport shapes that nation's ability to engage in foreign trade. Your own readiness or reluctance to register for the draft or to urge others to do so must be taken into account when your nation's leaders calculate their preparedness to use military means to secure the ends they seek.

Similarly, the acts of a wide range of public officials help shape the course of international relations. Local politicians, for example, may work hard to create conditions that will convince foreign investors to establish production facilities — and create jobs — in their communities, even when they would prefer to be able to do without the foreign capital. Jyoti Basu, chief minister of the Indian state of West Bengal, recently toured the United States and Europe with twenty-seven of Calcutta's top industrialists to publicize the city's political stability, skilled workforce, local democracy, falling birthrate and rising literacy. A lifelong Communist who has held his office for eighteen years, the 82-year-old Basu has accepted the pressures of global capitalism. "I am forced to do certain things," said the minister, conceding that, given present circumstances, "when PepsiCo came here and took over a sick company . . . it was very good. I'm not interested in their drinks but they've done good work in Punjab with food processing."[18]

Legislators and executives at the provincial level can also be significant actors in international relations. They can create conditions that foster or impede the development of export commodities, the demand for imported goods, the growth of defense industries, the willingness to accept refugee populations, or the establishment of cultural ties. National legislators perform all these roles as well, and often have the further responsibility of approving treaties, declaring wars, and appropriating the funds to carry out a nation's international commitments. As we have already noted, chief executives normally play a leading role in establishing as well as executing foreign policy, aided by a more or less vast bureaucratic apparatus devoted to that task. Nor is it uncommon for judges to have their say in this domain, ruling the terms of particular treaties valid or invalid, or judging the behavior of citizens lawful or unlawful according to its conformity with international agreements that have become the law of the land.

In recent years private groups and enterprises have taken an increasingly active role in international politics. In the European context, such organizations are referred to as *Eurogroups*. Although some authors, such as Ernst B. Haas, predicted that the growth of supranational bodies would lead automatically to federations of national interest groups, in practice most national associations have not yet been willing either to provide the necessary funding nor the necessary spirit of transnational cooperativeness to give such activities effective power. The result has been, especially in the realm of private business, a determination to go it alone. As Andrew McLaughlin, Grant Jordan, and William A. Maloney have shown, in such cases individual businesses do not hesitate to bring their own "distinct corporate interests" into the international arena.[19]

Nevertheless, among the various participants in international affairs, members of the world's executive branches and departments still hold the lead in making and carrying out the decisions that shape relations among nations. In doing so, however, they customarily rely on two other sets of actors whose work deserves closer scrutiny: the members of the **diplomatic corps** and their sometimes shadowy colleagues, the officers of the world's **intelligence agencies**.

Changing Rules of the Diplomatic Game

The job of the diplomat has changed a great deal during our century. One hundred years ago, the work was by and large a gentleman's game, played according to extremely formal rules by the frequently aristocratic representatives of chief executives who were themselves often autocratic potentates, accountable to no electorate. At the same time, existing modes of transportation and communication meant that diplomats were taken more seriously by their hosts as national spokespersons. It was impossible for other senior government officials to engage in impulsive globetrotting or to pick up a telephone and check out the information they were given by another nation's diplomats or by their own overseas representatives through their slow-moving couriers' pouches. Negotiations were often conducted in the greatest secrecy, and lip service at least was given to the idea that a diplomat's word of honor was as good as his bond.

The spread of democratic institutions, the development of much more efficient means of transportation and communication, and the emergence of the new and more compelling issues of interdependence discussed in the previous section have changed forever the world of the diplomat. In today's world the public is far better informed about diplomatic exchanges. Chief executives often serve as their own diplomats at summit meetings. At other times they send such high-ranking emissaries as foreign ministers and secretaries of state — officials who in the past stayed home and issued orders to others — to enter into negotiations with their counterparts overseas. The inevitable result is a lessening of the significance of the role played by resident diplomats, who now engage in a number of public relations tasks that would have seemed beneath their dignity in other days — putting in dutiful appearances at trade fairs, football games, and television talk shows.

Another difference in today's diplomatic game is the role of *third party nations* in disputes between other nations. It is now much more common for nondisputant nations to take a major role in international conflict resolution. Sometimes those outside the conflict consider themselves implicated in the dispute and seek to interfere in order to produce a satisfactory outcome. At other times the disputants themselves are more concerned about the possible effect of their debate on nonparticipants than they are about resolving matters between themselves.

The visits of U.S. secretaries of state to the Middle East in the late 1980s and the 1990s provide a good case study for several of these developments. The persistent efforts of George Shultz, James A. Baker, and Warren Christopher to find solutions for the points of discord between Israel and the Arab states offer excellent examples of the high-ranking statesman serving as diplomat, of a third-party nation (the United States) taking part in the diplomatic negotiations between two other nations, of an effort to use diplomacy to impress yet other parties, and of the tendency to conduct diplomacy far more openly than in the past. In recent years it has also provided an interesting insight into how the activities of diplomats may be shaped not only by their own governments but by other interests within the nations they represent. While seriously pursuing peace negotiations, the Clinton administration has at the same time put more and more emphasis on "dollar diplomacy" in the Middle East, seeking to improve U.S. business opportunities in the area and to launch projects such as "Partnership for Growth," an economic agreement initiated with Egypt in 1995 in order to increase U.S. investment in Egypt, boost contacts between the two countries' private sectors, and intensify trade flows.

Leon Hadar believes the new stress on trade (over aid) is owing to the nature of U.S. electoral politics; he claims the administration is working to serve "the interests of the most powerful and skillful players in the political game in Washington, those who can deliver votes, raise funds, and manipulate the media."[20] According to Hadar, this means paying particular attention to Saudi Arabia, a wealthy nation whose purchases of U.S. goods can "create jobs in key electoral states" and to Israel, a nation befriended by Jewish-Americans whose votes are critical, often in the same states.[21] Others take a more positive view of the same tendencies, seeing the development of business links with and within the Middle East as in fact a crucial step in achieving peace: "Israel used to be a nation of 3 million surrounded by 40 million enemies. Now, it's a nation of 5 million surrounded by 60 million customers."[22] Of course, diplomats have always been involved in questions of international trade as well as questions of war and peace, but the ever-growing global economy makes the link between the two clearer now than ever before.

Summit level diplomacy. In 1993, the prime ministers of Japan (Morihiro Hosakawa) and Great Britain (John Major) reviewed Japanese troops during the G7 meeting held in Japan that year — and discuss questions of mutual interest to their two nations. (© 1993 Jose Caldeira/Black Star)

This link is very strongly apparent in the meetings of the Group of Seven, commonly referred to as G-7, an annual meeting of the prime ministers and presidents of the world's largest industrial nations. The agenda of these summit meetings always includes many matters of economic concern with global significance, such as the development of an international telecommunications system or the creation of a worldwide emergency fund for nations on the verge of bankruptcy.[23]

Intelligence versus Espionage

To deal effectively with one another, the policymakers of the world's nations must be well informed about one another. Some information is readily acquired, either by specialists at home or by experts in the diplomatic corps abroad. A trip to the library, reading the newspapers, paying a few friendly visits, or simply making an open request for the facts may be all that is necessary. However, when relations between nations are unfriendly or when the information in question concerns the military materiel and procedures necessary to maintain security against foreign attack or internal subversion, the inquiring party is likely to encounter a formidable wall of secrecy. In the sometimes strange language of international relations, gathering information about another nation is called gathering *intelligence*. If the other nation would prefer that the information not be known and it must therefore be gathered by covert means, the attempts to acquire it are called *espionage*.

Whether operating openly or covertly, intelligence agencies do not, by their nature, seek publicity. We have probably all heard of the U.S. Central Intelligence Agency (CIA) and the Soviet Committee of State Security (better known as the KGB), but how many of us know that it was the Mossad, Israel's intelligence agency, that rescued 103 hostages from terrorists at Entebbe, Uganda, on July 4, 1976? Or that it was Australia's Security Intelligence Organization (ASIO) that arranged for the defection of Russian diplomat Vladimir Petrov and his wife in 1954 and kept them under protection ever after? Even the British intelligence agency is not well known, despite the popularity of the spy stories that come from that nation's presses. We may know what the fictitious British agent James Bond calls his boss, but who knows the real name of the British agency? It is, simply, the British Secret Intelligence Service.

The proclivity of intelligence agencies for secrecy is closely related to another of their characteristics: a readiness to intervene in the internal political or economic processes of other nations based on the information they have gained. International jurisprudence generally takes a dim view of such behavior. "The basic principle of international law," notes one specialist in that area, "is that of respect by each sovereign state for the territorial integrity and political independence of others." [24] However, this principle is often set aside in time of war — spying during wartime has greater legitimacy than spying during peacetime. This may prove to be of small comfort to any captured spy: "A spy, if captured in the act, can be executed after trial," say the experts. However, "his activities are not dishonorable, his government is not violating law in sending him, and his act is not, therefore, a war crime. Espionage is a legitimate belligerent operation." [25]

The more difficult problems with the ethics of intelligence operations arise in times of peace. The tangled history of the CIA over the past twenty years illustrates how hard it has been for U.S. citizens to decide what they really believe an intelligence agency should be authorized to do when the nation is not at war but has key interests abroad. The revelation that agents of the CIA regularly planned and carried out assassinations, bombings, and other violent activities, up to and including the overthrow of popularly elected governments, stimulated public condemnation in 1974 and a number of congressional investigations, leading to the formation in 1976 of two additional oversight committees, one in each house, and to the passage in 1978 of the Foreign Intelligence Surveillance Act insisting that federal warrants be issued before electronic surveillance could be used in suspected cases of foreign espionage, terrorism, and sabotage.

By 1981, however, the year Ronald Reagan came to office, public opinion had shifted again and new administration's determination to "revive" the CIA met with strong approval. The agency steadily regained some of its former liberty of action and its reputation as "an aggressive Cold War weapon." It also resumed the practice of hiding some of its more delicate and controversial operations from Congress itself, including its involvement in the Iran-Contra scandal (the secret and illegal transfer of profits made from the sale of arms to Iran to guerrilla groups fighting the established government in Nicaragua) in the mid-1980s. The scandal caused by the revelation of these activities and the agency's failure to prepare the government or the nation for the collapse of the Soviet Union and the consequent revolutionary change in the politics of Europe undermined the agency's newly restored reputation.

Once again, however, the agency has made a comeback. Democratic president Bill Clinton promoted the position of agency director to a cabinet-level post, insisting that that official should play a stronger role in setting national security policy and at the same time making clear his approval of industrial espionage. The battle for economic supremacy having replaced the Cold War, the secrets to be discovered are now in the business world. (As one observer put it, "You want a spy, the CIA's got spies for you.") At the same time, the agency launched a new effort to improve its standing in Congress, asking its agents to develop better personal ties with members of that body, and to educate themselves regarding their "special interest areas."[26]

ORGANIZING INTERNATIONAL POLITICS

Two factors making political relations between nations difficult are the unpredictability of significant economic, social, and political events and the impossibility of foreseeing the impact of such events on international relations. Gathering good intelligence helps reduce the element of surprise, and maintaining diplomatic relations improves the international community's chances of responding effectively to sudden crises. Another way the nations of the world attempt to gain some mastery over the course of history is by making pacts with one another — agreeing to engage in certain activities or promising to do so in the event of certain other developments. Such pacts may be made between as few as two nations. They may take the form of regional organizations, and such associations may make and remake the terms of their relationship with further pacts. Or the pacts among nations may assume worldwide proportions.

Treaties: Functionally Limited Pacts

The treaty is a time-honored means of organizing the relations between nations. The Stele of Vultures, a document that records the terms of peace insisted upon by Eannatum of Lagash in Babylonia after he defeated the

A treaty made in the hope of ending war. The presidents of Serbia (Slobodan Milosevic), Bosnia (Alija Izetbegovic), and Croatia (Franjo Tudjman) sign the Dayton accords, November, 1995. (Mikhail Shultz/Sygma)

city-state of Umma, was written nearly 4,500 years ago. Another almost equally ancient treaty that archaeologists have discovered is a friendship treaty between the city-states of Lagash and Uruk. The best known of the ancient agreements is the treaty made 3,200 years ago by the Hittite king Hattusilis III and Ramses II of Egypt after the battle of Gadesh.[27]

Treaties are made for a wide range of reasons. They may be intended to offer assurance to the signatories that if one of them is attacked the others will come to its aid, as in the North Atlantic Treaty signed by the United States and eleven other nations in 1949, in which the partners agree to consider an armed attack against one or more of them in Europe or North America an attack against them all. The role — and possible expanded membership — of NATO has been under serious discussion since the fall of the Soviet Union and the end of the Cold War. Will those against whom the alliance was formed now join it as cooperative members? Will the alliance become an agency for keeping or restoring peace in the world's trouble spots? Or are other functions likely to develop? At the present time, it seems reasonable to predict only that, as in the case of the CIA, the functions of this institution are likely to continue to change in response to changing circumstances, while the body itself remains in place.[28]

Treaties may also be made in an effort to reduce the chance of war, as in the series of arms limitations agreements between the United States and the Soviet Union toward the end of the Cold War (see p. 467). Treaties may be made at the conclusion of a war, spelling out the terms of dominion of one nation over another, as when the Fulani people conquered the Mande people of west Africa in the middle of the eighteenth century and demanded that the Mande respect the laws of Islam or turn over their land to those who did.[29] Or the terms of peace may be considerably less demanding, as at the conclusion of the Gulf War, when little more was actually demanded of Iraq than its withdrawal from Kuwait and its leader Saddam Hussein was allowed to remain in power.[30]

Treaties are also made for purely peaceful purposes, often in the realm of international trade. The scope of such treaties may be broad indeed; the principal signatories (Canada, the United States, and Mexico) of the North American Free Trade Agreement (NAFTA) have a combined population of 370 million people and gross domestic product of $6.8 trillion. The main provision in NAFTA is a schedule of tariff reduction on manufactured goods that will lead to their total elimination by the year 2009. The signatories are still unsure what the long-term effects on their economies will be, especially in the case of Mexico, where some see the likelihood of vastly increased foreign investment as making that nation the main beneficiary of the treaty and others insist that poorer Mexicans will be forced out of their own economy, losing their land and their jobs to the economic "readjustments" made necessary by the treaty.[31]

Treaties may also be much more limited in scope, such as those that settle border disputes between two nations or clarify the conditions under which the citizens of one nation may visit or emigrate to the other. Yet even such limited pacts may well have wide significance. When Germany and Poland signed a 1991 treaty fixing the borders between them, they were seeking to end centuries of debate, mistreatment of each other's emigrating citizens, and frequent armed aggression. The signing of this treaty was seen as a key moment in the creation of a "common European house" in the postcommunist era.[32]

Treaties made for economic or cultural purposes are often intended to ensure not only that the question at hand will be satisfactorily resolved but also that relations between the parties will remain peaceful in the future. Such a wish is not always well founded. The fact that Great Britain and Argentina were able to agree in 1974 on the "Supply and Marketing in the Falkland Islands of Argentine Petroleum-Based Products" did not prevent those nations from going to war over possession of the islands in 1982, and it remains to be seen if the 1991 economic treaty between the United States and Argentina, which provides for the repatriation of U.S. profits and sets standards for the expropriation of U.S. property, will be more successful.[33]

Regional Organizations

Often even the simplest treaties entail the establishment of some form of organization to carry out their provisions. More elaborate treaties necessitate more elaborate structures, and if these in turn prove successful, they

BOX 13.3

MAJOR REGIONAL ORGANIZATIONS FORMED SINCE WORLD WAR II

Year	Organization
1947	Economic Commission for Europe (EEC)
1948	Organization of American States (OAS)
1949	North Atlantic Treaty Organization (NATO)
1949	Council for Mutual Economic Assistance (COMECON)
1952	Australia, New Zealand, United States Security Treaty Organization (ANZUS)
1955	Warsaw Treaty of Friendship, Cooperation and Mutual Assistance
1957	European Economic Community (the Common Market)
1960	Central American Common Market (CACM)
1960	Organization of Arab Petroleum Exporting Countries (OPEC)
1961	Organization of Economic Cooperation and Development (OECD)
1963	Organization of African Unity (OAU)
1967	Association of Southeast Asian Nations (ASEAN)
1973	Caribbean Community (CARICOM)
1975	Economic Community of West African States (ECOWAS)
1991	Commonwealth of Independent States (CIS)
1991	Southern African Development Community (SADC)
1991	Southern Cone Common Market (MERCOSUR) (Argentina, Brazil, Paraguay, Uruguay)
1992	Council of the Baltic Sea States (CBSS)
1992	European Union (evolved from European Community)
1995	North American Free Trade Agreement (NAFTA)

Source: *The World Factbook 1995* (Washington, D.C.: Central Intelligence Agency, 1995), pp. 485–521 and *Europa Yearbook, 1987*, vol. 1 (London: Europa Publications, 1987), pp. 90–211. Reprinted by permission.

sometimes inspire the formulation of further treaties and further structures. In some cases the process thus begun can lead to the formation of new states, as formerly distinct entities move from functional cooperation to national integration. It is easy enough to find historical examples; contemporary Italy, Germany, and Switzerland were all formed after a long period of treatymaking between independent principalities. But can it still happen today? What are the chief regional organizations of today? What are the chances that new national entities will emerge from them?

The list in Box 13.3 answers the first question. Here we will examine some of the possible answers to the second question by looking at two examples: the European Union and the Organization of African Unity (OAU).

The European Union   A condition of the American Marshall Plan, initiated after World War II to assist in the rebuilding of Europe, was that the recipients work out a single plan for the distribution of any aid received. In response, French foreign minister Robert Schumann proposed the creation of a single authority to control the production of coal and steel. In 1952, France, former West Germany, Italy, Belgium, Luxembourg, and the Netherlands signed the European Coal and Steel Community Treaty. This was no simple treaty; although its terms covered only coal and steel, the well-known intention of at least some of the signers was to develop eventually a wider-ranging European Common Market — and possibly even a single European nation, roughly equal to the Soviet Union and the United States in territory, population, and natural resources.

In the first years of the ECSC's existence, the partners made rapid progress toward these goals — so rapid that in 1957 the Treaty of Rome was signed, creating the European Economic Community (EEC). The EEC abolished all customs duties among the member countries and established a Council of Ministers, an Executive Commission, and a Court of Justice. Ten years later, in 1967, a European Parliament was added. However, for the first twelve years of its existence the European Parliament was a non-elected body with no legislative functions. Representatives were appointed by the member nations as they saw fit, and the parliament's function was simply to oversee the work of the Executive Commission. The parliament had the power to force the resignation of the commission by a two-thirds vote, and in 1975 it gained the power to amend any draft budget submitted to it by the Council of Ministers. But not until 1979 did Europe hold its first direct elections to this parliament, and many of those elected had campaigned by promising to prevent any expansion of the parliament's power that might threaten national prerogatives or sovereignty.

It was almost the end of the twentieth century before whatever hopes the European Community held for a united Europe could be viewed as anything but that: hopes. The worldwide economic recession that began with the oil shortages of 1973 was sharply felt by most of the member states (now including the Denmark, Greece, Ireland, Portugal, Spain, and the United Kingdom as well as the original six; Austria, Finland, and Sweden have voted to seek membership as well). It also had the effect of worsening economic relations among them. Former patterns of protectionism began to reestablish themselves, and the members' commitment to free trade among themselves was "chipped away by squabbles over wine, sheep, fruit, and other sensitive items" as individual governments tried to protect native producers against cheap imports.

By the end of the 1980s, however, the twelve partners had agreed that as of 1992 they would eliminate all internal commercial, financial, and customs barriers, thereby creating a truly common market. And when the time came, they may have faltered a bit, but they have nonetheless moved ahead determinedly. In December 1991 and then again in February 1992, the twelve met and produced the Treaty of Maastricht, named after the small Dutch town in which they met and going far beyond the trade agreements originally envisaged. The new treaty called for massive changes in the nature of the community, laying out in detail the steps to be taken toward a new Economic and Monetary Union (EMU) and a new political union (European Union). In the very near future, said the treaty, Europe would have a single currency, a common foreign and defense policy, and common citizenship.

It was not easy to get all the representatives to agree on the details, and the means taken to do so added new meanings to old words in the vocabulary of federalism: Spain, Portugal, Greece, and Ireland had to be reassured with promises of *cohesion*, which now means that states that are to live together should all be of roughly the same economic strength, and that the richer states should make contributions as necessary to the poorer ones, to achieve that end. Once cohesion is achieved, the next step will be *convergence*: Germany, the member state most concerned to assure financial stability and responsibility, insisted that the new Economic and Monetary Union (EMU) should not be formed until at least seven of the members had "converged," meeting fixed criteria regarding rates of inflation, interest rates, national budget deficits, public debt ratio to GDP, and currency stability. Only then would a state be eligible to join EMU, tentatively set for 1996, and use the new single European currency. To reassure the British, always the problem child of the twelve, the treaty gave strong promises to respect *subsidiarity* — that is, to guarantee that no European laws would be made except in the domains specifically set aside for the community or when the objectives could be better realized at the supranational level than by the states acting individually. (To make this promise more secure, the treaty specified that in many areas, especially those of a fiscal nature, decisions could be made only by unanimous vote.) Also to please the British, the treaty gave new meaning to the procedure of *opting in*: Only those nations who wish to are obliged to share in joint making of social policy on such issues as working conditions, equal rights for men and women, social security, and treatment of immigrants. Eleven states immediately "opted in," and Britain's John Major went home happy to report that he had been able to sign without budging an inch (or even a centimeter) from the Thatcher legacy of subordinating social needs to the overriding needs of the British economy.[34]

The new treaty had to meet the test of several referenda and failed the first by a narrow margin, when the Danes voted against it on June 2, 1992.[35] The Irish voted yes by a very large margin a few weeks later, but the positive French vote in September was by a very slim majority. Some important changes were made in the treaty, and Denmark reversed its vote in the following year. In 1994, four other nations voted on whether or not to seek to join the Union: Austria voted yes heartily (66.4% approving), Finland was reasonably enthusiastic (56.9% in favor), Sweden agreed but rather reluctantly (52.2%), and Norway, in a vote that raised a new record for voter turnout, said "no" (by 52.3%).[36]

The road to unity is obviously not an easy one and there have been important setbacks, but progress nonetheless seems steady and sure. Ignoring dire warnings from a cynical new world that the effort to combine social protection with economic progress and fiscal stability is hopelessly out of date in an era of unrestrained free-marketeering, the old world continues to build a yet newer world, a united Europe.[37] By 1995, very few of the 373 million citizens of Europe thought of themselves as purely European; about a fourth of the Belgians, Germans, French, and Luxembourgers were ready to say they were "European first" and their own nationality second, and in every nation but Britain about 50 percent said that although they were their own nationality first, they were "European second." One analyst suggests that Europeans are after all accustomed to a sense of dual nationalism (for example, the Welsh who are British, the Bretons who are French, the Basques who are Spanish) and that it may be easier for them than it might be for others to accept the idea of divided loyalty and divided sovereignty.[38]

The Organization of African Unity   The Organization of African Unity (OAU) was formed in 1963, when thirty-one heads of African states met in Addis Ababa, Ethiopia. There was little agreement at this first meeting as the dignitaries present argued among themselves about whether the new organization should immediately form a common market and work to establish some form of pan-African union, take a much more gradual approach toward the same ends, or focus primarily on lending "unconditional support" to the African peoples still under colonial rule. The last position ultimately prevailed, as eloquently stated by Algeria's president, Ahmed Ben Bella: "Let us all die a little, so that the peoples still under colonial domination may be free and African unity may not be a vain word." The OAU took this mission as its prime reason for existence.[39] By 1983, twenty more nations had gained independence — many of them significantly aided by efforts of OAU member states — and joined the organization; and by 1991 there were fifty-one members states in the OAU.

Besides holding annual meetings, the OAU also organizes meetings on problems of special import, often in conjunction with the United Nations.[40] One such meeting was the International Symposium on Refugees and Problems of Forced Population Displacements held in Addis Ababa, Ethiopia in 1995. There are now approximately 7 million refugees in Africa, ten times the number twenty-five years ago. The OAU identified the root causes as including not only armed conflict and arms proliferation, but also natural disasters, the failures of governments, and poverty so severe that about two-thirds of Africa's population lives below the poverty line and thirty of the poorest countries in the world are on that continent.[41]

Working out of such desperate circumstances, it is little wonder the OAU has found it difficult to meet its own past commitments, in all domains. Yet the organization insists that Africans must "continue to sit down and take care of the problems themselves" and shows little tendency to

BOX 13.4

AFRICAN REGIONAL ASSOCIATIONS[a]

African Development Bank
Central African State Development Bank
East African Development Bank
West African Development Bank
West African Economic Community (CEAO)
Economic Community of West African States (ECOWAS)
Economic Community of Central African States (CEEAC)
Mano River Union (MRU)
Council of the Entente States
Central African Customs and Economic Union (UDEAC)
Economic Community of the Great Lakes Countries (CEPGL)
Southern African Development Coordination Conference (SADCC)
Inter-Governmental Authority on Drought and Development (IGADD)

[a] List does not include Arab regional associations.
Source: Arthur S. Banks, ed., *Political Handbook of the World* (Binghamton, N.Y.: CSA Publications, 1987), pp. 747–54; *The World Factbook 1991* (Washington, D.C.: Central Intelligence Agency, 1991), p. 371.

blame postcolonial exploitation of their resources by First World nations for the fact that Africa is "the only region in the world likely to experience an increase in absolute poverty over the next decade."[42]

Most of the states belonging to the OAU have also pursued their goals through other bodies, such as the United Nations' Economic Commission for Africa (ECA) and several smaller regional associations. There are now more than thirty regional associations in Africa. Among the most important are the sixteen-member Economic Community of West Africa (ECOWAS), focusing almost exclusively on economic ends, and the nine-member Southern African Development Coordination Conference (SADCC), still dedicated first and foremost to the independence of all African peoples (see Box 13.4).

The United Nations   No dream has held greater appeal for humankind than the dream of a united world. Confucius imagined a "Grand Union," Dante yearned for a world monarch, the anarchist Mikhail Bakunin sought a "United States of the World" based on "the right of voluntary union and the right of voluntary separation," and Marxists hoped that "the International Republic of Soviets" might one day be established.[43] Today a World Order Models Project (WOMP) periodically convenes, bringing together scholars from all the world's continents who attempt to devise what they refer to as "relevant utopias" — that is, plans for a world order that are rooted in present reality and so will not be dismissed as mere wishful thinking.[44]

But however strong the appeal of the idea of world government is, at present the institution of the nation-state remains the clearly dominant form of human organization. Intergovernmental organizations that attempt to deny this reality founder or fail to materialize. The ones that take it as a given are more likely to achieve a modicum of success. The United Nations is an example of this kind of more realistic international organization.

The people who drafted the United Nations charter were conscious of the need to recognize the continuing strength of nationalism and thereby avoid the fate of the League of Nations, the world's previous effort to establish international cooperation.[45] The new charter made it clear that no nation would be expected to commit its forces to a military action without internal deliberations and assent. It also avoided repeating what had proved to be another mistake of the League; instead of granting all nations equal voting power, as the League had done, the UN Charter gives the five major world powers (the United States, Russia, China, Great Britain, and France) permanent membership in the organization's strongest "action body," the Security Council, and provides each with the right of veto.[46]

The UN Charter, adopted in San Francisco in 1945 by fifty-one member states, is thus not the blueprint for a world state, nor is it intended to function as one. It is instead a set of rules governing a truly *international* organization, in which each nation's sovereignty is recognized and accepted. The United Nations was established to help preserve international peace and to foster international cooperation in addressing the social and economic problems that plague the human polity. The organization has six governing organs and a wide range of committees, programs, and agencies (see Figure 13.2).

The General Assembly   All the 184 member states of the United Nations are entitled to representation in the General Assembly. According to the United Nations' own description, this body discusses and makes recommendations on "any questions or any matters within the scope of the present Charter," controls the budget, and elects members to the five other governing organs. Originally intended to play a subordinate role to the Security Council, the General Assembly has become increasingly important in recent years as the unwillingness of the Security Council members to cooperate with one another and the veto power of that body's five permanent members have combined to produce successive stalemates in its deliberations. The General Assembly requires a two-thirds majority to decide on the most important matters, but that has on occasion proved easier than getting the Security Council to move of its own accord.[47]

Until 1970, the United States and its Western allies effectively controlled the General Assembly. When checked by Soviet vetoes in the Security Council, this bloc of nations could usually find a means to have its way on major issues. Since that time, however, power in the assembly has shifted away from the Western world, and it is now more likely for blocs

United Nations System

Main and other sessional committees

Standing committees and *ad hoc* bodies

Other subsidiary organs and related bodies

UNRWA—United Nations Relief and Works Agency

UNITAR—United Nations Institute for Training and Research

IAEA—International Atomic Energy Agency

UNCTAD—United Nations Conference on Trade and Development

UNICEF—United Nations Children's Fund

UNHCR—United Nations High Commissioner for Refugees

WFP—World Food Program (UN FAO)

UNDP—United Nations Development Program

INSTRAW—International Research and Training Institution for the Advancement of Women

UNEP—United Nations Environment Program

UNU—United Nations University

WFC—World Food Council

Regional commissions

Functional commissions

Sessional and standing committees

Expert, *ad hoc* and related bodies

WIPO—World Intellectual Property Organization

IFAD—International Fund for Agricultural Development

UNIDO—United Nations Industrial Development Organization

UNDOF—United Nations Disengagement Observer Force

UNFICYP—United Nations Peacekeeping Force in Cyprus

UNIFIL—United Nations Interim Force in Lebanon

UNMOGIP—United Nations Military Observer Group in India and Pakistan

UNSTO—United Nations Truce Supervision Organization in Palestine

Military Staff Committee

Standing committees and *ad hoc* bodies

GATT—General Agreement on Tariffs and Trade

ILO—International Labor Organization

FAO—Food and Agriculture Organization of the United Nations

UNESCO—United Nations Educational, Scientific and Cultural Organization

WHO—World Health Organization

IMF—International Monetary Fund

IBRD—International Bank for Reconstruction and Development

IDA—International Development Association

IFC—International Finance Corporation

ICAO—International Civil Aviation Organization

UPU—Universal Postal Union

ITU—International Telecommunication Union

WMO—World Meteorological Organization

IMO—International Marine Organization

Security Council

Secretariat

General Assembly

International Court of Justice

Trusteeship Council

Economic and Social Council

FIGURE 13.2   The Structure of the United Nations

Source: United Nations publication.

and counterblocs of small, medium, and large states to form and reform as the assembly moves from issue to issue. The Western powers have shifted their focus to other subsidiary bodies (see below).

The Security Council   The role of the Security Council is to maintain international peace and security. Besides its five permanent members (China, France, Russia, the United Kingdom, and the United States), the Security Council has ten members elected for nine-year terms according to rules that ensure geographic representativeness. The Security Council has the right to discuss any situation that threatens international peace, to make recommendations for the resolution of disputes, to require members to apply sanctions against other states, and to make recommendations concerning the regulation of national armaments. On substantive matters, all five permanent members plus four other member states must vote affirmatively — that is, each permanent member has the right to veto any proposal before the council.[48]

The Economic and Social Council   The fifty-four members of this body are elected by the General Assembly for three-year terms. Here, too, every effort must be made to ensure geographic representativeness. The function of the Economic and Social Council is to promote international cooperation in economic and social matters. The council is assisted by a large number of functional and regional commissions, such as the Population Commission and the Western Asia Commission, and by a wide range of specialized agencies, such as the World Health Organization (WHO), the International Monetary Fund (IMF), the United Nations Educational, Scientific, and Cultural Organization (UNESCO), and the General Agreement on Tariffs and Trade (GATT).[49]

The Trusteeship Council   The Trusteeship Council was originally established to assume the role formerly held by the League of Nations Mandate System after World War I. Eleven territories taken from Germany, Italy, and Japan after World War II (by no means all the world's colonies) were placed under its supervision, and the council was directed to promote their political, economic, social, and educational advancement while fostering "their progressive development toward self-government or independence." The council's task was so limited — and has been accomplished so thoroughly — that little remains to be done by this body. Its members are China, France, Russia, the United Kingdom, and the United States.[50]

The International Court of Justice   The fifteen judges of the International Court of Justice (often called the World Court) are elected by the General Assembly and the Security Council for nine-year terms. All must be from different nations. The court has jurisdiction only over cases the members agree to refer to it, but it may give advisory opinions when requested to do so by other UN bodies. The court has sought to establish a reputation for fair and expert deliberation and thus to win compliance with its decisions, but has not been entirely successful in either respect. The United States has been among those nations choosing to comply with World Court rulings only when convenient; a July 1987 ruling outlawing military and financial support for guerrillas opposing the Sandinista government in Nicaragua was repudiated on the grounds that the court had no legal jurisdiction over continuing armed conflicts.[51]

The Secretariat   The Secretariat is the bureaucratic apparatus of the United Nations. It is headed by the secretary-general, who is appointed by the General Assembly on the recommendation of the Security Council, and who is assisted by a worldwide staff of 23,000 persons.[52] The secretary-general has the additional responsibility of bringing to the attention of the organization any matter that seems to threaten international peace.[53]

How Successful Is the United Nations?   Any evaluation of the United Nations, as of most human labors, is likely to be based on the evaluator's hopes for it. Those who believed the United Nations would be a means of keeping perfect peace have been disappointed. Belligerent parties have often ignored its recommendations. Open acts of aggression have been condoned and even encouraged. The organization has never had an enforcement capability sufficient to serve as a genuine deterrent to aggression. It played almost no role in ameliorating or resolving the most serious conflict that has emerged since its birth, the Vietnam War.[54] Its peacekeeping mission in the former Yugoslavia was widely ruled a failure. In other conflicts the UN has found itself enmeshed in situations it can neither leave nor resolve: Blue-helmeted peacekeeping forces have been in the mountains of Kashmir since 1949, in Cypress since 1967, on the Golan Heights since 1974, and in Lebanon since 1978.

But real successes have also been achieved. For years, the UN presence in the Middle East helped keep that troublespot from triggering superpower confrontation. The organization made key contributions to a number of arms control measures: the partial nuclear test ban treaty, the banning of nuclear weapons from outer space and the seabed, and the Nuclear Nonproliferation Treaty. More recently the UN Observer Mission in El Salvador (ONUSAL) monitored a ceasefire and was involved in the entire restructuring of that nation's governing and socioeconomic structures at the end of its civil war. The UN Transitional Authority in Cambodia (UNTAC) supervised and verified the withdrawal of Vietnamese forces in 1992 and helped repatriate and resettle some 350,000 displaced Cambodians; it also eliminated millions of landmines, monitored human rights, and organized and supervised a national election in which 90 percent of the registered voters were able to take part in 1993.[55]

By their very nature, peacekeeping (or, perhaps more accurately, peace-establishing) missions are risky, complicated, costly, and unsure. Over a thousand men and women from more than forty countries have died while in the service of UN peacekeeping forces. The struggles emerging at the end of the Cold War era have greatly increased both the demand and the difficulty of success — by mid-1995, nearly 80,000 UN troops were involved in over 17 peacekeeping operations. In 1993 alone, the United Nations spent $3.7 billion on peacekeeping.[56]

The United Nations has also worked assiduously to improve the world's economic and social conditions. The World Health Organization virtually eradicated smallpox by 1980. The UN Relief and Works Agency has helped millions of refugees. The UN Human Rights Commission investigates situations in countries where human rights violations are believed to occur and other UN agencies are also active in this domain. Its Commission on the Status of Women, ECOSOC, the General Assembly, the UNHRC, and the UNDP Governing Council have all been active in working to improve the condition of women around the globe. Other agencies with important humanitarian and pragmatic accomplishments to their credit include the Food and Agriculture Organization (FAO), the International Telecommunication Union, the International Maritime Organization, the World Meteorological Organization, the International Civil Aviation Organization, and the International Atomic Energy Agency.[57]

But although every nation in the world has benefited in one way or another from such activities, the United Nations has nevertheless been disappointing to many. The shifting terms of the global economy naturally produce confusion and anger, and sometimes that anger is directed against the United Nations as well as against competing nations. Those who are negatively affected argue that the UN should broaden its interpretation of "unfair trade practices" and act to restrict practices in other nations that are making the old terms of trade impossible to maintain.[58] Others are simply ready and eager to make the most of the new opportunities and would like the UN to work in ways that are useful to them. Yet another group of UN watchers can be found among those who are concerned that the emerging global economy may create a global underclass containing the less fortunate members of all our polities; they believe the UN must work against that likelihood. In figuring out where they stand on these questions — and on the role they would like to see played by the United Nations — US citizens would do well to keep in mind that their own nation is by far the strongest member not only of the UN but also of such increasingly powerful international bodies as the International Monetary Fund, the World Bank, and the GATT (see Chapter 4). Its power is not likely to be severely affected by adverse votes in the General Assembly for a long time to come.

Meanwhile, despite the bad press and its sometimes genuinely disappointing performance, the United Nations continues to win strong support across the globe. An important accolade came in 1988 when the body won the Nobel Prize for peace, but this support has also been reflected at the level of ordinary citizens in the opinion polls that have been conducted by the agency in twenty-five nations every year since 1989. Recent polls have shown a strong awareness of the existence of the UN (at or above 90% in over half the countries) — even though less than 50 percent of the population in twenty-two of the twenty-five nations could remember having been taught about it in school. More significantly, a strong plurality of the respondents assessed the organization's performance as good (far fewer said it was poor; many said they did not know if it was good or poor). The main reason offered by the minority who thought the UN was performing poorly was that it did not have enough power and authority to do its job properly; others saw the organization as too dependent on great world powers and political blocs. It may be something of an exaggeration to claim that there has always been "general agreement by [the] peoples of the world that the United Nations is the only hope for international peace and security and that it is an essential institution for the advancement of social and economic development," but that the UN is "truly a symbol and instrument for peace and human progress" seems difficult to deny.[59]

THE CONDUCT OF INTERNATIONAL POLITICS: LAW VERSUS FORCE

The actors in international politics may be elected officials, diplomats, or secret agents. They may work individually or within complex organizational structures. In any case, their behavior — where it is not purely careerist and self-serving — is likely to be guided by respect for two often contradictory principles: the rule of law and the rule of superior force. In international relations guided by respect for law, the final appeal in any dispute is properly made to the World Court, where the principles of international law are developed and applied. In relations between nations that are governed by respect for superior force, the final appeal is likely to be to strength in battle — to warfare. The net result of the world's mixed adherence to these two principles is the web of power relationships at any given time: victor to defeated, colonizer to colonized, superpower to satellite, peer to peer.

International Law   The international actor guided by respect for the rule of law must sometimes make a difficult choice between national and international law. If the two are in conflict, the choice is very likely to be made in favor of the national law; at the present time, the surest protector of the cultural identity and military security of any state remains that state itself. Yet even the most resolutely autonomous state can no longer help but recognize the need for a modicum of global social order. New conditions that threaten the internal order of all nations but can only be solved on a global scale — such as international terrorism, control of outer space, exploitation of marine resources, the need for restraints on transnational corporations, and pollution of the biosphere — force the evolution of new international law.

And although this new law evolves within a tradition of respect for the sovereignty of individual nation-states, it is often only by showing respect for those rules that the nations of the world can have any hope of there being sufficient order and prosperity to permit any of them to pursue their separate ends. One of the clearest signs of how well this principle is now understood appeared in 1994 when the writers of the new Russian constitution expressly included treaties and customary international law in their domestic legal system. In areas such as human rights, the writers of the constitution formulated Russian domestic law by making direct reference to international law.[60]

Thus the body of international law continues to grow, gradually receiving greater and greater acceptance. The International Law Commission, an auxiliary of the United Nations General Assembly, has taken on the job of codifying international law in a wide range of fields. More specialized groups, such as the International Labour Organization and the Intergovernmental Maritime Consultative Organization, have helped to spell out accepted principles of law in their respective domains. Drawing from established customs, generally accepted principles of law, and specific treaties or conventions, the writers of international law have established rules to govern relations between nations. These rules cover such matters as the recognition by states of one another's sovereignty (including the granting of diplomatic immunity), the establishment of frontiers on land and water, the acquisition and loss of territory, the human rights of aliens and citizens, the making of treaties, the responsibilities of international organizations, the arbitration of third parties in international disputes, the conditions for the legal use of force, and the conditions governing nuclear testing.

Warfare: The Politics of Force

When you see millions of the mouthless dead
Across your dreams in pale battalion go,
Say not soft things as other men have said,
That you'll remember. For you need not so.
Give them not praise. For, deaf, how should they know
It is not curses heaped on each gashed head?
Nor tears. Their blind eyes see not your tears flow.
Nor honour. It is easy to be dead.[61]

The attitude of Charles Sorley, later killed at the age of 19 in the Battle of Loos in World War I, was not typical of the young men Britain sent to fight in that war. He refused to accept what another poet who shared his views referred to as "the old Lie" — that it is sweet and proper to die for one's country (*dulce et decorum est pro patria mori*). A more common response in those days — and still not unknown in our own cynical times — was that of Sorley's fellow poet in arms, Rupert Brooke.

Now, God be thanked who has matched us with His hour
And caught our youth, and wakened us from sleeping,
With hand made sure, clear eye and sharpened power

> To turn, as swimmers into cleanness leaping.
> Glad from a world grown old and cold and weary.
> Leave the sick hearts that honour could not move,
> And half-men, and their dirty songs and dreary,
> And all the little emptiness of love! [62]

What causes human beings to prefer to settle disputes by the use of armed force? Theoreticians of war suggest almost as many plausible explanations as there have been wars. We will consider only the following condensed list, giving each rationale for war the name of the author or scholar most commonly associated with it.

The Brooke Argument   War provides an opportunity to exercise some of the finer human qualities not called for in peacetime: self-sacrifice, courage, heroism, and devotion to a cause larger than oneself.

The Hobbesian Argument   War is the natural condition of humankind; the state of nature is a time of "war of all against all." [63]

The Clausewitz Argument   War is the continuation of politics by other means. This often-cited argument from the early nineteenth century reads in full: "War is not a mere act of policy but a true political instrument, a continuation of political activity by other means. What remains peculiar to war is simply the peculiar nature of its means." [64]

The Freudian Argument   Humankind is innately, genetically predisposed to aggressive behavior as a way of discharging accumulated stress, asserting leadership, supplanting parents or breaking free of the restraints they impose, or relieving boredom. [65]

The Marxist Argument   War is a way of acquiring economic benefits from other states. The victors acquire access to raw materials, living space, cheap labor, expanded markets. [66]

The C. Wright Mills Argument   War is a way to acquire economic benefits from one's own political system. The industrialists who make war-related materials and the professional warriors who seek an opportunity to prove their worth combine forces in a "military-industrial complex" to manipulate public opinion and pressure elected officials to take the path of war. [67]

The Margaret Mead Argument   War is a cultural habit that, once learned, is passed on from generation to generation. If children are taught to engage in simulated acts of violence, exposed to stories in which violence plays an important part (whether they are told by grandmothers or broadcast on television sets), and encouraged to emulate the bellicose acts of their elders, their society will tend to settle conflicts with other states by means of war. [68]

Beyond Arguments: The Control of War   It is impossible to state with certainty what causes war, but we can say with considerable confidence that the Hobbesian argument is wrong. There is a good deal of evidence that earlier societies were, on the average, less warlike than so-called modern states — that the incidence and severity of wars has, paradoxically, increased with the evolution of civilization. This phenomenon seems to be related to the development of fixed settlements and the consequent need to assert and expand control of territory. The technological advances that began in the fifteenth century have steadily improved (if that is the word) the capacity of humans to slaughter one another and have led to ever greater expenditures on arms and ever greater numbers of men and women serving in the military. Thus, it is no surprise that by far the greatest share of the work of diplomats, regional organizations, and the United Nations is devoted directly or indirectly to the attempt to avoid, limit, or end wars. For most of our present century, war theoreticians have tended to recommend one of two approaches to the men and women who are employed in this most crucial task. Unfortunately, the assumptions on which both are based are not always matched by reality, as the maelstrom of change, often violently produced, into which we have been spun at century's end makes all too clear.

The first approach to the control of war is to encourage the mutual development of the power to make war. A world in which every nation is fairly equally armed should, the theory goes, be a nation in which no nation would dare risk armed attack. Struck by the relative peacefulness of Europe during the latter part of the nineteenth century, war historians pointed out that during those years the powers of the major European states were in rough equilibrium, and for this happy situation they coined the term **balance of power**. (Others have since pointed out that it was also a period when these states were directing their military efforts elsewhere, particularly in expanding imperialistic control over the land masses of Africa and Southeast Asia; when the United States was rent by a most terrible civil war, and when revolutionary leaders competed with imperial and military dictatorships in setting new records for bloodshed in Latin America. Nevertheless, the balance-of-power theory gained considerable credence.)

After World War II and the development of nuclear bombs, it became fashionable to speak of *deterrence* rather than balance of power. The idea of being able to prevent war by building such a massive and threatening arsenal of nuclear weapons that no one would dare attack seems at first fundamentally different from the idea of establishing a power equilibrium. But in practice deterrence theory seems to have become balance-of-power theory written in megatons. As we have seen, for forty years the two major superpowers relied on the fact of each other's power as well as their own; because the Soviet Union had its own arsenal of nuclear weapons, the United States could count on it to understand the probable meaning of particular American advances in defensive or offensive weaponry and to be suitably "deterred" — and vice versa. Other nations accepted the argument

and sought either to shelter under the protective wing of one of the superpowers or to develop their own deterrence force.

Even before the collapse of the Soviet Union, however, it was quite clear
that balanced nuclear power might deter nations from engaging in nuclear
warfare but had little or no impact on their willingness to engage in conventional warfare. We were very much back where we started, minus the
billions of dollars and thousands of sleepless nights squandered on the nuclear nightmare. Russia has been working hard to unload the Soviet nuclear
arsenal, but other nations are, as we saw earlier (pp. 467–469), scrambling
to take up any slack, both in nuclear and conventional arms. The United
States is slowly decreasing its own military establishment, including its nuclear stockpile, but nevertheless now maintains an apparently vast superiority to all other nations. What has happened to the balance of power?

According to a recent analysis that draws on several recent studies, what
has happened is that deterrence simply no longer works: "A great power's
capability and credibility, backed by the threat of the use of superior military force, is quite often insufficient to deter," say Don M. Snider and
Gregory Grant. But it is not only classical deterrence strategy that no
longer seems to apply. Snider and Grant identify five central strategic concepts — deterrence, collective security, power projection (e.g., declaring
readiness to defend allies), forward presence (stationing forces outside the
United States), and reconstitution (rebuilding diminished military capabilities rapidly in times of crisis) — and point out the inadequacies of each
in the new world created by the dissolution of the Warsaw Pact, the withdrawal of Soviet armies from eastern Europe, the reunification of Germany,
the breakup of the Soviet Union, and the fracturing of polity after polity
into warring factions of nationality versus nationality, guerillas versus regular army, ins versus outs. The problem now is not so simple as how to keep
two superpowers from engaging in nuclear war; it is how to prepare to
respond at any and all times to "disparate crises and regional contingen-
cies."[69] Does this mean that in the present era the only hope for controlling
war is to encourage the United States in its new role as global policeman,
on duty twenty-four hours a day, stretching its resources beyond their limit
at a time when domestic needs clamor for attention — and in the process
making as many enemies as friends?

Before we reluctantly say yes, let us consider the second commonly recommended means of controlling our species' potentially fatal tendency to
resolve its disputes by force of arms: seeking both to improve our understanding of one another and ourselves and to develop the skills that permit
peaceful negotiation and settlement of disputes. Increased diplomatic contact, cultural exchanges, better codified international law, and intergovernmental organizations that work on substantive problems before they
become the basis for war are some of the ways we try to put this method
to work. Academic studies designed to test hypotheses derived from the
theories about the causes of war are another.

Some of the most interesting work in this area has been done by political scientists using game theory (see Chapter 1). Game theorists operate on the principle that when sovereign states interact, the strategy of each side depends on guesses and information about the other side's probable strategy, just as in any other game. If the situation is **zero-sum** — that is, if one state's gain can only be at the expense of another state — then peace can probably be maintained if the state with the apparent advantage will agree to settle for a minimally acceptable gain. In a nonzero-sum situation, where both sides can do better by taking a cooperative approach, the only requirement is to establish the rules for such cooperation and for distribution of the rewards it brings. Furthermore, it may be possible to transform a zero-sum situation into a nonzero-sum situation by introducing the prospect of benefits other than those that are the bone of contention between the two states — benefits that can be achieved by cooperation in a wider range of activities, including the matter at hand. For example, if Tunisia and Algeria were on the brink of war over a border dispute (in which land gained by one would inevitably be lost by the other), game theorists might recommend that the parties renegotiate customs duties as well. Then whichever state gives up the contested land might deem itself adequately compensated by the lowered tariffs on its exports to the other and drop all talk of settling the matter by force of arms.

However, although such approaches seem more promising than those evolving from deterrence theory, here too a note of caution is in order. Such tactics may sometimes work between sovereign nations, but what about the internal battles between those who are rich and powerful and those who would like to take their place and have nothing but the force of arms with which to make their point? Furthermore, some disputes between nations may be possible to resolve by material tradeoffs, but not all. If what is at stake is a people's right to practice a religion, to maintain a dearly held conviction of racial superiority, to engage in the practices of a traditional culture however distasteful to others, to follow blindly a leader believed to have godlike qualities, or simply to live apart, surrounded by those who speak the same language and think the same thoughts, and let the rest of the world go hang, then watch out: The rational exchanges of a rational human polity may have no persuasive powers whatsoever. The struggles we are witnessing today provide clear and painful illustration of how badly we need new thinking on the important problem of bringing peace to our planet.

SUMMARY AND CONCLUSION

Contemporary issues of international politics are multiple and complex. The proliferation of arms, the protection of human rights, the international impact of ethnic nationalism, and the ever more serious need to protect our environment are only a few of the problems requiring our urgent, global attention. Diplomats and secret agents pursue the quest for solutions while at the same time seeking to maximize national advantage. Treaties and regional organizations formed around the globe bind us to one another in economic, cultural, and defensive agreements that strengthen not only our interdependence but also our ability to meet our social and material needs while discouraging would-be aggressors. Lawyers steadily clarify and augment the body of law that gives us a means of resolving our international disputes peacefully and fairly. Social scientists study the possible causes of war and develop new methods for resolving conflicts. Some write books like this, hoping to make it ever more obvious that in today's world *we* must mean all of us, if it is to have any meaning at all.

Of course, none of this is enough. Our problems are immense, and the amazing events of recent years have not lightened our load, however heartening this era of dramatic change may have seemed at first. In the next chapter we will look at some of the major developments in recent world politics, both those that we know very well and those that are taking place more gradually, but perhaps with even greater impact on our lives. We will try to face candidly the ones that undermine our hopes for the future of the human polity, as well as explore the ones that give us hope.

As we take on the challenges of this final chapter, perhaps it will help us to bear in mind a point that was made in Chapter 1: We have only been working on the task of settled, social civilization for 5,000 years. If anthropologists are correct that our species took its present form about 35,000 years ago, then it took us 30,000 years (give or take a millennium) just to get to that point. Still, however rapid our recent progress has been when viewed metahistorically, we may not have a great deal of time left. Given the success of the perverse efforts we have made to develop the means of destroying ourselves altogether, it is possible that the advances we have made in the last 5,000 years may prove to be too little, too late. Then again, the very magnitude of the "success" we have achieved in preparing for our own destruction may force us not only to save ourselves but also to create a stable and harmonious international order while we are about it.

Selected Readings

Bledsoe, Robert L. and Boleslaw A. Boczek. *The International Law Dictionary*. Santa Barbara, Calif.: ABC-Clio, 1987. Defines international political concepts and describes various international treaties.

Chan, Stephan. *Issues in International Relations: A View from Africa*. London: Macmillan, 1987. Examines international relations from an African perspective, discussing the new international economic order, dependency, interdependency and state security.

Diehl, Paul Francis. *International Peacekeeping*. Balti-

more: Johns Hopkins University Press, 1993. Provides an historical background to international peacekeeping and examines recent peacekeeping operations to determine the elements necessary for success.

Ellis, Anthony, ed. *Ethics and International Relations*. Manchester, England: Manchester University Press, 1986. A series of articles on ethical aspects of international relations. Topics discussed include the applicability of the word *moral* to state entities, international intervention, and nuclear deterrence.

Forsythe, David P. *The Internationalization of Human*

Rights. Lexington, Mass.: Lexington Books, 1991. Discusses the protection of human rights in international law, the United Nations, the Organization of African States, the United States, and private international organizations such as the Red Cross.

Hartung, William D. *And Weapons for All.* New York: HarperCollins, 1994. Detailed study of U.S. arms trade policies, making clear how international, political and industrial factors contribute to the proliferation of U.S. weapons worldwide.

Lundestad, Geir and Odd Arne Westad. *Beyond the Cold War: New Dimensions in International Relations.* Oxford: Oxford University Press, 1993. A collection of writings on the future of world politics.

Robinson, Thomas W. and David Shambaugh, eds. *Chinese Foreign Policy: Theory and Practice.* Oxford University Press, 1994. The articles in this volume make clear the many issues influencing Chinese foreign policy decisions.

Schiavone, Giuseppe. *International Organizations: A Dictionary and Directory.* New York: St. Martin's Press, 1993. Provides profiles of over 200 international organizations.

Segal, Gerald. *The World Affairs Companion: The Essential One-Volume Guide to Global Issues.* New York: Simon and Schuster, 1991. Analyzes key issues in international affairs, with useful maps and charts.

Notes

1. *New York Times,* 17 May 1995, A1. See also *World Press Review* 42 (July 1995): 4.
2. *Le Monde,* 18 June 1992, 1.
3. Leonard S. Spector, *The Undeclared Bomb* (Cambridge, Mass.: Ballinger, 1988); Patrick Glynn, "Bombs Away," *The New Republic,* 205, no. 18 (28 Oct. 1991): 13–16.
4. *New York Times,* 11 Aug. 1991, A10; 16 Nov. 1991, A5.
5. "Post Cold-War Nuclear, Security Issues Debated in Disarmament Forum," *U.N. Chronicle* (March 1995): 76–75.
6. Mel Gurtow, *Global Politics in the Human Interest* (Boulder, Colo.: Lynne Rienner, 1988); *Time International* (22 June 1992): 19.
7. Amnesty International, *Political Killings by Governments* (London: Amnesty International Publications, 1983), pp. 15–25; *International Herald*

Tribune, 22 June 1992, 1, 4; *Time International* (22 June 1992): 38.

8. Jonathan Power, *Amnesty International: The Human Rights Story* (New York: McGraw-Hill, 1981), p. 6. Incidents of torture in recent years have been reported for Turkey, China, Syria, India, Peru, the former Soviet republic of Georgia, Israel, and Myanmar. See *Country Report of Human Rights Practices for 1991* (Washington, D.C.: U.S. Government Printing Office, 1991); and Jeri Luber, "Cruel and Usual Punishment," *New York Review of Books* (10 July 1989): 34–35.
9. For a sober and thoughtful study of the problems facing the most recently created of these organizations, see Claude E. Welch, Jr., "The African Commission on Human and Peoples' Rights: A Five Year Report and Assessment," *Human Rights Quarterly* 14, no. 1 (Feb. 1991): 43–61.
10. Karin von Hippel, "The Resurgence of Nationalism and Its International Implications," *The Washington Quarterly* 17, no. 4 (Autumn 1994): 185–200.
11. Ibid., p. 190.
12. Charles G. Boyd, "Making Peace with the Guilty: the Truth about Bosnia," *Foreign Affairs* 74, no. 5 (Sept.-Oct. 1995): 22–39.
13. Ted Robert Gurr and Barbara Harff, *Ethnic Conflict in World Politics,* (Boulder, Colo: Westview Press, 1994), pp. 152–53.
14. Lester R. Brown, Christopher Flavin, and Edward C. Wolf, "Earth's Vital Signs," *The Futurist* (July-Aug. 1988): 13–20.
15. Ronald A. Taylor, "Eastern Europe: The World's Greatest Polluter," *Europe* (Oct. 1990): 17–19.
16. *Le Monde,* 16 June 1992, 1, 14. See also "The 'Earth Summit' on Population," *Population and Development Review* 18, no. 3 (Sept. 1992): 571–82.
17. "The U.N. Convention on the Law of the Sea: A Chronology," *U.N. Chronicle* (March 1995): 10–12, and Michael Stocking, "The Quest for World Environmental Cooperation: The Case of the UN Global Environmental Monitoring System," *Journal of Development Studies* 31, no. 2 (Dec. 1994): 368–70.
18. Hamish McDonald, "The Big Switch: Calcutta's Ruling Communists Give Capitalism a Chance," *Far Eastern Economic Review* (29 June 1995): 58–61.
19. Andrew McLaughlin, Grant Jordan, and William

A. Maloney, "Corporate Lobbying in the European Community," *Journal of Common Market Studies* 31, no. 2 (June 1993): 191–212.

20. Leon T. Haddar, "Muddling through in the New World Disorder — and in the Middle East," *Journal of Palestine Studies* 23, no. 4 (Summer 1994): 62–68.

21. Ibid.

22. An Israeli businessmen quoted by Robert Lenzner in "Let's Talk Business: Middle East/North Africa Economic Summit," *Forbes* 154, no. 13 (5 Dec. 1994): 161.

23. Nigel Tutt and Orla Ryan, "Gore opens G-7 Meeting with Promise of Open U. S. Telecom Market," *Electronics* 68, no. 5 (13 March 1995): 12; David E. Sanger, "International Business: Big Powers Plan a World Economic Bailout Fund," *New York Times*, 8 June 1995, 1.

24. Quincy Wright, "Espionage and the Doctrine of Non-intervention in Internal Affairs," in Roland J. Stanger, ed., *Essays on Espionage and International Law* (Columbus: Ohio State University Press, 1962), p. 3.

25. Ibid., p. 11.

26. Ray S. Cline, *The CIA Under Reagan, Bush and Casey* (Washington, D.C.: Acropolis Books, 1981); Scott D. Breckinridge, *The CIA and the U.S. Intelligence System* (Boulder, Colo.: Westview, 1986); Rhodri Jeffreys-Jones, *The CIA and American Democracy* (New Haven: Yale University Press, 1989); Steve H. Hanke, "Common Cause: What's This New Love Affair Between President Clinton and the CIA?" *Forbes* 155, no. 8 (10 April 1995): 7; Tim Weiner, "CIA Mission: Strengthen Ties on Capitol Hill," *New York Times*, 21 Feb. 1995, 1.

27. J. A. Thompson, *The Ancient Near Eastern Treaties and the Old Testament* (London: Tyndale Press, 1963), pp. 9, 11.

28. Stanley R. Sloan, "Nato's Future in a New Europe: An American Perspective," *International Affairs* 66, no. 3 (July 1990): 495–511.

29. Ousmane Poreko, "Evolution sociale chez les peuls du Fouta-Djalon," *Etudes Guinéennes, Les Recherches Africaines* 4 (Oct.-Dec. 1961): 78.

30. For relevant articles on Iraq's continuing military power after the war, see *International Herald Tribune*, 30 June 1991, B1; and *New York Times*, 16 April 1992, A3, A20.

31. Andreas Falke and Hung Q. Tran, "NAFTA and the European Union: Two Important Economic Regions with a Solid Basis for Cooperation," *Deutschland* (October 1994): 18–21; John Ross, "Mexico: Historic Turning Point," *Global Exchanges* (Summer 1994): 1–6.

32. *Washington Post*, 18 June 1991, A12.

33. *New York Times*, 15 Nov. 1991, A17.

34. *The Economist*, 14–20 Dec. 1991, 51–54 and 29 Jan. 1991, 64; *Le Monde*, 8 Feb. 1992, 1, 6, 8, 9.

35. *Le Monde*, 16 June 1992, 7.

36. Pertti Pesonen, "Three Nordic Referenda on EU Membership," *Scandinavian Review* 82, no. 3 (Winter 1994): 4–11.

37. For a typical example of new world nay-saying, see Walter Goldstein, "EC: Euro-Stalling," *Foreign Policy* 85 (Winter 1991–1992): 129–47.

38. "More-or-Less European Union," *Economist* (26 Aug. 1995): 46.

39. Seth Kitange, "Towards a Pan-African Community," *Africa News* 20, no. 13 (28 Mar. 1983): 5.

40. The terms of association between the OAU and the UN were formalized in UN Resolution 48/25 in November 1993. See Department of Public Information of the United Nations, "Cooperation Between OAU and the UN System," *Yearbook of the United Nations 1993*, vol. 47 (Dordrecht: Martinus Nijhoff, 1993), pp. 304–306.

41. Peter Tran, "The OAU/UNHCR International Symposium: Refugees and Problems of Forced Population Displacements in Africa," *Migration World Magazine* 23, nos. 1-2 (Jan.-April 1995): 23–27.

42. An assessment made by the World Bank in 1993, cited in ibid.

43. Gerard J. Mangone, *The Idea and Practice of World Government* (New York: Columbia University Press, 1951), pp. 3–9.

44. For the concept of world governance, see James Dilloway, *Is World Order Evolving?* (New York: Pergamon Press, 1986); Samuel S. Kim, *The Quest for a Just World Order* (Boulder, Colo.: Westview Press, 1984); and Meghnad Desai, "Global Governance," in Meghnad Desai and Paul Redfern, eds., *Global Governance: Ethics and Economics of the World Order* (London and N.Y.: Pinter, 1995), 6–21.

45. In fact, the League's language calling for collective action against aggressor states was extremely vague and required near unanimity among the members. As a result, the clauses

were seldom invoked, and never successfully in any major conflict.

46. Robert E. Riggs and Jack C. Plano, *The United Nations: International Organization and World Politics* (Chicago: Dorsey Press, 1988), p. 38.

47. Peter Calvocoressi, "Peace, the Security Council, and the Individual," in G. R. Berridge and A. Jennings, eds., *Diplomacy at the U.N.* (London: Macmillan, 1985), pp. 22–24, and Thomas Hovet, Jr., and Erica Hovet, *A Chronology and Fact Book of the United Nations, 1941–1985* (Dobbs Ferry, N.Y.: Ocean Publications, 1986), pp. 143–46.

48. The ten nonpermanent members of the Security Council must include five members from Africa and Asia, one from eastern Europe, two from Latin America, and two from western Europe and other states. Riggs and Plano, *United Nations*, pp. 38–39. See also *Background Notes: United Nations* (Washington, D.C.: Bureau of Public Affairs, U.S. State Department, 1994), p. 2.

49. *Background Notes: United Nations* (Washington, D.C.: Bureau of Public Affairs, U.S. State Department, 1994), p. 2.

50. *Ibid.* The last territory under the control of the Trusteeship Council, the Federated States of Micronesia, was granted internal self-government on November 3, 1986, but the United States, which provides over 90 percent of government revenue and pays compensation for its continuing military presence, still controls some aspects of its foreign affairs.

51. *New York Times*, 1 Aug. 1987, A3.

52. *Background Notes: United Nations* (Washington, D.C.: Bureau of Public Affairs, U.S. State Department, 1994), p. 1.

53. Hovet and Hovet, *Chronology and Fact Book of the United Nations*, p. 163.

54. Riggs and Plano, *The United Nations*, p. 346.

55. Steve Burback, "The Blue Helmets: A History of United Nations Peacekeeping Forces," *Special Warfare* (January 1994): 2–6.

56. Ibid.

57. *Background Notes*, pp. 1–12.

58. Jagdish N. Bhagwati, *The World Trading System at Risk* (Worcester, U.K.: Harvester Wheatsheaf, Simon & Schuster, 1991), p. 20.

59. Fred Babi, Gerhard Haensel, and F. Lwanyantika Masha, "Public Opinion in the World about the United Nations," *Review of International Affairs* 42 (10 May 1991): 12–15.

60. Gennady M. Danilenko, "The New Russian Constitution and International Law," *American Journal of International Law* 88, no. 3 (July 1994): 451–70.

61. Charles Sorley, "Sonnet," from *Marlborough and Other Poems* (Cambridge: Cambridge University Press, 1916), p. 69. Quoted in Giovanni Costigan, "British Poetry of World War I," in L. L. Farrar, Jr., ed., *War: A Historical, Political and Social Study* (Santa Barbara, Calif.: ABC-Clio, 1978), p. 249.

62. Rupert Brooke, "1914," in *Collected Poems of Rupert Brooke* (New York: Dodd, Mead, 1915).

63. Thomas Hobbes, *Leviathan* (Oxford: Basil Blackwell, 1960).

64. Carl von Clausewitz, *On War*, ed. and trans. Michael Howard and Peter Paret (Princeton, N.J.: Princeton University Press, 1976), p. 87.

65. Roy L. Prosterman, "The Study of Lethal Human Conflict," in Farrar, *War*, pp. 14–17. It should be noted that Prosterman rejects all of these explanations except the quest to assert leadership, "Together, the frustrated, status-protecting, ideology-affirming leaders, and the obedient, ideology-accepting followers, make war" (p. 18). Prosterman also identifies Freud with the Hobbesian argument, but elsewhere Freud argued along the lines described here, in a fashion more consistent with his general trend of analysis.

66. Karl Marx, "The German Ideology," in Robert C. Tucker, ed., *The Marx-Engels Reader* (New York: W. W. Norton, 1972), pp. 115–16.

67. C. Wright Mills, *The Power Elite* (New York: Oxford University Press, 1956).

68. Margaret Mead, "Alternatives to War," in Morton Fried, Marvin Harris, and Robert Murphy, eds., *War: The Anthropology of Armed Conflict and Aggression* (Garden City, N.Y.: Natural History Press, 1968), pp. 215–28.

69. Don M. Snider and Gregory Grant, "The Future of Conventional Warfare and U.S. Military Strategy," *Washington Quarterly* 15, no. 1 (Winter 1992): 203–28.

14 Regime Change in the Human Polity

Prague is the capital of the Czech Republic, the larger and more western part of what used to be Czechoslovakia, in central Europe. It is a very old city that has weathered many crises, and many battles. A great old castle looms on a hilltop on its western edge, and the river Vltava runs through it. On the eastern side of the river is the Old Town, and further east yet is the New Town. Franz Kafka, whose novel *The Castle* tells far more about the negative aspects of modern bureaucracies than you found in Chapter 11, lived in Prague—you can go there and visit his tiny house, just below the castle. And when you roam around the city, you will see some of the world's most dazzling examples of every form of architecture: Roman, Gothic, Baroque, Rococo, Neo-classical, Art Nouveau, Modernist, and contemporary.

But if you drop your eyes down from the castle heights, and down too from the turrets, towers, and spires of the bridges, churches, and other wondrous buildings, what you will see in Prague today is: A hot dog stand. A young man selling toys. A shop selling souvenirs. A tour guide inviting you for a boat ride on the river. And yourself, the traveling student, multiplied a thousand thousand times. Prague is open to the world, and the world has discovered Prague—again. Capitalist enterprise runs rampant in its streets and up the sides of neon-lighted hotels. The city is alive, the money flows, the times are good.

Or thus it appears in Prague. The countryside does not look quite the same. As your train chugs in from the west, you are immediately struck by how utterly decrepit the rail yards are, and although the countryside is green and beautiful, the small towns you wind through on your way do not look much better. The people you see seem poor, but you notice they do not look sad or oppressed, just matter-of-fact as they go about their lives. Later someone may tell you, as someone did me, "Regimes come and go; the Czech peasant knows how to take it all in stride."

Regimes come and go. We live now in an era of massive regime change, from communism to democracy and capitalism, from single-party authoritarianism to multiparty democracy. What does it mean? Is it the triumph of democracy or the triumph of capitalism? Or is it both? What does it mean for individual lives? Surely not every citizen can "take it in stride"— not, for example, when regime change means massive ethnic cleansing— or genocide—as in former Yugoslavia or parts of Africa. And even in nations where the impact is less violent, regime change has its effects, produces it winners and its losers, gives the wheel of fortune a mighty spin. What is really going on?

Of course, we cannot fully answer such a question, but perhaps we can take a few steps in the right direction. In this chapter we will consider some of the key questions posed by the effort to establish democracy and capitalism where they did not exist before. We will look at some of the more striking kinds of regime change recently experienced, at nations that have moved from communism to capitalism and democracy (and at some that have moved part way back again); at those that resist such a change but find themselves making certain compromises nonetheless, and at nations busily setting up the outward marks of democracy whose conversion may be less total than it at first appears.

But we will not stay at the level of the nation-state. We need to take a look as well at the impact on the individual, and on particular groups as well, such as the newly rich, the newly poor, and those newly uncertain what the future will hold. We will give special attention to the impact of regime change on women. We will examine the effects of regime change on the citizens of stable democracies: Are they becoming more isolationist, refusing to take on problems that are not theirs? Or is the humanitarian instinct gaining ascendancy?

We will move as well to a perspective above the individual, and above the nation-state: What is the impact of massive regime change on the human polity at large? Has it strengthened (or was it caused by) the forces pushing us toward globalization? What new roles has it given to international institutions, not only those we studied in Chapter 13, but also private international organizations, including multinational businesses? Will it eventually produce a new system of international government composed of transnational regimes? Is it a first step toward the ultimate regime change, an international government that works?

We can do no more than begin to touch on the answers. But leaving important questions open is a good idea for an introductory text. What would be the point of an introduction that was also a conclusion? There is, after all, a whole world of political science out beyond this book, and out beyond the course for which it was assigned.

ESTABLISHING DEMOCRACY

The most striking characteristic of contemporary regime change is the fall of communism in state after state and the establishment of capitalism. The second most widespread change is the transformation of noncommunist but nonetheless authoritarian states into multiparty political systems. There are now more than a hundred nations with competitive elections in which at least some civil and political rights are protected.[1] More than thirty nations began the move to democracy between 1974 and 1990.[2] This is not, therefore, just a time of massive economic change; it is the hour of democracy.

But shifting to democracy cannot be done merely by deciding to do so. Many questions about democracy have never been fully resolved. What, after all, *is* a democracy? What can we count on a democracy to do? Can a democracy be established anywhere, given the determination to do so, or are there essential preconditions? What roles must be played by elites to make the effort a success? Is there anything outsiders can do to help? Once everything is set in motion, will the process be unstoppable, or will some of the new democracies falter and fail, littering the global landscape like half-finished homes planned by overly ambitious and underfinanced developers?

These important questions are being posed with ever greater urgency by political scientists and other scholars watching this era's events unfold. A brief look at some of the answers they offer will help shape and sharpen our investigation.

What Is a Democracy?

As our earlier discussions have presumably made clear, democracy is a political system, not an economic one. Although often present together, democracy and capitalism are far from synonymous, and indeed some scholars argue that the latter necessarily limits the possibility of fully achieving the former. In any case, the literal meaning of *democracy* is simply "rule by the people." In contemporary practice, it is often assumed that the way people rule is by voting in "free" elections—that is, elections with a secret ballot, universal suffrage (all or nearly all adult men and women are eligible to vote and allowed to vote without coercion or restriction), and more than one political party in the competition. A typical definition reflecting this certainty that free elections are all but synonymous with

Patterns of Democratization	Scores of the Physical Quality of Life Index 0 10 20 30 40 50 60 70 80 90 100	Number of Countries
Consistently nondemocratic		10
Inconsistently nondemocratic		59
Inconsistently democratic		23
Consistently democratic		23

FIGURE 14.1

Patterns of Democratization and the Physical Quality of Life

Source: Dol Chull Shin, "Political Democracy and the Quality of Citizens' Lives: A Cross-National Study," *Journal of Developing Societies* 5 (Jan.-April 1989): p. 37. Leiden, The Netherlands: E.J. Brill, 1989. Reprinted by permission.

democracy is the one offered by Philippe Schmitter and Terry Lynn Karl: "Modern political democracy is a system of governance in which rulers are held accountable for their actions in the public realm by citizens, acting indirectly through the competition and cooperation of their elected representatives."[3]

Other authors have been more demanding. In addition to free elections, Robert Dahl lists effective participation, control of agenda, and enlightened understanding as necessary criteria.[4] Peter Merkl agrees that parties and elections are "common structural attributes and criteria" of democracy, but adds civil, political, and social rights: Citizens in democracies have the right to petition government, to exercise free speech (including access to a free press), and to assemble and organize for democratic political purposes.[5] George Munda Carew, focusing on regime changes in the multi-ethnic political communities of Africa, points out that free elections are not sufficient to prevent unfair treatment of minorities; a true democracy must also respect "the fairness principle" and function within a "culture of solidarity, fellow feeling and fair play."[6]

What Can We Count on a Democracy to Do?

Even when a regime meets the more difficult criteria set for democracy, we should not expect heaven on earth. Overall, the physical quality of life is clearly better in democracies (see Figure 14.1), but many have argued that the quality of life permits the establishment of democracy, not vice versa.

Democracy does not guarantee social or economic equality, nor even a decent standard of living for all. It does not eliminate immorality or corruption: "Democratic politics involves, almost always, lots of unsavory characters, people whose views one finds unattractive, even antidemocratic, certainly unpalatable."[7] There is no solid evidence that democracies are more efficient economically or administratively than other forms of government, nor are they likely to "appear more orderly, consensual, stable or governable than the autocracies they replace."[8] Ensuring freedom of choice does not ensure its exercise; democratic government is not enough to protect us from the pressures of social conformism.

Democracy does, however, have two indisputable advantages over other forms of government. First, the idea of democracy is appealing; it is highly satisfactory to believe we are able to participate in creating and running our own government.[9] Second, and more substantively important, democracy provides a more peaceful way of processing conflict and effecting change than can be found in other systems: "Democracies have the capacity to modify their rules and institutions consensually in response to changing circumstances"—when we are on the losing side, the processes of democracy help us to "lose peacefully."[10] The contribution democratic processes make to peaceful adjudication of disputes carries over into the international arena; although democracies go to war, they rarely fight each other: one author goes so far as to assert that since 1816 "no democracy has fought another democracy."[11]

Are There Preconditions for Establishing a Democracy?

There is now a widespread conviction that all nations should adopt the democratic model. Is this a realistic hope? Can any nation become democratic "if it tries?" Or must certain conditions be in place before democracy can flourish? Georg Sorensen finds that four sets of preconditions have been posited by different authors—and that none of them holds absolutely true. Some have associated the development of democracy with modernization and wealth, others argue for the importance of having a political culture that emphasizes equalitarianism and tolerance, still others think a strong middle class is an essential precondition, and a final argument is that external factors (such as the amount of aid received or the extent of foreign control over a nation's economy) will inevitably play a powerful role in determining whether or not democracy is possible. Sorensen finds exceptions for every claim: "For every factor seen as conducive to democracy, counterexamples can be put forward" and reminds us as well that "in many countries, different preconditions may exist that point in different directions."[12] Seymour Martin Lipset, who was one of the first to argue the link between wealth and democracy, now says that "what new democracies need above all is efficacy, particularly in the economic area, but also in the polity."[13] According to Doh Chull Shin, most scholars now recognize that "no single factor is sufficient or necessary [and that] the emergence of democracy in a country is the result of a combination of causes."[14]

The Role of Elites in Establishing Democracy

The readiness to acknowledge that the birth of each new democracy may be the result of a different combination of factors has also permitted scholars to give more attention to the important role often played by specific actors—or kinds of actors—in the process. As Sorensen reminds us, "Democracy does not fall from heaven. It is brought about by individuals and groups, by social actors, who fight for it." Those who struggle to establish democracy are usually eager to attack the power and privileges of dominant groups. Even members of an existing authoritarian elite may see democracy as a means for taking power away from the more dominant members of their own group. Sorenson believes most transitions to democracy in recent years have been set up as a result of negotiations with dominant elites in the former regime.[15] If the pay-off to such elites is too great, and permits them to stay in power, how genuine is the new democracy?

What Can Outsiders Do to Help?

Is there a role for those in established democracies to play in helping other nations make this kind of regime change? The experts are, on the whole, dubious. Charles Tilly wonders if trying to promote democracy is not like trying to change the weather: "We can more or less understand the weather and its wide variation in different times and places, perhaps even affect it in small ways. However . . . no one seriously talks about promoting good weather." He believes external efforts are likely to have a chance of success when they take the specific circumstances of a particular system into consideration and are coordinated with internal activities working toward the same end. But he adds that it might be useful to have a "rapid strike force" capable of intervening to facilitate democratic change whenever an authoritarian system enters into a period of crisis.[16] Sidney Verba is equally cautious: "We do not know how to manage change, we do not know how in any precise way to create democracy out of nondemocracy . . . we can provide support, but whatever grows probably has to grow uncontrolled and grow outside our control in ways that are sometimes negative . . . I suppose what we do is to help and to hope for the best."[17]

Is Democracy Unstoppable Once Begun?

Here the answer from the scholars is unambiguous: no. They soberly remind us that the *consolidation* of democracy is a long and difficult business. To John Higley and Richard Gunther, consolidation means elite consensus on procedures plus extensive mass participation in elections; Juan Linz says it means that none of the major actors thinks there is any alternative to the democratic process as a way to gain power; and to Guy Hermet it means that a society can "no longer imagine any other possible regime."[18] In any case, no one thinks consolidation happens easily. Doh Chull Shin finds that the presently democratizing nations "tend to lack many factors that facilitate the process of democratization"; it is "uncertain," he says, "whether these democracies will continue to consolidate or whether they will regress into authoritarian rule."[19] Georg Sorensen is also pessimistic about the chances for what he calls "democratic deepening." He worries that the negotiations made with preexisting elites have made the new democracies "frail and unconsolidated and plagued by acute social and economic problems"; he allows a few exceptions (South Korea, Taiwan) but concludes that "the odds seem to weigh heavily against the further development and consolidation of the frail democratic openings that have taken place in recent years."[20]

Will the passionate striving of the human spirit for the right to control its own destiny overcome the dire forebodings of the experts? Will the economic gains possible when governments (and the massive resources they control, either directly or by the impact of the laws they write and enforce) change hands regularly be sufficient to motivate elites to continue the struggle to install this system of governance? Will international businesses provide the motive power, eager to foster the worldwide establishment of a kind of regime which is basically stable and thoroughly familiar? It is certainly too soon to know which, if any, of these forces may give the lie to our pessimistic pundits. But while we wait to find out, we can take a closer look at some of the actual transitions that have been taking place, and their impact on us all.

KINDS OF TRANSITIONS

As we have already pointed out, the major form of regime change in recent years has been from authoritarian to democratic. This change has taken place in two kinds of authoritarian systems, communist and noncommunist; in the former it has been accompanied by a change to a capitalist economic system. But not all regime change has been to democracy; as we will see, in some cases communist states have shifted a long way towards free market capitalism while making little or no political change. And we will take another brief look at the case of Peru here to remind ourselves that regime change can still sometimes go in the opposite direction, from democracy to authoritarian rule.

Transitions from Communism to Democracy and Free Market Capitalism

The changes produced by the fall of communism beginning in 1989 have been the most dramatic and have seized the lion's share of the world's attention. All the component states of the Soviet Union and all the former satellites of that state in eastern and central Europe have shifted to democracy and have introduced a capitalist economic system.

What does this mean in practice? In all cases, it means the overnight introduction of competitive elections with a multiparty system and the slightly more gradual (and more partial) introduction of a market economy and private enterprise. What it does not mean is that all the former elites have been banished from power. Some of them have never left power, whereas others have begun to find their way back under new party labels. The changes have been radical, but the changes themselves have changed.

At the same time, those communist nations that have so far resisted overt radical regime change—China, North Korea, and North Vietnam as well as Cuba—have also been making some surprising changes, particularly in the nature of their economies. Let us examine this complex pattern of change in somewhat closer detail.

Political and Economic Change in Eastern and Central Europe: The Polish Case Of course, every case is different, but a brief examination of the recent history of Poland will give us some interesting illustrations of the kinds of changes that have taken place in eastern and central Europe.

Poland is an interesting case because the move toward democratization began long before the fall of the Berlin Wall in 1989 and the rapid sequence of revolutionary overthrow of other communist regimes in the succeeding months. The trade union Solidarnosc and the Catholic Church had been putting pressure on the communist leadership for many years, and that leadership had been making concessions to that pressure, including the introduction of quasifree elections in June of 1989. It surprised no one when Lech Walesa, the leader of Solidarnosc and an electrician by trade, became the president of the new regime in 1990; when the new Sejm (the lower house of the Polish legislature) was turned over to a strong anticommunist majority; and when the nation embarked on a vigorous promarket reform program. Yet a mere three years later, in September 1993, the parties with roots in Solidarnosc were soundly defeated and their leaders were ousted from parliament; in the presidential elections of 1995, Walesa himself lost his bid for reelection and was replaced by Aleksander Kwasniewski, a former communist.[21]

What caused the shift back to leaders and ideas that seemed to have been so thoroughly discredited? There were a number of causes. One was the failure of Solidarnosc to hold together. Once the enemy, the former communist party, had been vanquished—and the enemy's best friend, the Soviet Union, had fallen apart—Solidarnosc lacked the focus that had held it together and internal power struggles tore it apart. The two principal factions were led by President Walesa and his erstwhile ally, Tadeusz Mazowiecki, prime minister in the first Solidarnosc government. The split began almost immediately after victory, when the two men ran against each other in the 1990 presidential election. The new electoral system, commendably open and democratic, also played its part; anyone could form a party and it sometimes seemed as if everyone did. By 1992, Poland had over 132 parties; by 1995, the number had grown to over 200. "Only" twenty-nine parties won seats in the 1991 elections to the Sejm, but the strongest of these had only 12.31 percent of the vote and sixty-two seats.

Another cause was that the new economic system, rather than bringing the optimistically expected instant improvement to the lives of the Polish people, imposed new rigors on most of them. The reform program of Finance Minister Leszek Balcerowicz was pushed forward vigorously, some

Ex-communist Aleksander Kwasniewski, the new president of Poland, waves to his supporters as he stands next to his wife Jolanta, after taking the lead in the first ballot in November, 1995. (Reuters/Peter Andrews/Archive Photos)

said ruthlessly. Price controls were eliminated and the market became the basis of all major economic activities. Although the state industrial sector did not disappear overnight, privatization flourished: Over 900 state-owned companies were sold off, and by 1995 the private sector accounted for 45 percent of the country's gross domestic product (GDP), employed 60 percent of the labor force, and included 1.5 million firms. Positive results were readily apparent: Inflation was reduced to a "mere" 38 percent by the end of 1993 (having reached 640% at the beginning of 1990) and economic growth moved into the highly respectable 4 percent to 5 percent range. Foreign aid was pouring in, 50 percent of the nation's foreign debt was canceled, and the International Monetary Fund was offering some $700 million in loans.

But as we have seen in other cases, what looks like national economic recovery to outsiders may look like something very different to those inside who are stuggling to make ends meet. There were more goods available, but less money to buy them with: By 1993, the average real wage was 25 percent below the 1989 level (the drop was 40 percent for industrial workers and 66% for farmers), public employees' wages were fixed (regard-less of inflation), unemployment was at 15.7 percent (above 20% in thir-teen of the forty-nine provinces) and a third of the people, many of them elderly, were living below the poverty line. All told, these categories, con-sisting of those least able to take advantage of the reforms and the newly free market, account for well over 50 percent of the Polish population.[22]

By 1993, the political tide was beginning to turn. There were 7,213 strikes in April and May of that year, and on May 28 the Sejm voted the existing cabinet out of power. President Walesa called for new elections and in September the two ex-communist parties, the Democratic Left Al-liance (SLD) and the Polish Peasant Party (PSL), won 171 and 132 seats, respectively, in the 460-member body, as well as 73 of the 100 seats in the Senate.[23]

The improvement in the national economy continued: By 1995, annual Polish exports were at $20 billion, imports at $23 billion, and Western foreign investment at $1 billion. The situation for some of the general population also improved: By the end of 1994, unemployment fell slightly (to 14%), real wages rose slightly (by 3.4%), and inflation was down to 22 percent.[24] But this was not enough to give Lech Walesa, who had lost credibility not only by the unsatisfactory performance of the economy but also by adopting an increasingly coarse and demagogic style, a second term in the presidency. At the end of 1995, Aleksander Kwasniewski, the leader of the Democratic Left Alliance, forced Walesa into a runoff and in December of that year the former communist won, taking 51.7 percent of the vote.[25]

Had Poland returned to communism? Not at all, said Kwasniewski: "Communism is a thing of the past. It is not possible for it to return and there is no sense in its coming back."[26] Kwasniewski, described as a "deep-dyed, deideologized pragmatist," claims he is too young (41 years old at the time of his election) to be held responsible for the errors of the past regime, and has an upper middle-class family income. He is, he says, a social democrat. Although he favors reducing unemployment, building in-expensive municipal housing, and "taking into account the interests of la-bor veterans," he supports the entry of Poland into NATO and Europe, promises to continue the market reforms, and is expected to continue the policy of fighting inflation, reducing state spending, encouraging privati-zation, and bringing in more foreign capital.[27]

A Universal Move Back to the Left?   Although the details vary greatly, the general picture is very much the same in other ex-communist states. New parties led by former communists are now in power in Hungary and Bulgaria and the governments of the Czech Republic and Slovakia are in-creasingly dependent on ex-communist and/or social democratic support.[28] The Czech case—the three-party conservative coalition won only 99 of the 200 seats in the Czech parliament in the elections of June 1996—was perhaps the most surprising, since in that nation real wages have risen, not fallen, and unemployment is low. But the government has introduced means testing for social security payments, mass privatization has produced a "tiny, ingrown elite," and tales of government corruption "fill the newspapers."[29]

The Czech tale replicates the Polish story also in that the leader of the leftist opposition is in no way eager to return to the past: Milos Zerman, leader of the left-leaning Social Democratic Party that is now the second largest party in parliament, calls for more, not less privatization, especially in banking; his hope is for a "socially and ecologically orientated market economy."[30]

In general, in all the former Soviet satellite states ex-communists now present themselves as reformers who will ensure that the burden of reform is more equitably shared, not as unregenerate believers determined to turn back the clock. Communism is out; social democracy is in.

Transitions from Communism toward Free Market Capitalism

The pressures for change exerted by an ever-stronger international market economy are also being felt in still-communist nations like China, North Korea, North Vietnam, and Cuba. In these nations massive political regime change has not yet taken place, but economic changes have been profound.

Such changes began in the three Asian states long before the fall of the Berlin Wall. The beginning of China's economic reform dates back to 1978, and in fact 1989 brought a three-year setback, as the Tiananmen uprising on behalf of democratic politics in June of that year persuaded Chinese leaders to adopt more conservative economic policies as well as to heighten political oppression.[31] Despite this temporary slowdown, the economy of the People's Republic of China grew by more than an average of 9 percent per year from 1978 through 1995, with particularly spectacular growth since 1990; the gross domestic product in 1993 was $545 billion (see Figure 14.2).[32]

The decision to compete in the world market has brought massive change to China, but so far it has not brought serious political change.[33] The communist party-state still rules. This means, in turn, that the economic system has not simply become a free enterprise system; it is what the Chinese call a "socialist market economy." Foreign investment has grown, and so has the private sector, but according to David S. G. Goodman, the most spectacular growth has been in what is known as the "collective sector." This sector includes collectively owned enterprises that are heavily controlled by—but for the most part not owned by—the state. They now account for 35.7 percent of the gross value of industrial output (the state accounts for 52.9 percent, private enterprise for 5.7 percent and "other and foreign-involved" for 5.7 percent) and the official prediction is that they will account for 47.7 percent by the year 2000. Goodman identifies six kinds of collectives, from large-scale enterprises like the West

FIGURE 14.2   **China's Real GDP Growth, 1987–94**

Source: "China," in *U.S. Global Trade Outlook 1995–2000* (Washington, D.C.: U.S. Department of Commerce, 1995), p. 74.

Lake District Dragon Well Tea Company (see Box 14.1) to local government collectives to share-based cooperatives. What they have in common is that "each must operate within the market economy but is also inextricably part of the party-state."[34] This dual identity shapes every form of economic development in China: acquiring raw materials, securing bank credits, and finding markets still depends on personal connections with state officials. Is this a new form of corporatism? A socialist market economy, as the Chinese claim? Or a transitional hybrid economy resulting from the effort of a massive communist system to maintain total political control while effecting the transition to capitalism? And will economic change eventually force matching political change? It will be interesting to watch and see what the answers to these questions will be.

The tendency for the state to maintain a very high level of both ownership and control while steadily pushing the economy toward the market and away from central planning is also found in North Vietnam, North Korea, and Cuba.[35] In the latter two cases, special factors add further complications: In North Korea, the expectation of eventual reunification with fully capitalist South Korea overshadows everything, especially since the death in 1994 of "Beloved Leader" Kim Il Sung; in Cuba, the efforts of the state to improve its condition after the loss of Soviet support by permitting a measure of growth in the private sector (with an emphasis on tourism) have been all but canceled out by the deleterious effects of the U.S. embargo and the passage in 1995 of the Helms-Burton law that levies such punishments as cancelation of U.S. visas on foreign investors who profit

BOX 14.1

THE WORKINGS OF A LARGE-SCALE COLLECTIVE IN A SOCIALIST MARKET ECONOMY: CHINA'S WEST LAKE DISTRICT DRAGON WELL TEA COMPANY

[A] successfully reformed large-scale collective is the West Lake District Dragon Well Tea Company. The Hangzhou green tea plantations are famous throughout at least the Chinese speaking world, and Dragon Well Tea is probably the most famous of Hangzhou's teas. Tea in East China can be compared with wine in Burgundy, both in appreciation and in its cultivation and production. Many small producers in a very few select and nominated areas are the only ones able to produce Dragon Well Tea. Before 1949 there were some twelve villages that produced Dragon Well Tea, but by 1980 this had declined to only two. Nonetheless, those two villages maintained the traditions of tea cultivation, including the intergenerational transfer of knowledge.

The Tea Company, very much like a Burgundian *négociant,* buys the tea from the growers, which it then processes and markets. By the early 1980s the local tea industry had been badly run-down despite any lingering reputation. In 1984 the local Dragon Well villages decided to engage in reform on their own behalf. They appointed a native son, trained tea taster and producer previously working in the Trade Section of the Village Government, to reorganize the collective in order to develop and market Dragon Well Tea and the local industry. By any standard, the enterprise has been a great success. In 1984, 13 persons were employed in the company itself, which had a turnover of 210,000 yuan RMB. By 1991, the collective employed 134 people and had a turnover of more than 10 million yuan RMB. More significant is the collective's impact on the local economy: the number of tea villages has already increased to five, and there are plans to replant still more former tea areas.

The funding of the Tea Company is of particular interest. Initially, it had been structured as an early reform-era form of the 'share-based cooperative' introduced later. As a collective with local government support the Tea Company was successfully able to negotiate a 30,000-yuan RMB loan from the Agricultural Bank. The remaining 20,000 yuan RMB of the original capital was to be provided by the workforce. The collective agreed to pay the workforce a dividend, which would be higher than the prevailing bank interest. Unfortunately for the implementation of any collectivist ideology, the Tax Office insisted that tax had to be paid before any dividends were declared. In the first year of operation there was insufficient profit to ensure the dividend payout, and as a result the workers withdrew their capital.

The Tea Company is now funded on a system of workers' pledges. All members of the workforce are assigned a proportion of the total enterprise capital according to their position in the company and their wage. Local government fixes a target for the enterprise profit in the coming year which is calculated according to a three-year moving average. If the target is 25 percent met, the workforce then shares the next 27 percent of the profit target before taxes are paid. If the target is not met, the workforce must compensate the local government. In either case reward or compensation is calculated according to the individual worker's pledge, or notional share of the total enterprise capital.

Source: David S. G. Goodman, "Collectives and Connectives, Capitalism and Corporatism: Structural Change in China," special issue on "Enterprise Reform in Post-Socialist Societies," *Journal of Communist Studies and Transition Politics* 11, no. 1 (March 1995): 19–20. Reprinted by permission of Frank Cass, Publisher.

from properties expropriated from American citizens or companies after Fidel Castro took power in 1959.[36]

Transitions from Noncommunist Authoritarian Rule to Democracy

Transitions from noncommunist authoritarian rule to democracy have taken place in Italy and Germany after World War II, and in Portgual, Spain, and Greece more recently.[37] Here, however, we will look at this form of transition only in Africa and Latin America.

In Africa   In the first twenty years (roughly 1960 to 1980) after achieving political independence from colonial rule, most of the new African states were ruled by single-party or military dictators, often supported by the former colonial powers in exchange for continuing privileged access to these nations' cheap labor and raw materials. But in the 1980s regime change came to Africa, and by the mid-1990s multiparty elections had been introduced in a majority of African political systems: In 1996 alone, national elections were to be held in eighteen countries, and eight more were scheduled for 1997.[38]

What caused the change? Certainly world opinion played a part. So did domestic opinion as "declining living standards . . . arbitrary and bad government, corruption and a breakdown of law and order" caused Africans to lose patience with their rulers.[39] But this is a good time to remember the words of Greg Sorensen who has insisted that what causes the introduction of democracy is the determination of the powerful to establish it (see earlier, p. 512).

In the African case, two sets of the "powerful" were at work. The first were the organizers of the "structural adjustment" programs of the World Bank and International Monetary Fund. Able to promise massive loans in exchange for economic liberalization (improving conditions for foreign investment) and political reform (introducing free elections that, besides introducing formal democracy, could also be expected eventually to loosen the grip of the autocrats), these international powers made a strong appeal to the second group of powerholders, internal elites whose grip was becoming shaky as their nations' increasing fiscal decline reduced the resources they required (such as foreign exchange, local currency, and government contracts) to make the necessary patronage rewards to their supporters.[40] Although the dramatic events in eastern Europe and the Soviet Union and the more gradual shift from military to parliamentary rule in Latin America heightened global certainty that "democracy and capitalism are progressing irresistibly, and in tandem," close observers have pointed out that in Africa as elsewhere in the world there are reasons to doubt that the truth is as cheerfully simple as that.[41]

First, the move to democracy in these regimes is not only led by elites, it has often been less than popular with the general population, because it is linked with efforts to impose the austerity programs demanded by the IMF as part of structural adjustment. Second, although leaders may

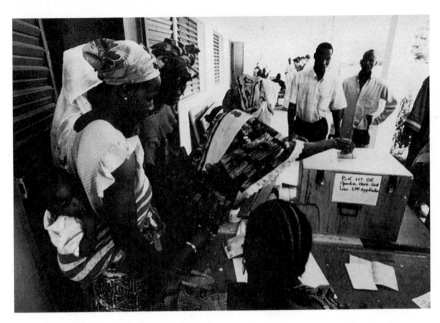

Multiparty elections in Africa. Here Ivory Coast women vote at a polling station north of the capital of Abidjan in the October 1995 presidential election. (AFP/ Bettmann)

change, they continue to be members of the African elite; "lawyers, university lecturers, bankers, businessmen, professionals, and former officials of international institutions" predominate in the new governments and in the parties.[42] Furthermore, elections do not necessarily produce leadership change. Clever autocrats also know how to make "adjustments." When protests escalated in his country in 1990 and international pressures grew, the late Félix Houphouet-Boigny of the Ivory Coast moved swiftly to master the new situation. He "announced a suspension of many of the planned austerity moves, legalized opposition parties, and called presidential and legislative elections for October and November. . . . Thanks to this swift initiative, [his party's] advantages as the state party, and the opposition's fragmentation, [he and his party] won the elections handily."[43] Similarly, Flight Lieutenant Jerry Rawlings, the former air force pilot who had seized power illegally twice in Ghana, proved himself adept at the new game. After calling for free elections, he waited until three weeks before election day to announce his own candidacy. By that time, the opposition was split in three and incapable of uniting in so short a time: Rawlings took 58.3 percent of the vote and was sworn in as president of Ghana's Fourth Republic on January 7, 1993.[44]

President Yoweri Museveni of Uganda was yet another long-time ruler

BOX 14.2   **"FREE ELECTIONS" IN THE SUDAN**

The Islamic military government in the Sudan, led by Lieutenant General Omar Ahmed al-Bashir and the National Islamic Front, a fundamentalist party led by Dr. Hassan al-Turabi, staged its own version of "free" elections in 1995. Political parties were allowed to form, but not to campaign. Forty-two candidates registered for the presidency, and 900 for the 275 seats in parliament. Candidates were given twelve days to campaign in a nation one-fourth the size of the United States. The government paid for and printed one piece of campaign literature for each candidate for the presidency, and allowed each candidate one 15-minute spot on the state-owned television and radio station. Each candidate was also given a symbol (examples included a fan, a table, an elephant, a rifle, a razor blade) because the government insisted there were too many illiterate people to allow words on the ballots; officials in polling places were allowed to "help" voters tick off the "right" symbol if they were confused.

To no one's surprise, the principal opposition parties called for a boycott and General Bashir was reelected president, winning 4,181,784 of the 5,525,280 votes cast. According to the cheerful victor, the results made it clear that "the Sudanese people had decided to move ahead along the path of popular consultative democracy." According to the opposition, only 5% of the population had voted.

Sources: *New York Times*, 11 March 1996, A5, and "Sudan," *Defense and Foreign Affairs* (March 1996), p. 14.

not about to be swept aside as he made the required bow in the direction of democracy. Political parties were authorized, but they were not allowed to raise funds or to hold meetings, and all candidates were required to run as independents during the five-week presidential campaign in 1996. Museveni took 76 percent of the vote.[45] In other cases, such as Egypt and Jordan, the present leaders have been able to introduce democratic reforms that are modest in the extreme and in no way threaten their own control[46] (see Box 14.2).

Even the most dubious observers admit, however, that things have changed in Africa. Openly autocratic rule is no longer acceptable in most nations, opposition parties do exist, the press seems freer to criticize those in power, and associations such as trade unions and women's groups are taking a renewed interest in the political game. It may still be only a game, and one that has little real meaning yet for the vast majority of Africa's population. Continuing and severe economic hardship plus ethnic rivalries that can erupt in mass violence make the task of democratic consolidation more difficult here than in Europe.[47] But something has changed. It is too soon to be certain the change will hold, and deepen, but it is also too soon to be certain that the change will fail.

In Latin America   The situation in Latin America is similar to that in Africa in several respects. As in Africa, this continent also experienced a massive turn away from dictatorship in the 1980s; over two-thirds of Latin American people were living under military rule in 1979, but by 1993, "not a single military regime remained in Central or South America or the Spanish-speaking Caribbean"[48] (see Table 14.1). As in Africa, a severe need for economic bailout (here owing largely to the impossibility of keeping up payments on foreign loans—that is, to the international debt crisis discussed in Chapter 4) helped convince endangered elites they would have to accept neoliberal economic strategies of reducing government regulation, privatizing public enterprises, and shrinking the size of the state in order to qualify for further foreign aid and loans.[49] As in Africa, democracy has been "pared to the bone" and is largely limited to its "electoral dimension" leaving social needs "at the bottom of the agenda."[50] As in Africa, certain groups, generally those already better placed in the social system, have prospered with the change while the poor have grown poorer. As in Africa, intermediary representative groups (opposition parties, trade unions, other associations of civil society) have not yet gained sufficient strength as "channels of interest mediation [to be able to] renegotiate with society the terms of political representation."[51] And finally, as in Africa, although the overall results have been dubious and disappointing, one can find some grounds for hope, as we will see.

There is, however, one key difference in the nature of Latin American regime change, and that is the far more powerful role of the military, both before and after the changes that have taken place. Although military regimes were in power in many nations on both continents throughout the 1960s and 1970s, those in Latin America were far less limited by poverty and the inhibiting conditions of postcolonial trade and aid than their African counterparts; at the same time, these nations were far more determined to "obliterate the political left and roll back decades of labor gains" (few such gains had yet been made in Africa).[52]

TABLE 14.1   **Transitions to Civilian Government in Latin America**

Ecuador	1979	Uruguay	1984
Peru	1980	Brazil	1985
Honduras	1982	Guatemala	1986
Bolivia	1982	Chile	1990
Argentina	1983	Paraguay	1993
El Salvador	1984		

Source: Brian Loveman, "'Protected Democracies' and Military Guardianship: Political Transitions in Latin America, 1978–1993," *Journal of InterAmerican Studies and World Affairs* 36, no. 2 (Summer 1994): 106.

The exceptional power of the Latin American military did not come to an end with the introduction of formal democracy, and the new governments have been described as keen to avoid "any policy initiative that might provoke a new military coup." Although they have sometimes reduced the size of the military, they have often granted, explicitly or tacitly, immunity to members of the armed forces known to have engaged in extreme acts of oppression during their time in power, have incorporated many of the antidemocratic and anticivil libertarian institutions and practices of the past regimes into contemporary constitutions, and have given the military a range of powers which more established democracies would never countenance. The result, according to Brian Loveman, is that these are "protected" democracies—which is to say, regimes in which the military is given the role of "protecting" the new system from its own excesses and/or in which the civilian authorities have accepted military definitions of what constitutes such an excess. Loveman concludes that in most of these nations military coups are no longer a threat, because they are not necessary: "Protected democracy provides a handy legal rationale for the military to assert themselves in a variety of acceptable ways. . . . Beneath the veneer of elected civilian government, both authoritarian legal institutions and a political mission for the armed forces have been consolidated"[53] (see Table 14.2).

Nevertheless, as in Africa, the new regimes do provide some grounds for hope. They may not have had "any significant effect on the great and increasing inqualities" of their economies or societies," and it may be true that "the dice are probably loaded in favor of repeated iterations of shaky and relatively short-lived democracy and ever-uglier authoritarian rule," as Guillermo O'Donnell sadly observes.[54] Yet O'Donnell himself is willing to hope he may be wrong and bases that hope on the fact that "most political and cultural forces of any weight now attribute high intrinsic value to the achievement and consolidation of political democracy." He reminds us that when democracies are first established anywhere, it is usually with a great deal of pessimism, uncertainty, and even reluctance. Like Sorensen, he points out the importance of the motives of elites—it is, he says, when the main political, social, and religious forces conclude "that the costs of trying to eliminate each other [exceed] the costs of tolerating each other's differences" that true democracy has a chance.[55] Although the grounds for hope seem slight indeed, perhaps that moment is on its way in Latin America.[56]

A Transition from "Protected Democracy" to Authoritarianism and Back Again: The Case of Peru   Unfortunately, however, the difficulty of deepening Latin American democracy has been given striking illustration in the case of Peru. As we have noted earlier (see p. 339, Chapter 9), the president, Alberto Fujimori, announced an *autogolpe* ("self-coup") on April 5, 1992, giving himself the power to rule by decree. The constitution was suspended and the legislature was closed down. Fujimori had become im-

TABLE 14.2

Military Limitations on Transition to Elected Government in Selected Latin American Nations

Argentina	Least successful case for military controlling transition, but gradual reassertion of military presence as civilian governments make concessions after mutinies and coup attempts 1985–1992.
Bolivia	Military retains basic prerogatives; no trials for human rights violations, except prosecution of ex-president García Meza and 47 collaborators on various charges.
Brazil	Military maintains almost all prerogatives and relative service autonomy; no Defense Ministry permitted. Intelligence agencies (SNI) and National Security Council also retain much autonomy despite later name changes and reorganization. Military fails to control transition election entirely, but active participation in elaborating 1988 Constitution ensures broad constitutional mission, participation in policymaking affecting "national security" (e.g. labor and agrarian reform policy) and continued relative autonomy.
Chile	Transition according to 1980 Constitution. Small concessions to opposition in 1989 reforms, but also implementation before President Aylwin takes office of *leyes de amarre* (group of laws, decrees, and organic laws which further limit authority of incoming government in many policy areas, including new organic laws for armed forces and national police just prior to transition).
Ecuador	Military monitors plebiscite on alternative constitutions; impedes participation of certain candidates in transition election; manipulates recount on first round of 1978 presidential election; assures respect for institutional prerogatives of armed forces and participation in naming defense minister.
El Salvador	Army retains most prerogatives; country under state of siege for most of 1984–1993, involving broad military jurisdiction over civilians. Minimal civilian authority over military. Peace Accord between government and FMLN in 1992 calls for civilian role in reforming military education through a new Consejo Académico Cívico-Militar and in reviewing cases of officers accused of human rights abuses for their dismissal (*depuracíon*).
Guatemala	Military creates *Tribunal Supremo Electoral* to control transition election and devises new election laws. Calls constituent assembly (1984) to adopt a new constitution. Obtains confirmation of decrees of junta and guarantees against trials for human rights abuses. President Cerezo claims he has "30% of the power" (the army has the rest).
Paraguay	Military retains all previous prerogatives; 1991 armed forces law stipulates "autonomy" of armed forces, Congress cannot pass laws on military unless previously approved by president; pre-election rumors that if *Colorado* party candidate Carlos Wasmosy lost, the armed forces would seize power. Various election irregularities.
Uruguay	Military vetoes candidacy of most popular presidential candidate; key opposition leaders in jail; informal guarantees of military prerogatives; SIFA (Armed Forces Intelligence Service) continues surveillance of civilian politicians, activists, labor leaders, and media.

Source: Drawn from Brian Loveman, "'Protected Democracies' and Military Guardianship: Political Transitions in Latin America, 1978–1993," *Journal of InterAmerican Studies and World Affairs* 36, no. 2 (Summer 1994): 120–121.

patient with the reluctance of the Peruvian Congress to implement the economic austerity measures required by the IMF and the World Bank, or to take the counterinsurgency measures he had urged against Shining Path, a revolutionary movement that had caused the loss of over 25,000 lives between 1980 and 1992 and that seemed to be growing stronger every day.

The hesitation of the lawmakers to pass the economic legislation sought by Fujimori had clearly been linked to the condition of the Peruvian people. With only 15.6 percent of the economically active workforce employed full time at the minimum wage or above and half the population living below the poverty level, many members of the legislature doubted that further cuts in public spending could be made. It was also not difficult to understand their reluctance to adopt the counterinsurgency measures Fujimori had proposed, linked as these were to efforts to give the armed forces dangerous new powers in many areas. Restrictions on journalists were to be tightened, the state would have the right to confiscate property on grounds of national security, special military courts would be set up to try terrorist suspects, and it would become impossible to try military officials in civilian courts for human rights violations.[57]

In the days following his coup, Fujimori took these and similar steps on his own (including dismissing thirteen members of the Supreme Court and more than 100 judges and prosecutors).[58] To the president's surprise, the fact that he was following policies the international community had recommended, such as introducing neoliberal economic measures and strengthening the fight against both the terrorists and the drug cartel, did not bring a positive response from that community. On the contrary: The U.S. suspended aid, the IMF postponed a $222 million loan, and other South American governments suspended cooperation with Peru.

Fujimori soon learned what was wrong—it was his open repudiation of democracy. Although no foreign nation was demanding that he relinquish power or even change his major policies, there was general agreement that his methods were too blunt. As one senior U.S. State Department official put it, Peru would have to "get that democratic feeling back."[59] The president was a quick study—before his first month in dictatorial power was up, he had announced that he would hold a plebiscite within six months and called for a "national dialogue for peace and development." Although Fujimori was opposed to political parties, which he saw as overly powerful, politicizing everything, not internally democratic, and serving only narrow interests, he urged them to take part in elections for a constituent assembly that would also serve as a legislature until a new constitution could take effect.

Fujimori's own party, Cambio 90, won a majority of seats in the new assembly in the November elections, partly because two other major parties boycotted the election, but also because so many Peruvian voters had been disappointed by the performance of the previous ostensibly democratic government and believed that Peru needed "stronger government to

Alberto Fujimori, the president of Peru who strengthened his power by staging a "self-coup," outlines his government strategy in a news conference. (Reuters/Anibal Solimano/Archive Photos)

deal with the chaos, insecurity and corruption that had become a part of daily life."[60]

Once given this democratic ratification for the abolition of democracy, Fujimori could pursue his program. Interestingly enough, he was not backed by the entire military, despite the measures he took on their behalf.[61] But his gains were strong: Terrorism was significantly reduced after the capture of the head and seven other top leaders of Shining Path; inflation, which had run at 40 percent per month, was down to 15 percent per year by 1994; and economic growth was up to 12.9 percent that year.[62] Privatization of the economy moved along rapidly, often into the hands of foreign investors, thereby helping to build foreign exchange reserves of $7 billion. A U.S. debt restructuring plan (the Brady plan) reduced the total foreign private debt by nearly half. The constitution Fujimori had sought, giving stronger powers to the executive and the military, was approved in the fall of 1993 by a yes vote of 52 percent; Fujimori was elected to a second term (something that would have been impossible under the old constitution) in April 1995 by a vote of 64 percent; and his party took 67 of 120 seats in the new legislature. These impressive electoral results were owing in part to clever strategies used to encourage opposition candidates and new parties—the thirteen competitors for the presidency and the nineteen opposition parties seeking legislative seats thoroughly divided the opposition vote—but on the whole the election was seen as "free and fair despite some local irregularities."[63]

But not all the signs are positive. The country's growth rate, although still strong, had fallen to 6.7 percent by the mid-1990's and was expected to keep falling; the economy is in a recession "produced by major cuts in public spending that are needed to meet debt payments." Furthermore, aside from some improvements in the availability of electricity and water, the condition of the ordinary people of Peru is little changed. As of mid-1996, 85 percent of the workforce still did not have full time jobs, 55 percent lived in poverty, and "the influx of foreign companies and investment into Peru [had] produced no perceptible job growth." Yet the president's approval rating, while dropping, still stood at 60 percent.[64] Apparently the results of Fujimori's tenure do not seem worse than what most Peruvians knew under the "protected democracy" in place before he gave himself such extensive powers, and most see no good reason to believe that the fragmented and largely discredited political opposition would be able to do better. At present writing, democracy that goes deeper than the "democratic feeling" provided by competitive elections does not seem to be an option in Peru.

REGIME CHANGE AND THE INDIVIDUAL

The case of Peru might seem to suggest that regime change does not necessarily make a significant change in the lives of individuals. But this is not generally the case, and it is worth while to take some time now to examine a few of the more significant kinds of changes that can occur in private lives when regimes come and go.

Winners v. Losers: The Newly Rich, the Newly Poor

The shift to democracy may be limited to electoral formalism in many nations; the shift to capitalism is, however, likely to have far-reaching effects almost immediately. Of course, authoritarian communism did not eliminate economic inequity and most noncommunist authoritarian states did not even seriously aspire to do so; what is new under worldwide market capitalism is not that such inequities exist, but that different people are getting rich—and getting poor.

We have not said much in this chapter about regime change in Russia,

FIGURE 14.3

A Guide to Privatization in Russia. Russian Regions Ranked by Level of Privatization, February 1994[a]

[a]Determined by the ratio of number of enterprises privatized to the number of enterprises subject to privatization under the official program; regions coded as privatizing "over 100%," such as the City of St. Petersburg, privatized more enterprises than required by the state.

Source: Elisabeth Rubinfien, "Divide and Conquer: Russia Demands a Regional Approach," *Central European Economic Review* 2, no. 2 (Spring 1994): 13. Reprinted b permission of Central European Economic Review, © 1944 Dow Jones & Company, Inc. All Rights Reserved Worldwide.

partly because the process in that complex land is so unpredictable that tomorrow's headlines are likely to contradict any generalizations we might venture today. However, in recent years Russia has provided us with a wealth of examples to illustrate the impact on individual lives of a sharp shift to free market practices. Economic liberalization, including drastic cuts in public spending and extensive privatization of state-owned firms, has proceeded at a rapid pace (see Figure 14.3), while overall productivity has taken a sharp dip (down 36% between 1989 and 1993) and inflation has only recently begun to come under control.[65] Such macrolevel changes do not fail to touch the lives of individuals. There are exciting opportunities for those well positioned to take advantage of them. Oleg Polumordvininov, who sells Japanese electronic space heaters and other appliances he buys in Vladivostok, happily reports a "kind of trading frenzy" and his fellow trader Alexandr V. Levin, who buys Russian pig iron, lead concentrate, and raw materials for Japan and sells Japanese consumer goods, forklifts, trucks, and electronics to Russia, is also enthusiastic: "When you succeed, wealth multiplies very quickly."[66] Thirty-six-year old Nikolai Panchenko would surely agree: his new house in Zubchaninovka is a "colossal, turreted, walled-off brick mansion" complete with enormous bedrooms, a sauna and swimming pool in the basement, stained glass windows upstairs, and a marble entrance hall with a massive crystal chandelier. Prior to the fall of the Soviet state, he and his father were engaged in illegal speculation in consumer goods; Panchenko senior spent nine years in prison for selling sheepskin hats and nylon raincoats. But now Nikolai's 77-year-old father "watches with satisfaction as [his son] expands his business, opening a food store, dealing in car parts and importing consumer goods from Europe— all of it legal."[67]

That's nice for the Panchenkos and the other successful traders, but not everyone fares so well. Take the case of Viktor Popov, one of the world's leading experts in cell biophysics for the past twenty-three years, whose laboratory now has less than 5 percent the funding it used to have, with "no money for equipment, for new journals, for computers" and who is one of several leading Soviet scientists seeking to supplement their incomes by tutoring American high school students during the summer.[68] Or consider the plight of Yefim and Olga Hayut, young doctors in Tver, Russia, who earn a combined monthly salary of 1,000 rubles. The elimination of virtually all price controls by Russian President Boris Yeltsin in 1992 reduced the value of this income, formerly sufficient to feed the Hayuts and their two children, to the equivalent of less than $10 a month. "Our profession will always be needed," says Yefim, "but I'm not sure this profession will always be able to feed me."[69]

Enterprising capitalists assisted by foreign investors and investments are frequently winners in the new regimes (for the extent of foreign investment in Russia, see Figure 14.4). Professionals like Viktor Popov and Yefim Hayut appear to be, at least for now, clearly on the losing side. Others, like Vera Simyonova, a 38-year-old cleaning woman, are out-and-out losers. Simyonova was never wealthy, but the food packages and other state assistance she used to receive from the old centrally controlled economic system now no longer come her way. Her income of 200 rubles is far below the poverty line (1,900 rubles a month), and to support herself and her mentally handicapped 14-year-old son she now goes, with hundreds of others like herself, to the outdoor market in the town of Tishinsky every day to try to sell whatever personal belongings she can, including canned food in her cupboard left over from the days of subsidized prices. Simyonova is not a fan of regime change: "Under Brezhnev," she says, referring to the days when hardliner Leonid Brezhnev was the Soviet leader, "everything was cheap. We could live."[70]

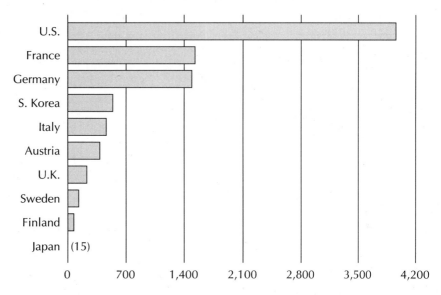

FIGURE 14.4   **Foreign Investment in Russia. Value of Investments Between January 1990 and September 1993 (in $US Millions)**

Source: Elisabeth Rubinfien, "Divide and Conquer: Russia Demands a Regional Approach," *Central European Economic Review* 2, no. 2 (Spring 1994): 12.

Women and Regime Change

As the case of Vera Simyonova and her son suggests, women and children are often particularly vulnerable to the impact of regime change on individual lives. Lynne Haney summarizes some of the changes in eastern Europe: the closing of child care centers and curtailment of maternity leave spending as part of cuts in government spending; the emphasis on the role of women as consumers in the new market economies (fashion magazines, home improvement guides), the spread of pornography as a result of the new freedom of the press (and the new license to focus on profit at the expense of other values); and the tendency of the new democratic parliaments to be almost exclusively male.[71]

As regime change has led to the reduction of government employees, women workers in the public sector have often been fired in disproportionate numbers. Over two-thirds of Russia's unemployed are women, and women are far more likely than men to be required to take extended holidays without pay or at the minimum wage, or to leave the workforce altogether. In an interview given in 1993, Gennady Melikyan, Russia's labor minister, was unconcerned: "Why should we employ women when men are out of work? It's better that men work and women take care of children and do housework." Foreign observers have noted that "sexual harassment in the workplace is rampant in today's Russia," but although there are laws in place against such acts, cases that are reported are normally neither denounced nor investigated.[72]

(Jeff Danziger © *The Christian Science Monitor*)

It should be remembered, however, that women's role was far from idyllic under communism. Although women entered the labor force en masse, they still spent nearly three times longer on household tasks than men and held the lower skilled and lower paid jobs. In Hungary, they earned on average only 72 percent of what men were paid for equal work. In the Soviet Union, vocational training schools were segregated and provided different kinds of training for girls and boys. And one author insists, Polish men still "kissed women's hands, [but] never did a jot of housework."[73]

Furthermore, most women did not change their image of themselves during the communist era in ways that are familiar to Western women. According to observers, they needed to work and enjoyed working, but they were usually ready to agree with those who claimed that work was less important to a woman than to a man. Lynne Haney quotes a Hungarian sociologist she interviewed in 1987: "I know what to do at the workplace. I do it without concern. My husband is so concerned about work. Not me. . . . This struggle does not concern me."[74]

BOX 14.3   WOMEN BEFORE AND AFTER THE REGIME CHANGE IN POLAND

WALBRZYCH, Poland — The workers of the state-owned Porcelana china factory went on strike in 1980 against the evils of communism and in favor of political liberation. In 1993, the workers of the privately owned Porcelana china factory went on strike against the evils of capitalism and in favor of women's liberation.

The first strike took a decade to show results. The second might take longer. Communism was no picnic, but it gave women standing at work and security at home.

Now they have got stress at work and strife at home. Poles are so aggrieved at how capitalism has been thrust on them that in September they voted the old order's descendants back into power. Polish women have reason to feel more aggrieved than most.

The two-month strike . . . was about layoffs and low pay. The company agreed to think those things over, and work resumed in August. But at root, the strike was also about ownership: The women of Porcelana believe they got a better shake from the state. [Their boss] wholeheartedly agrees: "Day care. Holiday resorts. Subsidies for single mothers," he says. "These women got all kinds of assistance. It was a custom. A habit. They got soft treatment from management. Now they have lost these grants. This factory pays only for work done."

Source: Barry Newman, "Women in Poland Find Little Liberation in Shift to Democracy," *Wall Street Journal*, 19 Nov. 1993, 1, and A11. Reprinted by permission of The Wall Street Journal, © 1993 Dow Jones & Company, Inc. All Rights Reserved Worldwide.

Such attitudes, carried forward into the present period, have clearly made it more difficult for women to fight for rights that are now ever more reduced. But there are a few signs of change. In her postrevolution research, Haney found some younger and better-educated Hungarian women who "flirted with notions of equality" and Barry Newman notes that in Poland, where the overall situation is much the same (see Box 14.3), some women are becoming owners of small businesses, women academics have succeeded in changing the law calling for their mandatory retirement at age 60, and have begun to introduce women's studies courses, and women's magazines now run stories advising readers, "Don't be afraid of success."[75]

The Impact of Regime Change on Individuals in Stable Democracies

There are, of course, many other kinds of individuals whose lives are thrown in turmoil by regime change: children, members of minority groups, and refugees of all ages, to name only a few. We have mentioned some of the effects on such groups in earlier chapters and today's newspapers, magazines, and broadcast reports are only too replete with stories giving the often sad details—our failure to treat these groups here is thus no indication they are not of the utmost importance. We conclude this section with a brief look at what regime change has meant to a different kind of group: the citizens of stable democracies.

How have those of us who live in regimes unaffected by massive regime change been responding to the news we receive of these events? There are several possible replies, all of them correct for different people at different times: We pay no attention, we seek ways to profit from the change, we become anxious that such changes will endanger our own well-being and try to take preventive steps, or we try to find ways to help make the transitions of other regimes go as smoothly and painlessly as possible. Those who pay no attention often have little or no information and/or are deeply concerned about problems at home. Others are far more aware of the connections between what happens abroad and the chance of profits at home: one-third of the gross domestic product and one-third of the jobs in the North Carolina congressional district of Republican Representative Mark Sanford depend on foreign trade; not suprisingly, Sanford reports, "Most of the people in my district would say we need to stay connected with the rest of the world."[76]

Others take a more fearful stance. In nations that have been attracting large numbers of the refugees forced out by regime changes at home, members of the local population may turn against foreign asylum seekers and try to take steps to keep them out. Far-right groups in France and Germany have taken extremist steps, attacking individual refugees and campaigning for office on anti-immigrant platforms, and even the more moderate governments of both nations have reduced the ease of access for immigrant populations.[77] There are, however, others who are unhappy with current rates of immigration but think a different approach is in order. Prime Minister Poul Nyrup Rasmussen of Denmark argues that the best way for European nations to keep immigrants out is to provide more aid to other nations: "If you don't help the Third World, if you don't help northern Africa, if you don't help eastern and central Europe with a little part of your welfare, then you will have these poor people in our society," says Rasmussen.[78]

William Pfaff believes that the failure of the Western powers to take positive steps to end the civil war that erupted in the midst of regime change in the former Yugoslavia was owing to a general tendency of the citizens and governments of democracies to become excessively complacent: "We say that because the democracies are virtuous they will always win out in the end. . . . Democracies don't like sacrifices, or the politicians who demand them . . . Democracies don't want their comfort or profits interfered with."[79] Still others believe the general public is willing to try to help but suffers from misinformation. For example, recent polls show that a majority of U.S. citizens would be willing to spend more than 1 percent of the annual budget on foreign aid; however, they believe that the amount that is actually being spent is fifteen to twenty times that figure. In point of fact, the United States spends only about 1 percent on foreign aid, the lowest percentage of gross national product that any of the developed nations disburses.[80]

REGIME CHANGE AND INTERNATIONAL INSTITUTIONS

Whatever the perspective of citizens inside regimes, most observers are forced to agree that the problems raised by change on such a massive scale cannot all be solved by individual nations. As we have noted several times, international forces are involved in facilitating the economic and political changes under way; they are also involved in trying to correct the mistakes that have been made and bring relief to those whose lives have been shattered. And all of them are themselves affected by the scope of change— the roles they play are seldom what they were before 1989. Here we will consider, briefly and in general terms, the impact of regime change on international government organizations, international nongovernment organizations, and international business.

International Government Institutions

The international government organizations most profoundly affected by the sweeping regime changes of the past few years have been the previously "subglobal" economic organizations such as the IMF, the World Bank, and the General Agreement on Tariffs and Trade (GATT). All now boast virtually universal membership and have, as we have seen, played a very strong role in shaping the economies of the new regimes. The number of countries seeking IMF funds to rehabilitate their economies has risen to ninety (from sixty-three in 1989). The powerful agency continues to operate with no public or professional scrutiny; its meetings are closed and the minutes are not made public—even the amount of money the fund has to lend is never announced.[81]

Other groupings that have no aspirations to universality, such as the European Community, the Organization for Economic Cooperation and Development (OECD), and the Association of South East Asian Nations (ASEAN), have also been able, since 1989, to broaden their membership and to look ahead to yet a wider scope for action, as political reasons for declining membership have disappeared and the economic necessity of not being left behind has become ever more apparent.[82]

As we saw in Chapter 13, the United Nations has had a difficult time in the post–Cold War years, unprepared as it was to assume so massive and so difficult a peacekeeping role in lands where regime change was the first step to civil war. But its efforts to meet the challenge have met with some success, as we have seen, and it has often been particularly effective in providing the humanitarian aid that is so essential a step to rehabilitation of wartorn polities.

International military alliances such as NATO and the Warsaw Pact have been the most profoundly affected agencies of international governance. The latter lost all reason for existence and disappeared; the former has assumed peacekeeping functions of its own, particularly in ex-Yugoslavia, and is being urged to bring in new members from East and Central Europe, and possibly even Russia and other former Soviet states.[83]

International Nongovernment Organizations

Private international organizations seeking to improve the human condition by attacking particular problems are gathering more international recognition and support; at the same time, they often find the problems on which they focus to be ever more massive and intractable. As Peter J. Spiro says, "Environmentalists, human rights activists, women, children, animal rights advocates, consumers, the disabled, gays, and indigenous peoples have all gone international. . . . These groups have developed distinct agendas at the global level, and in the form of nongovernmental organizations (NGOs) they are working with increasing sophistication to further these interests in international institutions." The "explosion" in the number of such groups—there are now some 14,500 international nongovernmental organizations (NGOs)—has been made possible by the greater ease of travel and more rapid communication (including the fax and the Internet). It has been made necessary by the global nature of the problems we face today, many of which are directly linked to the recent upheavals caused by regime change.[84]

Not all NGOs work by bringing pressure to bear on official international agencies. Sometimes they work alone, sometimes they seek to pressure national governments, sometimes they seek to arouse public opinion—and, of course, the same agency may combine several methods. When the Human Rights Watch issued its report for 1995, it called upon the United Nations to be less committed to neutrality, more prepared to act forcefully when "faced with genocide and mass slaughter." At the same time, the organization made a sharp attack on the governments of the United States, Germany, France, Canada, and Australia for putting "geopolitical designs and commercial motives" ahead of concern for human rights abuses and for "hawking trade and investment deals while relegating human rights to the ineffectual realm of private diplomacy."[85]

In other cases, the relationship is reversed and government aid programs seek out the NGOs, believing that funneling public assistance through such agencies may be a better way of reaching "the poorest." However, observers find little evidence that NGOs are able to reach the neediest any better than well-meaning government bureaucrats (although they may do so more cost effectively) and point out the danger to such groups of being coopted by officialdom, thereby losing their legitimacy as independent and effective agents of social transformation. Naturally enough, the groups themselves tend to welcome the opportunity to expand their funding and effectiveness.[86]

International Business

In the best of all semantic worlds, we would recognize that transnational corporations are also NGOs, albeit profit-seeking NGOs. However, scholarly usage forbids us to call them that; the acronym of choice is TNC. As you may have noticed, the first qualification for the study of international relations today is an ability to master the acronyms. It isn't fair to change them in midstream, and so we will stick with TNC.[87]

The causal relationship between TNCs and contemporary regime

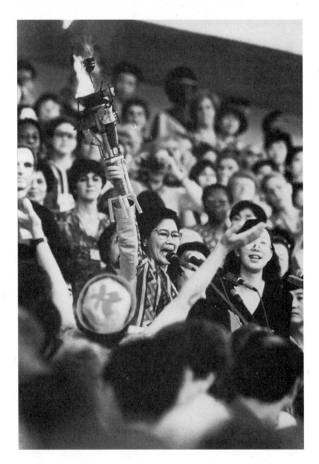

International Non-government Organizations. The United Nations Women's Convention, held in Beijing, China, in September of 1995, brought together representatives from women's organizations around the world. (Corbis-Bettmann)

change is clearly reciprocal. International business interests have strongly influenced the decisions of the international funding agencies that are so actively shaping the new economies; the investment opportunities thus produced have in turn revolutionized the international business world. The rush to privatize has opened investment opportunities to businesses as well as to individuals. The readiness of new regimes to welcome foreign owners as well as investors has led to the building of new plants in cities never considered before.[88] At the same time, the liberalization of trade means that it is often not necessary to build such plants in order to be multinational—key steps in the production and distribution of many products are now routinely "outsourced" to entrepreneurs in other lands, where lower wage costs and "less restrictive" labor practices contribute to higher profits.

One of the most interesting developments in the relationship between transnational businesses and regime change is the new link between some TNCs and large-scale international development banks (IDBs). We have often mentioned the two most important banks of this type, the World Bank and the International Monetary Fund; two others with major funding are the International Finance Corporation (affiliated with the World Bank) and the Inter-American Development Bank. The announced mission of such banks, which are put together by the governments of nation-states and financed by taxpayers, is to help less developed nations (LDCs) out of chronic poverty. Each year they generate about $30 billion in contracts.

Such contracts are more and more likely to go to private entrepreneurs rather than to the governments concerned. "The Cold War's demise removes the philosophical underpinnings for the earlier support of government intervention," says one former top official of the World Bank. By this he means that it is no longer necessary to make loans directly to governments to keep them from "going communist." In addition, the banks are now beginning to align themselves more openly with private investment funds in the First World, serving as advisors and sometimes entering into cofinancing of projects that are likely to bring those private investors profits as high as 25 percent a year.[89] To understand how this process works, read Box 14.4.

The competition for TNC investment monies has also had a profound effect on First World nations, now engaged in sometimes drastic recreations of themselves. New Zealand is an interesting example. Long ruled by a socialist party, the new New Zealand is now completing a massive privatization program and has little concern for the nationality of the buyers of the formerly state-owned enterprises. As one CEO (whose forestry business snapped up the state timber operation during privatization and was then itself acquired by the International Paper Company) says, "We think internationally now." Today, over half of New Zealand's stock market capitalization is foreign money. But attracting foreign investors has meant downsizing the labor force and reducing workers' rights and services "that were once taken for granted." The Employment Contracts Act of 1991 gives employers in New Zealand the right to negotiate directly with employees; since its adoption, "union membership has plunged 38 percent through layoffs."[90]

Richard J. Barnet has written one of the most scathing attacks on the effect TNCs are having on the economy and labor force of the United States. Outraged by the fact that "the world's 358 billionaires have a combined net worth of $760 billion, equal to that of the bottom 45 percent of the world population . . . the average CEO in the United States now brings home about 149 times the average factory worker's pay . . . an estimated 18 percent of American workers with full-time jobs earn poverty-level wages; [and] since 1973, the number of American children living in poverty has increased by 50 percent," Barnet puts the blame squarely on

BOX 14.4   **INTERNATIONAL DEVELOPMENT — OF WHAT, FOR WHOM?**

The Inter-American Development Bank is owned by forty-six nations. Its mission is to reduce the chronic poverty of Latin America, and it loans billions of dollars to private businesses in those nations. In the fall of 1995 the bank entered into a "first-of-its-kind" alliance with a private group of investors, including Lloyd M. Bentsen, U.S. Secretary of the Treasury in 1993 and 1994 and a former governor of the bank, now a private businessman. The alliance will provide a "billion-dollar investment fund banked by giant corporations and pension funds. They hope to realize profits of as much as 25 percent a year by investing in Latin American power projects, telecommunications systems and toll roads." The agreement with the Inter-American Development Bank will include "information sharing and possible co-financing," according to Mr. Bentsen. Many of the managers of the investment group formerly held high positions in this or other independent development banks (IDBs), including the World Bank.

Jerome Booth, head of emerging markets research for a private bank, points out that the fund's natural emphasis on profitseeking may distort the kind of development pursued. He believes that banks like the Inter-American Development Bank should just be "in the business of helping development of countries, typically things like water, sanitation, health and education, not toll roads, telecommunications or power stations."

The bank's president, Enrique V. Iglesias, recognizes that the new alliance could pose some problems. He promises that the bank will "prod Mr. Bentsen's fund to follow its lead and invest in the region's neediest countries. But he . . . fears 'money will only flow to the best projects' since Mr. Bentsen's fund's stated intention is to make 80 percent of its investments in the region's six richest countries."

Louis T. Wells, professor of International Management at Harvard Business School, says, "It's going to be questioned in the host country where somebody is going to say we could have raised this money a lot cheaper. It's an interesting dilemma."

Donald Strombon, a business consultant in Washington, D.C., isn't worried. He says forming links with the IDBs is good business: "The multilateral development banks do $30 billion a year in contracts awarded by borrowers, and . . . give out another $4–$5 billion in consulting contracts. It's a very sizable market."

Moeen Qureshi, a former top official of the World Bank and identified as the "brains" behind the new alliance, agrees with Strombon and points out the advantages of working through an IDB: "The risk is lower with the presence of a multilateral institution. Governments will think twice about reneging on an obligation where a public institution is involved."

Source: Drawn from Jeff Gerth, "In Post-Cold-War Washington, Development Is a Hot Business," *New York Times*, 25 May 1996, 1, 6.

the "stateless corporations" of the world, who are, he says, just "walking away from the enormous public problems their private decisions create for American society." Gone are the good old days when "big companies created tens of millions of well-paid jobs, provided health care and pensions, and brought women and minorities into the work force." Now "a global pool of bargain labor is available to companies making virtually anything" and "about a third of the jobs in the United States are at risk to . . . low-wage workers . . . elsewhere." Strikes don't work anymore—"Management now wields the more credible threat: Take it or we leave"—and only 12 percent of the U.S. workforce in private industry is now organized for collective bargaining. American workers in the "superstar" category "bring home a fortune every year," but the median earnings of the professional class and most entertainers are staying flat, and the real wages of low-ranked workers like janitors, bank tellers, and back-office employees in brokerage houses have fallen 15 percent or more. Layoffs and CEO salaries are up, often in tandem (twenty-three of the nation's top "job-slashers" received raises averaging 30 percent in 1993). The corporate share of federal income taxes has fallen from 23 percent in the 1950s to 9.2 percent in 1991 as TNCS have improved their competitiveness by going "stateless" and basing their accounting operations in tax havens abroad.

Barnet does not offer any easy cures. He thinks the dependency of both political parties and their leaders on "the obscenely expensive, never-ending campaign that now defines American politics" means that even in the United States free elections are not enough to guarantee that those chosen will be able to carry out their programs (he cites the failures of Clinton's health care reform and job creation programs, which he ascribes to the "medical-industrial complex" and the bond market, respectively). Furthermore, it is hard to get the message out, says Barnet: "[The] rage and the fury found almost everywhere . . . is directed almost exclusively at government because the mainstream media . . . never target global corporations as major contributors to the nation's socio-economic woes, and because even if they did, the business behemoths would seem beyond reach."[91]

A. G. Kefalas agrees that the TNCS now have amazing power, surpassing that of the nation-state, and describes them as "at the center of the entire world-reshaping scheme." But Kefalas has hopes that Barnet does not seem to share. He outlines three ways of looking at TNCs—pessimistic, optimistic, and melioristic (it can get better)—and tends to take a point of view somewhere between the second and the third positions. International businesses are, Kefalas says, "a potent and potentially valuable force that must be integrated into" the process of building a new world order that brings "a more equitable distribution of material wealth." He is confident the nation-states of the world "share the goals of establishing world security, increasing world productivity, stabilizing the world populations, sustaining economic growth, creating equitable conditions for development and promoting world monetary stability," and he is sure international business possesses "great potential for facilitating the accomplishment of these goals." Kefalas therefore recommends recognizing such businesses as "full-fledged partners" in the work at hand, and he urges the businesses themselves to "engage in a process of self-assessment in order to bring [their] philosophies, policies, and operating procedures in line with the idea of an interdependent world of diverse but unified societies."[92]

The ideas of Kefalas are reassuring; those of Barnet are tough to take. Both writers agree that we are giving too little attention to the power these giants now wield over our lives. Kefalas's point that TNCs are helping to bring a more equitable distribution of material wealth may have some rough truth to it, but when your company moves its business to another land, it is hard to be joyous about the fact that a fraction of what was your salary now goes to someone who still lives in poverty. Barnet's point about our growing inability to keep control of our own governments, given the dependency of elected leaders on those who paid for their campaigns, is one I have made in this book (see Chapters 7 and 8) and one with which many others agree. As we have seen throughout this chapter, it is difficult to deepen democracy in the nations that have recently adopted free elections; Barnet reminds us it may be time to take soundings on the profundity of those democracies we take for granted, including our own. Kefalas's recommendation to take TNCs in as full partners seems a bit behind the times, inasmuch as they appear already to be senior partners, and it is difficult to find realistic grounds for his pious hope they will engage in "self-assessment" and reform. Both agree there are serious problems to resolve.

CONCLUSION

But the human polity never gives up. There must be a way out of the complex and interwoven dilemmas that have followed so swiftly and dishearteningly on the regime changes that initially promised such a brave new world. There must be something the individuals who make up the human polity—like you, like me—can do to insist that change be followed by change, that the problems that have emerged must be solved, and to help find the solutions. What must we do? What can we do?

Our first job, it seems to me, is to know what our values are and figure out which of them matter the most. Can you make a list of your values? Can you figure out which comes first, which last? Are you willing to sacrifice one on behalf of another that is higher on your list?

A second, and equally important, job is for us all to develop a new and deeper respect for the truth, as well as we are able to determine what that strange animal may be. "Reason from evidence" is easy to say, not so easy to do. We need to act on our values, of course, but we must not let serving them cause us to deny obvious realities or entertain unreal hopes that all our woes will somehow magically just go away. There is real work to be done.

That being so, the next thing to do is to choose a task and choose a way to work on it. We cannot all do everything, but every one of us can make some kind of contribution. Really working on one small part of one small problem is surely better than *thinking* about working on everything. Maybe you will join others who are trying to do the same thing—that's a good way to learn what works and to maximize the effect of the work you do. But you may be a loner, at least for now, and that's okay. Everyone can find a way to help.

But suppose the public service work you decide to do just makes the job chosen by that guy who sits on the other side of the classroom harder to do? We don't all have the same values, we do sometimes work at cross-purposes. There is no total cure for this, but there are a couple of partial ones. Keeping respect for the truth (see earlier) means hearing what "that guy" has to say and basing your defense of what you are trying to do on the most solid facts you can find. You two may find you can work together after all.

The other partial cure for the tendency of human beings to cancel each other out is for us all to learn to keep a new thought constantly in mind: *connectedness*. By this I do not mean only that the human polity consists of all the world's peoples, ever more dependent on one another for their well-being (so be nice). I mean something a bit more tangible than that. To see what connectedness means, pick up a copy of today's newspaper and make a list of all the headlines having to do with national or international news. Then ask yourself what each one has to do with all the others. Anything? Everything? Try it and see. Then think about how the problem you have decided to work on is connected to other problems and other efforts (not all of them benign). If you do this, chances are you will find a way to work on your problem that is less likely to be at cross-purposes with the work of others who share your general hopes for a better and fairer world.

While you are doing all this, you may as well give some thought to what you think the role of international institutions should be and how to get them to play it. Would it be best to follow the Kefalas approach and join efforts that seek to persuade the TNCs of the importance of self-reform? Or is that unreasonable in a world where "noncompetitive" today can mean "nonexistent" tomorrow? Would it be better to work to strengthen international governance institutions whose reach might eventually match that of the TNCs? Or is any form of business regulation simply antithetical to your values?

Whatever you decide and whatever you do, a final thought to keep in mind, or so it seems to me, is the need to work where and when we can. This is a tricky one. Whether they end up working in the schools, the government, or the business world, political scientists have tough work to do that may or may not be related to saving the world. Academic freedom is all well and good, but no department head is going to hand out many accolades or promotions to teachers or professors whose work seems biased and oblivious of different points of view. No senior government bureaucrat or elected official needs to hear daily lectures from junior staff about how important it is to build international governance institutions that work, given the frailty of the nation-state. And no boss in private business is likely to keep paying a junior employee who insists day after day that the company has a social responsibility to avoid layoffs at home and make sure its investments abroad are creating jobs with good pay and good working conditions and not extracting unreasonable profits. No matter what their field of employ, most junior employees do well to keep most of their sociopolitical activism for after hours. Otherwise, they may end up having *only* after hours.

But you are not always going to be a junior employee, are you? Someday you will be that tenured teacher, that senior bureaucrat, or that boss, right? And what then? Well, for one thing, by then you should have a better idea what kinds of recommendations and activities on behalf of your beliefs are reasonable and appropriate in your line of work. If you say, "None," then answer me this: How will the behaviors of governments or businesses ever improve if living and breathing social scientists, bureaucrats, elected officials, and businessmen and women take no responsibility beyond that of earning a living wage? Let us hope that when you reach a more senior position, you will make a point of taking **connectedness** seriously, in every aspect of your own life as well as in the way you read the headlines.

Who can tell if you will? Not I. But I can hope. And only thus, it seems to me, can any of us hope for the creation of a human polity in which all humanity has a home. This new ethic—this very *old* ethic—must somehow be made to grow and thrive in all our connected worlds. Making this happen is a tremendous challenge. And an absolute necessity.

Selected Readings

Adelman, Sammy and Abdul Paliwala. *Law and Crisis in the Third World*. London: Hans Zell, 1993. Essays examining the major issues in law and development in light of changes in the world system.

Barnet, Richard J. and John Cavanagh. *Global Dreams: Imperial Corporations in the New World Order*. New York: Simon and Schuster, 1994. The rise of multinational corporations, with a discussion of how transanational business is affecting the standard of living throughout the world.

Cameron, Maxwell A. *Democracy and Authoritarianism in Peru: Political Coalitions and Social Change*. New York: St. Martin's Press, 1994. Discussion and analysis of the recent political history of Peru.

Dahl, Robert A. *Democracy and its Critics*. New Haven: Yale University Press, 1989. A detailed overview of the history of democracy from ancient Greece to modern times.

Hogan, Michael J. *The End of the Cold War: Its Meaning and Implications*. Cambridge, England: Cambridge University Press, 1992. A collection of articles discussing the significance of the end of the Cold War.

Jarausch, Konrad Hugo. *The Rush to German Unity*. Oxford: Oxford University Press, 1994. Provides an interesting chronicle of the events leading to the unification of West and East Germany.

Markoff, John. *Waves of Democracy: Social Movements and Political Change*. Thousand Oaks, CA.: Pine Forge Press, 1996. An attempt to locate current efforts of democratization within an historical context, giving special emphasis to the role of social movements in this process.

Moreno, David. *The Struggle for Peace in Central America.* Gainesville, Florida: University Press of Florida, 1994. A political history of peace and social justice movements in Central America.

Sorensen, Georg. *Democracy and Democratization: Processes and Prospects in a Changing World.* Boulder, Colo.: Westview Press, 1993. Reviews the elements of democracy and discusses new systems that may result from the changing world order.

Stokes, Gale. *The Walls Came Tumbling Down: The Collapse of Communism in Eastern Europe.* Oxford: Oxford University Press, 1993. Examines the decline and fall of communism in Eastern Europe, beginning in 1965 and carrying forward to the present day.

Notes

1. Carole Pateman, "Democracy and Democratization," *International Political Science Review* 17, no. 1 (1996): 5–12. As Pateman points out, "Never before has democracy been so popular" (p. 5).
2. Georg Sorensen, *Democracy and Democratization: Processes and Prospects in a Changing World,* (Boulder, Colo.: Westview Press, 1993), p. 31.
3. Philippe C. Schmitter and Terry Lynn Karl, "What Democracy Is . . . And Is Not," in Larry Diamond and Marc F. Plattner, *The Global Resurgence of Democracy* (Baltimore: Johns Hopkins University Press, 1993), p. 40.
4. Robert A. Dahl, *Democracy and Its Critics* (New Haven: Yale University Press, 1989), pp. 106–115.
5. Peter H. Merkl, "Which Are Today's Democracies?" *International Social Science Journal* 136 (May 1993): 257–58.
6. George Munda Carew, "Development Theory and the Promise of Democracy: The Future of Postcolonial African States," *Africa Today* 40, no. 4 (1993): 46–50.
7. Sidney Verba, "A Research Perspective" in "Threats to Democracy: Plenary Session IV," Commission on Behavioral and Social Sciences and Education, National Research Council, *The Transition to Democracy: Proceedings of a Workshop* (Washington, D.C.: National Academy Press, 1991), p. 78.

8. Schmitter and Karl, "What Democracy Is," p. 49.
9. Philippe Braud, *Le Suffrage universel contre la démocratie* (Paris: Presses Universitaires de France, 1980) et *Le Jardin des délices démocratiques* (Paris: Presses de la Fondation Nationale des Sciences Politiques, 1991).
10. Schmitter and Karl, "What Democracy Is," p. 51; Jane Mansbridge, "Politics," in "What Is a Democracy? Plenary Session I," Commission on Behavioral and Social Sciences and Education, *Transition to Democracy,* p. 6.
11. Mansbridge, "Politics," p. 5. Mansbridge bases this statement on unpublished data from the Yale Human Relations Area Files on 186 societies. She notes it requires us to presume that Germany was a monarchy in World War I and a dictatorship in World War II and that Lebanon in 1967 was a military regime. We might add that the statement also requires us to ignore civil wars within democracies and the readiness of other democracies to come to the aid of one side or the other in such internal battles.
12. Sorensen, *Democracy and Democratization,* pp. 25–28.
13. Seymour Martin Lipset, "The Social Requisites of Democracy Revisited," *American Sociological Review* 59 (Feb. 1994): 1.
14. Doh Chull Sin, "On The Third Wave of Democratization: A Synthesis and Evaluation of Recent Theory and Research," *World Politics* 47, no. 1 (Oct. 1994): 151.
15. Sorensen, *Democracy and Democratization,* pp. 29–30. Such negotiations mean, he argues, that the new regimes' ability to introduce social and economic reform measures—measures which might harm the interests of the elites—will necessarily be restricted.
16. Charles Tilly, "Overview," in "Comment and Synthesis: Plenary Session III," *Transition to Democracy,* pp. 60–61; see also p. 25.
17. Verba, "Research Perspective," pp. 82–83.
18. These authors are cited by Shin, "On the Third Wave," pp. 144–45.
19. Ibid., p. 137.
20. Sorensen, *Democracy and Democratization,* pp. 40, 61–62.
21. *New York Times,* 21 Nov. 1995, A14.
22. Kenneth Ka-Lok Chan, "Poland at the Crossroads: The 1993 General Election," *Europe-Asia Studies* 47, no. 1 (1995): 125–27.

23. "Nostalgia Wins the Day in Poland," *New States-man and Society* (1 Oct. 1993): 20–21.

24. Ray Taras, "The End of the Walesa Era in Poland," *Current History* 95, no. 599 (March 1996): 127.

25. "Kwasniewski Wins: Political Lessons Explored," *The Current Digest of the Post-Soviet Press* 47, no. 47 (1995): 15–17.

26. *New York Times*, 6 Nov. 1995, A3.

27. "Kwasniewski Wins," *Current Digest*, pp. 16–17.

28. For some representative accounts, see Patrick H. O'Neil, "Hungary's Hesitant Transition," *Current History* 95, no. 599 (March 1996): 135–39; Barnabas Racz and Istvan Kukorelli, "The 'Second-Generation' Post-communist Elections in Hungary in 1994," *Europe-Asia Studies* 47, no. 2 (March 1995): 251–79; "Bulgaria, Back under Ex-Communism," *The Economist* (7 Jan. 1995): 43–44; Samuel Abraham, "Early Elections in Slovakia: A State of Deadlock," *Government and Opposition* 30, no. 1 (1995): 86–100; "Czechs Prepare to Vote," *The Economist* (25 May 1996): 58.

29. "Czech Republic: Surprise," *The Economist* (8 June 1996): 52–53.

30. Ibid.

31. Kate Hannan, "Reforming China's State Enterprises, 1984–93," special issue on "Enterprise Reform in Post-Socialist Societies," *Journal of Communist Studies and Transition Politics* 11, no. 1 (March 1995): 33–55.

32. David S. G. Goodman, "Collectives and Connectives, Capitalism and Corporatism: Structural Change in China," special issue on "Enterprise Reform in Post-Socialist Societies," *Journal of Communist Studies and Transition Politics* 11, no. 1 (March 1995): 12–32.

33. Shen Tong, "The Next Revolution," *New York Times*, 1 Sept. 1992, A15.

34. Goodman, "Collectives and Connectives," p. 19.

35. Melanie Beresford, "The North Vietnamese State-Owned Industrial Sector: Continuity and Change," Special Issue on "Enterprise Reform in Post-Socialist States," *Journal of Communist Studies and Transition Politics* 11, no. 1 (March 1995): 56–76.

36. "Kim Jong Il's Inheritance," *The Economist* (16 July 1994): 19–21; Susan Hurlich, "Letter from Havana: Capitalist Ways—Cubans Dabble in Free-Enterprise Markets," *Macleans* (21 Aug. 1995): 22–23; Joel Simon, "Despite U.S. Coercion, Cuba Dips Toe into Capitalist Zones," *Christian Science Monitor*, 16 July 1996, 1, 18.

37. Some of these cases are treated in Guillermo O'Donnell, Philippe C. Schmitter, and Laurence Whitehead, eds., *Transitions from Authoritarian Rule: Prospects for Democracy* (Baltimore: Johns Hopkins University Press, 1986).

38. "Democracy, African-Style," *The Economist* (3 Feb. 1996): 17.

39. "Democracy in Africa," *The Economist* (22 Feb. 1992): 17–20.

40. Jeffrey Herbst, "The Dilemmas of Explaining Political Upheaval: Ghana in Comparative Perspective," in Jennifer A. Widner, ed., *Economic Change and Political Liberalization in Sub-Saharan Africa* (Baltimore: Johns Hopkins University Press, 1994), p. 194. Herbst highlights urban populations and military and security forces as the two groups whose interests must be addressed for African leadership to stay in power.

41. Ernest Harsch, "Structural Adjustment and Africa's Democracy Movements," *Africa Today* 40, no. 4 (1993): 8.

42. Ibid., p. 23.

43. Ibid., p. 19.

44. Herbst, "Dilemmas," p. 185.

45. James C. McKinley, Jr., "After a String of Dictators, Ugandans Vote Once Again," *New York Times*, 10 May 1996, A3; Susan Linnee, "Incumbent Wins Big in Uganda," *San Francisco Chronicle*, 11 May 1996, A8.

46. Gawdat Bahgat, "Democracy in the Arab World: An Elitist Approach, "*International Relations* 12, no. 2 (Aug. 1994): 49–60.

47. John F. Clark, "Elections, Leadership and Democracy in Congo," *Africa Today* (third quarter 1994): 41–60.

48. Brian Loveman, "'Protected Democracies' and Military Guardianship: Political Transitions in Latin America, 1978–1993," *Journal of Inter-American Studies and World Affairs* 36, no. 2 (Summer 1994): 105–89. Quote from p. 105.

49. Ibid., p. 114.

50. Loveman, "'Protected Democracies,'" p. 115; Carlos M. Vilas, "Latin America in the 'New World Order': Prospects for Democracy," *International Journal of Politics, Culture and Society* 8, no. 2 (1994): 275.

51. Frances Hagopian, "After Regime Change: Au-

thoritarian Legacies, Political Representation and the Democratic Future of South America," a review article in *World Politics* 45 (April 1993): 464–500. Quote from p. 500.

52. Ibid, p. 467. In general, Hagopian stresses the need to examine each regime separately, particularly when attempting to assess the impact of the period of military rule.

53. Loveman, "'Protected Democracies,'" pp. 123–25, 157–58.

54. Guillermo O'Donnell, "Introduction to the Latin American Cases," in Guillermo O'Donnell, Philippe C. Schmitter, and Laurence Whitehead, eds., *Transitions from Authoritarian Rule: Prospects for Democracy* (Baltimore: Johns Hopkins University Press, 1986), pp. 14–15.

55. Ibid., p. 15.

56. Scott Mainwaring is another author who rejects all-encompassing pessimism, assessing democratic reforms in Chile as successful and pointing to some gains in Brazil and Uruguay. Mainwaring appears to accept, however, the truncated version of democracy that other authors cited here repudiate. See his "Democracy in Brazil and the Southern Cone: Achievements and Problems," *Journal of Interamerican Studies and World Affairs* 37, no. 1 (1995): 113–179.

57. Maxwell A. Cameron, *Democracy and Authoritarianism in Peru* (New York: St. Martin's Press, 1994), p. 149.

58. The significance of trying civilians in military courts was brought home to the U.S. public in early 1996 when New Yorker Lori Helene Berenson, whose trial was closed to the public and whose lawyers were not allowed to cross-examine witnesses or challenge key evidence, was convicted of treason in Peru by such a court, and sentenced to life in prison. *New York Times*, 14 Jan. 1996, pp. 4, 6.

59. Quoted (anonymously) by Cameron, *Democracy and Authoritarianism*, p. 155.

60. Ibid., p. 145.

61. These measures included a blanket amnesty for all human rights abuses committed from May 1980 to June 1995, as part of the struggle against terrorism. For an interesting perspective by a general forced to retire by Fujimoro for his dissident views, see Alberto Arciniega Huby, "Civil-Military Relations and a Democratic Peru," *Orbis: A Journal of World Affairs* 38, no. 1 (Winter 1994): 109–17. Much of the debate within the military seems to have centered on how to deal with the peasants making their livelihood growing coca, the base of cocaine, and with the strength of the Shining Path among this group. Arciniega favored recognizing that the peasants "were forced into this sector by the severe nature of national economic and social realities" and fighting the problem by providing alternative employment (p. 116).

62. David Scott Palmer, "'Fujipopulism' and Peru's Progress," *Current History* (Feb. 1996): 70–75.

63. Palmer, "'Fujipopulism'" pp. 73, 75.

64. *New York Times*, 19 May 1996, 4.

65. Terence Roth, "Gap Widens Between Winners and Losers," *Central European Economic Review* 2, no. 2 (Spring 1994): 5–7.

66. Mark M. Nelson, "Russia's Far East Attracts Intrepid Western Investors," *Central European Economic Review* 2, no. 2 (Spring 1994): 14. As the title of the article suggests, the opportunities Polumordvinov and Levin have depend in large part on the presence of foreign investors—and investments.

67. Lee Hockstader, "Spending Russia's New Money:Lavish Mansions are Sprouting Next to Communist-Era Hovels," *Washington Post*, 23 June 1994, A18. Not all the rich new capitalists are *newly* rich; see John Pomfret, "In E. Europe, Old Comrades are New Rich," *Washington Post*, 30 April 1994, A1, a news story about the ability of former communist party members to make the shift to the free enterprise system. ("People who made it in the old regime are going to make it in the new one too.")

68. Michael Specter, "Russia's Elite Scientists Turn High School Tutors," *New York Times*, 25 July 1994, p. A1.

69. Carey Goldberg, "Husband-Wife Doctors Join Russia's Poor," *Los Angeles Times*, 25 Jan. 1992, A1, A6.

70. Margaret Shapiro, "Moscow's Hard-Luck Flea Markets," *Washington Post*, 15 Feb. 1992, A1, A35.

71. Lynne Haney, "From Proud Worker to Good Mother: Women, the State and Regime Change in Hungary," *Frontiers* 14, no. 3: (1994), 113–50.

72. "The Human Rights Watch Global Report on Women's Human Rights," *Human Rights Watch* (Aug. 1995): 307, 316.

73. Barry Newman, "Women in Poland Find Little

Liberation in Shift to Democracy," *Wall Street Journal*, 19 Nov. 1993, 1.

74. Haney, "From Proud Worker," p. 128.

75. Ibid., p. 144; Newman, "Women in Poland," pp. 1, A11.

76. George Moffett, "Despite Threats, America Turns Its Gaze Inward," *Christian Science Monitor*, 5 June 1996, 1, 10.

77. *New York Times*, 13 June 1995, A4; *Los Angeles Times*, 8 Dec. 1992, p. A27.

78. *New York Times*, 10 March 1995, A5.

79. William Pfaff, "The Complacent Democracies, The International Community and the War in the former Yugoslavia," *New York Review of Books* July 15, 1993, 17.

80. *Christian Science Monitor*, 5 May 1995, 1, 5.

81. Jeff Gerth and Elaine Sciolino, "I.M.F. Head: He Speaks, and Money Talks," *New York Times*, 2 April 1996, A1.

82. Nicholas Bayne, "International Economic Relations After the Cold War," *Government and Opposition* 29, no. 1 (Winter 1994): 3–21.

83. *New York Times*, 24 Nov. 1994, A6. For an argument against expanding NATO, see Charles A. Kupchan, "Expand NATO—and Split Europe," *New York Times*, 27 Nov. 1994, 11. For a scholarly analysis of the link between regime change and alliances in general, see Randolph M. Siverson and Harvey Starr, "Regime Change and the Restructuring of Alliances," *American Journal of Political Science* 38 (Feb. 1994): 145–61.

84. Peter J. Spiro, "New Global Communities: Non-governmental Organizations in International Decision-Making Institutions," *Washington Quarterly* 18, no. 1 (1994): 45–56.

85. *New York Times*, 11 Dec. 1994, 10.

86. Michael Edwards and David Hulme, "NGO Performance and Accountability in the Post-Cold War World," *Journal of International Development* 7, no. 6 (1995): 849–56. See also Roger Charlton and Roy May, "NGOs, Politics, Projects and Probity: A Policy Implementation Perspective," *Third World Quarterly* 16, no. 2 (1995): 237–55.

87. Which, of course, used to be the MNC, the multinational corporation. Think about the difference between *multi* and *trans*. What does it tell you about the process of globalization that it has seemed necessary to make this change?

88. "Coca-Cola Moves to Broaden Business in the Soviet Union," *Wall Street Journal*, 30 Aug. 1991, A3.

89. Jeff Gerth, "In Post-Cold-War Washington, Development Is a Hot Business," *New York Times*, 25 May 1996, 1, 6.

90. *Wall Street Journal*, 2 Oct. 1995, R16, R22.

91. Richard J. Barnet, "Stateless Corporations: Lords of the Economy," *The Nation* 259, no. 21 (19 Dec. 1994): 754–57. Barnet also points out that the world's 200 largest corporations now control more than a fourth of the world's economic activity. This article is drawn from Richard Barnet and John Cavanagh, *Global Dreams: Imperial Corporations and the New World Order* (New York: Simon and Schuster, 1994

92. A. G. Kefalas, "The Global Corporation: Its Role in the New World Order," *National Forum* (Fall 1992): 26–30.

GLOSSARY

A teacher I know has an answer for students who complain that he sometimes uses words they don't understand: "I'm sorry," he says sympathetically, "I just wish there were a book somewhere that could tell you the meanings of all the words in the English language."

Unlike a dictionary, a glossary is not comprehensive and does not give all possible meanings of the terms listed. But this glossary *will* help you understand each term as it is used in this book. For a fuller definition, please do consult your dictionary.

Ad hoc coalition. A temporary organization created to allow several political organizations to pool their resources in a joint effort in which all are interested.

Administrative law. The rules and decisions of administrative agencies.

Admiralty and maritime law. Law governing shipping and water-borne commerce.

Aggregation of interests. The gathering and compromising of different points of view on a topic in order to facilitate the making of policy. Often seen as a prime function of political parties.

Alienation. The condition of being withdrawn and detached from oneself and/or society. A concept developed by Karl Marx describing the tendency of factory workers to see themselves as mere extensions of their machines.

American government. The subfield of political science devoted to the study of the political processes and institutions of the United States.

Amorphous groups. Groups of individuals who share an interest and act on its behalf in a way that indirectly affects government policy.

Anarchism. An ideology stressing belief in the ability of men and women to establish functioning social communities without need for the apparatus of the state and dedicated to the overthrow of existing states by revolution.

Anomy. The condition of being without values; normless.

Apartheid. The South African system of strict racial segregation, maintained by that nation's minority government of white supremacists. Under apartheid, black Africans were required to live in isolated "homelands" and other nonwhite populations were confined to particular neighborhoods within the cities.

Apathy. The condition of being without interest, unconcerned, indifferent.

Apprentice. A person who works in a trade or an art for a more experienced tradesman or artist in return for instruction.

Arms control. Using diplomacy in order to obtain international agreements that limit the production and/or use of nuclear weaponry.

Ascription. A basis for leadership recruitment, specifically, the placing of persons in positions of leadership because their possession of other characteristics (e.g., placement in a lineage system) leads one to believe they must have the necessary qualities to rule.

Associational group. A fully organized group formed specifically to represent the interests of its members.

Attitudes. General, often unverbalized sets of feelings that incline the person holding them to adopt particular specific beliefs and opinions.

Authoritarian system. A political system in which the power of the rulers is virtually unlimited, although this power is not always exercised in all domains. See also totalitarian system.

Authority. The right to exercise the power and influence of a particular position that comes from having been placed in that position according to regular, known, and widely accepted procedures. A person in such a position.

Authority figures. Persons whose positions carry such authority—the boss, the landlord, the military commander—that they may continue to shape political choices for us in adulthood as they did in childhood.

Balance of payments.   The relationship between the payments received by a nation for goods it exports to other nations and the payments made to other nations for goods it imports.

Balance of power.   The theory that the best way to prevent war is to ensure that the major nations of the world remain roughly "balanced" in the power each has to wage war successfully. See also deterrence.

Band.   A nomadic group of families that live and move together and that determine together how goods shall be shared, what individual behavior is permissible, and what religious ceremonies shall be performed.

Behavioral approach.   A way of studying politics that focuses on how an individual acts politically and that seeks explanations for that behavior within that individual.

Belief.   The conviction that a certain thing is true or false. See also opinion.

Bicameral legislature.   A legislature with two houses, usually an upper house and a lower house. See also unicameral legislature.

Bureaucracy.   The administration of government through departments and subdivisions managed by sets of appointed officials following fixed rules of procedure.

Bureaucrat.   A government employee responsible for carrying out some aspects of the administrative work of government according to fixed rules of procedure.

Bureaucratic.   A tendency to follow rules closely, without regard for differences in rank or circumstance of the persons to whom they apply. Often used pejoratively to refer to someone who insists on following a routine in a mechanical way, insisting on proper forms and petty rules.

Bureaucratic drift.   A movement away from control by elected representatives of the people they serve.

Cabinet.   A body composed of the heads of the most important subdivisions of a nation's executive branch and led by the nation's chief executive. Its functions are normally to advise the chief executive and to assist in the formulation of legislation to be proposed to the national legislative body. In a presidential system the cabinet is under the control of the president and is responsible to that leader, whereas in parliamentary and presidential-parliamentary systems its ultimate responsibility is to the legislature.

Cadre parties.   Political parties with small, loosely affili-

ated memberships, a co-opted elite leadership with little control over the base, and weak communication links.

Capitalism.   An economic system in which individuals are free to invest their savings (capital) as they wish, to purchase goods and hire labor in order to develop private enterprise, and to reinvest profits (also capital) in such businesses or in those of other citizens.

Cartel.   Associations of businesses formed in the early twentieth century to establish national or international monopolies over particular raw materials or manufactured goods.

Catchall party.   A party that makes concrete, pragmatic short-range promises to fulfill the immediate interests of as many voters as possible.

Center-periphery relations.   Relations between a polity's central government and the governments of provincial and local units. See also periphery.

Ceremonial leader.   See chief of state.

Charisma.   Having the gift of leadership and being recognized as having that gift.

Chief executive.   The most powerful leader in a given polity's executive branch—usually the most powerful leader in the state. Normally a prime minister or president.

Chief of state.   The official who performs the ceremonial roles of government leadership. Normally a hereditary monarch or an elected but relatively powerless president. In a presidential system, the functions of chief of state and chief executive are combined.

City-state.   An early form of political community, a polity seldom larger in population or area than a medium-size city of today but constituting at the same time a sovereign state.

Civic culture.   A culture in which citizens combine a commitment to moderate political participation with a belief in the legitimacy of officialdom and a tendency toward parochialism.

Civic training.   Teaching the facts about a political system and the procedures for participating in that system as a citizen. See also political indoctrination.

Civil law.   Law governing unfair (but not criminal) behavior that affects only other individuals, not the community. Civil law calls for retribution to the offended party, not punishment on behalf of the public order.

Civilian supremacy.   The principle that civilian leadership shall be maintained over the armed forces of a polity.

Class.   A kind of group identity, normally based on differences in level of income, level of education, and kind of occupation, sometimes also based on differences in accent, dress, and kinds of material acquitions desired and purchased.

Clientelistic linkage.   The connection between citizens and political leaders that takes place when the former offer electoral support in exchange for material rewards provided by the latter.

Clientelistic parties.   Parties in which leaders make sure their followers receive certain material benefits for their support but do not encourage them to express opinions on matters of policy.

Codified law.   Laws that have been set down in writing in conjunction with other laws. Edicts, treaties, decrees, legislative enactments, and judicial precedents are among the forms of law that may be codified. See also statutory law.

Colonialism.   The system by which a nation maintains control over a distant territory in order to exploit that territory's resources. See also neocolonialism.

Committee system.   The use of specialized or standing committees by legislative bodies to organize and facilitate their work.

Common law.   Law made by using the rulings of judges in earlier cases as precedents. Sometimes referred to as "judge-made law." See also precedent.

Common law legal culture.   The making of judicial decisions by reference to previous judicial decisions. Dominant throughout the British Commonwealth, in the United States, and in other former British colonies.

Communications media.   A term referring to the technical devices employed in mass communication, typically including newspapers, magazines, radio, and television. Commonly known as the media.

Communism.   A form of socialism emphasizing the absolute abolition of private property, economic equality, rule by the workers (the proletariat), and access to power by armed revolution. Subcategories of communism include Marxism, Leninism, and Maoism.

Comparative government.   The subfield of political science devoted to the study of foreign polities, using the comparative method.

Confederal system.   A system of government in which the units are independent states that have decided to join together in a formal alliance, acting as a single unit for some limited purpose, but not for others.

Confederation.   A system of government in which nearly all powers are reserved to the constituent units of the nation—that is, to the states, provinces, or cantons.

Conservatism.   An ideology that stresses conserving what exists; takes a nonegalitarian view of human nature; and holds order, continuity, loyalty, protection of individual freedoms, piety, and nationalism as its highest values.

Constituency.   All the people, especially voters, served by a particular elected official, especially a legislator. The district of such a group of voters.

Constitution.   A set of rules prescribing the institutions and procedures of government and having precedence over all other rules in a given polity.

Constitutional law.   A nation's constitution and the body of judicial rulings about the meaning of the constitution. The subfield of political science devoted to the study of the institutions and procedures of government as these are formally prescribed in constitutions and explicated in judicial rulings.

Co-optation.   Granting prestigious appointments or other benefits to one whose support is sought but not yet certain, as a means of securing that support.

Corporate guilds.   Organizations formed in Europe in the sixteenth century to regulate the social, economic, and political affairs of craftsmen when such workers—masters, journeymen, and apprentices—found themselves able to live independently from the feudal system.

Corporatism.   An economic system in which formal ownership of the means of production remains in private hands, but the state requires that all industries and other productive enterprises be grouped into units according to the function performed. See also neocorporatism.

Coup d'état.   A French term meaning overthrow of the state, normally by armed force. A coup is different from a revolution in that it usually entails replacement of the top leadership of a regime by another narrow elite, and is not based on a mass movement.

Criminal law.   Law governing crimes. Criminal law views an act of crime as an offense against the public order and therefore deserving of punishment by society.

Cultural relativism.   The idea that each society sets its own standards in accordance with its own culture, and that what is correct in one society may be repugnant in another.

Cultural values.   Values shared by a group of people.

Culture.   The ideas and customs of a given people in a given period.

Decentralization.   The process of breaking up the concentration of power in the central government and allocating some portion of that power to provincial and local units.

Decree.   A rule issued by a leader in a given polity's executive branch and having the force of law.

Delegation of power.   The practice of ceding to one branch of government powers that are constitutionally assigned to another, most commonly from the legislative branch to the executive branch.

Demagogue. A person who gains public office by appealing to fears and prejudices, and then uses the power of office for personal gain.

Democracy. Rule by the people. A system of government in which all adults not disqualified by criminal behavior or mental incapacity have the right and the means to exercise some form of genuine control over government. The means of ensuring democratic government normally include the protection of individual liberties, free elections, and political equality.

Democratic socialism. An ideology espousing the principles of socialism but stressing the need to achieve and exercise power democratically.

Deterrence. The theory that the best way to prevent nuclear war is to build up such a massive and threatening arsenal of nuclear weapons that no other nation will dare to attack. See also balance of power.

Dialectical materialism. The Marxist theory that human history is evolving through stages characterized by different modes of production and different allocations of power to control the means of production. Movement from stage to stage is by dialectics: The status quo is the thesis, the effort to impose its opposite is the antithesis, and the eventual compromise between old and new is the synthesis—which becomes, in turn, the new thesis.

Dictatorship. A political system in which power is concentrated in the hands of a single individual and is maintained by the autocratic exercise of that power; often characterized by the development of a cult of personality around the dictator.

Diplomat. A representative of a government who conducts relations with another government in the interests of his or her own nation.

Diplomatic corps. The group of diplomats for each country.

Direct democracy. Government immediately by the people, as contrasted to government by elected representatives or by charismatic or dictatorial autocrats.

Directive linkage. The connection between citizens and political leaders that exists when the latter maintain control over the former, either by coercion or by manipulation.

Directive parties. Parties that link voters to government by helping the government maintain coercive control over its subjects.

Division of labor. The assignment of different tasks to different persons in a community.

Domestic law. The body of laws that nations apply within their own territories.

Economic and Social Council. A United Nations organization whose function is to promote international cooperation in economic and social matters.

Economic development. The transformation of natural resources (the nation's own or those imported from other nations as raw materials) into ever more valuable processed goods, the improvement of services, and the marketing of those goods and services in order to enhance the material well-being of the nation's people.

Economic equality. The condition that exists when all citizens have approximately the same amount of material wealth.

Economy. A system of producing, distributing, and consuming wealth.

Elected board (council). The most common rulemaking body of local government.

Electoral system. The rules and regulations governing how citizens vote in a polity.

Empire. A polity composed of numerous smaller polities that maintain their own identities but have come under the sway of another polity, usually through warfare.

Equality. Having the same fundamental needs as well as the same rights under the law. Such rights may be political, economic, and/or social.

Equity law. Law designed to supplement the common law by providing relief when the operation of the law will wreak irremediable harm; an example is the injunction.

Espionage. The act of gathering information about another nation that the nation prefers not be known; spying.

Ethnic group. A self-identified group with distinctive racial and/or national characteristics and a shared set of beliefs and values.

Executive veto. A veto by the person in the highest government position.

Extraconstitutional forces. Forces outside the formal government by a polity that are nevertheless strong enough to shape public policy.

Extraconstitutional power. Power exercised by the government when groups external to the government are able to pressure the agents of the government into a situation in which they feel they have no choice but to comply.

Fascism. A far-right ideology based on the principle that race, nationalism, and absolute obedience to authoritarian leadership are the highest values.

Federal system. A system of government in which certain powers are reserved to the central government but others are constitutionally reserved to the governments of the nation's constituent parts—that is, to the states, provinces, or cantons.

Feedback.   A term used in political systems analysis to denote the transmission of information, rewards, or punishments from one element of a system to another, as a form of response to input from that element. See also input.

Feudalism.   A system in which the political leaders, large landholders, and the serfs who worked the land were linked by mutual political and economic dependency. Wealth, and thereby political power, was based on agricultural production.

Freedom.   The condition of being able to act without restraint.

Functional regionalism.   A form of regionalism, often temporary, established to deal with a single problem; more limited in scope than structural regionalism.

General Assembly.   The organization of the United Nations to which each of the member states sends a representative and which has the power to make recommendations in the name of the United Nations if a two-thirds vote can be obtained.

Government.   The institutions responsible for making and carrying out the laws of a polity and for adjudicating disputes that arise under those laws. The arena in which political choices are made manifest. In political systems analysis, the decision-making apparatus that receives inputs and emits outputs.

Guerrilla warfare.   The attempt to accomplish political change by training and arming a band of revolutionaries who live in hiding, preferably in difficult and well-forested terrain; who attempt to recruit others to their cause; and who make only limited attacks on the forces of the state until the balance of power between themselves and the state is sufficiently equal to permit open warfare. See also terrorist political organization.

Head of state.   In a parliamentary system, the nation's monarch or president.

Hegemonic party system.   A system in which there is more than a single party but one party has established pronounced and continuing dominance.

Ideological party.   A party of true believers who gradually rally others to their cause.

Ideology.   A comprehensive set of beliefs and attitudes about social and economic institutions and processes.

Imperialism.   The policy and practice of forming and maintaining an empire by the conquest of other countries and the establishment of colonies.

Indirect election.   An election in which only those who have already been elected to another post are entitled to vote.

Indoctrination.   Overt instruction in a body of beliefs.

Industrialism.   A social and economic system characterized by large industries, machine production, and the concentration of workers in cities.

Inflation.   An increase in the amount of money in circulation, resulting in a relatively sharp and sudden fall in its value and a rise in prices.

Influence.   The ability to affect the behavior of another. See also power.

Initiative.   A provision in a polity's electoral system that permits citizens to vote directly on specific proposals for new legislation, provided a certain number of citizens petition for the opportunity to do so.

Injunction.   A court order issued to prevent an action until the offended party has had time to prepare and present a fuller legal argument that the action should not take place.

Input.   A term used in political systems analysis to denote the support and demands coming to governments from such forces as public opinion, interest groups, and political parties. See also feedback.

Institution.   A structure with established, important functions to perform; with well-specified roles for carrying out those functions; and with a clear set of rules governing the relationship between the people who occupy those roles.

Intelligence agency.   A government office assigned the task of gathering information about other nations in order to assist a nation's decision-makers in the formulation of foreign policy and the safeguarding of national security.

Interest.   A clearly identified personal stake in a decision or the outcome of an event.

Interest group.   An organization whose main purpose is to affect the operation of government by persuading key persons in government to act in accordance with the group's interests.

International Court of Justice.   The judicial branch of the United Nations, with jurisdiction only over cases the members of that body agree to refer to it. Sometimes called the World Court.

International law.   The law that applies in relationships between nations, or between the citizens of one nation and either the government or the individual citizens of another nation.

International relations.   The relationships between nations. The subfield of political science devoted to the study of relationships between nations.

International terrorism.   Terrorism directed by criticism of one nation against those of another in an effort to alter relations between political systems.

Iron law of oligarchy.   According to Robert Michels, the natural tendency of people in organizations to divide into those who lead and those who follow.

Journeyman.   A craftsman who has completed an apprenticeship and is now a qualified worker for another.

Judicial activism.   The use of judicial review to overrule both legislative statute and court decision.

Judicial independence.   The protection of the judiciary, usually by constitutional guarantees, from interference by the other branches of government in the conduct of its work.

Judicial review.   The power of a judiciary to review legislative and executive enactments in order to decide whether or not they conform with a polity's constitution and to declare such enactments null and void where they are found not in conformance with that constitution.

Judiciary.   The branch of government concerned with adjudicating disputes that arise under the law.

Justice.   Fair treatment under the law. As such, justice is the possible (but not inevitable) result of decisions made by those who have been granted authority to determine what constitutes fair treatment.

Kinship system.   A means of ordering sociopolitical relationships in which each person's right to use a parcel of land and to own cattle or other property is determined by his or her place in the family lineage.

Laissez faire.   A French term meaning "let them do as they will." A laissez-faire economy is one in which government stays out of the world of business as much as possible.

Law.   A regulation established by public authorities and backed by the collective power of the polity to which it applies.

Left.   A term used to describe political ideas comparatively. Those on the political left tend to take a more posi-

tive view of human nature and to be convinced that change and progress are necessary and possible to improve the human condition. See also right.

Legal cultures.   Regional variations in the evolution and application of the law.

Legislative veto.   A device developed by the U.S. Congress to permit it to delegate certain of its powers to the president but to retain the power to veto that leader's rulings in the delegated domain. Recently declared unconstitutional by the U.S. Supreme Court.

Legislature.   A body of persons given the responsibility and power to make laws for a polity.

Legitimacy.   The condition of being considered correct and proper. See also political legitimacy.

Liberalism.   An ideology that sees the role of government as protecting individual liberties while at the same time ensuring everyone the chance to lead the best possible life and to fulfill his or her individual potential.

Liberty.   The absence of constraint.

Linkage.   The connection between one political unit (e.g., citizen, political organization, level of government, nation-state) and another.

Lobbying.   Seeking to influence public officials by direct personal contact; often attempted in the lobbies of public buildings by the paid representatives (lobbyists) of groups or individuals.

Local government.   Subnational government that is under the jurisdiction of provincial and national (and sometimes regional) government and that is within the reach of the citizens it governs.

Mass parties.   Political parties with large, dues-paying memberships. These parties are centralized, bureaucratic, and have strong communication links running throughout the organization.

Master.   A sixteenth century leader of a corporate guild who negotiated political and economic matters on behalf of those who worked under him.

Material benefits.   Goods and services made available to an interest group's members.

Mercantilism.   A theory urging that the state use its powers openly to provide the best possible conditions for private entrepreneurs to carry on their business, thereby identifying the interest of the state with that of private business.

Minister.   A high officer appointed to head a segment of government.

Minority government.   In a multiparty parliamentary system, a cabinet composed of representatives of parties that have, altogether, only a minority of seats in the legislature.

Mixed economy.   An economy based on a mixture of public and private ownership of the means of production, and on considerable public regulation of the private sector.

Model.   An imitation of something that is or that is thought to be or that may someday come to be; a representation of the essence of the subject.

Moderate pluralism.   A system in which numerous parties are only moderately differentiated from each other ideologically.

Motion of censure.   A motion made in parliamentary and presidential-parliamentary systems to remove a prime minister and his or her cabinet from office.

Multiparty party system.   A party system with more than two parties.

Municipal council.   A body of individuals, usually elected, whose duty it is to make the laws (ordinances) of local government. Sometimes also responsible for electing a mayor or appointing a city manager.

Municipal law.   Collective name for local ordinances.

Nation.   A relatively large group of people who feel they belong together by virtue of sharing one or more traits such as race, language, culture, history, or a set of customs and traditions.

Nationalism.   A collective identity shared by the citizens of a polity; the belief that national interests are more important than international considerations.

Nation-state.   A polity in which all citizens share a sense of common identity (nationhood) and in which subunits, if any, are wholly or partly under the domain of a central government. See also state.

Natural law.   Law based on laws that already exist in nature and that have been, according to some philosophers, implanted there by a divine creator. Those who believe in natural law believe it is discoverable by "right reason" and is binding on everyone. See also positive law.

Natural law legal culture.   Basing judicial decisions on the precepts of religious and philosophical thought. Found throughout the Islamic world and often also found in coexistence with more modern legal cultures, especially at the local level, as in many villages in India and in non-Islamic African nations.

Natural resources.   The material wealth that can be drawn from a nation's natural environment.

Neighborhood association.   A group of citizens who gather together to seek to influence government to make changes of benefit to their immediate neighborhood—or not to make changes that will be detrimental to their neighborhood.

Neocolonialism.   A system for maintaining the economic dependence of one state on another while permitting it to acquire or maintain its political independence. The usual methods are the establishment of cooperative political leadership in the dependent nation, backed up by the promise of military assistance from the dominant nation, and the creation of trade agreements beneficial to the dominant nation and to the indigenous elite. See also colonialism.

Neocorporatism.   An economic system in which the state gives official recognition to different interests by establishing boards of representatives to advise the government and grants subsidies or enacts supportive legislation favoring those that are cooperative with the state. See also corporatism.

Norms.   The values or standards that an individual, a group, or a social system decide to apply to the facts of a situation.

Oligarchy.   Rule by the few, usually in their own behalf. The iron law of oligarchy is the tendency of all organizations to divide into those who lead and those who follow.

OPEC.   The Organization of Petroleum Exporting Countries. An international organization formed to promote the interests of the world's major oil-producing states. Its members include Algeria, Ecuador, Gabon, Indonesia, Iran, Iraq, Kuwait, Libya, Nigeria, Qator, Saudi Arabia, Venezuela, and the United Arab Emirates.

Opinion.   The conviction that a certain thing is probably true, often combined with an evaluation. See also belief.

Order.   The condition of peace and serenity, in which everything appears to be functioning properly.

Ordinance.   A ruling made by a local government body; sometimes referred to as municipal law.

Organization.   A body of persons working together in a structured way to achieve a specific purpose.

Ostracism.   The exclusion of an individual from a group.

Outputs.   A term used in political systems analysis to denote the work produced by governments: laws (including ordinances and proclamations), the steps taken to implement laws, and the decisions made to settle disputes that arise under the law.

Pardon. The constitutional right of a chief executive to cancel punishments decreed by jurists, including those in military tribunals.

Parliament. A national legislative body, normally composed of an upper house and a lower house. See also parliamentary system.

Parliamentary system. A system of government in which the national legislature (parliament) is linked to the national bureaucracy by the fact that both are ruled by the same body, the cabinet, which is itself responsible to the legislature. See also cabinet and parliament.

Parochialism. The tendency to withdraw into the private sphere; to be concerned only with matters in one's own immediate area and to take a narrow, limited, and provincial outlook on life.

Participatory democracy. Self leadership; a government ruled immediately by the people, not by their representatives.

Participatory linkage. The connection between citizens and organizations (including governments) that exists when the former are directly involved in the decision-making processes of the latter.

Participatory parties. Political parties in which members are aided in participating directly in policymaking processes.

Particularistic party. A party that identifies completely with the interest of a particular social group.

Party primary. An election held to choose the person who will stand as a political party's nominee for an elective post.

Party system. Political system defined by the number of parties that operate within it.

Patronage. Jobs, honorary positions, or other material rewards given in exchange for political support. Sometimes referred to as "the spoils of office."

Periphery. Provincial and local governments, as contrasted to the "center" (the national government).

Phenomenology. An approach to the study of politics that focuses on change and the events (the *phenomena*) that led up to that change. It is an inquiry into the causes of a significant change in a political system.

Planned economy. An economy guided by the state in accordance with a general plan.

Pluralism. A condition in which all groups within a polity have an equal right and opportunity to form, put forward their points of view, win adherents, and influence decision makers. Under such circumstances, polity is the result of a pluralistic struggle for power. Pluralist theorists argue that such a condition actually exists in western democracies and, further, that the net result is the fairest possible form of government.

Polarized pluralism. A party system in which the parties are ideologically separated by vast distances.

Policy-responsive linkage. A connection between citizens and political leaders in which the decisions of the latter are responsive to the views of the former.

Policy-responsive parties. Parties in which members work to ensure that policy is made in the interests of their supporters, but that are not directly under the control of those members.

Political appointment. An appointment to government office that is made by someone already serving in another government position.

Political behavior. The subfield of political science devoted to the study of political attitudes and acts.

Political bias. Partiality on the part of the media, expressed through the media's deliberately shaping the content and presentation of the news so as to favor certain political interests, actors, practices, and/or ideas over others.

Political consultant. Political operatives who help candidates deal with all aspects of campaign politics.

Political culture. A set of political values, beliefs, and attitudes that is widely shared throughout a polity.

Political documents. Forms of the written word that are studied by political scientists; namely, constitutions, statutory laws, judicial decisions, party statutes and platforms, leaders' speeches and memoirs, records of legislative proceedings, newspaper accounts of political happenings, and the like.

Political economy. The relationship between economic conditions and the political choices we make. The subfield of political science devoted to the study of the relationship between economic and political factors.

Political equality. The condition that exists when all citizens have an equal right to participate in the political process and to be treated equally in it.

Political event. An event that affects the right to allocate scarce resources in a polity.

Political indoctrination. Teaching a specific political ideology in order to rationalize and justify the behavior of a particular political regime. See also civic training.

Political legitimacy. The condition of being considered correct and proper in the exercise of political power. See also legitimacy.

Political organization. An organization that is not itself a government agency but whose main purpose is to affect the operation of government. The subfield of political science devoted to the study of nongovernmental organizations that seek to influence government.

Political party. An organization that seeks to place representatives in government by nominating candidates to stand for election, claiming that power so won will be exercised in the public interest.

Political party system. The identification of political systems according to the number of parties they have and the concentration or dispersion of power among the parties. Common types include the one-party system; the hegemonic party system (more than one party, but one is dominant over all the others); the two-party system; and the multiparty system.

Political socialization. The ongoing processes through which citizens acquire—and amend—their personal views of the political world.

Political system. A structure with interdependent parts that deals with political matters.

Political systems analysis. An analytical framework that treats political units (particularly political organizations and nation-states) as systems composed of interdependent parts and explores the relationships among those parts.

Political theory. The subfield of political science devoted to the study of political philosophy, including the formulation of concepts, categories, and logical explanations of political phenomena.

Politics. The process that determines who shall occupy roles of leadership in government and how the power of government shall be exercised. The authoritative allocation of scarce resources throughout a polity.

Polity. A state, or any society with an organized government. Any group of persons who have some form of political relationship with one another. The interdependence of human beings around the globe has created a worldwide polity, the human polity.

Polls. Studies of the opinions of the public, or of selected portions thereof, normally based on interviews with a random sample of the group in question.

Positive law. Law made by humans, pragmatically, to meet specific needs. See also natural law.

Power. The ability to control the behavior of others by threatening and/or carrying out severe sanctions if that behavior is other than compliant. See also influence.

Pragmatic-bargaining party. A party that aggregates interests through negotiations, which reach unconcernedly across conflicting values.

Precedent. A court case used as an example to be followed in succeeding similar cases. See also common law.

Precinct. An electoral subdivision of a city, usually comprising a few blocks. See also ward.

Predictions. The content of well-founded speculation on the part of political scientists about the feared or hoped-for events of the future.

Presidential-parliamentary system. A system of government in which the chief executive is elected directly by the people and in turn appoints a prime minister who must be approved by the parliament (the national legislature) before taking responsibility, with his or her cabinet, for carrying out the laws of the land and developing legislative proposals to put before the parliament. In this system, the prime minister is responsible to both the president and the parliament. Sometimes referred to as a quasi-presidential system.

Presidential system. A system of government in which the chief executive is elected directly by the people, is responsible for carrying out the laws of the land, and has only advisory powers with respect to the actual content of those laws, which are made by a separate legislative body whose members are elected independently of the president.

Pressure methods. The means groups use to exert pressure on government.

Pressure points. The levels and branches of government that groups seek to influence.

Prime minister. The chief executive in a parliamentary system and the second in command in a presidential-parliamentary system. A prime minister is chosen by the ceremonial chief of state in the former system and by the president in the latter. He or she must be approved by parliament in both systems and normally leads the party with the most seats in parliament.

Progress. The condition of advancing toward a better state; improvement.

Proportional representation. An electoral system that gives each political party contesting an election a number of seats (usually in a legislature) roughly proportionate to the number of votes its candidates received in combination.

Protectionism. The policy of sheltering domestic producers—both agricultural and industrial—by adopting government policies that shield them from the competition of the world market. The favored methods of protectionism are the imposition of high tariffs on imported goods, the establishment of price supports for domestic goods, insistence on trade agreements favoring domestic businesses, and setting quotas on the amount of certain foreign goods that may be imported.

Proximate forces. Forces we encounter in person, such as family, teachers, and bosses (as contrasted to nonproximate forces, such as historical figures, political leaders, and the media).

Public administration. The subfield of political science devoted to the study of the bureaucratic processes and institutions of government.

Public agenda. The list of political issues that are normally of concern to almost everyone in a nation during a political campaign.

Public interest group. A group that claims to work for a cause that is in the public's interest, not its own. See also special interest group.

Public opinion. The collective nature of a body of individual opinions.

Public opinion poll. A study of the opinions held by a representative sample of the entire population.

Purposive benefits. The satisfaction some members of interest groups get from working on behalf of a value or cause in which they believe.

Quasi-presidential system. See presidential-parliamentary system.

Recall election. A special election held when a sufficient number of voters petition to remove an official (usually an elected official) from office.

Recruitment. The process of finding, persuading, and training candidates to run for electoral office. Often seen as a major function of political parties.

Referendum. A provision in a polity's electoral system enabling a group of citizens to "refer" a piece of legislation passed by the government to the voting public, provided a sufficient number of citizens petition for the right to do so.

Regionalism. A level of intermediate government below the level of the national government and usually (but not always) above the level of the province. See also structural regionalism and functional regionalism.

Representative leadership. Leadership based on the right of the people to choose certain individuals to attend to matters of state on their behalf.

Revolutionary one-party system. A single party that is used as the chief instrument for taking over an existing political system and effecting revolutionary change in all social, economic, and political relationships.

Right. A term used to describe political ideas comparatively. Those on the political right place greater stress on the importance of maintaining tradition and order than those on the political left. See also left.

Romano-Germanic legal culture. The making of judicial decisions by reference to codes of law based on the Roman tradition. Common in most of Europe, all of Latin America, the nations of West and Central Africa formerly under French dominion, and in the Canadian province of Quebec and the American state of Louisiana.

Rule of law. The principle that the regulation of social behavior shall take place under laws that apply equally to all.

Ruling. An interpretation, usually by a judicial body, of a regulation, decree, ordinance, or law.

Secret society. A group of lay persons who share a common religion, who hold secret ceremonies to reinforce the sense of solidarity with the group, and who commonly engage in social, charitable, and/or political activities they believe to be consistent with their religion.

Security Council. The organization of the United Nations in which the United States, Russia, China, Great Britain, and France have permanent membership, each with the right of veto. Intended to be the chief decision-making body of the United Nations, the Security Council has so frequently been prevented from acting by its members' use of their right to veto that power has increasingly shifted to the General Assembly.

Separation of powers. The constitutional establishment of three branches of government—legislative, executive, and judicial—each with separate and independent bases of support, terms of office, and powers of office.

Simulation. A process in which computer technology is used to gather all available information about a subject, form a model of that subject, and then manipulate that model by introducing other factors and examining their impact on it. See also model.

Single-party system. A political system in which only one political party is allowed.

Social equality. The condition that exists when every citizen has the right to be treated as a social equal, at least with respect to one's basic characteristics and needs.

Socialism. An ideology that holds that human beings readily engage in cooperative social activity and that the state, controlled by the workers, should own or at least control the means of production. An economic system in which the state controls all or most of the means of production.

Socialist legal culture. The making of judicial decisions by reference to the law code of the former Union of Soviet

Socialist Republics, a code characterized by its explicit use of the law to serve political purposes.

Socialization.   The process by which values are passed on clearly and persuasively by those who hold them to those who do not; the inculcation of values.

Sociocultural values.   Values derived from membership in a particular social group, such as pride in a way of life, in shared traditions, and in the group culture.

Solidary benefits.   The benefits provided by an interest group when it gives its members a sense of belonging, a chance to socialize with others, and/or improved social status.

Sovereignty.   The power of a polity to make decisions that cannot be overruled by any other body.

Special interest group.   A group that works exclusively for the interests of its own members. See also public interest group.

Specialized committee.   A legislative committee that is responsible for bills having to do with a specific area of policy, such as agriculture or health. See also standing committee.

Spontaneous groups.   Groups of organized individuals who act together politically and deliberately, but in an unconventional and often violent fashion.

Stagflation.   An economic condition in which prices are inflated yet at the same time growth is slowed.

Standing committee.   A legislative committee that is not limited in scope, to which different kinds of bills may be referred. See also specialized committee.

Stare decisis.   A Latin phrase meaning "let the decision stand," referring to the practice in common law legal cultures of basing decisions in contemporary cases on those made in earlier similar cases.

State.   A structure that has the legal right to make rules that are binding over a given population within a given territory. See also city-state and nation-state.

Statutory law.   Written law, including legislation, treaties, executive orders, decrees, and codes of law. See also codified law.

Strict construction.   The practice of adhering closely to the letter of the law as found in a constitution or statute.

Structural-functional approach.   A way of studying politics that focuses on the political functions that must be carried out in every political system and that seeks to discover which structures do, in fact, perform these tasks.

Structural regionalism.   A form of regionalism in which provincial units are grouped in regions by constitutional fiat and are expected to be permanent additions to the body politic. See also functional regionalism.

Structure.   A set of patterned role relationships.

Subnational government.   Government below the level of the nation; regional, provincial, and local government.

Subversion.   Any act designed to interfere with an established government by covert means, usually with a view to accomplishing its destruction.

Suffrage.   The right to vote in political elections.

Surrogate.   A person who takes the place of another and stands in for that person. In politics, surrogates often stand in for the chief executive in public ceremonies or for political candidates in election rallies.

Syndicalism.   An ideology that argues that the trade union should replace the state, allowing workers to assume control of their own affairs, and that this should be accomplished via a general strike of nationwide proportions.

System.   A structure all of whose parts are interrelated, so that a change in one part means a change in all.

Technocratic elite.   Leaders in government and the private sector with high level and up to date skills in production and/or management.

Technological development.   The use of high level and up to date skills to improve processes of transforming natural resources into useful goods and services.

Terrorist organization.   An organization that attempts to change the operation of government by using violence to induce fear of the consequences of *not* changing and/or provoking the authorities to respond so oppressively as to lose legitimacy in the eyes of the general public.

Theocracy.   A government ruled by religious leaders who claim to have divine authority for their edicts.

Totalitarian system.   A political system in which the authorities have unlimited power and attempt to exercise it over all domains of life; authoritarianism carried to the ultimate extreme.

Transnational corporation.   A cluster of businesses located in several different nations but commonly owned and managed. An independent network of fiscal, research, productive, and distributive institutions, often with gross annual sales larger than the gross national products of many nations.

Treaty.   A document signed by representatives of two or more nations that sets the terms for relations between those nations with regard to particular matters.

Two-party system.   A system in which two parties compete for an absolute majority that is within the reach of either.

Unicameral legislature. A legislature with only one house, as in the state of Nebraska in the United States. See also bicameral legislature.

Unitary system. A political system in which all the powers of government are reserved to the central government. That government may delegate the exercise of those powers to subunits but can revoke such delegation at any time.

Urban politics and government. The subfield of political science devoted to the study of politics and government in cities.

Value. A serious and deeply held normative principle with wide applicability.

Veto. The constitutional right of a ruler to reject bills passed by a legislative body.

Vote of confidence. A vote taken in a parliamentary or presidential-parliamentary system to demonstrate the legislature's continued confidence—or lack of confidence—in the prime minister and his or her cabinet. Usually called for by the prime minister during a period of crisis. If the vote is lost, the government is normally dissolved, and new elections are held.

Ward. An electoral and sometimes also an administrative subunit of a city. See also precinct.

Workers' council. A council of workers' representatives, usually elected, whose duty it is to take an active part in management decisions, particularly as these affect the interests of the workers. Established by the company and often (especially in socialist systems) mandated by the state, the workers' council should not be confused with the independent trade union, although the two may have shared leadership.

Xenophobia. The fear or hatred of anything foreign or strange.

Zero-sum. A term taken from game theory, used to describe a situation in which the gain of one player (e.g., politician or nation) can only be at the expense of another player.

INDEX

ALASKA
(U.S.)

CANADA

UNITED STATES

MEXICO

GUATEMALA
EL SALVADOR

COSTA RICA

PANAMA

PACIFIC OCEAN

Equator

WESTERN
SAMOA

TONGA

Midway Is.

Hawaiian Is.

Easter Is.

Galapagos Is.

GREENLAND
(DENMARK)

ICELAND

IRELA

PORTUGA

Azores

ATLANTIC OCEAN

WESTERN
SAHARA
(MOROCCO)

Bermuda

BAHAMAS

DOMINICAN REP.
CUBA
JAMAICA   HAITI
BELIZE   Puerto Rico   Virgin Is.
HONDURAS
NICARAGUA

ST. CHRISTOPHER AND NEVIS
ANTIGUA AND BARBUDA
DOMINICA
BARBADOS
ST. LUCIA
GRENADA   ST. VINCENT AND
                    THE GRENADINES

TRINIDAD AND TOBAGO

VENEZUELA   GUYANA

FR. GUIANA

COLOMBIA   SURINAM

ECUADOR

PERU

BRAZIL

BOLIVIA

PARAGUAY

CHILE

URUGUAY

ARGENTINA

Falkland Is.

CAPE
VERDE

SENEGAL
GAMBIA
GUINEA-BISSAU   GUINEA

SIERRA
LEONE
LIBERIA

MAURIT

EQ

SAO TO

80°N

60°N

40°N

20°N

0°

20°S

40°S

60°S

80°S

160°W   140°W   120°W   100°W   80°W   60°W   40°W   20°W